INTIMATE EMPIRES

INTIMATE EMPIRES

BODY, RACE, AND GENDER IN THE MODERN WORLD

Tracey Rizzo and
Steven Gerontakis

New York   Oxford
OXFORD UNIVERSITY PRESS

Oxford University Press is a department of the University of Oxford.
It furthers the University's objective of excellence in research,
scholarship, and education by publishing worldwide.

Oxford   New York
Auckland   Cape Town   Dar es Salaam   Hong Kong   Karachi
Kuala Lumpur   Madrid   Melbourne   Mexico City   Nairobi
New Delhi   Shanghai   Taipei   Toronto

With offices in
Argentina   Austria   Brazil   Chile   Czech Republic   France   Greece
Guatemala   Hungary   Italy   Japan   Poland   Portugal   Singapore
South Korea   Switzerland   Thailand   Turkey   Ukraine   Vietnam

For titles covered by Section 112 of the US Higher Education
Opportunity Act, please visit www.oup.com/us/he for the
latest information about pricing and alternate formats.

Published by Oxford University Press
198 Madison Avenue, New York, New York 10016
http://www.oup.com

Library of Congress Cataloging-in-Publication Data

Names: Rizzo, Tracey. | Gerontakis, Steven.
Title: Intimate empires : body, race, and gender in the modern world / Tracey
    Rizzo and Steven Gerontakis (University of North Carolina, Asheville).
Description: New York : Oxford University Press, 2016. | Includes
    bibliographical references and index.
Identifiers: LCCN 2015020912 | ISBN 9780199978342 (paperback : acid-free
    paper)
Subjects: LCSH: Imperialism--Social aspects--History. | Colonization--Social
    aspects--History. | Human body--Social aspects--History. | Race--Social
    aspects--History. | Sex role--Social aspects--History. |
    Masculinity--Social aspects--History. | Femininity--Social
    aspects--History. | Identity (Psychology)--Social aspects--History.
Classification: LCC JV105 .R59 2016 | DDC 306.2--dc23 LC record available
    at http://lccn.loc.gov/2015020912

Printing number: 9 8 7 6 5 4 3 2

Printed in Canada
on acid-free paper

FRONTISPIECE: *France Offering the Dove of Peace to Five Continents,* central fresco in the Palais
de la Porte Dorée, 1931 Colonial Exposition, Paris, France.

To Judith P. Zinsser, a daring genius for our times

BRIEF TABLE OF CONTENTS

Detailed Table of Contents ix
List of Maps xiii
Acknowledgments xv
Maps xvii

INTRODUCTION 1

CHAPTER ONE THE GENDER OF EMPIRE:
MASCULINITIES 12

CHAPTER TWO THE GENDER OF EMPIRE:
FEMININITIES 62

CHAPTER THREE THE INSTITUTIONS OF EMPIRE 111

CHAPTER FOUR THE ARTIFACTS OF EMPIRE 157

CHAPTER FIVE THE RACE OF EMPIRE 205

CHAPTER SIX THE END OF EMPIRE 257

CONCLUSION 303

Glossary 313
Notes 317
Bibliography 361
Credits 381
Index 383

DETAILED TABLE
OF CONTENTS

Brief Table of Contents   *vii*
List of Maps   *xiii*
Acknowledgments   *xv*
Maps   *xvii*

INTRODUCTION   1
Imperialism: an Overview   3
Coverage   6
Historiography   8
Legacy of Empire   11

CHAPTER ONE   THE GENDER OF EMPIRE:
MASCULINITIES   12
Vignette: James Cook of Britain and the Pacific   12
Interracial Sex   14
    Empire as Playground   15
    Taming the Frontiers   17
    Transgressing Boundaries   20
Imperial Men   23
    Social Darwinism   23
    Making Boys into Men   24
    Turning Men into Colonists   28
Warriors   31
    Western Militaries   31
    Martial Races   34
    Colonial Militaries   36
Colonized Masses   40
    Slaves   41
    Laborers   45

Colonized Elites   47
   Horizontal Alliances   48
   Subalterns   51
Bridging the Divide   53
   International Sports   53
   Anti-Imperialism   56
Conclusion   59

CHAPTER TWO   THE GENDER OF EMPIRE:
FEMININITIES   62
Vignette: Ahyssa of Senegal and Saint-Domingue   62
Virtue in Cross-Cultural Contexts   64
   East versus West   65
   Melodramas   66
   Interracial Romance   68
Colonized Women   72
   Slaves   73
   Prostitutes   77
   Indentured Servants   80
The Colonial Household   83
   Settling   84
   Managing   85
   Children   88
Independent Women   90
   Nurses and Teachers   91
   Travelers and Collectors   94
   Pleasure Seekers   96
Feminism   99
   Trans-Pacific   99
   All-India   101
   Pan-Islamic   105
Conclusion   109

CHAPTER THREE   THE INSTITUTIONS OF EMPIRE   111
Vignette: Emily Ruete of Zanzibar and Germany   111
Global Christianity   113
   Missions   113
   Converts   120
   Organizations   125
Schools   129
   Early Childhood Education   130
   Curriculum   131
   Teachers   134
   Boarding Schools   136
Achieving Status   139
   Political Culture   139

Citizenship   143
Combatting Hybridity   146
　　Voluntary Segregation   147
　　Legal Segregation   148
　　Separatist Movements   151
Conclusion   154

CHAPTER FOUR　　THE ARTIFACTS OF EMPIRE   157
Vignette: Mata Hari of Indonesia and Paris   157
　　Collectibles   160
　　Furnishings in the Metropole   160
　　Furnishings in the Colonies   162
　　Pets   164
Wearables   168
　　Clothing in the Metropole   168
　　Clothing in the Colonies   170
　　Cosmetics   173
Edibles   176
　　Foods   176
　　Drink   180
Spectacle   183
　　People as Objects of Study   183
　　Circuses, Fairs, and Expositions   186
Western Art   190
　　Painting   190
　　Performing Arts   194
Exotic Erotica   198
　　Postcards   198
　　Ancient Texts   199
　　Scientific Texts   201
Conclusion   203

CHAPTER FIVE　　THE RACE OF EMPIRE   205
Vignette: Olaudah Equiano of Nigeria and London   205
Perfectibility   207
　　Theories of Progress   208
　　Race, Climate, and Evolution   210
Altered Bodies   213
　　Body Marking   213
　　Foot Binding   216
　　Witchcraft   218
　　Yoga   220
Managing Reproduction   223
　　Infanticide   223
　　Abortion   225

Contraception   228
Sterilization   230
Immigration   232
Managing Illness and Health   234
  Treating the Body   235
  Treating the Baby   238
  Treating the Mind   241
Managing Sexuality   243
  Gender Variance   243
  Sexually Transmitted Diseases   247
  Antimasturbation Campaigns   251
  Female Circumcision   253
Conclusion   255

CHAPTER SIX   THE END OF EMPIRE   257
Vignette: Toussaint Louverture of Haiti and France   257
Contained Conflicts   260
  Early Revolutions   261
  Failed Insurrections   262
  Millenarianism   269
Mass Movements   273
  Liberal Nationalism   274
  Marxism   279
  Civil Disobedience   283
Transfers of Power   286
  European Militaries   286
  Japanese-Sponsored Forces   288
  Independence Armies   290
Ending Settler Colonies   291
  British Kenya   292
  French Algeria   293
Postcolonialism?   296
  Non-Alignment   296
  United Nations   298
  Westoxification   300
Conclusion   300

CONCLUSION   303

Glossary   313
Notes   317
Bibliography   361
Credits   381
Index   383

LIST OF MAPS

European Overseas Empires in the Atlantic, c. 1750   xix

Empires and Patterns of World Trade, 1914   xx

European Population Movements, 1750–1914   xxi

Migration Routes from China and India in the Nineteenth Century   xxi

Empire as Playground   xxii

Select Practices of Embodiment   xxiii

European Empires, 1936   xxiv

Resistance and Revolution   xxv

Decolonization in Asia and Africa, 1945–1999   xxvi

ACKNOWLEDGMENTS

This book is dedicated to Judith Zinsser, a dear friend and mentor of over twenty years. She has dared throughout her career to trespass limitations, whether personal or within the field. Her brilliant work, beginning with the magisterial *History of Their Own*, shows all of us how vital interpretive synthesis can be: how it opens the world of scholarship to students and shifts the research field in new directions. Her commitment to women's history, from her early work at the United Nations International School to her presidency of the World History Association, gendered a field that resisted for many years. She then dared to become the world expert on scientist and philosophe Émilie du Châtelet, a subject befitting the maverick that she is. Pursuing an unconventional career path, she modeled for so many students how it is never too late to heed the call of the academy. Experienced in the pleasures and dangers of coauthorship, she also nurtured us through the rough spots. She urged us to undertake this project and offered both tough critique and half of her library to support its unfolding. Mere mortals that we are, neither of us as daring or as genius, we could not write the book that she would, but her insights have truly enhanced our text. In fact, it would not even exist without her example and friendship.

We wish to thank Charles Cavaliere, our editor at Oxford University Press, who grabbed our concept and knew its potential before we did. His enthusiasm for the project never flagged, even when ours did. We are so fortunate to have in Charles that rare breed of editor who is a learned intellect in his own right. All of the staff at Oxford University Press has been a pleasure to work with. Lynn Luecken has been more than patient, creative, and warm. The reviewers of the proposal and of the manuscript reshaped it to be the book that it is today. We especially acknowledge the enthusiasm and close attention of Bonnie Smith. We were exceptionally fortunate to have one of the leading historians of our time take such an interest in this project.

Research and editorial support in our hometown of Asheville shepherded the book through its final stages. We thank Naomi Friedman, a thorough and thoroughly creative development editor; Amanda Glenn-Bradley, a tireless reference librarian who secured obscure materials at the eleventh hour; Nancy Hayes, who patiently processed hundreds of interlibrary loan requests; and Chelsea Beresford, who helped fact-check the final manuscript. Above all, we thank the insights of the many UNCA students who course-tested the manuscript, notably Brooke Weston, Laura Engel, Tammy McDaniel, Andrew Simons, Chloe Gagin, Christopher Cowart, Linnea Conway, and Bryan Smith. Seeing through their eyes, as best we could, made it a better book.

We thank Daniel Pierce, Chair of the History Department at UNCA, for all manner of moral and material support. We were inspired by his model of producing first-rate scholarship despite his many commitments to teaching and service, not to mention his large family. Support from UNCA also included a generous grant from the University Research Council. Scholars who critiqued the project from inception to sendoff included Eric Roubinek, William Spellman, and Alice Weldon. Their diverse knowledge base expanded our thinking in countless directions. We are also grateful for the very many edifying suggestions provided by several outside reviewers commissioned by Oxford University Press. Our thanks to Sandrine Sanos, Texas A & M University; Bonnie G. Smith, Rutgers University; and Victoria Thompson, Arizona State University.

We also thank Ken Banks, an accomplished historian and teacher in his own right, who managed three children when their mother was less available to them, and whose support in the project's later stages was unwavering.

Finally, we thank each other. Before meeting, we had conceptualized similar books but never had the spark to bring them to fruition. The remarkable complementarity of our interests and aptitudes, the passions we shared that we didn't even know about, and the intensity of our first months of collaboration bore miraculous fruit. Oxford University Press was the first and only publisher that we approached within weeks of beginning our collaboration. Our travails notwithstanding, we managed to sustain that passion for three busy years, remarkably short given the scope of the book we have produced and the obstacles we have overcome.

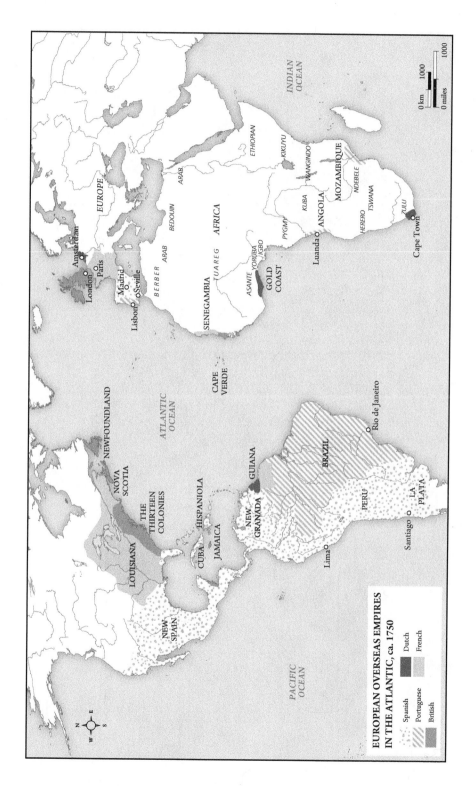

EUROPEAN OVERSEAS EMPIRES
IN THE ATLANTIC, ca. 1750

Spanish · · · · ·   Dutch

Portuguese ////   French

British

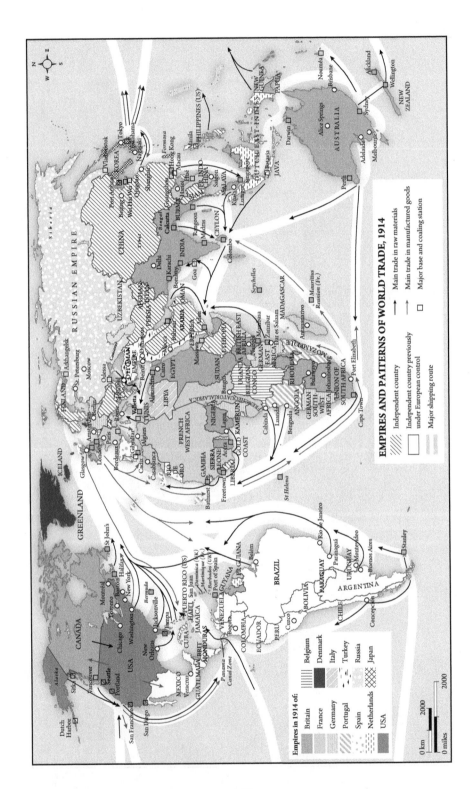

EMPIRES AND PATTERNS OF WORLD TRADE, 1914

Empires in 1914 of:

Britain
France
Germany
Portugal
Spain
Netherlands
USA

Belgium
Denmark
Italy
Turkey
Russia
Japan

Independent country

Independent country previously under European control

Major shipping route

Main trade in raw materials

Main trade in manufactured goods

Major base and coaling station

0 km   2000

0 miles   2000

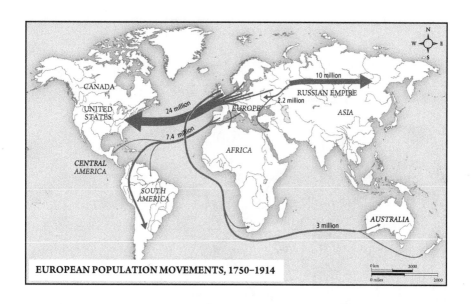

EUROPEAN POPULATION MOVEMENTS, 1750–1914

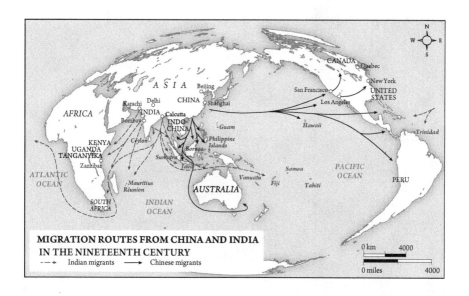

MIGRATION ROUTES FROM CHINA AND INDIA IN THE NINETEENTH CENTURY

- - - → Indian migrants   ⟶ Chinese migrants

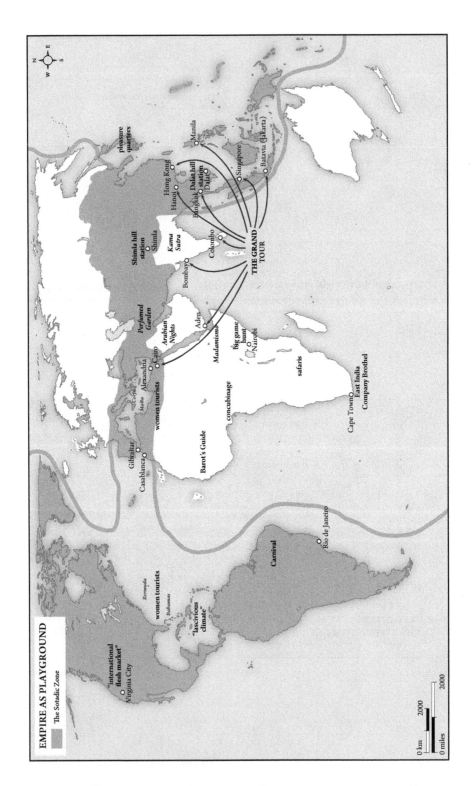

EMPIRE AS PLAYGROUND

■ The Sotadic Zone

"international
flesh market"
Virginia City

women tourists

"lascivious
climate"

Carnival

Rio de Janeiro

Bermuda

Bahamas

Casablanca
Gibraltar
Corfu
Malta
Alexandria

women tourists

Barot's Guide

Perfumed
Garden

Arabian
Nights

Cairo

concubinage

Aden

Madamismo

big game
hunt
Nairobi

safaris

East India
Company Brothel

Cape Town

Shimla hill
station
Shimla

Kama
Sutra

Bombay

Colombo

THE GRAND
TOUR

pleasure
quarters

Hanoi

Hong Kong

Bangkok
Dalat

Dalat hill
station

Singapore

Batavia (Jakarta)

Manila

0 km   2000
0 miles   2000

xx

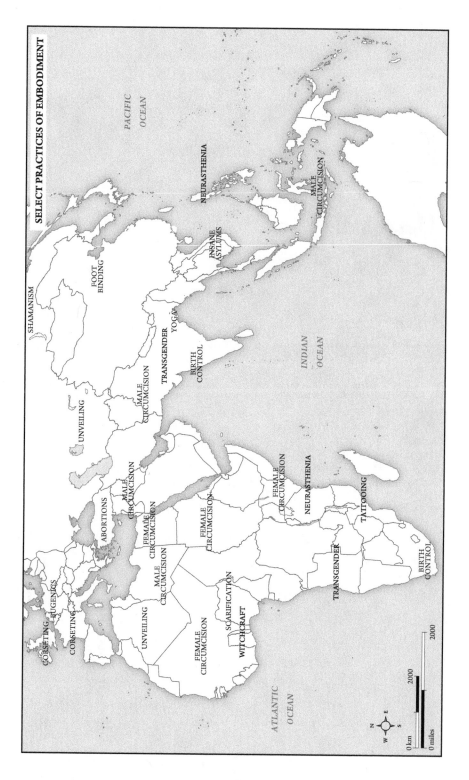

SELECT PRACTICES OF EMBODIMENT

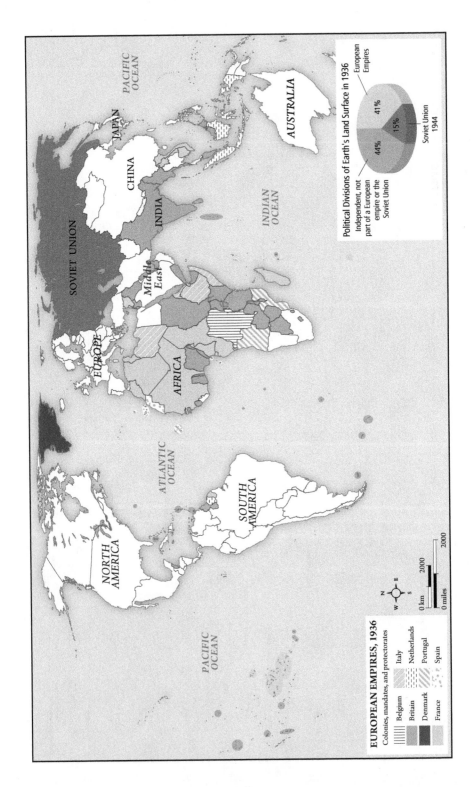

EUROPEAN EMPIRES, 1936

Colonies, mandates, and protectorates

Belgium
Britain
Denmark
France
Italy
Netherlands
Portugal
Spain

Political Divisions of Earth's Land Surface in 1936

European Empires 41%

Independent, not part of a European empire or the Soviet Union 44%

Soviet Union 1944 15%

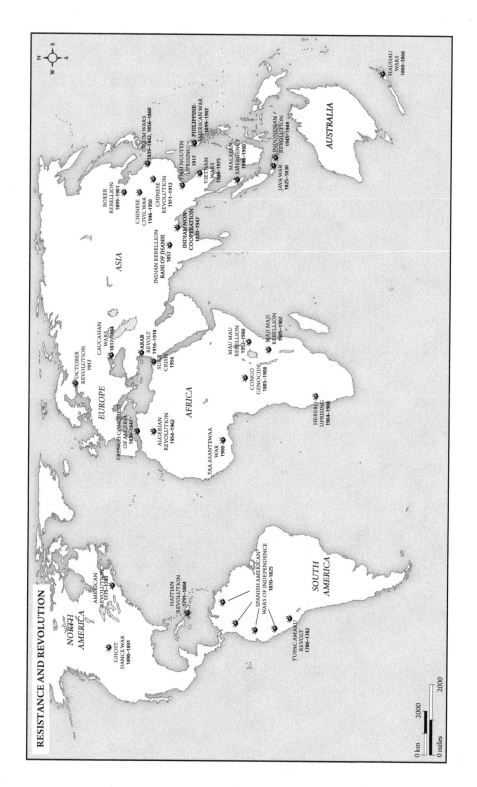

RESISTANCE AND REVOLUTION

NORTH AMERICA

EUROPE

ASIA

AFRICA

SOUTH AMERICA

AUSTRALIA

AMERICAN REVOLUTION 1775–1783

GHOST DANCE WAR 1890–1891

HAITIAN REVOLUTION 1791–1804

SPANISH AMERICAN WARS OF INDEPENDENCE 1810–1825

TUPAC AMARU REVOLT 1780–1782

OCTOBER REVOLUTION 1917

FRENCH CONQUEST OF ALGERIA 1830–1847

ALGERIAN REVOLUTION 1954–1962

CAUCASIAN WARS 1817–1864

ARAB REVOLT 1916–1918

SUEZ CRISIS 1956

YAA ASANTEWAA WAR 1900

CONGO GENOCIDE 1885–1908

MAU MAU REBELLION 1952–1960

MAJI MAJI REBELLION 1905–1907

HERERO UPRISING 1904–1908

BOXER REBELLION 1899–1901

CHINESE CIVIL WAR 1946–1950

CHINESE REVOLUTION 1911–1912

INDIAN REBELLION RANI OF JHANSI 1857

INDIAN NON COOPERATION 1920–1947

OPIUM WARS 1839–1842, 1856–1860

HAI NGUYEN UPRISING 1917

PHILIPPINE AMERICAN WAR 1899–1902

VIETNAM WARS 1946–1975

MALAYAN EMERGENCY 1948–1960

INDONESIAN REVOLUTION 1945–1949

JAVA WAR 1825–1830

HAUHAU WARS 1860–1866

0 km   2000

0 miles   2000

xxiii

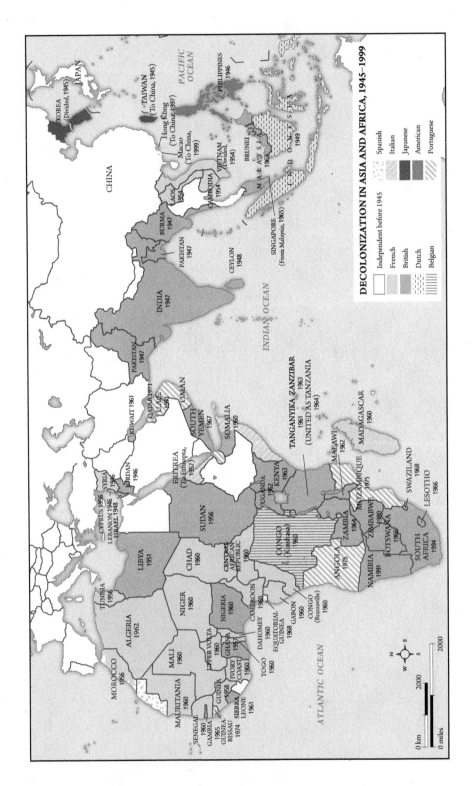

DECOLONIZATION IN ASIA AND AFRICA, 1945–1999

Independent before 1945
French
British
Dutch
Belgian
Spanish
Italian
Japanese
American
Portuguese

PACIFIC OCEAN

JAPAN

KOREA (Divided, 1945)

TAIWAN (To China, 1945)

CHINA

Hong Kong (To China, 1997)
Macao (To China, 1999)

PHILIPPINES 1946

BURMA 1947

LAOS 1954

CAMBODIA 1954

VIETNAM (Divided, 1954)

BRUNEI 1963

I N D O N E S I A 1949

M A L A Y S I A

SINGAPORE (From Malaysia, 1965)

PAKISTAN 1947

CEYLON 1948

INDIA 1947

PAKISTAN 1947

INDIAN OCEAN

QATAR 1971
U.A.E. 1971
OMAN

KUWAIT 1961

SOUTH YEMEN 1967

SOMALIA 1960

JORDAN 1946

ERITREA (To Ethiopia, 1952)

SYRIA 1946
LEBANON 1946
ISRAEL 1948
CYPRUS 1956

UGANDA 1962

KENYA 1963

TANGANYIKA ZANZIBAR 1961 1963 (UNITED AS TANZANIA 1964)

MADAGASCAR 1960

MALAWI 1962

MOZAMBIQUE 1975

SWAZILAND 1968

LESOTHO 1966

SUDAN 1956

LIBYA 1951

CHAD 1960

CENTRAL AFRICAN REPUBLIC 1960

CONGO (Kinshasa) 1960

ZAMBIA 1964

ZIMBABWE 1980

BOTSWANA 1966

NAMIBIA 1991

ANGOLA 1975

SOUTH AFRICA 1994

TUNISIA 1956

ALGERIA 1962

NIGER 1960

NIGERIA 1960

CAMEROON 1960

GABON 1960

CONGO (Brazzaville) 1960

EQUATORIAL GUINEA 1968

MOROCCO 1956

MALI 1960

UPPER VOLTA 1960

GHANA 1957

IVORY COAST 1960

DAHOMEY 1960

TOGO 1960

MAURITANIA 1960

SENEGAL 1960
GAMBIA 1965
GUINEA BISSAU 1974
GUINEA 1958
SIERRA LEONE 1961

ATLANTIC OCEAN

N
W E
S

0 km   2000
0 miles   2000

xxiv

BODIES IN CONTACT— BODIES IN MOTION

Vivid images of bodies in motion, rendered realistic, abstract, or grotesque, invite us into people's experiences of imperialism. Although most of these images were created by Europeans or North Americans, they can be read as more than the representation of passive subjects. An interaction between bodies preceded the product. Those interactions are the subject of this book. To get at them we must read behind the image and against the grain of the interpretation that the maker intended. By representing Europe as a white female, both Moll (Plate 1) and Ducos de la Haille (frontispiece), whose works were nearly 200 years apart, locate power in whiteness yet neutralize that power by personifying it as a woman. Europa represents benevolent imperialism, not manly conquest, and so the world's peoples are attracted to her. But were they? Do we reveal ambivalences when we read against the grain?

These allegorical representations stand in contrast to scenes from real life. Comparing depictions of women and men enables further reading against the grain. Women are differently positioned in the racial hierarchy of the Caribbean (Plate 2), engaged in commerce while free men of color and enslaved men prepare for battle. Toussaint Louverture and Dutty Boukman are portrayed as revolutionary heroes who achieved Haiti's triumphant ousting of the French (Plates 3 and 4). The image of the women reads almost as a snapshot taken in the moment of transaction, whereas the images of the men were depicted afterward by victors telling the story of national greatness. There is even more complexity in a German depiction of the German army's triumph over the Herero of Namibia in 1904 (Plate 5). Without reading against the grain, we simply see the Germans as victors, the way the artist intended. But when we set the image in its context, 1936, we recall that by then Germany had lost World War I, along with all of its colonies, and the Nazis were in power. Why would a defeated people retell a moment of bygone triumph? What did the past triumph of whites over blacks in 1904 mean in 1936? Reading against the grain yields greater insights when we juxtapose images.

We can also read monuments against the grain. The Catholic Cathedral built by the French in Vietnam illustrates the intermingling of cultures at the height of the imperial age. Its modern presence is testament to an imperial power that was both victorious and defeated (Plate 6). Japan, which was never colonized by Europeans, fascinated the Western painters who adopted the artistic techniques of Japanese woodcuts (Plates 7 and 8). Viewing Japanese paintings next to the cathedral in Saigon enables us to see how the conquered Vietnamese influenced Western culture differently from the independent Japanese. *Japonisme* influenced more homely spaces as well. Elites acquired exotic goods to display their worldliness (Plate 9), whereas the Samoan Taupou girl (Plate 10) is herself an exotic good included in an American travelogue. But if we read against the grain, we see her as more than that. She gazes at us with an enigmatic smile. Transactions went both ways, as consumers all over the world bought American products like Egyptian Brown Face Powder (Plate 11). Imperialism itself was marketed in the centennial celebration of the French occupation of Algeria (Plate 12). If we read against the grain, we resist superficial delight in the harmonious whole and notice the underlying tensions. Bodies in contact and bodies in motion attracted consumers to circuses and fairs, including the "Barnum & Bailey Greatest Show on Earth" that created artificial versions of exotic peoples, structures, and animals (Plate 13). Fears about the effects on health of bodies in contact and bodies in motion were also advertised—and lampooned. The exotic yet exhausting tango dance was a product of imperialism, as was the modern ailment of neurasthenia (Plate 14).

Advertisements, allegories, and national mythologies are easier to read than visually obscure images of even more obscure subjects, like Catlin's painting of the Native American Berdache (Plate 15). Yet fascination with sexual minorities marked the Age of Empire to the point where sexual minorities now make it the subject of parody during the Carnival in Rio (Plate 16). When we juxtapose images from very different times and places we read them against the grain of what their makers intended. By contemplating bodies in motion, we glimpse the intimate lives of people during the modern Age of Empire.

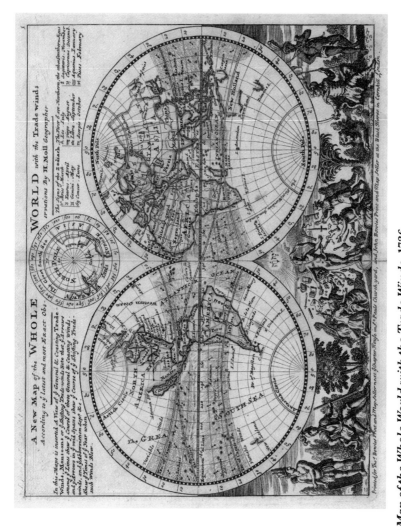

Plate 1. *A New Map of the Whole World with the Trade Winds,* 1736
Mapmakers like Herman Moll (1654–1732) decorated their maps with representatives of the world's peoples paying homage to Europa, represented as a goddess.

Plate 2. Agostino Brunias (1730–1796) *Mulatto Girl*
Multiracial populations in the Caribbean increased in the Age of Empire. Mixed-race women could enjoy privileges and esteem as in this sympathetic depiction by Italian painter Brunias.

TOUSSAINT LOUVERTURE
Chef des Noirs Insurgés de Saint Domingue.
A Paris chez Jean rue Jean de Beauvais N° 10.

Plate 3.   Toussaint Louverture on horseback, engraving
Hero of the successful slave rebellion that ended France's occupation of Haiti in
1804, Toussaint Louverture (1743–1803) inspired freedom fighters everywhere for
over a century.

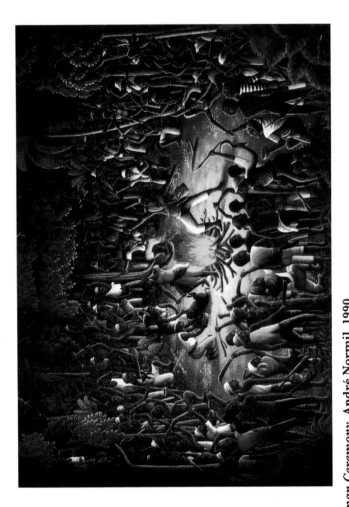

Plate 4. *Bois Caïman Ceremony*, André Normil, 1990
In 1791, voodoo priest Dutty Boukman called on slaves in Haiti to rise up and break their chains during this ceremony. Narratives emphasized the significance of the sacrificial black pig whose bristles conveyed special powers.

Plate 5. *German Troops Fight the Herero,* c. 1904
Painting by Richard Knötel (1857–1914), published in a 1936 book. This nostalgic depiction of the genocidal suppression of the Herero uprising in German Southwest Africa (Namibia) circulated in 1936 after Germany had lost its colonies.

Plate 6.   Notre Dame Basilica, Saigon
European governments commissioned structures that combined European and local
elements, such as this Catholic cathedral in Vietnam.

Plate 7.   Vincent Van Gogh (1853–1890), Enchantillon, 1887
European masters revolutionized their genre due to the influence of Japanese techniques and themes.

Plate 8. Helen Hyde (1868–1919), *Blossom Time in Tokyo,* **1914**
American artists like Helen Hyde used Japanese techniques like the woodblock print
to depict nostalgic scenes of traditional Japanese festivals.

Plate 9.   "The New Necklace," William McGregor Paxton, 1910
European and North American elites adopted Eastern fashions and furnishings,
including wallpaper with Japanese motifs.

Plate 10. *Samoan Taupou Girl,* **1896**
Travelers populated their accounts with images of the people they encountered. This young Samoan woman is shown in traditional dress, and in her full humanity, not just as an object.

Alluring Perfection

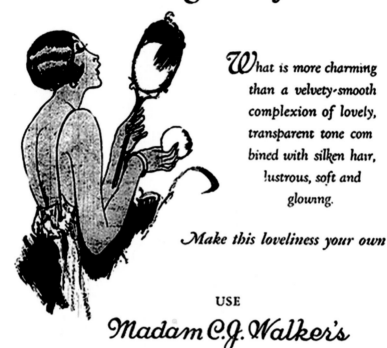

What is more charming than a velvety-smooth complexion of lovely, transparent tone combined with silken hair, lustrous, soft and glowing.

Make this loveliness your own

USE

Madam C. J. Walker's

EGYPTIAN BROWN FACE POWDER

GLOSSINE

Clinging, invisible and adorably perfumed. Imparts an olive tint to fair complexions and harmonizes bewitchingly with the darker skins. For sale by Walker agents everywhere.

Oils and softens dry, brittle hair. Imparts a rich, healthy lustre. In dispensable for bobbed or long hair and unsurpassed in the opinion of social leaders and well groomed gentlemen. For sale by Walker agents and good drug stores.

Plate 11.   Egyptian Brown Face Powder
African American entrepreneur Madam C. J. Walker (1867–1919) marketed cosmetics worldwide, including Egyptian brown face powder to counter the trend in skin lightening.

Plate 12.   Celebrating the centennial of France's occupation of Algeria
Commemorating 100 years of its occupation of Algeria, this French poster celebrates
the fusion of cultures, typical of European arrogance during its imperial apex.

Plate 13.   Barnum & Bailey, *Realistic Jungle Menagerie*
Bringing together exotic people, plants, and animals in artificial environments, the
Barnum & Bailey shows substituted clichés and entertainment for meaningful cul-
tural exchange.

Plate 14.   Le Tango Neurasthenique, 1900
Syncretic forms of sport and leisure derived from exotic and hot climates led to fears
about their enfeebling effects in this satirical depiction.

Plate 15.   George Catlin (1796–1872) *Dance to the Berdache*
Anthropologists in North America chronicled the gender diversity of indigenous
Americans. Among the Plains Indians, two-spirit people were thought to be both
male and female.

Plate 16.   Rio Carnival 2012, Queen's Diamond Jubilee
Former subjects of the British Empire parody the Age of Empire in a contemporary
Rio Carnival.

Introduction

A woman, almost saintly, dispenses justice (or is it healing?) to other women. She is draped in white and red, fully clothed and diminutive, quite white, while the others are mostly brown, nude, and buxom. Almost lost in a riot of color and activity, black women peek out from lush greenery. The sailing ships, the ocean, and the doves overhead set the stage. Except for a small skyscraper in one corner, the image is one of sexualized primitivity. Only off to the side do men appear, clothed in their ethnic costumes. Rather than bodies on display, they are engaged in their various tasks, looking away from the women and from the viewer. Every-where in evidence are "whites of an olive tint and yellows of a pale visage, blacks with skin of shining ebony, lemon Orientals . . . all the races, all the languages, all the costumes, all the vocations. And over this crowd from Babel, swarming and guttural, over the palaces and the huts in the billowing Vincennes greenery, the tricolor flag snaps in the pale sky, the symbol of the unity of the French Colonial Empire."[1] Journalists thus rhapsodized the opening of the Colonial Exposition of 1931 in Paris's Bois de Vincennes. Pierre Ducos de la Haille (1889–1972) painted the scene at the entry to the Palais de la Porte Dorée, the expo's only permanent building. Spread across three floor-to-ceiling frescoes, Haille titled the piece *France Offering the Dove of Peace to Five Continents* (see frontispiece).

It is the historian's privilege and burden to note the irony of that confidence, so arrogantly expressed not even a generation after the truly global blood bath of World War I, not even a generation before the European empires imploded. *Intimate Empires* offers an interpretive synthesis of recent scholarship on inter-sections between gender, race, and empire from the mid-eighteenth to the mid-twentieth centuries. It attempts to untangle the embodied experiences and representations of people all over the world in the era of Europe's global domi-nance. Studies of intimate experiences complicate narratives of imperialism that have traditionally revolved around political and economic developments and thus obscured the ways in which ordinary people ignored, survived, co-opted, or even subverted imperialists and their institutions. Ducos de la Haille's portrayal

1

of the continents of the world as voluptuous women, appropriately racialized, for larger-than-life public display, reminds us of the centrality of the body to the imperial project. We discuss the development and coproduction of metropolitan and colonial identities alike, incorporating art, children's literature, cookbooks, and sport in addition to migration, missionary work, and legal trials. Whether ravaged by disease, wearing imported cottons, or physically engaged—as lovers, coworkers, or prisoners of war—bodies experienced intersecting cultures viscerally and literally. In one of the frescoes, a nun bandages a boy's wound; in another, a doctor administers vaccine. The soothing image of benevolent imperialism was meant to paper over the memory of violent conflict. A frieze at the entrance to the pavilion assured visitors of France's positive influence in the world. The caption below the frieze depicted French conquests as salvation: salvation of Indochina and North Africa from pirates, and of the rest of their African holdings, from extinction. Placing the caption below fleshy and vibrant bodies, the organizers educated the public by tantalizing them. The very familiarity, even intimacy, of bodily experience across cultures and centuries renders the cold abstractions of imperialism tender and human even as they provoke feelings of disgust and grief triggered by enormous suffering.

In a book of this length, we cannot possibly do justice to the complexities of modern identity formations, but we can move them from the periphery to the center. Organized thematically, each of the six chapters moves from the mid-eighteenth through the mid-twentieth centuries to unfold an aspect of identity. Masculinity as a global construct, produced in tandem with racial hierarchies, is the subject of Chapter 1. European men ushered in imperial relations when they traversed the globe in the modern era. Culturally specific forms of masculinity came into conflict with each other whether on the beaches of Hawaii or the battlefields of World War I. Men engaged with men in the Age of Empire but they also engaged with women. Their encounters with native women spark the shift to Chapter 2 in which we explore modern feminine identities, from European norms through the myriad ways that women everywhere empowered themselves and suffered in the face of increasingly militant and racist patriarchal structures in colony and metropole. Women crafted a range of responses to imperial constraints and opportunities, often in the sphere of intimate life which included interracial sex. The proliferation of such hybrid identities is the subject of Chapter 3, including mixed-race people and people whose lives were structured by imperial institutions, including citizenship laws, proselytization, education, and, more broadly still, the adoption and adaptation of Western modernity by whole societies. In Chapter 4, we focus on material culture and performance because hybridity is perhaps most visually evident in the artifacts of empire, from the homely culture of cookery and decoration through mass-produced fashions and cosmetics to the avant-garde culture of art and erotica. Some cultural practices transformed the body itself. These are the subject of Chapter 5 in which we contrast different forms of managing the racialized body, from tattoos to circumcision, through birth control and campaigns to restore bodily integrity such as the transnational movement to end Chinese foot binding. In each case, body discipline was expected of colonizers and colonized alike through the imposition of regimens that were healthful, oppressive or deadly. These regimens occasionally provoked massive resistance. In Chapter 6, we describe the dismantling of European empires through several stages: contained conflicts punctured every empire during the eighteenth and nineteenth centuries; the interwar years saw the growth of mass movements and a collective effort to achieve self-determination; by World War II most empires entered two decades of successful transfers of power, some peaceful, many violent. All pivoted on gender: the militant muscularity of armed anticolonial movements contrasted with the asexual asceticism of passive resistance. We conclude that contestations over the body are one of the most enduring legacies of the Age of Empire. Whether in the United Nations Universal Declaration of Human Rights or in global consumer culture, the battles continue over freedom of gender and sexual expression and disparities in health and wealth between the former imperialist nations and their former colonies.

IMPERIALISM: AN OVERVIEW

The closely related terms "imperialism" and "colonialism" are often used interchangeably. Colonialism refers to when one nation conquers another and exercises direct rule over the inhabitants of the conquered territory. Colonies include settler populations that immigrate to the colony, some unwillingly as slaves or convicts, and indigenous peoples ruled by colonial officials appointed by the conquering nation. [Imperialism refers to the process of creating an empire by asserting political, social, cultural, and economic domination over subjugated peoples.] Imperial nations project power not only through formal sovereignty over conquered regions but also through informal mechanisms of military, economic, or political domination of other nations on a regional or a global scale. Imperialism can be thought of as the ideology of empire whereas colonialism can be thought of as the practice of empire, with a dynamic interaction between the two. In Ducos de la Haille's fresco, the activity of colonists, such as administering vaccine, signifies colonialism, whereas the depiction of continents as women signifies imperialism.

The era of modern imperialism differs from previous eras because of the development of mercantilism and, later, capitalism. Figure I.1 illustrates the use of gender, race, and empire to promote European economic interests, always the primary incentive for establishing colonies. Competition for colonies in the early modern world pitted seaborne empires against each other, especially the Spanish, French, and the British who competed for dominance in the Americas. Their economies depended on securing access to resources and markets, and therefore access to the sea. Their rivalry erupted in the Seven Years War (1756–1763), a war on four continents, which resulted in the defeat of the French in North America. The Seven Years War also led to the American Revolution when the French sought

THE FORMULA OF BRITISH CONQUEST

PEAR'S SOAP IS THE BEST

Figure I.1 Advertising in and of Africa

Commercial interests dominated imperial exchange, capitalizing on popular colonial images to generate revenue.

revenge by supporting American colonists in their revolt against England. The United States became a new Western imperial power in its own right, its westward expansion and eventual overseas projects similar to the European empires of the nineteenth and twentieth centuries. Inspired by the American Revolution, Latin American Revolutions in the early nineteenth century ended the Spanish Empire while the Portuguese Empire shifted away from the Americas to its African holdings of Angola and Mozambique. The British loss of the thirteen colonies was compensated for by its westward expansion in Canada and its deepening involvement in India. At the end of the Napoleonic Wars in 1815, Europeans adhered to a balance-of-power strategy in diplomatic affairs, determined to prevent the dominance of any one country. Colonies were central to this strategy. Territorial gain by one country was countered with comparable gains by rivals. And so the century proceeded through the colonization of most of Africa, predominantly by the French and the British, but joined by smaller or newer countries including Italy, Belgium, and Germany. In fact, Chancellor Otto von Bismarck (1815–1898), the Prussian leader of the newly united Germany, was determined to rapidly establish a German global empire to compete for superpower status with France and Britain. He organized the Berlin Conference of 1884–1885, which sparked the "Scramble for Africa." Fourteen European nations and the United States divided up the parts of Africa that were not already under colonial rule. Within a decade of the meeting, the only remaining independent nation was Ethiopia, which defeated Italy in 1896 with the help of Russia and France. Italy would avenge this affront in 1936.

Deepening encroachment into China, whose own land-based empire was in decline, contrasted with the more direct colonization of Southeast Asia, with only Siam (Thailand) maintaining its independence. In the early twentieth century, Japan became a modern empire, expanding into Korea and China, threatening French control of Indochina, and impeding Russian ambitions in Asia. Japan's swift rise, along with Germany's, upset the global balance of power, ultimately contributing to the outbreak of both World Wars. Meanwhile, defeat by the Japanese checked Russia's expansion until the Russian Revolution of 1917, which ended the reign of the tsars and established the Soviet Union.

Like the Qing Empire in China, the Ottoman Empire entered a state of decline in the nineteenth century. From its peak in the eighteenth century as a Mediterranean power controlling much of North Africa and the Middle East, the Ottoman Empire lost province after province to the French and the British in the nineteenth century. Following its collapse after its defeat in World War I, a scramble for territories in the oil-rich Middle East ensued as France and Britain secured areas of influence under the oversight of the newly created League of Nations. But Germany, Italy, and Japan were similarly determined to continue to expand their empires during the 1930s, eventually leading to World War II.

These power plays between and within empires resulted in a very uneven distribution of influence. In 1800, 35 percent of the world's peoples lived in areas controlled by Europeans. This figure rose to 85 percent by 1914. The rapid spread of the modern empires is often attributed to economic motives for imperialism: demand for new sources of raw materials and new markets, the use of colonies for strategic advantage, and the containment of rivals. Yet, more pertinent to this book is another set of motives for European expansion characterized as liberal imperialism. Originating in Enlightenment ideas of progress, liberal imperialists believed that the best fruits of European civilization needed to be shared with "primitive" peoples still living in "darkness." The Marquis de Condorcet (1743–1794) was its most eloquent spokesman. "The sun will shine only on free men who know no other master but their reason," he declared, as the spread of Enlightenment would eventually bring freedom to all.[2] He believed that progress through science would eradicate disease and perhaps even mortality itself. He argued education would ultimately triumph over ignorance, superstition, and prejudice, even war. Nineteenth-century liberals sought to bring about his predictions by using imperialism not to subjugate but to liberate through vaccines, literacy, and women's rights. Many Christians, some of them liberal, were among the first to establish schools and hospitals, but they also brought the gospel, not part of Condorcet's very secular vision. Missionaries preached the benefits of European civilization more persuasively than mining companies. They occasionally became apologists for subjugation, but their commitment to justice and Christian brotherhood also antagonized private companies and governments when missionaries exposed abuse of native peoples. Liberals across the globe broadly agreed on a program of reform based on scientific knowledge, the elimination of prejudice, and steadily expanding rights, but it depended on a limited conception of the citizen as a rights-bearing individual whose pursuit of freedom might conflict with tradition.

In Britain, traditional imperialists who saw no need to justify their pursuit of strategic advantage and economic gain called liberal imperialists "limps," but liberals never saw their agenda as a weaker version of conventional imperialism. It was not merely cover for economic exploitation or for military conquest, although the coincidence of benign literacy campaigns with ruthless resource extraction sometimes made it difficult to tell the difference. Underlying both justifications for imperialism was a belief that colonized people were lacking and therefore unable to transition to modernity without European intervention. By the late nineteenth century, some colonized elites, trained in European universities, embraced this concept and adapted liberalism to more directly address local issues such as polygamy or the caste system. They also used it to indict the hypocrisy of being deprived of the right to national self-determination by European liberal imperialists. The willingness by some colonized elites to appropriate Western institutions and culture, to fashion something new and hybrid out of them, suggests that they too learned to see their own cultures as deficient but that they also might wield the master's tools to bring down the master's house.[3] This further complicates the binary of colonizer and colonized and illustrates how colonized people carved out a range of possible encounters with European liberalism.

COVERAGE

Because their rivalry drove international developments in the period under study, and because they controlled the largest and most diverse empires, we analyze the French and British Empires more extensively than others. Historians and postcolonial writers of the British Empire have been at the forefront of the study of intimate life, producing a rich and varied literature for every region Britain controlled: primarily India, but also much of Africa, the Caribbean, and outposts in China and the Pacific. The availability of primary sources in English also contributes to historians' emphasis on the British Empire. Yet because our aim is to describe modern identity formation as a feature of world history at the roots of globalization, we include other major European empires where relevant: the Dutch especially, followed by the German and Belgian, and to a lesser degree the empires of Spain, Portugal, and Italy. Moreover, most scholars and activists identify the United States as a Western empire whose contours resemble those of the European empires. Indeed, by including America in his fresco (the blond woman beside a skyscraper) Ducos de la Haille made this point while attracting the ire of the expo organizers who charged him with representing French greatness and not Western civilization in general. Due to space limitations, we could not explore the United States in depth, but we compare and contrast specific US case studies where applicable. In Figure I.2, for example, American philanthropic societies undertake a humanitarian role in the world. Finally, although we do not aim to write a comprehensive survey of world empires, we draw from the Russian, Japanese, and Ottoman Empires to illustrate broader points where appropriate. In each of them an influential liberal elite developed who urged the adoption of Western ideas or institutions, enabling us to illustrate the global reach and force of European imperialism beyond the countries that it directly occupied.

A range of possibilities for inclusion emerged from the form and stage of imperialism. Colonial settlement differed from military occupation, the French

Empire differed from the Dutch Empire, and so on. Although a book of this length cannot delve into all of these variations, we suggest points of contact and overarching trajectories that enable a comparative approach. In settler colonies, by example, interracial relationships tended to be more limited and communities more segregated. Settlers established durable European institutions seeking to transplant their homelands and preempt the formation of hybrid forms of cultural expression and identity. The reach of the state is another central factor distinguishing forms of empire. In the early stages of empire, where state institutions were weak or absent and corporations were small, traders and missionaries integrated themselves into local communities. Only after mixed-race populations developed and more officials and settlers arrived did this general pattern give way to intolerance. Some empires limited access to citizenship, but the more liberal of them gradually erased racial disqualifications. On the other hand, the relative scarcity of state institutions and missions meant that the rapacious practices of private companies remained unchecked. Some colonies were ruled directly, others indirectly, although most maintained some form of local organization to stabilize imperial rule. Ideologies of empire differed significantly. Some nations undertook a civilizing mission to fully convert colonized people, at least elites, to Western modernity. Others had more limited aims, usually resource extraction or diplomatic advantage. These ideologies changed over time and followed a general trajectory toward secularism much like what took place in Europe itself.

Figure I.2 International Humanitarian Relief
American charitable organizations raised funds to contribute relief to the victims of the Armenian genocide at the end of World War I.

Simplifying complexity is the risky business of textbooks. In a text of this length, we paint with broad brush strokes. We trust that readers have enough familiarity with world history to understand that unique, particular, and local conditions *always* undermine generalizations but seldom to a lethal degree. And so we still make them. We have noted differences where they are crucial but organized the material thematically, to discern broad trends or patterns in intimate relations that enable comparison and tentative conclusions. *Intimate Empires* is an interpretive synthesis. We acknowledge that it is one of many possible interpretations based on a broad but ultimately subjective sampling of the latest scholarship. In our commitment to feature that scholarship, we generally illustrate well-known topics with less-well-known examples.

HISTORIOGRAPHY

In the last two decades, studies of modern imperialism have offered a more sustained consideration of gender and sexuality. Indeed, this book could not have been written otherwise. Historians of empire now study personal life, including sexual, family, and labor relations. Moreover, some engage feminist, postcolonial, queer, and disability theory to explain identity formation at the level of the body itself, revealing how expressions of embodied difference were produced by imperialism. Foundational to these approaches is the work of French philosopher Michel Foucault (1926–1984) who excavated the roots of modernity in eighteenth-century discourses on madness and sexuality.[4] His work has sparked generations of scholarship, much of it extending or modifying his conclusions, but his central insights remain compelling: that power is productive rather than repressive of identity and that the body is the site of knowledge production. This definition of power restores agency to those normally seen as victims while also pointing to the subtler forms of oppression that occur at the level of the body itself. Although Foucault did not extend his analysis explicitly to imperialism, others did so. In *Race and the Education of Desire: Foucault's* History of Sexuality *and the Colonial Order of Things* (1995), Ann Laura Stoler identified the colonial family, especially its intimate relations with local servants, as the site where knowledge about bodies, race, and gender intermingled.[5] Following Foucault, she argued that power emanates from multiple locations including the bodies of Dutch children and Indonesian nannies. One of her interview subjects, Ibu Rubi, described how nannies were not supposed to hold children because "later they'd smell of [our] sweat. . . . The sweat of Javanese is different you know."[6] Rubi likewise found Dutch sweat offensive "cause they eat butter, milk, cheese."[7] Yet servants did hold children, and colonial realities made the enforcement of such prohibitions all but impossible.

Meanwhile, some women's historians focused on restoring influential women to imperial history. For example, Flora Shaw, Lady Lugard (1852–1929) is now properly credited with coining the name "Nigeria" as well as working behind the scenes to prevent scandals in British West Africa. Helen Callaway and Dorothy Helly recount Shaw's story in *Western Women and Imperialism: Complicity and Resistance* (1992), edited by Nupur Chaudhuri and Margaret Strobel.[8] This volume introduced a now classic collection of essays mainly focused on European and North American women's activities overseas, including nurses, missionaries, travelers, activists, and spies. The essays often considered the degree to which women supported or challenged imperialism. Many studies followed, with some more expressly addressing issues of gendered embodiment. Nancy Rose Hunt explored the intersection of race, gender, and body in the intimate sphere in *A Colonial Lexicon: Of Birth Ritual, Medicalization, and Mobility in the Congo* (1999).[9] Her research on the collision between Belgian and Congolese women over breastfeeding demonstrates how differing racial constructions led to culturally specific forms of femininity. Belgians advocated scientific childrearing practices, like early weaning, to facilitate early individuation, while Congolese families insisted, "We can't let the child cry like the whites."[10]

While these studies considered gender broadly, their subjects were still primarily women. Indeed, if the Paris frescoes are typical, the obsession with sexualized native women justifies this focus. On the other hand, their nakedness before the male gaze invites comparable scrutiny of imperial masculinity. Adventurers and explorers have long populated traditional histories of European empire, but historians only recently began to focus more study on their sex lives and gendered identities. Ronald Hyam broke new ground with his publication *Empire and Sexuality: The British Experience* (1990), covering the British Empire in the nineteenth and twentieth centuries.[11] He alleged that the sexual desires and frustrations of powerful British men influenced colonial policy. As much as straight men, gay Europeans fashioned imperial identities for greater freedom. Robert Aldrich's *Colonialism and Homosexuality* (2003) identified the colonies as spaces that provide opportunity for Europe's sexual minorities to explore their identities.[12] Exploring opaque sources for clues, he argued that empire could serve as "playground" not just for straight men. Moving to a study of colonial masculinity, Mrinalini Sinha published *Colonial Masculinity: The 'Manly Englishman' and the 'Effeminate Bengali' in the Late Nineteenth Century* (1995), the subtitle indicating how these masculinities produced one another.[13] She traced the intersections between race and gender in a series of controversies in late-nineteenth-century India. Debates over child marriage and polygamy were as much about masculinity as femininity. Indian and British men and women used the thriving Indian press to debate imperial politics when proposed legislation threatened to disrupt intimate relations. Central to these debates was the image of the helpless Indian woman who needed rescue from decadent Indian men by British guardians, both male and female. That the "effeminate" Bengali male could also be predatory shows the incoherence of orientalist clichés.

Sinha applied the insights of Edward Said who theorized that Europeans produced knowledge about the "Orient" as a way of defining themselves. Clearly Ducos de la Haille's frescoes tell us more about French views of themselves than about the subjects of their gaze. In his now classic work *Orientalism* (1978), Said demonstrated how early European orientalists, enamored of exotic Middle Eastern and Asian cultures, reduced complexity to cliché in their massive scholarly works.[14] From reverence of otherworldly Hindu Brahmins to voyeuristic interest in the supposedly hypersexual masters of the harem and their lascivious concubines, these racial caricatures were thoroughly gendered. In this process, Europeans constructed gendered notions of race. Besides Arabs and Asians, Europeans depicted Pacific peoples as exotic "others" when they began to theorize that human—and gender—difference derived from climate variation. Thus, European ideas about race developed in tandem with European imperialism.

Non-Europeans contested those ideas throughout the Age of Empire and offered critiques of whiteness. In 1920, African American historian and activist W. E. B. Du Bois (1868–1963) was among the first to describe that relationship when he observed "whiteness is the ownership of the earth."[15] He was also one of the first critics to pivot from reflections on his own experience of being a racialized other to a sustained analysis of the impact of imperialism on identity. A later generation of critics in Europe's former colonies reflected on their diverse experiences under imperialism. Scholars such as Gayatri Spivak and Homi Bhabha focused on intermediate identities, racial melancholia, and belonging.[16] Collectively, the work of dozens of postcolonial authors and filmmakers has influenced the writing of imperial histories because they offered an indispensable vocabulary and interpretive framework for accessing the perspectives of people typically absent from the historical archive. They carved out a space for the "subaltern" to speak, some openly condemning imperial rule, but most expressing some degree of ambivalence. Indeed, Bhabha theorized specifically about ambivalence in *The Location of Culture* (1994).[17] He wrote about the mimic man whose performance of "Europeanness" both allures and frightens the colonialist. The subaltern experiences ambivalence in his simultaneous attraction to and revulsion for the colonizer.

Characterized by such ambivalence, mimicry, and hybridity, subaltern experience is the result of cultural contacts at the level of the body. Even the most privileged colonized people internalized the Westerner as an intimate stranger, simultaneously a target of love and hate according to Ashis Nandy in *The Intimate Enemy: Loss and Recovery of Self under Colonialism* (1983).[18] Because it is lodged in the mind, the West can be seen as an uninvited guest at weddings and funerals, in all of the most private and public rites of passage. In *Fantasia: An Algerian Cavalcade* (1985), Algerian author and filmmaker Assia Djebar described her ambivalence toward the French and their language, which brought liberation from the patriarchal Muslim family but also the internal colonization of the mind. "Speaking of oneself in a language other than that of the elders is indeed to unveil oneself, not only to emerge from childhood but to leave it, never to return. Such incidental unveiling is tantamount to stripping oneself naked."[19] Writing in French, which she called the stepmother tongue, seemed a betrayal and yet also a fulfillment as she chronicled enemy rule in the enemy language. Uncovering the subtler forms of racism that structured their lives, postcolonial scholars also variously celebrated or condemned the degree to which transcultural routes supplanted traditional roots. Hybridity might become a hated thing, or it might be cause for celebration, especially when it is a springboard to a new kind of cosmopolitanism. Although the purpose of this text precludes sustained treatment of postcolonial theory, we draw on their insights and experiences.

LEGACY OF EMPIRE

The reverberation of these empires in intimate life is still evident today: three-fifths of the world's population live in areas once governed by Europeans, and, despite the small size of Britain, English is the most widely spoken language in the world after Mandarin, the principal language of vast China. But the influence of imperialism has more subtle and deeper routes: population transfers, consumer culture, and international activism were cause and consequence of the spread of European influence. It underpins contemporary globalization and contributes to instability in many parts of the world. It finds expression in world music and film, in the global popularity of soccer, and in the successes of human rights campaigns at the United Nations. In short, to understand the world of the twenty-first century, one must go back to the world of the eighteenth century. Today, when we watch Bollywood films or protest rape camps in Congo, we are reminded of the centrality of the body in colonial and postcolonial realities alike.

ONE

THE GENDER OF EMPIRE
Masculinities

James Cook of Britain and the Pacific

[English sailors] had taken into their heads that the Natives of this Island were sodomites. This opinion they grounded on one of the Natives endeavouring to entice certain of our People into the Woods for a purpose I need not mention . . . [Yet] no person had been attempted who had not either a softness in his features, or whose employment it was to Carry bundles of one kind or other which is the Office of their own Women.

—William Wales, journal entry, August 13, 1774

For William Wales (1734–1798), the lead astronomer on the Second Voyage to the Pacific helmed by Captain James Cook (1728–1779), the social signals of manhood and of sexual availability expressed by the Melanesian natives of Vanuatu differed greatly from those of his fellow British sailors. From 1768 until his death in Hawaii in 1779, Cook led three voyages into the Pacific, opening a new frontier to British expansion and charting a new course for the so-called civilizing mission of empire. In Vanuatu society, carrying bundles was women's work; so, men who did such tasks, particularly young single men in service to other men, were viewed as transgender or sexually receptive. Wales put this observation to the test, playing a rather cruel joke on a young British sailor: "The Man who carried Mr. Forster's Plant Bag had . . . been two or three times attempted, and he happening to go into the Bushes on some occasion or other . . . I pointed it out to the Natives who sat round us, with a sort of sly look & significant action . . . on which two of them Jump'd up and were following him with great glee."[1]

Pacific exploration in the Age of Empire resulted in first encounters between very different cultures. These encounters illustrate how manhood is defined by the social roles that men are expected to perform in a given culture. Mr. Forster's assistant received sexual advances from Vanuatu men because his tasks as a junior

British sailor were those of a woman in Vanuatu culture. Yet the incident also re-veals how gestures, signals, and attitudes may cross cultural bounds. "Some of our Party bursting out into a laugh . . . called out Erramange! Erramange! (It's a Man! It's a Man!) on which the others returned, very much abashed on the Occasion."[2] In this case, the British sailors were able to communicate that the junior sailor was in fact not sexually available to other men. Although the roles that a man must per-form to show he is a real man vary from one culture to the next, they tend to have common themes that converge when men from different cultures are brought to-gether, often producing a new hybrid set of masculine norms.

In this chapter, we explore the production of modern masculinities during the Age of Empire. Although people are conditioned to regard their gender as visceral and innate, it operates more as an ideology formed by the cultural images, myths, discourses, and practices that define manhood and womanhood in a given society.[3] Four key developments during the Age of Empire shaped the social constructs that defined masculine norms in the modern West—and that were variously adopted or rejected by men in the non-Western world.[4] First, the rise of secular culture rede-fined masculinity as a character trait marked by rationality, with Western civiliza-tion seen as the bearer of reason to a less civilized world. Second, empires were forged by conquest carried out by a certain class of single men, mostly soldiers drawn from the middle and lower classes whose masculine values often clashed with those of conquered native men. The victors then gained the privilege of char-acterizing the masculinity of those subjected to their rule, at least until the success-ful liberation movements that brought the Age of Empire to a close. Third, the economics of empire produced a homogenizing ethic of capitalist masculinity in the metropolitan centers, including a division of roles for men and women into sepa-rate spheres. This close association between explorer masculinity and capitalist economics can be seen in Figure 1.1. The economics of empire also produced new forms of masculinity in colonial spaces, most significantly through the institu-tion of slavery and in the mass migration of settlers and workers. Finally, Euro-pean wars tied to imperial rivalries turned martial prowess and individual valor into character traits available to all men, whereas before they had generally been reserved for a more narrow social elite.

Europeans ranked the world's men on a scale of masculine to feminine, belong-ing to warlike martial races or to docile non-martial races. Joseph Banks (1743–1820), the senior naturalist on the First Voyage (1768–1771), wrote of the crew's great curiosity to meet the natives of Africa's southern Cape region during a stopover in 1771. "The Hottentots, so frequently spoken of by travellers, . . . are generally represented as the outcast of the human species, a race whose intellectual faculties are so little superior to those of beasts, that some have been inclined to suppose them more nearly related to baboons than to men."[5] In 1780, William Hodges (1744–1797), the official painter of the Second Voyage (1772–1775), traveled to India and recorded his impression of native men in the narrative of his journey. "They are delicately framed, their hands in particular are more like those of tender

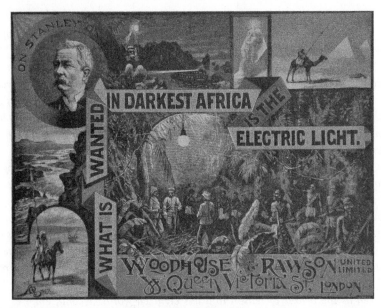

Figure 1.1. "Electricity for Darkest Africa"
The figure of the famous Henry Morton Stanley was used to promote a global vision
of Western progress and products symbolized by electric light.

*females. . . . Correspondent to this delicacy of appearance are their manners, mild,
tranquil, and sedulously attentive."*[6] *Such portrayals of the world's men created a
master narrative of empire, one designed to place the European man in a superior
position and to thereby justify the so-called civilizing mission of empire. There were
of course variations between empires and certainly individual exceptions. Indeed,
Banks was unconvinced about the alleged low intellect of the Hottentots, noting
that almost all of them spoke fluent Dutch, whereas local Dutch settlers were
unable to master the native Khoikhoi language. The actual practice of empire often
undermined and contradicted the narrow stereotypes of race and gender.*

INTERRACIAL SEX

White men engaged in a wide range of relations with native peoples after first
contact. As Captain Cook's crew described it, first contacts were often sexual. In
the many accounts of their voyages, an image emerges of "Empire as Playground."
Publication of their travel writings spread this image but also spread stereotypes.
Men "Taming the Frontiers" of empire had a similar experience until missionaries, governments, and settlers began to reconstruct European family norms in
the colonies, sometimes even with local women. But for men seeking to have
sexual relations with other men, "Transgressing Boundaries," the colonies provided opportunities for both experimentation and durable relationships.

Empire as Playground

Access to local men and women varied greatly from one culture to the next. European reactions to that access also varied. Local circumstances and individual personalities therefore resulted in a range of experiences that undermine generalities in much the same way that they subtly undermined imperialism.

James Cook was the paragon of a new type of British national hero, the enlightened explorer who merged science with adventure and manly action with sensible restraint.[7] By contrast, the common British seamen who sailed with Cook into Tahiti's Botany Bay were a hard lot by any measure. George Forster (1754–1794), the senior naturalist on the HMS *Resolution* during the First Voyage, constantly remarked about the crew's excesses: their swearing, drinking, violence, sexual appetites, and "inhuman propensity to destroy the poor harmless people of the South Seas."[8] Their rite of passage was the lash, which "made the man" aboard the long ocean voyages, earning him a badge of honor among crewmates if he took his whipping with stoic manly spirit.[9] Any behavior deemed unmanly or effeminate was antithetical to the homosociality of life aboard the ship, and sexual urges were most disruptive in a confined setting where men bunked together for years at a time.[10] The norm of restrained manliness aboard the ship met its opposite when the ship made landfall. In Tahiti, crew members were shocked at the open sexuality of natives who wished to consummate an alliance via public sexual intercourse between native women and British sailors.

The three-month layover of Cook's crew in Tahiti was marked by a frenetic sexual and material commerce. For the British, this was a traffic in women, whom they regarded as insatiable nymphs, practically demanding sexual favors in exchange for iron trinkets. For the Tahitians, this was a traffic in men: first an attempt to integrate the powerful foreigners into their cultural system; then a means of gaining supernatural power; and finally a mercenary exchange for iron wealth, more precious than gold on the metal-poor Pacific Islands.[11] For European audiences, the wildly popular accounts of these exotic voyages sealed the reputation of Tahitian women as licentious vixens. Tahitian men were in turn defined as passive and unmanly, being unable or unwilling to guard their women's honor.

Other crews had met a similar reception. When the British crew of the HMS *Dolphin* made landfall in Tahiti the year before Cook's arrival, ship's master George Robertson (1731–1799) recorded the first encounter in his log:

> I was tould [*sic*] by one of the Young Gentlemen that a new sort of trade took up the most of their attention this day, but it might be more properly called the old trade, he says a Dear Irish boy one of our marins [*sic*] was the first that began the trade, for which he got a very severe [thrashing] from the Liberty men for not beginning in a more decent manner, in some house or at the back of some bush or tree, Padys excuse was the fear of losing the Honour of having the first.[12]

French Admiral Louis Antoine de Bougainville (1729–1811) similarly described his arrival at Tahiti a few months later, writing that one crewman was immediately stripped by a crowd of Tahitians, "tumultuously examining every part of his body . . . desiring him to content those desires" with a girl on the spot.[13] The episode reveals how white explorers could themselves be targets of violation.

Ironically, the all-male crews of Western vessels proved to be an object of suspicion or even ridicule for Polynesians, who met the homosociality of British sailors with skepticism about British virility. On the Third Voyage (1776–1780), Lieutenant James King (1750–1784) reported how the arrival of the *Resolution* in Hawaii "puzzled them exceedingly, our having no women with us; together with our quiet conduct, and unwarlike appearance."[14] When Hawaiian men traveled by land or by sea, they were accompanied by women, and so they were perplexed by the curious strangers who had no women. Much like the Tahitians with Bougainville's crew, the Hawaiians tried to inspect the bodies of the British sailors to confirm that their parts were in working order. Their skepticism grew when some of the men declined offers of sex.

Hawaiians practiced rather different forms of homosociality. Most vexing to the British were the *āikane*, young warrior acolytes who took pride in their status as sexual companions to Hawaiian chiefs and other men of high rank. The warlike *āikane* posed a major challenge to European sexual and gender norms in an era when homoeroticism was thought of as unmanly. This was especially true when Hawaiian chiefs offered prized hogs in exchange for select British crewmen or when *āikane* youths expressed sexual desire for British officers. For their part, British men evidently did little to dissuade the Hawaiian men, instead taking advantage of the attention and signaling their own availability. As Lieutenant King reported, with remarkable complacency about such open homoeroticism, "It was ridiculous enough to see them stroking the sides, and patting the bellies of the sailors (who were certainly much improved in the sleekness of their looks) . . . On my part, I spared no endeavours to conciliate their affections, and gain their esteem; and I had the good fortune to succeed so far, that . . . I was strongly solicited to remain behind, not without offers of the most flattering kind."[15] In many Oceanic cultures, male-to-male sexual exchange was thought to transmit power and virility.

King's account reveals how Europeans in the eighteenth century thought of men having sex with men as the immoral act of sodomy, an optional matter of personal choice, rather than as an innate homosexual identity, which was not even named for another century.[16] The *āikane* challenged British expectations, being both masculine warriors and willing to have sexual relations with men.[17] By comparison, the transgender cross-dressing *mahu* of Tahiti received little attention in journals of the Cook voyages, since they fit neatly into the association of same-sex desire with effeminacy that was emerging in Europe at the time. Lieutenant King expressed the general view of Tahitian men when he compared them to the more robust men of Tonga: "The men here fall far short in my Idea, in shape, air, sweetness & manliness . . . they are effeminately and loosely made."[18]

At the other extreme, Cook and Forster described Vanuatu masculinity as "savage" and overly hostile, which they attributed to how isolated the natives of that island were from the "feminine softness" of civilization.[19]

For many European men, the appeal of the imperial project was not national prestige or racial rejuvenation but rather their near boundless sexual access to native peoples. Dr. Jonathan Troup's (1764–1799) journal of his exploits in Roseau, the capital of Dominica where he practiced medicine from 1789 to 1791, reveals how colonists transgressed metropolitan standards of sexual propriety and racial integrity. Both the white Creole masters of Dominica's plantation society, ceded to Britain by France in 1763, as well as the merchants and sailors who routinely passed through, engaged in a freewheeling lifestyle of racial admixture and sexual exploitation. Despite contracting gonorrhea less than a month after his arrival, Troup continued to frequent Roseau's mulatto balls, where he could "make love to a number of girls in my drunkenness . . . what can a young man do here to loose his time in evenings, he can't apply to books. Whores & money must be his Rescuer [*sic*] & cause of most of his misfortunes."[20] At a time when British gender and racial identities were destabilized, Troup recorded his anxiety over whether his Caribbean debauchery would inhibit his reentry into respectable British masculinity.[21]

In 1834, Captain Edward Sellon (1818–1866) expressed no such reservations when describing his own exploits upon arriving in India: "I now commenced a regular course of fucking with native women. They understand in perfection all the arts and wiles of love, are capable of gratifying any tastes, and in face and figure they are unsurpassed by any women in the world . . . It is impossible to describe the enjoyment I experienced in the arms of these syrens."[22] Whatever stereotypes proliferated about native people, some white men came to admire if not prefer the company of colonized women who they deemed superior to European women.

Taming the Frontiers

The frontier differed from the receptive Pacific societies encountered by Cook and from the sensuous Indian and Caribbean societies that attracted Troup and Sellon. The frontier mentality pivoted on conquest instead of delight and ruthlessness instead of refinement. Only the presence of women, European or native, could refine the rough frontiersman and sustain empire.

In the vast stretches of the Russian frontier, Cossack horsemen spearheaded the Russian Empire's expansion, with their fierce reputation for rape, pillage, and drunken revelry. Russian officers described nomadic Central Asian peoples as "wild, untamed horses" devoted to "savage customs."[23] Whereas the Cossacks were seen as crude, backward, and unruly by comparison to urban Russians, they were at the vanguard of the civilizing mission when set against these "savage" natives on the frontier. In the captivity narrative *Prisoner of the Caucasus* (1822), poet and novelist Alexander Pushkin (1799–1837) dramatized the dangers of the wild frontier. He depicted the native Circassian as a fierce, rugged "predator . . . born for war," but he also exalted the imagined freedom and simplicity of tribal life.[24] Once the Caucasus tribesmen were pacified, Russian portrayals shifted toward the earth-as-female metaphor. In 1832, Alexander Bestuzhev (1797–1837) wrote of his desire to ravish the Caucasus: "The time will come when [men] will descend on you, and their sweat will intoxicate you . . . They will settle into your secret canyons and gorges, cover you with social life's dusty siftings, pollute you . . . drill mines and stone quarries through your heart . . . turn you inside out, pervert you and crop you."[25]

By the latter part of the century, when the region had been tamed, Russian travelers sought to experience its frontier past. Although the Central Asian Railroad enabled their travel, and symbolized Russia's taming of the region, the harshness of the environment was part of the appeal. Russian men succumbed to the environment while women attempted to keep them, and themselves, civilized. "Unfortunately our male companions have completely given up washing and simply complain that they must carry with them additional freight in the form of soap and towels."[26] The men were quicker to give up the trappings of civilization, going native in their new environment. The women held out longer: "We more and more resemble female travelers in wild places: our new Circassian coats are frayed, our hands are terribly burned and coarsened: all coquettishness has had to be postponed for a more appropriate situation, we are concerned only with preserving some kind of tidiness, while it is warm, we have succeeded; they say that further, in the Pamirs, it will be necessary to forget even about this."[27] Though tamed, the frontier land remained rugged, and this only enhanced its allure for tourists seeking an authentic wilderness experience away from civilization.

From the eighteenth century onward, the British Empire experienced far more extensive settlement than any other. The minimal social and legal restraints of frontier spaces, along with their harsh living conditions, created a setting of endemic violence and moral license. As the *Brisbane Courier* remarked about Australia's Queensland frontier in 1867, "Men, who if they were in Sydney or Melbourne, would attend church and be ornaments of society, are to be seen with their shirts off, doing astonishing feats of fisticuffs."[28] Although a man could earn the respect of his fellows through displays of physical prowess or versatile skills in roughing it, the unstable, perilous frontier environment and the vagabond lifestyle of pioneer men made lasting friendships rare.

Symbols of class distinction tended to swiftly break down, and the intense, although fleeting, "mateship" that prevailed when men were thrown together by circumstance depended on an informal, egalitarian code of honor.[29] The most important tests of manhood were cliché: spinning tall tales to while away the hours, drinking and brawling at saloons, and carousing shamelessly with women of ill repute. In *Vicissitudes of Bush Life in Australia and New Zealand* (1891), Dugald Ferguson (1833—1920) described being "shut in by the rude surroundings of bush life without the refining effects of female society . . . the deeper feelings of my nature had been left to harden and contract from the want of sympathy to exercise and keep them expanded."[30] Those white women who did brave the rigors of early frontier society, to say nothing of native women caught in the crossfire, were seen as objects for sexual abuse rather than as maidens and matrons of civilized refinement.[31]

Frontier masculinity steadily gave way to a more civilized settler masculinity that was patterned according to metropolitan norms. *Philosopher Dick* (1891), a novel by George Chamier (1842–1915) based on his own experience as a cadet at Canterbury, New Zealand, presents this transition almost literally, and specifically due to the influence of settler women. "One hears a lot about the humanising and refining influence of woman, and there really appears to be something in it. There is a great improvement apparent in the manners of our fellows. They can't, indeed, give up all their bad habits at once, but they try to control their feelings even at the risk of personal discomfort."[32] Chamier described how the mere presence of a woman changed the men's behavior overnight when a married couple moved into the men's house at a large sheep station. "Unfortunately the boys have been so accustomed to swearing . . . that at present they are almost denied any sort of blasphemy, which must be very hard upon them. Conversation at the kitchen table flags very much in consequence, and my bashful mates appear to be reduced to monosyllables and to casting sheep's eyes at the all-absorbing damsel. Yet they seem to like it."[33] To be sure, the conversion of frontier masculinities into settler masculinities rarely involved such a smooth transition. Some frontiersmen resisted the civilizing efforts of colonial officials and missionaries and derided those who settled into domestic stability. In John Bell's novel, *In the Shadow of the Bush* (1899), men who married gave in to their "womanish nature," needing to be cared for by a woman, rendering them vulnerable to abuse by more hardened men.[34]

Governments, missionaries, and some settlers promoted durable relationships, even with native women, as a way to tame the frontiers and frontiersmen. Whereas most colonial officials were relatively circumspect in their public comments about interracial sex, there were exceptions who openly described it as a way to ease the transition into colonial spaces. In 1902, Louis Barot (1873–1951) issued a guide for Frenchmen in the imperial service that promoted "a temporary union with a well-chosen native woman."[35] As late as the 1940s, new arrivals in French West Africa were advised to "get yourself a little 'wife' . . . a sleeping dictionary, you know? It's the only way to learn . . . what happens under these blue veils."[36] Such liaisons were not only useful for learning the local language and customs but might also keep colonial men from the vices that often prevailed in frontier settings. "The European who has a native wife, if she is not too unintelligent, finally becomes a little attached to her; she diverts him, cares for him, dispels boredom and sometimes prevents him from indulging in alcoholism or sexual debauchery, which are unfortunately so common in hot countries."[37] Barot's advice reflected a specifically colonial moral code quite different from the prevailing view in the metropole. He countered that it was absurd to expect men in the French colonial service to have "the moral strength necessary to endure two years of absolute continence."[38] Therefore, it was basic common sense to channel male sexuality in a productive way since unbridled sexual license was the inevitable alternative.

Max Buchner (1846–1921), Germany's first commissioner in Cameroon, recommended concubinage for basically the same reasons: "The eternal feminine, also under dark skin, is an excellent charm against low spirits, to which one is so vulnerable in the solitude of Africa. Apart from these values for the soul, there are also practical advantages of personal safety. Having an intimate black girlfriend protects one from various dangers."[39] Buchner went on to mock German missionaries who opposed such unions, adding his belief that native women often took the lead in seducing German men. "What the pious missionaries so often claim, namely that their female lambs are exposed to the pursuit of immoral company employees who use devilish arts of seduction, is usually the other way around."[40]

The morality of such relationships was subject to spirited debate, especially in the metropole. Some critics, like the cartoonist in Figure 1.2, believed that the unbridled power white men had over black women would transform them into incurable sadists. Nonetheless, colonial authorities generally turned a blind eye to the casual sexual adventures of European men. Their concerns focused on interracial marriage, especially when German men lobbied to gain citizenship rights for their mixed-race children. After 1904, when native rebellions in German Africa made all race-mixing suspect, officials banned civil marriage between whites and natives, although they were well aware that unions between German men and native women would not cease. Oskar Hintrager (1871–1960), the deputy governor of German Southwest Africa (modern Namibia), stated that he was satisfied so long as interracial unions "stand outside the law, as contradictory to the state's interest."[41]

Transgressing Boundaries

The domestication that relationships with women promised did not appeal to some European men who sought escape from those very norms in the colonies. Whether they wanted to explore the playground or settle into a long-term relationship, colonies provided ample opportunities for Western men to engage in sexual relations with other men.

In 1906, English novelist E. M. Forster (1879–1970) developed his lifelong passion for India after he fell in love with Syed Ross Masood (1889–1937), an Indian student he was tutoring at Oxford University. The letters they exchanged over the next several years reveal how Forster associated empire with an opportunity to embrace his sexuality: "If you knew how much I loved you and how I long to be alone with you in that romantic part of the world . . . Let us get far away from the conventional crowd, and let us wander aimless if we can, like two pieces of wood on the ocean."[42] On a trip to India to visit Masood in 1912, Forster finally realized that the young man did not share his feelings. Soon after, Forster began *A Passage to India* (1924) about the difficulty of friendship across lines of race and culture,

Die Macht der Gewohnheit

Figure 1.2.   Simplicissimus, "Power of Habit," 1904
Some critics of imperialism published lampoons against the worst of its effects. This German cartoon, read from top to bottom, alleges that the man overseas becomes an incurable sadist.

with his lead character Aziz based on Masood. Forster did not come to terms with his homosexuality until late in life, losing his virginity at age thirty-nine to a passing soldier on a beach in Alexandria.[43]

Many were far less diffident, such as French Marshal Hubert Lyautey (1854–1934), dubbed the French "Empire-Builder" on the cover of *Time* magazine in May 1931. Lyautey's missives were often full of sexual innuendo, as when he wrote of colonial cadets in Casablanca: "If I like to surround myself with youths, it is not, of course, because I want joyful talk and frivolity—which, by the way, is no longer their custom—but because the young act with youthfulness and with action, and before ending the day, after the heavy quotidian tasks, nothing equals this happy bath of fertile and creative sap."[44] Whether ambivalent or forthright, situational or devoted, the exotic expanses of empire attracted men of all sexual orientations.

Yet governments worried about how homosexual behavior might compromise claims to moral superiority over colonized people. In 1910, a scandal unfolded in German East Africa when Governor Albrecht von Rechenberg (1861–1935) filed a suit for defamation in response to newspaper allegations that he had engaged in sexual relations with African manservants and Arab prostitutes. Although the charge of sexual deviancy was certainly a concern, the greater cause for alarm involved how such activities undermined European masculine authority in the eyes of the native population.[45] To settle the matter, Rechenberg went so far as to testify that he had not had any sex at all during his four years in the colony. Meanwhile, Willy von Roy (b. 1873), the newspaper editor who first leaked the rumors, blamed "the fever" for his confusion of facts when cross-examined.[46] Several others were indicted in similar cases, including the chief customs officer, whose excuse was overwork and lack of exercise, and a tax director who took early retirement, citing the "deterioration of his nerves due to life in the tropics."[47]

These cases reveal a world of malicious gossip and backstabbing among white men on the verge of nervous breakdown. They not only accused each other of sexual immorality but also of embezzlement, bribery, spying, and defamation. Because the evidence was tainted, the judge ruled in favor of Rechenberg in the libel case and sentenced Roy to a six-month prison term. Nonetheless, their social world featured outings to male brothels and a cross-dressing Arab man known as Daughter Hamiss, who allegedly serviced the governor in his mansion.[48] Rechenberg's enemies even bribed witnesses to testify that the governor routinely sodomized his servant Max, allegedly to the point that the man suffered injury and illness.[49]

The verdict effectively shielded white elites from public scrutiny by natives. The judge wrote, "This principle [the right to respect] has to be even more valid in a territory where the rule of the white race over the subject colored race is based on authority and where any communication to blacks about actual lapses on the part of whites is frowned upon."[50] None of the private details of these men's lives—from their fevers and nervous exhaustion to their dalliances with prostitutes and even rape of manservants—belonged in the public sphere. In four recorded cases when European men were expelled by German colonial governors for engaging in sexual acts with native men, three from German New Guinea and one from Cameroon, the relevant ordinances permitted the exile of undesirable elements "for the maintenance of public peace, security, and order and for the prevention of . . . existing threats."[51] The express judgment of all these cases was that the men in question lacked the "moral energy" to restrain their "criminal inclination" and, more importantly, that they would lead colonized natives to question the masculine integrity of European colonizers.[52]

White men raped and otherwise exploited native people sexually, but they also loved and reciprocated even when cross-cultural barriers caused misunderstanding. Their diverse experiences, chronicled privately or recorded in trial records and newspapers, contributed to a transfer of knowledge about the world's diverse sexual practices and constructions of masculinity. Although racial distinctions hardened over the course of the nineteenth century, intimacies across the color line sometimes undermined them.

IMPERIAL MEN

Despite the frequent crossings of the color line, European claims to racial superiority were closely connected to the development of European masculinity in the nineteenth century. "Social Darwinism," the application of the theory of evolution to Western social institutions, advanced the idea that rigid social divisions between men and women signaled a higher degree of civilization. The world's cultures were then ranked on the basis of men's roles as protectors and laborers. By the late nineteenth century, "Making Boys into Men" fit for imperial rule generated boys' adventure literature, which instilled racial hierarchies at a young age. To build their bodies for rule, scouting and fitness movements reached out to boys from all social classes, illustrating that imperial manliness was not just the prerogative of the elite. For the next phase, "Turning Men into Colonists," empires promoted migration to the colonies through settlement or military service. These many and varied interventions in the development of Western masculinity illustrate the centrality of race and empire to the construction of modern gender identity.

Social Darwinism

In the nineteenth century, Western administrators, ethnologists, missionaries, and travelers increasingly promoted the separation of men and women into distinct spheres. On one hand, the utilitarian masculine was marked by reason, self-control, industry, and physical prowess; on the other hand, the ornamental feminine was marked by beauty, modesty, tenderness, chastity, and emotional care. This narrow, middle-class ideal was rarely realized in practice, even in Europe. In the colonies, its imposition was impossible, but imperialists nonetheless ranked the cultures they encountered on the basis of gender roles.

In *The Origin of the Distinction of Ranks* (1771), Scottish philosopher John Millar (1735–1801) expounded on a basic premise of Enlightenment social theory: the notion that women's leisure was a reward of men's industry and therefore a measure of the degree of civilization in a society. The affluence of advanced society freed women from the need to labor outside the home so that they could devote themselves only to what "is thought conducive to the ornament of private life . . . trained up in the practice of all the domestic virtues."[53] In his journal of Cook's Second Voyage, naturalist Johann Reinhold Forster (1729–1798) similarly held up the condition of women as revealing the degree of civilization or barbarism in the various Pacific peoples that he encountered: "For the more the women are esteemed in a nation, and enjoy an equality of rights with the men, the more it appears that the original harshness of manners is softened, the more the people are capable of tender feelings, mutual attachment, and social virtues, which naturally lead them towards the blessings of civilization."[54]

English philosopher and biologist Herbert Spencer (1820–1903), who introduced the concept of "survival of the fittest," imported this ideal of separate spheres into Darwin's theory of evolution. In 1877, Spencer published an influential article in New York's *Popular Science Monthly* in which he expounded on the idea: "Up from the lowest savagery civilization has, among other results, brought about an increasing exemption of women from bread-winning labor, and that in the highest societies they have become most restricted to domestic duties and the rearing of children."[55] If a society was unable or unwilling to adapt to the gender norms required by modern civilization, as defined by Western standards, its people were doomed to inexorable decline and eventual extinction.

By the end of the nineteenth century, the imperial iconography of deviant men and debauched women had hardened into the ideology of social Darwinism, which placed societies on an evolutionary scale of civilization. The fitness of a society was commonly defined by its gender roles and sexual norms, which were now seen as a reflection of the innate racial qualities of its people. In *Psychopathia Sexualis* (1886), Austrian sexologist Richard von Krafft-Ebing (1840–1902) asserted that "the higher the development of the race, the stronger [the] contrasts between men and women."[56] With the Western gender binaries as the yardstick of civilization, colonized peoples were effectively neutered: African women were no more refined than African men; Asian men had no more self-restraint than Asian women; both were equally unfit in the struggle between civilizations. The effeminate Asian man and the hypervirile African man were thus not seen as separate constructs but as part of a unified coding of race and gender, which made the European white man the ideal balance of masculinity.[57]

Making Boys into Men

Balanced masculinity had nonetheless to be taught, especially to lower-class boys. From adventure stories to scouting and sports, modern European boy culture included a sense of racial superiority, sportsmanship, team spirit, upright conduct, and contempt for effeminacy.[58] Although geared toward all boys, the target audience was the upper-class boy whose rule over others was his birthright.

Around 1870, the emergence of boy's adventure stories in Britain marked a sea shift in models of imperial manhood, typified by the empire novels of Rudyard Kipling (1865–1936), H. Rider Haggard (1856–1925), and G. A. Henty (1832–1902). As framed by Henty, the standard formula was designed to "teach them patriotism [and] inspire them with faith in the divinely ordered mission of their country and their race . . . illustrated by bright personal examples of morality."[59] In these formulaic plot lines, some setback at home generally sent the boy hero to seek his fortune in imperial spaces, where his "pluck" and "fighting spirit" prevailed to save his comrades from menacing natives.[60] These tales portrayed a hierarchy of racial evolution, with Europeans at the top, followed by Asian peoples, and finally Africans. Infantilizing Africans, Henty described them as being: "Just like children. . . . They are always laughing or quarreling. They are good-natured and passionate, indolent, but will work hard for a time; clever up to a certain point, densely stupid beyond. The intelligence of an average negro is about equal to that of a European child of ten years old. . . . They are absolutely without originality, absolutely without inventive power."[61] Geared toward European boys, these stories ingrained the imperialist racial hierarchy from a young age.

In Kipling's novel *Kim* (1901), the boy hero is the orphaned son of an Irish officer stationed in India who identifies with the Indians and Tibetans that take him in. Yet his European heritage shines through, as he was "more awake and more excited than anyone" around him.[62] Kim is drawn into "The Great Game," the imperial rivalry between Britain and Russia in Central Asia, outwitting Russian secret agents and heroically saving the day for the British Empire before he even reaches manhood. This sort of adventure tale, popularized by hundreds of dime novels and illustrated in *Boy's Own* story papers in Britain, the United States, and Australia, defined imperial manhood for boys throughout the English-speaking world in the first half of the twentieth century.

German adventure stories similarly framed the world in hierarchies of civilization, where Europeans had a duty to intervene and lift up those who were deemed less civilized. The ability to spread Western progress, values, and technology was the very measure of German advancement. Youth journals such as *The Faithful Comrade* tied the raising of brave, daring, hard-working, and innovative men at home with Germany's imperial stature in the world, defined by a struggle for national survival.[63] A typical story is *The Slave Caravan* (1889) by Karl May (1842–1912) in which the hero, German naturalist Emil Schwartz, confronts Arab slavers who trade in both hapless African natives and any Europeans that cross their path. The European comrades use their resourceful courage and exceptional fighting skills to defeat the evil slavers and to free the prisoners. This portrayal of selfless, valiant German men bringing order and progress to chaotic, benighted colonial spaces was a core theme of German stories for boys in the decades leading up to World War I.[64]

This imagery was reinforced by the elaborate ethnographic toy sets that appeared around 1910, such as the "Indian Village" and "Life-Africa," which featured the popular markers of frontier spaces. Native men were all attired as spear-bearing warriors in animal skins and feathered headdresses, guarding women in exotic outfits that carried goods on their heads and tended naked children. Nearby, uniformed white officers stood guard in watchtowers and military tents, a clear symbol of racial hierarchy and colonial authority, the only thing standing against the wild disarray of the frontier.[65]

The Scouting movement that emerged in the early twentieth century, after Robert Baden-Powell (1857–1941) published *Scouting for Boys* (1908), depicted the ideal of imperial boyhood as an ideology of muscular Christianity, social Darwinism, and romantic militarism. Drawing on empire novels, guides on self-reliant middle-class manhood such as *Self-Help* (1859) by Samuel Smiles (1812–1904), and from his own military background, Baden-Powell opened the way for any British boy to engage the imperial project:

> Besides war scouts, there are also peace scouts, *i.e.,* men who in peace time carry out work which requires the same kind of abilities. These are the frontiersmen of all parts of our Empire. The "trappers" of North America, hunters of Central Africa, the British pioneers, explorers, and missionaries over Asia and all the wild parts of the world, the bushmen and drovers of Australia, the constabulary of North-West Canada and of South Africa—all are peace scouts, real *men* in every sense of the word, and thoroughly up in scout craft.[66]

Baden-Powell initially planned to call his scouts The Young Knights of Empire, trained expressly for military service, but settled on the more populist appeal of The Boy Scouts, aiming for the widest possible audience.[67]

Scouting spread rapidly in both Europe and North America, and eventually their colonies, as a solution to the supposed crisis of manliness brought on by the degenerative and feminizing effects of industrial urban life. Much as elite boarding schools placed upper-class boys in an all-male setting, Scouting aimed to remove middle-class boys from the feminine domestic sphere so as to revive their manly character by reconnecting them to primal nature. Holding that only trial by fire on the battlefield made a man worthy of mentoring boys, Baden-Powell asserted that "Manliness can only be taught by men, and not by those who are half men, half old women."[68] A free, adventurous life outside the stifling home atmosphere, full of frontier lore drawn from remote corners of empire, became a powerful fantasy for middle-class youths, readily translated into the militarist norms of imperial manhood.[69]

For older boys, the playing fields and lecture halls of elite boarding schools shaped imperial bodies and attitudes. The rise of social Darwinism equated the fitness of a nation to the virility and vitality of its men, who were pitted against the men of all other nations. In 1886, the nationalist *Saturday Review* weekly newspaper proclaimed that:

> To the boy or to the community alike, the constant reliance upon another for aid in difficulties, guidance in perplexities, shelter from temptations, fatally weakens the fibre of the character. Boys, like nations, can only attain to the genuine stout self-reliance which is true manliness by battling for themselves against their difficulties, and forming their own characters by the light of their own blunders and their own troubles. . . . The object of the public school is to introduce a boy early to the world, that he may be trained in due time for the struggle that lies before him.[70]

In this view, British sportsmanship was the source of military superiority over imperial rivals due to the combination of physical strength and moral character required to excel on both the playing field and the battle field. In 1895, James Welldon (1854–1937), the headmaster of Harrow School, asserted that: "Englishmen are not superior to Frenchmen or Germans in brains or industry or the science and apparatus of war; but they are superior in the health and temper which games impart . . . the very qualities which win the day in peace or war. . . . In the history of the British Empire it is written that England has owed her sovereignty to her sports."[71] The nexus between athletic prowess and military valor readily extended to the imperial enterprise, where physical energy and mental discipline were essential to the rigors of conquest and control.

French reformers similarly turned to athletics as the way to revitalize the masculine body after they lost to the Germans in the Franco-Prussian War (1870–1871). They were inspired by Britain's elite school system and its promotion of the sports ethic as the foundation of personal character, team spirit, and national strength. In 1882, Minister for Public Education Jules Ferry (1832–1893) ordered the teaching of gymnastics in all schools as the way to build robust military bodies and to train youth in martial discipline. Albert Surier (1871–1944), editor of the influential *La Culture Physique* bodybuilding magazine, called it "a warrior education . . . to remake France in its very flesh."[72] Surier argued that this "tonic of heroism" was needed not just in war but also in civilian life for a man to be a "virile" husband, father, and citizen.[73] Otherwise, he would be an "effeminate, puny runt . . . a ridiculous parasite" that no woman could take seriously.[74]

The diffusion of the sports ethic also fostered nationalism among European peoples ruled by other Europeans. In Finland, the fitness movement emerged from military conscription in the late nineteenth century as a form of resistance to integration within the Russian Empire, which conquered Finland in 1809. In the 1890s, Ivar Wilskman (1854–1932) pioneered Finland's gymnastics program as a way to build civic society and to promote Finnish nationalist aspirations. In his view, national regeneration depended on strong youth and sturdy men cultivated from the working classes rather than the aristocracy. Without physical fitness, their minds would atrophy and Finnish culture would decay. As Wilskman put it, "Physical degeneration is followed with the certainty of a natural law by apathy in culture."[75] In his view, civilization did not weaken the national body, as other theorists of degeneracy believed, but rather made it stronger. The key was individual initiative to combat the deleterious effects of factory work, poverty, and alcoholism. Gymnastics improved physical health by promoting "regular and unhindered digestion, the generation of blood and its circulation, breathing, solid nerve function and expulsion of useless bodily fluids . . . flexibility, civil decency and a strong will able to perform noble tasks."[76] The Gymnastics College even held beauty contests for naked gymnasts to promote national pride.

Conversely, the degenerate youth was described as pale and feeble, with slender hands, slim legs, gaping eyes, and a flabby mouth. He frequented theaters and cabarets where he would "applaud half-naked female dancers with a cigar in his mouth."[77] At the turn of the twentieth century, schools throughout Finland set standards for fitness and hygiene. By 1912, Finland boasted over ten thousand gymnasts and won medals at the Stockholm Olympics. In 1918, emboldened Finnish nationalists won their independence from the Russian Empire.

Boys saw role models in the plucky protagonists in children's literature, trained for leadership in the Scouts, and toned their physiques through gymnastics. They were then encouraged to serve their countries as immigrants and as servicemen.

Turning Men into Colonists

Governments promoted colonial settlement as a masculine enterprise where European men could leave behind the stifling confines of modern industrial society. Opportunities for social and economic advancement promised working-class or peasant men the opportunity to rise above their humble origins and even to rule others. In addition to material enticements, such as land grants and increased salaries, colonial men aspired to a higher status than they had in the mother country.

Promoters of the French colonial project, such as Raoul Serène (1909–1980), a Scout organizer in Indochina, emphasized how in the colonies "all French are somebody, all French have the right to consideration, to respect, to a rank . . . to servants, because all French are on a mission."[78] French settler masculinity was valorized as a source of national virility and vitality. In a 1907 speech at Oran, Algeria, Marshal Lyautey proclaimed that "Not only because of a taste for adventure and travel am I a committed colonialist. . . . I have found in our colonies . . . the finest practical school where, as in a crucible, our race can be tempered and recast. . . . Underneath their uniforms . . . you find men, real men . . . the terrain *par excellence* of energy, rejuvenation, and fecundity . . . [the] complete man."[79] Promoters of empire supposed that metropolitan men had degenerated and looked to the colonies for national regeneration.

As with all the empires, French colonial spaces featured a variety of men—soldiers, settlers, traders, explorers, civil servants, missionaries—each fitted with a distinctive masculine stereotype. The nexus between them was the premise that any common Frenchman could escape the drudgery and anonymity of the metropole and make a man of himself in the colonies. In a 1938 article, Serène quoted a barber who assured a nervous immigrant setting off for Vietnam: "For your house, Madame, you will have three servants: a *bep* for the kitchen, a boy for the service of the house, a coolie for the garden."[80] A European barber could expect little compensation and even less respect in the metropole. In the colonies, class fluidity and upward mobility remained a central draw throughout the Age of Empire.

But the barber had to be trained for rule. The masculine ideal for Frenchmen embarking on the colonial enterprise was promoted in books, speeches, pamphlets, expositions, and, later, in patriotic films and music. Louis Barot's guide to French West Africa vividly portrayed this new archetype of French manliness. "The true colonial must be intelligent, and thus moral, educated, patient, and observant. He must speak well, remain controlled in his actions, and be just in his evaluations, and firm in his decisions."[81] This vision of masculinity presumed the gender and racial superiority of colonial men, but, lacking class superiority, he would only represent France if he comported himself as middle class:

> Obliged to face new demands at any moment, the colonialist contrives to be a jack-of-all-trades, and in this virile scramble—where he must combat nature, humans, and disease—only strongly cast characters will be able to resist and to impose themselves. Life in the bush, with its dangers, fatigue, and surprises, its wild charm and its breadth of action, emancipates, revivifies, and consecrates the energies that lie dormant in the well-springs of European civilization.[82]

In the settler enclaves of the German Empire, "imperial patriarchs" acquired status by amassing land and livestock while skillfully navigating colonial social networks between settlers and natives, often through interracial marriage.[83] Newer arrivals tried to rein in the autonomy of the patriarchs and to enact strict limits on sexual relations between German settler men and native women. Paul Rohrbach (1869–1956), the settlement commissioner for German Southwest Africa, believed the colonies created an "overseas type of German" who could infuse the German fatherland with a sense of liberty, self-reliance, and patriotism. Rohrbach proclaimed that "in the colony every individual has his own importance; at home he is only a number."[84] Newer arrivals did not challenge the basic tenet of dominant imperial manhood so much as they wished to extend the benefits to a broader cross section of German settler men.

Colonial men did not always display the kind of masculinity governments wanted. In East Africa, Italians established settlements late in the nineteenth century. Poverty among southern Italians increased immigration, but the poor peasants set a bad example for the natives. In 1911, one official complained: "Since the Italian must be respected by the natives, it is necessary that European migration be limited. It should comprise only craftsmen, people who can supervise the work of the native workers, or people who have some capital. . . . We thus tried to discourage the mass of proletarians and people who do not have any skills from migration to Eritrea, because they would be in a social condition lower than that of the natives. There are already Italians of this sort in the colony."[85] To promote the image of the superior European, the law prohibited Italians from having sex with native women, borrowing money from Eritreans, carrying the bags of natives, or being drunk in public.

Italian men arrived with visions of the wealth and power they would wield. The reality on the ground was something else. More than eighty petitioners demonstrated against the colonial government in 1911 after some of their land was expropriated to compensate Eritrean landowners. Officials logged the grievances of the petitioners. Their remarks reveal the new kind of colonial masculinity that attracted them to the colony but which was nothing more than an illusion:

> One of the colonists who signed [the petition] expressed his surprise because the government had not enslaved the native population. Another concessionaire, who complained about labor shortages, was astonished because the government did not force the native to work in the concessions of the whites. "It is

pointless," he argued, "that they grant us land, if they leave the natives free to
work their own land, while we are lacking a labor force. Why did we sacrifice so
many lives and so much money if the Italian has to come here to work? If one
wants to work, one goes to America."[86]

To be a man in the colonies was to enjoy white privilege by being unburdened
from work and by controlling other people's labor. Colonists were outraged that
natives would be free to work their own land and to accumulate wealth beyond
what was possible for the newly arrived. They expected economic privileges from
the racial superiority they claimed as a birthright.

In contrast to the rugged frontiersmen and imperial patriarchs who settled
empire, the bureaucrats who managed it demonstrated their masculinity through
a punishing work ethic and compulsive self-control. Tropical neurasthenia was
the label given to the mental and physical exhaustion to which male colonialists
might succumb; the men implicated in the Rechenberg scandal all complained of
it to varying degrees. While the ill-defined condition was also identified in North
American and European cities and traced to the frenetic pace of modern life, the
climate supposedly made it worse in the tropics.

American diplomat Nicholas Roosevelt (1893–1982) called it "Philippinitis" in
1926, writing that "there are certain psychopathic and neurasthenic effects of
living in the tropics," the result of "nerves frazzled from heavy, hot moisture."[87]
For men who claimed mastery over others based on physical superiority, this
admission of fragility reveals how neurasthenia marked a specific form of masculinity. Even as doctors doubted the claims of sufferers to a previously unnamed
disease, men insisted on its reality.[88] Blaming neurasthenia on overwork in a hot
climate enabled the sufferer to prove his obsessive commitment to his job while
reinforcing the idea that climate enfeebled the subject population. To control it,
medical officers recommended avoiding any sort of indulgence, even cool-water
bathing.[89] Many who fell victim to neurasthenia, such as Manila Director of
Health Victor Heiser (1873–1972), blamed it on thankless work among ungrate-
ful natives. In 1908, he complained of the futility of trying to overcome "the passive resistance of the Oriental to health measures."[90] The ultimate cure for
neurasthenia was returning to a temperate climate.

Some populations were thought too sensitive to live in the tropics at all. Dr.
Louis Fales (1869–1937) worried over white children raised in the Philippines. In
1907, he wrote, "Born of neurasthenic parents, they will inherit an organism
lacking in nerve force. . . . In a generation or two there will result a race with little
resemblance to the mother stock, small, puny, weak-minded, in fact a degenerate
race."[91] Neurasthenia was the male bureaucrat's disease. Soldiers did not complain of it. Their physical activity, as opposed to the "brain work" of functionar-
ies, seemed to make them immune. American women were thought to
"menstruate more abundantly" in the Philippines than in the United States, but
few women complained of neurasthenia.[92]

As psychoanalysis came to dominate the study and treatment of nervous conditions, male sufferers became increasingly silent about them. Colonel Fielding

Garrison (1870–1935), a doctor dispatched to the Philippines in 1922, described his state as lethargic, forgetful, and even homicidal, although the latter was more of a dry joke.[93] Garrison self-diagnosed by reading the texts of psychoanalyst Sigmund Freud (1856–1939). His journal included scribbles about the heredity of homosexuality, the temptation of cute secretaries who "sit in your lap," the clever race of Jews, and a prostitute in a fur coat.[94] He apparently identified his frustrated libido as the root cause of his nervous disorder, but there was no clinical, let alone public, space for him to explore it. By the 1920s, complaints of neurasthenia began to vanish, suggesting that this former badge of manly overwork was now a sign of deficient manhood to be hidden.[95]

Imperial masculinity evolved from the exotic dalliances of Captain Cook's crewmen with Polynesians of both sexes to the repressed bureaucrats in Tanzania and the Philippines who became more ashamed of their sexual desires. As metropolitan governments strained to restrict interracial sex they limited white men's sphere of action: the civilizing process acted on them as well. While male colonists performed a variety of roles, barbers, farmers, and bureaucrats alike had to demonstrate their racial fitness for rule. But realities on the ground, including intimacies, undercut the integrity of imperial rule.

WARRIORS

Whereas the management of empire required hard-working bureaucrats, conquering and sustaining empire required sheer force. Imperial governments needed disciplined men for "Western Militaries." This keystone of modern masculinity developed against the backdrop of empire and the racialized domination of others. Those others were ranked along a civilization hierarchy with the so-called "Martial Races" near the top. Although their methods may have been savage in the eyes of Europeans, their bravery demonstrated a level of masculinity worthy of respect. Some might even be recruited into "Colonial Militaries," although bitterness about their subordination to whites could become a source of rebellion.

Western Militaries

Modern military masculinity emerged between the American and French Revolutions of the late eighteenth century and the World Wars of the mid-twentieth century. To be sure, many of the qualities deemed inherent to warrior masculinity remain universal and unaltered over the long course of history: personal bravery, a willingness to sacrifice for the cause, and dread of dishonor. The key shift that took place in Western society during the nineteenth century involved a democratizing of martial valor and heroism, which was no longer the domain of mercenary armies led by aristocrats but accessible to all men through the institution of the citizen-soldier.[96] On one hand, the advent of mass conscription was built on the premise that military service conferred political rights. On the other, the virilization of the citizen-soldier fused manhood with nationalism, making the practice of citizenship a function of masculinity that in turn gave all men an equal claim on the nation through military service.[97]

Modern warfare involved reconciling a set of paradoxes that arose when the state machine of war met the individual soldier. These included the moral claims of a civilizing mission that harnessed the energies of barbarism, the rational maneuvers of strategy that depended on the irrational compulsion of heroism, and the increasing reliance on advanced technology wielded by fallible male bodies.[98]

In 1798, the invasion of Egypt by French Emperor Napoleon Bonaparte (1769–1821) provided an early illustration of this tension between civilized national interests and the visceral warrior mythos. Napoleon justified his campaign in Egypt as a strategic move to control trade routes and eventually push the British out of India. He defeated the Mamluk warrior elites of Egypt with superior logistics and technology, much like he had swept away the remnants of medieval military orders in Europe. Yet Napoleon also reveled in the mythopoetic confrontation with a gloried past, his subjugation of the land of the Pharaohs in the model of Alexander the Great and Julius Caesar. In victory, Napoleon even appropriated Mamluk masculinity in the most literal sense, gaining his own personal Mamluk bodyguard, the imposing warrior Roustam Raza (1783–1845), who stayed in close attendance to Napoleon until the end of his reign, arguably domesticated but still a fearsome symbol of raw manhood.[99]

Imperial heroes like Napoleon justified the imperial project, personified national greatness, and became models of service and self-sacrifice.[100] At the turn of the nineteenth century, the romantic prototype of the British military hero was Lord Horatio Nelson (1758–1805), a consummately English admiral who was fatally wounded during his victorious encounter with Napoleon's fleet at the Battle of Trafalgar (1805). Nelson personified the eternal warrior, destined for greatness because of his upper-class birth and related sense of honor.

Illustrating the shift away from the nobility's monopoly on leadership, if not mythical status, T. E. Lawrence (1888–1935) was the archetype of a rather different hero. Lawrence was the illegitimate son of an Irish peer, an Oxford scholar whose first love was archaeology, and his five-foot-four stature repulsed British recruiters. Known as the Blond Bedouin, he immersed himself in Arab culture, organized a guerrilla force of Bedouin horsemen, and overthrew the Ottoman Empire in the Levant with a dashing set of maneuvers far removed from the grueling carnage of Europe's trenches in World War I.[101] He adopted Arabian dress and cultivated celebrity with widely circulated photos such as Figure 1.3.

In private, Lawrence was deeply fractured, haunted by the experience of otherness after years of living as an Arab and the trauma of being sexually assaulted when taken captive by Turkish guards in 1916. He wrote of how, "Sometimes these selves would converse in the void; and then madness was very near, as I believe it would be near the man who could see things through the veils at once of two customs, two educations, two environments."[102] He articulated the kind of hybrid identity described by many colonized people. As a public icon, Lawrence portrayed a newly egalitarian form of military manhood, forged by self-made

Figure 1.3.   Portrait of T.E. Lawrence seated in Arab dress with dagger
British officer T.E. Lawrence donned an Arab disguise to secure the cooperation of
Arabs with the British in World War I.

merit and sheer force of will, the personal embodiment of British imperialism.
His introspective writing stood in sharp contrast to the public bravado of imperial rulers.

When German Kaiser Wilhelm II (1859–1941) dispatched the East Asia
Squadron to suppress the Chinese Boxer Rebellion (1889–1901), his infamous
"Hun Speech" (1900) reflected a pervasive German belief in racial superiority,
manifest in superior Western military arms and ethics. "I send you out so that you
will demonstrate, first, your traditional German efficiency, second, the sacrifice,
braveness, and joyful bearing of all discomfort, and, third, the honor and fame of
our weapons and flags. . . . As the Huns a thousand years ago . . . made a name for
themselves that has lasted mightily in memory, so may the name 'Germany' be
known in China, such that no Chinese will ever again even dare to look askance
at a German."[103] The myriad ways in which military masculinity penetrated
social life, both in cultivating boys for military service and as a bridge between

metropolitan and colonial spaces, operated to make "civilized barbarism" a hall-mark of the imperial enterprise as a whole.[104]

By the time Nazi Germany geared up for World War II, the hypermasculine image of the soldier had become synonymous with manhood, a reflection of the fitness of the state, with men as machines set against both imperial rivals and the colonial other. When Adolf Hitler (1889–1945) founded the Hitler Youth in 1933, he declared the often unspoken tenet that training in imperial manhood began in childhood: "In my castles of the Teutonic Order a youth will grow up before which the world will tremble. I want a brutal, domineering, fearless, cruel youth. . . . The free, splendid beast of prey must once again flash from its eye. . . . That is how I will eradicate thousands of years of human domestication. . . . That is how I will create the New Order."[105] Indoctrinated from childhood, the Nazi soldier's individual will was to dissolve into the military unit, replaced by a readi-ness to kill those whose racial inferiority or deficient manhood had been drilled into his head. The Nazi war machine was the imperial order taken to its extreme, stripped of all pretense of the civilizing mission, an instrument of absolute de-struction destined by its horrific carnage to set the stage for the end of empire.

Martial Races

Eradicating centuries of domestication implied that natural man had more of the warrior in him than the modern civilized man. European explorers believed they found natural warriors among some of the people they first encountered. Al-though they may have enjoyed the more accommodating people who offered up their women, and sometimes men, for enjoyment by explorers, Europeans stig-matized them for a lack of warrior manliness. Conversely, the warriors they met were far from solicitous, which impressed explorers who deemed their peoples to be martial races.

When they arrived in New Zealand in 1769, the crew of the HMS *Endeavour* was challenged by the native Maori at every turn. The tattooed, athletic, combat-ive Maori were the embodiment of a "warrior race," fiercely protective of their lands and their women, which convinced the British of their "cultural capacity" as a sort of premodern version of enlightened Europeans.[106]. By the logic of impe-rial manhood, this violent reception was seen as a mark of higher civilization. After the cessation of hostilities, the British negotiated with the Maori. The an-nexation of New Zealand was set out by the Treaty of Waitangi (1840). In the British ranking of native peoples, only warriors deemed capable of civilization could be party to a negotiation between men.[107]

In India, British forces clashed with the Mughals, India's Muslim ruling caste, who succeeded in unmanning British forces in the eighteenth century. Accord-ing to William Watts (1722–1764), the Mughals "are a robust, stately, and . . . fair people . . . they are naturally vain, affect shew [sic] and pomp in everything, are much addicted to luxury, fierce, oppressive, and, for the most part, very rapa-cious."[108] After a British force was defeated and captured in 1780 by the Kingdom of Mysore, captivity narratives dwelled on the vulnerability of British men in thrall to such imposing warriors. Several hundred British prisoners, including senior army and naval officers, were restrained, forcibly circumcised, and adorned with slave earrings. The youngest men were turned into *ramzanis* at the sultan's court: dancing boys who wore female costumes. In London press reports, the men's bodies became an emblem of national humiliation and emasculation, irreversibly "othered" by their physical mutilation. In the words of one ensign recorded in the captivity journal of Colonel Cromwell Massey (1742–1845), "I lost with the foreskin of my yard all those benefits of a Christian and Englishman which were and ever shall be my greatest glory."[109] Some British captives volunteered for the conversion ordeal to gain relative freedom in service to the sultan, others described years of anguish at the loss of their manhood, but all of them cast Indians as equal to Europeans in terms of masculine prowess.[110]

Far from the racist portrayals that dominated a century later, early British accounts depicted Indian civilization as a rival of European civilization and regarded its martial castes as imposing and fearsome. Indeed, the British developed an elaborate literature on the martial skills of various Indian peoples, which were supposedly inherited, and then issued detailed recruiting manuals based on that racial hierarchy. These British hierarchies of martial and non-martial races would later be adapted by other imperial administrators to the peoples that they ruled, most notably by the Dutch and the French in Southeast Asia.[111]

In Africa, the British admired those warriors whose martial ethic resembled their own and who sustained their resistance to imperial rule. The Zulu of South Africa, who valiantly resisted British control, were praised for their "remarkable system of unremitting discipline," which made them "honest, brave and wise . . . not a mongrel but a man of repute, not a debased savage but an intelligent being . . . a man of right with an undeniably just and overwhelmingly strong claim to be dealt with as such."[112] The British also respected the Asante of Ghana for their empire building and the Maasai of Kenya for their imposing physical stature. Yet, they were nonetheless characterized as intractably aggressive and primordial, and therefore not worth the effort to civilize. The British solution was to cordon off unmanageable men in tribal preserves or autonomous kingdoms where they would not disrupt the project of empire.

In French West Africa, the Tuareg occupied a similar position, viewed with fascinated respect by the French and generally given wide berth in the remote expanses of the Sahara. The Tuareg presented a particularly interesting case of gendered social scripting with their unusual practice of veiling men rather than women. Whereas the veil was elsewhere seen as a marker of feminine subordination, among Tuareg men it conferred a fearsome aura of inscrutable and unpredictable danger. The veiling ceremony marked the passage of a Tuareg boy into manhood, after which he would only be seen unveiled by his sexual companions. The indigo veils served as "props in a masquerade" to remind men "of the need for caution and self-control" and to "create ambiguity rather than rigidly fix individuals in social space."[113] The Tuareg, like the Zulu, defied the racist conventions of empire and highlighted the contradictions of imperial discourses, which colonial authorities dealt with by sidelining and avoiding them whenever possible.

When the Dutch were expanding their colonial possessions in the East Indies (modern Indonesia) during the Java War (1825–1830), they regarded the Muslim Javanese as fierce, sturdy, elusive warriors. In the words of one Dutch officer who served in the 1820s, "The Javanese is invincible in his way of warfare. He marches through rivers, clambers over the rocks, hides away in caves and woods, where he keeps himself alive with the leaves of the trees. He attacks his enemies in mountain passes and he descends upon them from ambushes; fatigue is unknown to him."[114] Yet, by the turn of the twentieth century, the Javanese were regarded as a second-rank reserve force. Dutch officers asserted that the Javanese had "no fighting instincts," saying that they were "meek, disloyal, untrustworthy, and cowardly men—peasants instead of warriors."[115] By contrast, the Dutch portrayed the Christian Ambonese from the outlying Molucca Islands as valiant, heroic, and loyal subjects of the Dutch Empire.[116]

This reversal provides a remarkable example of historical revisionism and fabricated mythology. The Ambonese had been pacified under European rule since 1512 and refused to enlist in the colonial army or to leave their home islands in the Moluccas for most of the nineteenth century. Only in the mid-1870s did the Dutch begin a systematic effort to create an artificial myth of the "martial caste" of the Ambonese as a way to limit their dependence on the Javanese.[117] Dutch military officials sent recruitment parties to promote tales of Ambonese martial prowess; offered an enlistment bounty for the cooperation of Ambonese chiefs; and provided higher pay, better pensions, and more favorable treatment to Ambonese recruits than to those from other parts of Indonesia. By the late 1890s, the Ambonese embraced the fabricated self-image of an age-old military tradition, even casting themselves in biblical terms as "people of the covenant" with a God-given bond to the Dutch.[118]

Europeans viewed the martial races with respect after engaging them in combat, even when they were humiliated as in the case of the British at Mysore. By the nineteenth century, when the superiority of European firearms enabled swifter defeat, African warriors were still applauded for their bravery but were seen as remnants of the premodern world. In some areas, like the Dutch East Indies, favored warrior groups were enticed to side with European colonizers over their rivals and gradually evolved into modern colonial militaries.

Colonial Militaries

European forces recruited mercenaries from among the local population or rival groups into colonial militaries, which would help pacify local resistance. Elite local leadership, such as the sepoys in India, initially maintained allegiance to the empire they served, some even proudly serving in the World Wars. As they evolved, they became international, bringing together soldiers from various outposts of empire (see Figure 1.4). Their skills and sense of entitlement, in addition

Figure 1.4.   French colonial soldiers in WWI German prison camp
This photo illustrates the global nature of World War I and its relationship to imperialism. Troops from every continent fought all over the world as armies drew men
from diverse backgrounds closer together.

to their loyalty, also made them a volatile force, ripe for rebellion against their
colonial masters.

Black soldiers recruited from Dutch possessions in the Caribbean and West
Africa were an important component of Dutch military power in the East Indies.
In 1831, a recruitment station was opened in present-day Ghana, then still a
Dutch colony, with the idea that expensive European units and unreliable Indonesian soldiers in the Dutch East Indies could be replaced with cheap and loyal
Africans. The pilot project drew mixed reviews of African martial skills, although
the Dutch attributed the setback to a lack of education rather than to an innate
African deficiency, even debating the prospect of recruiting African Americans
from the United States. As one Dutch report explained, "That the *Africans* were
not popular in the artillery and therefore speedily only assigned to the infantry
must be attributed to their low intelligence. They were, however, *African*, half-
savage, Negroes. That on the contrary the American, the more civilized, *English-*,
French-, or *Dutch*-speaking Negroes are intelligent enough for the artillery weapons is apparent."[119]

In the 1870s and 1880s, the Dutch mounted a more successful recruitment
drive for black soldiers in both the Caribbean and Africa, offering a path to Dutch
citizenship as a way to attract high-quality recruits. The black soldiers of the
Dutch East Indies soon found themselves classed with Europeans by locals, who
called them Black Hollanders, and many served with great distinction.[120] The
most decorated was Jan Kooi (b. 1849), who received Holland's oldest and highest
medal for saving the life of his captain in one battle and of his lieutenant in another. In 1882, Kooi retired to his native Ghana, but many Black Hollanders married local wives and settled in central Java.

Nearly all of the Black Hollanders remained loyal to the Netherlands during World War II and the subsequent Indonesian Revolution (1945–1949), fighting first against the Japanese and then against Indonesian nationalists. The new Indonesian government forced the Indo-Africans to emigrate in 1949, along with all others who were classified as Dutch citizens, which was how they identified themselves. In the words of a patriotic hymn echoed by Indo-African applicants for refuge in the Netherlands, "pure Dutch blood flows through our veins."[121] The Black Hollanders and their Javanese wives were resettled in Holland as Dutch citizens, a prime example of the novel hybrid identities created by the Age of Empire.

Although colonial militaries could be a source of support for the colonial state, they could also engender resistance or outright rebellion, threatening to destabilize the entire imperial project. In 1917, units of the native Garde Indigène of French Indochina joined the Thai Nguyen Uprising, one of the earliest mass actions against French rule in Vietnam. The Garde Indigène represented the coercive and divisive policies of the imperial state, designed to cordon off some men from others, empowering them to use violence against their countrymen who opposed the colonial state. They were concentrated in Thai Nguyen, the site of Indochina's largest penitentiary, which housed hundreds of political prisoners and draft evaders who refused to serve the French Empire in World War I. The prison rebellion began when armed guardsmen released Luong Ngoc Quyen (1885–1917), Vietnam's leading nationalist and founder of the Vietnamese Restoration Society. Ordinary criminals, united with political prisoners and guardsmen, killed wardens, seized the arsenal, and captured the town of Thai Nguyen, killing both French officials and native collaborators.

The rebels issued a proclamation that highlighted a litany of abuses suffered at the hands of the French. "At this moment, our enemy is under attack in Europe. They requisition our men and use them like a high wall to protect them from bullets. They take our goods to provision their troops. Over there, our compatriots are overwhelmed with work and those who die are not given decent burials. Our widows and orphans cry in their homes; our old fathers cry along the road."[122] They emphasized both the cruelty and the vulnerability of the enemy, as World War I had forced many French troops to redeploy from Vietnam to Europe. Indeed, troops from around the Empire served in the trenches of Europe. The rebels concluded with a call to arms: "We appeal to men animated by a spirit of liberty and independence. We are forming battalions of liberation soldiers and we begin in Thai Nguyen province. . . . We are all brothers in the countries of Annam, intelligent men to whom education has been able to suggest some useful measures. Men of good health, aid us with your arms."[123]

The French crushed the rebellion after five days with a bombing campaign that razed the town, killing hundreds and dispersing the leaders of the rebellion. A crackdown on the press followed as colonial officials tried to quell settler concerns about a larger anti-French plot, especially alarmed by the appeal of the rebellion to native guardsmen and local laborers. They blamed the revolt on the deceased Quyen who they claimed twisted ordinary grievances into a nationalist uprising.

They also blamed the rebellion of guardsmen on their sadistic superior officer Auguste Darles (1876–1940). According to one report, "When . . . Darles came to inspect the corvée, he typically beat the gardes and prisoners with a large stick if the work failed to meet his standards."[124] His sadism was well known, as he attacked not just wardens and prisoners but civil servants as well. He attacked the wives of those he sought to punish, including allegations of rape. It was therefore unsurprising that the Gardes united with the inmates to seize control of the town. Indeed, Garde service often attracted would-be insurgents. "We, men of arms, have never stopped thinking of the misfortune of our people, even while living peacefully in our village. So many times we have had the intention to raise our swords and behead our enemies, but have instead been reduced to impotence because we failed to seize the proper moment. This is why we resigned ourselves to enter into the Garde Indigène."[125] These "impotent" men served the state with self-hatred, a powder keg bound to ignite at the right moment.

Colonial authorities feared the men in uniform who might at any time turn against them. They also feared the consequences of contact between native servicemen and European women. The deployment of thousands of colonial soldiers to the various fronts in the World Wars created widespread anxieties that interracial sex would undermine the imperial racial hierarchy. This was nowhere more prominent than in the Rhineland valley of Germany, occupied by French forces, including African colonial troops, after World War I. The new German government petitioned the victors to remove the troops. "For German women and children—boys and men—these wild people are a dreadful danger. . . . More and more cases are coming to light in which colored troops have defiled German women and children, injuring, even killing, resisters."[126] Propaganda posters depicted oversized African men clutching helpless nude women in their brutish hands (see Figure 1.5).

During World War II, British officials made strenuous efforts to keep African troops from having social or sexual relations with white or Arab women, at times resorting to absurd tall tales. As one Rhodesian soldier recalled of his training in North Africa, "We were to stay away from local women as we were told that the Germans had poisoned the women, which would result in your penis falling off if you engaged in sexual intercourse with them."[127] Soldiers from the King's African Rifles of Kenya, who were deployed in India, complained that local women were told by the British that Africans had penises "down to their knees" that would severely damage or kill any woman who had sex with them.[128] No matter how respected colonial soldiers were, stereotypes about black male sexuality persisted.

Indeed, at least some colonial soldiers viewed sex with white women as a way to avenge the violation of their own native women or to assert their masculinity over the metropole, a personal version of the contest between imperial and antiimperial power.[129] A Vietnamese colonial soldier stationed in France during the

"Jumbo": a poster intended to depict the stationing of Black French soldiers in Germany after 1918

Figure 1.5. "Jumbo" defiling German women
Germans propagandized against the allied occupation imposed by the victors after World War I. French colonial troops were among those stationed in the Rhineland.

interwar years put this in graphic terms in a 1926 letter written after he received oral sex from a French prostitute: "I forced the motherland of the Metropole (France) to suck the dicks of all Annamites. . . . It's my vengeance against the despicable people."[130]

COLONIZED MASSES

Although tens of thousands of colonized men served in colonial militaries during previous centuries, their numbers swelling during the World Wars, the majority of colonized men worked as "Slaves" on plantations, or as "Laborers" on farms, in mining camps, laying rail track, or toiling in factories. To secure their labor, imperialists emasculated and degraded them in ways great and small, from torturing slaves to referring to grown men as boys. The colonized masses resisted and adapted showing a multiplicity of responses and the uniqueness of local conditions. Only gradually did their circumstances improve toward the end of the Age of Empire.

Slaves

The system of chattel slavery was a thoroughly gendered enterprise where the forced labor of defeated African warriors on New World plantations revolved around the conquest and control of the black male body. The physical dimension of slavery, from the initial stripping and chaining to the horrific Middle Passage across the Atlantic to the savage corporal punishments meted out for resistance, was designed to systematically emasculate black men.[131] This total control of human property influenced how Europeans later tried to control other subjected populations.

The diary of Thomas Thistlewood (1721–1786), an English planter in Jamaica, chronicles the endemic violence and degradation that marked the institution of slavery:

> Wednesday, 28th January, 1756—Had Derby well whipped, and made Egypt shit in his mouth.
>
> Friday, 30th July, 1756: Punch catched [*sic*] at Salt River and brought home. Flogged him and Quacoo well, and then washed and rubbed in salt pickle, lime juice and bird pepper; also whipped Hector for losing his hoe; made New Negro Joe piss in his eyes and mouth.
>
> End of October 1756—A Stout Negro man of Dr Lock's is now gibbetted alive in the Square . . . a resolute rebel.[132]

Thistlewood remarkably described his methods as moderate in comparison to the other masters and overseers who populate his diary.[133]

The regime of the slave system reduced the enslaved to the status of a beast, bought and sold as a commodity, subject almost entirely to the whims of their owners. Caribbean plantations were among the more brutal slave environments where most slaves were worked to death within a few years of arrival and easily replaced by a constant stream of human cargo. The number of African slaves arriving in the Americas soared during the eighteenth century, rising to more than 80,000 per year in the 1780s.[134] However, in much of the Atlantic world, slaves were valued for their fitness, and even those slave masters with the least sense of humanity had a financial incentive not to damage their property.

The imagery, language, and practices of slavery were designed to strip away any concept of black leadership or heroism so as to justify the subordination of black men.[135] Similarly, black male bodies were portrayed as exotic, violent, over-sexed, and irresponsible, therefore in need of control and subject to exploitation.[136] Enslaved black men were thus kept and kept down by the white men who fed, clothed, and sheltered them, and who strictly regulated what little social life they were permitted.[137] Prior to their enslavement, African men expressed their masculinity in the same broad social roles as the European men who enslaved them: the ability to protect their community, to amass property and wealth, and to provide for their families. The denial of these roles reduced enslaved men to a social status associated with immaturity and femininity.

In *An Account of Jamaica* (1808), planter John Stewart described the Quashee slave personality as "gay, happy-go-lucky, frivolous, and cheerful . . . commonly submissive, capable at times of grateful attachments where uniformly well treated . . . possessed of passions not only strong but ungovernable; a temper extremely irascible; a disposition indolent, selfish, and deceitful; fond of joyous sociality; riotous mirth and extravagant show."[138] This Quashee stereotype portrayed enslaved black men as inherently and inescapably unmanly, stuck in a preadolescent state of arrested development, "docile but irresponsible, loyal but lazy, humble but chronically given to lying and stealing; his behaviour was full of infantile silliness and his talk inflated by childish exaggeration."[139] In colonies such as Jamaica, where the race of the mother decided the race of the child, enslaved black men were even more socially invisible due to the denial of fatherhood, one of the few aspects of masculinity available to slaves in more stable communities elsewhere.

The mental abuse of chattel slavery stemmed from three great terrors of the slave system: the trauma of the auction block; the bite of the whip; and the threat of sexual assault, what African American abolitionist Frederick Douglass (1818–1895) called "outrages, deep, dark and nameless."[140] The greatest fear for many slaves was not the whip but the slave auction, which at any moment could uproot their tenuous family life and underscore their status as property. In *Narrative of the Life of Frederick Douglass* (1845), Douglass recalled his experience of being auctioned as a boy: "We were all ranked together at the valuation. Men and women, old and young, married and single, were ranked with horses, sheep, and swine. There were horses and men, cattle and women, pigs and children, all holding the same rank in the scale of being."[141] In *Twelve Years a Slave* (1853), Solomon Northup (1808–1863), a free-born African American from New York who was abducted and sold into slavery in 1841, used the same metaphor in recalling a slave reduced to being whipped by the ten-year-old son of his owner. The boy "looked upon the black man simply as an animal. . . . To work like his father's mules—to be whipped and kicked and scourged through life—to address the white man with hat in hand, and eyes bent servilely on the earth, in his mind, was the natural and proper destiny of the slave."[142] Finally, the sexual assault that was a fixture in the lives of enslaved women was also a threat to enslaved men. In *Incidents in the Life of a Slave Girl* (1861), Harriett Jacobs (1813–1897) narrated life on a North Carolina plantation before her escape in 1835. Jacobs described a slave master who "took into his head the strangest freaks of despotism," and regularly forced himself on her fellow fugitive Luke, leaving him "a mere degraded wreck of manhood."[143]

Slaves exerted agency in multiple ways, from the daily refusals to work to inciting full-scale rebellion. One of the simplest ways to reclaim agency was to exit the system altogether. In the mid-eighteenth century, French historian Antoine-Simon Le Page du Pratz (d. 1775) described how many Africans brought to

Louisiana during the early period of French rule either committed suicide or ran away. "Some of them have killed or drowned themselves and many have fled. . . . In this case they attempt to return to their homes and think it possible to live in the woods with fruits which they expect to be everywhere similar to those at home; they even think that they will get home by roaming around the sea."[144] Some runaways stayed in the vicinity of their former plantations, armed with stolen rifles and returning nightly to procure supplies with the complicity of female slaves. In 1940, ex-slave Albert Patterson (b. 1850) gave an oral narrative to the Louisiana Writers' Project in which he described their tactics: "If a nigger hide in de woods, he'd come in at night to get [a] meal. They bore a little hole in the floor, and they break into de meat house too. De dogs couldn't catch dem nohow 'cause they put bay leaves on de bottom of their feet and shoes. . . . That way a man could come and see his family."[145]

Over the decades, the maroon communities of runaway slaves that emerged in the bayous and cypress swamps set up their own subsistence economy, cultivating crops, hunting, fishing, and bartering goods with other maroon settlements and even poor whites. As with much of the Atlantic slave world, "marronage" remained a constant feature of slave societies, described in 1854 by *La Meschachébé* newspaper. "The number of maroon Negroes is considerable on all the . . . Coast. These gentlemen are so sure not to be threatened they build cabins in the woods, very close to the habitations where they live in quietude."[146] Although planters sometimes organized hunting parties, they generally ignored the more established maroon settlements, fearing that a concerted campaign may spark a general slave uprising.

The Interesting Narrative (1789), by Olaudah Equiano (1745–1797), was the first published account of the horrors of slavery from the point of view of a former slave. Equiano narrates his life as a slave after being kidnapped from Nigeria's Igboland at age eleven and later as a free Englishman after his emancipation in 1767. *The Interesting Narrative* revolves around his path toward adopting a specifically male English identity, which began shortly after his capture. "I no longer looked upon [white men] as spirits, but as men superior to us; and therefore I had the stronger desire to resemble them; to imbibe their spirit, and imitate their manners."[147] Although Equiano was no doubt aware that the vast majority of slaves were field laborers, not tradesmen, his argument for emancipation routinely portrayed the industry and value of enslaved men, to place them on the same level as their English counterparts. "I suppose nine tenths of the mechanics throughout the West Indies are negro slaves; and I well know the coopers among them earn two dollars a day; the carpenters the same, and oftentimes more; as also the masons, smiths, and fishermen. . . . I have known many slaves whose masters would not take a thousand pounds current for them."[148] The more highly trained slaves were most valued not just by their masters but also by Equiano, who associated masculine identity with skilled, profitable labor.

Equiano includes several vignettes to present himself as more of a proper Englishman than some of his fellow English, at one point expressing surprise at his ill treatment by a merchant who refused to honor Equiano's sale of goods on credit. "I was astonished at this usage from a person who was in the situation of a gentleman, but I had no alternative; and was therefore obliged to submit."[149] Equiano's mastery of English masculine norms allowed him to subvert the racial component of Englishness by emphasizing its gendered aspect, laying claim to the rights of Englishmen for himself and for all enslaved African men by demonstrating their common humanity, civilization, and manhood.[150]

The resounding success of Equiano's narrative reflected how effectively he demolished the Quashee stereotype of black juvenile effeminacy, extant under various names throughout the Atlantic world. British women's rights advocate Mary Wollstonecraft (1759–1797) captured the prevailing view of Equiano among intellectuals of the Enlightenment in her review of *The Interesting Narrative*. "The life of an African, written by himself, is certainly a curiousity, as it has been a favourite philosophic whim to degrade the numerous nations, on whom the sunbeams more directly dart, below the common level of humanity and hastily conclude that nature, by making them inferior to the rest of the human race, designed to stamp them with a mark of slavery."[151] Wollstonecraft asserted that even if Equiano did not rise to the superior capacity of a philosopher of the Enlightenment, which she clearly believed he did, then at a bare minimum his literary work and his personal attributes ranked him no lower than any ordinary Englishman. "We shall only observe, that if these volumes do not exhibit extraordinary intellectual powers, sufficient to wipe off the stigma . . . the activity and ingenuity, which conspicuously appear in the character of [Equiano], place him on a par with the general mass of men, who fill the subordinate stations in a more civilised society than that which he was thrown into at his birth."[152]

Equiano's narrative helped influence the British parliament to halt the Atlantic slave trade in 1807 and to eventually abolish slavery throughout the British Empire in 1833. Notably, although *The Interesting Narrative* was translated into Dutch, German, and Russian within five years of its first English printing, it was not translated into Spanish or French until the 1980s. The striking absence of a similar literary tradition of slave narratives in the Spanish or French Empires, parts of which maintained slavery until the 1890s, testifies to the subversive power of such firsthand accounts to enact social change and to combat societal amnesia.[153]

Slave narratives routinely assert that the reclaiming of black agency could only begin after casting off the portrayal of blacks as servile, ignorant, and bestial. Equiano's *Interesting Narrative* set the standard for the genre, written in part to chronicle the abuse of slaves but even more so to assert the intelligence and capability of the once-enslaved authors. The genre functioned as a coming-of-age narrative, which often began with a literal renaming to symbolize rebirth as a free citizen, an assertion of personal autonomy in mind and body. The black masculine identities that emerged after emancipation were thus defined by their degree of freedom from the mental conditioning of enslavement, what Douglass describes as being "myself within the circle: so that I neither saw nor heard as those without might see and hear."[154]

In *The Souls of Black Folk* (1903), a landmark set of essays on the social status of African Americans after emancipation, W. E. B. Du Bois (1868–1963) wrote of his fragmented identity as a distinctly embodied state. "It is a peculiar sensation, this double-consciousness, this sense of always looking at one's self through the eyes of others, of measuring one's soul by the tape of a world that looks on in amused contempt and pity. One ever feels his two-ness,—an American, a Negro; two souls, two thoughts, two unreconciled strivings; two warring ideals in one dark body, whose dogged strength alone keeps it from being torn asunder."[155] Du Bois framed this conflict between external racist stereotypes and internal sense of self as the central feature of African American masculinity: "The history of the American Negro is the history of this strife,—this longing to attain self-conscious manhood, to merge his double self into a better and truer self."[156] Formerly enslaved men could resolve the ambiguities of their racialized identities by affirming an unequivocal masculinity.

Laborers

By the modern imperial period, centuries of maligning African masculinity underpinned an ideology of racial superiority that spilled over to all nonwhites. Stereotypes of inferiority and arrested development led to the White Man's Burden, the ideology that whites were obliged to raise so-called savages up to the highest level of civilization they could attain.

In 1899, Rudyard Kipling published his poem "The White Man's Burden" in New York City's leading periodical, *McClure's Magazine*, where he called on the United States to accept its heritage as an imperial power. Kipling's ode to high imperialism urged the ascendant industrial powerhouse to fully engage the global stage of European empire. It remains widely regarded as the ultimate distillation of the gendered racial ideology of the Age of Empire:

> Take up the White Man's burden—
> Send forth the best ye breed—
> Go, bind your sons to exile
> To serve your captives' need;
> To wait, in heavy harness,
> On fluttered folk and wild—
> Your new-caught sullen peoples,
> Half devil and half child.[157]

Kipling's poem arrived at a pivotal moment. A week before, the United States signed the treaty that ended the Spanish-American War (1898), inheriting imperial sovereignty over Puerto Rico, Cuba, Guam, and the Philippines. At the outbreak of the Philippine-American War (1899–1902), future President Theodore Roosevelt (1858–1919) copied the poem in a letter to his confidante Senator Henry Cabot Lodge (1850–1924), saying that it was "rather poor poetry, but good sense

More Like His Dad Every Day.

Figure 1.6.   "More like his Dad Everyday"
With the US occupation of Guam in 1898, American educators, doctors, and officials believed they must bring the fruits of civilization to a childlike people.

from the expansionist standpoint."[158] When depicted as "half child," colonized males, rendered as boys, looked up to their imperial fathers (see Figure 1.6). "Half devils," on the other hand, sought to destroy their fathers and preyed on their women. In this artificial dichotomy, the child image effeminizes the man while the devil image renders him hypervirile.

Filipinos were hardly the only recipients of the white man's interventions. The ideology of white intervention structured relations in every colony, especially in the newly carved out African colonies in the 1880s and 1890s. For the great majority of Africans, the most significant feature of the colonial period was the drastic reorientation of the labor market, focused increasingly around urban development in the administrative centers of empire, the road and rail networks built to open up the interior of Africa, and the mining centers or plantation regions that fueled the colonial economy. The broad racial stereotypes that defined empire were daily reinforced by petty displays of dominance, such as the "hammock tradition" of Nigeria where white colonial overseers were routinely transported on hammocks carried by African men who were officially titled "hammock boys."[159]

In a 1975 interview, one former mineworker recalled the grave insult to men who had wives, children, and positions of authority and respect in their home village being constantly referred to as boys. "Then all African workers were titled boy, for example, timber man was called timber boy, peak [man] called peak boy, tub man called tub boy. Everything, boy, boy! Only the Europeans were called overman and foreman."[160] These daily slights were a regular source of strife and protest, but changes mainly came in the late imperial era, especially during World War II when the war effort made empires more dependent than ever on African labor and African soldiers. In 1941, for instance, the Nigerian coal industry issued a directive that "the designation 'men' must be substituted for 'boys' in all communications referring to the Colliery labour either collectively or individually. No person employed by this department must be addressed as 'boy.'"[161] This was, of course, too little too late.

If not rendered as boys, African men were depicted as devils. In *Black Skin, White Masks* (1952), Martiniquan psychoanalyst and black nationalist Frantz Fanon (1925–1961) identified white sexual anxiety as one of the roots of the devil stereotype: "In relation to the Negro, everything takes place on the genital level."[162] In this paradigm, black masculinity was arrested in perpetual sexual adolescence, whereas only white masculinity could mature into fully actualized manhood. Yet, in Fanon's view, imperial fantasies about black manhood were more a reflection of white fears that civilized urban life attenuated the virility of white manhood. "Every intellectual gain requires a loss in sexual potential. The civilized white man retains an irrational longing for unusual eras of sexual license, of orgiastic scenes, of unpunished rapes. . . . For the majority of white men the Negro represents the sexual instinct (in its raw state) . . . the incarnation of a genital potency beyond all moralities and prohibitions."[163]

The colonized subject depicted as a reckless adolescent represented raw masculinity, unhindered by the trappings of civilization. Although he experienced it as a burden, only the mature white man could bring that civilization. Fanon's identification of white ambivalence helps to explain the deep roots and durability of stereotypes about black male sexuality, whether of the slave or the laborer.

COLONIZED ELITES

Securing access to labor, slave or free, often required the cooperation of local elites. Securing access to resources could be accomplished by compelling heads of state to sign treaties so that direct occupation was unnecessary. Such "Horizontal Alliances" typically lasted until client states insisted on greater autonomy. Meiji Japan was the first and most dramatic example of a client state achieving autonomy. Indirect rule was more formal and of greater duration in the British

Empire in part because of the extensive employment of "Subalterns" who carried out the everyday tasks of empire. Each group negotiated its distinctive masculine identity in relation to that of the white imperialist.

Horizontal Alliances

Alliances with Western imperial powers were only horizontal to the degree that they left local political structures relatively undisturbed. In late imperialism, imperial governments attempted to obtain what they wanted—labor, trading privileges, raw materials—by aligning themselves with non-Western powerful men. These alliances took a variety of forms with Japan negotiating the most equitable arrangement. In 1853, American Commodore Matthew Perry (1794–1858) sailed four warships into Tokyo Bay and opened fire, forcing Japan to end its two centuries old policy of isolation from the outside world. Within two decades, most Japanese people accepted the premise that resisting Western imperialism required emulating Western economic and military success. The Meiji Period (1868–1912) slogan *wakon yôsai* (Japanese spirit, Western science) symbolized the new Japanese man, a hybrid of Westernized social norms and traditional Japanese ideals.[164]

The first stage of Westernization required the overthrow of the old samurai order and its replacement with a modern monarchy. The old order did no go quietly, determined to preserve a distinctly Japanese form of masculinity. During the 1860s, in the twilight of Tokugawa Japan, the World Renewal cult drew together a motley assemblage of defiant cross-dressers, kabuki actors, fallen samurai, and a host of other dissident outcasts. Inspired by anti-Western restoration ideology and the revelry of sun-goddess worship, they romped gaudily about the countryside and cavorted drunkenly through the towns, staging orgies in back alleys and chanting the rouse to freedom, *eejanaika, eejanaika*: "We'll do as we bloody-well like!"[165] This populist movement, loosely united under banners of liberation and empowerment, danced up and down the main road from Tokyo to Kyoto, then finally descended into the "smashings" of 1867. This proved to be the last gasp of Tokugawa hedonism, as the Japanese militia opened fire to disperse the riots and officials responded with the Meiji Restoration program in 1868. Meiji reformers swiftly suppressed Tokugawa social norms, such as esteem for male homoeroticism and gender ambiguity, which were seen as incompatible with Western-style modernity.[166]

By early 1871, Japanese men were lining up and even camping out overnight to buy the translation of *Self-Help* (1859) by Samuel Smiles, ushering in a novel Japanese adaptation of Victorian masculinity. A new discourse of "self-cultivation" and "upright ethics" embodied the Meiji gender ideal in which a man's personal success depended on his adoption of Western middle-class practices and values.[167] The Western perception of Japan as a garden of sexual delights became a symbol of national disgrace. In that context, Eigo Fukai (1871–1945), editor of *The Far East* journal, expressed his contempt for the tea girls depicted in *The Geisha*

(1896), an English musical comedy. "Our country is simply a play-ground for globe-trotters, our people a band of cheerful, merry playfellows. . . . Light-hearted friends of Japan find in these lines the most happy features of the country, and overlook the gross injustice done in the play to the Japanese nation."[168] After Meiji authorities dismantled the prostitution network for foreign visitors that same year, the manly samurai swordsman replaced the sultry geisha girl as the foremost embodiment of Japan on the world stage.

In a crucial shift from the elite warrior caste system of the past, Meiji officials reframed service in the new Army of the Greater Japanese Empire as the birthright and obligation of all Japanese men. The 1872 edict that enacted universal conscription expressly invoked the Western citizen-soldier as the model for Japanese men. "In this way, everyone should endeavor to repay one's country. The Occidentals call military obligation 'blood tax,' for it is one's repayment in life-blood to one's country. . . . It follows, therefore, that the law providing for a militia is the law of nature and not an accidental man-made law."[169] The inscription of a new gender ideology to produce imperial soldiers was seen as essential to Japan's power and prestige as it sought to challenge Western empires on their own terms.

By the turn of the twentieth century, public schools promoted revived ideals of the samurai ethic, recast as essential for both military valor and economic prowess. Educator Nitobe Inazō's (1862–1933) influential text *Bushidō: Soul of Japan* (1900) described the ancient samurai code as "a law written on the fleshly tablets of the heart. . . . Scratch a Japanese of the most advanced ideas, and he will show a samurai."[170] The Meiji Restoration thus combined the citizen-soldier with the samurai ethic to rapidly become a military superpower that rivaled the Western powers. The expansion of the Japanese Empire was personified as an aspiring man desperate to join the imperialist men's club (see Figure 1.7). Japan's resounding

Figure 1.7. Japan wants in the men's club
Although Japan modernized its economy, government, and culture in the late nineteenth century, it was still seen as inferior in the eyes of some European rulers.

defeat of a European empire in the Russo-Japanese War (1905) shocked the world and proclaimed its emergence as an imperial power in its own right.

By 1907, the American author of *My Japanese Wife* (1895) noted with regret how much Japan had changed in just a dozen years: "Japan can no longer be thought of as what a humorist once called 'the kingdom of the two G's—the land of gardens and geishas.'"[171] Japan's shift from erotic subject of empire to martial agent of empire produced a renewed sense of confidence in Japanese traditions that led to their steady revival in the lead up to World War II. By the 1930s, Emperor Hirohito (1901–1989) became the embodiment of a nation at war whose "radiant aura" guided Japanese soldiers doing battle in China.[172]

After the bombing of Pearl Harbor in 1941 set Japan at war with the Western Allies, imagery of the emperor's divine purity, bathed with a heavenly glow in propaganda films and posters, unified the nation and transcended the "corrupting influences" of the West.[173] This divine spark, carried in all Japanese men by virtue of their supposed blood relation to the imperial line, was believed to make them more than a match against the impressive physiques of Americans and Australians, "just big bodies, with small hearts."[174] As one mother wrote in a letter to her son during World War II: "You are my son—and yet you are not my son. You are the son of the Emperor. Your body is not yours—it belongs to the Emperor. Therefore you must take good care of yourself."[175] The militarized body of the Japanese man dissolved into the imperial war machine, but illustrating the malleability of masculine norms, a renewed model of masculinity swiftly emerged after Japan's defeat in 1945. The salaryman once again replaced the soldier as Japan's masculine ideal, reflected in the term "corporate warrior" to describe the men tasked with turning Japan into an economic superpower.[176]

The British Empire depended on horizontal alliances with local elites, hereditary rulers seen as kings often on par with the British Crown. Nigeria Governor Claude Macdonald (1852–1915) asserted in 1904, "A great chief is a very valuable possession; his authority is an instrument of the greatest public utility, which it is most desirable to retain in full force."[177] With the pace and extent of the scramble for Africa, this was the only practical way to rule. Treaties in Malaya and Fiji also recognized traditional elites while laying out their obligations to the British. These alliances were marked by public displays of power full of pomp and circumstance. Parades and pageants were held on the occasion of anniversaries, birthdays, royal jubilees, or initiations into honor societies. Leaders recognized by the British were invited to join the prestigious Order of Saint Michael and Saint George. Their membership carried medals and ribbons and was celebrated publicly. Along with British members of the order, sheikhs, emirs, sultans, and paramount chiefs would variously be named CMG, KCMG, or GCMG, depending on their rank. CMG stood for "Call Me God"; KCMG for "Kindly Call Me God"; and GCMG for "God Calls Me God."[178]

But the reign of such Gods would be short-lived. As in Meiji Japan, liberal capitalism elevated a new class of leaders. As an administrator in Sudan explained in the 1930s, "The chiefs represent the Past. The educated classes represent the Present."[179]

Subalterns

Few members of the educated class would wield the power of a chief. Networks of civil servants, especially in India, carried out the mandates of the British. British elites initially and derisively described the Bengali civil servant, known as *babu*, in contrast to British imperial masculinity. Thomas Babington Macaulay (1800–1859), a member of the Empire's Supreme Council of India during the 1830s, described them: "The physical organization of the Bengalee is feeble even to effeminacy. He lives in a constant vapour bath. His pursuits are sedentary, his limbs delicate, his movements languid. During many ages he has been trampled upon by men of bolder and more hardy breeds. Courage, independence, veracity are qualities to which his constitution and his situation are equally unfavourable."[180] Macaulay concluded by drawing the parallel between outward physical traits and inner character that so often typified imperial discourse. "His mind bears a singular analogy to his body. It is weak even to helplessness for purposes of manly resistance; but its suppleness and its tact move the children of sterner climates to admiration, not unmingled with contempt."[181] After the failed Indian Rebellion (1857) led to direct British rule under the Raj, even the so-called martial races of India became subject to British paternalism, referred to as "tykes, little highlanders, little Gurkhs" by British soldiers.[182]

But as they became more modern and Western in their dress, comportment, education, and outlook, members of the Indian Civil Service (ICS) administered the Raj effectively. One of them recalled, "We young people were put in charge of districts and ruled a million people at the age of thirty or less with no questions asked, accountable to nobody except our seniors in the service. . . . So you really felt like you were king of your district, wherever you were."[183] Even colonized masculinity under the Raj entailed supreme and unchecked rule over others. To gain appointment to such positions, applicants had to attend the right schools; they also had to be a "good all-rounder, good with the gun, good on horseback."[184] Subalterns, in short, were expected to aspire to Britishness, and entrusted to manage the Empire, but would often find further advancement closed to them.

As early as the 1860s, leaders and intellectuals in Bengal began to pursue a regeneration of Bengali manhood, promoting Indian male prowess through a revival of traditional gymnasium culture. Bengali nationalist Bankim Chatterjee (1838–1894) called the *babu* stereotype the Indian Stigma and used his poems and novels to turn colonialist discourses back against the British. Social reformer Swami Vivekananda (1863–1902) promoted a manly physique as the key to anti-British resistance with this admonition: "You will be nearer to God through football than through the *Bhagwad Gita*."[185]

On July 30, 1911, *The Bengali*, a nationalist newspaper of Calcutta, published a poem to celebrate the electrifying victory of the Mohun Bagan soccer club, with

Figure 1.8.   British sports in the British Empire
British colonists introduced their sports ethic and their sports such as cricket and polo throughout the British Empire. By the early twentieth century, athletes from colonized peoples made the sports their own.

its roster of Hindu Bengalis, over East York, a British military team. "Thanks my friends of football renown, / For bringing the British teams down / A victory grand to behold, / Serene and noble-bright and bold—'The Mohun Bagans.'"[186] Subaltern victories on the field asserted manly equality with imperialists and contributed to smoother relations, as seen in Figure 1.8. The victory was pivotal for Indian nationalists who had long struggled against the perception of emasculation created by Western narratives of deficient Hindu manhood, which were bolstered by the demilitarization policies of the British Raj. The event made international headlines when Reuters news service observed that despite bitter sectarian differences, even the rival Moslem Sporting Club "went almost mad," waving their shirts in the air and "rolling on the ground" to celebrate "the victory of their Hindu brethren. . . . For the first time in the history of Indian Football, a core Bengali team, Mohun Bagan, won the IFA Shield by defeating a competent White team."[187]

As a rival to the nonsectarian Indian National Congress, the Hindu Mahasabha was founded in Amritsar as India's first Hindu nationalist party in 1914. It agitated for independence from Britain and defended Hindu interests against the All India Muslim League. A central aim of the Hindu Mahasabha was to "improve the physique of the Hindus and promote martial spirit amongst them by establishing military schools and organizing volunteer corps."[188] In 1923, the Mahasabha aimed to reclaim Hindus that had converted to Islam or Christianity. A closely associated program organized Hindus to defend their community. Both strategies glorified India's ancient war epics and the traditional Kshatriya warrior caste. In contrast to Gandhi's nonviolent and gender-neutral approach, the Hindu Mahasabha elected the nationalist firebrand Vinayak Savarkar (1883–1966) as its president at the start of World War II, running under the slogan "Hinduize all Politics and Militarize Hindudom!"[189]

Independence politics in the interwar years challenged both the horizontal and vertical structures of imperial rule as a new generation envisioned a different way of organizing public life and a different way of being masculine. Adopting Western forms of masculinity, whether as officials, as soldiers, or as laborers, colonized men compelled the respect of the colonizer. Sports were central to shifting perceptions of native men away from the weak civil servant and toward a newly empowered masculinity.

BRIDGING THE DIVIDE

Colonized men often looked to athletics to reclaim masculinity and to assert their right to independence. "International Sports" developed to bridge the divide between nations whose antagonism and claims to superiority were mediated on the field. Although athletes chiefly represented their nations, other men bridged national and even racial divides with their "Anti-Imperialism" writings and activism. These different strategies for realigning masculine identity away from racial hierarchies reveal how multiple responses to imperialism prevailed and that local conditions opened certain opportunities while foreclosing others.

International Sports

Over the course of the twentieth century, the sports arena became a prime venue where non-Western men could compete with Western men on an equal footing, thereby undermining perceptions of superior European manhood through much of the colonial and postcolonial world.

Supporters of the French imperial project recognized the symbolic power of colonial athletics early and sought to appropriate the diffusion of the Western sports ethic so that it would work in the service of empire. In the 1890s, the founder of the modern Olympic Games, Pierre de Coubertin (1863–1937), became the foremost champion of French athleticism as the means to restore the health of the French race. A fervent supporter of French colonialism, Coubertin promoted athletics both to instill imperial values at home and to bind French colonial subjects to the metropole: "Sport is a vigorous instrument of discipline. It engenders all kinds of good social qualities such as hygiene, cleanliness, order, and self-control. Would it not be better for the natives to be in possession of such qualities and would they not be thus more easily handled than otherwise?"[190] Whereas the British used the sports ethic to reinforce stereotypes of dominant colonizers and subservient colonized, under Coubertin's guidance the French turned athletic contests into a vehicle of cultural imperialism. The Olympic Games not only showcased French manhood on the international stage but were also used to promote the civilizing mission when colonial subjects competed under the French flag.

In the 1920s, French colonial officials issued regulations to ensure that no sporting contest would set the colonizers against the colonized, following guidelines from the metropolitan physical education bureau, which stated "that races be separated . . . lest jealousies arise likely to cause unfortunate incidents."[191] At the same time, colonized men were encouraged to join official sports leagues as an alternative to native fitness clubs that might foster anti-imperial activism, an initiative that met with mixed results.

In French Africa, memories of conscription during World War I made locals reluctant to engage in any activity that resembled military training supervised by the French army. By contrast, the Vietnamese opened a college of physical education at Hanoi in 1919, promoted as a way to counter feelings of racial humiliation and inferiority.[192] During the interwar years, French sports leagues funded colonial athletes as a way to present the Empire in a favorable light, yet reactions to athletic achievements by colonial subjects exposed French ambivalence about their success. At the 1928 Olympics in Amsterdam, Algerian-born Boughèra El Ouafi (1898–1959) won the marathon, France's only gold medal of those games. The publicity director of the French Athletic Federation noted that "Our dusky-hued comrade, with the frizzy hair . . . this little Algerian . . . has come to the rescue of the mother country France."[193] The Communist Party newspaper *L'Humanité* depicted the event as an indictment of middle-class French manhood, writing under the mocking headline, "At last, a French victory! But ironically it's that of the Arab, El Ouafi."[194] However, attitudes did gradually change so that by 1956, when Algerian-born Alain Mimoun (1921–2013) won the marathon at the Melbourne Olympics, he was celebrated as a French national hero. Ironically this took place during the opening years of the Algerian War of Independence (1954–1962).

Many nations eventually adopted a given sport as an emblem of national prowess, such as cricket in India, baseball in Japan, and wrestling in Turkey, each of which reflected certain ideals of athletic masculinity in their respective society. In the early twentieth century, the sport of polo took on this role for Argentina, where the *gaucho* horseman of the Pampas grasslands was seen as the national embodiment of masculinity, with his attributes of physical vigor, sexual prowess, and fraternal brotherhood.[195] Adopted from the British, Argentine polo converted and hybridized *gaucho* masculinity, by "civilizing" the violent *gaucho* equestrian games and turning the national icon into a source of international pride. When Argentina won the polo championship at the 1924 Olympics in Paris, an Argentine polo player asserted that his nation's victory over their British and American counterparts reflected this innate *gaucho* toughness, in terms of greater Argentine stamina and a more natural affinity to riding. "We have much more temperament than they; we are real fighters due, perhaps, to an atavistic gaucho instinct which is still in our veins and is manifested in many of the things we do. I believe, in sum, that Europeans will suffer a lot of defeats in the hands of the savages."[196] Reclaiming the savage in this self-ironic gesture is a hallmark of the postcolonial ethos.

This embodiment of Argentine national pride extended even to the rugged *gaucho* horses, a hybrid creole breed favored for its mixture of discipline and coarseness. "In the Argentinian pony, the creole blood has been kept; when pure-bloods have mixed with mares of our places, this blood is a heritage of freedom and of a brave existence in the desert. . . . The history of the heroism of the creole horse is well known, it is enough to say that his body is well-formed, that his organs are of steel and that he has benefited from the natural environment."[197] The character of Argentine horses provided an analog to idealized Argentine manhood, which turned racism on its head in its reverence for multiracial hybridity.

Whereas polo was the foremost athletic conduit for Argentina's elite men, football was the main arena for the creation of a hybrid national masculinity throughout Latin America in which men could embody national values and attributes regardless of social class or ethnic origin. In the 1920s, journalists at the Buenos Aires sports weekly *El Gráfico* used the concept of *lo criollo* to describe the essence of Argentine football players, seen as more innovative, spontaneous, and adaptable than their methodical European opponents. "When our immigrant country receives in its breast the great migrations of all races, it has assimilated qualities from each of them and has amalgamated them, giving them its own mark. This is the new race that European intellectuals talk about when they come to study the psychology of our people and cannot find a clear-cut defining characteristic because we have something from each civilization without belonging typically to any of them."[198] When Brazil reached the semifinals of the 1938 FIFA World Cup in France, Brazilian sociologist Gilberto Freyre (1900–1987) expressed similar sentiments in an interview for Rio de Janeiro's *Correio da Manhã* newspaper: "Our style of playing football seems to contrast to the European style because of a set of characteristics such as surprise, craftiness, shrewdness, readiness, and I shall even say individual brilliance and spontaneity, all of which express our mulattoism."[199] Much like his Argentine counterparts, Freyre depicted Brazilian football success as the embodiment of Brazilian racial and cultural hybridity. "Our passes . . . our tricks . . . that something which is related to dance, to capoeira, mark the Brazilian style of football, which rounds and sweetens the game the British invented, the game which they and other Europeans play in such an acute and angular way—all this seems to express . . . the flamboyant and at the same time shrewd mulattoism, which can today be detected in every true affirmation of Brazil."[200] The hybrids of Latin American football had a transgressive quality that subverted the European model of football as a sport of collective discipline. In Latin America, football was more a showcase of individual prowess and willpower, reflecting the improvised "school of the street" rather than the orderly self-restraint of the school room.[201] It enabled athletes to claim a formally derided classification as a source of pride.

Although sports teams continued to be organized by nationality, and their contests pitted nations against each other, the commitment to healthy competition on a level playing field enabled a spirit of internationalism that slowly broke down imperial and racial hierarchies in the twentieth century.

Anti-Imperialism

Internationalism stoked anti-imperialist sentiments even in the eighteenth century. The recognition that imperialism was incompatible with Enlightenment liberalism, including natural rights and toleration, fed a continuous critique of imperialism in and outside the West. As more voices of the colonized engaged this critique, allegiances among colonized people generated a massive force for resistance that would ultimately topple the Western empires.

Criticism of European imperialism could come from unlikely places. In 1773, Captain James Cook wrote about the Polynesian people he encountered on his Pacific voyages: "What is still more to our Shame civilized Christians, we debauch their Morals already too prone to vice and we interduce [sic] among them wants and perhaps diseases which they never before knew and which serves only to disturb that happy tranquility they and their fore Fathers had injoy'd. If any one denies the truth of this assertion let him tell me what the Natives of the whole extent of America have gained by the commerce they have had with Europeans."[202] Only a few years after first contact, Cook honestly observed the effects of imperialism. Abandoning the pretense to uplifting savages to a higher stage of civilization, Cook perpetuated the trope of the noble savage who enjoyed an uncorrupted existence until Europeans brought greed and shame along with physical deterioration.[203]

During the eighteenth century, Enlightenment thinkers in Western Europe set forth the doctrine of rights that would eventually prevail throughout much of the world, at least in principle if not in practice. Whereas most focused their efforts specifically on ending the scourge of slavery, some went further to condemn the imperial enterprise as a whole. In 1780, French philosopher Denis Diderot (1713–1784) published several anti-imperialist essays in the encyclopedic *Philosophical and Political History of European Settlements and Commerce in the Two Indies.* Diderot focused especially on how the project of empire altered the character of the imperialists and violated the agency of the peoples that they encountered. "Beyond the Equator a man is neither English, Dutch, French, Spanish, nor Portuguese.... He is a domestic tiger returning to the forest; the thirst of blood takes hold of him once more."[204] In forgetting his nationality, he forgets his humanity and devolves to the level of a bloodthirsty animal. Instead of conquering the savage, he becomes the savage. "Savage Europeans! You doubted at first whether the inhabitants of the regions you had just discovered were not animals which you might slay without remorse because they were black, and you were white."[205] Even before the hardened racial hierarchies associated with social Darwinism, Diderot bluntly denounced the emphasis on distinctions based on phenotype.

Meanwhile, German philosopher Immanuel Kant (1724–1804), further rejected the prevailing view that Europeans had a right of conquest by virtue of racial or cultural superiority. Kant asserted that "*Freedom . . .* insofar as it can coexist with the freedom of every other in accordance with a universal law, is the only original right belonging to every man by virtue of his humanity. . . . The *right of citizens of the world*, insofar as individuals and states, standing in the relation of externally affecting one another, are to be regarded as citizens of a universal state of mankind."[206] Whereas Kant affirmed that the resistance of non-Europeans established their right to ownership of their lands, Diderot went further, arguing that with "reason, and with no offence against the laws of humanity and justice, that people could expel and kill me if I seized women, children and property; if I infringed [on] its civil liberty; if I restricted its religious opinions; if I claimed to give it laws; if I wished to make it my slave. Then I would be only one more wild animal in its vicinity, and no more pity would be due to me than to a tiger."[207] The hypocrisy of Europeans was denounced by other Europeans even at the dawn of the modern Age of Empire. The incompatibility between imperialism and liberalism would render both vulnerable to critique. The contradictions between them eventually led to the dissolution of empires.

Set off by the Scramble for Africa a century later, dissident voices continued to reject the imperial world order and its conflation of whiteness with civilized manhood. As a leader of the American Anti-Imperialist League, author Mark Twain (1835–1910) satirized the U.S. colonial war in the Philippines, writing in 1901 to the tune of the patriotic Battle Hymn of the Republic: "Mine eyes have seen the orgy of the launching of the Sword; / He is searching out the hoardings where the stranger's wealth is stored; / He hath loosed his fateful lightnings, and with woe and death has scored; / His lust is marching on."[208] On cards that were distributed by the Anti-Imperialist League, Twain linked the Philippine-American War to China's Boxer Rebellion (1899–1901) and the South African Boer War (1899–1902), European imperial ventures that were widely criticized in the United States: "I bring you the stately matron called CHRISTENDOM— returning bedraggled, besmirched and dishonored from pirate raids in Kiaochow, Manchuria, South Africa and the Philippines; with her soul full of meanness, her pocket full of boodle and her mouth full of pious hypocrisies. Give her soap and a towel, but hide the looking-glass."[209] Twain's statements against the rising tide of jingoism in the United States created a sensation that led the press to question whether the quintessentially American satirist was sincere in his opposition to the imperial enterprise. Perhaps most controversial was Twain's description of Filipino rebel leader Emilio Aguinaldo (1869–1964) as a "patriot" fighting for "the highest and noblest of all causes."[210] By contrast, President Roosevelt was "clearly insane . . . and insanest upon war and its supreme glories."[211] By attributing equal rights of liberty and self-defense to colonial peoples as those claimed by imperial peoples, Twain's writings fit into the same tradition of anti-imperialism stretching back to Equiano and other Enlightenment opponents of empire.

Meanwhile, African American social activists responded to Kipling's ode to empire by pointing out America's legacy of internal imperialism, with emancipated ex-slaves still deeply oppressed by the Jim Crow system of racial segregation.

In 1899, African American clergyman Henry Johnson (b. 1857) issued his response, "The Black Man's Burden," which situated the Philippine-American War within the broader trajectory of American empire:

Pile on the Black Man's Burden,
'Tis nearest at your door,
Why heed long bleeding Cuba
Or dark Hawaii's shore;
Halt ye your fearless armies
Which menace feeble folks,
Who fight with clubs and arrows
And brook your rifles' smoke.

Pile on the Black Man's burden,
His wail with laughter drown,
You've sealed the Red Man's problem
And now deal with the Brown.
In vain you seek to end it
With bullet, blood or death,
Better by far defend it
With honor's holy breath.[212]

The National Afro-American Council took an anti-imperialist stance at its 1899 meeting, and two black anti-imperialist leagues were founded the same year. The one in Chicago even named itself the Black Man's Burden Society.[213] Outbreaks of racial violence against black veterans of the Philippines War and even reports of African American defectors joining Aguinaldo's insurgents led many to argue that black soldiers should not help white soldiers defeat other people of color.

Yet black anti-imperialism was far from universal. Wilberforce University classics professor William Scarborough (1852–1926) spoke for many aspiring black men when he argued in 1901 that African American colonization of "our new possessions" remained the one opportunity for "black manhood [to] stand erect and unhindered, and . . . enlarge respect for itself."[214] Poet James McGirt (1874–1930) even wrote a remarkable short story, "In Love as in War" (1907), about a Filipina princess Quinaldo who chooses a black suitor over a white suitor. The black enlisted man Sarge is so manly he arouses the passion of every Filipina who spies his glorious physique, leaving the white officer Vaughn "defeated and enraged" by his black rival's superior manhood.[215] The Philippines is personified in feminine form by Quinaldo, eager to be possessed by a black man. At least in the tale of "In Love as in War," the discourses of black manhood were not so different from the discourses of white manhood after all.

Anticolonial writers similarly invoked possession of the white woman as a metaphor for asserting a masculine identity born of revenge. Frantz Fanon described this longing of the native man: "The gaze that the colonized subject casts at the [settler town] is a look of lust . . . of sitting at the colonist's table and sleeping in his bed, preferably with his wife. The colonized man is an envious man."[216] In *The Wretched of the Earth* (1961), Fanon places violence at the core of reclaiming masculine agency for the colonized masses. "This violent praxis is totalizing since each individual represents a violent link in the great chain, in the almighty body of violence rearing up in reaction to the primary violence of the colonizer. . . . At the individual level, violence is a cleansing force. It rids the colonized of their inferiority complex."[217] The wretched of the earth form a united body to avenge centuries of cruelty and humiliation, seizing the only power left to them, that of brute force. But the colonized elite are estranged from the masses by their collaboration with empire, becoming an impotent tool of the master. In Fanon's view, the colonized intellectual has only words partly rendered in the master's tongue: "A permanent dialogue with itself, an increasingly obnoxious narcissism [that] inevitably paved the way for a virtual delirium where intellectual thought turns into agony."[218] He suffers from his intermediate position, attempting to translate the wishes of the people for the master. As their spokesman, he also becomes a target for reprisals and torture, yet "when the colonized subject is tortured, when his wife is killed or raped, he complains to no one."[219] For Fanon, the colonized man is emasculated by his inability to protect his women. He does not report these violations because they are of no consequence to the imperial state. His rage is therefore compounded by his invisibility. Only when he joins the almighty body of violence can he reclaim his manhood.

Whereas early critics of imperialism sought to bridge the divide, more militant critics in the twentieth century believed the divide was too deep and only violence would liberate the wretched of the earth, men whose masculinity had been systematically degraded for two centuries.

CONCLUSION

In the imperial imagination, manhood and whiteness were closely associated and produced in conjunction with one another. The first encounters of empire established narratives of race and gender that included the feminization of nature and, by extension, the feminization of indigenous peoples who were believed by Europeans to be closer to nature. Over the course of the nineteenth century, this hardened into an ideology of social Darwinism that ranked peoples on a scale of civilization and justified the civilizing mission of empire.

In the metropole, imperial bodies were shaped by fitness regimes while imperial attitudes were socially constructed through schools, toys, and youth leagues. This included a new form of military manhood with the rise of the citizen-soldier, who by virtue of his service shared equally in the rights and responsibilities of citizenship and conquest. These imperial values were in turn exported into colonial spaces, where the virtually lawless frontiers of empire were steadily domesticated, in large part by the arrival of missionaries and, later, European women settlers. Frontier masculinities evolved into settler masculinities shaped by many of the same institutions that originated in the metropole. For many men of empire, the chief attraction of colonial spaces was the fantasy of empire as playground, abounding with opportunities for sexual adventure. However, colonial officials might succumb to neurasthenia, mental and physical exhaustion attributed to being overworked in tropical climates, a badge of honor showing their commitment to the imperial project yet also exposing the vulnerability of imperial manhood.

For non-Western men, the experience of empire and the masculinities produced by and in reaction to imperialism were quite different. The slave system transported millions of Africans to plantations in the Americas, reduced to a dependent state of enslaved manhood. Yet slaves resisted and adapted the institutions of slavery, seeking to reclaim agency in various ways. They established communities of ex-slaves, launched armed uprisings, and fostered a hybrid culture that retained many elements of their diverse African points of origin. Other non-Western men forged an array of responses to imperialism. Some ethnic groups were deemed unmanageable and marginalized while others were drawn into the colonial labor market. For the latter, this produced a sort of dual masculinity, where men were respected in their home villages within traditional male roles but then disparaged in the Eurocentric workplace.

Modern masculine identities evolved over time and in conjunction with racialized and imperial hierarchies. Moreover, they evolved increasingly in opposition to feminine identities, which were similarly located in imperial and racial hierarchies. The modern gender order, pivoting on the utilitarian masculine as opposed to the ornamental feminine, informed Western views of the other and, once exported, transformed intimate relations in every culture.

TIMELINE

1769:	Captain James Cook makes landfall on Tahiti
1774:	William Wales describes Vanuatu sexual advances on British sailors
1780:	British captives forcibly circumcised in India
1789–1791:	Jonathan Troup carouses with the women of Dominica
1811:	Largest slave uprising in the United States takes place in Louisiana
1831:	Dutch East Indies begins recruiting colonial soldiers in Africa
1864:	Herbert Spencer coins the phrase "survival of the fittest"
1867–1868:	Smashings in Japan set off Meiji westernizing reforms
1899:	Mark Twain joins Anti-Imperialist League to protest Filipino War
1908:	Robert Baden-Powell publishes Scouting for Boys
1910:	German East Africa Governor Rechenberg accused of sodomy

1912: Finnish gymnasts medal at the Stockholm Olympics

1916–1918: T.E. Lawrence leads Arab Revolt against Ottoman Empire

1917: Garde Indigène joins prison uprising in French Indochina

1928: Ahmed Boughèra El Ouafi wins marathon at the Amsterdam Olympics

1941: Nigerian coal industry prohibits calling African men "boys"

TWO

THE GENDER OF EMPIRE
Femininities

Ahyssa of Senegal and Saint-Domingue

> To judge the value of liberty to a Moor by how it might inspire
> a Negro is to subscribe to a flawed notion; we know the status
> of the Negro in his own country; among the Arabs what a dif-
> ference! . . . Independent and desirous of a happiness which
> stems from their love of mediocrity, the mere appearance of
> subjection horrifies them. And who will not love men who, in
> their original simplicity, cherish virtues without knowing the
> means for hiding dangerous vices!
> —Moreau de Saint-Méry, *Causes Célèbres*, 1774

*In 1774, Moreau de Saint-Méry (1750–1819), a Creole lawyer from Martinique,
relayed the plight of his client Ahyssa (Aisha), an enslaved Arab in French Saint-
Domingue (modern Haiti), by situating her right to liberty in a racial hierarchy.[1]
He persuaded the court that her race determined her access to freedom. Moreau
represented the Arab as a kind of noble savage, simplistic yet lovable, inclined
toward virtue. He foreclosed oft-cited arguments that freeing one slave would cause
all to rebel by placing Ahyssa in a superior position vis-à-vis Africans, who implicitly did not understand liberty. Europeans deemed Arabs inappropriate for slavery
because of their biological and cultural proximity to Europeans. He mentioned
their straight hair and fair skin, although some Arab colonists, he added, had
become darker living in sub-Saharan Africa. In his rhetoric, liberty was neither
universally desired nor applicable. Ahyssa won her freedom thanks to the deployment of Enlightenment concepts of liberty, the colonial racial hierarchy, and her
own complex embodiment. Hers is an eighteenth-century story, transnational,
public, and gendered. In this chapter, we examine the role of race, and particularly
interracial sex, in producing modern feminine identities in the increasingly complex racial societies of the eighteenth through twentieth centuries.*

Ahyssa's case illustrates how the colonies functioned as laboratories where the forces of early globalization destabilized race, class, and gender hierarchies in the early modern era. Ahyssa lived in Senegal where her family engaged in the gum trade. Kidnapped and sold into slavery in 1763, she eventually fell into the hands of Joseph Cassarouy (d. 1774) who took her to Saint-Domingue and promptly named her Colombe. Enslavement entailed the total loss of identity, starting with her name. Moreau insisted she should never have been enslaved in the first place, reminding the court that Arabs also engaged in the slave trade. He added that Cassarouy nonetheless treated her well, and that she performed only the work of her sex, "which ours would call amusements."[2] In his will, Cassarouy stipulated that Ahyssa be freed upon his death, but the executor of the will determined that she either had to be sold to liquidate the inheritance or be given to the principal heir, Cassarouy's brother. Once transferred to the brother by court order, Ahyssa suffered many cruelties including being beaten and raped, ultimately resulting in her pregnancy. She escaped and obtained legal counsel. In 1776, the high court at Cap-Français nullified the original bill of sale and declared her free. They bypassed rather than disputed the letter of Cassarouy's will and determined that, as an Arab, she should not have been enslaved in the first place.[3]

Throughout Europe and its colonies in the late eighteenth century, some women won liberation from tyrannical masters, husbands, and fathers. Lawyers emphasized their innate virtue and their helplessness before the courts, where they would find a "father in the heart of each magistrate."[4] But this paternalistic rhetoric would paradoxically exclude them from many rights for more than a century. As democratic ideals spread through revolutions in the late eighteenth century, new constitutions formally excluded women as a group on the basis of their gender, perpetuating an increasingly sentimentalized version of the nuclear family. In this sense, gender was both contingent and universal. On the one hand, climates and cultures produced distinct femininities and masculinities. On the other hand, the categories "man" and "woman" came to represent biologically determined and oppositional identities ordered in a hierarchy. Feminists responded to this paradox by perpetuating another: they demanded access to "man" as a citizenship category on the basis of their membership in the category "woman." In this chapter, we will examine how such essentialized identities spread across the globe alongside imperialism and the multiplicity of responses by women who adopted or contested them.

Gender is foundational to the construction of modern categories of race and class as well as the institutions of slavery, imperialism, and the state. Figure 2.1 shows little gender differentiation among plantation slaves despite European constructs of the gender divide. Assumptions about essential differences between men and women informed analyses of other differences and enabled masculinity and femininity to be applied as markers, ranking people according to their degree of manliness. The power of gender as a category of analysis not only urges the inclusion of women in the historical narrative, but it exposes the social construction of identities and institutions.[5] Viewed through this lens, Ahyssa's case illustrates the existence of a paradox as well as its successful resolution, at least in her case.

Figure 2.1.   Slaves cutting sugar, Antigua
The harsh conditions of plantation agriculture, especially where sugar was produced in Brazil and the Caribbean, led to high mortality rates. Male and female slaves toiled together equally.

Ahyssa's status as an Arab, neither black nor white, created a wedge in the racial hierarchy. Her gender, emphasized to win the sympathy of magistrates, enabled Moreau to advocate for her liberty while leaving the slave system and patriarchal family intact. To preserve her virtuous reputation, Moreau skimmed over the implied long-term sexual relationship between Cassarouy and Ahyssa while emphasizing her rape by his brother. This enabled him to win the sympathies of the magistrate for a virtuous but abused woman. Some women similarly won their cases in Europe when lawyers urged paternalistic magistrates to wield the law against abusers on their behalf. Yet the particularities of climate and culture generated debates about the circumstances most likely to promote virtue.

VIRTUE IN CROSS-CULTURAL CONTEXTS

Articulating Muslim views of women's virtue, travelers to the West from Muslim countries generally found Western women's freedom of movement to detract from their virtue while commentators on women's seclusion throughout much of Asia thought the opposite, resulting in an enduring "East versus West" binary. At the same time, "Melodramas" brought characters from different cultures into contact whose assumptions about virtue were challenged. Travelers and novelists explored and foreclosed possibilities for "Interracial Romance" that proliferated on the frontiers of empire. Native women who had relationships with European traders and settlers often directly experienced tensions over cultural norms. Initially empowered as intermediaries with whites, many later gravitated toward Western norms, especially if they converted to Christianity, indicating a multiplicity of responses to imperialism, the role of intimacy in complicating relations with colonizers, and a trajectory toward assimilation into a European gender norm.

East versus West

Ahyssa was a Muslim who did not convert to Catholicism. If she had converted, Moreau would have used this to move the magistrates. Instead, he described her as a Moor or an Arab to defer attention from her religious identification. By the time of her trial, there was a longstanding association of Islam with poor treatment of women. Thomas Paine (1737–1809), British radical and pamphleteer of the American Revolution, summarized this in 1775: "All Asia is covered with prisons, where beauty in bondage waits the caprices of a master. The multitude of women there assembled have no will, no inclinations but his. . . . There the most gloomy tyranny has subjected them to creatures [eunuchs], who, being of neither sex, are a dishonor to both: There, in short, their education tends only to debase them; their virtues are forced."[6] The image of the women enslaved to a master's sexual passion stoked orientalist stereotypes for centuries. By the eighteenth century, such images informed the development of international feminism, which increasingly placed virtue in sexual purity and autonomous action. Like many feminists of his era, Paine promoted friendship and companionate marriage as the best form of relations between the sexes and the fount of honor and virtue.

Some Muslim commentators viewed the easy companionship of men and women as destructive of gender difference as well as honor and virtue in both sexes. In their view, only the seclusion of women protected their virtue. Ahmad al-Ghazzāl (d. 1777), Morocco's ambassador to Spain, reported on Spanish customs in 1766: "The women are very much addicted to conversation and conviviality with men other than their husbands, in company or in private. They are not restrained from going wherever they think fit. It often happens that a Christian returns to his home and finds his wife or his daughter or his sister in the company of another Christian, a stranger, drinking together and leaning against one another. He is delighted with this. . . . [God] save us from the wretched state of these infidels who are devoid of manly jealousy."[7] This formulation reveals how masculinity and femininity were productive of each other. In his view, jealousy and possession of women constituted masculinity. Infidels were therefore effeminate and implicitly controlled by licentious women who then became masculinized in their occupation of public space and command of men. Greater mobility of women in the public sphere did not signal the progress of civilization but rather its corruption.

This view was not held solely by Muslim traditionalists. Modernizers who sought to introduce legal reforms and a modern economy believed that traditional gender roles preserved a distinctive cultural identity amid rapid change. Egyptian Rifa'a al-Tahtawi (1801–1873) stated this connection in *A Paris Profile* (1839). Dispatched to France by Muhammad Ali (1769–1849), a reformer known as the founder of modern Egypt, he aimed to bring the best of Western civilization to the Muslim world. He found much in France worthy of emulation, including the French esteem of science. Although he shared the French abhorrence of homosexuality, he did not find them to be a moral people: "Among their immoral traits is the lack of chastity among the women and the absence of male protection of the women's honor."[8] He described Paris as a "paradise for women" because men slavishly submitted to them.[9]

Melodramas

As people across diverse cultures came into contact with each other in the eighteenth century, they expressed curiosity about the degree of their shared humanity as well as their different ways of expressing masculinity and femininity. Europeans accessed a wide array of sources about other cultures, including legal briefs like Moreau's, travelogues like Captain James Cook's (1728–1779), ethnographies about native peoples in the Americas, and various works of fiction. Debates ensued about which cultures best promoted women's virtue. In the context of the sentimental melodrama, an eighteenth-century phenomenon, some European authors posited that virtue was the keystone of essential femininity. Less likely to travel, much less publish their travelogues, female authors in Europe expressed their views through fiction reflecting the degree to which the literary public sphere was gendered. Nonetheless, their fiction reflected a familiarity with other cultures. They wrote about intimate life, placing women of varying ethnicities in situations in which their virtue would be tormented but then reaffirmed. They universalized metropolitan constructions of the virtuous feminine, absorbing racial and cultural differences in the process.

Françoise de Graffigny (1695–1758) related the story of Zilia, an Inca princess kidnapped and brought to France, in her epistolary novel, *Letters from a Peruvian Woman* (1747). Zilia recounted being cruelly torn from her native Peru by the evil Spaniards and then recaptured on the high seas by the more chivalrous French. Reprinted more than one hundred times and in many languages, the book was highly influential in spreading knowledge about the Inca and modern feminine identity for over a century. Zilia's evolution from noble savage to learned French woman enabled Graffigny to critique European strictures against women's mobility. Zilia expressed astonishment and despair at French customs that might appear alien if not barbarous to a native of Peru. In one scene, a guest to whom she has been presented "had the audacity to put his hand on my breast, I pushed him away with a surprise and indignation that let him know I was better schooled than he in the rules of civilized behavior."[10] In another, she struggled to don restrictive French dress, leaving behind her simple Incan shift. Seeing herself in the mirror, she became a Frenchwoman, shedding the distinctive dress that drew "discomforting attention."[11] Admiration of her beauty took the place of gawking. Indeed her French captor and benefactor, enamored of her as a native, fell hopelessly in love when she appeared more French. Nonetheless, she refused marriage to him, preferring to retire to her French country house with a full library. Zilia was thus a liberated woman, as the novel undermines the traditional marriage plot, to the dismay of many readers. But the subtext is that interracial sex was taboo, and an exiled Peruvian could only end up as a spinster. French ideas about exotic women pivoted on ambivalence about heroines such as Zilia. She was alluring, yet also asexual, independent, and dedicated to reading. Her gender status can be read as ambiguous.

Relaying another story about the ambivalence of exposure to French culture, Claire de Duras (1777–1828) published *Ourika* in 1823, locating virtue in an African protagonist whose exoticism was tamed by her French upbringing. The novel relayed the allegedly true story of a love-struck Senegalese girl gifted to a Parisian family as a child. Rescued from slavery and raised as a wealthy Parisian, Ourika first experienced prejudice as a teen at a ball. Doomed to the margins of European society because of her race, she was supposed to be grateful to be liberated from slavery. She descended into melancholy when she realized she would never be able to consummate her unrequited love for the son of her benefactor. Confronted by the taboos against interracial love, she lamented having been saved from plantation slavery where she could at least have had "a poor hut of my own . . . a partner in my life, children of my own race."[12] With no other recourse, she became a nun but nonetheless eventually died of a broken heart. On her deathbed, she wished that her little infant body had died in her homeland, covered by a "handful of African sand."[13] Duras's critique of racial prejudice and her psychological study of a black girl's coming of age in Europe exposed the paradox of a supposedly universal femininity still structured by her particular physical and racial locations. Readers were moved to compassion by her plight, but the heroine's tragic end reinforced taboos against interracial sex, thereby safely shoring up European domesticity. The object of her affection, Charles, married a proper Frenchwoman, oblivious to the feelings he inspired in Ourika. Wishing Charles and his new bride well, she demonstrated how virtue could trump desire and died in peace.

Cuban author Gertrudis Gómez de Avellaneda (1814–1873) told a similar story in *Sab*, published in 1841, but with an interesting gender reversal. One of the only abolitionist novels written by a woman in Latin America in the nineteenth century, *Sab* was first published in Madrid and banned in Cuba until 1914. Like Ourika, Sab, a male mulatto house slave and a Catholic, died tragically, a "sublime martyr of love," at the moment when his beloved Carlota marries Enrique Otway, a Jewish businessman.[14] The daughter of Sab's master, Carlota, and Sab were close in age and temperament. Since childhood, they enjoyed a close friendship and Carlota treated him as an equal. Sab praised her virtue and in his quiet devotion to her proved his. This contrasted strongly with her suitor's economic preoccupations, which Sab believed would doom Carlota to an unhappy marriage. Avellaneda positioned the slave as both more devoted and also morally superior to the businessman. His virtue and devotion was his only consolation as he died of a broken heart on her wedding night. In his dying moments, he wrote a letter to be posthumously delivered to her, professing his feelings. He lamented that the position of the slave and the woman are not so different: "Oh, women! Poor, blind victims! Like slaves, they patiently drag their chains and bow their heads under the yoke of human laws. With no other guide than an untutored and trusting heart, they choose a master for life. The slave can at least change masters, can even hope to buy his freedom some day if he can save enough money, but a woman, when she lifts her careworn hands and mistreated brow to beg for release, hears the monstrous, deathly voice which cries out to her: 'In the grave.'"[15] Because divorce was illegal in Catholic countries, wives could only escape their marital chains in death. Like Duras, Avellaneda explored longing for interracial love, which ends in the tragic death of the protagonist. By telling the story from an enslaved man's perspective, she universalized the despair of ill-fated love and the consolation of tormented virtue.

These tragic protagonists, victims of the slave system and racism, embodied virtue more profoundly than the white characters, thus challenging racial hierarchies. They embodied metropolitan constructions of the heroic masculine and virtuous feminine, absorbing racial and cultural differences. Each also moved beyond traditional gender expectations by not living happily ever after in domestic bliss. Dying of a broken heart was indeed a standard convention of European romanticism but orienting the narrative to an abolitionist agenda was not.

Interracial Romance

As novelists and travelers explored and foreclosed possibilities for interracial romance, they collectively constructed a normative femininity that both reflected and influenced real life. During the period they were written, from about 1750 to 1850, exploration and settlement in the Americas, Australia, and Africa brought European men into contact with diverse peoples whose gender practices were often quite different from theirs. White men throughout the European empires engaged in relations with local women to gain access to local customs and languages. Unions could be consensual or compulsory, temporary or permanent. When they were few in number, these men might assimilate into local cultures. But increased European presence, especially that of missionaries, gradually transformed local gender practices into something more hybrid. Local women experimented with a range of possibilities as they interacted with white men: native women on the frontiers might serve as invaluable intermediaries, empowering themselves in the process. But the increased influence of missionaries sometimes resulted in the adoption of Western family formations and ideas about women's virtue.

In North America, interracial marriages accounted for 75 percent of all marriages in the Upper Great Lakes region between 1765 and 1838.[16] Women sometimes wielded considerable influence in these unions. In his travels in the Southeast colonies of North America, William Bartram (1739–1823), a Philadelphia naturalist, chronicled Native–British relations from 1773 to 1777. He enticed readers with his descriptions of sylvan nymphs available for sexual adventure, but moved beyond clichés when he described the complex ways in which native women structured relations with whites.[17] He described enduring unions among the Cherokee of North Carolina marked by sincere love and esteem on the part of both partners. Cherokee women energetically promoted the interests of their husbands, which included mediation when conflicts between the two peoples arose. But sometimes "beautiful savages" manipulated white men to their material advantage. Bartram described a Seminole woman who seduced a North Carolina trader, now poor and emaciated, by "these powerful graces she has so artfully played upon her beguiled and vanquished lover, and unhappy slave, as to have already drained him of all his possessions, which she dishonestly distributes amongst her savage relations."[18] Whether or not her intentions were indeed dishonest, she apparently structured the relationship to her material benefit. As for her husband, "enslaved" by desire, he threatened to kill her or himself but instead drowned his sorrows in brandy.[19]

Although temporary unions were more common among Indians, and sometimes advantageous to traders, some white men craved Christian union and endeavored to convert their wives to Christianity and European domesticity. Irish trader James Adair (1709–1783) wrote in 1775 of an Englishman who courted the Cherokee Dark-Lanthorn: "Observing that marriages were commonly of a short duration in that wanton female government, he flattered himself of ingrossing her affections, could he be so happy as to get her sanctified by one of our own beloved men with a large quantity of holy water in baptism—and be taught the conjugal duty, by virtue of her new Christian name, when they were married anew."[20] For such men, Christian marriage would put an end to "wanton female government" in the family and in the community. But Dark-Lanthorn would have none of it. To the cleric whose speech she patiently listened to, translated by her husband, she concluded, "Very well, that's a good speech," although "troublesome and light," and that the cleric was an "Evil Spirit."[21]

Similar to fur trading cultures to the south, Russian traders in Alaska assimilated into native Alutiiq culture through intermarriage. However, Russian traders initially took Alutiiq women as hostages until native men brought their quota of pelts. British explorer George Vancouver (1757–1798) encountered them on a voyage to the North Pacific Ocean in 1794 and wrote that the Russians "appeared to be perfectly content to live after the manner of the native Indians of the country; partaking with equal relish and appetite their . . . food, adopting the same fashion, and using the same materials for their apparel."[22] Shortly thereafter, missionaries arrived and by the early nineteenth century joined company officials in encouraging legal marriage. Alutiiq wives gradually adopted European clothing, especially on conversion to Christianity, and used urine to whiten their skin.[23] These unions resulted in a mixed-race population. One missionary described the mixed-race offspring as gifted, and another wrote in 1825 that "they constitute a link uniting

Russians and islanders, humanity and savagery, and education and ignorance."[24] Company officials paid for European educations in Siberia in exchange for ten years work for the company. As mothers to the children of white men, Alutiiq women integrated colonists into their culture and saw a rise in their status as their sons rose through the company.

These women's status declined in other ways, however, especially when compared to native Alaskans before the arrival of whites. Anthropologists note the shift of storage lockers from the interior to the exterior of the dwelling, suggesting that women's exclusive control over provisions, such as seal meat, diminished after white traders placed a market value on them. In the traditional Yup'ik Eskimo family, men brought the catch to women who preserved and distributed the food, which included providing for extended family and ceremonial uses.[25] Storage pits were traditionally located in the women's areas of the village, but after the arrival of Russian traders they gradually shifted to the men's areas. The shift can be attributed to the colonists' preference for trading with men as well as to a decline in warfare. Local men's route to status shifted away from warfare to trade. Above all, it signals the shift to more limited domestic roles for women whose family lives began to resemble those of their European counterparts.

In German Southwest Africa (modern Namibia), missionaries and commanders initially encouraged interracial relationships. Lutheran missionaries from the Rhineland were among the first Europeans to establish permanent settlements in the region. Heinrich Schmelen (1776–1848) established a station in 1814 and shortly thereafter married one of his first Nama converts, Zara Hendricks (1793–1831).[26] Together they alphabetized the Nama language and translated the Bible. Their daughter also married a missionary, and her household became a "model for all the whites living in Damaraland."[27] In the 1880s, Carl Büttner (1848–1893), mission inspector of the Evangelical Missionary Society and an official in German Southwest Africa, praised the legacy of the family and urged German men to form proper German families with local women. But rather than emphasizing the advantages to men, he emphasized their responsibilities, both to the women they had relations with and to greater Germany. As Germans-in-law, Africans would "feel secure and happy as genuine subjects and denizens of the German Empire," and German interests would best be served by such moral alliances.[28] Mother of seven children, Zara oversaw the marriages of her daughters to missionaries and her sons rise in military or teaching careers. Büttner praised their central role "in the development of this land and one can only wish that there be more like it."[29] Local women in partnership with white men proved indispensable to the spread of Christianity. Conversely, Büttner disparaged native people that refused to convert. He scorned their paganism and referenced their practice of keeping women in common as a mark of their barbarism.[30]

By the next generation, a more racist government would strip women like Zara Schmelen and her mixed-race children of their legal status and identification as Germans. Farmer Carl Becker defended his family and protested these measures in a letter to the government from 1909. He expressed his pride in taking care of his family instead of abandoning them the way many white men did. He cited the family's many contributions to the colony. He concluded: "If my civic rights remain denied me, if my marriage is not recognized in law, it will finish my joy and pride in the country which I have served with all my strength these many years. . . . Nevertheless, there is no power in this world which will make me leave my wife, who has been a true companion for the past twelve years."[31] Genuine ties of affection drew white settlers and native people together, exposing the power of intimacy to undercut racial hierarchies.

Elite local women also proved indispensable to the state. In Nelson, on the South Island of New Zealand, intermarriage between whites and Maoris had stabilized relations for at least a generation. Descended from Maori nobility and married to a half-caste, Huria Matenga (1842–1909), also known by her Christian name Julia Martin, was a successful farmer and substantial landowner who maintained a Western-style dwelling overlooking the bay, complete with manicured lawns in the English fashion. Her home enabled cultural exchange, in her private life and personal taste, but also in public display, a visible testament to her embrace of British imperialism and a literal meeting space where whites and Maoris comingled. Matenga and other Maori risked their lives at sea to rescue ten stranded members of a British ship's crew in a storm in 1863. In a ceremony commemorating their bravery in service to the British Empire, officials awarded silver watches to the men who participated in the rescue. Because she organized the party, Matenga received the gold, with English engraved on one side and Maori on the other. As the British master of ceremonies proclaimed, "Englishmen know no distinction when rewarding conspicuous merit. . . . Mankind—no matter what colour or race—are knit together by the feelings of our common nature . . . you have made yourself worthy of the recognition of all noble-minded men by your praiseworthy deed."[32]

The ceremony provided an opportunity to advertise the supposed racial harmony of the British Empire and its generosity, even fellowship, toward subject peoples. A monetary award accompanied the watch, but Nelson Province Superintendent John Perry Robinson (1810–1865) insisted that this was not a money payment for services rendered "but as an evidence of the gratitude of the Government for their good and Christian act of saving life, even at the risk of their own."[33] By attaching universal good to the Christian faith, officials used the occasion to promote the colonizer's religion while celebrating common humanity. Although honored as the heroine of the rescue, Matenga remained silent while her husband, whose father was a British whaler and trader, accepted the award on her behalf. This womanly virtue only made her more of a heroine in the eyes of the British. A subject of children's literature and national myth, Matenga lived on, variously depicted as a romantic maiden, a masculinized tribal woman, or the last of a dying race. The real Matenga recedes from the record just as she did from the stage when she received her laurels.

Native women on the frontiers of empire sometimes experienced empowerment through their relations with European men. Whereas their femininity might initially be called into question by new arrivals unfamiliar with their

Figure 2.2.   Zitkala-Sa portrait
Zitkala-Sa (1876–1938), whose father was white and mother Lakota, was given the
name Gertrude Bonnin when she was removed to a boarding school. In her outlook
and appearance, she merged indigenous and European femininities.

gender systems, women like Dark-Lanthorn gained status and material privileges
through their association with white traders. They negotiated the absorption of
newcomers into their cultures, many of whom went native. After the arrival of
missionaries, however, their gradual embrace of Christianity often meant adoption of European gender norms (see Figure 2.2). Some nonetheless infused their
new family formations with vestiges of native practice, creating hybrid forms of
intimate life. As with the Schmelen family, their mixed-race daughters might
gradually erase their blackness in phenotype and in culture, only to have it rein-
scribed during the later more virulently racist phase of European imperialism,
particularly in the German Empire.

COLONIZED WOMEN

In the period before colonies became deeply rooted, frontier women had a range
of options when traders arrived into their communities, especially after they
converted to Christianity or otherwise adopted and adapted to the outsider.

Their mixed-race offspring might also enjoy social mobility for a time. These options were rarely available to other colonized women. "Slaves" suffered cruelty but might gradually improve their lives through strategic alliances with men, forming abolitionist movements or launching slave rebellions. Observers questioned their virtue when they entered into sexual relationships for any reason but love. "Prostitutes" entered the commercial sex trade as sex slaves or as voluntary immigrants and madams who empowered themselves through sex work. "Indentured Servants" may have also engaged in prostitution but eventually had other options for making money in agriculture, manufacturing, and domestic service, trades similarly practiced by women colonized in their own countries. Their productive labor notwithstanding, a general trajectory toward widespread adoption of the monogamous nuclear family suggests that—despite the adoption of temporary survival strategies—many women adapted hybrid forms of European domesticity, their Christianity and maternity demonstrating their innate virtue. In this way, gender norms tempered cultural differences.

Slaves

Whether transported to the plantations of the Caribbean or sold into sexual slavery, as was the case with Ahyssa and most non-African slaves, women suffered sexual violence, bearing the offspring of unions with masters, in addition to the other degradations of enslavement. Commentators rarely described them as virtuous, although a devout Christian like Mary Prince (b. 1788) of Barbados won her freedom after an upstanding white man testified both to her master's cruelty as well as to her virtuous character. "Indeed, she always appeared to me to be a slave of superior intelligence and respectability; and I always understood such to be her general character in the place."[34] Slave societies of the Caribbean developed the most multiracial populations of the eighteenth century in which early arrivals—men in the military, agriculture, commerce, and eventually administration—entered into relationships with enslaved women. As Ahyssa's story illustrates, these societies had become racially complex, with immigrants, free and enslaved, from many parts of the world disrupting the black/white binary. Like Prince, some former slaves became abolitionists, whereas others might become plantation mistresses in their own right. Creating options often depended on the whims of the master. Although coercion occurred more often than not, evidence of slave women entering into liaisons with white men suggests that this could be a liberation strategy, as can be seen in the case of Petite-Nanon, a domestic servant enslaved to Nicolas de la Fargue (d. 1744), a wealthy French merchant residing in Saint-Domingue.

La Fargue stipulated in his last will and testament that his five slaves should be freed and that his nephew Jean Guerre (d. 1763) should inherit his fortune. The will also named substitute heirs, the brothers Jamet, in case Guerre left no legitimate heirs. In the meantime, Guerre entered into a sexual relationship with Petite-Nanon, a house slave with whom he had two children. In 1744, she and the other slaves gained their freedom after La Fargue's death and the couple married in 1755, now the parents of five children. When Guerre died in 1763 the substitute heirs, François and Pierre Jamet, filed a lawsuit against Petite-Nanon charging that her children could never claim their great-uncle's inheritance because the union lacked legitimacy due to her lack of baptism. They did not question the children's right to inherit their father's wealth. However, as substitute heirs they insisted on their right to inherit La Fargue's assets. Significantly, they based their objection to the marriage on religion rather than race. In fact, Petite-Nanon claimed adherence to Catholicism, although she apparently had never been baptized. The high court at Port-de-Paix upheld the marriage and the inheritance, and condemned the Jamets to pay the cost of the suit.

A lengthy appeal process followed. This time, the Jamet's lawyer invoked threats of slave rebellion to keep Petite-Nanon in her place. He insisted that free blacks and mulattos should in every case be excluded from the privileges enjoyed by whites, especially the right of inheritance. He reasoned that the safety of whites demanded it because the success of some ex-slaves might inspire others to break their chains. In 1773, the magistrates finally upheld the initial verdict, and the children of Jean Guerre and his legal wife Petite-Nanon enjoyed the fortune of their father as well as that of their former master La Fargue. The Catholicism of both spouses apparently superseded the interracial character of the marriage.[35]

As the population of free people of color expanded throughout the Caribbean in the eighteenth century, metropolitan officials and planters alike became increasingly nervous about the stability of white power. In 1761, Jamaica passed the first comprehensive legislation to contain miscegenation, specifically striking down inheritance privileges. "Bequests tend greatly to destroy the Distinction, requisite and absolutely necessary . . . between white Persons and Negroes . . . and Mulattoes," according to Lovell Stanhope (1720–1783), the British agent whose policies angered planters and merchants who believed their intimate relationships were none of the government's business.[36] According to Stanhope, white men's infatuation with women of color might be tolerated, but not the transfer of property to such "Savages or their Bastard spurious progeny."[37] He worried about the "ascendency which the Mulattoes, especially the females, have already in that Country over dissolute Minds."[38]

In societies where white women were few in number, mixed-race women enjoyed an elevated status. Some even frequented the governor's mansion. For example, Lady Maria Nugent (1771–1834), wife of the governor of Jamaica, preferred the company of mixed-race women, "in-betweeners," to other whites.[39] In a diary entry from 1802, she described a sumptuous meal of jerked hog, followed by a crab pot stewed with peppers, okra, ham, and spices. She added, "I was really sicker than usual, at seeing such a profusion of eatables, and rejoiced to get to my own room, and, after my usual levee of black and brown ladies, to go to bed."[40] Nugent also fraternized with black men, including dancing with one at a ball at the governor's residence. Other society women were known to have sexual relations with black men, despite the considerable scandal this could cause.[41]

These warm relations notwithstanding, no significant white abolitionist movement formed in the Caribbean. Rather, African and mixed-race women led the way. Mary Prince joined the Moravian Church and with their support published a narrative of her life, the first female-authored slave narrative to be published in Great Britain. Sarah Ann Gill (1795–1866), also of Barbados, campaigned through the Methodist Church against slavery on the basis of its incompatibility with Christian morality. This led whites to destroy her church in 1823, forcing Gill to preach from her house. Within a year the Church reassigned her to South Africa where she continued her abolitionism.[42] Sisters Elizabeth Hart Thwaites (1772–1833) and Anne Hart Gilbert (1773–1833) of Antigua also fought against slavery, emphasizing how it dehumanized women and destroyed family ties. They linked slavery to prostitution in a comprehensive condemnation of male vice. Working through the Methodist Church, the Hart sisters generated self-help strategies like the Ladies Negro Education Society.[43] Finally, enslaved women acted as leaders in slave revolts in addition to their everyday acts of resistance. Nanny Grigg inspired the slave revolt of 1816 in Barbados, for example, urging men to take up arms following the example of Haiti.[44] The condemnation of male vice enabled abolitionists and feminists alike to elevate female virtue as the corrective. While acknowledging the unique cultures and degradations suffered by slaves, they articulated universal femininity as a platform for their activism, eventually joined by white abolitionist women in North America.

The Atlantic slave system was something of an anomaly. In most slave systems, women were primarily trafficked into some form of sexual servitude. Arab slavery in the Ottoman Empire included the trafficking of white Caucasian women, a practice that outraged the Western world. International contests over control of the Caucasus border provinces between Russia and Turkey destabilized and impoverished the region in the early nineteenth century and spiked the numbers of the enslaved, including debtors who sold themselves or their children, hoping for a better life. Local traders transported their captives across the Black Sea to slave markets in Constantinople. White sex slaves were trafficked through Constantinople to destinations as far flung as Latin America and India.[45]

For example, in 1852, Semsigul was sold to an Egyptian merchant, Deli Mehmet. She would in turn be resold at a slave market in Cairo. She became pregnant en route after he raped her. Mehmet did not disclose the pregnancy when he sold her in Cairo. The buyer returned her as damaged goods. Mehmet then beat her and force fed her poisons to cause an abortion. After this failed, a neighbor took her in, telling Mehmet she would procure a proper abortion. Instead, she took care of Semsigul until she gave birth. The neighbor sent the infant away and told Semsigul that he was dead. She was forced to return to Mehmet who tried to sell her again without success. She ran away to the police and relayed her story, alleging that Mehmet and his wife sold her illegally and caused her to lose the baby. The record ends there, but her resolve to obtain justice reveals avenues for empowerment even to those most disempowered.[46]

Although the plight of the white slave garnered the most international attention, the majority of slaves in the Ottoman Empire were in fact not white. Abolitionists in Europe sensationalized the plight of white slaves to propagandize
against all forms of slavery, but Ottoman defenders of slavery emphasized the
high status of harem women, likening their enslavement to arranged marriages
in the West.[47] As elsewhere, status usually followed the color line, with white
women made into harem wives and brown and black slaves from the Arab world
and from East Africa consigned to sexual servitude and menial household labor.[48]
For them as well, pregnancy could prove disastrous. An enslaved African woman
in Syria fled to the British consulate in Damascus in 1863. She had been badly
beaten by her owner and his brother, both of whom acknowledged having sex
with her. As neither wanted the responsibility of the child, they jointly tried to
induce abortion through beatings. The consulate turned her over to the Ottoman
governor-general who granted her asylum during the term of her pregnancy and
then freedom afterward.[49] This was consistent with Islamic law. When enforced,
it enabled freedom for women fleeing abuse, especially when pregnant.

Arab slavery persisted through the nineteenth century. Slavery within Africa
only ended with the colonization of West Africa by the British and the French in
the 1890s. Similar to the Ottoman trade, women featured prominently in African
slave systems because they performed more services, including sexual, and could
be used to secure male slaves attached to them. The arrival of whites who claimed
to bring the end of slavery, such as the British in Ghana, complicated the situation of young women, some of whom, like Abina Mansah, appealed her case to
court. Abina's enslavement was itself produced by abolition as the slave owners
among the defeated Asante knew that young women would be less likely to
demand their rights than other enslaved populations. But Abina understood that
after 1876 all people would be free. In her trial she explained: "I heard that master
(meaning white man) had said we were all free. Yet I had been sold and I had no
will of my own and I could not look after my body and health: that I am a slave
and I would therefore come and complain."[50] To her this meant that they would
be paid for their work, which she was not, and would have greater personal autonomy, regarding marriage choice for instance, which she did not. Indeed, it was
when her master arranged a marriage for her that she finally ran away. The trial
pitted her lawyer, a Christian convert who believed in the British civilizing mission, against Gold Coast financial interests who feared her liberation could spark
widespread rebellion. Their lawyers insisted that Abina had never been enslaved
in the first place because she did not witness an exchange of money. She therefore
lost her case but was not required to return to her master. Such ambiguous ver-
dicts punctuate the Age of Empire.

Elsewhere in West Africa, French commanders lured male slaves off of large
estates offering freedom in exchange for military service as well as female slaves
who provided material support and companionship to their French liberators.
But, as with Abina, it was unclear what freedom meant for these women.
Missionaries complained of French men who kept women as mistresses, including

girls as young as ten years old. They also obtained slaves after conquest, as was customary in some African societies. After a definitive victory in 1898, the French obtained nearly three thousand slaves, including hundreds of women from the harem, many of whom were emancipated only to be awarded to loyal allies.[51]

Even though the French formally abolished slavery in 1848, emancipation in the colonies came gradually. Meanwhile, runaways sought refuge in Christian missions or government offices, often to be sent back, as the French did not want to disturb native institutions. Gradually, however, policies and institutions developed, including liberty villages, to emancipate those who could pay a tax, those whose masters did not claim them, and those who were sold to missions that would then free them. Some of the most devoted converts were slave women who achieved freedom this way. Missions arranged marriages for them with recent male converts. As their numbers increased during the great exodus of nearly one million slaves throughout French West Africa, the French passed decrees promoting emancipation. Women sought to recover lost children and mission networks assisted with family reconstruction, complicated by the fact that men migrated to the cities and mines for work.

Some women fled to Christian missions to escape husbands. In one region, 69 percent of slave litigants were such women. The courts recognized Fanta Kone's freedom from her husband, for example, because she resided with her original family. Women's bids for independence were more successful when they belonged to a family as long as there was no record of legal marriage. One family ransomed their daughter back from her captor husband by giving him two cows.[52] Women in sexual servitude could also secure custody of their children as long as no legal marriage existed. Guine Toukoula got her children back in 1912.[53]

Like Ahyssa, enslaved women pursued paths to empowerment through the legal system, showing the multiplicity of responses to imperial violence. Maternity sometimes required legal intervention and the courts proved sympathetic in these cases, especially when litigants presented themselves as virtuous mothers and converts to Christianity. Local circumstances could undercut the brutality of slavery and the law.

Prostitutes

Some enslaved women were forced into prostitution. Others turned to it out of economic need, others out of a desire for independence and higher wages than they would receive in most other forms of paid work. Faced with the increased presence of imperialists in their communities, there was constant demand for commercial sex. European men living abroad seldom served in one locale for more than a few years, so they were unlikely to relocate their families, if they were married, or to form enduring attachments with native women. Therefore, many forms of commercial sex developed, most highly regulated by the late nineteenth century.

In the eighteenth century, the Dutch East India Company established a large brothel of female sex slaves in Cape Town for its employees, who passed through on their way to India, Southeast Asia, and the Far East.[54] Sex workers similarly streamed into the brothels of large urban centers such as Bombay, Singapore, and Hong Kong, catering to an assortment of local men, immigrant laborers, and European travelers. To be sure, British authorities in particular attempted to impose racial boundaries even on the sex trade. When they captured Cape Town from the Dutch in 1806, the British immediately imported white prostitutes to replace the black slaves.[55] In many parts of the British Empire, bordellos were officially classified based on the race of workers and clients. The "first-class" brothels, many of which employed only European women, were reserved for an elite white clientele. The "second-class" brothels offered up both white and native prostitutes to lower-level white men. The mostly unregulated "third-class" brothels were those frequented by native customers.[56]

The women who worked in the commercial sex trade came from many walks of life and entered in and out of sex work as economic need arose. As civil servant Francis Mayne (1827–1872) in India wrote in 1870, "The women who walk the road every evening to the west of the Cawnpore Cantonment, the coolie women and milk sellers, who are employed at the barracks in the day time, all of them married women, and by repute respectable household women, are as much common prostitutes as the most habitual professionals."[57] While this statement reveals Mayne's perceptions about women's occupation of public space, it also describes a reality for many women who sold sexual services: they did so occasionally, in addition to their other jobs and often despite being married. Native women who provided sexual services for pay likely understood their work differently from the colonial state.

Prostitution was prevalent in Hong Kong as a military outpost of the British Empire. In 1870, the chief magistrate estimated that five of every six women worked in the trade. Doctor Pang Ui-Shang, who treated patients with venereal disease, estimated that only 25 percent of the female population was "respectable."[58] Whereas some women, and especially girls, may have been trafficked to Hong Kong, some went voluntarily, seeking fortune. Liu Zhang wrote of her plans in 1891: "I am willing to go with Dai Yan Tong. He is a con-man, 29 years old. If he makes money I hope he will give some to me so that I can buy two or three girls and open a brothel and be the female boss. This is what my heart really wants."[59] Liu Zhang saw becoming a brothel keeper as a legitimate career aspiration. Some prostitutes became brothel keepers: some as young as nineteen, some as old as sixty. Only women kept brothels in Hong Kong, and this was the only sector of the economy where women could function as independent business operators. Once acquiring a building and a license, they purchased girls; provided clothing, jewelry, and a room at minimum; and then split the earnings. The larger the staff, the larger the profits: an investor with thirty-seven girls in her employ made back her investment within six months. One strategy to maximize profits was to buy preteen girls, who could be had as young as two years old for $2, compared to $150 for a teen. Raising her to puberty, brothel keepers made back their costs from the high deflowering fees wealthy clients would pay.[60]

Some prostitutes left China, settling on the US frontiers to improve their lives. Chinese women populated the early settlements of the West, including Virginia City, Nevada, where by 1870 they were a majority of all prostitutes.[61] Some had been sold into sex slavery before departing China, others were lured overseas by pimps, and still others immigrated voluntarily, either intent on becoming prostitutes or falling into it once other options evaporated. In Virginia City, Alfred Doten (1829–1903), a local journalist, recorded a visit to a well-known Chinese prostitute in his diary: "Went with Sam Glessner down to Chinatown—drank at Tom Poo's—went to Mary's house—we were in her room with her—she gave us each a cake left over from the holiday of yesterday—filled with nuts and sweetmeats—we laid on bed with her + smoked opium with her—a little boy some 2 yrs sleeping there, belonging to one of her women—long + interesting chat with her."[62] This entry illustrates the multilayered exchanges that could take place involving food, drugs, and conversation in addition to sex. In Doten's voluminous diary there is little overt racism, although white prostitutes charged higher fees and moved about society a bit more freely. Some became quite wealthy and were noted for their philanthropy. This path was not open to Chinese immigrants. Nevada historian Mary Mathews (1834–1903) complained that no respectable women come to the United States from China.[63] But, as seen elsewhere, deepening prejudice led to legal measures against interracial sex, in this case laws restricting Chinese immigration in the 1870s and 1880s.

But men still sought Asian prostitutes, and other Asians sought opportunities. Like their Chinese counterparts, poor Japanese farmers whose livelihoods were rapidly disappearing as Japan modernized in the nineteenth century sold their daughters. Others immigrated voluntarily. Procurers recruited them with stories of wealth and likely marriage to rich Americans. Hirakawa Tōkichi and his wife relocated to Seattle where they managed a profitable brothel in the early 1890s. When they returned to their Japanese village with their newly acquired wealth, they built an expansive house with a tiled roof. Dazzled neighbors called it "the American House."[64] The desire to escape poverty and get rich quick motivated many to immigrate, married and single. Some accompanied husbands but entered prostitution once in the United States because of poverty or a desire to divorce. One of eight children, Yamada Waka (1879–1957) immigrated to Vancouver and then Seattle to help her family save its sugar beet farm. There she was forced into prostitution under the name "Oyae of Arabia."[65] Her name doubly exoticized her but also rendered it meaningless, a sham even.

Generally, prostitutes congregated in red-light districts. Some were segregated by race as in Virginia City, or integrated in the case of Seattle's Deadline district. One Japanese tourist described it as "an international flesh market" in 1911, where some five hundred women of diverse origins and ethnicities solicited clients.[66] Despite the multiracial character of such districts, the trade was racially stratified. In San Francisco, for example, clients paid according to race: "$1.00 for native-born girls; $0.75 for French women; $0.50 for Chinese, Japanese, and black prostitutes; and $0.25 for Mexican women."[67] This trans-Pacific client base was multiracial as well. Many Asians hired prostitutes, but white women generally refused to serve them. Because demands for whites remained stable, outpacing supply on the West Coast, white prostitutes maintained greater control of the conditions of their labor. Governments variously attempted to regulate and then abolish the trade, often with little success.

The desirability of white prostitutes and metropolitan fears about race mixing led some governments to import them to military bases in Africa. While Eritrea had long attracted Italian immigrants, the mixed-race population was small in the early twentieth century. After Italy's invasion of Ethiopia in 1935, more Italian men entered into relationships with local women and greater penalties followed when Fascist Italy embraced race purity as official policy. As the military population increased, some local women voluntarily entered into concubinage with Italian soldiers for material and status advantages in a practice of high-class prostitution called *madamismo*. Known to Italians as "Black Venuses" thanks to the decades-long trade in erotica, madams commanded both respect and recognition of their autonomy in the patron–client networks they controlled. The Italian government condemned such relationships as "a violation of the prestige of the white race" in the Racial Laws of 1938.[68] The offspring of such unions could not gain citizenship, even in cases where their fathers intended to recognize them. When it came to maintaining racial purity, the state disregarded European male autonomy. In a circular letter to all Italian residents, Governor Guglielmo Nasi (1879–1971) insisted, "Aut Imperium aut Voluptas" (Either Empire or Pleasure).[69] Constructing interracial sex as damaging to the cause of empire, the government imported French prostitutes to service Italian men, transported by rail in what were called "Venus cars."[70] Previously, cohabitation with an African woman could cost a European man his military commission. By 1937, it became a criminal offense punishable by five years in prison. Meanwhile, punishments of white women who had relations with African men included public whipping and incarceration in concentration camps.

Women engaged in the increasingly global sex trade occupied a spectrum of experience from child enslavement to autonomy and wealth. Prostitution was a feature of imperialism from first contact and is arguably the site of its most flagrant contradictions. The sexualization of exotic women and their association with more animal forms of embodiment invited desire as well as disgust. The dependence of imperial men on local women meant that intimacy constantly sabotaged efforts to maintain segregation and the illusion of European moral superiority. At the same time, some local women maintained control of the conditions of their work.

Indentured Servants

European governments settled many colonies with convict labor, using colonies as repositories for poor and criminal whites. Those who were deemed undesirable at home could be useful abroad helping to accomplish imperial objectives by establishing white settlements among natives. Australia was developed in this way. Many more men than women immigrated, leading to skewed opportunities and perceptions. Local officials in Australia described women convicts as sexually dissolute, "lower than the brutes, a disgrace to all animal existence."[71] Lieutenant Ralph Clark (1762–1794) exclaimed at the arrival of the *Lady Juliana* convict transport in 1791, "No, no—surely not! My God—not more of those damned whores! Never have I known worse women!"[72] But in fact the stereotype of "damned whores" erases the complexity of Australian women's experiences. The punishments they endured reveal a brutal equality between poor men and women, including hard labor sentences and corporal punishment. Flogging remained legal until 1817. Afterward, head shaving and solitary confinement took the place of bodily torment, but head shaving in particular desexualized women. Poor and without status in Britain, they became homesteaders in Australia. During their term of indenture, their children were placed in orphanages. Some newly freed women determined to get them back and reclaim their maternity, the basis for virtuous feminine identity throughout the British Empire. After their term of indenture ended, many self-identified by other trades, although for survival they may have occasionally engaged in prostitution.

By the 1840s, lesbian subcultures developed in sex-segregated factories, such that officials documented it as a dangerous problem, once again perpetuating the association between lower-class status and deviant sexuality. Poor women generally were thought to be less capable of virtue, regardless of race. In 1842, John Hutchinson (1793–1866), the superintendent of Hobart Factory, reported five women "dancing perfectly naked, and making obscene attitudes towards each other, they were also singing and shouting and making use of most disgusting language. There was a sixth woman but I could not positively swear to her, the disgusting attitudes towards each other were in imitation of men and women together."[73] Although the women claimed to be joking, their "dirty, beastly action" resulted in a sentence of one year's hard labor for all but one of the women.[74] Officials proclaimed that "sexual lapses of women must ever be held more deplorable than those of a man simply because the offence in the woman's case causes more harm within her environment and more rapid and permanent injury to her own more delicate moral and intellectual fibre."[75] Moreover, the sexual license of women, especially lesbianism, withheld white women's procreative potential from a minority population in need of white babies and also because it evoked the specter of women living independently without men.

Women who lived without men or who only entered into temporary unions with them were suspected of prostitution throughout the British Empire. In the nineteenth century, the arrival of hundreds of thousands of South Asian indentured servants in Jamaica and other Anglo-Caribbean possessions complicated the racial hierarchy, especially because many more men than women immigrated, which resulted in complex racial intermingling. These men entered into relationships with black women or mixed-race women more often than with white women, still relatively few in number. Because of their own relatively small numbers, Indian women immigrants entered into relationships with other Indians and with whites as a survival strategy but on their own terms. One woman explained, "When the last immigrant ship came in I took a *Papa*. I will keep him as long as he treats me well. If he does not treat me well, I shall send him off at once; that's the right way, is it not?"[76] Such choices empowered women and prevailed in locales where the ratio of women to men was skewed to the women's advantage. Because these unions existed outside the law, men and women alike moved in and out of them.

British missionaries found the calculation underlying these temporary unions shocking. The British government responded by enticing Indian men to form durable families with land allocations, thus rewarding men's agricultural labor while shunting women off to the domestic sphere and replicating European family structures and feminine identities for all races. They cultivated virtue among immigrant women by enticing them out of the labor force and into monogamous procreative unions with men of their own race. Laborers from India migrated to the Caribbean as indentured servants to work plantations, including sugar, coffee, and cocoa. Figure 2.3 shows the suitability of women's generally smaller hands and frames for certain kinds of harvesting.

Figure 2.3. Women picking tea
Women's agricultural labor was essential to the growth of the global economy. Tea plantations employed thousands as the global demand for tea escalated during the Age of Empire.

A gender division of labor meant that workforces included up to 25 percent women. Photographs from the first decade of the twentieth century from chocolate companies Rowntree and Cadbury reveal that women removed and sorted cocoa beans from pods. Indian women feature disproportionately in the photographs because of their exotic appeal. In actuality, the majority of women working in cocoa production were still African in origin. Families might work as units, with men harvesting trees and replanting the fields, and children picking off bugs and sifting cocoa. Their living arrangement maintained the family as a unit of production. Workers normally resided in company barracks on estates but cultivated their own vegetable patches. All workers "danced" the beans to remove pulp.[77] Government reports documented pay scales, skewed in favor of men because of the nature of tasks performed, but also show that some women performed men's tasks and owned their own tools for this purpose. "Princess Wallace . . . provided her own hoe and cutlass and used one of each per year. She also kept eight fowls, and was a member of a Friendly Society."[78] Women worked as long and as hard as men at harvest time when the gender division of labor gave way. A male farmer in Guyana said, "When there is a push, the woman does work equal and straight with me."[79]

Some women even owned estates—51 of 635 cocoa estates in Trinidad in 1905, for example. Indian women especially valued land ownership as a marker of status and independence. One landowner described her mother's strategies for acquiring a large estate and what it meant to her: "My mother first buy seven acres of land in Sangre Grande [in 1917]. . . . That was cocoa land that she start to work for sheself. In the 1930s, . . . she start to rent 100 acres from the Mendez Estate, a cocoa estate in north Manzanilla. She eventually buy the 100 acres from the owners . . . she give plenty people work on the cocoa."[80] Through large scale farming, some women could operate their businesses and their lives on their own terms. Conversely, in Guyana, gender differences were more pronounced on small farms where women reported an aversion to doing men's work, their feminine identity increasingly defined by domesticity.

THE COLONIAL HOUSEHOLD

Gender and race informed women's relationships with each other, as household managers and servants within the household. While structured by race and class, women's interactions within the intimate sphere of the home fostered a multiplicity of responses and occasionally undercut imperial power structures. Among the first white women to immigrate voluntarily to colonies were the wives of missionaries, planters, and later civil servants. "Settling" on the frontiers, white women played multiple roles, often those normally occupied by men. This explains in part why frontier women in the United States gained the vote in the late nineteenth century and why New Zealand was the first country to grant women's suffrage in 1893. "Managing" servants developed as settlers established themselves permanently and class stratification occurred, marked by large staffs of servants. "Children" of settler families perhaps experienced the most intimate relationships with local people. Accounts of such relationships from the servant's perspective differ significantly from that of the child.

Settling

During the first wave of massive migrations out of Europe to settle the Americas, poor or persecuted Europeans voluntarily immigrated, sometimes as whole families. Governments interested in securing their colonies promoted white settlements to create neo-Europes. In 1778, the Spanish Crown sent two hundred poor families to Patagonia, on the southern end of South America. José Cornide (1734–1803) proposed to cultivate cotton there, employing whole families, including women. He cited the "extreme fecundity" of Galician women in particular who could not feed their children at home and who contributed to overpopulation in Spain. In his view, such fecundity was just what this uncultivated and unpopulated land needed.[81] Over a five-year period, thirteen separate ships transported the families, who in the end totaled 1,921 men, women, and children, including 81 of the most desperately poor children who arrived to board the ship completely naked and ill.[82] So committed to the enterprise was the government that it provided maternity and child care both before boarding and on ship, including one Caesarian section that the mother actually survived.[83] Indeed, healthcare on board was better than it would be on either side of the voyage. Most passengers survived, including children under two years old.

Upon arrival, most settlers took up residence in what is known today as Uruguay, few ever making it to Patagonia due to war with native peoples and disease. But their presence transformed Montevideo from a wild-west frontier town to one more conducive to Spanish family life. The daughters of settlers enjoyed attention from the mainly male population, permitting the Crown to claim that it had put an end to interracial relationships. Spanish commitment to women and children made the enterprise more successful than other colonization schemes in Spain and other European empires, demonstrating the centrality of gender to the imperial project.

Where settlers established plantation agriculture, hierarchical race and gender relations structured household life. Households, particularly plantation households, could be places of male brutality. Survival generated surprising alliances on a Caribbean plantation, for example, as detailed in one legal case in which the litigants were referred to only by last initial to protect their identities. Madame N of Saint-Domingue married Monsieur N in 1759. Monsieur N's alleged brutality ranged from beating his three daughters to subjecting his wife to degradation—including locking her in a closet for up to eight days and feeding her only crusts of bread and water. Her lawyer depicted him as a brutal Creole who allegedly allowed his slaves to die of malnourishment, neglect, and overwork, to the point where he dissipated his fortune replacing them. To survive this brutality, alliances emerged between the women of the household, especially between Madame N and the slave who nursed her children. Indeed, this woman evidently saved Madame N's life more than once when her husband attempted to kill her. Her lawyer then elaborated on her friendship with her husband's concubine, who had taken up residence on the plantation. "One understands how, in similar circumstances, one desires to make friends, and above all a woman has more need of that sweet affection which can sometimes result in a tender and sincere liaison between two persons of the [fair] sex."[84] He went on to report that when the wet nurse tending the concubine's baby ran out of milk, Madame N urged her father to procure another. Although the record does not mention the race of the concubine, she was likely black, possibly even a slave, as she resided on the plantation. At the very least, she would have been a mixed-race woman given the island's demographics.

Male slaves also intervened on Madame N's behalf. On one occasion, her husband beat a child in her arms, knocking her to the ground. He ordered a slave to bring his pistol. The slave's refusal probably saved her life. This final attempt on Madame N's life drove her to file for separation in 1770. Monsieur N contested the decision. Deploying the whole arsenal of stereotypes against white women in the Caribbean, Monsieur N's lawyer concluded that, "A husband is, for such women, only an instrument of their vanity, a slave to their tastes."[85] He added that the "lasciviousness of the climate" made white women weak, lazy, and sensual.[86] He alleged that Madame N's rescue by a male slave verged on adultery, the ultimate subversion of Monsieur N's male/master prerogative because neither white women nor black men could be trusted. As further proof, he cited his wife's interest in African cooking, learned from a male slave, but to no avail. When the high court at Cap-Français affirmed the earlier decision, the separation became final in 1785, twenty-six years after they married.

This case shows how interracial intermingling charged every relationship in the intimate sphere with pleasures and dangers. From kitchen help to wet-nursing, women befriended and betrayed each other. Especially where allegations of adultery erupted, whole communities could be mobilized along racial and class lines. Where women lived isolated from communities on plantations or in sparsely populated villages, solidarity could sometimes protect and even empower women. Solidarity emerged when women's differences from each other were blurred by their vulnerability to brutal men, but solidarity did not imply equality.

Managing

Managing homes, plantations, laborers, and servants, colonizing women empowered themselves and extended their influence beyond the home. Madame N managed the plantation well when her husband left for a seven-year sojourn in France, a factor that worked in her favor in court. European settler women generally engaged in a wider variety of roles than they would have at home. Gradually these roles included the moral uplift of settler and native populations. According to Caroline Chisholm (1808–1877), an English advocate for the welfare of women immigrants to Australia, "For all the clergy you can despatch, all the schoolmasters you can appoint, all the churches you can build, and all the books you can export, will never do much good without what a gentleman in that Colony very appropriately called 'God's police'—wives and little children—good and virtuous women."[87] Some early settlers fit the bill. Georgiana Molloy (1805–1843) married a pastor in England and settled in Augusta, Australia. Her voluminous correspondence describes her benevolent influence on the people her husband ministered to and the difficulties early pioneers faced. She presents an early example of "God's police." However, in addition to raising a large family (she died after the birth of her seventh child), she collected and labeled the first compendium of botanical specimens for the colony, demonstrating the variety of roles that frontier women could occupy.

Molloy's correspondence includes descriptions of lower-class whites who populated "this iniquitous Colony" and of her daily encounters with Aboriginals.[88] "One morning . . . about 20 natives came about and seeing potatoes in the garden and being instructed in the use of them by one that had been domesticated with some settlers, they were anxious to attack them. . . . I had Sabina in my arms, no servant or any one near me. . . . I was afraid to show fear and smiled."[89] They threatened her but then left. Managing meant protecting her children and embodying her superiority over the natives who could be dangerous. Her recourse to her womanly and motherly smile resolved the situation more effectively than firearms. Such influence became part of the national identity of Australia. In 1915, Australia became the first nation to form a female police unit, tasked not with fighting criminals but "in patrolling dance halls, parks, beaches and other places where young people congregate."[90] They also urged purity for men, best inspired by the white women they would marry: "Bright, educated, companionable, capable women will make cheerful, economical homes, keep the men from gambling and other bad habits, render embezzlement and speculation unnecessary and generally purify life."[91] Settler women usually had only their supposed racial superiority as a means of controlling subservient people, but sometimes they used violence as well.

Women's letters from South Africa about relations with servants reveal a surprising degree of intimacy, self-reflection, and even self-irony. In 1861, Lucie Duff-Gordon (1821–1869) recorded being laughed at by a servant whom she threatened with corporal punishment: "I begged him to be patient; on which he bonneted himself in a violent way, and started off at a pantomime walk. I told him, 'Ik sal je slaan' (I'll beat you) which is the last resource. He went off into the grandest guffaw I ever beheld, and was most anxious to fetch the 'sjambok' . . . for me to try. 'Oh yah, yah, yah, I like see Missis 'slaan Jack,' and roars of laughter."[92] Others admitted to difficulty carrying out threats of punishment but came to see corporal punishment as the most effective way to control domestic labor. "Boxing Boxer's ears was a trial to me, I confess, but I came to that at last, and repeated the dose when I once discovered its efficacy. I had been before but a poor thing in his estimation. I rose . . . at the end of the process full fifty per cent in his estimation."[93] Such emasculation also infantilized male servants. In 1875, Harriet Roche (1835–1921) treated her servants as misbehaved children who would only understand the rod. At the other extreme, her contemporary Mary Anne Barker (1831–1911) wrote of Maria, "She is so inexpressibly quaint about it all that one has neither the heart nor the command of countenance necessary to scold."[94] So Maria not only escaped physical discipline but also verbal abuse or even scolding. Indeed, some women wrote about the high quality of their native servants compared to those in Britain.

In a 1901 letter home, American teacher Philinda Rand (1876–1972), employed in the Philippines after the US invasion of 1899, described punishing her Filipino servant Francisco for ignoring her orders. When forced to kneel for two hours, he "wept for one hour and now is meekness itself. He does not even walk down stairs without permission."[95] She added, "I never realized also how true it is that they are, as Kipling says, 'half devil and half child.'"[96] Control also extended to gazing or even spying on their servants. For women who likely would have had very little opportunity to see scantily clad men, being surrounded by them was both a pleasure and a danger. Rand wrote in her diary about her "picturesque" cook who had a "pair of magnificently shaped legs" and about a servant's friend who visited "without any garments whatever, except the clout," and was "glistening with water and made a fine bronze statue as he stood with a pail in his hand."[97] Rand enjoyed the power she had over handsome men. Although her mission as a teacher was racial uplift, her practices, her gaze, and her willingness to disclose them reveals the pleasures and privilege offered by racial dominance.

Being a teacher, Rand could not employ a large staff of servants at home, but women's withdrawal from physical labor was especially important as a marker of their virtue and respectability. In 1929, Dutch journalist Beata van Helsdingen-Schoevers (1886–1920) proclaimed, "Isn't it true, every European woman in the Indies is a lady?"[98] This perhaps ironic statement testified to the upward class mobility that race privilege enabled for white immigrants. Furthermore, "a decent European [man or woman] does not perform manual labour or housework because of his prestige, and in the second place it is far too hot to do so."[99] Women who may have toiled back home on farms or in factories could supervise the labor of others, rendered inferior because of their labor in addition to their race. Europeans claimed that the inhospitable climate justified their exemption from manual labor as well as their refusal to assimilate into local culture. Such ladies perceived themselves to be a civilizing influence in the colonies, worthy of deference. In 1917, Maria Nittel-de Wolff van Wester-rode (1884–1945) described the necessity of white women's residence overseas. "Certainly in his heart the Native . . . also has respect for the European woman, whom he perceives as a personality, standing above him in culture, development and morality."[100]

Dutch women could obtain professional training to learn how to manage their staffs, either by attending the Colonial School for Girls and Women in The Hague or by studying training manuals. Pupils at the colonial school studied the Malay language, tropical hygiene, tropical medicine, food, and ethnology. The curriculum aimed to sufficiently familiarize students with local culture such that they would not be afraid of "natives, wild beasts and serpents."[101] In such exotic environments, white women enjoyed racial privilege even as they performed traditional gender roles: as wives, teachers, and household managers. Some experienced greater autonomy than they would have at home, while others were isolated on remote farmsteads or plantations subject to male brutality. They occasionally formed intimate relationships with neighbors and servants, though such friendships could be undermined by rivalry for the attention of men and children.

Children

Domestic servants had the most intimate and sustained interactions with European colonists, particularly children. As a symbol of their improved class status, white immigrants to the colonies hired as many servants as they could to perform even the most intimate of family tasks. In early colonial India, white women with infants hired native servants to nurse them. Wet nurses sold their milk to white families with nurslings, depriving their own of the milk. So deprived, these children commonly died. Mary Martha Sherwood (1775–1851) published a memoir of her time there between 1805 and 1815. She recalled a saying, "White child is good, black child his slave."[102] Race and poverty determined which children mattered, which would survive. White children might never know the sacrifice their existence exacted on the women they were closest to.

The use of Indian wet nurses, and the bodily intimacy it entailed, caused anxiety. Frederick Corbyn (1791–1853), author of *Management and Diseases of Infants under the Influence of the Climate of India* (1828), worried that: "Persons who generally eat opium, and smoke a poisonous narcotic, called bhang; who will promise to abide solely and wholly by the food given to them from their mistress's table, or to that which is prepared by the lady's cook; but will obtain, by an insidious contrivance, garlic, ghee, etc., and partake of the most sour and acrid vegetables; all of which the poor little infant sucks to a certain degree in the milk."[103] This was generally thought to be a contributing factor to the relative laziness of European children outside of Europe. Manual authors depicted them as uncouth and spoiled by doting caregivers who were more similar to the children than to adult authority figures. Although stereotypical, these depictions reveal a frustration with Indian agency, as servants clearly exerted influence far beyond their basic job descriptions.

Similar prohibitions existed elsewhere and were equally ineffectual. Indonesian servants recalled being told not to hold children. Ibu Rubi sarcastically explained the fear of the parents that "later they'd smell of [our] sweat. . . . The sweat of Javanese is different you know."[104] Because the division of labor reflected the traditional Javanese separation of the inner world of women (child care, cooking) from the outer world of men (serving, running errands), women were therefore closest to the food and also to the children. Figure 2.4 is a testament to the power of intimacy to transcend prohibitions.

Figure 2.4. Jantje and Agnes in the care of Baboe Mina, Surabaya, 1915
Female servants took care of European children, sometimes developing close relationships as suggested in this photo from Dutch Java.

An Indo-Dutch woman, Lin Scholte (1921–1997) recalled being nestled in a sling worn by nanny Bibi Koetis who rocked her to sleep while singing: "I still remember how heavenly I found that . . . [nestled] flat against her body, rolling with her slow rocking gait, with the veil-like material of her [blouse] gently grazing my cheek and her humming resonating in her breast so that I could feel it with the rise and fall of her voice. It was as if she flowed through me."[105] Dutch memoirists often wrote about nannies, these being their most intimate adult companions from childhood. But other servants could also exert fascination. Ernest Hillen (b. 1934) recalled the family gardener in Indonesia: "Manang wore faded khaki shorts that used to be my father's, no shirt, and a straw hat that hid his eyes. His large flat feet had spaces between the toes because he didn't have to wear shoes. . . . I wanted feet like that, and his shiny brown skin, and I tried to walk bow-legged like him."[106] He liked that Manang smelled of different kinds of smoke and moved with a relaxing gait.

These warm feelings may not have been reciprocated. Indonesian servants spoke about their work when interviewed decades later. By the 1930s, placement services connected employees to employers connoting a level of professionalism.[107] Some described their work in straightforward factual terms—what tasks they performed, what they were paid. Some described being welcomed as members of the family. Ibu Tinem liked working for her family who treated her like one of their own children. She commented favorably on being kept neat and clean and watched over when she received letters from a suitor. Her placement in their family was an escape from village poverty and a stepmother's cruelty, offering security that disappeared during the Japanese occupation of the country during World War II.[108] Others told stories of abuse. Ibu Sastro described being fired when she refused her employer's sexual advances. "So he wanted that, but I didn't want it. 'I'll give you money later, if you want' [he said]. . . . I didn't say anything, I was afraid."[109] Her sudden disappearance troubled the children. The result was that parents sought to limit intimacy with servants. A 1906 housekeeping manual urged mothers, "If we take care that our children hear a cultured, pure speech there is no reason to despair of forming good Dutch-speaking people; teach them that their place is in the family circle, and not in or near the servants' quarters; . . . teach our children as quickly as possible to care for themselves."[110] Servants might become part of the family or disappear without a trace. European children raised by local caregivers developed intimate ties but also received conflicting messages about that intimacy. Their mothers may have immigrated to the colonies to expand their own options beyond the domestic sphere, relegating childrearing to others, yet they also expected their children to develop European identities. These conflicts illustrate the range of responses to imperial intimacies for both colonizer and colonized.

INDEPENDENT WOMEN

For those women who embraced the opportunities that the colonies provided, time overseas enabled the transgression of metropolitan norms. "Nurses and Teachers" occupied traditional roles but still became world travelers and enjoyed a greater degree of autonomy than they would in those same professions back home. "Travelers and Collectors" undertook world travel and residence overseas for its own sake. As more European women obtained advanced degrees, independent incomes, and successful careers, more explored the world for reasons similar to imperial men. "Pleasure Seekers" included socialites who might go so far as to marry non-white men. Others came from working-class immigrant families. The most adventurous were the most inclined to transgress norms, especially sexual ones.

Nurses and Teachers

This trajectory can be seen in callings in which women embarked on enterprises relatively unsupervised. Male anxieties about their autonomy led to the bureaucratizing of their professions, especially in nursing. Following the example of the already iconic Florence Nightingale (1820–1910), British women left for West Africa in the latter part of the nineteenth century to engage in nursing. Nightingale opposed the professionalization of the field, arguing that feminine sensibilities were the most important qualification for tending British men overseas. The chief medical officer of the Gold Coast agreed, writing in 1896 that, "Good looks and a cheerful disposition conjoined go a long way in the successful management of cases of illness in this Colony; indeed in my experience of practice here, I have found that a tender touch, a sympathetic look . . . have done more good to their patients than the drugs, or other therapeutic measures prescribed by them."[111] But Mary Chamberlain (1864–1957) founded the Colonial Nursing Association to certify that only adequately trained nurses were sent out and that they be of appropriate moral character as well, with "sound religious and moral principles. . . . The girl who merely wishes to escape from the restrictions of home or life in England, who desires to place first 'seeing the world' and 'enjoying life'" need not apply.[112] After scandal erupted involving the younger nurses, the association went so far as to recruit only "lady nurses" of "mature years and less attractive appearance."[113] Professionalization also meant better pay. Feminists supported the professionalization of nursing as an avenue to women's independent employment. They were quicker to realize that recruiting "lady nurses" meant enabling middle-class and married women's paid employment, something the more conservative members of the nursing association rejected. Local associations and even colonial governments preferred "trained nurses of the servant girl class or members of a nursing religious sisterhood."[114] Lady vocationists and career nurses made too many demands, insisting on negotiating their terms for work and better pay. They rejected the title Matron to describe the superior nurse, preferring Senior Sister instead.

Similar conflicts erupted in Dar es Salam. Frieda von Bülow (1857–1909) used nursing as a vehicle for adventure travel, evidently never intending on doing much healthcare when she immigrated to German East Africa (modern Tanzania). The consul reported to the foreign office that "Miss von Bülow herself admits she knows nothing about nursing."[115] Instead, she excelled at organizing and fundraising and saw entertainment as a great service to German imperialism. As cofounder of the German National Women's League, Bülow saw the colonies as the space where women could achieve personal as well as national glory. But league officials complained that she squandered their treasury to "spend it there with the gentlemen on her pleasure."[116] Bülow's story pitted two very different versions of imperial femininity against each other: the matrons who intended to bring civilization as virtuous and upright exemplars of European femininity and the new women in search of adventure and autonomy, sexual and otherwise.

Bülow sensationally engaged in a love affair with Carl Peters (1856–1918), the founder of the German East Africa Company. He was infamous for his racism and brutality, eventually sanctioned for the rape, torture, and murder of Africans that he employed, including his African mistress and her lover. Bülow promoted the vision of a superior man, like Peters, who would spread German nationalism across the globe, even breaking metropolitan laws to do so. She thus stood by him: "I know that you can be brutal, and I certainly don't love brutality. But I also know that this brutality is almost inseparable from certain qualities that are rare and of the highest value, and that it is necessary in some situations."[117] When their affair ended, Bülow played the role of caregiver and adviser. She went so far as to recommend Peters marry a Jew for her millions, and, recalling his sadism, she reminded him that "all of them stand poor treatment excellently. So you would get along."[118] Given her deep anti-Semitism and dread of racial contamination, it is unlikely that Bülow was serious. Once free of Peters, she wrote fiction and managed her own estate, acquired in part through the contacts she had in the colony's wealthiest circles, contacts made when she worked for the nurses association.

Nurses generally cared for other whites. Teachers, on the other hand, generally tutored native children. Their demeanor and relationships therefore had to be even more carefully monitored. Teachers were among the first to be dispatched to the Philippines once the US occupation began in 1901. Inspired by Theodore Roosevelt's (1858–1919) invocation to undertake "The Strenuous Life" (1899) and bring civilization to savages, hundreds of teachers signed up. Mary Helen Fee (d. 1935) described her excitement: "I was going to see the world, and I was one of an army of enthusiasts enlisted to instruct our little brown brother, and to pass the torch of Occidental knowledge several degrees east of the international date-line."[119] Fee was one of more than five hundred teachers who left from San Francisco. More than one-third of this group was women, three-fourths of whom were single.[120] Another five hundred arrived within a year. Debates ensued about whether single women should even be allowed to serve overseas. Because they interacted more directly with colonial populations than other personnel, civilian or military, officials feared for their safety and morals. Furthermore, they were not connected to a religious order or private company. They represented the best of American Empire, according to the government, especially women who symbolized benevolent and peaceful uplift. This uplift included instruction in English and basic math and science. Advanced studies took the form of gender-specific vocational instruction: boys were trained in carpentry and agriculture, girls in lace, hat, and basket-making.[121]

The government was so committed to educating the population that it offered double the salary paid for the same work in the United States.[122] Financial gain attracted some teachers, as did the opportunity to travel and even to prove women's capabilities. Lisette Seidensticker (d. 1904) wanted to "refute the intimations of certain eminent professors that women are not fitted" for work overseas.[123] The feminists among them enjoyed demonstrating to locals that they could drive alone at night and carry pistols. Some took the opportunity to pursue their other interests, including ethnography, psychology, or botany. Like nurses, they brought not only their training but also their feminine sensibilities, which signaled a shift in colonial policy away from violence and toward moral persuasion. Once local teachers supplanted them, they became supervisors and school officials, enjoying authority they would likely have been denied at home. Still, some sought the adventure of the frontier. Fee asked to be transferred to a Native American reservation where she could more directly carry out the civilizing mission.[124]

Some European women were so committed to their goals as educators that they left family and homeland behind, and even religion. Irishwoman Margaret Noble (1867–1911) described her conversion to Hinduism in 1904: "Always I had this burning voice within, but nothing to utter. How often and often I have sat down, pen in hand, to speak, and there was no speech. And now, there is no end to it! As surely I am fitted for my world—so surely is my world in need of me, waiting, ready. The arrow has found its own place in the bow."[125] Attachment to another language and culture impelled her to utter previously suppressed speech. She found liberation in a new language, converted to Hinduism, and became a teacher. She took the name Sister Nivedita, "she who has been dedicated."[126] She likened her decision in 1895 to follow the guru Swami Vivekananda (1863–1902) to Nirvana, defined as "The Uncreated Flame itself we long for, without symbol or veil or barrier."[127] She moved between two cultures, enjoying both a Western woman's freedom of movement and the Eastern traditions that connected her to Indian women. Yet she retained white privilege and could have returned to Ireland and her roots.

Living in slums, Nivedita gained credibility with Indian women for whom she opened schools. Committed to a bicultural curriculum, she taught Bengali and English side by side in her school for girls. Pupils studied the geography and history of India in addition to that of England. She included sewing and needlework so that her pupils would have possibilities for useful employment. Orthodox Hindu parents allowed their children to go to the school in their neighborhood because Nivedita modeled the discipline expected of a Hindu woman. Her impeccable reputation and thoroughly Hindu identity gained her access to secluded women as well. She provided in-home education for married women observing purdah, the Muslim requirement that women remain at home, sequestered from men. While in Calcutta, she also engaged in relief work during plague epidemics. But she remained independent from any religious order or educational institution. This independence enabled her to join forces with Bengali nationalists. However, when she was threatened with arrest in 1907, she returned to England, exercising the white privilege she had never lost. She resumed residency in India in 1909 and remained there until her death in 1911. Although her school suffered from underfunding and sometimes very limited enrollment, its name is still used today.[128]

Travelers and Collectors

Women like Sister Nivedita traveled abroad to fulfill a religious calling. Many colonial teachers and nurses professed a similar dedication to serving others. Travelers and collectors ventured overseas for less lofty reasons. Margaret Fountaine (1862–1940), a renowned butterfly collector, traveled through sixty countries on six continents (see Figure 2.5). She collected until her death in Trinidad at age seventy-eight. Her collection of twenty-two thousand specimens remains on display in Norwich, England. Heir to her uncle's large fortune, she valued the freedom enabled by her money but also by her lack of attachments. "Freedom is the crowning joy of life. Thank God there are few on earth I really care for; I would there were none. I want to see all I can of this beautiful world before I have to leave it, and life is so distressingly short . . . it is the affections that tie us down to one spot."[129] Insect and plant specimen collecting was a legitimate pursuit for a Victorian woman of means. It signaled her engagement, not with peoples and cultures, but with the delicate side of nature. It was one of the major ways women both benefited from and facilitated imperialism.

In Syria, Fountaine began a life-long love affair in 1900 with a married man fifteen years her junior, her Greek-Egyptian assistant and guide Khalil Neimy (1877–1928). She kept it a secret, only allowing her diary to be opened posthumously in 1978. She likened love to conquest and records that she initially resisted

Figure 2.5. Margaret Fountaine
British butterfly collector Margaret Fountaine explored the world with her Syrian assistant and lover Khalil Neimy. Her adventure travel and scientific study illustrated the possibilities for women opened up by imperialism.

his advances, but "the very audacity of the man overcame my sense of all that was right and proper. Why are men such animals?"[130] Elsewhere her diary attests to an enduring affection between the couple that lasted until his death in 1928. "The roving spirit and love of the wilderness drew us closely together in a bond of union in spite of our widely different spheres of life, race and individuality, in a way that was often quite inexplicable to most of those who knew us."[131] Neimy was a naturalist in his own right, and the collection today bears both of their names. Fountaine escaped sanction due to her discretion and to the increasing prevalence of the so-called spinster abroad, the stereotypical wealthy Victorian lady traveler who lived life on her own terms.

British explorer Mary Hall (1857–1912) traveled throughout East and South Africa because she could and because it was there: "In 1904, when South Africa was still uppermost in all minds, I decided to turn my steps in that direction."[132] Her account of her travels includes many sublime, mundane and hilarious encounters with Africans, but at least once she acknowledged that her porters "never doubted the omnipotence of the white skin to overcome every difficulty."[133] But race privilege could only get her so far. As a woman alone, she believed her vulnerability enabled her to enter into more equitable relationships with Africans than a white man could. She described how far a "little courtesy" got her in the company of sultans and herdsmen alike.[134] She recounted one near-combat situation when her courtesy literally disarmed a "dusky chief" and his men in East Africa over the apparent conscription of one of his men by the two soldiers escorting her.[135] She apologized and offered a compromise that the man in question be allowed to accompany them only as far as the next river. Once they came to terms, the "dusky chief" allowed her to photograph him, thus documenting "one of the most thrilling incidents of my life."[136] Eight miles on, he sent her a goat as a present. The chief's high status enabled this exchange among equals, her gender beneath his, his race beneath hers. Although, as an upper-class woman, she described her porters as children, she was not above play herself. When they made haste into Blantyre, Malawi, supporting her in a hammock strung across a pole, they "assumed the same hilarity they had displayed at the start, and we approached the hotel in great form" such that she tumbled out of it "more or less in public" and appeared as "a disorganised mass at the onlookers' feet."[137]

Hall's sense of humor and self-mockery undercut the social distance her class privilege might have dictated when relating to servants. Other women brought a seriousness of purpose to their travel. By the 1930s, women did not need to be carried in a hammock to see Africa. The automobile enabled women to undertake long-distance road trips. A new woman who enjoyed the open road, German journalist Louise Diel (1893–1967) trekked through Ethiopia after the Italian invasion in 1936. Far from traveling for its own sake, Diel was instrumental in forging an alliance between the German Nazis and Italian Fascists in the 1930s. She published *Women under Italian Fascism* in 1933 and later a book on dictator Benito Mussolini (1883–1945) that was endorsed by high-ranking

Nazi officials. *"Behold Our New Empire"–Mussolini* (1939) was "successful as a record of high-speed travel and industrious enquiry."[138] In her introduction, she announced "I feel not a little proud, and consider myself exceedingly fortunate, to be the first of my sex in the writing profession to have set eyes upon Abyssinia since the change. I travelled alone, taking with me, in lieu of companions, a camera and a typewriter. . . . In discussing my third visit to Africa—the first took me to Libya, a second to Tunis—Signor Mussolini said: 'You will find a good deal less 'Africa' than you expect.' We shall see how correct he was."[139]

Diel praised Italian colonialism for carving out a place for Italy under the African sun and assured readers that Mussolini wished the same for Germany. For Diel, civilization included policies against racial mixing. Like other imperialists of her time, assuring Italian men of access to white women was the solution. "It is bound to be seen that all laws and measures of precaution would be futile if an insufficient number of white women were not prevailed upon to settle in East Africa. In the long run, only the family and family life can remove the danger of racial intermingling and ensure successful development of the Empire."[140] It was through Diel that Africa came to serve as the nexus between the visions of the two regimes. However, her support for women's independence as well as personal connections to Jews and Catholics garnered the regime's ire in the 1940s.[141]

Pleasure Seekers

Except for Diel, few of these women did much for the cause of empire. Governments formed recruitment societies to attract more "reputable" women to the colonies.[142] The French, for example, founded the French Society for the Immigration of Women in 1897. In that year, it received five hundred requests by women predominantly from the lower middle class. Unlike the pastor's or the diplomat's wife, most of these women listed independent professions, especially after World War I. However, instead of virtuous and prolific wives dedicated to the civilizing mission, critics saw women perpetuating racial condescension, a taste for luxury, and an aversion to hard work. Officials and tourists alike alleged the "vacuity of their minds, the emptiness of their souls, their lives!"[143] Male observers contrasted the natural, simple beauty of shy native women, with their "doe eyes," to the gaudily dressed immigrants, "their make-up sliding off with their sweat."[144] For French West Africa, the founder of the women's immigration society, Comte Gabriel d'Haussonville (1843–1924), urged that better sorts of women immigrate, classifying women immigrants to the colonies in three types: "A handful of devoted wives of civil servants, wishing their husbands had been appointed elsewhere; used-up entertainers who can no longer get billings anywhere in the home country; and religious sisters or nuns."[145] In this way the colonies could be repositories for nonconforming women just as they had been for nonconforming men. Such immigrants failed to uphold white femininity as constructed in the metropole.

Like Diel, Russian Isabelle Eberhardt (1877–1904) ended up advancing the political interests of an imperial power. Eberhardt immigrated to Algeria in 1897, converted to Islam, took multiple Arab lovers, cross-dressed, and smoked hashish. The scandalous identity she constructed reveals the degree to which imperial spaces enabled experimentation and the degree to which modern identities were self-fashioned and influenced by climate and local customs. Marrying an Arab Muslim, she accessed French citizenship, illustrating the ironies of intersecting identities at the intersections of world history. Because she could pass as an Arab, the French state used Eberhardt as a spy during one of its later pacification campaigns. To achieve its objective of a continuous vast French Empire in West Africa, the government needed control of Morocco. Instead of costly wars, the state now forged alliances with local elites. Eberhardt accomplished this in her relations with Sidi Brahim, head sheik of the powerful Qadiriyya Sufi order in Morocco. Posing as a Sufi mystic, having previously attached herself to the order, she sought study with the sheik who promptly gave her an isolated cell in which to pray. By now a celebrity, Eberhardt could not maintain the disguise. He knew her true identity and tried to compel her to live the role she had only played at. Nonetheless, she secured the alliance, but drowned in the desert at age twenty-seven on her way back to Algeria.[146] Eberhardt's flaunting of convention contributed to her success as a spy. By drawing attention to herself, she permitted the government to use her.

In her novelized memoir, Marguerite Duras (1914–1996) chronicled the cynical pleasure-seeking of a rebellious daughter. Her mother Marie Donnadieu (1877–1956) immigrated to Vietnam with her husband. After his early death she was forced to raise their three children by herself on a teacher's salary. Duras proclaimed her determination to enjoy a better life. She described her mother's plainness against the sophistication to which she, as a modern girl coming of age in 1920s Saigon, aspired: "My mother, my love, her incredible ungainliness, with her cotton stockings darned by Dô, in the tropics she still thinks you have to wear stockings to be a lady, a headmistress, her dreadful shapeless dresses, mended by Dô, she's still straight out of her Picardy farm full of female cousins, thinks you ought to wear everything till it's worn out . . . her shoes are down-at-heel, she walks awkwardly, painfully, her hair's drawn back tight into a bun like a Chinese woman's, we're ashamed of her."[147] Dô, the Vietnamese maidservant, raised by nuns and nearly raped by one of Duras's brothers, remained loyal to her mistress, even relocating to France with her later in life. She had been trained as a seamstress and rendered sackcloth into frocks for Marguerite with pleats and Peter Pan collars. Marguerite hated their formlessness and borrowed a brother's belt to shape them to her figure. The modern girl in the colonies rejected traditions from Europe, especially rural traditions. She also rejected her mother. Yet Duras's mother also knew her modern girl daughter had a future that involved money. "That's why, though she doesn't know it, that's why the mother lets the girl go out dressed like a child prostitute" in her gold-lamé shoes and man's broad brim hat.[148] She also wore makeup at age fifteen. "I use Crème Tokalon, and try to camouflage the freckles on my cheeks, under the eyes. On top of the Crème Tokalon I put natural-color powder—Houbigant. The powder is my mother's, she wears it to go to government receptions. That day I've got lipstick on too, dark red, cherry, as the fashion was then."[149] She described how men looked at her, as they did all white women in the colonies, and girls too, as young as twelve years old.

At age fifteen, Duras began a clandestine love affair with a wealthy and older Chinese businessman. Her daring not only broke with tradition, with the mother, but also with feminine virtue and white privilege. For a white woman, illicit interracial sex was the last frontier of respectability. Yet it was her very whiteness that enabled this transgression. The love affair began when the elegant man offered her a cigarette on a ferry and told her about his student days in Paris and his father's opium addiction. He took her to his apartment with its ultramodern furniture, an appropriate setting for the modern girl's deflowering. She attributed his trembling to her whiteness. When he professed love, "She says nothing. Suddenly, all at once, she knows, knows that he doesn't understand . . . such perverseness. And that he can never move fast enough to catch her."[150] She told him she came for his money, which he duly gave her. Her descriptions of him border on orientalist: thin and vulnerable, hairless, not much of a man except for the penis. Intimidated by his father, "He often weeps because he can't find the strength to love beyond fear."[151] When her mother accused her of prostituting herself with him, she lied, even when her mother searched her body for traces of a Chinese scent. She appealed to her mother's racism to dispel the suspicions. "How could I, I say, with a Chinese, how could I do that with a Chinese, so ugly, such a weakling?"[152] Duras's scandalous affairs, and her graphic accounts of them, made her a modern girl on the margins. She concludes *The Lover* with meditations on her white schoolmate's breasts: she wanted to eat them.

Elite Western women also sought sexual leisure in Mediterranean cities, on Caribbean beaches, and in the Grand Tour of colonial hotels. By the 1880s, women tourists outnumbered men in Southern Europe and North Africa, both of which gained a reputation for romantic female getaways.[153] They flocked to Caribbean islands with their steamer trunks, where many rented spacious beach homes and tapped young black men to service them for the duration, often seeking out the same man year after year. The locals all knew which youth paired up with which lady tourist, so when the ships docked there was rowdy teasing: "Simon, your mudder com!"[154] In the 1920s, the palatial hotels that became a fixture of colonial tourism—such as Cairo's Shepheard's Hotel, Colombo's Grand Oriental Hotel, Hanoi's Hotel Métropole, and Jakarta's Hotel des Indies— provided another venue where temporary sexual encounters between Western travelers and native peoples transgressed norms of race, gender, and sexuality. As noted delicately by a Ceylon travel guide, "In the hotels, passengers frequently make the mistake of supposing they are attended by maid instead of men servants."[155]

Most white women kept their sexual indiscretions to themselves: Fountaine revealed hers to no one but her diary, Duras denied it during the time, and Eberhardt dwelled far outside polite society. Yet more transgressive were the white women who married their non-white suitors and mothered mixed-race children. A high-profile case erupted in Australia in 1915 when wealthy socialite Molly Fink (1894–1967) married the Indian Raja of Pudukkottai (1875–1928). The *Melbourne Punch* reported that, "Mrs. Newly Wed brought her coffee-coloured prince to proudly present him to her envious acquaintances. What was her surprise to find them not envious! All agree that he is a charming and cultured man to meet—but not to marry.... Several calls which the newly-married pair have paid have not been a huge success."[156] Social ostracism and gossip isolated the couple. Speculation about the coloration of their firstborn appeared in the news as well. The mixed-race population that emerged from Asian immigration to Australia in the late nineteenth century led to limits imposed by the Immigration Restriction Act (1901). Their marriage took place in an era of pronounced xenophobia.[157]

FEMINISM

White women who hired male prostitutes may not have seen their behavior as feminist, but independent European women enjoyed the benefits when feminists opened up access to wealth management and higher education. They in turn extended a shift in European attitudes that enabled single women to experience empire on their own terms. As part of a knowledge transfer circulating between West and East, modern feminists also joined forces regionally and globally to challenge patriarchy in all its guises. For some feminists this also entailed challenging imperialism. Activists gradually developed a transnational feminist politics that could cross racial and religious boundaries. Women claimed citizenship equal to men and analyzed gender roles. Their interracial organizing also enabled them to articulate the ways in which race and gender are coproduced and socially constructed. Originally they cooperated in intraregional associations, such as the "Trans-Pacific," the "All-India," and the "Pan-Islamic." Whereas feminist consciousness developed during the eighteenth century in many cultures, transnational feminist political mobilization emerged in the nineteenth century as part of the antislavery movement. Other causes incited global activism, including child marriage and polygamy, which often led logically to feminist analysis and organizing. Transnational activism might give way to nationalist anticolonial agitation, although some feminists maintained a commitment to internationalism through the peace movement or communism. Their many approaches to gender equality reveal the multiplicity of responses to imperialism and how intimate relations, including friendship, undercut imperial rule.

Trans-Pacific

Raden Ajeng Kartini (1879–1904) launched feminism in modern Indonesia. She began a correspondence with Estella Zeehandelaar (1874–1936), a Dutch peer, in 1899. She conveyed the prejudice she experienced as an Indonesian: "What have

I not suffered as a child at school through the ill will of the teachers and of many of my fellow pupils?"[158] She castigated the imperialists who complained of native laziness and idiocy, but did nothing to educate them. White civil servants with pretensions to nobility especially incurred her ridicule. "The European makes himself ridiculous in our eyes whenever he demands from us those tokens of respect to which our own rulers alone have the right."[159] These included being shaded by a native holding a golden umbrella and being kissed on the feet by submissive natives. But in another letter she proclaimed, "I love the Hollanders very, very much, and I am grateful for everything that we have gained through them" particularly how they favored the Javanese nobility, of which she was a member.[160] "Father sent a note to the Government on the subject of education. O Stella, I wish that you could read it. You must know that many of the native rulers rejoice at the actions of the Government. The Javanese nobles are in favor with the Government here and in the Motherland, and everything possible is done to help them, and to make them blossom to perfection."[161] She thus drew attention, perhaps unwittingly, to the class prejudice of the Dutch. But Kartini was a feminist first and foremost; rarely did she espouse nationalist leanings. She predicted violent strife but for the woman's cause. "While this agitation among the men is on the [table], that will be the time for the women to rise up and let themselves be heard. Poor men—you will have your hands full."[162] Kartini and Zeehandelaar developed a friendship that transcended race. "I am no Javanese, no child of the despised brown race to you; and to me you do not belong to that white race around us that holds the Javanese up to scorn and ridicule. You are white to me in your understanding of the truth, white in heart and soul."[163] Although she died shortly after giving birth at age twenty-five, her copious letters assured the survival of her ideas and her reputation as one of Indonesia's founding feminists. By the 1920s, nearly every Indonesian town had a women's organization, some eventually named after Kartini. Like Kartini, they advocated women's access to education and monogamy while critiquing Indonesian patriarchy. Like Kartini, their relationship to Dutch colonialism was ambivalent.

When transnational feminist organizing developed in earnest, interracial friendship could facilitate an ambitious women's rights agenda. Indeed, New Zealand was the first nation to grant full women's suffrage in 1893. Still, "the devil which leads to a feeling of superiority and arrogance" needed to be exorcised, according to New Zealander Elsie Andrews (1888–1948) who co-organized a New Zealand delegation to attend the Pan-Pacific Women's Conference in 1934.[164] She knew that even the best-intentioned white women could fall into maternalist condescension toward their supposed racial inferiors. Andrews's interracial friendship with Maori Victoria Amohau Bennett (1888–1975) illustrates the racial harmony of New Zealand but also the struggle against the subtler racism of liberal activists. Of mixed-race descent, Bennett traced her Maori lineage to her maternal grandmother. Educated in an elite boarding school and a Christian, Bennett became active in women's issues through the YWCA. In a 1934 letter to the YWCA periodical *New Zealand Girl*, she encouraged women to commit to Christian ideals of service and of standing "united and unafraid."[165] By then a mother of three, she served as the YWCA acting president in 1936.

Together they attended the annual meeting of the Pan-Pacific Women's Association held in 1934 in Hawaii. The Maori members of the delegation obtained an audience with Hawaii's princess Abigail Kawānanakoa (1903–1961). Kissing the princess's hand, Andrews joined a brown sisterhood, reversing her racial position. Andrews believed in British imperialism and pitied the fate of native Hawaiians. This strengthened her determination that British tutelage would help the Maori to preserve their heritage. Yet the success of the Maori delegation in the "Brown Pacific"—in their space and on their terms—foreshadowed the end of empire, which Andrews would live to see.[166] Bennett helped Andrews translate her speech into Maori and to learn a native dance, which, Andrews wrote, degenerated into burlesque when performed by a clumsy outsider. Andrews thus remained at the margins, despite her role in organizing the conference. Andrews and Bennett became fast friends on the long sea journey, but Andrews apparently hid her lesbianism, which drove another wedge into their interracial understanding. She described learning of Bennett's "purple past without giving away my own."[167] Purple, as applied to Bennett, clearly implied her mixed-race blood, whereas Andrews's subversion was sexual. Her letters written to her partner during the conference also indicate a level of homoeroticism and the allure of interracial sex, as elsewhere glimpsed only to be foreclosed, but now in the context of international movements for women and for the autonomy of colonized peoples.[168]

All-India

Women reached across national and racial divides by forming large regional organizations like the Pan Pacific. Other ways of cutting across divides included pan-Muslim movements. Like Kartini in Indonesia, some Muslim feminists in India criticized polygamy and the seclusion of women. Because this was practiced by Hindus as well, trans- or all-India organizing also united women across sectarian lines. Print in English aided this process, as seen in Figure 2.6.

Rokeya Sakhawat Hossain (1880–1932), a Muslim educator and feminist from Bengal, India, devoted her life to the education of girls, founding and directing a school in her name and also several organizations. However, her first attempt foundered over the issue of purdah, which required that girls never be visible to male strangers. Hossain found it difficult to allow them to observe purdah and be transported to school by bus. She contrived to cover the windows, but the bus became so hot that students vomited or fainted. When she opened the windows and the curtains fluttered, parents complained that purdah had been violated and that she was suffocating them alive in "the moving black hole of Calcutta."[169] After this effort failed, Hossain concluded, "On behalf of the women imprisoned in seclusion, I wish to say: Oh why did I come to this miserable world, why was I born in a purdah country!"[170] Hossain published this account, among others, in

CONTENTS.

                                                                    PAGE
Ourselves   25
Queen Victoria and Queen Alexandra.—(Illustrated)   26
Social Intercourse between European and Indian Ladies   ..   29
Col. Meadows Taylor's " Seeta ": A Study   31
The Vedic Wife   34
In the Forest :—A Poem   36
"A Little Child shall lead them":—A Hindu Story   37
Pundita Ramabai and her Work.—(Illustrated)   40
Miss Marie Corelli on " Sovran Woman "   43
Friendly Chats between Ourselves :—The Home   45
Seriousness : A Fancy   45
The Low-Caste Wife: A Sketch from Life   48
An Indian Lady's Appreciation   49
Editorial Notes:—Women's Work in the Handicrafts; Miss Ghosal
        on the Education of Indian Girls   50
Things Seen :—The Marina   52
Indian Cookery   52
Correspondence :—Lady Ampthill's Women's Memorial to Queen
        Victoria · The Maharani's Girls' College, Mysore ; A Famous Indian
        Lady   53
News and Notes   55

Figure 2.6. Indian Ladies magazine
Indian and British women collaborated to produce periodical literature of interest to both populations.

The Secluded Ones (1928). Some critics reacted harshly, echoing a recurrent charge from her detractors that "to her everything Indian is bad and everything Euro-American is good."[171] Accusations of being too Western could silence feminists in an era of emergent anti-imperialism. But the relative gains made by non-Muslim Indian women, including liberal Hindus, indicted the purdah system. As girls' schools proliferated at the end of the nineteenth century, tens of thousands of Indian women completed higher education and entered professions. Few of these degree holders were Muslim.[172]

Hossein is best known as the author of *Sultana's Dream* (1908), a utopian short story in which the gender order is reversed. In her futuristic society, complete with flying cars, men are secluded. As a result there is no crime. Typical of feminist politics of the era, *Sultana's Dream* combines gender equality with gender essentialism in which the seclusion of men and the liberation of womanly qualities lead to a better world. Indeed, this woman's paradise was the result of warfare in which most of the men were killed and the defeated veterans welcomed into seclusion by the women who assumed leadership roles in their absence. Women professors, who had mastered solar power, pushed back the enemy with their marvelous display of the harnessed sun's power. They were then left to live in peace.[173] Hossain's radicalism was but one form of Muslim feminism.

While Muslim feminists shared a commitment to women's education they differed on the central issue of seclusion. The female ruler of Bhopal in India, Sultan Shahjahan Begum (1838–1901), undertook three European tours as she contemplated reforming the position of women. One of the founders of the All-India Muslim Ladies Conference in 1914, she advocated for women's education like others of her generation. But she also defended purdah, especially after her visits to Europe. She concluded that "a woman gains more pleasure from caring for her family than anything else" and noted the "blot on the escutcheon of Western civilisation" wrought by too much freedom for women: divorces, marital turmoil, abandoned women and children.[174] She hoped to take a balanced approach, borrowing the good from the West and leaving behind the evil. She perpetuated the modern construction of femininity along cultural and racial binaries where modesty and virtue follow from women's entrenchment in the family, best assured by seclusion. In her view, freedom of movement made women lascivious.

Hindu feminists gained access to education more readily than did Muslim feminists. One of the most notable Hindu feminists of the period was Sarojini Naidu (1879–1949) who wrote poetry in English. Born into an educated Bengali family, she studied in London and then at Cambridge. Her poem published in 1912 is a paean to a Hindu spring fertility festival but ends with a widow's lament: "For my sad life is doomed to be, alas, / Ruined and sere like sorrow-trodden grass, / My heart hath grown, plucked by the wind of grief, / Akin to fallen flower and faded leaf, / Akin to every lone and withered thing / That hath foregone the kisses of the spring."[175] Patronized by the literati of London as a young woman, she originally composed verses that "were Western in feeling and in imagery" rendering her a "machine-made imitator of the English classics," according to Edmund Gosse (1849–1928), one of Britain's most famous poets and critics of the time.[176] Gosse mentored her during her London sojourn when she was sixteen. He implored her to offer "some revelation of the heart of India, some sincere penetrating analysis of native passion, of the principles of antique religion and of such mysterious intimations as stirred the soul of the East long before the West had begun to dream that it had a soul."[177] He grasped that her success would rest on her claim to Indian authenticity. "She springs from the very soil of India; her spirit, although it employs the English language as its vehicle, has no other tie with the West."[178]

Known as the Nightingale of India, Naidu went on to a career in politics. She organized women of the Indian diaspora, culminating in her leadership at the

East African Indian Congress meeting in Kenya in 1924. The congress formally protested South Africa's Class Areas Bill, which legislated the racial segregation of Indian South Africans, native South Africans having been segregated a year previous. Mahatma Gandhi (1869–1948), the hero of Indian nationalism, sent Naidu in his place, as he was ill from a recent prison term. During her three months there, she was celebrated as "a living testimony of the heights to which a woman can rise."[179] South African feminist Zainunnisa "Cissie" Gool (1897–1963) continued: "She has been a warning to Europeans, a lesson to the non-European, and a glorious inspiration to the dark races of Africa."[180] Upon her return to India, she became the first Indian woman to preside over the Indian National Congress in 1925. Like Gandhi, she participated in acts of civil disobedience for which she was imprisoned.

More active in local issues, Muthulakshmi Reddi (1886–1968), daughter of a college president in Madras, obtained an education equivalent to her male peers and became Madras's first woman doctor. She rejected her mother's Hinduism as superstitious yet retained her commitment to caregiving, but in a secular, scientific context. Having personally struggled against the structural limitations placed on women, she joined or led a variety of reform movements on behalf of women. These included raising the age of consent for girls, ending the practice of "marrying" young girls to temples, ending caste segregation of girls' hostels, and widening access to education, including vocational schools for reformed prostitutes. As a doctor who worked with poor and low-caste women, she identified women's lack of empowerment as a source of disease and early mortality.[181] She worked in maternity, juvenile, and widows' institutions, some administered by the Children's Aid Society jointly created in 1908 by wealthy British and Indian philanthropists. She traced the sources of mental and physical disability to gender-specific neglect and abuse. She started a massive slum rehabilitation program in cooperation with the YWCA and the Bishop of Madras. This multiethnic and transnational cooperation expanded under the auspices of the Women's Indian Association, which she founded. Many doctors and medical personnel participated: Dr. Mary Poonen Lukose (1886–1976), an Indian gynecologist of Syrian Christian descent; American missionaries Ida Scudder (1870–1960) and Anna Sarah Kugler (1862–1930); Dr. Alexandrina MacPhail (1860–1946), a Scottish woman who established a hospital in Madras; and Dr. Rahmathunnisa Begum (b. 1902), who cofounded the Muslim Women's Association in 1928.[182] She also was instrumental in organizing an All-Asian Women's Conference in 1931, which was more anticolonialist than her other endeavors.

Like other feminists of her generation, Reddi's position on marriage reform reflected the rise of heterosexual monogamy as a sign of modernity. She wrote in an undated letter, likely in 1927, "The ideal of monogamous life has been preached and practised by all good men and women of the world and hence the love of one man to one woman has evoked the noblest and loftiest of sentiments, [and] has been the central theme of our epic poems."[183] From this standpoint she campaigned against temple marriages in which low-caste girls dedicated to ritual service, known as devadasis, wedded a temple god and lived their lives as ritual performers and dancers, some entering into liaisons with male patrons of the temple, some subsequently forming families, some remaining celibate. In 1927, the Women's Indian Association condemned temple marriage along with prostitution. Reddi reserved special pity for the devadasis who she saw as patriarchy's greatest victims. She decried a double standard that heaped shame on them while honoring the men who patronized them. Even more, "These devadasis are not the victims of their own inclinations as ordinary prostitutes are, but rather the victims of custom, which teaches them to practice vice as their caste dharma."[184] She went on to sponsor the Madras Hindu Religious Endowments Act (1929), which allowed devadasis to keep their land grants in exchange for a rent payment instead of obligatory temple service.[185]

She even urged Gandhi: "I place the honour of an innocent girl—saving her from an inevitable life of shame and immorality even above that of Swaraj [self-rule]."[186] Devadasis organized in protest, but Reddi insisted: "As for the local devadasis' protest, they are all a set of prostitutes who have been set up by their keepers."[187] Instead she cited the letters of support she got from temple women who happily left the service once their lands had been enfranchised. Viewing temple women as backward and superstitious unfortunates who could only be reintegrated into the dominant society via marriage and vocational school, she energetically opened opportunities for them. She counted many successes by the late 1930s, which included former devadasis entering the professions but above all marriage. "Almost all of them got married and settled into a respectable life" to the extent that by 1937 her organization was no longer needed.[188] Within ten years, the practice of temple marriage was rendered illegal.

Pan-Islamic

While activists in India and New Zealand made significant gains for women, feminists met with greater obstacles in the Islamic world. Periods of Western-style reform were generally followed by a conservative religious backlash except in those areas that became nominally secular such as Turkey and Central Asia under Soviet rule.

In the Ottoman heartland of Asia Minor, modernizers during the *Tanzimat* reform period (1839–1876) criticized the oppressive patriarchy of Turkish family customs. In 1860, Ibrahim Sinasi's (1826–1871) satirical play *Poet's Wedding*, the first Turkish theater production written in Western style, attacked the arranged marriage system. During the 1870s, reformer Ahmet Mithat Efendi (1844–1912) advocated women's education and covered a wide range of women's issues in his treatises, most notably *Women's Philosophy* (1870). Meanwhile, Grand Vizier Mehmet Ali Pasha (1815–1871) called for outright adoption of the French legal code, including its secular, liberal provisions on family law and the rights of women. However, the wholesale reforms advocated by Francophile modernizers were successfully resisted by Ottoman religious authorities, led by Turkey's leading

Islamic scholar Ahmet Cevdet Pasha (1822–1895). *Tanzimat* reformers secured but a few modest legal rights for women and opened a handful of women's vocational schools by 1888, when the reactionary backlash shut down the reform commission and blocked further reforms. Ironically, Cevdet Pasha's daughter Fatma Aliye Topuz (1862–1936) became a pioneer of women's rights when she published *Women of Islam* (1891), a critique of Turkish patriarchy. Topuz went on to write five Western-style novels featuring self-reliant heroines, became a regular contributor to Istanbul's weekly *Ladies Own Gazette*, and founded the Society for Supporting Ottoman Women in 1897.[189]

The forging of the New Woman was put on hold until after the Turkish Republic was proclaimed in 1923, when President Kemal Atatürk (1881–1938) took up the cause as an explicit rejection of the Ottoman past. Revered as the savior of modern Turkey from Ottoman defeat in World War I, Atatürk enacted sweeping changes in gender relations that were achieved only gradually, if at all, in the rest of the Muslim world. In the diary he kept during the war, Atatürk recorded his view that educated mothers were crucial toward Turkish modernity, that women's liberation was a just goal in itself, and that gender equality would also benefit men. "Leading a common life with women will have a good effect on men's morals, thoughts, and feelings. There is an inborn tendency towards the attraction of mutual affection."[190] During the Turkish War of Independence (1919–1923), Atatürk spoke of teachers as officers in the army of education, adding that women must be even better educated than men to dispel backward Ottoman customs and cultivate the modern citizens of Turkey.[191] Soon after taking power, Atatürk carried his message of reform to the deeply conservative villages of the Turkish hinterland, proclaiming that "We will become civilized. . . . We will march forward. . . . Civilization is a fearful fire which consumes those who ignore it."[192] The avalanche of reforms included the adoption of a new family code based on Swiss law, the founding of girls' institutes with the express mission of instilling Western values, and universal women's suffrage in 1934.

By contrast, French women did not obtain the vote until 1944. To strengthen the demand for women's suffrage, the French Union for Women's Suffrage reached out to feminist organizations in French North Africa. Figure 2.7 shows the differences between these cultures in women's clothing. Affiliated with the International Women's Suffrage Association, it claimed up to one hundred thousand members during the interwar years. Their newspaper, *La Française*, featured regular stories on the plight of North African Muslim women whose lives were structured by both Islamic restrictions and privileges. They understood that ignorance and patriarchy were more repressive to women than Islam per se. In 1926, one author concluded, "Nearly all indigenous women suffer not only from their social and familial situations, but also from an intellectual inferiority that we can barely imagine."[193] Such attitudes justified French women's intervention in the lives of their Arab sisters. This could include medical care. Marthe Bertheaume (1878–1963), a doctor, wrote in 1923, "Women have largely contributed to the

Figure 2.7. French woman meets Algerian women
The differences between Western and Eastern women were often signaled by their clothing. Yet some women overcame superficial divides to forge a transnational feminist movement.

expansion of French influence, by undertaking both a humanitarian and moral mission. We know that the system of imprisonment strictly observed in Arab families deprives women and young children of all medical assistance administered by men."[194] Women thus had a special role to play in the deployment of France's civilizing mission. They should be compensated with the suffrage, according to the paper.

The paper occasionally allowed Muslim women to speak for themselves. In 1924, it described Tunisian feminist Manoubia Ouertani who "with rare courage denounced, before an audience composed partly of her peers, the servile situation forced upon Muslim women, and called for a liberation of the women of Africa similar to that of Turkish women."[195] Feminists in Algeria founded the Muslim Housekeeping School in 1935. Meanwhile, Tunisian Tawhida Ben Cheikh (1909–2010) was the first Muslim woman in North Africa to earn a medical degree. Centrifugal forces thus collided over the uplift of North African women—one Eurocentric and the other indigenous.[196] White women in the colonies came to resent metropolitan intrusion, insisting that it took years to understand the Muslim world and that inflammatory tactics, such as featuring unveiled Muslim women as public speakers, would only further alienate a restive population.

Archeologist Jeanne Alquier wrote in 1935, "I will never cease repeating that the metropolitan French must not meddle in the Muslim affairs of Algeria. With the best intentions in the world they risk causing a lot of harm. One must live a long time with the Arabs to know them a little. It is not those who came to sow discord who will have their throats slit the day of the riot."[197] Alquier's prediction would ultimately come true but not because French feminists made much headway there. Ultimately French rhetoric in favor of the emancipation of Muslim women was just that. Even in areas under direct French rule, such as Algeria, the French government did not disturb Muslim family law.

Unlike the Western empires that generally favored religious tolerance in the areas they ruled, the Soviet Union aimed to eliminate religion altogether. It therefore adopted far more aggressive policies in its Muslim provinces. According to one Soviet feminist, "The woman within her family is considered a slave, her husband is the lord of all things, he decides everything and jeers at her."[198] Soviet feminists passed laws banning child marriage and polygamy, enabled women to access divorce, and expanded educational opportunities. Although Central Asia had developed a discourse of feminist reform, the imposition of women's emancipation by an imperial power generated nationalist opposition and undercut local feminist movement. Bourgeois feminist Muslims in other countries such as Turkey and Afghanistan had already instigated similar reforms, more successful to the degree that their reforms were in the service of nationalist modernity.

Communists in Central Asia worried that the contagion of emancipatory ideas would alienate women from communism if they were not proactive. Halmirad Sahetmiradov (1898–1937), head of the Turkmen Communist Party, warned that "there is a danger that kulaks, mullahs and ishans [Sufi leaders] may . . . turn women against us, saying, 'look, Turkey and Persia are backward states and are adopting such laws, but the Soviet regime is not doing anything for you.'"[199] This lent urgency to Soviet efforts, which were made rapidly and forcefully. To overcome resistance, Soviet police prosecuted men who refused to allow wives and daughters to go to school.[200] The mass public unveilings of 1927 generated the most opposition.[201] These tensions came to a violent head when traditionalists brutally murdered some two thousand women in Uzbekistan who participated in the unveilings. Turkmen women were murdered for attempting to get divorces or for joining the Communist Party. For these crimes, sixty men were found guilty and thirty-five put to death.[202] The Soviets alienated local men, defensive of religious and especially family traditions. At the same time, Soviet state centrism also alienated local liberals, among them feminist organizations who were forbidden to meet after the occupation. They even alienated local Communists who distanced themselves from the issue, strengthening the impression that women's emancipation was an imposition from Moscow. Within a decade, Soviet Premier Joseph Stalin (1878–1953) scaled back women's emancipation throughout the Soviet Empire and purged Sahetmiradov from the Communist Party.

CONCLUSION

Conflicts over women's roles continue to pit East and West, Muslims and Christians, and traditionalists and modernists against each other. But even as an eighteenth-century gender order began to structure women's lives globally, women developed a range of strategies for empowering themselves. Ahyssa, the Muslim slave woman whose story opened this chapter, gained liberty because of, not despite, her brown skin. More than a century later, brown-skinned women from Samoa to India negotiated multiple axes of identity and, as in the case of Victoria Bennett, entered into alliances with white women to promote the intertwined causes of feminism and national self-determination. Ahyssa never enjoyed political rights because of her gender. A century and a half later most of these women would. Elite women like Indian doctor Muthulakshmi Reddi benefited from access to education and used their international connections through organizations like the YWCA to improve all women's lives. But despite a clear trajectory of progress, colonized women, especially poor women, bore the brunt of imperialist exploitation across the globe for at least three centuries as productive and reproductive laborers on Caribbean plantations, in Hong Kong's brothels, or in private homes in South Africa and elsewhere.

Yet the intimacies they experienced served as a measure of the power they could wield as cultural intermediaries. Former slave Petite-Nanon and Cherokee Dark-Lanthorn managed to negotiate love relationships on their terms. Women of African descent, like Princess Wallace who owned her own cocoa plantation or Fanta Kone who secured her freedom in a West African liberty village, used the tools of imperialism to their own advantage. White dependence on their skills as translators, mediators, caregivers, laborers, and lovers never lessened during the period under study, despite the gradual arrival of more white women into colonial spaces who took on some of these functions. Indeed, white women's arrival expanded the demand for domestic service and increased the intimacy between servants such as Indonesian nanny Ibu Rubi and the children she was not supposed to hold.

A preoccupation with a wide range of interracial relationships therefore dominates the archives of empire, whether in the increasing strictures in custom and in law, or in private letters sent home. White women who precluded interracial relationships in the fiction they wrote two hundred years ago might well have engaged in them a century later. And the thriving commercial sex trade suggests that interracial sex was a problem in name only. Even the boldness of women as different from each other as Duras, Eberhardt, and Fountaine attests to improved opportunities for women in every sphere. The global proliferation of a multiracial population is a testament to the centrality of these intimacies to the imperial project. Transnational itineraries increased dramatically over the course of the long nineteenth century, enabling a level of mobility unprecedented in history. Because men made up the majority of migrants for most of that period, their relations with local women embodied and perpetuated intersecting identities at the intersections of world history.

TIMELINE

1776	Ahyssa wins freedom from slavery in Saint-Domingue
1785	Dame N wins legal separation from abusive husband in Saint-Domingue
1792	George Vancouver's voyage to the North Pacific
1816	Nanny Grigg inspires slave revolt in Barbados
1826–1831	Rifa'a al-Tahtawi visits Paris on behalf of the Egyptian government
1831	Former slave Mary Prince publishes her autobiography
1839–1876	*Tanzimat* reforms in the Ottoman Empire
1841	Australian women sentenced for dirty and beastly actions
1863	Maori Huria Matenga rescues drowning sailors in New Zealand
1890s	European powers abolish slavery in West Africa
1901	More than 500 US teachers leave for the Philippines after United States pacifies its new colony
1904	Irishwoman Margaret Noble converts to Hinduism
1908	British and Indian philanthropists create Children's Aid Society
1914	All India Muslim Ladies Conference
1915	Australia is the first nation to form a female police unit
1919–1923	Turkish War of Independence
1927	Mass public unveilings in Soviet-ruled Turkmenistan
1934	Interracial New Zealand delegation attends Pan-Pacific Women's Conference in Hawaii
1938	Italian government passes racial laws in East Africa

THREE

THE INSTITUTIONS OF EMPIRE

Emily Ruete of Zanzibar and Germany

> I left my home a complete Arab woman and a good Muslim and
> what am I now? A bad Christian, and somewhat more than half
> a German.
>
> —Emily Ruete, *Memoirs of an Arabian Princess*, 1886

In 1866, Salme bint Sa'id (1844–1924) left Zanzibar for Germany along with her German lover, a spice trader. An unintended pregnancy required marriage and conversion to Christianity. No longer an Arabian princess, she changed her name to Emily Ruete. Ambivalent about her choices, she wrote her memoir in the 1880s to convey her experience of her motherland to her Arab-German children and to express her hybrid identity.[1] She claimed the authority to speak about the East, too often represented as "the land of fairy-tales" by the writer who relies on "second-hand accounts of the French or German waiters at his hotel, or from sailors and donkey boys."[2] Determined to challenge orientalist clichés about Arab women, Ruete successfully navigated her hybrid identity, writing about her roots and routes in German for a curious audience. Ruete's memoir occasionally called out German racism: in one episode, a German woman touched her "negro-hair" out of curiosity.[3] Bicultural, multilingual, and transnational, Ruete's life was one border crossing after another. Transnational itineraries forge layers of identity over top of roots, but they also destabilize "essential" identities. "Roots" derived from nature, organic and biologically determined, are juxtaposed against culturally produced itineraries or "routes."[4] The condition of being uprooted can lead to longing or liberation or both.[5] In this chapter, we explore the complex identities produced by imperial institutions.

Ruete was the youngest of thirty-six children, born to the sultan of Zanzibar and a Circassian concubine. Her mother was a slave, a circumstance that she described as a matter of fact: "She must have come into my father's possession at a tender age,

as she lost her first tooth at his home."[6] The sultan had "secondary wives, number-
ing seventy-five at his death, [that] he had bought from time to time."[7] Even before
her association with Heinrich, the princess developed a hybrid identity through the
acquisition of European material goods delivered by ship, including textiles and
toys. She enjoyed the uncut cloth that could be fashioned into loose fitting shifts
worn by men and women equally. She praised the simplicity of the Arab woman's
dress and critiqued European women's extravagance. "Lacing, that injurious,
abominable habit, is one to which the Oriental female has not yet succumbed."[8] Yet
in her portraits in European dress, she clearly wore a corset. She raised her children
as Germans, explaining, "I would have wished my children to be brought up in the
Arab way if circumstances had been the opposite. . . . I, of course, am an Arab
woman to the core. Outwardly, I indeed am totally 'à la franca,' but the inside
remained the same and did not let itself be reformed so easily."[9]

Ruete's unconventional routes hint at the unconventional life she led, even as a
child. Envying her brothers, she secretly taught herself to write, unusual even for a
princess of her rank. She also learned how to ride a horse and shoot firearms from
one of her brothers. Her affair with her neighbor Heinrich, and resulting pregnancy and exile, caused permanent estrangement from family and homeland.
Heinrich's death in a tram accident in Hamburg when their children were still
young left her in poverty. She had thought her hybrid identity would count for
something, but once widowed, "The fact that an Arab woman had married a
German, and that a Muslim woman had become a Christian, was such an indif-
ferent matter that nobody cared about it. . . . Here it is said everywhere: 'every man
for himself.' If by chance you are not a man, the mere nationality of your husband
is of very little help to you."[10] The legal status of women was tied to that of their
husbands, but this counted for little in the face of cultural difference. Although she
desired to return home a widow with small children, she determined to honor her
husband's memory by raising his children as Germans. When they were older, she
migrated yet again, first to London and then to Lebanon and Palestine. She asserted that the British understood Arabs better than the Germans given the duration and extent of their empire.

Such ambivalence is characteristic of the attitudes colonized people held toward
imperialists and their own complex identities. Whereas some enthusiastically embraced the religion, language, and law of the colonizers, others bitterly opposed it.
Most, like Ruete, occupied a middle position. In this chapter, we explore that intermediate space by analyzing the institutions that fostered hybrid identities: the
church, the school, and the state. We consider the many ways that people forged
multilayered identities: in relationships with colonizers, as mixed-race persons,
and as immigrants. We deploy concepts formulated by postcolonial authors such
as racial melancholia, liminality, hybridity, and mimicry to untangle intersecting
identities. We describe how transnational routes undermined traditional roots,
enabling a painful experience and a joyful experience. Hybridity was sometimes
embraced, sometimes accepted, sometimes resisted by individuals or by whole
societies. Some attempted to undo hybridity by segregating neighborhoods and

institutions. Some pan-nationalist, separatist, and anti-imperial movements also opposed hybridity, believing that a rejection of whiteness at the level of the body was the only way to survive imperialism. The diversity of these movements attests to the multiplicity of responses to the imperial experience even as their very existence attests to the power of hybridity to undo imperialism.

GLOBAL CHRISTIANITY

No force in the modern world was more responsible for fostering hybrid identities than global Christianity. "Missions" generally predated governmental institutions and began converting people to Christ from the founding of Christianity, escalating with imperialism in the modern era. Already in 1910 there were nearly 612 million Christians worldwide. By 2010, the number was just over two and a quarter billion. In 1910, 93 percent of all Christians lived in Europe or the Americas. In 2010, only 52 percent did. Expansion into Asia was eclipsed in the twentieth century by phenomenal growth in Africa: 9 percent of the population of sub-Saharan Africa was Christian in 1910; one hundred years later, it was 63 percent. Today there are twice as many Protestants in Nigeria as there are in Germany and twice as many Catholics in Brazil as there are in Italy.[11] "Converts" worldwide have made Christianity their own producing hybrid and syncretic forms of belief and practice. Many launched criticism of imperialism from their position as Christians. Nonsectarian Christian "Organizations" also challenged racial hierarchies and gender divides, especially when headed by native leadership. As Ruete's case illustrates, complicated entanglements as much as sincere embrace of the Gospel swelled the numbers of Christians across the globe from the eighteenth through the twentieth centuries.

Missions

Sometimes missionary activity provoked brutal persecutions, as in Vietnam; sometimes persecutions resulted in state intervention if not full-fledged European military occupation. Once European rule was established, converts enjoyed certain legal protections, access to education, and greater economic opportunities. Converts might in turn become missionaries, teachers, or healthcare workers, facilitating the work of European imperialism on behalf of the relatively fewer white people residing in the colonies. Many converts blended Christian beliefs and practices with their local traditions, just as many missionaries forged a middle ground between seemingly alien religions. Religious difference pivoted on issues of body and gender, especially when Christianity's traditional duality between body and soul encountered the embodied religious practices of many of the world's peoples. Overseas missionary work attracted Protestants and Catholics, and men and women. In some cases, missionaries arrived before formal colonization took place, and their agendas developed independently from the state.

Anne-Marie Javouhey (1799–1851) saw more of the world than most other European women. As a nun and founder of the Sisters of Saint Joseph of Cluny in France, she extended the order across the globe: Reunion Island in the Indian Ocean, Senegal on the west coast of Africa, Guiana in South America, India, Tahiti, and Madagascar. Her most ambitious undertaking, for which she was known as the "mother of the blacks," was the utopian community at Mana in French Guiana.[12] Although she had successfully founded missions among settler populations elsewhere, her ambition to create a godly community led to the choice of Mana in 1827. Isolated from the settler community in Guiana's capital, Cayenne, Mana was located near the Amazon and the only other people living nearby were escaped slaves in maroon communities. Vividly illustrating intersecting identities at the intersections of world history, she sought to create a little French village in South America populated by French immigrants and people of African descent. Still recovering from the French Revolution's assault on Catholicism, the restored French monarchy dedicated itself to the revitalization of religious life in France and abroad. The Crown backed the community, providing land and infrastructure, but otherwise left the settlement completely in her charge. Forty-one French men arrived in August 1828, accompanied by five wives and ten children. They received land with livestock and eighteen months' worth of rations in exchange for three to five years labor. Thirty of the thirty-six nuns who accompanied her were young and devoted to hard agricultural work in addition to teaching.[13] Despite a promising start, the settlement foundered after the European settlers found the material circumstances too challenging, particularly the gender ratio. There were no marriage partners for the European men and the quasi-monastic routines as well as isolation from other settlements drove many away. The number of settlers dwindled by half in the first four years.

Javouhey then reconceptualized Mana to serve as a haven for runaway slaves. The government began moving slaves from Cayenne to Mana and also transporting those seized on illegal slave ships, the trade having been outlawed in 1817. By 1836, there were over five hundred black inhabitants to about two dozen whites. Javouhey described herself as a "mother in the middle of her large family."[14] In addition to her maternal posture, Javouhey administered the colony with full authority, a fact that made skeptics in France nervous. Even more disturbing was the prospect of an ever-growing population of newly freed blacks whose very presence might inspire slave rebellion elsewhere in Guiana and across the Caribbean. Nonetheless, the colony prospered, and by 1838, she described it as a "pretty village in France."[15] It also resembled a cloister in that girls and young women lived separately from men, mixing only for work and religious instruction. This protected residents from the "vicious habits to which they were so unfortunately previously inclined."[16] Unlike other abolitionists, she favored immediate equality for emancipated slaves at Mana aged twenty-three and older, although some worthy individuals could be emancipated earlier. Mass emancipation followed mass baptisms. She gave newly freed people a new pair of shoes, the right to wear shoes being associated with freedom, in addition to individual plots of land. She measured their progress toward civilization in terms of the fruitfulness of the land they cultivated and the goods they acquired, "fishing boats and especially parasols" befitting free people.[17] Yet she also wrote that "the more one acquires civilization, the more malice grows" and of her preference for the woods of South America to the streets of Paris.[18] Javouhey ran her own godly community for twenty years. Eventually, a more secular French government took over the administration of the community, nervous about a woman wielding so much power and about the degree of democratic participation it enabled for blacks. Many of her more progressive measures were swiftly repealed by the male officials appointed directly from France to take her place.

French Catholicism thrived in the 1830s, helping to explain Javouhey's success. With the full support of the Restoration Monarchy after the definitive end of the French Revolution and the large financial contributions of the reinvigorated nobility, foreign missions proliferated. Catholicism had established missions in Vietnam as early as the seventeenth century. It was so prevalent that in 1833, Emperor Minh Mang (1791–1841) banned Catholicism and began an increasingly violent campaign to eradicate it. The torture and murder of French and Vietnamese priests in the 1830s, however, only served to inspire others. Evoking embodied images of blood and seed, French Catholics promised the Vietnamese that their suffering would not be in vain. "Your churches will not be abandoned, the blood of your holy Confessors will become, as in the first ages, the fruitful seed of Christians. . . . We give you base and terrestrial gold and you, you give us back martyrs and protectors in Heaven."[19] Hundreds of Vietnamese Catholics gathered to bid their priests farewell as they approached their martyrdom.

When asked why Catholicism appealed to them so, one woman answered, "They preach to our husbands to flee from gambling, drunkenness, and the vices that dishonour or ruin families; they teach women to be humble, modest, chaste, and submissive to their husbands."[20] Catholicism dovetailed with traditional Vietnamese beliefs about respect and obedience owed to others in hierarchical relationships. However, its emphasis on equality of souls and the accessibility of the afterlife to all appealed to those who, in their culture, manifested their bad karma by their poverty and disease, especially leprosy. It also attracted soldiers because those who died violent or lonely deaths would wander forever as ghosts if they did not receive the proper funerary rites, according to Mahayana Buddhism, the religion of the majority.[21]

By the 1840s when the persecutions ended, waves of baptisms increased the flock by several thousand per year through the 1850s.[22] The now solvent Church could better provide for the martyrs' families, distribute alms to the poor, and most importantly bribe officials. But the increasing wealth of some landowning Catholics attracted official ire, and the government renewed persecutions in the 1850s. Baptisms soared in the midst of the turmoil, and Catholics offered new forms of magical intercession to combat it, including holy water, crucifixes, and saints' medals. In 1853, villagers whose traditional intercessions could not rid their village of arsons attributed to evil spirits begged the local priest to exorcise the village. He called forth fifteen of the village's Catholic grandmothers and their granddaughters to hold a vigil for three days and nights, chanting and sprinkling holy water throughout the village. The arsons ceased, causing local officials to admire the religion's efficacy. "If the old women and young girls have so much virtue, what then must be the power of the priests and bishops of this religion."[23]

Some non-Christians who witnessed such miracles respected or even feared Christians, their ghosts, and their relics. Tales abounded about the bad luck or worse that resulted from the theft of a martyr's possessions. As reported in a Propagation of the Faith newsletter of 1833, those who handled the chalice of a martyred priest allegedly all went blind.[24] Others, including non-Christians, gathered around the site of a martyrdom to dip cloths in the martyr's blood, later to be used to heal the sick or ward off evil. If the potency of Catholicism was so great, perhaps the ghosts of the martyred would torment the living. This caused some, even officials, to invoke the traditional intercessions of their own faith to protect them from the vengeance of Christian ghosts. One official, when forced to hand over priests to the authorities, slaughtered a sacrificial pig, pleading, "It is not my fault, the injustice must be imputed to the orders that I carry out; let the punishment for this injustice fall on its authors!"[25] Catholicism thus stimulated even non-Catholics to develop hybrid practices illustrating how all local people responded to the presence of European institutions.

The personality of the missionary influenced his success or failure among local people. The charismatic martyrs of Vietnam developed international reputations while attracting people to the faith. The relationship status of the missionary was also a factor, heavily debated among mission boards. Rarely does the historical record leave traces of the romantic lives of missionaries, let alone priests. While celibate priests undoubtedly experienced and incited their own erotic longings, marriageable Protestant missionaries presented both possibilities and risks to the institutions they served. Single, the danger that they might enter into an interracial intimate relationship was countered by the attraction of local women to the missionary and thereby to the faith. Married, they modeled possibilities for white settlement and European family formations but also the risk that their wives would distract them from their ministry. Mission boards throughout the world debated whether to allow missionaries to marry. Lutherans generally required an initial period of celibacy so the missionary could focus on his work. He might however have a fiancé destined to join him. This was the case of Frieda Keysser (1875–1957) and Carl Strehlow (1871–1922). Their letters written during their courtship between 1892 and 1895, when Carl was stationed in central Australia awaiting his bride-to-be to reach the age of maturity when she could join him, reveal the eroticism evoked by the foreign environment and the freedom it lent its visitors. In one letter, Strehlow linked the hot climate to heightened desire: "I rather think that the heat especially makes the blood flow more vigorously, which is a good sign for love. I also believe that the two of us, you and I, will love each other much more deeply and passionately than if we had gotten married in Germany."[26]

Belief that the climate stoked desire gave mission boards—and wives and girlfriends back home—cause for concern. Carl attempted to disavow any erotic relations when the board published a photo of him with a beautiful black woman named Rebecka: "I have already been teased often with the black woman standing next to me in the photograph; especially because she snuggles up against me a bit; but you don't have to get jealous, because she has already been married for a while, [and] already has 4 children, the oldest of whom is 10 years old."[27] But he added that "Rebecka herself is one of the prettiest of her race here; you may thus really be a little jealous, dear Frieda."[28] She replied that she was relieved that Rebecka was married, suggesting that her marital status would be a stronger safeguard against Carl's philandering than her race. But marriage practices among Aboriginals, even converts, did not always include fidelity. For his part, Carl condemned interracial sex in his correspondence with officials. He urged that a German horse-driver in an open relationship with a black woman be fired. "For when white people employed by the mission go whoring with black women, then our real mission work is for nothing, and will never bear fruits."[29] Furthermore, such relations made a mockery of German claims to moral superiority, especially when German men abandoned their mixed-race children: "What impact does their life have on the blacks if each of these 'heroes' leaves a half-caste at the mission? While the chaps disappear when it's time [for the birth of their half-caste children], the disgrace remains attached to the [mission] station, and it is no surprise when people, although they are no better themselves, joke about it and say that the mission itself ensures the existence of half-castes."[30]

If interracial sex was discouraged, it was not unheard of, even for missionaries. Carl did not condemn it per se but insisted in another letter that German men marry these women and legitimize the children. Fears about miscegenation gradually prompted Protestant mission boards to send wives into the field as a way to limit the development of a hybrid population and also to promote the European family model. But the self-disclosure in Carl's letters reveals possibly widespread, if private, acknowledgment of interracial desire.

Ironically, the South Australian Baptist Missionary Society left the proselytizing of Aboriginals to the Germans and sent Australian missionaries to India instead. The early Australian missionaries favored Indians over Aboriginals, believing that the latter were hopelessly pagan and primitive. Ellen Arnold (1858–1931) and Marie Gilbert (1856–1926), the first women missionaries sent out from Australia, arrived in East Bengal in 1882 specifically to proselytize in the women's secluded quarters. Prior to 1882, the society raised money to sponsor native preachers in Bengal since the Baptist faith had attracted converts for decades. But Australian women missionaries wanted to minister directly to "our dear Bengali sisters" and also to see the world.[31] Seeing Indian women as capable of uplift, they participated in what was becoming a transnational rescue movement. They studied Bengali for a year while the society built their dwelling. Three others joined in 1885. So successful was their work that they became known as the Five Barley Loaves, a biblical reference.

More women than men went out: fifty-four women to sixteen men between 1882–1913.[32] Indicating how faith might supersede nationality, the women identified variously as Australian, British, English, or White, but above all as Baptist.[33] The missionaries published their travel accounts in the society's magazine *Truth and Progress*. They combined their fascination with the exotic other and moral ruminations about women's status. In 1886, Marie Gilbert described the women's secluded quarters: "Each lady has her own little cell, where she and her children live, never going outside of the court . . . still, they seem very contented."[34] Their reports notably lacked stereotypes of secluded women as lascivious sex slaves or as morose castoffs, suggesting that some Christians could see native women in their full humanity.

Indeed, they regarded Indians highly. Ellen Arnold wrote in 1894, "We met with real Australian hospitality in this jungly place, the people of the house turning out of their own bed to give us a chance of sleeping."[35] This followed an evening of singing and bible reading at the home of a convert who was the first patient of Baptist doctor Laura Hope (1868–1952). In fact, mission work, health care, and teaching often went hand in hand. Once established at their mission station in Faridpur, they worked alongside native preachers. Gilbert and Arnold wrote of their experiences, largely refraining from stating any prejudice. They described meeting a fifteen-year-old woman "very contented and cheerful. She had been married five years."[36] They made no comment on child marriage, possibly seeing their work as saving souls one at a time rather than transforming gender norms. Still, they never lost sight of their superiority as Christians committed to raising others up to their level. For these missionaries, the experience of hybridity included their challenge to the purely British administration of India. As Australians, they were also subjects of the British Empire; they asserted their difference from the mother country while allying with its other subjects. Indian and Australian solidarity as Baptists enabled the crafting of a transnational, even subversive, identity.

Some mission boards believed that Westerners of African descent from the Americas might best reach their brethren in Africa. Like Baptists in India, they could develop camaraderie with other colonized people. Nonetheless, like their white counterparts, most middle-class African Americans or Afro-Caribbeans believed that Africans needed to be civilized and Christianized. Benjamin Ousley (1855–1931), born a slave in Mississippi, earned a BA and MA from Fisk University and a BD degree from Oberlin Theological Seminary. He became the first ordained African American minister to be sent abroad by the American Board of Commissioners for Foreign Missions. Reflective of their middle-class identification, particularly after having left behind the experience of slavery, missionaries decried African women's agricultural work as inappropriate for women. Ousley wanted African women to adopt Western gender roles. He wrote of his frustration in working with the women of Portuguese Mozambique, "It is sad, but nevertheless true, that woman seems more degraded here, and harder to reach, than man.... We often commiserate the degraded condition of these poor women; yet they do not appreciate our pity, or even desire to live different lives."[37] Missionaries also condemned polygamy as well as the relative lack of clothing and more open sexual expression of Africans.

Ousley's wife Henrietta Bailey (1852–1941) was also born to slave parents in Mississippi. A member of the African Methodist Episcopal Church, Bailey studied in Knoxville, Tennessee. She accompanied her husband to the East Central African mission from 1884 to 1893. Ousley was the first black woman sent out. Upon arrival, the couple noted the difficulties imposed on all foreigners by the Portuguese government, which included limiting them to religious instruction in certain districts surrounding the mission. Governments knew that missionaries presented an alternative source of authority and could critique imperialist policies. The Ousleys learned to speak the local language and within a year had about fifty students in their school. Nancy Jones (b. 1860) of Tennessee, the first single woman to be sent out, joined them in the Mozambique mission. She claimed she was instructed by the Lord to do the work of Christ in Africa. "He directs my mind and heart to Africa, the land of my Forefathers."[38] Jones openly criticized the Portuguese government for depriving people at its work camps of food. She concluded it would be better "if this country was in the hands of a more judicious government."[39] Declining health finally forced the Ousleys to repatriate to the United States in 1893. Jones carried on their work, although segregation policies in the United States influenced African missions. At a new station in Southern Rhodesia, several white missionaries refused to live with her, finally leading to her resignation in 1897.

Missionaries like Jones who learned local languages and customs attracted more converts and earned respect in their communities. William Henry Sheppard (1865–1927), an African American missionary from Virginia who proselytized among the Kuba in Belgian Congo, donning their dress and learning their language, was among the first to expose the atrocities committed there in the first decade of the twentieth century. Known by the Kuba as the "black white man," his life illustrates how Westerners abroad might develop their own hybrid identities.[40] He used his ability to move between cultures as a means for achieving one goal of Westernization—Christianization—while undercutting another: exploitation of labor for profit. The Kasai Rubber Company committed atrocities tantamount to genocide in the first decade of the twentieth century. Sheppard published his accounts of the atrocities, which included witnessing the curing of eighty-one severed right hands to be preserved as proof of the company's disciplinary policies. The company sued him for libel in a Belgian court in 1909. The media coverage of the trial drew further attention to the atrocities and mobilized activists in and outside of Belgium. International pressure finally forced the Belgian government to intervene and end the company's reign of terror. As for Sheppard, he was finally acquitted. After twenty-two bouts of malaria, he returned home, donating his collection of Kuba artifacts to his alma mater, Hampton University in Virginia.

Converts

Like Sheppard, successful missionaries rooted themselves in local communities and combatted cross-cultural misunderstandings and prejudice. Converts, like missionaries, adopted hybrid identities, sometimes disavowing their own cultures in their pursuit of social advancement or their embrace of the Gospel. In Latin America, converts grafted Christian saint days onto native festivities and then overlaid them with influences brought over by West African slaves. Converts in India used their outsider perspective to critique Hinduism and Islam, especially oppression of women and the caste system. Conversely, converts in Papua New Guinea critiqued British racism on the basis of their Catholicism. Throughout Southern Africa, Christians merged their native traditions with Christianity, producing hybrid forms of religious expression. While Christianity as a Western institution challenged native beliefs and practices, these examples show a multiplicity of responses to this foreign influence. The close relationships that might develop between Christians regardless of race and gender also illustrate how intimacy could undercut oppressive rule.

In 1893, Colombian historian Rufino Gutiérrez (1854–1923) recorded his travels through the isolated villages in the hot, humid jungles of the Pacific coast, far from the urban centers of Columbia's social life. In the village of Altaquer, he encountered an animated procession led by a Catholic priest to mark the fiesta of Our Lady of Las Lajas, held to the beat of bass drums, flutes, and tambourines, with masked revelers adorned in a brilliant array of headdresses, flowers, streamers, and sashes. Gutiérrez remarked on his mortified local guide, who noted that the fiesta-goers were but "semi-civilized Indians," fearful that his cosmopolitan guests would condemn the customs of his land:

> What timidity! Perhaps he did not know that in our pueblos which are called civilized, beginning with Bogota, also are celebrated religious and patriotic fiestas with processions, masking, dances, banners, sashes, and flowers. In the dances organized by the Indians the women took no part and when they presented themselves in public they were modestly covered; in our dances some of the women are painted more than the nobles of the rivers, and expose their flesh to the air almost like the naked damsels of the Patia.[41]

Gutiérrez added that the burlesques endured despite solemn efforts to suppress them over the centuries, reviving the "melancholy spirit" of natives who had been forced to give up their exuberant, sensuous festivals for the more severe doctrines of the Catholic Church.[42]

Although the colonizing Portuguese imported the original Shrovetide procession to mark the start of Lent, Rio de Janeiro's Carnival evolved over the centuries to reflect the agency of multicultural Brazilians. This included slaves and their descendants when African and Amerindian spiritual beliefs fused with the dominant Catholic faith. The most popular Orisha cult devoted to Yemanjá, the Yoruba mother goddess and queen of the ocean, took on attributes of native Amazonian river spirits, as well as Our Lady of Rosario, an incarnation of the Virgin Mary that focused on the mystery of life in all its joys and sorrows.[43] In its purest form, Orisha worship morphed into the Candomblé religion, best known for rituals where women mediums used rhythmic dances set to samba-reggae beats to enter a trance-like state so as to channel the Orisha spirits. When slaves were permitted to join in the Portuguese Shrovetide festival, they Africanized it with Orisha displays and Candomblé step dance, using the liberty of Carnival to reclaim their ethnic identity and to parody their masters. In this way, religious expression subverted imperial power structures.

In Latin America, Christianity became the majority religion in part because of its capacity to accommodate other traditions. Where Christianity was a minority religion, like India, converts risked ostracism or worse. Indian development economist and educator Malcolm Adiseshiah (1910–1994) described his father's rebellious conversion from Hinduism to Anglicanism. He defied his parents who went so far as to take him to court for disobeying their authority, a move that represents how thoroughly ingrained English law had become in India. "When the Magistrate asked him: 'Why have you become a Christian?' he quoted a verse from the Bible: 'There is no other God on earth except Jesus Christ.'"[44] Rejecting the polytheism of Hinduism, some converts agreed with missionaries that the faiths they had grown up with oppressed some members of the population, particularly women.

Although Adiseshiah maintained the family's Anglicanism, he condemned British prejudice toward other faiths. He blamed Victorian prudery more than racial prejudice for British phobia about Hindu eroticism. The British saw Hindu virgins performing the ceremonial dance of South India as vulgar prostitutes and temple statuary as licentious and corrupting. Perceiving Hinduism to be sex saturated, the missionaries "asked us Christians to keep out of that," but Adiseshiah defended ceremonial dances and statuary as cultural artifacts.[45] Indian Christianity was not as accommodating of the burlesque as Latin American Christianity.

Some Indian feminist Christians embraced what they saw as Christianity's relatively higher status for women. Krupabai Satthianadhan (1862–1894) challenged the foundations of patriarchy by decrying the Indian preference for sons: the male child was a "petted, spoiled despot, or a selfish ease-loving lord."[46] She hailed Christ as the "saviour" of "deserted wives, prostitutes, and widows."[47] Pandita Ramabai (1858–1922) was an upper-caste convert and a feminist who published travel writing in the late nineteenth century. Her moment of conversion came during a visit to Britain when she witnessed mission work with prostitutes.[48] Ramabai did not identify with any specific Christian sect. Her interfaith approach astounded American audiences when she went on a lecture tour in 1886. The *Philadelphia Evening Bulletin* reported, "And when the earnest little lady suddenly closed her address by asking an American company of educated and refined men and women to join with her in a moment's silent prayer 'to the Great Father of all the nations of the earth' in behalf of the millions of her Hindoo sisters to whose cause she has given her life, there was something almost startling in the strangeness of the unique situation."[49] Her lectures were well attended, and she interacted with the major women's reformers of the era, including leaders in the Society for the Prevention of Cruelty to Animals and Women's Christian Temperance Union. She praised the United States for its progressive hybridity and saw it as an alternative model to the British. The tour and her widely circulating memoir of it positioned her as a transnational interfaith activist whose vision was broader than the nationalist anti-imperialism of her Indian contemporaries.[50]

Satthianadhan and Ramabai maintained Hindu food, clothing, and other customs, forging a hybrid identity by choice. They also challenged both British and Indian norms for women. Ramabai taught carpentry and masonry, while Satthianadhan noted the racism of later missionaries. In her view, these newer, more detached missionaries "would not convert a Hindu in a thousand years!"[51] Like Ramabai and Satthianadhan, many converts in turn became teachers and missionaries, finding it difficult to work within conservative missions.

Converts faced different challenges in other British colonies, especially those that were rigidly stratified by race. Segregationist policies generally arrived much later than missions. The goal of the former was to contain native populations within hardened racialized categories; the goal of the latter was to make them Christian and in that sense more egalitarian. In Papua New Guinea, a Melanesian island north of Australia, Father Louis Vangeke (1904–1982), became the first Papuan Catholic to be ordained a priest in 1937. Emerging from the increasingly racist and segregationist policies of the time, sumptuary laws required Papuans to be naked above the waist, clothing being a marker of whiteness. Papuans were also forbidden to consume alcohol. Vangeke by law would have had to perform mass half-naked and refuse the Communion wine, which directly contradicted the mandates of his order and of his own conscience. When one vigilant parishioner insisted that these laws be followed, Vangeke's bishop wrote directly to Governor Hubert Murray (1861–1940): "Though being a pure native . . . he is living with us on same footing as his European confreres, sharing with them house, meals and everything without any difference."[52] Interracial fraternization in shared living quarters enabled hybrid identities to flourish as bodies came into contact in the name of Christ. Their brotherhood made not only segregated treatment of Vangeke personally unacceptable but also emblematic of state intolerance of religious observance. Testifying to a basic equality across race lines, the Catholic Church petitioned for a relaxation of these regulations but only succeeded in changing the laws during World War II.

These dress codes placed all native converts in awkward, even absurd situations. Native men and women were not permitted to wear any clothing above the waist. Women who wore dresses to Sunday service therefore violated the law. A village constable in Metoreia even demanded the women remove their dresses before entering church.[53] But the outcry of parishioners protected the converts' right to dress in a European manner. Those who adopted hybrid identities could be caught between the democratizing aspects of European influence, in this case church attendance, and the segregationist aspects, with their very existence exposing the unsustainability of those contradictions.

Undermining such sumptuary laws, mission stations promoted weekly sewing classes as early as the 1830s because clothing was associated with conversion, resulting initially in more women converts than men throughout Africa.[54] Converts became known as "dressed" women.[55] Covering the body was a sign of godliness and was associated with clean living in general. In South Africa, women's prayer unions known as Manyanos, proliferated in the early twentieth century. In the Manyano rules published in 1916, the white president of the Native Women's Association admonished women to "(a) Sweep and clean the house every day. (b) Keep your things and your family clean and good. (c) If you have children teach them the Christian faith. Do not let them run naked."[56] The Methodist missionary newsletter *Foreign Field* waxed poetic about the enthusiasm of the women's prayer unions, which in Transvaal alone increased from seven in 1907 to eight hundred in 1913 to ten thousand by the start of World War II.[57] Newsletters repeatedly described female converts' desire to preach, but cautioned, "One hesitates to quench and discourage their eagerness to pray . . . yet it is so much mixed up with a sort of excitement and it is so bad for women, mostly mothers of families, to get into the habit of being out all night."[58]

These converts embraced Christianity in their own way, blending spiritual practice from their own traditions in ways that alarmed mission boards. Apparently some prayer unions sewed uniforms for their children to show to which faith they adhered: Anglican or Methodist. By 1936, the mission board formally objected to the obsession with clothing. "Considering the multiplicity of 'uniforms' seen in Native country, members of the Mothers' Union would be well advised to make their homes distinctive, and keep their clothes commonplace."[59] Competitive displays of faith through clothing, excessive singing, or preaching at all night prayer meetings were deemed unladylike.

In Johannesburg, the local economy revolved around beer making, but this means of livelihood was forbidden to converts. One convert who adhered to the increasingly rigid rules of the prayer unions complained in 1930: "It's almost impossible for us to live decently in Johannesburg . . . The temptation to sell this stuff [beer] is too strong. All the women around here are making a lot of money; buying pianos and gramophones and silk dresses. Because I am a Christian and try to go straight, I have to stand here day after day and kill myself washing."[60] Modern South Africans displayed their wealth by adorning the body with silk and by acquiring other markers of middle-class consumerism. Members of Christian sects that rejected worldliness found their beliefs incompatible with materialistic norms that accompanied Westernization. This led some to flock to the more lenient African Methodist Episcopal Church (AME), an African American Church that increased its missionary efforts in the early twentieth century. The AME Church assumed a more radical political stance as well. Some respectable Christian housewives became activists against proto-apartheid legislation, leading to female anti-pass demonstrations in 1913 in Bloemfontein and demonstrating against residential permits in 1929 in Potchefstroom.[61]

In neighboring Rhodesia (modern Zimbabwe) converts resolved these contradictions on their own by fusing Christian beliefs and practices with local traditions, sometimes in defiance of white clerics and white law. The Brethren in Christ Church (BICC) established itself among Rhodesia's Ndebele people in the late nineteenth century. The Brethren renounced worldliness. Missionaries regarded any form of dancing as Satanic, heathen, or pagan, including ritual wedding dances. Missionary Frances Davidson (1860–1935) described the dancing she saw at Mapane in 1905 as "wild orgies," while another missionary, Adda Engle (1869–1960), asserted that same year, "If ever I saw the works of darkness, I saw it then."[62] Yet another noted that, "the bridal party comes in dancing in a way that can cause longing of the flesh . . . this type of dancing is bad for men and women."[63] African converts did not always abide by these restrictive practices. Marriage among the Ndebele involved the unity of two kin groups, most of whom were unlikely to be Christian. In Mayezane, up to a thousand people attended Sunday services, and some five hundred might attend the wedding of a prominent villager. Traditional weddings included much drinking, dancing, and revelry, as well as the ritual slaughter of a sacrificial beast.

The BICC also banned fancy dress and jewelry, including wedding rings. Brides usually observed these strictures because it resembled the Ndebele admonition for wives to not "be a chatter box."[64] But men displayed their status through ornamentation as they shifted away from rituals of scarification, as shown in Figure 3.1. Some wore black ties and top hats, white gloves, and held white canes, and flowers. With the introduction of a cash economy and wage labor, African men who formerly exhibited prestige through body modification now wore elegant clothes.

Figure 3.1.   Brethren in Christ wedding in Zimbabwe, 1937
The wedding ceremonies of African Christians show their commitment to plain dress for women and fancier dress for men. The parties after the ceremonies were more rooted in their traditional cultures than that of the missionaries.

The Ndebele therefore adopted those Christian regulations that suited them. Even those converts who entered the clergy blended traditions in their own lives. In 1934, village pastor Ngeleza Sibinda held a simple ceremony for his own wedding but then allowed dancing, which "carried on all night."[65] Church superiors ordered him to confess before the congregation the next day. Sanction could include being suspended from church membership for up to a year, although this was an unlikely punishment for a pastor or his bride whose plain dress, portrayed in their wedding photograph, suggests that she adhered more strictly to Brethren doctrine.

Furthermore, the BICC limited the prospects for African leadership in the church and disdained African aspirations to higher education, which the Brethren deemed to be signs of worldliness. Their condemnation of wedding rites risked further alienating prominent Ndebele men, especially with the increasing reach in Southern Africa of the worldlier AME Church, which also promoted black equality.[66] To retain membership, the Brethren had to compromise. Looking the other way when nocturnal worldly festivities broke forth after weddings was one response. Eventually, even more compromises were required as Christian denominations competed for souls. Converts leveraged this, and the church finally allowed blacks to become full ministers in 1944. The annual BICC report boasted, "It must come as a satisfaction to the Home Church to know that there are now fully ordained ministers from among the converts of Africa's sons. These men's fathers were pagan savages, it was in this atmosphere that they were born and reared to young manhood."[67] The report did not state that occasional reversions to so-called pagan savagery might accompany wedding festivities.

Due to the prevalence of polygamy, many men did not convert despite their participation in church activities. In the 1930s, Dlodlo Mpofu attended Sunday school and gave financial contributions but did not convert because he had twenty wives. He also found the sermons "patronizing."[68] Yet his son converted and hosted a hybrid wedding ceremony, showing how the reach of Christianity was far greater than the number of converts alone. How many others supported churches financially and attended without joining is hard to know. But the story of Mpofu and his son illustrates how colonized peoples accessed Christianity differently, assimilating some norms and traditions into hybrid identities and demonstrating the range of responses to Western institutions.

Organizations

In addition to churches and mission boards, other Christian organizations attracted adherents in Africa. International and nondenominational, they were uniquely poised to foster transnational and hybrid identities. They were also not bound to ally themselves with any government. They nonetheless became embroiled in local politics and could use their influence to support imperial rule or to translate internationalism into anticolonialism. Scouting organizations, segregated by gender, imparted European gender norms but nonetheless generally broke down racial boundaries. Though formally apolitical, the YMCA similarly entered the fray of imperial politics, especially in racially-segregated South Africa.

In the interwar years, the Boy Scouts and Girl Guides grew in number, and in branches, across the British Empire. Scouting in the colonies appealed to native children who suffered from "over-civilization," according to a 1938 pamphlet, and who "need an outlet for their more primitive instincts."[69] Scouting attracted boys and girls of all races across the empire, but in South Africa the organization had to adapt to a segregated society, divided not just by race but also class, creed, and gender. By 1911, Africans, Indians, and mixed-race "Cape Coloureds" applied for Scout membership but were rejected. By 1915, the association told applicants that "it had been found expedient to exclude native and Coloured lads."[70] Because the Scouts in South Africa would not allow race-specific auxiliaries, parallel scouting groups emerged, including the Pathfinders for African boys and the Wayfarers for African girls. Separate groups formed for Jews, Indians, and "Cape Coloureds."

Segregation did not align with Scout policy elsewhere in the British Empire. Indeed, it disregarded Robert Baden-Powell's Fourth Scout Law: "A Scout is a friend to all, and a brother to every other Scout, no matter to what country, class, or creed, the other may belong."[71] In India, Annie Besant (1847–1933) formed an integrated Girl Guides troop that toured South Africa to great consternation. In Malaya and Jamaica, interracial Guide troops proliferated during the 1920s. Internationally minded Scout officials objected to South African segregation. In 1929, one Scout leader noted how, "The pathetic faces of those little black boys trying to look like Scouts almost moved my wife to tears, especially in view of the fact that she heard that the police had, two or three days before, locked them up for the night for carrying staves without permission. Natives are not allowed to carry staves."[72]

This put the Scouting movement in a difficult position. Splinter groups that imitated the Scouts risked contamination of the brand. Full integration risked alienating Afrikaner elites, including powerful mining companies who contributed funds to the Pathfinders and Wayfarers. The Scouts shared some materials with these groups whose structure and policies were modeled after the Scouts, but they withheld use of the official uniform. The groups also had different mottos— "Be Prepared" for Scouts; "Forward" for Pathfinders; "Upward" for Wayfarers— connoting the civilizing mission.[73] By the 1930s, organized protests by Pathfinders and Wayfarers who were repeatedly denied admission into regular troops drew international attention. In an extraordinary display of teen activism, some Scouts in England demanded to be admitted to Pathfinder troops as a way of showing solidarity. They became pen pals with Pathfinders and Wayfarers and mingled with them at international conferences.[74]

Instead of following the lead of the membership, the South African Scouting organization reached out to white Afrikaners who had typically rejected British institutions, especially the more elite of them. Olave Baden-Powell (1889–1977) described the situation in 1936: "The Guide Association felt that it was important to try and get the Afrikaans speaking people into Guides, to bring the two WHITE races together as a first step."[75] But Afrikaners refused and formed the Voortrekkers, a whites-only organization comparable to the Scouts. Baden-Powell recognized that this could potentially free the Scouts and Guides from perpetuating segregation, but she had her own reasons for separating the races. One was the protection of imperiled white girlhood, not just from presumed black male predation, but also from black girls. "The reason for this is that the feeling of insecurity where the natives are concerned and the very real dangers to white girls, lack of control, etc. make it quite definitely not safe for black and white girls to meet on equal footing, as would be inevitable if one had native Guides."[76] The danger lay in the potential transmission of "undesirable habits, manners, and customs."[77] By 1936, grassroots pressure produced some results, and the Guides led the way in amalgamation, creating a separate but equal hybrid group: the Wayfarer-Guides. Afrikaner members resigned in protest.

This tension chafed against the idealistic mission that some white leaders embraced. With a population of over three hundred thousand poor whites, Scouting had the potential to save youth from delinquency. Olave Baden-Powell explicitly stated this goal in a 1931 report: "Havanga has seven Troops of Dutch boys, sons of poor whites (Dutch) on relief work in forests in Sabia District. . . . They are most difficult to deal with having no character, parents averse to their going into camp for fear of accidents which might disable them from wage earning. None of them earn anything and suffering under 'inferiority complex' don't try to work. They are a growing problem which we should do well to address."[78] Yet troops were usually middle class, and such stereotypes deterred poorer children from joining, especially in South Africa.

Similarly caught in the proto-apartheid politics of the 1930s, the YMCA was also active in South Africa. Max Yergan (1892–1975) was the first person of African descent allowed to represent the YMCA. Originally committed to the uplift of colonized people, especially those in the ancestral homeland of Africa, African Americans like Max Yergan became radicalized by their time in the field. For Yergan, this meant a gradual embrace of Marxism and Pan-Africanism. Born in Raleigh, North Carolina, Yergan experienced the Jim Crow South in his youth. He first served as a chaplain in Bangalore, India, and then in East Africa during World War I. Praised for his service, in 1921 he sought the post of YMCA Secretary in South Africa, but the South African board was reticent. Frederick Bridgman (1869–1925), an American adviser to the all-white South African YMCA, cautioned, "If he belongs to the Du Bois school as regards claiming and forcing recognition of negro rights, then he should not come here. But if he has the attitude which Booker Washington was usually credited with, then by tact and patience and inherent worth, there is no reason why he should not gradually and increasingly gain the confidence and goodwill of a large class of whites."[79] Similarity to Washington was enough for some members of the board to approve Yergan's application, but others, including American YMCA director John Mott (1865–1925), feared the incendiary consequences of sending African Americans to work in South Africa. "There is a pretty strong prejudice in most quarters against the American Coloured man. . . . Moreover, recently the newspapers have given a good deal of prominence to the egregious antics of [Marcus] Garvey and Co. and that has not tended to weaken the prejudice."[80] Yergan's tributes to Booker T. Washington (1856–1915) in his sermons and his support of Washington's Hampton and Tuskegee institutes were sufficient credentials for the YMCA to appoint him, a breakthrough for the YMCA.

Yergan relocated his family to Fort Hare Native College, founded just five years before. Committed to the YMCA's goals of promoting Christianity, fostering interracial cooperation, and abstaining from radical politics, Yergan supervised the growth of branches of the Student Christian Association in the 1920s throughout South Africa. His wife Susie Wiseman Yergan (1893–1971) organized sewing circles and homemaking groups, which also provided a forum for professional women to network. Officially committed to nonracialism and accommodation, the Yergans nonetheless covertly maintained connections with Du Bois and the NAACP. Yergan described his own form of double consciousness: "I travel, I talk, I listen, I see, I shed tears, I plan, I am insulted by low bred whites, I go hungry at times; because I am a Black man wearing a collar and tie and talking grammatical English, and withal somewhat modest and unassuming, I am stared at. I wonder what the whites think."[81] The Yergans' nationality, level of education, and middle-class appearance rendered them liminal, not fitting in to any premade identities. On the other hand, black South Africans welcomed them. Christianity had deep roots throughout Africa by this time, its indigenization well underway. Because the YMCA did not ally to any one Christian faith, it was well positioned to facilitate the development of a uniquely African Christianity.

Yet Yergan believed that the YMCA should take a firmer stand to challenge white supremacy. Labor organizing began in earnest in the 1920s, spreading socialist ideas. Yergan wondered to what degree socialism could be compatible with Christianity and began to emphasize the social gospel of Jesus in his teaching. In 1932 he wrote, "I have no desire to contrast Christianity with communism, but I cannot refrain from observing that communism offers to Christianity its supreme opportunity as a force for social regeneration, and there is no place in the world where this is more true than here in Africa."[82] That same year, he proposed a more comprehensive curriculum at Fort Hare that would examine native customs. It expressly targeted animism and witchcraft as the root of native backwardness. But he deemed his efforts fruitless as a more racist government took power. "I cannot go on in the face of this failure of so-called liberalism which is condoning the increasing political and economic repression of the Africans."[83] Disillusioned, he joined Paul Robeson (1898–1976) and other radical intellectuals from the African diaspora in founding the International Committee on African Affairs in 1937, later called the Council on African Affairs, to which he attached himself for twelve years.

Yergan's gradual embrace of radical politics stemmed from his recognition that Christian institutions, if not sentiments, would not sufficiently challenge racist structures. Although many Christians from all parts of the world worked within the Church to advance a social justice agenda, many more simply adapted it to their increasingly hybrid lives. Their relationships across the color line could break down stereotypes and advance the brotherhood of man. Meanwhile, their promotion of Western gender norms created opportunities for women and foreclosed others.

SCHOOLS

From Javouhey to Nivedita to Yergan, people motivated by their faith established schools all over the world, from Guiana to India to South Africa. Missions and eventually governments established schools in the peripheries of empire. As shown in Figure 3.2, missionaries generally established the first schools. Some were restricted

Figure 3.2. Missionary teachers in New Guinea
Many missionaries established schools prior to and independent of colonial governments. They taught the gospel in addition to literacy and employable skills.

to white settler children. Some were specifically geared to the uplift of native children. Some were, surprisingly, mixed. "Early Childhood Education," where it existed, generally saw wide-ranging opportunities for talented boys and even girls. But an increasingly Western "Curriculum" could be alienating. Even where liberal imperialists touted the benefits of schooling the native population, the reach of education was limited. In French Algeria, merely 10 percent of the native population was literate when the colony won independence in 1962.[84] In the Dutch East Indies, as late as 1930 the literacy rate stood at 10 percent for men and less than 2 percent for women.[85] Although better by comparison, in rural areas of India, the literacy rate remained between 10 percent and 25 percent depending on location. Nonetheless, in India the raw numbers reveal progress in girls' education especially: between 1863 and 1890, the number of schools for girls grew from 92 to 2,238 and the number of pupils from 2,486 to 78,865.[86] "Teachers" drawn from the ranks of the talented native population gradually expanded literacy to a broader spectrum of the population. The highest school attendance was, perhaps ironically, in the "Boarding Schools," which housed native children removed from their families in Australia and the United States. Catholic boarding schools in French West Africa and Italian East Africa claimed to rescue abandoned or orphaned children, but their missions were not terribly different from those of their more secular counterparts. Colonized individuals debated the legacy of schooling even more than that of Christianity because of the degree to which it colonized the mind, on one hand, and opened up opportunities on the other.

Early Childhood Education

In 1831, Dr. John Philip (1775–1851), Superintendent of the London Missionary Society in South Africa, described the purpose of early childhood education, provided by missionaries throughout the British Empire in the early nineteenth century to children age one to seven: "The children of barbarous tribes . . . [might] raise up to cultivate and humanise their parents, and become the elements of a society that will soon be able to supply its own wants, advocate their own rights, and diffuse the blessings of civilisation among the tribes in the interior of Africa."[87] Identifying the home as the source of prejudice and superstition, many missionaries saw preparation for self-governance as the goal of education, transforming the child into a bridge between civilization and savagery. The British East India Company initially barred missionaries from engaging in educational activities, fearing that they would make trouble. But by 1830, the company helped fund the first infant school in Calcutta with forty-eight pupils of age eight or younger. The school was immersive, meeting daily from nine to five, with a lunch break of curry and rice. Rhapsodic about its success, Calcutta Bishop John Turner (1786–1831) wrote, "Every human heart must rejoice to see so many infants snatched like 'fronds from the fire' and placed in an institution where their innocent and tender minds will be trained up in the fear of the Lord, and in habits of order, cleanliness and usefulness."[88] The school foundered, however, until local teachers' aides could be trained to mediate between the children and the teachers, translating cultures and languages across the divide.

Elsewhere, William Brown (1809–1898) of New Zealand did not despair of finding such aides: "If one native in the tribe can read and write, he will not be long in teaching the others. The desire to obtain this information engrosses their whole thoughts and they will continue for days with their slates in their hands."[89] He wrote this in 1845, about a dozen years after the first school had opened in Paihia. Settler children, increasingly numerous, attended alongside Maori children, boys and girls together. Some teachers praised the superior abilities of the Maori children, which they attributed to local childrearing practices. Shortly after his arrival in 1832, Anglican missionary Joseph Mathews (1808–1895) explained: "The custom of the Chiefs is, to make known every thing of importance to the child. I have noticed the principal Chief of Kaitaia talking to his little boy as though the child was able to give him advice. The father would steadfastly look his son in the face, while describing the scene which took place. And his son would as earnestly behold the father, and show, by strict attention, that every word was digested."[90] Matthews and others thus recognized native curiosity and intelligence. The teachers described how their "little wild pupils were all noise and play" at first, but soon adapted to the schoolroom setting.[91] Teachers were determined to keep the children engaged and their method entailed gentle correction, aimed to win the children's love. An 1829 instruction manual noted, "They will attend to you because they love you."[92] These close relationships brought the colonizers' culture into the individual psyche and the indigenous home.

Curriculum

Learning the colonizer's language was one of the first and most essential purposes of colonial education. Creating a commonly used language in cultures that spoke a diversity of languages facilitated imperial relations. Defending imperial languages against hybridization was another. European purists might disparage the hybridizing effects of living in such cultures in which distinct identities disappear. Writing about Rio de Janeiro in the 1850s—"with its houses of all nations"— French expatriate Adèle Toussaint-Samson (1826–1911) described the dissipation of European émigrés, manifested in their unintelligible language.[93] "As they had, during their twenty or thirty years' sojourn in Brazil, about unlearned the little French they had ever known, and knowing still less the language of the country they had inhabited for so many years, they spoke an impossible idiom, insensible mixture of two tongues enamelled with such strange phrases that I thought I heard Chinese or Hebrew."[94] And maybe she did.

In other cultures, Europeans safeguarded their languages as a way to maintain their distinctiveness. Feminist Raden Adjeng Kartini (1879–1904) wrote in the early twentieth century that Hollanders did not wish to speak to Javanese in Dutch: "Why do many Hollanders find it unpleasant to converse with us in their own language? Oh yes, now I understand; Dutch is too beautiful to be spoken by a brown mouth. . . . Oh, now I understand why they are opposed to the education of the Javanese. When the Javanese becomes educated then he will no longer say amen to everything that is suggested to him by his superiors."[95] Yet the diversity of ethnicities created the need for a common language. Kartini wrote, "Is it presumptuous of Father to call attention to the fact that African and Ambonese children may go directly to the European schools, without understanding a word of Dutch?"[96] Kartini's description of the status of the Dutch language in the schools reveals both how multicultural Indonesian schools were and how rudimentary the comprehension of Dutch and the ambivalence of the colonizers. Functioning in the colonizer's language was essential to serving him but could also facilitate autonomy.

Generally, only elite children had access to the colonizer's language. For Algerian author Assia Djebar (1936–2015), this access came through her unconventional Muslim father, a teacher in a secular school. Calling French her stepmother tongue, Djebar recounted growing up under the French occupation in the 1940s and the dilemmas of using their language as a tool for personal and eventually national liberation. "Speaking of oneself in a language other than that of the elders is indeed to unveil oneself, not only to emerge from childhood but to leave it, never to return. Such incidental unveiling is tantamount to stripping oneself naked."[97] Access to French entailed access to Western modernity. When queried by other women about her daughter's freedom of movement, Djebar's mother responded that "she reads," as if this signifier contained within it all of Western modernity and its subversive, even treacherous, potential.[98] Where children did have access to schools, instruction in the colonizer's language enabled pupils from diverse parts of their countries and from different backgrounds to communicate in a common language. In Algeria, Berber, Arabic, and French existed side by side. Associating Arabic, the mother tongue, with the world of childhood, Djebar became a professional writer and historian who taught French in the United States. Indeed, she wrote her memoir in French, but remarked on the irony: "This language was formerly used to entomb my people. . . . By laying myself bare in this language I start a fire which may consume me."[99]

In India, where hundreds of languages were spoken, English helped perhaps ironically to create an Indian national identity. For some, English even imparted a transnational identity, far grander than the small island country from which it sprang. Indian poet Harindranath Chattopadhyay (1923–1988) insisted, "I didn't choose English; English chose me. I took to English as a duck takes to water."[100] Colonial subjects could discover the England of Shakespeare, for them transcendent and uncontaminated by the petty bureaucrats of British India, but it came at a cost. According to Romesh Thapar (1922–1987), "We were really turned into the children of colonialism . . . it deprived me of my contact with my own cultural past."[101] Another prominent journalist, Khushwant Singh (1915–2014), specifically targets English, which "cut me off from Punjabi and Urdu," mother tongues that he had to relearn as an adult, so overpowering was the stepmother tongue.[102]

This emerged among successful elites who recognized benefits to European rule. Access to the most prestigious positions in the British Raj, particularly membership in the civil service, required being steeped in the European literary canon. The top training schools oriented the curriculum to the passage of the Indian civil service examination. Families organized their children's education and sometimes their own lives to achieve this end. Some even immigrated to Britain so that their children could attend a British boarding school. Schoolmasters introduced them to Latin and Greek as well as to the history and philosophy of the Greco-Roman world. They did not study science or economics, which some later lamented as an impediment to Indian-owned commercial and manufacturing enterprises. After passing the civil service examination, a career aspirant would spend a probationary year at Oxford or Cambridge. He would then be introduced to British history and literature. More important, graduates were expected to be good horsemen and to master British social graces. The goal was "being a good all-rounder, good with the gun, good on horseback."[103] If a prospect didn't measure up, "then you were consigned to the judiciary, which wasn't regarded as a very glorious career in those days."[104] Governors back in India favored those trainees who could play a good game of tennis. Hence, schools taught more than core subjects; they imparted and imposed British masculine identity.

Indians studied the Eurocentric geography curriculum. In an Indian girls' school of the early twentieth century, the geography textbook began thus: "Our country is an island."[105] Teachers lamented their inability to obtain books of more relevance and had to make do with British castoffs. Some teachers drew their students' attention to this most basic disrespect for India. Djebar experienced something similar: "I learn the names of birds I've never seen, trees I shall take ten years or more to identify, lists of flowers and plants that I shall never smell until I travel north of the Mediterranean."[106] Seemingly culturally neutral information, like plant identification, became a means of colonizing the mind. More overt representations of normative gender relations illustrated children's books of vocabulary and sociological or mathematical concepts: "Settings and episodes in children's books are nothing but theoretical concepts; in the French family the mother comes to fetch her daughter or son from school; in the French street, the parents walk quite naturally side by side."[107] French comportment revealed a very different set of gender relations from those of Djebar's native Algeria.

Similarly in German Togo, the geography and history of Germany featured on a 1909 exam given in a German missionary school: "What are the names of Germany's most important mountains? What are the names of the most important rivers in Germany and in what direction do they run?"[108] The subject on the essay portion of the exam promoted imperialism even more blatantly: "What good things have the Europeans brought us?"[109] And under the history section of the exam, students were asked to name those men who had especially supported the government of Kaiser Wilhelm I (1797–1888). This example clearly documents the complicity of missionaries in a Eurocentric vision of the civilizing process. At the same time, teachers understood that success in the German Empire required a basic understanding of Germany's geography, government, and history in addition to the heroic German men who supposedly brought civilization.

German government ambivalence about educating native children constructed de facto segregation: mission schools taught native children while colonial government schools taught German settler children. In 1891, the Pan-German League committed funds for the latter, pledging to train the next generation of colonial administrators. Its policy called for: "Raising of the fund for German schools in foreign countries to 500,000 marks; [a] division in [the] foreign office to be created to deal with these schools; creation of [a] pension fund for their teachers; [and] standard German textbooks to be supplied to these schools."[110] The Pan-German League also recommended the expansion of railways, reorganization of the Navy, subsidies to German steamship lines, and the dispatch of commercial consuls throughout the world. That schooling for German children resident overseas would be listed among these conventional and ambitious imperialistic goals reveals the degree to which the cultivation of German nationalism rested not only on managing school curricula but also on cordoning off white Germans from native and mixed-race children who attended mission schools—another example of metropolitan anxieties about the protection of national identity from hybridity.

Teachers

Segregation required white teachers for white children and native or mixed-race teachers for nonwhites. Teacher training schools, whether secular or religious, aimed to cultivate a native cadre of educators, as seen in Figure 3.3. Teachers

Figure 3.3. Algerian school
French teachers instructed Algerian pupils. Once French rule was secure some of the pupils went on to become teachers themselves.

emerged from the ranks of talented local people, such as Assia Djebar's father, Tahar Imalhayène, who gravitated toward the French camp for economic reasons. "It was some time before I realized how poor my father's family was. My father started attending the French school fairly late, did brilliantly in all his classes . . . [and] by becoming a teacher he was able to offer his mother and sisters some security."[111] The first generation often came from humble origins. An announcement from a teacher training school in 1905 read, "We are seeking intelligent young people, with open minds and a lively curiosity . . . a flexible mind always attracts the attention of the examiners no matter what his origin."[112] The announcement indicates equality of opportunity based on merit. Teaching was one of the few vehicles for class mobility open to native people. Of twenty students admitted in the first year, six came directly from tribal schools. Imalhayène would likely have been among this cadre. He intended to raise his daughter to continue the family's ascent. Although Djebar understood his ambitions and acknowledged the benefits of a Western education, she still expressed dismay at his decision to estrange her from her religious, familial, and maternal customs. It was the mothers and grandmothers who kept tradition, secluded as they were. About her grandmother, otherwise stifled, she wrote that "when she danced, she became indubitably queen of the city. Cocooned in that primitive music, she drew her daily strength before our very eyes."[113] But Djebar could not experience such religious ecstasy. By entering French public space, she left behind the Muslim women's world. "Thus, my father, the schoolteacher, for whom a French education provided a means of escape from his family's poverty, had probably 'given' me before I was nubile—did not certain fathers abandon their daughters to an unknown suitor, or, as in my case, deliver them into the enemy camp?"[114] Djebar wondered if she was the sacrificial object in a negotiation between enemies, her father securing his own status unaware of the consequences that it would have for her.

Native educators, central to the colonization of the mind, often became European in orientation and thereby facilitated this transition for children. One founder of a training school in Algeria wrote, "The native intellectuals are the best intermediaries between France and the Moslem masses; their knowledge of the various milieus, their culture, their respectability, their independence, their impartiality, their attachment to France, are so many guarantees for the public powers."[115] At the same time, students at teacher training schools understood that there would always be a racial glass ceiling. Sometimes a Western-oriented native drew scorn when "he takes himself for a Frenchman."[116] But if they remained too close to their native roots, they were dismissed as too Arab.

Elsewhere in Muslim North Africa, teacher Nabawiya Musa (1890–1951) was the first Egyptian woman to become a school principal and chief inspector at the Ministry of Education. Rebellious as a child and envious of her brother's education, Musa implored her brother to teach her how to read and write. On her own she enrolled at the Al-Saniya Girls' School. Once she entered the teaching profession, she discovered that her male counterparts earned more money, so she insisted on full access to the training that would determine her salary. She received it and became the first woman to successfully earn the necessary credential in 1907. Despite her radicalism, she maintained her adherence to Islam, wearing the hijab with a European suit jacket and tie, outwardly exhibiting her hybrid identity. She similarly combined her European training with her religious affiliation to articulate anticolonial demands, starting in her own workplace. As part of a growing nationalist movement in Egypt in the early twentieth century, she drew attention to the Anglicization of staffing in which British teachers even taught Arabic grammar.[117] After being denied the opportunity to practice law, since women were not permitted to take the bar exam, she criticized the Ministry of Education and was dismissed. Undeterred, she then opened a private school for girls in Alexandria. Insisting on their own authority as producers of knowledge about their own languages and cultures, such educators made the case against continued imperial rule. Musa's hybridity manifested in an unconventional life. She never married, rare among Muslim women of the time. Although she successfully crusaded for female education, she opposed the unveiling campaigns then underway by her feminist colleagues, thus navigating the tension between modernity and tradition.

Boarding Schools

Mixed-race children faced a different set of obstacles. Anxious that their whiteness through the father would give them pretensions, but even more that their indigeneity through the mother would debase them, Australian officials removed so-called half-castes from their homes at an early age to civilize them. "No doubt the mothers would object," said territorial administrator Samuel Mitchell (1852–1926) in 1911, but "the future of the children I think should outweigh all other considerations."[118] In other words, the mandate to educate extended the white man's burden, a sacrifice on the part of the colonizer required by humanitarian concern for the future of the colonized. The sacrifice would also have to be made by the children's' mothers, whose ties of affection would otherwise condemn the child to remain in a state of supposed savagery.

The boarding schools were located at Darwin, capital of Australia's remote Northern Territory, and at Alice Springs in Australia's desert outback. School matrons processed boarders on arrival, giving them new clothes, a new name, and sometimes a new birth date. Their hair might be cut or heads shaved. Protector of Aborigines Cecil Cook (1897–1985), who held appointment from 1927–1939, sought to teach inmates "a high appreciation of the principles of hygiene and industrial cleanliness."[119] Boys, dressed in khaki, became skilled in pastoral industry. Girls, in blue uniforms, trained for domestic service where they would learn civilization from the whites they served. Children assembled in lines for everything, even bathing. June Barker (1935–2012) recalled, "Your life was governed by the bell. The first bell would go [off at] morning, you would have to go down to the treatment room: that's where you would get your cod-liver oil and eyes done every day. . . . The bell would ring for school; the bell would ring for rations; a mournful bell would ring for funerals. . . . You got to know the different sounds in the bell."[120]

Whiteness may have been the most salient item in the curriculum. "It was drummed into our heads that we were white," recalled a former student, though experience in the outside world often proved otherwise.[121] "They tried to make us act like white kids but at the same time we had to give up our seat for a white-fella."[122] Whiteness was equated first and foremost to cleanliness. Lacking suffi-cient resources for proper hygiene, bodily inspections took place regularly. This emphasis on pupil cleanliness stood in stark contrast to the deplorable conditions of the facilities: forty-four children boarded in a three-room house in Darwin. Lack of funding and persistent racism undermined lofty principles.[123] Removed from her family at age six, Daisy Ruddick (1915–2002) lived at a "Half-Caste Home" in Darwin in the 1920s. She recalled that the matron was "good at keeping us clean."[124] She later became a nurse and married a white man. Through marriage and profession, she achieved the whiteness that the schools had set as their goal. Nonetheless, for Ruddick, the process of whitening came at the cost of her family of origin and her Aboriginal identity. Ruddick's experience was common. An esti-mated one-tenth to one-third of all mixed-race children in Australia were removed from their families and placed in boarding schools. In the Northern Territory, more than half of all mixed-race children were housed in boarding schools.[125] Those who married "white," as did Ruddick, achieved the goal of assimilation, which some Australians saw as destiny. Auber Octavius Neville (1875–1954), Pro-tector of Aborigines in Western Australia, asked in 1937, "Are we to have one million blacks in the Commonwealth or are we going to merge them into our white community and eventually forget that there were any Aborigines in Australia?"[126] This melting pot version of assimilation strived to eliminate, not celebrate, multi-culturalism. In some ways more radical, this version assumed race could be refash-ioned. Blackness would disappear, at least as a political category, and possibly as a racial characterization as well. This might literally be accomplished through inter-racial sex. Neville further explained that to "breed out the colour" posed no risk to whites because Aboriginals were "a people already allied to us by association, con-sanguinity, and ancestry" who "predate us in some vague Caucasian direction."[127] More than Africans, Pacific natives, thought to be vaguely related to the white race, could be made European.

Reformers intervened on behalf of mixed-race children on the presumption that they had been abandoned by their fathers and were unwanted by their mothers. The governor of Niger in French West Africa, Jean-François Toby (1900–1964), argued for the humane treatment of mixed-race people: "The French administra-tion considers the métis question from a sentimental point of view. It is in the nature of the French, who are not steeped in racial prejudice, to take pity on these little children, often deserted by their father through cowardice or necessity, and abandoned by their mother, and whose lot is indeed pitiful. That is why orphan-ages for métis are generously open to children in every colony, and they are cared for there with complete devotion by those in charge of them."[128] Schools welcomed girls and boys alike, deeming the education of girls especially important because of the influence they would have on others. In 1917, Georges Hardy (1884–1972) insisted, "When we bring a boy to the French school, we gain an individual; when we bring a girl there, we gain an individual multiplied by the number of children she will have."[129]

Though well-intentioned, these interventions fostered a legacy of ambivalence, if not outright despair. Barthélémy Chaupin, the secretary of a society representing West African métis in the late 1940s, described the racial melancholia prevalent among the graduates of boarding schools. Left at home, the child "would all the same have benefited from the maternal tenderness which, whatever anyone says, has a great influence on children. Numerous examples demonstrate it: at times a bitter melancholy, a deep spiritual sadness spontaneously overcomes them."[130] Although access to French and Frenchness might facilitate professional success in French institutions, boarded children suffered the loss of connection to local community, culture, and, first and foremost, the family.

Anxious about the possibility that schools might facilitate anticolonial activity, some administrations limited access to schooling. Religious boarding schools in the Italian colony of Eritrea, on the Horn of Africa, educated Catholic mixed-race students only, mostly sons of local Catholic notables not recognized by the Italian parent. After visiting a parochial school in Massawa during the first decade of the twentieth century, Governor Ferdinando Martini (1841–1928) wrote in his diary that, "In my opinion, the blacks are more alert than us, and the superiority of the whites, on which every colonial regime is based, proves in the schools not to hold water."[131] Hence the decision to *not* provide a more extensive educational system to natives was racially motivated but with an ironic twist. In this case, recognition of their abilities foreclosed campaigns for their improvement. Italian colonial administrators feared that white rule might be defeated by the talented members of the colonized population who wielded the master's tools.

As elsewhere, perceived abandonment of mixed-race children justified intervention by missions.[132] By 1940, laws prohibited Italian men from recognizing the offspring of interracial unions. Moreover, the designation "orphan" rendered native mothers invisible, and Fascist racism foreclosed even the little that had been achieved by the mission schools. By decree, "The métis child assumes the status of the native parent and he/she is considered native to all intents and purposes: he/she can no longer be recognized by the parent citizen, nor can he/she use the name of the parent. He/she must be maintained, educated, and instructed at the exclusive cost of the native parent. Institutes, schools, colleges, special boarding houses for métis children, even if of a conventional nature, are forbidden."[133] The severity of these laws could be attributed to Fascist racial policies as well as the goals of Italian imperial ambitions in Africa, which had never really endorsed a civilizing mission. Fascist racism suppressed even the mission schools, and the net number of students graduating declined.

Native teachers and pupils appropriated European education for their own ends while critiquing its reach. Whereas some adopted imperial languages and job opportunities with gusto, others rejected them. Most occupied a middle ground illustrating the multiplicity of responses to imperial institutions. Mixed-race persons, especially those who attended special schools, articulated the intermediate status that they would always occupy.

ACHIEVING STATUS

Colonial governments struggled with the liminal status of mixed-race people. In most empires, mixed-race persons would later enjoy the privileges of full citizenship, but in the nineteenth and early twentieth centuries informal networks of power operated to allow mobility to only select colonial subjects. Where formal imperial institutions were undeveloped or where they were in competition, local men could acquire a measure of status. "Political Culture" included newspapers, professional organizations, and clubs, constituting an alternative public sphere accessible to some native men. When empires finally began the long process of enfranchisement, the more cosmopolitan a society, the earlier the path to "Citizenship" for men. A woman's access to citizenship lagged everywhere, often tied to that of her husband if she had one.

Political Culture

In the early stages of empire, the formal structures of political power were either absent or fluid. Native or immigrant men could achieve status more easily in the early part of the nineteenth century than they could later. Immigration to Canada from other parts of the British Empire meant that mixed-race persons from the Caribbean and India joined the land grabs that began in the 1850s. Pioneers and refugees intermingled with native others, producing a mixed-race population in the Americas known variously as mulatto, colored, or métis. James Douglas (1803–1877), the illegitimate son of a Scottish sugar planter in British Guyana and a free woman of color, eventually became British Columbia's first governor in 1858. A fur trader for the Hudson's Bay Company, Douglas married Amelia Connolly (1812–1890), the daughter of an Irish-born trader and a Cree woman. Their intersecting racial identities, and especially their brown skin, raised the ire of some metropolitan imperialists but did not block Douglas's career success. His acceptance by white society did not hinder his ambitions for people of color. He recruited black Jamaicans into British Columbia's police force and welcomed black immigrants from California. It was left to his wife and daughters to adopt white identities in the governor's mansion. The family's integration continued apace as their daughters married white men and adopted Victorian manners and rituals, such as afternoon tea. The family's ability to negotiate multiple axes of identity demonstrates how empire functioned on the ground and how metropolitan conventions had limited relevance in the farthest-flung spaces of empire. Yet, as British Columbia became more "respectable," so did its governors, thus illustrating an imperial trajectory seen elsewhere. The governors who succeeded Douglas were white.[134]

By the twentieth century, immigrants to Canada demanded more rights as British subjects and used political institutions and the press to assert their claims. Restrictive immigration laws incurred special ire. Male migrants from India were not allowed to bring their families because of the fear they would stay. They formed the Ghadar Party, which would become an anti-imperialist organization, to bring pressure on the provincial government in Ontario. The *Toronto Star* newspaper endorsed colonized women's immigration in an editorial in 1912 but not on the basis of immigrants' rights: "A married Sikh with a wife and baby in his cottage will be a far better Sikh than a glowering, morose, and wronged Sikh leading a lonely life and disapproving of all he sees around him. The man should not be here if his wife is not."[135] As elsewhere, wives of one's own race were deemed essential to the containment of male sexuality. These sentiments bordered on the hysterical after a murder of a white woman in Victoria in 1914. An editorial in the *Victoria Daily Colonist* observed that "the disposition of the body and the callousness of the murderer indicates a phase of character which is exceedingly rare among people of our own race. . . . In an article of our last Sunday section, the writer suggested the segregation of the Sikhs from the rest of the community."[136] Yet segregating Sikhs would not have prevented the murder: the perpetrator was Chinese.

But in the context of the "Yellow Peril," a term used widely to connote the threat posed by Asian immigration, white fears of Asian population growth and particularly racial intermixing led to generic prejudice toward all Asians. A 1902 royal commission on Chinese and Japanese immigration reported that: "The number of Chinese who have intermarried with whites is greater than the number of Jews who have married with Gentiles. It is possible that the coming here of Chinese in large numbers might result in bringing about conditions similar to those now prevalent in the Southern United States."[137] Raising the specter of the white supremacist's worst nightmare, nonwhite men raping white women, Senator James Lougheed (1854–1925), leader of the Conservative Party in Parliament, promoted Chinese women's immigration in a 1911 speech: "It would be much better that they have the opportunity of debauching their own women."[138] Immigration quotas were eased, particularly for women, in part due to the active political engagement of Asian immigrants in Canada's largest cities. But fears of interracial sex and the belief in the stability of the nuclear family were the main reasons legislatures shifted their position.

In British India, the political public sphere was dominated by the colonial social clubs, leisure sites where informal networks of power enabled the functioning of colonial administration. Initially these clubs limited membership to whites only. But by the last quarter of the nineteenth century, Indian elites and their British supporters pressed for integration. The first experiment with integration did not last long. The chief magistrate of Calcutta, James Hume (d. 1862), opened the Cosmopolitan Club in 1860. It closed within a year. The next attempt, the India Club, lasted longer. It aimed to provide a "place where gentlemen, both native and European, could freely mix, independent of their social, political, and religious differences."[139] Although the club attracted some European members initially, its clientele became exclusively Indian, reflecting the racial attitudes of the period. Visiting the India Club in the 1880s, Member of Parliament Wilfred Scawen Blunt (1840–1922) explained that "the bitterness of feeling is now so great that, with the exception of two or three secretaries in attendance on Indian princes I was the only Englishman present."[140] The last decades of the nineteenth century saw the formation of the Indian National Congress and sustained calls for the British to grant greater autonomy. But as more Indian elites occupied positions in business, government, and the military, more pressure to Indianize colonial administration created a more receptive climate for integrating the clubs by the second decade of the twentieth century.

British clubs began to lift their bans on Indian membership. Some granted only honorary membership, whereas others provided partial access to the club's facilities. At the Calcutta Club, only Indians who did not keep their wives in seclusion were allowed to access the ladies' annex where balls were held, indicating how ideas about native sexuality continued to structure men's access to the political public sphere.[141] Even where there were no formal prohibitions against interracial mingling, attitudes prevented it. Social occasions were in practice segregated by race and gender: "For instance, at a Government House ball, one would not ask an English lady to dance. And hardly any British officers would ask any Indian lady to the floor. And all the Indians, including the ministers and very senior officials, would be sitting on one side, and the British would be on the other side."[142] Such awkwardness began to expose the futility of using the clubs at all. Former Indian members described the banality of the clubs. Bridge was a favorite activity there "because in bridge you don't have to make any conversation or establish any personal rapport with anybody."[143] As nationalist politics became more militant in the 1930s, the political public sphere shifted away from the clubs, now attended only by the old guard that was becoming increasingly obsolete.

By contrast, in colonies where the population of whites was small, colonial administration depended on the cooperation of local elites (see Figure 3.4). Hybrid institutions formed to facilitate governance, such

Figure 3.4.   East African leader
Even in the German Empire, cooperation with local elites was essential to administration. In German East Africa (Tanzania), regular councils were conducted in Swahili.

as the district councils in German East Africa established in 1890. Each district officer assembled dozens of local notables in weekly meetings that deliberated on all matters of law, including regulations and taxation, and had the authority to mete out and execute punishments.[144] Subjects could bring complaints; therefore, the district council might be called to meet more often as need arose. This practice assured the integration of German rule into daily life. Councils met in rural areas as well as the larger coastal cities, with business primarily conducted in Swahili. The arrangement of bodies in the council halls reveals that even in German East Africa political legitimacy was a process of negotiation with variously empowered local participants. The district officer sat at the center, flanked on either side by local men, sitting in rows. Members of the public stood behind them, forming an outer circle. The halls were gazebo-like structures, circular with thatched roofs, their decorative accents quoting local not German design. This was a formal affair, with both German and local men dressed in their most formal attire. Military personnel were also in attendance, including African soldiers in the German colonial army.

Punishments, usually floggings, were public spectacles, held on the spot after the meeting adjourned. Although the district officer alone served as jury and judge, subjects could present their cases and local notables could advise the officer. Nonnatives, that is, those who racially resembled Germans, were entitled to due process; whereas natives were judged "based on the legal principles of the civilized nations, common sense and local customs and traditions."[145] Hybrid laws applied to hybrid people, including Japanese residents in cosmopolitan Dar es Salaam, who fell under the native category because they were not white. Women might be present when they were accused, or as family members of the accused, but generally the administration of colonial justice was a male affair. Nonetheless, advisory bodies enabled the expansion of the political public sphere and validated traditional elites while also displaying imperial power to silent onlookers of both sexes.

The situation was more complicated in Germany's Pacific colonies. English settlement preceded the Germans in Samoa. Efforts to apply German laws and the German language therefore met with hostility. Moreover, colonial wars over the Samoan Islands resulted in its partition between the United States and Germany. Under German rule, patriarchs of local families and large estates saw their privileges challenged by a metropolitan government that wanted to promote large-scale immigration of poorer Germans. Castigating early settlers as morally debased, revealed by their high rates of interracial concubinage, Governor Wilhelm Solf (1862–1936) went so far as to decry interracial marriages as "tasteless and an insult to white women . . . because they prostitute the essence and moral value of the marital bond."[146] A ban followed with exceptions for colonial subjects who spoke European languages and adopted European lifestyles. Solf justified these exceptions on the basis of the racial similarity between Samoans and Germans. Some mixed-race individuals lived variously as European or Samoan depending on the circumstance and could invoke either set of laws to suit their case. Deputy Governor

Heinrich Schnee (1871–1949) described meeting one such man: "To my great astonishment, a tall man in Samoan dress, that is, with bare chest, who had a completely European appearance, apart from bronze-toned skin, and with a very intelligent demeanor, presented himself to me as village chief."[147] He went on to explain that he had lived as a European until inheriting the office of chief from his mother. He told Schnee that "he was perfectly happy and had no wish to appear as a European ever again."[148] Once again proximity to whiteness, not only in parentage but in behavior, carried special privileges, but other privileges, such as the chiefdom passed down through the mother, carried more weight. Solf desired to impose order on this chaos and issued a further decree that required the registration of all "Mixed-Bloods."[149] By 1910, the government banned interracial marriages.

At the same time, missionary societies attempted to improve the status of half-castes, as they were called in Samoa. In the largest city, Apia, they had their own classrooms and gained access to imperialist languages and upward mobility. They could get jobs as clerks, interpreters, and policemen. They could frequent bars, bowling alleys, and billiard halls. Only the wealthiest could go to balls, polo matches, and dance clubs, one of the latter started by American author Robert Louis Stevenson (1850–1894). There were also half-caste churches.[150] When they could claim status as foreigners, half-castes appealed to embassies for support. German half-caste William Laban (b. 1876) appealed successfully to the German consulate and a German warship when a local chief prevented his occupation of a small islet.[151] This event illustrates an unusual benefit to half-castes: they could move between cultures, sometimes pitting them against each other, to secure their status. Some complied with orders to register for this reason. If they had American fathers, even African American fathers, they were eligible for American citizenship, as were their mothers, even if they were illegitimate.[152] As the interracial hierarchy became more complex, the Samoan language developed words to distinguish between British half-castes, German half-castes, and American half-castes.[153]

Citizenship

Accessing citizenship varied from colony to colony and was generally achieved piecemeal. Before World War II, most empires restricted access to citizenship on the basis of race and gender. The Dutch empire was one of the earliest empires to gradually introduce citizenship to its subjects. By the 1880s, nearly half of the European male population in the Dutch East Indies—tens of thousands—cohabitated with Asian women. To regularize these relationships, the Mixed Marriage Law (1898) decreed that a woman's legal status followed that of her husband.[154] Some women resisted, preferring the relative autonomy provided by their nonlegal status. For many, becoming European would limit access to property or divorce. In the Southeast Asian islands of Borneo, Sumatra, Java, and New Guinea, the Dutch had exerted control since the seventeenth century, but the East Indies had attracted Asian immigrants for centuries, especially from China (see Figure 3.5). Such intra-Asian

Figure 3.5. Chinese laborers in Dutch Indonesia, 1854
Chinese immigrants throughout the Pacific took menial jobs including transporting Indonesian elites.

diversity complicated attempts to regulate interracial sex, including the ban on intermarriage between Christians and non-Christians on the books from 1617 to 1848. By 1930, 1.2 million "racially ambiguous" Chinese resided in the Dutch East Indies.[155] This included Catholic Filipino-Chinese persons who could claim some degree of Europeanness. Hence, drop-of-blood qualifications for citizenship proved to be impossible to calculate, let alone enforce. The government ultimately removed race qualifications in the constitution of 1918 as part of a strategy to bring all people under the aegis of the state. According to Izak Alexander Nederburgh (1861–1941), a colonial jurist writing in 1898, "in the civilized world, no one may be without a relationship to the state."[156]

Preferring a hierarchical process for accessing citizenship to naturalization en masse, the Dutch East Indies developed three tiers of citizenship. Dating from the early nineteenth century, the relevant legal statute remained in effect until World War II. It laid out the three categories of residents in the colony: European, Native, and so-called Foreign Oriental, and the privileges attending each. In law, this meant being subject to different codes and therefore punishments, and tried in different courts. Taxes, voting, and terms of military service were all accessed differently depending on these categories. Europeans generally enjoyed better funded schools and thereby career prospects leading to higher pay, higher pensions, and the heritability of those pensions. Furthermore, the likelihood of marrying another "European" followed from all of these things.[157]

Because Indonesia had attracted wealthy immigrants across the Pacific, including Japanese, Turks, and Siamese, Dutch law enabled certain Asians to be legally "European," separating the designation from national origin and phenotype and signifying degrees of modernity or civilization deemed similar to those of Europe. Even some Africans gained the designation: approximately three thousand soldiers from the Gold Coast served in the Dutch colonial army, attracted in part by the government's offer of full European citizenship. Those who established families in Indonesia after their term of service transferred their citizenship to their wives and children, regardless of their ethnicity.[158]

The statute also allowed for Natives and Foreign Orientals to become "equated Europeans" by means of an application process. In the 1920s, there were 3,608 equations out of a total "European" population of about 245,000. The practice steadily increased so that by 1939 there were some 900 equations annually.[159] Equation depended on the demonstration of cultural competencies. Bureaucratic forms asked precise questions: "Does he speak and write Dutch or any other European language? Which schools has he attended and what grade has he reached in that educational institution? Has he passed any exams? Has the applicant enjoyed an upbringing in Europe or has he been raised in these parts in a European environment as a European?"[160] Applicants went on to describe relations with Europeans, travel to Europe, and their wealth and profession. Being a Christian could also improve one's chances. Male applicants could gain equation for their family members if they met the criteria. Because a wife's identity was tied to her husband's, her lack of any of the criteria did not have a negative impact on the family's application. Native women, fully rooted in their traditional cultures, could only gain the status of "European" through marriage.[161] Statutes thus redefined "European," separating it from race and nationality, and precluding direct access to the native female, tying gender to race.

The French also enabled the ascent of mixed-race persons possibly because of the loss of their most valuable colony, Haiti, in the eighteenth century. Colonial officials knew that such individuals linked the colonized majority to ruling elites. As such, they could foster cooperation or rebellion. Imperial policies therefore focused on the often small mixed-race colonial populations. In 1911, Arthur Girault (1865–1931), an authority on colonial law, issued a warning about mixed-race people in French West Africa: "Rejected by all sides, they will become *déclassés*, and, I would add, the most dangerous *déclassés* from the point of view of maintaining European domination. . . . The basic reason for France's loss in the eighteenth century of Saint-Domingue, which was her finest colony, was the division of whites and mulattoes."[162] Girault understood that upwardly mobile, mixed-race individuals would always constitute a potentially subversive segment of the population. Division among elites with common class interests, purely on the basis of race, assured their fall from power. Therefore, securing class divisions, more than racial divisions, was the key to success. A Dahomey school inspector explained further:

> We must treat them as Europeans, something I wish to happen. However, we must not forget that even in Europe, there is a world of difference between the children of a labourer, those of a skilled worker, and those of a banker. To treat them in the manner of a white child from a very well-to-do family would be to develop aspirations in them which they would not all be able to satisfy. . . . After a happy childhood, these people will be embittered potential communists.[163]

In other words, European-style class stratification must also be enforced among populations of color. Elites must be carefully cultivated, but the fostering of equal aspirations regardless of class would lead to a crisis of rising expectations among those who might be attracted to communist support for national self-determination and the abolition of capitalism.

For this reason, governments generally rejected naturalization en masse, preferring to rank potential citizens on the basis of the cultural competencies they possessed. Thus, the French decree of September 1928 facilitated the recognition of citizen status, which included all mixed-race people, regardless of whether they had been recognized by their fathers. However, the decree required colonial subjects to petition for this recognition. Between 1928 and 1944 only 372 people successfully petitioned in all of French West Africa. Upwardly mobile civil servants constituted the bulk of the petitioners. For them, recognition meant a salary boost because they then qualified for the same supplement as Europeans. Male petitioners thus outnumbered female. In 1934, by example, four women successfully petitioned, compared to eighty men. Two women petitioners were rejected because they had married black men.[164] Their failure attests to a gender double standard: a successful petitioner in Guinea retroactively regularized his marriage to a black woman. Both she and their children thereby also became French citizens. As seen in case after case in every empire, a wife's status followed the husband's regardless of the cultural competencies she possessed. A mixed-race woman who married a black man descended into blackness, while a black woman who married a mixed-race man approached whiteness, illustrating the relative fixity of gender as compared to the relative fluidity of race. As in other spheres, gender categories hardened while racial ones eased.

COMBATTING HYBRIDITY

But some groups insisted on hardening racial categories, indeed separating the races. Cartoons like Figure 3.6 illustrate white anxieties about the degeneracy that would supposedly follow racial admixture. As fears about white women's sexual vulnerability as well as their claims to sexual autonomy spread, mandates to cordon off whiteness stoked calls for whites-only laws and whites-only spaces. "Voluntary Segregation" occurred when Europeans fled to cooler climates and founded hill stations away from malaria and natives. But when this approach proved ineffective against interdependence, governments passed "Legal Segregation" to stave off greater integration and race mixing, and Europeans passed laws segregating institutions and neighborhoods. Yet European imperialism facilitated the transnational itineraries of millions of individuals, which meant that in some locales populations became too diverse and too mobile for strict segregation by race to be effectively implemented, despite strenuous efforts. Protecting whiteness was not the only motive for combatting hybridity. "Separatist Movements," including Pan-Africanism, called attention to what they perceived as the degrading effects of intermingling with whites.

Figure 3.6.   "A Little Australian Christmas Party of the Future," 1909
Satirical depictions of mixed-race families both acknowledged the reality of interracial intimacies and provoked measures to prevent them, such as segregation.

In response, they sought to defend their identity and culture by limiting contact with whites.

Voluntary Segregation

Europeans segregated themselves as their empires became more established. To escape the heat and its perceived dangers, including malaria, they built hill stations, such as Penang Hill in Malaya. As more civilians and their families relocated to colonies in the twentieth century, they sought more of the comforts of home, including reproducing their own livestock and agriculture in addition to architecture and clothing. Some hill stations therefore evolved into cities. Leisure activities could be recreated, such as golf, tennis, croquet, and even hiking once suitable pines grew large enough to create a semblance of a forest.[165] In India, the scale and function of Shimla, the summer capital of the British Raj in Northern India established in 1864, attracted more women and children than India's cities or cantonments. It functioned to reproduce the British social world literally and figuratively. By the late nineteenth century, when railway lines facilitated access, the stations became full-fledged cities with churches, governor's mansions, fountains, statues, and other monuments to imperial power. After the completion of the church in 1876, novelist Constance Cumming (1837–1924) exclaimed, "here for once mosques and temples have retired into the background."[166] But such expansion required labor, and during periods of rapid development conditions worsened, making the hill towns as dirty and overcrowded as their lowland counterparts. Such conditions escalated after World War I when better-off

British subjects returned to England, causing property values to drop, followed by an influx of middle-class Indian buyers.[167]

Dalat, the French hill station in Vietnam, was founded in 1897 as a sanitarium but quickly grew to become a major tourist destination. One account from 1908 enthusiastically declared, "After the suffocating climb through the forests of fevers and death, the air becomes lighter, we find a pine-covered mountainous region. It is as if one were inhaling France itself."[168] Jean le Pichon (1906–1995) went further in 1943: "Dalat . . . has become a large resort, where colonials can be themselves again, where anemic children can, under temperate climes, prepare to become men."[169] Beyond recovering health, Dalat's residents recovered their Frenchness and their masculinity. The air allegedly made people who were formerly languishing take up exercise and intellectual pursuits. Opportunities for exercise included tennis, diving, canoeing, polo, hiking, and big game hunting, the latter being the only exotic activity. At night there was gambling, although the government attempted to ban it. There were also "Saigon beauties" whose hairstyles were covered by the colonial press alongside the death of an Indochinese militiaman in a canoeing accident.[170] The 1935 headline was "Easter celebrations in Dalat."[171] The presence of Saigon's beauties, as well as the thousands of Vietnamese laborers required to cater to French needs, meant that racially exclusive enclaves were unsustainable.

At first, laborers came and went. In 1922, Deputy Commandant Robert Delavignette (1897–1976) wrote in a similar manner about Zinder, the capital of Niger in French West Africa:

> The natives in our city, the colonial city, were guards and orderlies, cooks and their scullions, boys with their "small boys" who worked the punkahs [fans]; and women for our need, prostitutes for a night, or concubines for a tour, sometimes servant-mistresses for a lifetime. For the threescore of us Europeans, there were about three hundred servants; a mysterious company, who did what they had to do without bringing us any real contact with the neighbouring world from which they came. And, though they lived with their families in restricted quarters in our buildings, they would slip out at times to recapture in the native city the life which they lacked among us.[172]

As these cities expanded, more affluent natives acquired property or otherwise established themselves permanently. This even included the ruling elite: Vietnam's last Emperor Bao Dai (1913–1997) vacationed at Dalat.

Legal Segregation

Because whites depended on native labor, voluntary segregation was never complete. Governments therefore passed laws to limit natives' freedom of movement, ability to work, and choice in clothing. In Papua New Guinea, male indentured servants in the city were confined to barracks at 9 p.m. by an ordinance issued in 1906. A 1925 ordinance required confinement by dusk.[173] This resulted in segregation of town from country, enforced by a five mile corridor or no-man's land between the urban core and surrounding villages. Harsher laws reflected increased racial panic, especially where domestic servants worked in private homes. The White Women's Protection Ordinance (1926) carried the death penalty for rape or even attempted rape.[174] In 1930, a delegation to Governor Hubert Murray (1861–1940) insisted that "natives must be taught that this is a European Town and not a native playground."[175] Only indentured servants had contact with both white and black communities, the former in the city, the latter in the villages. Indentured servants vastly outnumbered whites: 1,500 whites to 10,000 indentured servants in Papua; 4,500 whites to 40,000 indentured servants in New Guinea by 1939.[176] Tens of thousands of natives thus moved from village to city for work on a daily basis. Whites seldom moved in the opposite direction, yet so relentless was the logic of the cordon that laws developed to limit the movement of whites out of the city. By 1954, ordinances barred whites from black villages after 9 p.m., supposedly to protect native women from white predators.[177] In both cases, then, the sexual threat from men was exploited to justify segregation.

The segregation of Aboriginal men in Darwin, Australia, reflected the deep fears of the "Black Peril," the widespread belief that black men in proximity to white women would commit sexual assault.[178] By the 1930s, in the relatively small town of Darwin, Aboriginal and mixed-race men had to register with the police, be fingerprinted, and wear identity tags. They were subjected to curfew laws that restricted them from leaving their compounds from 9 p.m. to 8 a.m.[179] They could only attend films previewed by the magistrate and with his permission. The curfew included Darwin's Chinatown where gambling was rife. Humanitarian rhetoric occasionally justified these measures as protective: the Aboriginal was too vulnerable to the corruptions of modern life and ought to adhere to his traditions in the compound. But more oft-cited reasons were the spread of disease and the protection of white women. By day, Aboriginal men labored in town where, as couriers, they had access to white homes. Reports of rape as early as the 1870s prompted these laws, whether or not the charges were true. Assumptions about native male sexuality made every man a potential rapist and every white woman a potential victim. When an alleged rape riveted the community in 1938, tensions between white vigilantes and white humanitarians came to a head over every aspect of the case, from the alleged victim's truthfulness to the use of police coercion to extract a confession to the biased trial and punishment. The Northern Territory Aboriginal Ordinance (1918) outlawed floggings and reduced the penalty for rape: a convicted rapist would get only a seven-year prison term. Vigilantes were outraged and threatened to take matters into their own hands, while activists on behalf of the accused demanded a fair trial, pointing out the white man's greater propensity to use violence. They cited the many more instances of white men assaulting Aboriginal women with impunity.[180]

Eventually convicted of attempted rape, Packsaddle was thus caught between two constructions of his sexuality. One narrative showed the benefits of the civilizing process: gainfully employed and entrusted with domestic service, he illustrated the degree to which he had risen above his native savagery. But the compounds ironically undid the work of the civilizing mission by forcing him to return at night to its perceived backward and dirty ways. The opposing view accepted the failure of the civilizing mission as a given. Native people had to be thoroughly controlled, allowed to enter white society only for laboring under strict conditions. But no matter how strident the measures, this episode shows that it was impossible to combat hybridity. Laborers moved between at least two worlds, and those depending on their labor interacted with them in ways both restrained and intimate. Many years later, Cecil Cook (1897–1985), the medical officer in Darwin, said it was well known that the accuser had always treated Packsaddle as her "pet pussycat."[181] Moreover, demographic changes in Darwin made the town of 3,600 thoroughly hybrid. Packsaddle's delivery was from a Greek grocer who provided an alibi that the court refused to entertain. Nonetheless, this diversity destabilized the black/white divide and made some white women nervous. The local Women's Christian Temperance Union complained of Malays, South Asians, and even Japanese who allegedly were responsible for spreading venereal disease. They demanded that the Ministry of the Interior subject them to measures like those used to police Aboriginals.[182]

Segregation was even more complicated in larger cities. In the British Empire, the diaspora of hundreds of thousands of people from South and Southeast Asia during the era of British colonialism resulted in the formation of significant immigrant communities. Zoning strategies that segregated blacks from whites or Europeans from natives did not address their presence. Communities often lacked legal mechanisms for segregating them. In Southern Rhodesia, prosperous Indian immigrants had bought property in Bulawayo's white suburbs by the 1920s, much to the consternation of segregationist whites who tried to pass housing covenants precluding Indian owners from residing in their own properties. Colonial law classified Indians as citizens, and private owners could sell to any citizen. By 1930, segregation laws expelled Indians from African residential areas in an effort to contain blackness, stranding them in the inner city.[183]

To defend their access to white neighborhoods, elite Indians formed the Bulawayo British Indian Association (BBIA) arguing that they should not be forced to mingle with Africans who may have a deleterious effect on the morals of lower-caste Indians. They cited especially the "African women peril."[184] According to the BBIA president, mixed-race neighborhoods presented "a greater opportunity for and the danger of undue familiarity between Indian males and Native women in cases where men are separated from their wives and families."[185] Raising the specter of interracial sex as a downward trajectory—in this case, Indians descending the racial hierarchy—the BBIA president perpetuated white stereotypes about Africans. Their intermingling would result in "a disgrace to the Indian community that Indian children should be reared and trained among Natives," fearing that the presence of Africans may result in "contagion."[186]

Whites played the race card differently by arguing that the real threat of interracial sex was not that between Africans and Indians, as alleged by the BBIA. In 1934, prominent Bulawayo women's leader Mary McKeurtan (b. 1858) wrote to Prime Minister Godfrey Huggins (1883–1971), "Like every other woman in Rhodesia, I have a special interest in segregation, ultimately complete and final."[187] Echoing widely held views in white communities, she called for the physical cordoning off of whiteness to prevent sexual transgression. Another letter to the editor went further. This "Indignant White Grandmother" wrote to the *Bulawayo Chronicle* in 1947 that whites "as respectable, more highly civilised people object to being forced out of their homes by those who were definitely not their equals and to this end of the wedge, which will lead to sharing our schools, churches, buses, dance halls, sport, theatres and if the quality rules, eventually, mixed marriages."[188] She viewed Indians as less civilized and a source of contamination as well as desire, just as Indians had described the Africans with whom they did not want to intermingle. She concluded with an ironic tone: "Would you like to see your friend the Indian pushed out by a Hottentot or Bushmen who had somehow acquired the means to purchase his home over his head? . . . Actually the African has more right to own property among us, for at least the country did originally belong to him, not the Indians."[189] Indians breached the divide between black and white, thereby calling attention to racial segregation's untenability. Acknowledging the possible property claims of the native people that they displaced, whites would sooner cede their own rights to them than to supposed outsiders.

Separatist Movements

Imperialists introduced separatism through various strategies of containment such as boarding schools and reservations. Although some anti-imperialists fought for inclusion and integration, others believed that the establishment of separate ethnically defined communities would enable the preservation and indeed flourishing of native communities under threat of total absorption, if not extinction.

The Papuan curfew of 1954 that prevented white men from entering native compounds demonstrates that the recognition of the danger white men presented to black women was long in coming. The cordon would have been welcomed by separatists like Jamaican Marcus Garvey (1887–1940) who believed that full separation of whites from blacks was the only solution to global racial discrimination. Garvey called for a Pan-African movement that initiated a back-to-Africa settlement scheme, the Black Star Line, which ultimately failed. The sentiment that black safety and prosperity depended on autonomy from whites was widely held by intellectuals of the diaspora in the twentieth century. Even Max Yergan gravitated toward this position in the 1940s and Emily Ruete's eldest son, Rudolph Said-Ruete (1869–1946), supported a similar movement among Zionist Jews in Palestine, a community that he married into.[190]

In 1914, Garvey founded the Universal Negro Improvement Association with the slogan "Race First."[191] The movement organized parades, such as the one in Figure 3.7, to draw attention to global white supremacy. Garvey's goals were to

Figure 3.7.   Universal Negro Improvement Association (UNIA) Parade, 1924
Marcus Garvey's UNIA marched through the streets of Harlem drawing attention to
the connections between racism and imperialism.

encourage black economic independence by fostering black businesses patronized
by blacks, to promote a reunion of diaspora Africans in a new homeland in Africa,
and to discourage interracial mixing that diluted black purity and drew reproductive and economic resources away from the black community. Garvey advocated
absorption of light-skinned African Americans into the white community. He
viewed mixed-race people as the living testament to the biological impact of white
domination and by implication traitors to Black Nationalism. "That where our slave
masters were able to abuse our slave mothers and thereby create a hybrid bastardy,
we ourselves, at this time of freedom and culture, should not perpetuate the crime
of nature."[192] The narrative of defilement by the white man supposed that all mixed-
race people were somewhere in their lineage the offspring of rape. Intent on managing black women's sexuality, he condemned women's celibacy and use of birth
control as contributing to "race suicide."[193] Garvey's gender politics were anachro-
nistic for the 1920s, pivoting on the chivalrous protection of women by black men
whose masculine identities as soldiers, warriors, and leaders earned feminine reverence. The spectacle of his movement, including parades and military drills, attracted supporters. Yet financial and legal troubles derailed the project, with Garvey
jailed in the United States for mail fraud in 1925 and deported back to Jamaica in
1927. When he attempted to revive the movement in the late 1930s, other separatist
movements had already arisen that rested on women's subordination to men.
Indeed, Garvey boasted in 1937, "We were the first Fascists."[194]

Garvey's claim to be a Fascist on the basis of black purity and women's subordination reveals the imperative to manage race and gender central to both Italian Fascism and German Nazism. In 1938, Fascists in Italy published the *Manifesto of the Race*, which proclaimed, "with the creation of the Empire the Italian race has come into contact with other races; it should therefore be wary of any hybridism and contamination."[195] Rejecting the cultural and racial mixing prevalent in the modern world, totalitarian regimes implemented the most extreme measures to prevent it including criminalization, sterilization, concentration camps, and mass murder.

In most communities prejudice did not take on these extreme proportions. To be sure, anxiety about, if not outright rejection of, mixed-race children was widespread among native communities. In the 1930s in French Sudan, a saying went like this: "Dieu a fait le café, il a fait le lait, mais il n'a pas fait le café au lait" ("God made coffee, he made milk, but he did not make coffee mixed with milk").[196] This saying had also been common in Senegal for some time. Such attitudes could lead to the ostracizing of mixed-race children. In 1945, a Lobi woman named Waal-Hirèna was forced into a temporary union with a French official in Upper Volta (modern Burkina Faso). She was sent back home after she became pregnant. Although such pregnancies were usually aborted, Waal-Hirèna's mother let the child be born despite the Lobi spiritual belief that birthing mixed-race children led to damnation. For Waal-Hirèna, the birth turned her life into an "endless nightmare."[197] People gawked at her for daring to carry a "white" child to term. Her husband rejected the child, refusing to feed it, which led her to divorce him and in turn resulted in his suicide.

Recognizing the degree to which the modern world was segregated, even black delegates to the Council of French Equatorial Africa, formed after World War II, urged the mixed-race person to choose an identity. Stéphane Tchitchelle (1915–1984) stated plainly, "The métis is a European or he is an African. If he is a European, he only has to live with Europeans, or if, despite his skin colour, he considers himself an African, he only has to continue to live with us."[198] Despite the responsibility the nuns were taking for the children abandoned by the French, the privileging of the métis orphan came at the expense of black orphans in his view, and illustrated how imperialists continued to use a divide and conquer strategy. In January 1947, an unsigned editorial in Senegal's French-language newspaper *Réveil* asserted that: "It is the European who taught the métis that his personal dignity as a [mulatto] forbade him from assimilating to black society, or marrying a black woman if she was more cultivated than him. In this way ... the white man, not content merely to have turned his back on his paternal duties, seeks by his insinuations to detach the métis from the sole milieu in which it is possible for him to find a suspicion of happiness, from those who, far from turning their backs on him, have unconditionally adopted him as their own."[199] Likewise, Léopold Senghor (1906–2001), one of the founders of the Négritude movement, urged the métis to choose his African self, arguing that they would always be seen as such by white society and that the only defense against racial discrimination was the solidarity of all peoples of African descent. He called for métis to close their racially particular organizations: "What are we waiting for to be a united people?"[200]

But in response, some mixed-race people formed mutual aid societies and claimed their status as Eurafricans. Even for Eurafricans, hybridity was not an option. The founder of the Eurafrican Union, Nicolas Rigonaux, wrote in 1949, "A human being cannot belong simultaneously to two races and two civilizations; he must opt for one or the other or sink into the anonymous despair of an individual without social ties."[201] Eurafricans aspired to Frenchness, one of them describing his blackness as a "ball and chain."[202] Others urged African mothers to raise their children as French as possible. The society raised funds to support these children and their mothers and also formulated new citizenship laws and other privileges that mixed-race people could access. Once citizenship was finally granted, it therefore divided rather than rallied colonized peoples. Some embraced their new status and pledged their loyalty to the mother country. Many more determined to assert their national identity, even forming separatist movements, leaving mixed-race people in a liminal situation.

Efforts at combatting hybridity ultimately failed, although apartheid laws lasted beyond the Age of Empire. Although the general trend of openness between colonizer and colonized at first contact was followed by the hardening of racial and gender strictures, hybrid individuals and institutions destabilized those strictures into the twentieth century. Intimate relationships meant that "Saigon beauties" consorted with French men at Dalat while Australian women grew fond of Aboriginal men. Garvey could not attract enough support for his separatist movement because so many people of African descent claimed, and even valued, their mixed-race identities.

CONCLUSION

Imperialism enabled and sometimes required the formation of complex modern identities because it brought people in contact who never would have otherwise known each other. Emily Ruete, one of the Zanzibari sultan's thirty-six children, might never have left the harem, let alone the continent, if she had not fallen in love with a German spice merchant. And Heinrich never would have met an Arabian princess were it not for the expansion of global trade in the nineteenth century. They lived liminal and hybrid lives, moving between cultures and languages, raising mixed-race children who had to wrestle with their own hybrid identities. Not rooted to one place, their routes further layered new identities over top of their old ones. Emily converted to Christianity, as did millions of people all over the world in the modern era, enabling transnational axes of identity to transcend the nation. Australian missionaries and their Indian converts identified as Baptists first, subjects of the British Empire second, and only later by nationality. But Vietnamese Catholics did not mindlessly adopt the white man's creed. In a complex process of negotiation, which included adoption and rejection, they developed a form of religious belief and practice that drew from their cultural traditions, a phenomenon seen everywhere missionaries worked. The missionaries were themselves transformed in the process, a source of anxiety to metropolitan mission boards who, along with metropolitan governments, became increasingly intolerant of the interracial mingling required by their work. Yet the opposite was also true, as in Vangeke's case in which his white brothers in the priesthood demanded and secured equal treatment for him.

Schools too, some of them run by missionaries, enabled and required the formation of complex identities. Where even basic literacy was taught, pupils of necessity glimpsed different worlds. More advanced study required immersion in those worlds to the point where some colonized elites identified a form of schizophrenia, the internalization of different personalities to fit those different worlds. Djebar described her ambivalence toward French, the stepmother tongue, while Chattopadhyay separated the English language from the petty English bureaucrats ruling India, claiming it even as something that transcended one country and its people. Francophonie similarly united French speakers across the globe who made French theirs. Hybrid identities could be sources of pride and unity. But they could also be sources of shame and bitterness, particularly for some children forced into boarding schools who were totally deprived of contact with the language, customs, and especially the tenderness of their mother's milieu. Such schools supposed that mixed-race people could be made white, but, for many, acceptance in the white world proved elusive.

In the early twentieth century, colonial governments generally introduced citizenship to mixed-race people on the basis of their "Europeanness" and only later to all colonial subjects. This tiered process enabled some to access career opportunities, wealth, and status but at the cost of fragmenting colonized communities. In more traditional areas, mixed-race identity carried a stigma, and colonized people rejected local women who had "white" children. Whereas access to citizenship in some of the most cosmopolitan areas of the world, like Indonesia, served as a belated recognition of the futility of racial sorting, in more rural areas like Northern Australia racial sorting entailed everything from curfews to registration to wearing identification tags. This multiplicity of responses makes generalizations about imperialism all but impossible, but the fact that there was a multiplicity indicates the role of intimacy in forging complex identities and undercutting imperialism.

TIMELINE

1827	Sister Anne-Marie Javouhey founds a colony for escaped slaves in French Guiana
1830	British East India Company funds the first infant school in Calcutta
1833	Vietnamese Emperor Minh Mang bans Catholicism
1858	James Douglas, of mixed-race heritage, becomes British Columbia's first governor

1864	British establish hill station at Shimla in Northern India
1882	Baptist Church in Australia sends first missionaries to India, both of them women
1884	Benjamin Ousley is the first African American minister sent to Africa by Foreign Missions Board
1886	Hindu Feminist Pandita Ramabai tours United States for speaking engagements
1897	French establish Hill Station at Dalat in Vietnam
1906	Indigenous male indenture servants subject to curfew in Papua New Guinea
1912	Ban on interracial marriages in German Samoa
1914	Marcus Garvey founds Universal Negro Improvement Association
1915	Formal segregation of the Boy Scouts and Girl Guides in South Africa
1918	Dutch Indonesia removes racial qualifications for citizenship
1928	Decree in French West Africa allows petitions for citizenship regardless of race
1937	Father Louis Vangeke is the first Papuan Catholic to be ordained a priest
1937	African Americans Paul Robeson and Max Yergan help found Council on African Affairs
1954	Whites barred from entering black villages in Papua New Guinea after 9 p.m.

FOUR

THE ARTIFACTS OF EMPIRE

Mata Hari of Indonesia and Paris

My dance is a sacred poem in which each movement is a word
and whose every word is underlined by music. The temple in
which I dance can be vague or faithfully reproduced, as here
today. For I am the temple.

—Mata Hari, speaking at the Musée Guimet, 1905

*Opportunities for residence overseas, the consumption of material goods from all
over the world, and exposure to other cultures through mass media initiated a dynamic process of cultural exchange that is quintessentially modern. Few personified this process better than Mata Hari, a Dutch woman whose actual name was
Margaretha Zelle (1876–1917). Answering a personals ad in 1895, she married a
Dutch officer twenty years her senior stationed in Java, the main island of the
Dutch East Indies. After the birth of two children, one of whom may have been
poisoned by a servant or contracted venereal disease from his parents, Zelle's
tumultuous marriage fell apart and she ran off to Paris. An invention of the modern
world, Mata Hari became a sex worker and exotic dancer in brownface after her
divorce. She experimented with, became famous for, and was perhaps executed for
her performance of fluid ethnic, national, and sexual identities. Skepticism remains about whether she actually spied for the Germans during World War I.
Some argue that her death before a French firing squad was actually punishment
for a lifetime of sexual—and racial—transgression. In her own words, she, larger
than life, was the temple, vague or faithfully reproduced.[1] She insisted on her right
to self-representation and capitalized on her period of exotic residency to craft a
cosmopolitan identity. That identity depended on the transnational circulation of
goods: clothing and make-up most obviously. Her allure was also constituted indirectly through music, and the instruments that made it; through food and drugs,
and the ingredients and recipes that produced them; and through the occupation of*

*gendered space, from the harem to the brothel. In this chapter, we attempt to trace
these complex interactions at the level of the body: cosmetics and clothing; at the
level of the home: food, pets, and decoration; at the level of high culture: opera and
painting; and at the level of pop culture: cinema and pornography. We refer
throughout to the process of othering and appropriation known broadly as orientalism. This process went in multiple directions as consumer culture promoted
globalization and stereotypes but also fostered cross-cultural understanding.*

*Mata Hari means "dawn" or "rising sun" in Javanese, but the name also al-
ludes to a Hindu minor god, a servant of Shiva. Like much orientalist kitsch, her
name is an insensible amalgam of Eastern references. Although her sojourn in
Java inspired her art and the cultivation of an oriental identity, she acquired the
materials necessary for her transformation through Emile Guimet (1836–1918), a
French orientalist collector. In this instance, first-hand knowledge of Java and its
assimilation into a hybrid identity required a reconfiguring of that culture through
European appropriation and display. Guimet managed her early career, outfitting
her with authentic Indonesian clothes and even a spear for her more phallic performances. It is notable that her costume changes featured transvestism, where for
select audiences she dressed as a soldier in uniform. Guimet also collected instruments and recordings of Indonesian gamelan percussion instruments so Mata
Hari could practice her act.*

*Mata Hari knew how to work this inauthentic authenticity to her advantage.
With the physique of a tall European and the darkened skin, hair, and eyes of a
so-called Oriental, she played to male and sometimes female fantasies of the Asian
Other without subjecting them to the contamination of actual interracial sex.
In fact, in Indonesia people regularly mistook her for an Indo, a mixed-race person.
She choreographed her dances around Hindu themes, although she had no experience of Hinduism. "One must always translate the three stages which correspond
to the divine attributes of Brahma, Vishnu, and Siva—creation, fecundity, destruction. . . . By means of destruction toward creation through incarnation, that
is what I am dancing—that is what my dance is about."[2] Although fabricated, her
dances attracted the interest of Indian musicians touring Europe in the early
twentieth century. Sufi holy man and musician Inayat Khan (1882–1927) performed while she danced at a university in Paris, thereby legitimizing her claims
and situating their collaboration in the genre of world music. Perhaps ironically,
Khan went on to found a Sufi order in the Netherlands.*

*Mata Hari performed at the most elite clubs, and at private parties that in-
cluded diplomats and ambassadors (see Figure 4.1). Eroticizing the veil, Mata Hari
catered to Western obsessions with female covering—and uncovering. She admitted that
her talents as a dancer were dubious; people came for the nudity. "With every veil I
threw off, my success rose. Pretending to consider my dances very artistic and full of
character, thus praising my art, they came to see nudity, and that is still the case."[3] The
fetishizing of this particular article of clothing signifies multiple meanings. It serves as
marker of religious devotion, or from some perspectives, fanaticism; as boundary between the secluded female and voyeuristic if not predatory male; and as symbol of the*

Figure 4.1.   Mata Hari at the Musée Guimet, 1905
Exotic Dutch dancer Mata Hari dazzled audiences with her burlesque performances in a supposedly authentic Indian or Indonesian setting.

unknowable and ultimately unconquerable Orient. But it was all a ruse. Even as she exposed herself, she exposed the many fabrications on which European hegemony was based. She told conflicting stories about herself to the press—sometimes she identified as Indian, or Indo, or as the orphaned daughter of a temple dancer. She hypocritically heaped scorn on rivals who only pretended to be oriental. "Born in Java, in the midst of tropical vegetation, I have been taught from my earliest childhood the deep meaning of these dances which constitute a cult, a religion. Only those born and bred there become impregnated with their religious significance."[4] *Once she was in her thirties, and putting on weight, her career waned as younger, more professionally trained dancers seized the limelight. Her spate of wealthy lovers also gradually lost interest in her. With the outbreak of World War I, her border-crossing love affairs got her into trouble, and some evidence suggests she spied on the French for the Germans. She was executed by a French firing squad in 1917.*

Mata Hari's principal rival was American Loie Fuller (1862–1928) who also pretended to be oriental but with even fewer credentials than Mata Hari. During the Paris World's Fair of 1900, former French Prime Minister Jules Ferry (1832–1893) wryly noted that "All that interests the French about the Empire is the belly dance."[5] *Fuller performed Salome's Dance of the Seven Veils at the fair with a backdrop of colored lights mounted on rotating platforms. The press dubbed her "The Electricity Fairy."*[6] *Fuller's Salome act became the emblem of that World's Fair. Art critic Camille Mauclair (1872–1945) aptly summed up the escapist function of such orientalist fantasies in his review: "She rushes in to purify the place of all the agonizing human fury. After the dramatic expression of passion, after the last spasm of a desperate and convulsed humanity, she arrives, serene . . . like a messenger from heaven. . . . Loie Fuller tears us away from the destructive conflicts of life, from ordinary life, and takes us to the purifying countries of dreams."*[7] Audiences wanted to be dazzled and soothed rather than edified or challenged. Regardless, some used the orientalist lens to gaze critically back at what was wanting in their own cultures.

The consumption of globally produced goods enabled people throughout the world to claim vague familiarity with other cultures, if not connoisseurship. For many, the products inspired the creation of entirely new and modern hybrid artistic forms or consumer goods. Production and consumption went both ways, indicating how inextricably bound to the imperial project most people had become. Consumers in the colonies may have genuinely prized European-made objects and fads but may also have felt pressure to mark their own level of modernity by acquiring European goods. Consumers all over the world adopted Western fashions and cultural norms but always adapted them to their own milieu. By contrast, traditionalists attempted to signal authenticity by rejecting Western imports. Consumer goods thus performed the work of empire by both fostering hybridity and its opposite, and by mediating relationships between producers and consumers, colonizer and colonized. Above all, they are testament to multidirectional knowledge transfers that problematize a purely top-down approach to the study of imperialism.

COLLECTIBLES

Initially the province of the wealthy, collecting gradually became a pastime of the middle class who acquired useful and decorative items to signal their level of culture. "Furnishings in the Metropole" became increasingly global and therefore eclectic. Collecting was a way of bringing the imperial playground home. Collecting also contributed to the construction of European gender identities: the distinction between shopping (female) and collecting (male) spread throughout the world along with global consumer culture. The demand for such goods gradually shifted commerce from an export basis to domestic production, ironically undermining the allure of exotic items once their provenance was no longer exotic. "Furnishings in the Colonies" similarly reflected hybrid consumer tastes and practices. Consumers in the colonies responded to Western goods in a variety of ways, some emulating European wealth by displaying similar goods, others rejecting European practices that required special products like dishware. "Pets" from the colonies might also be collected by both metropolitan and colonial consumers, illustrating the sometimes strange routes by which modern identities were forged.

Furnishings in the Metropole

Metropolitan tastes absorbed foreign, especially oriental, goods from at least the fifteenth century. Mass production in the eighteenth century stoked a craze for porcelain china, which gradually made its way to the middle classes, unlike the luxury items of previous centuries. Thousands of goods crossed oceans and overland routes, from furniture to carpets and bric-a-brac. By the late nineteenth and early twentieth centuries, mass production enabled more people to consume more items from all over the world but at the same time made them less coveted.

By the late eighteenth century, even wallpaper could be mass produced. Because wallpaper could tell stories in ways other furnishings could not, it more literally translated imperialism for metropolitan pleasure and edification. Capitalizing on early interest in Pacific peoples and landscapes, French wallpaper manufacturer Joseph Dufour (1757–1827) mass produced panoramic prints as early as 1804. The scenes included Romantic landscapes with palm trees and sea shores but also natives in pastoral or amusing activities, including hunting, wrestling, dancing, and cooking.[8] Dufour promoted the wallpapers for instructional and not just decorative purposes. He wrote in a brochure accompanying the paper, "A mother will give effortless lessons in history and geography to her eager, inquisitive and intelligent daughter."[9] Dufour took erudition seriously and commissioned scenes that could be authenticated in Captain James Cook's (1728–1779) widely read travelogues. He further addressed women as the intended audience as he described the importance of the female subjects on the paper: "Women will be reassured that the art of disarming power and of subjugating force with weakness is a gift that belongs, in general, to all of the fair sex. In cities as in deserts, in the perpetual snow of the poles, as in places burnt by the sun, in whatever form she may appear, woman knows how to exert her influence and to make herself loved."[10] He chose to depict peaceful scenes, particularly warm familial relations. In fact, Dufour described the Nootka of the Pacific Northwest as ferocious and cruel savages in the brochure but chose to bypass warriors altogether on the paper and instead portrayed their women tanning fish. He gendered imperialism for gendered metropolitan spaces.

Dufour espoused loftier aims, documenting recently explored lands, but also commenting on human nature: "This decoration has been designed with the object of showing to the public the peoples encountered by the most recent explorers, and of using new comparisons to reveal the natural bonds of taste and enjoyment that exist between all men, whether they live in a state of civilisation or are at the outset of the use of their natural intelligence."[11] Although a civilization hierarchy is implied, what mattered more to Dufour was the universality these scenes depicted, the universality of natural intelligence and sociability. The scenes moved through different Pacific societies, with a focus on Tahitians, feasting and dancing for their king. Elsewhere on the twenty different panels, each eight feet high, Hawaiians board a canoe and Maoris are hiking while the Kanaks of New Caledonia pick bananas. To the other side, royalty from Palau, an island northwest of New Guinea, pose in clothes appropriate to their station. The queen, Dufour notes in his brochure, "displays all that is richest and most fashionable in these islands. That of the king is not so exquisite."[12] Gender norms thus appeared to be universal in the brochure: men dress plainly while women adorn themselves. The focus on kingship can be read as politically loaded in the early part of the nineteenth century, after the end of the French Bourbon monarchy and just as Emperor Napoleon Bonaparte (1769–1821) established his own hereditary line. Notably, the depiction of all of these Pacific peoples precluded French chauvinism because some of these lands were then occupied by the British. Produced as it was in the early nineteenth century, the wallpaper represents a version of colonialism that celebrated common humanity rather than national military glory or racial superiority. Accompanied by an educational brochure, it might even have incited genuine curiosity about the peoples that were depicted. At the same time, it trivialized them as decorative objects. Whatever else it enabled, ultimately the wallpaper was used to signify the good taste and cosmopolitanism of the purchaser.

Furnishings in the Colonies

Consumers in the colonies also bought exotic European goods to signal their wealth and worldliness. Like their European counterparts, the wealthier among them sought handcrafted items. Indeed, ornamentation facilitated horizontal alliances among colonizing and colonized elites. Indian maharajas collected British-made glass, creating such a demand that leading manufacturer F. & C. Osler began producing hookahs and other items exclusively for an Indian market. As depicted in Figure 4.2, crystal was all the more valued because of its craftsmanship and rarity. Only gradually did an Indian middle class begin purchasing more homely dishware. Osler established its reputation among Eastern rulers in 1847 when the ruler of Egypt, Ibrahim Pasha (1789–1848), commissioned two massive candelabras for Muhammad's tomb in Mecca.[13] Queen Victoria then commissioned an entire set of dishes in ruby glass, further stoking the firm's prestige and a heated competition for their wares with India's princes. So entrenched in the Indian market was Osler that in 1844, it opened its first showroom in Calcutta, one year before it opened a London showroom. It then began expanding into the Indian interior, perceived to be an untapped market full of fabulously wealthy people.

This expanded market emerged after the British unseated the Mughals in 1857. The British adapted Mughal formalities to legitimize their rule, which included regular assemblies with local notables that became opportunities for commercial exchange. Henry Pratt, Osler's Calcutta agent, described preparations for the Lahore assembly of 1880. "Mr. Persey has a choice collection of goods there and a small staff of men and I am sure he will use every effort to make it one. All the Punjab princes will be there and 400 little ones."[14] He later reported success with the Nawab of Bhawalpore making an impressive number of purchases. By the 1870s, European companies like Osler had clients in Punjab, Kashmir, and Hyderabad; princes in the states of Gwalior and Patiala were especially prolific buyers. Royal commissions included a monumental crystal fountain and a crystal bed.

Figure 4.2.   Cultural mixture
Elite consumers in India and elsewhere purchased luxury items such as this British-
made crystal and integrated them into their local milieu.

Osler also sold cheap mass-produced glassware, particularly lamp shades, to
a less affluent market.[15] It catered to a mass market, printing catalogs in English
but with prices in Indian rupees. They featured ready-mades such as flasks.[16] The
company's correspondence sometimes revealed a desire to bring European civilization to a wider audience of Indians. Henry Pratt wrote to Henry Osler in
1878, suggesting the time was right to introduce English dining customs and
dishware. "I am very anxious to introduce or to try to introduce native dinner
sets in crockery. I have been making enquiries about it and the result is favour-
able. The 'orthodox' Hindoos are not very likely to adopt innovation at first, but
'young Bengal' is not quite so strict as their fathers were. Most of them still
retain the native way of eating—with their fingers, but the old custom of smash-
ing pots and pans made of clay after they have been used once is not now considered so necessary as it used to be."[17] Product development depended on research
into local practices, particularly at their moment of transformation. Noting the
embrace of modernity by young Bengalis, Osler's agents kept a close watch on
these developments, and the company was quick to respond. Indeed they successfully introduced the same dishware they sold in Britain within a few years.
A gradual homogenization in consumer preferences enabled manufacturers to
produce for a global market.

Pets

As with other consumer goods, the imperial exchange in animals also brought peoples into contact: sometimes on more equal terms in the case of the nearly universally prized long-haired cats, sometimes as exploitation when Europeans stole royal Pekingese dogs from China's Forbidden City, and sometimes as an instigation to violence when crusaders against animal cruelty attacked the practices of native people. More than inanimate goods, pets embodied the cultures of their provenance, their strangeness marked by their apparent ahistoricity.

Europeans adopted exotic pets from all over the world. Early explorers and later travelers described an intra-Asian trade in long-haired cats that had been valued by Asian elites for centuries. British explorers charged with producing better maps of Central Asia in the nineteenth century commented on Persian cats, which had been introduced into Europe a century before. Mountstuart Elphinstone (1779–1859) wrote the following in 1815: "The cats must also be noticed, at least the long-haired species called boorauk, as they are exported in great number, and everywhere called Persian cats."[18] An American traveler to Central Asia in the 1870s described cats bound for India. "Cats were petted and protected, and beautiful specimens are frequently seen, especially the graceful creatures of the Bukharan breed, with long silky hair and bushy tails."[19] They arrived in India, as far as Calcutta, with camel caravans. Various travelers described their transport, twenty at a time, tethered together like horses. The cats were increasingly exported to the West as well. In 1871, Queen Victoria (1819–1901) stoked European demand when she bought two blue Persians at the first European cat show, held at the Crystal Palace in London. Soon, fashionable ladies wanted to have them and be photographed with them. Major Frederick Millingen (1836–1901), longtime resident in Kurdistan, described their general popularity throughout Asia but how "in Europe these animals are the pets of ladies."[20] So great was the demand for exports that the cats had become increasingly scarce in Central Asia. As European demand grew, domestic breeders overtook importers as primary suppliers. But as with other goods, domestic products never had the cachet of imports.[21] By 1893, Dr. Charles James Wills (1842–1912) advised, "If you want a Persian cat of the finest kind, you can best get one in Paris, at any of the numerous bird-shops on the quays."[22]

Part of the allure of the Persian, even the domestically bred version, was its association with the antiquity of Persia (modern Iran), described as "the land of pussycats and poverty" by Reverend Charles Stileman in *The Subjects of the Shah* (1902).[23] His book even featured the map of Iran illustrated in the shape of a cat resting on a cushion (see Figure 4.3). "It has its back towards Afghanistan and India, and its head towards Russia. The cushion keeps it from getting its feet wet in the Persian Gulf!"[24] In his view, the character of Persia was so feline that the title of its ruler, the Shah, was pronounced the same as *chat*, the French word for cat. Nasir al-Din Shah (1831–1896) played along with this popular association when asked why he dimmed the lights at night, replying that he did so "because

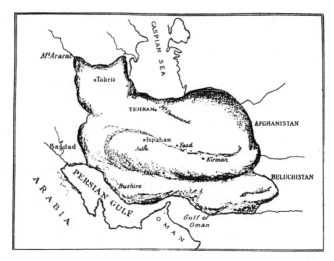

Figure 4.3.   Land of Pussycats, 1902
British author Charles Stileman pointed out how the contours of Persia (Iran) take the shape of a cat. This contributed to the orientalist association of Persia with its most famous export: the Persian cat.

the cat [Shah] sees better in the night."[25] Orientalists peddled stories of his obsession with the cats, elevating them to the status of favored wife, designating special eunuchs to guard his most favorite. His nephew described how "the cat was involved in running the country and deciding appointments and dismissals" and how Iran's best physicians, even the European ones, were called in when the cat fell ill.[26] Jealous wives allegedly saw to the murder of the Shah's beloved cat. His successor, although not as obsessed, did not challenge the association of Persia with felines. When traveling in France, his retinue was greeted by French onlookers with loud meows, to which they apparently replied in kind.[27]

During the first quarter of the twentieth century, Britain's fashionable ladies also used Pekingese lapdogs to convey their high status, worldliness, and good taste. The Pekingese had an aura of mystery about it, of allegedly imperial origin and evocative of Old China.[28] Aficionados went so far as to claim that the Pekingese retained a kind of race memory of his mystical origins as evident in his fear of thunderstorms and the tawny dog's rejection of any but yellow mates, yellow being the emperor's privileged color.[29] In her history of the breed, *The Lion Dog of Peking* (1931), Annie Coath Dixey (b. 1889) wrote

> How many people realize, as they walk abroad with that most uncannily clever four-footed friend, that they are in the company of one of an imperial race of the loftiest lineage, a race that for hundreds of years was never set eyes on by any but the most privileged persons of the royal court, a race that less than a hundred years ago was shrouded in mystery, the subject of endless speculation by Chinese and foreigners alike? . . . We of a modern civilization may be unaware of this, but the proud little Pekingese never forgets.[30]

As with many status objects, the difficulty in obtaining the dogs only enhanced their prestige. When the Chinese imperial family fled the Summer Palace after defeat at the hands of the British in 1860, plunderers seized their five Pekingese dogs among other precious objects. One of them, renamed Looty, was given to Queen Victoria.[31] Those stolen from China and taken to Britain via the black market were among the most prized, especially by women just entering the world of dog shows. In the women's magazine *Ladies' Field* one of the first articles in Britain about the dog in 1901 stated, "You might as well ask a Chinaman to give you his pig-tail as his dog—either would be an impossibility.... The plain truth is they have to be stolen."[32] Whereas British men bred and showed large breeds like the bull mastiff, women entered this man's world with toy dogs. The Kennel Club of Britain resented how "lady exhibitors swarmed to the front" of dog shows, "utterly swamping the male element."[33] Complaining that the club was "so unflinching in its rather unnecessarily anti-suffragette sort of loftiness," the ladies then formed their own branch enabling them to retain control of breed specifications and judging the competitions. Judges were even deemed "doggy suffragettes."[34]

When the Qing Empire fell in 1911, the dogs became even more valuable as did the race memory attributed to them. In their memoir *Our Sentimental Garden* (1914), Agnes Castle (1860–1922) and Egerton Castle (1858–1920) described their dog's reaction: "Loki will not believe that the Manchu masters have fallen in China (of course it is not from us that he has heard these distressing rumours), so he still demands as his right the best silk eiderdowns to lie upon, satin for his cushions, grilled kidney for his breakfast, freshly poured water in his bowl every time he wants to drink.... He sits up and waves his paws with imperious gesture; or else rolls over on his back and puts them together in an attitude of prayer."[35] Ironically, Britain became the center of Pekingese breeding to the extent that the dogs had to be reintroduced into China from British stock. Britain's theft of these representatives of Imperial China ironically became a salvation for these last living vestiges of Old China. As in Figure 4.4, collectors of Chinese items acquired clothing and other artifacts as well, the wealthiest even using them to adorn their children in Chinese styles.

In the view of elite Europeans, obsession with exotic pets marked a high level of civilization. British intervention on behalf of the Pekingese could be marshalled to support its claims to be defenders of civilizations and the weak. They rescued royal dogs and thereby the imagery of royal China from the forces of modernity. Europeans extended this protective role to all animals, as branches of the Society for the Prevention of Cruelty to Animals (SPCA) spread across Europe and North America in the nineteenth century. Branches also opened in Europe's colonies, where the protection of animals, domestic and wild, justified cruel punishments of people caught abusing animals and even their removal to create preserves for endangered species.

Settlers in Kenya brought their beloved pets with them, including an Irish setter in 1907. Some pets were so treasured that they accompanied their owners to church. By the 1920s, kennel clubs had formed in Nairobi. Less cuddly animals also inspired love. In *A Kenyan Farm Diary* (1930), Violet Mabel Carnegie (1892–1980) wrote of how her husband "loved" the family geese "with a blind devotion" and would never have any killed.[36] Settlers wrote that love for animals helped them survive difficult environments, reminding them of home. These values propelled the SPCA into legislative work. They gradually succeeded in introducing laws preventing the use of nose rings in oxen, for example, and in reforming Nairobi's slaughter house, which they called a "Municipal Torture Chamber" and "a disgrace to our so-called civilization."[37] They also promoted education by reprinting stories such as *Black Beauty* (1894), which inspired empathy for animals by telling about their suffering from the animal's perspective. Furthermore, members felt justified in inflicting violence on humans to

Figure 4.4. British girl in Chinese clothes with Pekingese dogs
The British craze for Chinese items extended to children's clothing and animals, especially the Pekingese dog, descended from the royal dogs of the defeated Qing emperors.

prevent them from hurting animals. Carnegie was herself tempted to inflict violence on a servant who blinded a sparrow, tying it down to serve as bait for larger animals he hoped to trap. She fired him, but "at the back of my mind I felt that more important still was to bring his cruelty home to him."[38] She refrained, not out of a sense of proportion but because in her view such an effort would be wasted. "With such a callous creature would physical punishment be of much use?"[39] Others did not refrain, and accounts of whites flogging Africans for animal cruelty, with or without legal sanction, underscore the persistent prejudice that only violence could reform them.

The next generation of whites were more likely to accept the full, if undeveloped, humanity of Africans who were deemed capable of empathy. They called for Swahili language pamphlets teaching empathy for animals, but they did not appear until an African section of the SPCA formed in 1945. Inspector Njoroge Kiania was praised for his work exposing animal cruelty whether committed by Africans, Indians, or British. During his tenure, a *Care of Animals* (1952) booklet appeared in which a dog pleaded: "Please feed us like friends because we love humans and guard your houses at night."[40] Membership in the African section numbered in the thousands in the 1940s and 1950s, proving to whites that Africans would evolve to European standards of civilization. In the process, both the African and white sections increasingly exposed the abuse of animals by whites, including those who trapped exotic animals for export to European zoos. They exposed merchants of African wildlife who fed live puppies to caged leopards and left caged monkeys dead alongside live monkeys and their own waste. Although white ranchers escaped serious penalties, the publicity served to make settlers and Europeans back home aware of the cost of putting exotic animals on display.[41]

The evolution of the SPCA in Kenya captures imperial processes in microcosm: white settlers imposing their cultural norms on native peoples, to the point of corporal punishment. This was followed by the rise to leadership of native people who then remade the organization on their terms, accepting but also modifying an imperial institution's original aims. Finally, the now hybrid institution exposed white rapaciousness. Over time, all imperial institutions would undergo such a process, illustrating how the politics of private life would eventually destabilize imperial rule.

WEARABLES

Privately held collectibles like glassware or wallpaper conveyed status to those privileged enough to access the private spaces of the home or palace. Clothing, on the other hand, immediately enabled the wearer to portray his or her level of cosmopolitanism and modernity, or, conversely, commitment to tradition. "Clothing in the Metropole," especially for women, absorbed the greatest diversity of new fabrics and styles. "Clothing in the Colonies," especially when worn by urban youths, enabled an instant rejection of tradition and embrace of modernity. "Cosmetics" also promised a youthful, modern look, but not merely a white one. Imports initially commanded the highest prices and thus conveyed the highest status. But as domestic production of imported goods facilitated their spread to a mass market, more people could acquire reproductions of the artifacts of empire. This range of modifications to personal appearance illustrates not merely a multiplicity of responses to imperialism but also the consumer's self-conscious development of a hybrid identity.

Clothing in the Metropole

Even before merchandisers, travelers spread fashion across the globe. Accenting clothing with artifacts from one's travels visibly represented taste, leisure, and wealth. It might also spark a desire for imitation. Travelers might bring items back home for gifts or even resale. Sales through personal contacts or even personal ads contributed to a more organic form of exchange than vast commercial enterprises.

Women sold their shawls in personal ads in British ladies' magazines such as the following in *The Englishwoman's Domestic Magazine* of July 1870: "I have just returned from India and have a handsome Punjaub shawl to dispose of i.e. to exchange for a couple of good dresses. . . . This shawl is made of the fine camel-hair, and beautifully worked all over in pine leaves patterns with a fringe."[42] Because of their adaptability to European dress, Indian shawls sold particularly well. In the 1820s, shawl emporiums appeared in London featuring only expensive shawls imported from Kashmir. By mid-century, paisley shawls were manufactured in England to appear Indian and sold at prices even the middle class could afford. Indian farmers exported raw cotton to Britain's factories, which made "Indian" garments and exported them back to India and throughout the world. Like Mata Hari, this owner could claim to possess, if not be, the genuine article, having resided abroad. The purchaser, on the other hand, could don this ornament to show off good taste and the means to afford an exotic luxury without ever having to leave the comforts of home.

While the shawl found an international audience, the sari never quite caught on. Early orientalists like Charles "Hindoo" Stuart (1758–1828) rhapsodized about the sari, urging British women to don this most alluring gown. A general who went native, so to speak, in the early nineteenth century, Hindoo Stuart wore Indian clothing and recommended everyone do the same. He described the conflict of industrial cultures with traditional ones by comparing the natural fitting sari with the confining bustle and corset. In his view, wearing iron busks made women highly susceptible to lightning strikes. "This is no laughing matter, ladies, for I am absolutely serious."[43] He concluded that discarding them would enhance the supply of iron for farmers in need of new wagon wheels. Following Stuart, more natural Asian women would frequently be positioned as mirrors to reflect negatively on the supposed excesses of European women. Nonetheless, some Eastern women, most notably in Japan, adopted the confining corset and bustle to signify their ascent up the civilization hierarchy.

At the same time, Western women adopted free-flowing Japanese kimonos. Although the kimono's influence in Europe predates the modern period, its widespread manufacture and distribution follows that of the shawl. Mary Crawford Fraser's (1851–1922) travelogue, *A Diplomatist's Wife in Japan: Letters from Home to Home* (1899), conveyed in its very title that she felt truly binational, equally at home in Japan and England. Almost with an anthropologist's eye, she relayed both the homely and the exotic, in the sphere of the intimate and of public spectacle. She collected Japanese dolls, which she described as "lovely women (I cannot help speaking as if they were living creatures), in poses light and dreamy as the swaying of the lotus stems moved by water. Their faces were pale and sweet, and there was a kind of tragic grace in the bent heads . . . all in robes stiff with gold and brilliant in colour . . . some gorgeously dressed."[44] She waxed poetic about their kimonos, which she added to her own wardrobe as well.

Such women transmitted material culture to and from the metropole. The preciousness of the artifacts sent home marked the consumer's elite and cultured status. Only the wealthiest consumers and global travelers could acquire genuine goods from the distant lands of empire. Elite status was rooted in authenticity even more when British factories cashed in on orientalism and produced cheap imitations for the middle class. By 1898, Liberty and Co. merchandisers produced kimonos for Western consumers, "the Shapes, Styles and Fittings adapted for Western use."[45]

Clothing in the Colonies

European women adopted patterns, fabrics, and sometimes entire outfits worn by native women throughout the world. Housekeeping manuals also advised European women how to dress. In Indonesia, the more traditional guides warned immigrants to avoid local clothing like the sarong and kebaya to prevent the risk of "going native."[46] Instead they should train their servants to sew European patterned dresses of white muslin, appropriate to the climate. These were looser fitting than similar dresses back home. Some oriental details were allowed, preferably from China or the Middle East to maintain distance from local culture. Wealthier women ordered their clothing from catalogs. Gerzon's, a prominent department store in the Netherlands, enjoyed a thriving mail-order business despite the four months it might take for packages to reach their destinations. By the 1930s, it opened branches in the Indonesian cities of Batavia and Surabaya.[47] Not only did fashions have to maintain the racial hierarchy but also the class hierarchy. The wife of a low ranking civil servant could not appear better dressed than his superior's wife. Indeed, the latter had the right to evaluate the length of a bathing suit before the junior woman could wear it.[48] Mail-order suppliers also shipped European foods in cans, lessening reliance on local foods. Rice, once a staple of everyone's diet, was generally consumed only on Sundays once applesauce and sauerkraut could be ordered in.[49]

Consumers throughout the world, including India, bought British-made Indian style saris in addition to shawls. By the 1920s, nationalists like Mahatma Gandhi (1869–1948) called for the burning of British-made goods. Shiva Dua recalls her dilemma over her deceased mother's sari: "I wore it a couple of times with a kind of mental conflict. . . . When the call came, and the crowd was just below our house, and the neighbours were throwing them things, immediately I decided that Mother was Mother, but the Mother Country was higher than Mother, and the sari must go, and I gave it."[50] The irony of burning a sari to signal rejection of British rule illustrates how the transnational circulation of goods both undercut and stoked nationalism.

For Gandhi, this rejection included his abandonment of the Western suit in favor of a dhoti, the traditional men's body wrapping in which he frequently appeared. In his view, the suit was a symbol of the civil servant who desperately wished to be British. Lampooned as servile, the Bengali *babus*, who could be lawyers, merchants, or even petty clerks, were the subject of an 1882 diatribe by Mokshodayani Mukhopadhyay (b. 1848), author and founder of a Bengali women's journal. "Alas, there goes the Bengali babu! / Cane in hand, wearing shoes, smoking a cheroot; / Some, sahib-fashion, are hatted and coated. / . . . / He longs to be fair, scrubs vigorously with soap; / . . . / Parts his hair in front in the style of Prince Albert."[51] In Mukhopadhyay's stereotype, those who served the Raj would stop at nothing to become proper Englishmen. More usually, elite men wore Western dress but fashioned a hybrid identity. Maori chief Wi Tako Ngatata (d. 1887), for example, sat for his portrait in full Western dress, his face covered in *moko* (Maori tattoos). As the first Maori elected to the upper house of New Zealand's legislative council in the 1870s, he attracted the attention of Czech portraitist Gottfried Lindauer (1839–1926) who was determined to record the authentic practices of New Zealand's native peoples.

Modern consumers believed they could adopt Western clothing without thereby exhibiting allegiance to the colonizer. Young women in the early part of the twentieth century generally rejected their mothers' traditional appearance, from whatever culture they came, and evolved a modern persona that was more global than culturally specific. They challenged bourgeois morality, sexism, and nationalism with their prohibitions against women's liberation and same sex and interracial desire. At the same time, the modern girl was a product of global capitalism, her identity constituted through display and consumerism. Her appearance marked shifts in the family away from producing to consuming units and away from paternal control of women's bodies to greater autonomy. But the shift away from citizen to consumer had consequences for women's politics and reinforced class differences between women. The rise of the United States as a leading producer of women's magazines, cosmetics, and fashions also anticipates corporate globalization and neo-imperialism, reminding us again of the centrality of the body to different iterations of empire.

In British Ceylon (modern Sri Lanka), traditional Buddhists decried modern fashion. As early as 1880, mission-educated anti-imperialist Anagarika Dharmapala (1864–1933) castigated Western dress, advocating a long flowing white gown with a white banian and shawl for men and women alike. His own mother wore this in 1884 on a pilgrimage to the Buddhist shrine Bodh Gaya in India.[52] Despite his admonition, more women adopted Western fashions. This escalated along with women's demands for suffrage in the 1920s. Some Sinhalese letter writers may have accepted women's suffrage, but not for modern girls. As one women's rights advocate asserted in a letter to the *Self Rule* nationalist daily in 1928: "Those who should not get the vote are the women who cut their hair, wear short *sarees* and dance *bailas* . . . a woman's hair is her most precious and noble ornament. How much I love my own hair!"[53] But critics went further, arguing that the suffrage was a foreign import. In 1929, one asserted that "our respectable ladies," the keepers of Sinhala "traditions" and Buddhist "culture," should be protected from rebellious, masculinized women who spread foreign "contagion" in the form of "a new civilization."[54] Women's activism for greater freedom was often met with patriarchal and anti-imperialist resistance, but fashion appears to have galvanized opposition the most. A letter in the form of a poem published in 1931 reads, "Declaring it's for the progress of country and race / Wearing short dresses and cutting her hair / Destroying her *vili* like shameless white hussies / Today's noble woman only destroys Lanka."[55]

Sinhalese women fought back and defended their claims for rights as well as their fashion choices in their own newspapers. Rupa Piyaseeli insisted in 1930, "Is it not the young man, who sniggers and lowers his eyes to check the length and width of a young girl's mini dress, who is more dangerous to civilized society?"[56] Locating danger in men's predatory voyeurism, Piyaseeli underscored the patriarchal imperative to control women's sexuality that animated the anti-suffrage movement. Traditionalists associated suffrage and women's rights more broadly with Western libertinism, despite the indigeneity as well as transnationalism of these movements.

Young men also began to adopt the latest Western fashions. In Tanzania, this included wearing eyeglasses, even in the absence of vision problems. In 1932, Rashidi Ali Meli wrote a letter to the editor in the *Mambo Leo* newspaper: "nowadays I see many youths who love wearing glasses . . . for the price of twenty cents without any reason, and if you ask them what does this mean, they would reply that [they] are part of the 'Culture.' But, fellows, is this Culture or ruin? And what is the sense of the word Culture?"[57] They also donned the standard Western suit, including trousers, white shirt, jacket, and tie. Instead of the sexual innuendo of the modern girl, the modern boy expressed his "culture" by dressing plainly, men's and women's styles diverging in sharp contrast to the more gender-neutral clothing of the traditional milieu. Above all, "culture" implied urban over rural and modern over traditional. For many, achieving the look entailed going into debt.

Some Tanzanian men attempted to innovate the suit, the resulting wide-leg trousers, as opposed to straight, and short jacket, as opposed to long, looking "ridiculous" in the words of another letter writer, Anton Yohana.[58] He pointed out that this was a copy of the British navy suit and broke all the rules of respectable fashion, concluding that Africans "would die" if they kept on "imitating" Europeans.[59] This navy style apparently mimicked a similar trend in Congo, which suggests that borrowing from Europeans occurred by means of trans-African cultural exchange. Traditionalists further decried other clothing styles in the paper, this time men's tight trousers. In a poem from 1954, Andrew Kunguru Mtendeje defended traditional Western dress against innovation: "We see Europeans, along with Indians, / When they stitch trousers, they make them large at the bottom, / Instead we make them tight, what kind of behaviour is this? / Tight trousers, where do they originate from?"[60] He concluded with a plea: "Dress in a honourable way, I stress this point again, / Even middle-aged people, imitate this, why on earth is that? / You obviously do not respect yourselves, please, my friends, / Tight trousers, where do they originate from?"[61]

After World War II, the trend accelerated as young people danced to 1950s music, adapting Western ballroom styles. One Tanzanian commentator celebrated the trend in a poem published in *Mambo Leo* from 1953: "Those who dance to it, are worthy people, / Respect is acquired through clothes and other things, / [Dance admirers] are not mandarin sellers, as in open markets, / Dance is a cheerful dance, and great fun."[62] By referencing traditional agriculture and commercial exchange, the author highlighted what it meant to be modern. Others specifically linked dance to the public accessing of whiteness, with clothing in particular being the only "immediately accessible part of white people's richness."[63] The physical proximity of men and women in the dance halls concerned traditional Muslims, but younger more modern ones embraced it.

Popular media, films and radio in the interwar years facilitated the spread of a global modern identity, if not imperialism itself. In his exposition on *African Nationalism* (1959), Zimbabwe independence leader Ndabaningi Sithole (1920–2000) pondered the enduring effect of initial contact with Europeans, who brought their wonders of modern technology, on both Africa's self-image and Western views of Africa:

> The first time he ever came into contact with the white man, the African was simply overwhelmed, overawed, puzzled, perplexed, mystified, and dazzled.... Motor-cars, motor cycles, bicycles, gramophones, telegraphy, the telephone, glittering Western clothes, new ways of ploughing and planting, added to the African's sense of curiosity and novelty. Never before had the African seen such things. They were beyond his comprehension; they were outside the realm of his experience. He saw. He wondered. He mused. . . . Here then the African came into contact with two-legged gods who chose to dwell among people instead of in the distant mountains.[64]

Material culture attracted the world's peoples to the West, which inspired god-like awe and commanded obedience, but also created a space for eventual liberation.

The commercial exchange of cosmetics and clothing facilitated by globally accessible advertisements, magazines, and films enabled people to fashion hybrid identities. Debates about clothing as a marker of modernity revealed the degree to which imperialism was an intimate experience. Personal appearance and other consumer choices became increasingly political as anti-imperialist movements became more widespread.

Cosmetics

The modern girl was initially white, especially when some corporations like Pepsodent, a brand of toothpaste, ran the exact same ads in newspapers all over the world, depicting the same women, their verbiage translated into many languages.[65] Even some locally produced products, like Afghan Snow, a skin-lightening emollient made in India, promised whiteness. But by the 1930s, some advertisers, especially where there were burgeoning nationalist movements, used images of local beauties (see Figure 4.5). Capitalist enterprises recognized, perhaps more quickly than imperial governments, that the mood in the colonies was no longer tolerant of hegemonic whiteness. Even Afghan Snow advertisements featured Asian eye slants on stylized line drawings of racially ambiguous women to suggest oriental beauty. At the same time, other products promised skin darkening to athletic white women who wanted to show off their tans. Modern girls enjoying athleticism or the outdoors in these ads hinted at same-sex desire.[66]

Figure 4.5. Cutex ad, China, 1937
US corporations marketed products globally by featuring local beauties. This ad in *Elegance* magazine contributed to a standardization of hygiene and beauty.

But ads generally shied away from overt sexual transgression.

In South Africa, manufacturers like Keppels sold cream, invoking protection against the climate as a way to safeguard light skin, thus skirting interwar segregationist politics. The African American owned Apex went further and marketed skin bleach in *Bantu World*, a South African newspaper published in the English, Xhosa, Zulu, Sotho, Tswana, Venda, Afrikaans, and Tsonga languages.[67] Other African American firms capitalized on a black-is-beautiful ideal. The C. J. Walker Company, run by prominent African American businesswoman, Madam C. J. Walker (1867–1919), marketed Egyptian Brown Face Powder to impart an "olive tint" to light skinned African American women and to harmonize "bewitchingly with darker skins."[68] Playing on the ahistorical allure of Egypt, entrepreneurs found ways to erase racial phenotype distinctions by promoting the beauty of generically brown skin.

Meanwhile, consumerism expanded in Muslim countries such as Egypt. In the nineteenth century, secluded Egyptian women received traveling saleswomen and tailors in their homes or later shopped by catalog.[69] The transformation of shopping and women's movement into public space was facilitated by broader changes. By the 1920s, Egypt had undergone a revolution and drafted a liberal constitution. As in the new Republic of Turkey, modern women symbolized the dramatic departure from tradition in some ads. Egypt was represented as a Modern Girl, albeit white, her unveiling a metaphor for the new Egypt.[70] In the years leading to nationalist triumph, Egyptian businesses thrived and European products were discouraged. A 1915 ad in the weekly news roundup, significantly called *Al-Sufur* (The Unveiling), promoted an Egyptian-owned Cairo department store as a "national store . . . bigger than the foreign ones."[71]

Another store marketed the latest undergarments by featuring a young woman with a curly bob, the international sign of the modern girl. Going still further in 1925, a line-drawn woman with a bob modeled a corset in an ad for the Barir Stores. The caption denoted who the ad was for when it asked, "Buying for the ladies of Egypt?"[72] Another corset ad was placed beside an article featuring feminist Huda Sha'arawi (1879–1947), recently returned from her notorious trip to the 1923 International Alliance of Women conference in Rome. Disembarking from the train at the Cairo railway station, she and other Muslim feminists removed their veils. The placement of the corset ad subtly suggested that liberated modern women were also sexually available and that her liberation from the veil might be replaced by her adoption of the corset. Occupying public space more readily than Muslims, Jews, Christians, and foreigners worked in department stores and could be depicted as modern girls in advertisements without overtly disturbing Islam. An ad for the Cairo branch of the French department store Bon Marché showed a modern girl behind the wheel of a car while a stylish Muslim woman stood by, indicating that both were welcome in the store and both were preoccupied with fashion.[73]

Ads for specific products, especially soap, used the modern girl, sometimes scantily clad, to demonstrate their product's efficacy. Afridol Soap played to Egyptian preference for light skin in its 1933 ad, which juxtaposed two dark-skinned women next to a light-skinned woman. The latter sits at her vanity, the mirror reflecting sunlight on her very white face. The soap promised to kill germs and protect the epidermis.[74] Only in a few cases did advertisers Asianize the models for their products. Istanbul Beauty Cream was one that drew the models with full lips, sharp noses, and slightly slanted eyes.[75] The tourism industry also used exotic beauties in line-drawn ads to promote travel, as in Figure 4.6.

Publications Issued by the
Official French Tourist Office
French Government

Édition de l'Office Algérien d'Action Economique et
Touristique du Gouvernement Général de l'Algérie
26, Boulevard Carnot - ALGER

Figure 4.6. Algerian tourism promotion
The image of young Muslim women smoking on a tourism promotion poster suggests how much travel to the colonies was associated with youth, sexuality, and carefree behavior.

EDIBLES

The consumption of food, drinks, and drugs has served as an intersection between cultures for centuries. Seemingly more neutral than fashion, homely "Foods" like the potato do not obviously carry cultural meanings or power relations. But their production, circulation, and reception involved people with different understandings of the symbolism of food, as well as of literally different tastes. Imbibing the world's spices, food and "Drink" has brought bodies into contact for centuries, driving the integration of economies and facilitating cross-cultural curiosity and interdependence. However, the industrialization of shipping, production, and marketing made exotic goods cheaper, more plentiful, and more global by the eighteenth century. Furthermore, governments became more adept at regulating, suppressing, or profiting from the consumption of such goods even as smugglers regularly outsmarted them.

Foods

In all cultures, the production, preparation, and consumption of food is associated with gender, race, and class. Abolitionists made this connection as early as the eighteenth century. Housewives understood this when the mass production of food stuffs and cookbooks transformed consumer's relationships to food. Immigrants longed for the foods of home even when they carried stigmas, illustrating how Europeans abroad also transformed the global cultural exchange.

Slaves toiling on the plantations of the Caribbean produced foods that achieved global distribution, notably sugar, rum, and coffee. The Atlantic system, made up of the export of slaves from West Africa in exchange for Caribbean sugar and North American cotton bound for European consumption, can perhaps be called the beginning of modern globalization. Abolitionists argued that West Africans would be more productive in that economy if allowed to be laborers and consumers. Famed abolitionist and former slave Olaudah Equiano (1745–1797) asserted at the end of his *Interesting Narrative* (1789) that African consumption of British goods would be more profitable than slavery and spread wealth across a larger segment of the population. "As the inhuman traffic of slavery is to be taken into the consideration of the British legislature, I doubt not, if a system of commerce was established in Africa, the demand for manufactures will most rapidly augment, as the native inhabitants will insensibly adopt the British fashions, manners, customs, &c. In proportion to the civilization, so will be the consumption of British manufactures."[76] He specifically refered to clothing, describing how primitive Britons also lacked clothing, but the spread of civilization also spread consumerism. This inevitably would come to Africa if the slave system ended.

Other abolitionists pointed to the global consumption of foods as a basis for ending slavery. Worried that the end of slavery would mean the end of access to the fruits of plantation agriculture, a German surgeon in Danish Guinea, Paul Erdmann Isert (1756–1789), wrote in a 1787 letter to his father, "Must we thus forego the sugar, coffee, chocolate & so many other products that our European luxury has made both necessary and indispensable? No—that would make as many Europeans unhappy as the number of Negroes that we would raise out of their misery. But how have our predecessors not had the wisdom to see that plantations of all commodities could be established in Africa itself? It is there that we could find abundant labour, & at the lowest cost, without mistreatment and making no one unhappy."[77] Isert couldn't bear the thought that the end of slavery would deprive Europeans of their favorite foods and so crafted a compromise. Isert was so determined to prove that cultivation in Africa would render the slave trade unnecessary that he founded a colony in what is now Ghana. He purchased the land and agreed to a monthly rent, relocated his family, began construction of dwellings, and planted vegetables, tobacco, and indigo. He also welcomed any locals to settle freely, but required Europeans to obtain permission. Despite this entrepreneurship, he and his family died from disease within a few months and the colony foundered. His brother-in-law delivered the eulogy, praising Isert's philanthropic spirit. He cited Isert's wish for the "products of India to flourish along the banks of the Volta" enabling local people to "appreciate knowledge and freedom" such that "Europeans would hurry there, not to rob the region for its people like before, but to share with them the fruits of the land."[78] His vision assumes a global economy in which Europeans and Africans work the land to produce for their own subsistence and also for export.

Gradually, the foods of Europe's colonies made their way into European cuisine. Europeans sometimes embraced exotic new foods with fervor. British men who served in India might bring their cooks back with them, or at least their recipes, while Indian immigrants to Britain opened Indian restaurants. The Hindoostane Coffee House opened in 1809 in London. Its proprietor, Sake Dean Mahomed (1759–1851), had served in the British Army and married an Irish woman. He proclaimed his restaurant would serve dishes "allowed by the greatest epicures to be unequalled to any curries ever made in England."[79] Male-owned niche restaurants and British men returning from service spread knowledge of curry in elite circles. But women accompanying husbands in civil or military service sent Indian foods and goods back home as gifts and later as a means of making money. This knowledge transfer stimulated an even greater demand roughly correlating to Britain's deepening involvement in India. Although known to Europeans at least as far back as the late seventeenth century, curry gained a wide audience when it appeared in British cookbooks such as *How to Cook or Serve Eggs in a Hundred Different Ways* (1825).[80] Later cookbooks further associated exotic cooking with the domestic sphere. In 1857, an anonymous poem later attributed to William Makepeace Thackeray (1811–1863) was published in *Punch's Poetical Cookery Book*. It expressed the delight Samiwel, the speaker, takes in watching his cook prepare the curry: "Three pounds of veal my darling girl prepares / And chops it nicely into little squares / Five onions next prepares the little minx / The biggest are the best her Samiwel thinks / . . . / What's next my dexterous little girl will do? / She pops the meat into the savory stew / With curry powder, tablespoonsfulls three / And milk a pint (the richest that may be)."[81] The end product is a "dish for emperors to feed upon."[82] Because *Punch* appealed to a mass audience, the girl may have been a daughter or wife instead of a paid cook. Suggesting adaptability to lesser budgets, the poem concluded that veal could be replaced by "Beef, mutton rabbit, if you wish / Lobsters, or prawns, or any kind of fish."[83] The centerpiece was the curry.

The mass circulation of cookbooks spread exotic cuisines across the Empire and across the globe. Curry made its way to US tables after the US Civil War (1861–1865) once ingredients could be purchased at the grocery instead of at the druggist. American women's magazines and cookbooks included the provenance of foreign recipes, with notes about geography and even politics. Purveyors of recipes used sales promotion as a way to educate American housewives about the world. This included the celebration of American empire. As a 1910 *Good House-keeping* piece noted, peppers had "become more common since the Spanish war, as they are used in our new territories so much that Americans are beginning to use them as the English learned curry from India."[84] By likening the US occupation of the Philippines to the crown jewel of the British Empire, the magazine implied that the United States now rivaled Britain as a global superpower. Magazines also celebrated American ingenuity. *The New York Tribune* recommended the enjoyment of guavas, available thanks to the "enterprising American canner who had planted his foot in Cuba and other Southern countries."[85] These exotic foods arrived via imperial conquest. Other cuisines arrived via immigration.

The foods of European immigrants such as Germans and Scandinavians were less exotic to most Americans, and more easily assimilated, but, gradually, US cooks began experimenting with Asian cuisines. In 1908, a *Ladies' Home Journal* article titled "Rice as the Chinese Prepare It" announced: "Here is the detailed process, learned first-hand from a Chinese restaurant proprietor."[86] Cooks with leisure time educated themselves to serve food that was as authentic as possible. In the realm of cuisine, immigrant knowledge was valued, but only that of some immigrants. A civilization hierarchy appeared in food writing in which French food indicated fine taste and luxury, other European foods came next, then Asian, but that of most indigenous peoples was used to indicate their savagery. Cookbook author Julia C. Andrews wrote in 1875, "The flesh of the sloth, lizard, alligator, snake, monkey, and kangaroo, are eaten in South America; the grasshopper is roasted and eaten by the North American Indian, and the eggs of various insects are prepared and eaten by other savages."[87] Even as many food writers peddled cheap stereotypes about peoples and cuisines they deemed racially inferior, others thought US cooks could learn not only tastes but also nutrition from foreign cuisines. According to an article in *Good Housekeeping* from 1910, in contrast to the Hindu, "the Occidental boils all the essence or life out of the vegetable and throws it away, retaining the mere waste for food."[88] By the early twentieth century, domestic scientists warned of the dangers of the unhealthy American diet, overly processed and dependent on sugar.

For European expatriates, fresh local foods were promoted as the key to good health. At Dalat, the hill station in Vietnam created for French settlers to recover their health by means of exercise, spas, and cool mountain air, food was a central attraction. The French could enjoy foods from home as well as fresh local foods. A 1935 newspaper reported, "At Dalat, there are papayas . . . but mostly strawberries, oranges, clementines, real lemons. . . . Vegetables are not canned, but rather fresh, beautiful, and cheap. It's largely for this reason that vitamin-deprived colonials recover their good health."[89] Familiar fruits cured homesickness, once cultivation finally succeeded. One visitor exclaimed on visiting an experimental farm in 1898, "During my stay I gorged myself on red lettuce, Brussels sprouts, radishes, green beans, tomatoes, carrots, . . . beets, sorrel, my dishes being garnished with a touch of parsley or chervil, all of which grow easily."[90]

European fruits were more easily replicated in the highlands of Dalat than familiar meats. Several attempts at raising sheep failed due to parasites and attacks by tigers.[91] The vulnerability of the sheep reminded Dalat's residents that Vietnam could never be France. On the other hand, a few of the several head of Breton milk cows imported to Dalat eventually acclimated, resulting in milk and cheese production in quantities sufficient to allow shipping to Vietnamese locations beyond Dalat. Cultivators of European foods hoped to expand their markets not just to other French people living throughout Indochina but also to wealthy and upwardly mobile Chinese and Vietnamese. Once free from the confines of the French enclave, the foods took on a life of their own, being appropriated and adapted by Asian consumers. A hybrid cuisine gradually developed including savory strawberry ice cream and artichoke tea. Cashing in on the demands of the French, Vietnamese growers also converted their fields to produce foods for a French market, including vineyards.[92] Ban Thaï, a Vietnamese pharmacist, opened a pastry shop in Dalat famed for its *mille-feuilles* and called the Pâtisserie Dauphinoise, evocative of traditional French cuisine.[93]

Some native people initially resisted European foods and food rituals. In the early part of the twentieth century, a porter in German East Africa revealed how he spent his earnings as a modern consumer: "I bought myself many things. I bought loincloths and shoulder cloths. I bought these cloths for three rupees. I also bought tobacco from the market and soap too. At the same time I bought manioc and groundnuts for the home journey. But none of us thought of buying sugar. Because when we saw sugar, we said: That is salt. None of us had ever seen white sugar."[94] But enterprising merchants anticipated global demand for popular globally produced products like sugar. Its gradual adoption caused anxiety. One Tswana elder blamed diet changes for the diseases that accompanied civilization: "Our forefathers did not use sugar because they were not civilised. They did not take tea. Tea is the cause of tuberculosis. It is the cause of various diseases that attack our people. Our native body does not agree with European food."[95] The embodied impact of cross-cultural contact illustrates the dislocation associated with the substitution of modernity for tradition.

By contrast to imported processed foods, local foods initially deemed exotic or even savage could serve as mediators between cultures when consumed across racial boundaries. The most compelling example of this is the sharing of the meat after a big game hunt. In his *Kenya Diary* (1957), British Colonel Richard

Meinertzhagen (1878–1967) recalled his days on safari as a young lieutenant in 1904: "When I arrived in the country I was obsessed by an unashamed blood-lust. Hunting is man's primitive instinct, and I indulged it and enjoyed it to the full. In Kenya's early days fresh meat was not easy to obtain. The African was loath to part with his stock and there was no European settler in the country who could provide meat. Also, when travelling with from 20 to 200 healthy Africans, all doing hard work, meat becomes almost an essential, and more than three-quarters of the animals I shot went to provide meat for hungry and deserving mouths."[96] He then divvied the meat up according to status, however, and those who worked the hardest and grumbled the least received the most. This hunter associated the hunt with masculinity and the sating of bloodlust, yet he was quick to add the utilitarian, even humanitarian, dimension: providing suste-nance to the people who accompanied him.

Drink

Some foods were associated with masculinity, others with femininity. Homely drinks such as tea, coffee, and even milk were signifiers of status, taste, and the global economy. Chocolate, coffee, and sex followed one from the other accord-ing to Moreau de Saint-Méry (1750–1819), chronicler of the French Caribbean. Attributing sexual decadence to the "lascivious climate," Moreau drew attention to the interconnectedness of stimulants in the global economy and their ability to transform bodies and cultures. Languid Creole women stereotypically overin-dulged in sex, even with their African servants. "They eat only chocolates, sweets, fruits, café-au-lait. Inactivity, too much sleep, poor diets, lively passions menace them; they lose their health and their ability to please rapidly."[97] Because climate and food altered behavior and looks as well as health, the European could lose his or her so-called natural superiority when overseas for too long.

More than other consumables, alcohol involved formal imperial politics be-cause of the high degree to which it was regulated. The production, circulation, and ultimately regulation of alcohol drove imperial relations even in the eighteenth century. When Alonso Gutiérrez sought permission in 1760 to open yet another tavern in Santiago de los Caballeros, the regional capital of the Captaincy General of Guatemala, he assured a nervous government that his stocks of Spanish wine and Peruvian distilled cane alcohol would not contribute to public drunkenness. The quality and price of his stocks all but guaranteed an elite, Spanish clientele. He persuaded town officials that he would purchase his license, whereas poorer con-sumers bought locally made and illegal, even adulterated, liquor.[98]

By then, hybrid forms of liquor, but also forms of drinking, were long estab-lished. Male Spaniards proved their machismo by engaging in frequent and sus-tained binge drinking, while the Mayans solidified kin and village ties within their disintegrating communities by drinking to the gods. The merger of these behav-iors, especially for Mayan converts to Catholicism, increased the amount of drunk-enness throughout the population. The many saints days were opportunities for festivals revolving around massive alcohol consumption. Henry Dunn (1800–1878) described the impact of "demon rum" on locals in his travel journals from 1828. Around the cauldron of fermenting sugar, "three or four dirty children were sitting on the ground, and two women, nearly naked, stretched on a mat, were singing, or rather howling in an advanced state of madness."[99]

To limit indigenous drunkenness, the town council initially prohibited natives, or even mestizos, from opening taverns and revoked the licenses of taverns that served them. Blacks could be served but not the indigenous Amerindians. But when the town coffers were empty, it proved lucrative to distribute licenses more widely. It was also argued that licensing would diminish the consumption of illegally made or contraband alcohol. To that end the town council also allowed tent shops to open temporarily on plazas for festival days.

This tension between the regulation of vice and the need for revenue structured the availability of alcohol in every century and every empire. So ubiquitous was the circulation of alcohol that consumption skyrocketed with deepening European involvement. Even after the end of the slave trade, when rum had often been bartered for African captives, alcohol still substituted for other forms of African currency. By 1885, bottles of gin replaced cowry shells as the main currency in Lagos, Nigeria. In 1907, cases of gin replaced iron bars as the standard of value throughout the colony. Gin was used to pay bride price as late as 1930.[100]

Such levels of consumption can be seen throughout Africa and not just in the British Empire. Even before Germany established an outpost of empire in West Africa, German liquor distributors exported large quantities of alcohol in the mid-nineteenth century. Half of all exports to Africa from Hamburg, Germany's largest port, were alcoholic drinks.[101] In Cameroon, alcohol consumption had long been the prerogative of prosperous men. Women and young men were formally excluded, and poor men could not afford to distill their own liquors let alone import them. Schnapps made from potatoes was the beverage of choice. Communist theorist Friedrich Engels (1820–1895) noted in 1876, "Potato spirits are for Prussia what iron and cotton goods are for England, the product that represents it on the world market."[102] Chiefs negotiated treaties to secure access to alcohol while poor laborers were often paid in liquor. Missionaries objected to the widespread deleterious effects of alcohol and pressured governments to restrict merchants. This had the effect of driving up prices and encouraging contraband.

Some native activists combatted alcoholism. Father William Wadé Harris (1860–1929), an ethnic Glebo from Liberia, converted two hundred thousand Africans to Christianity in the first decade of the twentieth century. He tolerated polygamy but otherwise advocated an improvement in women's status such as the end of segregating menstruating women. Above all, his message as he moved through West Africa was anti-alcohol. "I am coming to speak for all the peoples of this country, White or Black. No abuse of alcohol. Respect for Authority. I tolerate polygamy, but I forbid adultery. Thunder will speak, and the Angels will punish the World if it does not hear my words, which interpret the Word of God."[103] As a prophet, he claimed to be called directly by Jesus Christ to purge African religion of animism and to rid African communities of alcohol. When Father Peter Harrington (1889–1956), an Irish priest in Côte d'Ivoire, offered him a glass of wine, he asked for tea instead, explaining that the Archangel Gabriel instructed him to abstain from alcohol. Harrington later concluded, "This Archangel Gabriel of his . . . must have had a Chinese rather than a French or Spanish or Italian taste—perhaps even commercial interests in the Far East."[104] Disparagement of Harris was followed by all out persecution. His appeal was seen as subversive, and he was beaten, imprisoned, and finally forced out of Côte d'Ivoire.

Elsewhere in the French empire, French regulators insisted on overseeing alcohol importation and production for reasons of hygiene and to force competitors out of the market. Chinese producers dominated the Vietnamese market for alcohol distilled from rice. Even before France proclaimed its imperial rule of Vietnam, it intervened as early as 1864. The widespread consumption of alcohol distilled from rice offered a tempting target for cash-strapped regimes to collect revenues. First they introduced a sales tax and later required licensing. By 1874, the government of Emperor Tu Duc (1829–1883) cooperated with the French to extend licensing throughout the country.[105] Initially, native distilleries were not targeted, but Chinese importers were. In 1892, Albert Calmette (1863–1933) wrote in praise of regulations that excluded Chinese firms from bidding on sales monopolies and "will allow our compatriots finally to reclaim for their own profit, a monopoly that it is painful to see remain so long in foreign hands, in a country that we have paid for so dearly with our gold and our blood."[106]

The increasing reach of regulators, including night raids of villages, stimulated illegal production and smuggling, which in turn created a need for a larger customs office to thwart the black market. Alcohol regulation became the most familiar point of contact between the Vietnamese and the French; a Vietnamese person was five times more likely to meet a customs officer than a schoolteacher.[107] Alcohol thus came to represent the most contested terrain, with defenders of the right to produce, transport, and consume alcohol increasingly forming anticolonial movements. Ordinary consumers rebelled, insisting on the superior taste and affordability of traditionally produced alcoholic beverages, whereas the Vietnamese middle class preferred French champagne.

Other French liquors, like absinthe, achieved global appeal in part because it was thought to be an aphrodisiac. The drink of choice for the artists and writers of France's Belle Époque period (1871–1914), the level of absinthe consumption reveals a much more widespread phenomenon: 36 million liters a year in France alone by 1910. Moreover, exports reached destinations as diverse as San Francisco, Valparaiso, and Saigon.[108] Originally a medicine derived from wormwood, it countered intestinal parasites. Like many recreational drugs, it reveals the inexact nature of premodern pharmaceuticals whose purposes included pain relief first and foremost. Absinthe did in fact have hallucinogenic properties, and abuse of it alarmed public health officials and moralists. In August 1914, shortly after entering World War I, France issued an emergency decree banning sales.

Unsurprisingly, the contemporary revival of the drink recalls the romance of that era. "Absinthe Mata Hari" has been marketed as a "Bohemian" liqueur by an Austrian distillery since 1990. According to the vendor's website, this absinthe "has the same natural green color, grande wormwood (the subject of the controversy that led to the banning of absinthe) and louche effect of French style absinthe, but that is where *her* deception ends."[109] Tracing the history of absinthe, a contemporary connoisseur asked, "Did I mention that absinthe was also considered a 19th-century version of Viagra?"[110] The association of Mata Hari with deception and enhanced sexual performance is not surprising, nor is the use of her name for marketing purposes. This is one of the legacies of empire: consumerism. Even during her lifetime, her name brand sold, attached to tobacco among other products.

SPECTACLE

The consumption of globally produced food and drink lodged imperial relations in the body. The association of particular consumer products with gender and sexuality invited consumers to adopt a particular identity that some consumers resisted, especially when they retained a degree of control over production. To sell their products, manufacturers needed to sell imperialism itself at the many imperial spectacles that spread across the Western world. Advertisers introduced consumers to global products at circuses, fairs, and expositions while the curious, the voyeurs, and the scientists flocked to see "People as Objects of Study" in public or private performances or in ethnographic exhibits. "Circuses, Fairs, and Expositions" gradually proliferated for profit, as millions of visitors sought entertainment, if not edification. Visitors had a wide range of responses to imperial display, some merely amused, others validated in their pride of place in the hierarchy of civilization, and others inspired to critique and revise their own cultures.

People as Objects of Study

Slave markets had long subjected people to the public gaze. Buyers inspected the slave's body for fitness for work in what was ostensibly a purely economic transaction. Because they were held in public squares, slave markets were also spectacles. As those markets disappeared, other public displays emerged, subjecting people deemed to be curiosities or freaks to anonymous spectators and scientists.

Small-scale exhibitors brought people from all over the world to display for profit and education. One of the earliest and most notorious cases was the so-called Hottentot Venus. Sometime before 1810, kidnappers ambushed Saartjie "Sara" Baartman's (1789–1815) wedding party in Dutch South Africa and sold her to a black master in Cape Town, Hendrik Cesars. There she worked as a domestic servant until Cesars conspired with British military doctor Alexander Dunlop to send her to London to be displayed. The pair anticipated making a great fortune at her expense due to her apparently oversized buttocks and genitals. They called her the "Hottentot Venus" to indicate something of her provenance: Hottentot being a generic name for the Khoikhoi of South Africa, Venus equating her to the goddess of love. Once in London, she was displayed in a cage mostly naked except for feathers and beads to make her look more "savage." Abolitionists tried to free Baartman, but because she received a wage and consented to spurious contracts, the courts dismissed them. Indeed, the publicity only served to attract more attention. Thousands gathered to gawk, even in the fashionable Piccadilly district. In Paris, naturalist Georges Cuvier (1769–1832) studied her extensively while she was alive and even after she died. Cuvier praised her feminine qualities, similar to those of European women, and especially her modesty. Baartman had always insisted that her genitals be covered even when offered money. Once discharged, Baartman died young having become an alcoholic and possibly a prostitute. Cuvier carved up her body, including her genitals, for study and display. Her remains were only returned to South Africa in 2002.[111]

European obsession with racial otherness continued to subject women to scientific scrutiny. When explorer Franz Stuhlmann (1863–1928) brought two Aka Pygmy women to Berlin after freeing them from alleged cannibals, society ladies adopted them out of a sense of Christian charity. They meant to train them for domestic service but were persuaded to first display them at a fundraiser for the German Colonial Society and Women's Association for Nursing. Although some of the clubwomen in attendance expected to be charmed by Asmini and Chikanao, they instead saw them as stupid and childish, especially when they stuck their tongues out at onlookers. Asmini and Chikanao also refused to allow German men or women to look under their clothes. Male organizers of the display attributed this to a natural and universal feminine modesty, but female organizers responded that the pygmies only wanted to guard this marker of their ascent toward Europeanness.[112] European women located their gender superiority in their race, refusing not only common femininity with racialized others but even common humanity. Clara von Monts insisted that she "cannot believe that creatures who until 16 months ago wore *string* as their only dress, and two or three grass stalks pulled through a hole pierced in the upper lip as their only jewelry, can have *artificially* appropriated within the short time mentioned such a feeling of exaggerated decency."[113] Modesty was thus presented as natural to the European but artificial to the African, who could only mimic her European betters. Observers believed they could identify the biological as opposed to cultural root of racial difference by juxtaposing it against the universal feminine.

Displays of live people were eventually eclipsed by cultures and artifacts on display in European and North American museums. Meant to showcase the diversity of human civilizations and to enable anthropological work to proceed, the displays nonetheless depicted racial hierarchies by emphasizing technological achievement. The primitive man, represented by the totem pole, stood at the beginning of the origin story of the human species. As paleontologists situated early human evolution in Africa, proximity of early man to contemporary Africans inevitably lodged the association of primitivism with Africa. Some museums specifically stated that their mission was to spur man to greater progress by showing how far he had come. When the ethnology museum at the Trocadero Palace in Paris opened in 1878, its promoter claimed that the museum would showcase the efforts of man to "overcome the forces of nature, to better his situation, to attain progress."[114] On one hand, early man was celebrated for his ingenuity. On the other, peoples living in geographic proximity to him were indirectly disparaged for their failure to go yet further. Visitors proceeded through the rooms that featured discrete peoples, such as those from the Americas or Oceana, their artifacts arranged alongside human remains to show their cultures. Many museums, including the Smithsonian in the United States, opened in these years, all of them competing for the most complete fossil collections. Museums reflected the growing field of anthropology, its origins in Darwinian theories of evolution plainly manifest. As the field matured, and as more anthropologists began to question the racist typology of social Darwinism, museums aspired to greater diversity in their interpretation of the human story, or at least greater neutrality. They separated biology from culture when exploring difference. The Trocadero ethnology museum, for example, moved away from representing race via human remains and toward a celebration of diverse cultures by showcasing clothing, art, and other artifacts and by refraining from placing these in a hierarchical relation to each other. Indeed, the celebration of crafts (see Figure 4.7) could inspire curiosity if not admiration.

But some anthropologists maintained their emphasis on fossil evidence to tell the story of human evolution. When Paris's Museum of Man opened in 1938, it included a plaster cast of Sara Baartman's body as well as her skeleton. Nearby were photographs of women's breasts from around the world, including Europe, to illustrate human diversity.[115] Skulls from the three races—black, yellow, and white—were displayed alongside maps indicating where those people lived. More specialized displays, like that for Indochina, included skulls alongside traditional costume and artifacts, continuing the association of biology with culture, but nonetheless diminishing the weight placed on human remains.[116] The juxtaposition of culture and biology reflected tensions among museum staff, some of whom, like biologist Henri Neuville (1872–1946), insisted that studies of human physiology yielded no "formal racial distinctions" except those between "a masculine race and a feminine race," added to illustrate the absurdity of making any claims about racial difference.[117] But George Montandon (1879–1944), the chair of ethnology at Paris's College of Anthropology, defended the findings of racial science and criticized the museum for trying to cover them up: "A certain great museum pertaining to Man is stuffed full of cultural artifacts—of which a large number are wrongly labeled—in order to better extinguish racial facts, to silence, hide, and disperse cranial series—that is to say, [to silence] the demonstration of certain great racial circumstances. Jewish influence, in short, boycotts anything that exposes racial fact."[118] In other words, clothes covered the body, disguising racial difference in his view. To attribute this sleight of hand to Jewish influence

Figure 4.7.   Moroccan craft show poster, 1917
Europeans collected the traditional crafts of the countries they occupied. The possession of authentic artifacts of empires marked consumers as worldly.

in 1938 squarely placed Montandon's racial politics in line with the Nazis, with
whom he later collaborated.

Circuses, Fairs, and Expositions

Whereas ethnographic museums were curated by scholars and aimed to spread
scientific knowledge about humanity, tourist attractions such as the world's fairs
exposed more people to the world's cultures by means of entertainment. Smaller
in scale and less grandiose in ambition, circuses and congresses predated the
fairs and competed with them for visitors throughout the Age of Empire.

In 1874, Phineas Taylor Barnum (1810–1891) opened the Great Roman
Hippodrome in New York City and staged the Congress of Nations modeled after
Britain's Congress of Monarchs. Performers represented the monarchs of the
world and other world leaders under the banner "All Civilized Nations." They
entered the arena in elaborate chariots decorated with flags and in the style of

their place of origin. The Pope and Queen Victoria were represented alongside Chinese and Turkish rulers, past and present. The implied equality of world leaders irked some commentators. All of the actors were white despite P. T. Barnum's claim of featuring "the only genuine Zulus ever exhibited in America" found in places "where a white man never trod before."[119] The publicity alleged that other circuses were using African Americans as proxies. In the ten years between the two congresses, the shows became more blatantly racist, in parallel to wider social developments. Whereas Barnum positioned world leaders as equals in 1874, alleging to represent the most perfect humans he could procure, by 1884 he billed the show as representing "every rude barbarian presented exactly as described in history."[120] To achieve this end, he approached the US government for support and wrote of his intention to not only depict all of the races of man but also those "who possess extraordinary peculiarities, such as giants, dwarfs, singular disfigurements of the person, dexterity in the use of weapons, dancing, singing, juggling, unusual feats of strength or agility, &c."[121]

Freakishness included racial difference and disability as well as extraordinary talent. All of these othered bodies were classified as racial types in Barnum's London Ethnological Congress, a loftier title and aim than his New York circuses. In 1883, it claimed to include "Cannibals, Nubians, Zulus, Mohammedans, Pagans, Indians, Wild Men . . . Strange and Heathen Types of Human Beings."[122] Anthropologists and other tourists inspected people on display—their body markings, skin pigmentation, or skull size. A reporter for the *Chicago Tribune* remarked on the Australian Aboriginals' supposedly "gorillaish features."[123] Excessive hair by Western standards signaled animalism. Another London attraction was the Hairy Family of Burma, exhibited in 1887. Mah-Phoon and Mauge-Phoset were not displayed as singular curiosities, however, but as the "most weirdly, peculiar, distinct race of mankind of whom there is any trace or record."[124] Program notes claimed that their lineage went back four generations to Burmese royalty. Their hairiness was not seen to be an aberration. Instead, it supposedly proved that they were a heretofore undiscovered and separate race.

At international trade expositions and world's fairs, the achievements of civilized humanity were showcased alongside representations of primitive peoples to communicate even more unequivocally the wide chasm between primitive and civilized man. Hundreds of exhibitions and fairs took place primarily in Europe and North America between 1850 and 1950, but also in Europe's colonies of Canada and New Zealand, and even in Japan. One of the grandest and most famous, the 1889 Paris World's Fair, for which the Eiffel Tower was erected, commemorated France's Great Revolution of 1789. Gustave Eiffel (1832–1923) proclaimed that this would be France's Egyptian pyramid, a wonder of the world and a symbol of eternal France. In contrast to this claim, avant-garde visitors at the fair looked to "natural man" for inspiration, challenging or outright rejecting Europe's infatuation with itself. So influenced by the Javanese performances he saw at the Paris exposition (see Figure 4.8), Claude Debussy (1862–1918) infused impressionist piano music with oriental flavors.

Figure 4.8.   Indonesian gamelan musicians
When musicians from Dutch Indonesia performed traditional music for European
audiences at world's fairs, they introduced new possibilities for the transformation of
Western music.

For Debussy, these more natural peoples "learn music as easily as one learns
to breathe. Their school consists of the eternal rhythm of the sea, the wind in the
leaves, and a thousand other tiny noises, which they listen to with great care,
without ever having consulted any of those dubious treatises."[125] Thus, in addition to functioning as a paean to industrial civilization, the expositions also introduced alternatives to that civilization, undercutting the chauvinism they were
meant to foster. Exposure to non-Western music enabled one of Europe's most
renowned composers to revitalize Western music with oriental flavors. At the
same time, even elite fairgoers like Debussy resorted to romantic clichés when
describing something he loved.

Expositions included elaborate ethnographic exhibits of natural man from the
world's diverse civilizations, organized around civilization hierarchies that positioned industrial achievements on top. Whereas in previous decades, the expositions showcased the latest manufacturing and engineering technologies, by the
fin-de-siècle, spectacle and consumer goods displaced manufacturing. The technologies disappeared as did any other reference to the real world. Michel Corday
(1869–1937), a journalist covering the Paris World's Fair, lamented the replacement of the Gallery of Machines by an international food market. In his view, the
universal workshop that respected labor gave way to crass consumerism and "the
fattening joys of eating. No more sharp whistles, trembling, clacking transmission

belts; nothing being released except champagne corks."[126] The engineering behind the facades was now concealed. Visitors wanted to be dazzled by the magic of technologies they could not understand. Modern people increasingly defined themselves more as consumers and less as laborers, and were more interested in amusement than instruction.

During the Berlin Trade Show of 1896, which remained open for six months, trams transported more than seven million spectators to recreated civilizations replete with replicas of their monumental architecture, ponds, fountains, and baths.[127] Journalists at the time noted the sham and ruse perpetrated by displaying only the greatest marvels, but spectators went to colonial exhibitions to see the likes of the Taj Mahal, not the Great Famine of India. They flocked to exhibits of Germany's African possessions, all represented as one village, staffed by one hundred African contract workers from German Southwest Africa, German East Africa, and Togo and Cameroon in West Africa. Although some preferred to wear Western clothing when off duty, anthropologists insisted that they appear in authentic primitive attire. Nearly half of these performers were Swahili speakers, and likely Muslim, yet Islam was not represented as part of their culture.[128]

Implying that Cairo was a part of the German Empire, the Cairo display across the street from the African villages featured Islam as though it was frozen in time. According to one guidebook, passersby would observe "lazy" beggars, just as they would allegedly find them in the real Cairo. The book assured guests that these authentic Egyptians "do not arouse bad moods in the tourists of the Nile, but pleasure."[129] The implied pleasure was the economic status of tourists who could consume Egyptian antiquities at their leisure, taking no responsibility for the social—and imperial—causes of poverty. Portrayals of women also reinforced cultural stereotypes. While feminism took root in Germany, Arab women displayed their ethnicity, religiosity, and status in traditional style, ignoring Egypt's own nascent feminist movement. Some women in the display performed as servants at the lazy men's beck and call, men engaged in "sweet do-nothingness," while the dark eyes of the veiled women of the harem peered out on their Arabian knights.[130]

Specialized events could have a more feminist or trade-union orientation. To counter the trend toward greater consumerism and to honor the contributions of colonized people's labor to modernity, five hundred Dutch women organized a National Exhibition of Women's Labor in 1898 to celebrate the rise to the throne of eighteen-year-old Queen Wilhelmina (1880–1962). To manifest female solidarity across class and racial divides, the organizers chose to highlight labor and laborers' claims to citizenship. It attracted over ninety thousand visitors during its three month run, most of them women. Displays included real laborers performing their jobs, from machinists to typists to lace makers. A Javanese display featured thirty-seven Indonesians who demonstrated weaving, the batik style of dyeing cloth, and traditional dancing.[131] At the end of the show, the Javanese workers demanded their wages and passage home, refusing to go on to the next

show in Germany. Despite the profits their display produced, they had little negotiating power. Local labor organizations ignored their grievances when the
promoter failed to honor their contract. But in a show of female solidarity,
wealthy women philanthropists donated the funds.[132]

At the fairs, people gained superficial understanding of the world's peoples, but
attendance may have sparked a deeper encounter. Debussy's embrace of Javanese
music is one such example. While orientalist clichés marked its early attraction,
his infusion of Javanese instruments into his work shows how European impressionists borrowed from other cultures to reinvigorate Western music and art, rendering it hybrid if not global. Knowledge transfers from colonies to the metropole
in many ways validated cultures that were previously scorned.

WESTERN ART

Artists constantly look for new sources of inspiration, new techniques to invigorate
their artworks, and new styles to enrich their creative output. Western artists
adapted, blended, and absorbed non-Western art forms throughout the Age of
Empire. Even before the modern era, Spaniards fused Aztec styles such as high-still
reliefs and patterned ceramic tiling into the decorative elements of their cathedrals.
In the eighteenth century, whimsical Chinese motifs were embraced by the rococo
movement. "Painting" was revolutionized in the nineteenth century by exposure to
Japanese woodcuts, launching the *japonisme* movement among Impressionists. At
the turn of the twentieth century, modernist Primitivism emerged using the stylized glyphs, angular forms, and energetic silhouettes of African, Oceanic, and
Amerindian arts. "Performing Arts" such as opera and cinema similarly took inspiration from other cultures, especially when dramatizing intimate cultural conflicts.
Whereas some artists perpetuated clichés about exotic peoples, particularly women,
others attempted to depict a universal and complex humanity only accessible once
Europeans widened their creative lens.

Painting

In a classic knowledge transfer from East to West, Europeans became familiar
with Japanese art almost by happenstance. European Impressionist painters
were strongly influenced by the woodcuts of Katsushika Hokusai (1760–1849),
which first arrived in Europe in 1828. German physician Philipp Siebold
(1796–1866) acquired an album of the *Hokusai Sketches* (1814) while stationed
at the Dutch trading post in Nagasaki Bay. In 1856, the French etcher Félix
Bracquemond (1833–1914) serendipitously happened across a copy of the
Sketches that had been used as packing material for imported Chinese porce-
lains. He was so amazed by the vitality and fluidity of the Japanese artform that
he praised its virtues at every turn, setting off the *japonisme* craze that swept
through Impressionist art circles. The randomness of Bracquemond's discovery underscores how the transnational circulation of goods functioned to both

advance and to undermine European hegemony. Utilitarian objects destined for domestic female consumption inadvertently sparked an obsession with Japanese artwork, including erotica destined for clandestine male consumption, all because of throwaway packing material.[133]

In 1863, influential French art critic Edmond de Goncourt (1822–1896) wrote in his diary about his recent acquisition of erotic Japanese prints: "The other day I bought some albums of Japanese obscenities. They delight me, amuse me, and charm my eyes. I look on them as being beyond obscenity, which is there, yet seems not to be there, and which I do not see, so completely does it disappear into fantasy. The violence of the lines, the unexpected in the conjunctions . . . the picturesqueness, and, so to speak, the landscape of the genital parts."[134] Goncourt captured the allure and turmoil with which Europeans ventured into imperial spaces, often unsettled by the peculiar and the subversive, yet equally transfixed by exotic novelty. As European artists became familiar with the novel *Sketches*, known as the Floating World style in Japan, many were especially drawn to the fusion of the erotic and the macabre in the uniquely Japanese subgenre of *shokushu goukan*, literally "tentacle rape." The most famous by far was Hokusai's woodprint of two octopuses molesting a Japanese pearl diver, known in Europe as *The Dream of the Fisherman's Wife* (see Figure 4.9).

Impressionist painters adapted the Floating World aesthetic into ethereal portraits and translucent landscapes such as the delicate series of *Water Lilies* (1897–1926) by Claude Monet (1840–1926). French sculptor Auguste Rodin (1840–1917) uncovered his *japonisme* aesthetic in the corporeality of the flesh, full of texture and rhythm, accented by light and shadow. Goncourt wrote in his diary about first showing Hokusai's prints to Rodin, who was "full of admiration before the women's drooping heads, the broken lines of their necks, the rigid

Figure 4.9.   Katsushika Hokusai, *Dream of the Fisherman's Wife*, c. 1820
Japanese erotica influenced European artists to experiment with both form and content.

extension of arms, the contractions of feet, all the voluptuous and frenetic reality of coitus, all the sculptural twining of bodies melted and interlocked in the spasm of pleasure."[135] Rodin later described his renowned sculpture of *The Thinker* (1902) in strikingly similar terms: "What makes my *Thinker* think is that he thinks not only with his brain, with his knitted brow, his distended nostrils, and compressed lips, but with every muscle of his arms, back, and legs, with his clenched fist and gripping toes."[136] The *japonisme* styles that held the Parisian art world spellbound produced a dynamic array of artistic innovation well beyond its borders, inspiring such timeless works as *The Scream* (1895) by Norwegian Edvard Munch (1863–1944). Devoted *japonisants* even formed a secret society that dressed in brilliant kimonos when meeting to drink saké and eat with chopsticks off dinnerware designed after Hokusai's *Sketches*.[137]

Few artists embodied immersion in *japonisme* more than Dutch painter Vincent van Gogh (1853–1890), who discovered Japanese prints in Holland when reading Goncourt's novel *Chérie* (1848), whose hero first voiced the then-famous phrase "Japonaiserie forever!"[138] Two years later, in 1887, he saw Hokusai's *Sketches* on exhibit in Paris. Van Gogh wrote that the experience "gave birth to a day in that enchanting land, a day without shadow, filled with light . . . a fantasy disturbed by the light of reality, by the wintry sun of Paris."[139] Van Gogh adapted Japanese color schemes, brush strokes, and visual perspective in his compositions, eventually owning some five hundred Japanese prints in the brief remainder of his life. Van Gogh's famous *Portrait of Père Tanguy* (1887) integrates a mélange of Japanese and Impressionist art forms, placing the subject amid a sublime montage of Japanese prints, conveying the serenity that the painter sought in his own mental escape to Japan. In a letter to his brother in 1888, Van Gogh wrote that, "In a way all my work is founded on Japanese art. . . . Japanese art, decadent in its own country, takes root again among the French impressionist artists."[140] Indeed, Van Gogh moved to Arles in the south of France so that he could be closer to his vision of the Floating World, writing in one of his last letters, "I saw a magnificent and strange effect this evening. . . . Seen from above, [a boat] all shining and still wet with rain; the water was yellowish white and the clouds pearl grey, the sky violet with an orange streak in the west. . . . It was pure Hokusai."[141] Soon after, Van Gogh painted *Starry Night* (1889), a midnight view from his asylum room, an eternal homage to his love of Japan.

At the end of the nineteenth century, artists looked elsewhere for inspiration. In 1890, French Post-Impressionist painter Paul Gauguin (1848–1903) acheived his longtime dream of a studio in Tahiti, far from the artificiality and imposition that he felt in Europe. "There, in Tahiti, in the silent beautiful tropical nights, I will be able to listen to the sweet murmuring music of my heart's movements in loving harmony with the mysterious beings around me."[142] He soon married a young Tahitian girl Tehura that he described as if she were a painted vision. "Through her excessively see-through pink muslin dress, one could see the golden skin of her arms and shoulders. Her chest had two buttons pointing straight; her delightful face was not of a type that I had seen before anywhere on the island; she also had exceptional hair like a bush and slightly frizzy. In the sun all that was an orgy of chromium."[143] Halfway through his stay, Gauguin painted the *Tahitian Pastorals* (1892), a bold composition that sums up his mature style. It captured the plaintive scene of a Tahitian woman playing the flute, which he described in a poetic letter to a friend. "Complaining together, close or distant, my heart and the vivo sing. What is the musical savage thinking of on the shore, and to whom do [the] vivo's modulations go? Wild too, what is this wounded heart thinking of, and tell me for whom is it beating in this solitude?"[144] Running out of funds, Gauguin was forced to move back to France in 1893, yet Primitivist Oceanic motifs were evident throughout his last decade of artwork, most famously his *Two Tahitian Women* (1899) modeled after Polynesian wood carvings. In 1901, Gauguin set out on his final journey to the Marquesas Islands where he spent the last two years of his life.

Much like Gauguin, the long career of Spanish painter and sculptor Pablo Picasso (1881–1973) spanned an array of art movements, most notably the Cubist style that he founded, inspired by African sculpture and African masks. By the time Picasso arrived on the stage, *japonisme* had become conventional, even commodified, and so, for him, it represented constraint, not innovation.[145] In an interview given in 1937 to French novelist André Malraux (1901–1976), Picasso explained: "Van Gogh once said, 'Japanese art—we all had that in common.' For us it's the Negroes. . . . The masks weren't just like any other pieces of sculpture. Not at all. They were magic things."[146] For Picasso, the African masks of the 1907 ethnographic exhibit were a revelation of savage physicality, a celebration of life, in contrast to the contrivances of Western culture. So inspired, he painted *The Young Ladies of Avignon* (1907) depicting the angular bodies of French prostitutes, some of whose faces appear as African masks. "I understood; I too am against everything. I too believe that everything is unknown, that everything is an enemy! Everything! Not the details—women, children, babies, tobacco, playing—the whole of it! I understood what the Negroes use their sculptures for."[147] Picasso saw the masks as totems of individual expression, as a form of resistance against the encumbrance of tradition. He described them as personal fetishes and sacred weapons against hostile outside forces that would conquer the irrepressible spirit. "Spirits, the unconscious . . . emotion—they're all the same thing. I understood why I was a painter. All alone in that awful museum, with masks, dolls made by the redskins, dusty manikins. *Les Demoiselles d'Avignon* must have come to me that very day, but not at all because of forms; because it was my first exorcism painting—yes absolutely."[148] European painters borrowed from diverse cultures both for novel techniques and to explore taboo subject matter. The erotic imagery in *Dream of the Fisherman's Wife* hinted of violence as did the full frontal nudity of alienated prostitutes in *Les Demoiselles*. Even Gauguin's more soothing portraits of Tahitian beauties illustrate how exotic others enabled the projection of European male sexual fantasies onto the canvas.

Performing Arts

Although exposure to the creative works of other cultures revolutionized European art, it did not dislodge racial clichés. Indeed, it often perpetuated them. Even more than paintings, the dramatic arts were uniquely positioned to introduce audiences to strange exotic worlds. Representations of non-European exoticism extended far beyond fine art galleries and exhibition halls. The eclectic adaptation of Asian imagery and artifacts was pervasive throughout European cultural venues, from the elite opera houses of Rome and Vienna to the sumptuous Indian gardens and Persian pavilions of London to the carnival sideshows and traveling revues of German Bavaria. But the material culture of empire appealed only as long as the novelty. Once members of the public had been dazzled by an Indian garden or a Japanese woodcut, they moved on to the next big fad.

Opera, dance, and cinema were key venues through which representations of the world's peoples reached a mass audience. German composer Wolfgang Amadeus Mozart (1756–1791) drew on the already popular subject of the harem to produce *Abduction from the Seraglio* (1782), which featured the familiar motif of oriental women yearning for freedom from the confines of the harem. In Act Two, the heroine Konstanze's English maid proclaims, "Never you mind about the Pasha! Girls are not goods that can be given away as presents. I am an Englishwoman, born to be free, and defy anyone who would attempt to coerce me!"[149] Enacting a European narrative of triumph for true love, Mozart's hero Belmonte liberates his beloved Konstanze, "in Moorish lands a maiden fair," who has been sold by pirates to the Turkish Pasha.[150]

Interest in harem-themed art grew along with Egyptomania after Napoleon's invasion of Egypt in 1798, when scholars brought plundered Egyptian antiquities to Paris. In recognition of the cross-fertilization of Western art with Eastern themes, the Ottoman viceroy of Egypt, Ismail Pasha (1830–1895), commissioned Italian composer Giuseppe Verdi (1813–1901) to produce *Aida* (1871), which premiered at the Khedivial Opera House in Cairo. Far from the cliché harem trope, *Aida* was staged with all the grandeur of pharaonic Egypt, as seen in Figure 4.10. The plot of *Aida* is riveted on African star-crossed lovers: Aida, a captive Ethiopian princess, and the Egyptian captain of the royal guard, Radamès. Betrothed to the Pharaoh's daughter, Radamès is torn between his love for Aida and his loyalty to the Pharaoh. He meets a tragic end when his love is taken for treason since Ethiopia and Egypt are at war.[151] Rather than renounce Aida, he accepts his death sentence. The heroism of the African characters served as an antidote to more negative stereotypes, a victory enabled by the collaboration between Verdi and his Egyptian patrons.

Corresponding to the Impressionist fascination with Japan, Italian composer Giacomo Puccini (1858–1924) wrote *Madame Butterfly* (1904), an opera in which the tragic Japanese heroine, a young courtesan abandoned by her American lover, kills herself so that he can return to monogamy, "in real marriage" with his "real American wife" who will raise Butterfly's biracial son.[152] Having

Figure 4.10.   Verdi's *Aida* in Cairo
European artists produced works reflecting Egyptomania, the craze for all things
Egyptian, which lasted through and beyond the nineteenth century. Italian com-
poser Giuseppe Verdi staged his Egyptian themed opera in Cairo to wide acclaim.

renounced her Japanese heritage by converting to Christianity to marry a foreigner, yet without hope of acceptance into American society, Puccini's heroine
Cio-Cio-San, the titular Madame Butterfly, represents intersectionality at its most
ruinous: a defilement of Japanese customs by the predatory US Navy Lieutenant
Pinkerton.

Forbidden love and untimely death exoticized and sexualized contact between
different cultures in most of these European performances. While they presented
audiences with clichés and stoked perceptions of European greatness, they sometimes included subtle critique of imperialism. Cinema brought imagery of empire
to a mass audience. The Italian silent war film *Kif Tebbi* (1928), directed by Mario
Camerini (1895–1981), dramatizes Italy's conquest of Libya in 1912. The film centers on a romance between an Italian-educated Libyan and a nomad woman. The
hero chooses Italy over the Ottoman Empire in the war. The film gives one of the
more sensitive early cinematic portrayals of empire by telling the story from an
African perspective. Yet the Westernized male lead ultimately acts as a foil for the
barbaric native men and customs who threaten his naïve female companion, a
standard convention of colonial film. The film portrays the Italians as liberators
who free vulnerable Arabs from "evil Turks."[153] In the closing scene, the reunited
couple and their faithful servant watch the Turkish crescent come down, replaced
by the tricolor Italian flag. "It is Italy, Ismail whispers. And he holds his little

Figure 4.11.   *Sanders of the River*, 1935
Films also dramatized colonial encounters, including *Sanders of the River*, which starred African Americans playing Nigerians and Kenya's future president Jomo Kenyatta as an extra.

Arab girl, while nearby Taleb, astonished and moved, looks at the beautiful flag waving in the sun."[154] Although the message is squarely nationalist, the protagonists are African suggesting that their dilemma in the face of encroaching empire was deemed worthy of portrayal.

The civilizing mission is more blatantly racialized in the British film *Sanders of the River* (1935). Empire films depicted consensus between imperial rulers and their colonial subjects, in this case through the friendship between the strong but fair British Commissioner Sanders and the dutiful Nigerian chieftain Bosambo, played by African American singer and actor Paul Robeson (1898–1976), who appears in Figure 4.11. The peaceful colonial setting of the film is disrupted when the renegade King Mofalaba seeks to usurp the loyalty of Bosambo and lead a rebellion against the commissioner's valiant attempt to improve the lot of the natives by ending the trade in slaves, gin, and guns. *Sanders of the River* is a cinematic paragon of the "white man's burden," with the relationship between Sanders and Bosambo like that between a father and child, a projection of how Europeans viewed the imperial project as a whole.[155] The film also used the convention of a threatened female, revolving around Mofalaba's abduction of Bosambo's wife, which was how it was advertised for the masses: "A million mad savages fighting for one beautiful woman! Until three white comrades ALONE pitched into the fray and quelled the bloody revolt!"[156] Paul Robeson, who went on to become a major figure in the US Civil Rights Movement during the 1950s and 1960s, took the role of Bosambo thinking that it would help audiences understand and respect African culture. Robeson was furious to find that Bosambo had been changed in postproduction from a Nigerian leader into a "loyal lackey, dependent on his white master."[157] Robeson explained in an interview that "the imperialist angle" was inserted only during the last five days of shooting.[158] He again condemned the film in 1938, saying that "it is the only one of my films that can be shown in Italy and Germany, for it shows the Negro as Fascist States desire him—savage and childish."[159]

In Nazi propaganda films that pivoted on nostalgia for the African empire lost in World War I, Afro-German dancers performed as African "savages" in tropical set pieces meant to celebrate German greatness.[160] Erika Ngambi ul Kuo (b. 1915) reminisced about her acting career during World War II: "In the hope of regaining the old colonies after the war's end, many colonial films were made.... They needed colored people. We were hired and the wages were good. We got to travel abroad a lot. All the actors and everybody else were very nice to us. They definitely weren't Nazis."[161] Her sister and fellow actor Doris Reiprich (b. 1918) described how much fun they all had while filming as well as the dread of returning home to Nazi Germany. "It occurred to us once in a while that they could knock us mulattoes off while making a movie, all at one time. But where would they then have gotten other Africans? One time about two hundred to two hundred and fifty Black prisoners of war were brought in because they needed extras for a film. Black POWs from the United States besides. Those poor fellows were glad to be with us, since they got to eat and play football and were treated well."[162] By laughing at the absurdity of the situation and at the whites who staged it, the players enacted a strategy as old as oppression itself: the masters would not get precisely what they wanted on exactly their own terms.

These Afro-German actors represented the hybrid identities produced by imperialism, yet their very existence undermined the stability of white supremacy. In league with other diaspora Africans, muscular football-playing soldiers at that, they were "treated well" because whites depended on their cooperation, yet Reiprich's vignette reflects the ambivalence of the colonial situation. Always aware of their vulnerability—"they could knock us off"—the players performed with staged gestures that only hinted at mockery.[163] As the war ended, the sisters escaped and formed a dance troupe named South Sea Magic with fellow surviving actors, but many were far less fortunate.[164] Bayume Mohamed Husen (1904–1944), an actor from German East Africa, fought as a child soldier during World War I and "embodied the myth of the loyal Askari."[165] After the filming of *Carl Peters* (1941), he was denounced as a race traitor because of his relationship with a white woman and imprisoned in the Sachsenhausen concentration camp, where he died in 1944.

Afro-German actors crafted a range of responses to the dire threat of Nazism. While the films they made may have sated German nostalgia for empire and perpetuated stereotypes about Africans, actors attempted to maintain control over their work and a sense of self-irony. The more serious genres of opera and fine art also show potential for respectful cultural exchange, even though the final products might be shallow or opaque. Reading them against the grain, against the direction their creators intended, reveals complex processes of cultural interaction, resistance, and even intimacy.

· EXOTIC EROTICA

Like cinema, photography advanced the voyeuristic possibilities of empire to a mass audience, particularly through the proliferation of "Postcards" featuring nude or nearly nude natives. Whereas performing artists could occasionally negotiate the terms of their work and how they were portrayed, models posing for photographs were more objectified. Postcards also circulated more widely than other genres of erotica, such as translations of "Ancient Texts." The circulation of such texts revolutionized European sexology, which resulted in new "Scientific Texts" diffused globally by sexologists. This illustrates how imperialism facilitated the transfer of knowledge between multiple cultures in some ways to its own detriment. Originating from India and Arabia, titillating books and images attracted interest in other cultures and destabilized European approaches to sexuality.

Postcards

Photography swiftly created a transnational market for erotic albums and postcards. The earliest emergence of imperialist photography followed the trajectory of *japonisme*. When US Commodore Matthew Perry (1794–1858) forced the opening of Japan in 1854, he maintained the custom of having artists record the venture, a tradition that extended as far back as Captain Cook's Pacific voyages. Perry included a daguerreotypist who in 1856 presented a three-volume pictorial narrative of the expedition in the China Seas and Japan to the US Congress. These captivating images of the exciting and exotic new frontier in East Asia drew the notice of Italian war photographer Felice Beato (1832–1909), acclaimed for his dramatic images of the Crimean War (1853) and the Indian Rebellion (1857).[166] In 1863, Beato settled in Yokohama where he turned to a very different passion, a three-decade career of photographing Japanese beauties and geishas in both natural and posed settings.[167] "In all countries, the most interesting objects in the eyes of a stranger are the female population . . . she is gentle;—she is inviting;—she is very coy! . . . She will show you all her little toy-like treasures."[168] When Hokusai's woodprints became the prism through which most Europeans encountered Japan in the late nineteenth century, Beato began to recreate the ethereal Floating World scenes from the prints in evocative photographs that depicted the Japanese pleasure quarters as a refined erotic haven for adventurous, cosmopolitan Western men.[169]

Whereas Beato's beauties were clothed, censors allowed graphic images of colonized women's bare breasts, buttocks, and genitals so long as they advanced an ethnographic purpose. Even postcards of nude native men could be openly mailed if they were described as scholarly.[170] The same was true in the closely related advertising medium, where seductively posed Arab *sultanas* were used to peddle French cosmetics in the late nineteenth century, and scantily clad Polynesian "hula girls" were a fixture in the emergence of the twentieth-century tourist industry.[171]

However, while colonial peoples were a commodity of imperial sexual fantasy, women and native men were usually forbidden from being consumers of pornography. Graphic imagery was deemed too unsettling for the supposedly frail female psyche and was held to "poison the minds and stimulate the baser passions" of native men.[172] In 1911, for example, one judge framed the issue in *The Vigilance Record* of South Africa upon handing down a conviction to a man charged with selling obscene images to black men. "You have committed a grave breach of the law. What makes it still worse is this: you sold and showed these most filthy photos to the natives. What the effect on their minds will be I do not know. For you, a white man, to make a living out of the sale of this stamps you as a person of no character."[173] The judge situated the offense within the broader imperial project that depended on maintaining artificial hierarchies between white settlers and native subjects.

Ancient Texts

While dime novels and erotic postcards catered to a mass market, scholars cloaked their equally graphic writings beneath the mantle of anthropology. The translations of Eastern "harem novels" by Sir Richard Burton (1821–1890), most notably the *Kama Sutra* (1883) and the *Arabian Nights* (1885–1888), are among the most iconic and enduring of the orientalist texts. Early in life, Burton displayed a penchant for languages, a fascination with the exotic, and an iconoclasm that marked both his respectable scholarly work and his more risqué writings. He mastered several Romance languages while touring Europe in his late teens, had an affair with a young Gypsy woman, and engineered his own expulsion from Oxford in defiance of his father.[174] Following in the footsteps of so many alienated European men, he left to find his fortune in the Empire, enlisting as an officer with the British East India Company. Yet Burton did not travel far down the standard career path of British imperial agents. He apprenticed with a Brahmin master, which earned him the nickname "white nigger" from his fellow officers, and officially went undercover to investigate a male brothel in Karachi that was frequented by British soldiers.[175] After seven years in India, he got circumcised and memorized the Quran to disguise himself as a Muslim during a pilgrimage to Islamic holy sites where infidels were forbidden. Burton found fame and fortune in the vogue for true stories from the exotic East in 1885 when he published his popular account of the journey to Mecca and Medina. He then explored the Horn of Africa, where he was imprisoned by the Emir of Harar and impaled by a javelin during a skirmish with Somali warriors, volunteered to fight in the Crimean War, trekked to the Great Lakes of East Africa, and joined the British Foreign Service in 1861. He sailed the Congo River, explored the Brazilian

highlands, and finally served as consul to Damascus. With his cachet as an imperial adventurer, Burton cofounded the Anthropological Society of London in
1863, "to supply travellers with an organ which would rescue their observations
from the outer darkness of manuscript, and print their curious information on
social and sexual matters."[176]

In the late 1880s, Burton issued his ten-volume *Plain and Literal Translation
of the Arabian Nights' Entertainments* (1885–1888) in a private printing for several hundred subscribers of his underground Kama Shastra Society, which was
swiftly pirated and released to a general audience. Burton's translation replaced
the well-known, sanitized French translation of *Arabian Nights* by Antoine
Galland (1646–1715) and turned the *Arabian Nights* into one part pornographic
fairytale and one part ethnographic sex manual. Burton's *Arabian Nights*
became an instant sensation in Britain where the public was titillated and scan-
dalized by its graphic passages of forbidden erotica. He not only translated sections that had previously been censored as obscene but also inserted hundreds
of footnotes based on his wealth of personal knowledge about sexual behavior
throughout the world.

Moreover, the tenth volume of *Arabian Nights* featured Burton's "Terminal
Essay," the first treatise to be published in English regarding sex between males,
"what our [French] neighbours call *Le vice contre nature*—as if anything can be
contrary to nature which includes all things."[177] This implicit validation of sex
between men opened public dialogue in Britain about homosexuality just as
similar debates appeared on the Continent. The reason why this discourse could
emerge about "the love that dare not speak its name" was its justification as orientalist study of imperial cultures and colonial peoples.[178] In the "Terminal
Essay," Burton presented what he called the Sotadic Zone, which included the
Americas, North Africa, the Middle East, and East Asia. He claimed that in this
geographic realm climate and culture fostered male same-sex relations. Initially
defined by Burton as a narrow band of the Tropics, the Sotadic Zone underwent
drastic expansions and contractions as the essay progressed, even shifting tem-
porally to include Classical Greece and Rome. By the end of the essay, it covered
the entire Western Hemisphere and was thus incoherent from a geographic
standpoint, leaving the reader to deduce that arbitrary cultural factors were the
determining factor in sexual behavior.[179] The Sotadic Zone basically represented
the world beyond Christendom, both in time and place, its true bounds ultimately more theological than geographic.[180]

Critics labelled Burton's work pornographic. In 1885, John Morley (1828–1933)
wrote in The *Pall Mall Gazette*, "In the garden of western literature there are many
foul quagmires which must be faced by the explorer; but we have a legitimate—
nay, an imperative—interest in wading through them. Is there any reason why we
should laboriously import the gigantic muck heaps of other races, place them *très
curieux*, and charge a high price for the privilege of wallowing in them?"[181] Burton
replied that Western imperial power required familiarity with Eastern sexual customs, as stated in the preface to *Arabian Nights*. "Hence, when suddenly compelled

to assume the reins of government in Moslem lands, as Afghanistan in times past and Egypt at present, [England] fails after a fashion which scandalises her few (very few) friends; and her crass ignorance concerning the Oriental peoples which should most interest her, exposes her to the contempt of Europe as well as of the Eastern world."[182] Burton's descriptions of the supposed "true East" were in fact consulted by colonial officials when drafting imperial policies. For instance, his imagery of oversexed Africans helped lead colonial authorities in West Africa to the conclusion that it would be impossible to suppress local prostitution.[183]

Under the veneer of ethnographic science, Burton also translated two ancient Indian sex guides, the *Kama Sutra of Vatsyayana* (1883) and *Ananga-Ranga* (1885), as well as the Persian pillow book *Perfumed Garden of Sensual Delight* (1886). The *Kama Sutra* became a sensation not only in Britain but on the Continent as well, where editions were soon printed in Brussels and Paris. Burton's version of *Arabian Nights* also circulated in German and inspired a French translation by Joseph Mardrus (1868–1949), which swiftly appeared in Spanish and Italian. In the "Terminal Essay," Burton stated his reason for translating the Eastern sex manuals: to challenge what he viewed as the "silly prejudice and miserable hypocrisy" of Victorian Britain.[184] The Royal Geographical Society effectively provided the distancing and credentials necessary to start a public discussion of illicit sexuality, in much the same way that graphic postcards of colonial peoples were permitted as works of anthropology.

Scientific Texts

Sexology as a legitimate field of study emerged at the intersections of biology, psychology, and public health in late nineteenth century Europe. Anthropologists broadened the study of human sexuality by comparing practices in different cultures. Activists who sought increased acceptance of Europe's sexual minorities looked to other cultures. At the same time, defenders of racial hierarchies found the sexual practices of non-European cultures to be a measure of their barbarism. Out of this contestation emerged a body of literature that was widely adopted on the premise of promoting sexual health.

John Addington Symonds (1840–1893), a member of Burton's Cannibal Club since 1865, cited Burton's "Terminal Essay" as the authority on the subject of homosexuality. He persuaded Havelock Ellis (1859–1939) to author his pivotal study on *Sexual Inversion* (1896), which popularized the concept of the "sexual invert" who desired sex with other men as an inherent character type.[185] Ellis set his European cases amid an abundance of examples from Burton's Sotadic Zone, describing acquired homosexuality as a result of social acceptance. Because "homosexual practices" were "regarded with considerable indifference" among both "the lower races" and "the lower classes," Ellis concluded that "the uncultured man of civilization is linked to the savage," both of whom were prone to developing an acquired taste for homosexuality.[186] Ellis in turn routinely corresponded with Austro-German psychiatrist Richard von Krafft-Ebing (1840–1902)

who popularized the terms "homosexual" and "heterosexual" in his seminal text
Psychopathia Sexualis (1886).

Krafft-Ebing similarly drew a distinction between hereditary homosexuality
and acquired homosexuality, in his view the result of unchecked masturbation
leading to amoral self-indulgence.[187] According to Krafft-Ebing, "the savage races"
were still in an uncivilized stage of undifferentiated sexual gratification, while
"the greater sensuality of southern races as compared with the sexual needs of
those of the north is well known."[188] Moreover, because he held that Christianity
was singularly responsible for sexual morality, Europeans were "certainly far
beyond [the] sodomitic idolatry" of ancient Greece and less likely to acquire
homosexuality than "the polygamic races" of the Muslims.[189] In short, when a
Christian engaged in homosexual behavior, he was behaving either as a savage or
as a Muslim. To be sure, Krafft-Ebing was far more condemning of homosexuality
than were Ellis and Burton, but the common link between them was the use of
ethnography to define sexual norms in terms of white, European, middle-class
heterosexuality, while equating homosexuality with uncivilized or oversexed
peoples somewhere out beyond the horizons of European civilization.

The *Untrodden Fields of Anthropology* (1898), published by an anonymous
Frenchman under the pseudonym Dr. Jacobus X, cataloged an impressive variety
of sexual practices among a great array of peoples native to Asia, Africa, America,
and Oceania. Later condensed and reissued as *The Erogenous Zones of the World*
(1964), the detailed sexual ethnography shaped views of indigenous sexuality well
into the twentieth century, especially with regard to lesbian relations. Jacobus X
closed his work with "the Sapphic couples at Tahiti, formed of Vahinés having the
same tastes," which he believed to be the result of corruption by white men.[190] This
conflated both the racial and gender stereotypes of Western society, implying that
women had sex with women only due to the influence of men rather than of their
own initiative. Moreover, since Polynesians were thought to be in a more natural
state of being, they supposedly could not develop such customs on their own.

Although Jacobus X set out to create a sexual geography much like Burton's
Sotadic Zone, the bewildering range of practices he encountered led him to abandon the task, instead concluding that sexual behavior was an inborn racial trait.
"All that I simply wish to show is that the influence of race appears to me to be
predominant. We have seen the Asiatic of the Far East, a sodomite and a pederast;
the African Negro, simple in his tastes, a devotee of natural love; the Black, or
rather the Melanesian half-breed . . . a pederast when he cannot procure women;
the Maori, a plain lover of the natural Venus, but his Vahiné practising, since she
has come into contact with European civilization, the vices of Lesbos."[191] However, in an interesting twist on the standard narrative, revealing yet again the
variety and complexity of orientalist portrayals, Jacobus X compared Europeans
unfavorably to the more narrowly typecast peoples of the world. "In fact, to sum
up the whole, it is the European who fosters all kinds of genital depravity."[192]
Fixation on the sexual otherness of exotic peoples resulted in the perpetuation of
racist stereotypes in literature that was both pornographic and scientific. At the

same time, some sexologists critiqued European sex and gender norms and undermined European claims to racial superiority.

CONCLUSION

The erotic content of the transnational exchange of goods was sometimes overt, more often latent. The graphic woodcuts of Hokusai were the high art counterparts to Tokyo's red light district. The sexualization of Eastern women is manifest in the fashion for shawls as well as the passion for *Kama Sutra*. The tension between the absorption and containment of colonial peoples, customs, and products exposed fault lines in white supremacy. Europeans appropriated everything they conquered, but in so doing occasionally gained understanding of the cultures they exploited, even to the degree of supporting their independence. Colonized peoples gazed back and recreated cultural artifacts while demanding the right to self-representation. Whites who performed exotic identities, like Mata Hari or Richard Burton, capitalized on fluid identities created by European imperialism, but so did Africans who performed at world's fairs. To some degree, they all engaged in self-conscious mimicry with its subversive potential.

The homogenizing of taste is one of the more enduring outcomes of the Age of Empire. Wearing eyeglasses as a fashion statement or showing Asian pets at kennel clubs was novel at first but soon became commonplace. Initially the purview of elites in all cultures, eating, wearing, and exhibiting goods from all over the world spread to most economic groups thanks to mass production. Homogenization tends to erase distinctiveness, causing some defenders of tradition to reject the globalization of consumerism while others celebrate the opportunities for self-fashioning that it enables. Such transfers of knowledge illustrate the dynamic flow of information, goods, and people during the Age of Empire. Producers and consumers across the world mediated imperial relations through material culture. They were most disempowered when they were objects of display and global capitalism was the primary beneficiary of this exchange. Nonetheless, race, gender, and sexuality structured every level of the exchange and therefore enabled surprising possibilities for resistance and empowerment.

TIMELINE

1787	German surgeon founds colony for Africans and Danes in Danish Guinea
1809	Hindoostanee Coffee House opens in London
1844	British glass firm F. and C. Osler open their first showroom in Calcutta
1856	French etcher discovers Japanese erotica by Hokusai in packing material

1860	British soldiers loot five Pekingese dogs from the Forbidden City after China's defeat in the Arrow War, introducing them to Europe
1871	Queen Victoria buys two Persian cats at the first Occidental Cat Show in London
1871	Ismail Pasha of Egypt commissions Giuseppe Verdi to produce *Aida*
1874	P. T. Barnum opens the Great Roman Hippodrome in New York City
1878	Ethnology museum opens at the Trocadero Palace in Paris
1883	Richard Burton translates the *Kama Sutra* into English
1889	Van Gogh paints Japanese inspired *Starry Night*
1889	World's Fair opens in Paris, unveiling the new Eiffel Tower
1907	Pablo Picasso paints cubist-style *Young Ladies of Avignon*
1914	French government bans sales of absinthe at start of World War I
1917	Mata Hari accused of spying for Germans, executed by French firing squad
1923	Huda Shaarawi and fellow Muslim feminists remove their veils at the Rome Women's Conference
1938	Museum of Man opens in Paris
1945	African section of the Society for the Prevention of Cruelty to Animals formed in Kenya

FIVE

THE RACE OF EMPIRE

Olaudah Equiano of Nigeria and London

> As I was now amongst a people who had not their faces scarred,
> like some of the African nations where I had been, I was very
> glad I did not let them ornament me in that manner when I was
> with them.
>
> —Olaudah Equiano, *Interesting Narrative*, 1789

Former slave and abolitionist of Igbo origin, Olaudah Equiano published his autobiography in English in 1789. He contrasted the body modification practices of the Igbo, witnessed as a child, and English embodiment, experienced as a free man. Whereas scarification indicated status in Africa, it would forever attest to embodied difference in Europe.[1] The distance Equiano had traveled between his adolescent and adult selves can be traced as a transformation of his embodiment. Kidnapped as a youth in Africa, enslaved in the Caribbean and in the British Navy, Equiano bought his freedom at age nineteen and went on to become a hairdresser, traveler, and abolitionist. In his autobiography, The Interesting Narrative of Olaudah Equiano, *he relayed his origin story beginning with an ethnographic description of the Igbo centered on their bodily practices. "My father was one of those elders or chiefs I have spoken of, and was styled Embrenché; a term, as I remember, importing the highest distinction, and signifying in our language a mark of grandeur. This mark is conferred on the person entitled to it by cutting the skin across at the top of the forehead, and drawing it down to the eye-brows; and while it is in this situation applying a warm hand, and rubbing it until it shrinks up into a thick weal across the lower part of the forehead."[2] Such practices ultimately conferred masculine authority on powerful men, indicating the gendered function of diverse forms of body modification.*

Once in the new world, Equiano recounted the physical abuses endured by slaves whose minds and bodies were forever marked, if not disabled, by the experience of enslavement. At the same time, he described his own transformation into a

205

British gentleman. The Interesting Narrative *therefore introduces readers to many aspects of masculine embodiment within the imperial domain: scarification and circumcision, branding and abuse, comportment and martial skill. The* Interesting Narrative *was also central to the success of abolitionism, the first transnational movement to end subjected embodiment. In this chapter, we consider these and other forms of body modification resulting in the modern condition of complex embodiment.*

Grateful not to be scarified and hoping this would assist his smooth integration into white society, Equiano nonetheless felt the stigma of his blackness. While still a young adolescent, his master lodged him in England with a welcoming family. He observed how the face of their little white child became rosy when her mother washed her. "I therefore tried oftentimes myself if I could not by washing make my face of the same colour as my little play-mate (Mary), but it was all in vain; and I now began to be mortified at the difference in our complexions."[3] *Yet, in his homeland, a white African, likely albino, was seen as a deformity.*[4] *He concluded that what is deemed a beautiful complexion is subjective and recognized blackness for the stigma it carried in white society.*

After Equiano was a free man, his blackness still subjected him to discrimination and brutality. But he explained differences in skin pigmentation as a simple matter of climate, as did many of his eighteenth-century contemporaries. He described the gradual darkening of Spaniards who immigrated to the Americas or of Portuguese immigrants to Sierra Leone who through intermarriage with natives produced offspring with wooly hair. "These instances, and a great many more which might be adduced, while they shew [sic] how the complexions of the same persons vary in different climates, it is hoped may tend also to remove the prejudice that some conceive against the natives of Africa on account of their colour. Surely the minds of the Spaniards did not change with their complexions!"[5] *He attributed the low intellectual state of slaves of African descent to their condition—"Does not slavery itself depress the mind?"—and blamed Europeans for failing to see that "understanding is not confined to feature or colour."*[6] *He stated that intelligence was universal, but that cultural conditions shaped the uses to which that intelligence could be applied.*

Like many learned people in the European Enlightenment, Equiano believed in the inevitable spread of civilization. Starting from a common origin in the state of nature, all humans then began to differentiate based on climate and access to resources. For example, he cited a common origin for Jews and the Igbo because their cultural practices were strikingly similar, including circumcision and the seclusion of supposedly unclean menstruating women. To explain this, he cited a biblical authority who "deduces the pedigree of the Africans from Afer and Afra, the descendants of Abraham by Keturah his wife and concubine."[7] *He insisted that those who believed in inherent differences between humans based on skin color were ignorant. "Let the polished and haughty European recollect that his ancestors were once, like the Africans, uncivilized, and even barbarous."*[8] *Even as he explained the common origins of humanity, he also accepted that some had progressed out of a state of savagery faster than others.*

In this chapter, we explore the roots and effects of the ideologies of progress and disability in eighteenth-century theories of perfectibility. We examine how imperialism altered bodies—through decoration as symbols of political status, through campaigns to convey a normative standard of mental and physical health, and through initiatives aiming to eliminate some populations while propagating others. These ventures—to fight disease, to manage population, to improve the body— were essential to liberal imperialism and its desire and burden to uplift the world's "less civilized" peoples. The malleable and perfectible body pivoted on social constructions of race where whiteness was equated to a higher degree of control over one's body, especially one's sexuality. It was both cause and consequence of complex embodiment, a concept that acknowledges that bodies are both corporeal entities and social objects jointly constructed by biology and culture. The drive to improve the body by altering social forces has resulted in decreased infant mortality, a longer life expectancy for most people, and prompt interventions to halt epidemics. Transfers of knowledge between peoples have generally had a positive impact on standard measures of health.

At the same time, perfectibility also leads to ableism, an ideology that elevates the youthful white male body, free from disease or impairment, to normative status. The spectrum of ableism ranges from simple preference for able bodies to the sometimes dangerous and costly quest for perfectibility, and finally to the rejection of people whose bodies or behaviors do not conform. The range of responses to imperialism was greater to the degree that one possessed desirable physical and mental characteristics. Imperialism spread ableism through diverse means. For most of the world's population, ability equated to being a productive laborer whose body produced profit. Impairment was defined as the inability to do this. For women, ability equated to reproductive labor. Depending on the needs of the moment, imperial governments attempted to either promote or suppress the birth rate of certain segments of the population. Western healthcare workers set out across the globe to teach hygiene and appropriate family planning and to spread fitness culture and vaccines. In some places, local medical traditions were incorporated into Western biomedicine. More often they were suppressed. Meanwhile, imperialism disabled some colonial subjects through the physical impairments that resulted from armed conflict and exploitive labor practices. Above all else, Europeans reacted to increased contact with people from different cultures by seeking to exert control over them, particularly their sexuality and gender norms.

PERFECTIBILITY

Between 1750 and 1850, European naturalists developed modern concepts of race. Like Equiano, they queried the role of climate in creating different body types and different cultures. Some eighteenth-century naturalists believed in the common humanity of all, regardless of cultural differences (see Figure 5.1). "Theories of Progress" included racial mixing to improve humanity, underscoring the centrality of managed mating to perfectibility. Later naturalists, especially

Figure 5.1. "All Mortals are Equal"
Some Enlightenment thinkers posited the common humanity of all people while depicting their cultural differences.

Charles Darwin, theorized about the interplay between "Race, Climate, and Evolution" and identified randomness in the selection of traits and a diminished role for human agency in the evolution of the species. Mate selection played a role in evolution, but outcomes could not be so easily controlled. Originating in the Enlightenment, as modern empires began a new wave of expansion, such theories left divergent legacies into the twentieth century. Embrace of racial mixing gave way to criminalization, a cause and consequence of shifts in the biological understanding of race. As scientists situated race in biology rather than culture, the category became concrete and seemingly immutable. It was intimately linked to practices of gender and sexuality with distance from the European norm often measured in these terms.

Theories of Progress

Developments in European political philosophy fueled the program of reform known as the Enlightenment. Philosophers theorized about gender difference even as they famously argued for the rights of man, infusing European masculinity with political empowerment. They advanced the view that human nature was malleable and therefore shaped by environment. Marquis de Condorcet (1743–1794), a radical French philosopher, framed the idea of human perfectibility in his *Sketch for a Historical Picture of the Progress of the Human Mind* (1794). He rhapsodized that through education, the total and global perfectibility of man was possible, even imminent. "Will all nations one day attain that state of civilization which the most enlightened, the freest and the least burdened by prejudices, such as the French and the Anglo-Americans, have attained already? Will the vast gulf that separates these peoples from the slavery of nations under the rule of monarchs, from the barbarism of African tribes, from the ignorance of savages, little by little disappear?"[9] Like Equiano, he assumed it was merely a matter of time before all peoples adopted European civilization. Perfect human intelligence, health, and freedom would emanate out of Europe as the sunlight would shine only on free men. In *Progress of the Human Mind*, the perfection of the body issued inevitably from the progress of civilization. Through education, people would limit family size, aspiring to bequeath happiness to their offspring, "rather than foolishly to encumber the world with useless and wretched beings."[10] Educated people with access to family planning would rid the world of useless beings by not producing them in the first place. Condorcet asserted that the march of civilization would also erase disease and impairment, perhaps someday conquering mortality itself. The progressive advances in Europe would spread to other parts of the world, leading to the universal perfection of man.

Imperialism resulted in greater contact between the world's diverse peoples and inevitably in racial mixing, stimulating naturalists to speculate about its effects on the human species. Charles-Augustin Vandermonde (1727–1762) was born in Macao, a Chinese port city ruled by Portugal, to a French father, a physician on official appointment, and a Portuguese mother of Asian descent. He moved to Paris and became an eminent physician and a follower of the Comte de Buffon (1707–1788), a naturalist who historicized nature and developed the theory of monogenesis, that all humans descended from a common ancestor. He developed early theories of adaptation through reproduction. Vandermonde's *Essay on the Manner of Perfecting the Human Species* (1756) aimed to popularize Buffon's work, but in fact it went much further. Because the role of heredity was not well understood at the time, Vandermonde concluded that people with gout should not have children because "the germ of the gout is transmitted to the fetus, and the child is born with the body shrunken and the limbs deformed."[11] He nonetheless held that the transmission of traits may occur over several generations. Therefore, blind parents may not produce a blind child, but it would likely present at some point in the family tree. Breeders of cattle and dogs understood this principle and intervened to improve their stock "by simply manipulating the traits and attractions of their particles in cross-breeding. Should we not apply the same rule to humans?"[12]

Vandermonde advocated merging different ethnicities to produce the best result in humans. He cited the beauty and talent of people living in maritime cities such as Macao, which attracted people from all over the world. Conversely, he held that the supposed inbreeding of Jewish communities "could be one of the physical reasons that caused the degeneration of this people."[13] By beauty, he meant proportion and symmetry reflecting that of nature. He decried unnatural practices of body modification that destroyed proportionality, such as foot binding among the Chinese, corseting among the French, and blackened teeth among Indians. The strength and beauty of mulattoes in the New World proved that, left alone, sexual attraction will do nature's work. But he knew certain obstacles had to be overcome, the first of which was convincing people of the biology behind the phenomenon. He again invoked animal breeding by analogy. "By chance, organic particles of donkeys and mares attach to each other in a particularly strong way. And could not we say the same about the mulatto? Are not they in general those who execute the harder physical tasks?"[14] Other obstacles could be overcome with state intervention to promote and regulate interracial mating.

Of his experience with mixed-race people, Baron de Wimpffen (1748–1819) on his tour of Saint-Domingue (modern Haiti) in 1788–1790 marveled that "it has not already occurred to some ingenious speculator to monopolize . . . the fabrication of all mulattoes."[15] In fact, Governor General Gabriel de Bory (1720–1801) published an essay in the 1770s that called for extensive management of reproduction. Influenced by successful experiments in which domestic sheep were bred with the most separated "races" of sheep, the Moroccan and Tibetan, Bory asserted that breeding separate races led to the best outcome.[16] He sought to breed a mulatto race of soldiers who would defend the island against foreign threat and also from restive slaves while eliminating the hated conscription of whites.[17] To achieve this end, Bory proposed banning intermarriage between mulattoes and blacks while encouraging it between whites and mulattoes. For this scheme to work, all enslaved mulattoes would be freed.[18]

Race, Climate, and Evolution

Other scientists believed that the potential for perfectibility inherent in all people required the abolition of slavery. Johann Friedrich Blumenbach (1752–1840) developed the racial hierarchy that dominated nineteenth-century racial thinking, with Caucasians at the top and Africans at the bottom. He alleged that all of humanity originated from Europe and darkened in different climates because it is "very much more difficult for dark to become white."[19] His preference for Caucasians was, however, aesthetic, and he nonetheless insisted that his research proved the common humanity of all people. "No doubt can any longer remain but that we are with great probability right in referring all varieties of man . . . to one and the same species."[20] Because he accepted the view that all humans progressed from savagery to civilization at different rates, his taxonomy represents culture more than biology, but later naturalists and anthropologists lost this distinction when they invoked this hierarchy. He illustrated "racial geometry" by means of skulls but attributed differences to climate and culture.[21] He believed that Australian Aboriginals developed narrow eye slits because they were subjected to "constant clouds of gnats . . . contracting the natural face of the inhabitants."[22] These adaptations were then passed on to their descendants. "Almost all the diversity of the form of the head in different nations is to be attributed to the mode of life and to art."[23]

Changing environments would change people. He cited the achievements of former slaves to demonstrate the efficacy of education, and even the nobility of former slaves whose humanity survived the brutality of the slave system.

By the mid-nineteenth century, naturalists forged taxonomies similar to Blumenbach's illustrating biological, not cultural, difference. But evolutionary biology continued to demonstrate constant adaptability rather than fixity. Like Blumenbach, Charles Darwin (1809–1882) campaigned for the abolition of slavery, while others used Darwin's scientific findings to support notions of white supremacy. Unlike Blumenbach and many naturalists of the previous generation, he did not believe that progress from savagery to civilization was inevitable or linear. Rather, adaptations happened over long periods of time and more randomly. Darwin directly challenged Jean-Baptiste Lamarck (1744–1829) who believed that physical modifications acquired during one's lifetime could be selected for and passed down to the next generation. In Lamarcks's view, elephants, for example, stretched their trunks to reach water sources and then passed on longer trunks to their offspring. Darwin thought that adaptation happened independently of the behavior of animals. Elephants that randomly happened to have longer trunks were better suited for survival and then reproduced themselves, causing the shorter trunks to die off in the competition known as survival of the fittest. Darwin's voyages in South America revealed tremendous variety among plants, animals, and humans. He theorized that such variety indicated natural selection, the somewhat random and spontaneous development of traits best suited for survival in a given environment. For example, the indigenous people of Tierra del Fuego that he encountered in their native environment in 1834 had to adapt to a landscape of "a broken mass of wild rocks, lofty hills, and useless forests, & these are viewed through mists & endless storms. . . . How little can the higher powers of the mind come into play. . . . How little must the mind of one of these beings resemble that of an educated man."[24] Although he initially pondered their humanity, describing them as "greasy" and "without any dignity," he associated their characteristics with the harsh climate.[25] But they were obviously educable. The HMS *Beagle*'s captain, Robert FitzRoy (1805–1865) had brought four Fuegians to Britain the year before to demonstrate how savages could be civilized. In his drawings, FitzRoy positioned them as natural man, closer than whites in proximity to apes, but still human (see Figure 5.2). Darwin met them on their return trip in 1831. In *The Descent of Man* (1871) he recognized their common humanity. "I was incessantly struck, whilst living with the Fuegians on board the 'Beagle,' with the many little traits of character, showing how similar their minds were to ours."[26]

Because of their capabilities, Fuegians could be improved on, as demonstrated by their experience in England. This commitment to raising all of mankind to the same level of civilization resembles the views of Equiano or Condorcet. Like them, Darwin was a supporter of many liberal causes of his day. Progress could be achieved by social and political reform, not through a manipulation of biology. By the late nineteenth century, Darwin's cousin Francis Galton (1822–1911)

Figure 5.2.   Portraits drawn by Robert FitZroy, Captain of the HMS *Beagle*
Charles Darwin was not the only naturalist aboard the *Beagle* in his famous voyage around South America in the 1830s. Fitzroy's sketches of Fuegians reveal ambivalence about their humanity.

founded the first eugenics society, which came to promote aggressive intervention in human reproduction to prevent degeneracy, including healthy diet and exercise, but also sterilization of those deemed unfit.[27] Social Darwinists like Herbert Spencer (1820–1903) added the concept of "survival of the fittest" to Darwinism. Darwin himself first used it in 1869 for the fifth edition of *The Origin of Species*. Some of Darwin's comments in *The Descent of Man* suggest that he endorsed measures to curb the reproduction of the unfit. By example, he noted the utility of incarceration: "In regard to the moral qualities, some elimination of the worst dispositions is always in progress even in the most civilized nations. Malefactors are executed, or imprisoned for long periods, so that they cannot freely transmit their bad qualities."[28] Yet he did not suppose a direct transfer of criminality from parent to offspring but more vaguely implied that this transmission may be through example. He did not promote the rigid scientific racism of his popularizers and instead cited the barbarism and savagery of slave owners, those who abused animals, and those who inflicted misery on the poor. "If the misery of our poor be caused not by the laws of nature, but by our institutions, great is our sin."[29] Such a remark betrays a deep skepticism about the humanity of affluent whites and challenges the association of Darwin with the scientific racism of the late nineteenth century. Even among European naturalists there was a multiplicity of reactions to contact with other cultures. Familiarity with Fuegians aboard the *Beagle* influenced Darwin's ideas about racial difference, illustrating how intimacy challenged generalizations and complicated imperial thinking.

ALTERED BODIES

People all over the world have altered their bodies through ornamentation such as scarification and tattooing, through modification such as foot binding, or through physical regimes such as yoga. Many of these practices evolved to mark gender difference and to enhance physical attractiveness. The line between body and spirit is porous and culturally specific. Physical practices of "Body Marking," such as tattooing and scarification, widely practiced in the eighteenth century and even emulated by European explorers, generally disappeared as contacts with European civilization, especially Christianity, deepened. One of the more durable forms of body modification, Chinese "Foot Binding," was practiced by elites for nearly four hundred years and only yielded to an amalgam of influences including Chinese feminism, Christianity, and Marxism. Spiritual practices such as "Witchcraft" might also alter bodies, giving practitioners special powers to alter other people's bodies. Fitness regimes that infused physical with spiritual well-being, such as "Yoga," also altered people's bodies. For yogis, this went way beyond toned muscles. Rooted in ancient Hindu spirituality, the practice gradually evolved into modern exercise for many. All of these practices initially shocked Europeans who attempted to eradicate some of them. They adopted others, creating synthetic fitness cultures to improve health or to mark worldliness. In the case of the latter, a transfer of knowledge between the West and India and back launched one of the world's most popular fitness regimens.

Body Marking

People in different cultures in the eighteenth century marked their bodies with tattoos or scars to indicate status or belonging. Europeans marveled at these practices, exhibiting a mixture of delight and disgust. First contacts with the peoples of Oceania in the eighteenth century stimulated curiosity on the part of British and French explorers, some of whom, like Joseph Banks (1743–1820), had themselves tattooed by Tahitians. However, the arrival of missionaries beginning in 1797 ended that phase. John Muggridge Orsmond (1784–1856) wrote in 1849 that Tahiti was the "filthy Sodom of the South Seas" and condemned tattooing along with infanticide and human sacrifice as examples of their ungodly practices.[30] Missionaries saw tattooing as a means of mutilating or defiling the body, God's creation. The French administration, in cooperation with Tahiti's King Pomare II (1782–1821), introduced law codes in 1819, 1820, and 1822 that criminalized the practice. Penalties for such "ancient evil customs" included forced labor—road building for men and cloth making for women.[31] Repeat offenders had their tattoos blotted out and were subject to corporal punishment. In 1832, a youth who tried to tattoo another boy was condemned to be flogged by that boy "whom he had tried to seduce to a heathenish custom."[32] At the same time, courts increasingly used tattoos as public shaming, to identify prostitutes, adulterers, and other criminals.

Pomare II declared himself a Christian in 1812 and promoted the destruction of Tahitian religion, including idols. Some Tahitian converts to Christianity abandoned tattooing, one historic function of which was protection from evil spirits in which they no longer believed. Some preferred to demonstrate status by wearing gender-specific European clothing in place of tattooing, while others hid their tattoos as an act of subversion.[33] Some engaged in more blatant acts of resistance including the destruction of Christian icons and the formation of independent communities in the mountains. Their tattooing came to symbolize "revolt against the existing government."[34] Once tattooing transitioned from a rejection of Christianity and a sign of heathenism to an act of treason, the state determined to eliminate it, even after the influence of Christianity declined.

In Portuguese Mozambique, Swiss Presbyterian missionaries described the prevalence of tattooing and scarification among the Tsonga. However, their arrival in the 1880s came at a time when male tattooing was already in decline, as a majority of men migrated to South Africa for work, leaving behind traditional practices. These men abandoned tattooing and scarification; their only remaining method of body marking was pierced ears. For most of the century, internal strife and the gradual encroachment of the Portuguese, along with the arrival of missionaries, destabilized Tsonga communities. Thus Europeans saw Tsonga tattooing as feminine and decorative and situated women outside modernity. According to missionary Henri Alexandre Junod (1863–1934), women adopted these "ornamental mutilations . . . to make themselves prettier . . . as they think!"[35] But in a time of transition, tattooing became a way of demonstrating belonging and was subversive of Portuguese efforts to eliminate it.[36] Lise Nsumbane, born around 1910, recalled how teachers in the mission school beat girls who cut tattoos. The girls concealed them under clothing while at school and sported them once back at home.[37]

In fact, by the early twentieth century, women incorporated images of modernity into their tattoos: watches, scissors, keys, and waistcoats. Missionary and anthropologist Emily Dora Earthy (1874–1958) recorded interviews during the 1920s with women who "have the story of their lives written on their own flesh."[38] She detailed the ritualistic bloodletting they underwent and how a complex system of meaning was represented in the tattoos as texts but also in the hierarchies of tattoo artists and the spaces in which the act was done. Women told her what the tattoos meant to them: "If we see any object which particularly pleases us, we go home and have it tatued [sic] on our bodies—but if other people envy us, and want to make incisions like ours, we do not reveal where we have seen the object—for the spirit . . . of the thing remains with her who has made a representation of it on her body."[39] Women traditionally tattooed their entire bodies, including the genital area. Because incisions were made with fish hooks and broken glass, bumpy scars accompanied tattooing. Their prominence in the abdominal area (see Figure 5.3) suggests that men stroked the scars to achieve arousal, as women attested when interviewed.[40]

By the 1930s, tattooing occurred more commonly on the limbs, face, and chest. As needles came into greater use, more intricate designs could be tattooed

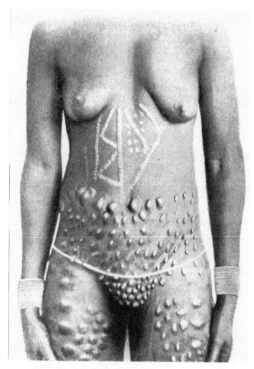

Figure 5.3. "Body Marking of a Portuguese East African Woman," 1924
Tsonga women of East Africa described their body marking practices to missionary anthropologist E. Dora Earthy who attempted to allow the women to speak for themselves in her compiled interviews.

on the face without causing significant scarring. As in Polynesia, the advent of this new tattoo technology transformed tattooing from an activity done by girls among friends to one carried out by men. Men returning from South African work camps brought notebooks full of new patterns and images that appealed to women who wanted tattoos like "the girls had over there," including images of industrial goods, like flower pots or beveled diamonds.[41] But the practice all but died out near mission stations where prohibitions were enforced, mixed-race populations formed, and some converts wanted to appear less savage.[42]

West African peoples, such as the Igbo described by Equiano, used scarification to indicate status and belonging. The instability caused by the slave trade, warfare, and the collapse of the Yoruba state meant that two dozen different ethnic and language groups intermingled, often inharmoniously, in the nineteenth century. Composite towns emerged, highly stratified and meant to recreate the communities that refugees and immigrants had left behind. The largest were Lagos and Ibadan in Nigeria. Before slavery ended in the 1890s, a majority of these town dwellers were slaves.[43] New communities were forged through marriage, particularly among elites who arranged marriages. Women combined the religious practices of their people with those of their husbands, forging new syncretic systems of belief but also undermining ethnic distinctiveness. Scarification was used to preserve distinctiveness in such circumstances. Osifekunde, an Ijebu Yoruba slave, explained its function in an 1839 interview with a French scholar: Marking "done for a fee by an artist [at] between ages six and seven, is a kind of insignia, a national badge, uniform for all individuals of the same group and different from one people to another so as to give each one a distinctive characteristic."[44] Beyond marking ethnicity, scars also indicated wealth and taste, as do all other forms of ornamentation. Those who could add color, thus mixing the genres of scarification and tattooing, were deemed more beautiful and wealthy. Indeed, the word for a poor person translated as "he who has no money to procure marks."[45] Moreover, people who did not hire a professional or whose bodies did not properly heal after the process were stigmatized as ugly or disabled.

People from Ife, a town in southwest Nigeria, were generally unmarked. In fact, popular lore told of their proud rejection of markings. "The face abhors the knife and must avoid it. The plain face condemns a marked one; I love my unmarked face. Woe unto the tattooer."[46] But assimilation into the dominant culture required elective scarification. The mother of Osundina was a slave who had converted to Christianity in 1892, so she did not mark her child. As an adult, Osundina had himself marked. Even foreigners seeking naturalization would have themselves scarred. Strangers could also be forcibly scarred. Robert Stone, a Baptist missionary stationed in Yorubaland from 1859 to 1861, described the perils: "These tell-tale marks on the face make it quite impossible for strangers to conceal their identity and slaves rarely escape to the interior on that account. . . . Gate keepers are thoroughly posted in this kind of lore and they know the nationality of every one passing through their gates."[47] Both Europeans and Yoruba thus associated scarification with ethnic, even national, identity. But, as the modern city continued to grow and its residents became increasingly distant from their cultures of origin, body markings came to be associated with rural people who lacked modernity.

Foot Binding

These examples demonstrate a general pattern whereby religious or governmental attempts to end body modifications generally failed. Only such forces of modernity as migration for work, urbanization, or global consumer culture contributed to their falling into disuse. In China, imperial governments were unsuccessful in their attempts to ban traditional practices such as foot binding that they deemed barbaric. Dating from the tenth century, the practice entailed the folding and binding of a young girl's toes and upper foot down toward the arch, thus creating a lotus shape and preventing further growth. Among elites, having a bound foot was a prerequisite for marriage and the girl's inability to walk well was part of her charm (see Figure 5.4). Eventually, British missionaries involved themselves in the cause at the behest of sixty Chinese Christian women in 1874. Their efforts resulted in the formation of the Heavenly Feet Society.

Figure 5.4.   Bound feet
Transnational activists joined Chinese feminists in decrying the ancient practice of binding the feet of Chinese girls. Despite laws against it, the practice persisted into the twentieth century.

One of the society's founders, Reverend John Macgowan (1835–1922), re-marked in *How England Saved China* (1913): "Many a savage tribe has shown barbaric ingenuity in the methods they have devised to disfigure and maim the human body, but it has been reserved for the Chinese people, with their great intelligence and with a highly developed civilization, to carry out such a system of mutilation as the world has never known in the long history of the past."[48] Admirers of Chinese civilization thus deployed stereotypes when evaluating the status of women and masked the agency of the Chinese who decried the practice. Above all, Macgowan was an evangelical. In his view, the natural intelligence of the Chinese mind was undercut by its immersion in idolatry.

In 1895, nine secular women from various countries launched the "Natural Feet Society" in Shanghai.[49] Led by Alicia Little (1845–1926), their approach was more secular and biomedical, focusing on the practice's unhygienic and deleteri-ous health effects. They attracted educated Chinese women, especially those who had been introduced to Western feminism on their travels to Europe and North America. For such feminists, Chinese masculinity was also to blame. Male preference for dainty feet contrasted the effeminacy of the scholar class against the warrior masculinity of the Qing.[50] Little's book *Intimate China* (1899) reveals ambivalences about femininity and her own status as a big-footed woman, a woman who could not be seen as a woman in China. Confounded by customs from using chopsticks to exchanging currency, Little explained that an English woman in China survives by apologizing for what she cannot understand. "And while she is in China, she must live in one constant state of being to blame."[51]Little's introspection and lack of self-confidence complicates stereotypes of self-righteous Europeans pushing an imperialist agenda.

Some activists worked independently. Qiu Jin (1875–1907), a leading opponent of foot binding, was executed in 1907 for her role in attempting to overthrow the last of the Qing emperors. Her radicalism included a passionate commitment to women's rights, which she believed could only be realized under a Western-style government. A devotee of the martial arts, Qiu left her abusive husband and their children to study in Japan in 1903. There she was introduced to a thriving feminist movement that had adopted a women's liberation program modeled on that of Western nations. She returned and became editor of a woman's magazine and principal of a girls' school. A poet, she channeled her sentiments into "Random Feelings":

> The sun and moon lusterless, heaven and earth grow dark;
> Submerged womankind—who will rescue them?
> Barrette and bracelet pawned to travel across the sea,
> Parting from kith and kin, I left my homeland.
> Freeing my bound feet, I washed away the poison of a thousand years,
> And, with agitated heart, awakened the souls of all the flowers.
> Alas, I have only a binding cloth woven of mermaid's silk,
> Half stained with blood, half with tears.[52]

Whereas some missionaries focused on rescue of the helpless victim, activists like Qiu empowered themselves and defended bodily integrity as a universal right. Using the language of rights, the liberal revolution that overthrew the Qing in 1911 made some headway against foot binding, but only under Communist rule later in the twentieth century did it finally end.

Witchcraft

Other practices proliferated, at least initially, as a way to cope with the dislocations produced by the spread of modernity. In the Gold Coast (modern Ghana), the Asante had traditionally practiced witchcraft. Yet decades of civil war, the destruction of the Asante kingdom with its state rituals to protect people from evil, and the emergence of a cash economy centered on cocoa created waves of panic that provoked widespread fear of witches. The rapid dissolution of traditional social and economic structures and the associated destabilization of matrilineal kin relations led to a dramatic increase in the demand for white magic to counter black magic. One chief who ordered the poisoning of Christians to compel them to identify witches explained: "What else could I do? The blessing has departed from our town. We work hard but never achieve anything. The fertility of the soil declines. Snails are nowhere to be seen nowadays—and they were our main trading product and the food we like most. Less children are born and more babies die. We are afflicted by many diseases. There must be witches about. Therefore I have told the fetish man to find the guilty ones."[53] The association of Christianity with witchcraft testified to the alien nature of the religion. Although its rituals bore some resemblance to witchcraft, Christian disavowal of Asante cosmology enabled it to provide sanctuary to accused witches. Several villagers from Bekwai wrote a letter to the Asante District Commissioner in 1930: "These losses in infants and mothers are the work of witches all over the country. It is regrettable to remark that the majority of the witches are refuged in the Christian churches of the Colony, notably in the Wesleyan Churches of the Colony."[54] According to the Asante, the witch's body was the site of her power, "believed to be an evil spirit found in the vagina of the witch, allowing her to attack the soul of her victims undetected, causing an endless number of ailments."[55]

Witch-finders constructed shrines, sold potions, performed rituals, and promulgated behavior codes that promised to empower their adherents against witchcraft. In 1935, the Tigare shrine promised that "Anyone who has undertaken to drink the medicine of the fetish Tigare is free from: 1. His or her cocoa farm becoming destroyed by any witchcraft; 2. His wife becoming deprived from breeding by witchcraft; 3. Becoming cursed by anyone with whom he or she has a dispute; 4. Becoming poisoned by anyone who may desire to do away with his or her life."[56] Whereas the witch might provide abortifacients, the witch-finder protected against barrenness, of the field or of the womb. Witch-finders increasingly targeted prosperous members of the community, individuals whose very prosperity set them apart from their kin group, especially once new inheritance laws pitted siblings against each other.

Meanwhile, the British in Ghana passed laws against witch-finding in 1906, 1922, and 1930, complaining of the erotic dancing and loud music at shrines and of their influence on new converts to Christianity.[57] These had little effect. Only when modern Western explanations for illness and misfortune prevailed did belief in witches and the need for witch-finding diminish. Possession might be an Asante explanation for mental illness, such as postpartum depression, prominent in accusations because of its critical location at the axes of birth, death, and sexuality. Villagers scrutinized the expectant mother, especially one caught between Western medicalization and traditional birth rituals and childrearing practices. One woman developed murderous inclinations toward her newborn and eventually all of her children and close kin. She believed it was punishment for cursing. "She thinks she is being punished by the *obosom* Tigari (whose medicine she has drunk) because she once cursed her husband's relatives to God for spoiling her plantain farm (all cursing is against Tigari's rules)."⁵⁸ Eventually, the forces of modernization, including urbanization and access to Western-influenced medical and educational systems, lessened the need for witch-finders. But among rural populations, belief in witches continued to exist.

Yoga

Traditional beliefs continued to exist in India as well, but elites adapted their yoga practice under colonialism. Yoga, infused with European calisthenics to promote greater strength and beauty, became less rooted in Hindu spirituality, especially in its sexual tantric incarnation.

When the British occupied India, they prohibited military bands made up of yogis that controlled trade routes. Ascetic trade soldiers became performers to make a living. They joined circuses and other spectaculars in India, Europe, and North America. Billed as boneless wonders who could contort themselves into impossible positions, they became associated with fire-eating sword swallowers.⁵⁹ But elite Hindu reformers in the late nineteenth century promoted yoga as serious exercise emanating from Hindu tradition and distanced themselves from ascetic buskers. The visit of Swami Vivekananda (1863–1902) to the Chicago World's Fair of 1893 signaled this transformation. His international English-language publication *Raja-Yoga* (1896) contributed to the globalizing of yoga. He emphasized the importance of breath, which he defined as "the infinite, omnipresent manifesting power of this universe."⁶⁰ Figure 5.5 depicts spiritual yoga. Tapping into this force

Figure 5.5. Morning Devotions
Originally associated with Hindu spirituality, yoga evolved into a fitness regime under the influence of British calisthenics.

required mastery over the body, which Vivekananda saw as a mechanism, borrowing from Western science, thereby diminishing yoga's association with Sanskrit physiology.[61] Those who could access this force would wield great power over others, as had all of the great spiritual leaders of the world. He associated breath with every form of power, including the steam engine and electricity.[62] He also diminished yoga's association with religion, enabling it to appeal across sectarian lines. In Britain and North America, late Victorian spiritualist movements adopted elements of Eastern practices that promoted neo-yoga, especially breathing, to achieve personal transcendence.

In India, physical culture transformed yoga into a regimen of spiritual and physical self-improvement. Do-it-yourself manuals proliferated with the rapid spread of cheap print media in the late nineteenth century. They promised initiates that they could become competent practitioners without studying under a master. Physicalist and scientific neo-yoga appealed to an increasingly fast-paced Bengal in particular, where traditional study under a master became incompatible with modern life.[63] A guidebook in Urdu by Jagannath Prashad included illustrations for postural exercises, instructions for proper breathing, and admonitions to never practice yoga in a moving train.[64] These guidebooks showed Sufi influences attesting to the internally hybrid Muslim and Hindu culture of North India. They were also increasingly severed from their association with tantra, the classic erotic version of yoga. Similarly, the use of intoxicants was discouraged, as bodily purity came to be the goal and intentional breathing was the path to self-control. A Sufi pamphlet titled *The Dervish's Secrets* (1898) recommended breathing through one nostril at a time to bring calm to tense situations, such as negotiating the purchase of a horse, elephant, or camel; searching for lost property; or learning if one was pregnant with a girl or a boy.[65]

By the twentieth century, yoga in India and the West became associated with eugenics. Western esoteric thought had a following in India, particularly through Annie Besant (1847–1933), an Irish proponent of birth control in India and ardent supporter of "positive" eugenics.[66] She believed yoga would speed up evolution by weeding out bad character traits in its adherents and thereby revive "what used to be called the Aryan Race."[67] In 1898, even Vivekananda associated yoga with evolution, preferring the term "involution" to allow for the role of the will in evolution. Self-mastery would lead not only to individual perfection but perfection across generations.[68] This was a misguided triumph of Lamarck over Darwin, the former allowing a role for the conscious production of traits to pass on. One of Vivekananda's followers, Aurobindo Ghose (1872–1950), was more explicit in 1915: "Man misuses heredity in the false conditions of his social life to transmit and perpetuate degeneracy. We must study the law of heredity, develop a science of Eugenics and use it wisely and remorselessly, with the remorseless wisdom of Nature."[69] Although spiritual in orientation, Ghose incorporated "negative" eugenics into his program, such as the elimination of the unfit through sterilization or placement in institutions.

Such ideas influenced the movement for birth control in the 1920s. Krishna Iyer (1894–1982), a physical culturist and Hatha yogi, put it bluntly in 1927:

"Will our women bring forth only healthful useful children to save our mother-land from this degeneration, from this slavery? . . . Physically deficient mothers and devitalized fathers [produce] helpless derelicts and weaklings."[70] Yoga could even improve the quality of a man's semen according to Swami Sri Yogendra (1897–1989), a materialist yogi who wanted to purge yoga of its spiritual roots. As late as 1954, American philosophy professor Raymond Piper (1888–1962) summarized the views of Chakravarti Rajagopalachari (1878–1972). "[He] gives a new social turn to the doctrine of rebirth: 'Let us be re-born purified and better than we are. If we all try thus, the world will ultimately be a world full of good men. This is the plan of Vedanta, the eugenics of souls, a scientific plan to bring into existence a better breed of men.'"[71]

Eugenics gave urgency to the physical fitness movements of the twentieth cen-tury, with a better breed of men seen as essential to nationalism. The rebuilding of Egyptian manhood, for example, and especially that of educated civil servants and young professionals, was deemed imperative to the cause of national liberation. In *The Present State of Egyptians* (1902), civil servant Muhammad Umar reflected on the prevailing view that superior physical fitness regimes were, "The reason for the rise and success of the European peoples—especially the English—who have achieved such obvious mastery through the strengthening of their muscles and the training of their bodies and their various parts."[72] In 1909, like-minded Egyptian social reformers founded the National Club for Physical Culture, de-signed to rejuvenate Egyptian manhood by revitalizing men's bodies. Of course, Egyptian nationalists did not merely mimic Western norms; they co-opted Euro-pean discourses and adapted them to native forms. They transformed the concept of *al-riyada*, an ancient Islamic tradition of mental training and physical disci-pline to reach a higher spiritual state, to instead signify sports and physical exer-cise as a means of building a manly character.[73] In 1911, an article in the nationalist *Freedom* newspaper, titled "Cultivate Your Bodies before Your Minds," promoted this new, modern Egyptian sensibility of *al-riyada*: "The nation's happiness rests on its youth. The men of tomorrow must care for their bodies properly. . . . Physical education will alter their cowardliness and indolence by raising within them a courageous and indefatigable spirit and by teaching them to love freedom and independence."[74] In a speech before the Egyptian General Assembly on February 6, 1919, the president of the National Club for Physical Culture proclaimed that the creation of sports clubs addressed both the lack of political solidarity and the lack of physical activity among Egypt's next generation of leaders. His words would prove prophetic. The following month, demonstrations by university students and urban professionals sparked the Egyptian Revolution of 1919, which swiftly spread through the countryside and eventually forced the British to grant Egypt nominal independence in 1922.[75]

Some practices of body modification adapted to the forces of modernity; most did not and were instead embraced as a marker of tradition or simply died out. Knowledge transfers initially contributed to misunderstanding the mean-ing of bodily practices, but greater familiarity undercut stereotypes about the otherness of their practitioners, illustrating how local encounters tempered generalizations. Committed to human perfectibility, activists across the globe combatted practices they saw as unhygienic while advocating those thought to improve the race.

MANAGING REPRODUCTION

Many body modification practices evolved to enhance sexual attractiveness, or even promote fertility. Imperial intervention in these practices largely substituted Western scientific knowledge about the body for more spiritual ones and individual responsibility over community regimes of self-control. But Christian epistemology also motivated interventions, especially in the case of "Infanticide," "Abortion," and "Contraception." Governments generally promoted population growth, although eugenic policies resulted in the compulsory "Sterilization" of those deemed unfit. When promoting the birth rate through conventional means failed, governments regulated their "Immigration" programs to improve their nation's vitality. To control reproduction on their own terms, many people simply continued their traditions in a more clandestine manner, demonstrating the malleability of responses and resistance strategies practiced around the world.

Infanticide

In the absence of access to birth control, women in many cultures resorted to infanticide to rid themselves of unwanted offspring. In eighteenth century Europe, lawyers believed that murdering mothers were victims of temporary insanity and should therefore not suffer the death penalty. Reformers aimed to alleviate women's desperation by creating depositories for infants, holding seducers accountable, and, by the twentieth century, educating women about their fertility. This led to an overall decline in the number of convictions for infanticide in most European countries.[76] In the colonies, women continued to commit infanticide but for reasons colonizers could not readily understand.

In slave societies, sparing the child from the experience of enslavement could be seen as an act of mercy, even as it deprived the master of control over women's bodies. In the gold mines of Spanish Barbacoas, modern Columbia, slaves also murdered children so that they would be arrested and even executed, their only way out of the mining camps. Six infanticides between 1789 and 1798 drew attention to the cruel treatment of mine workers and led to a government investigation of working conditions. Two slaves, Bernardo and Manuel Salvador, testified to the horrific conditions and even threatened that if conditions did not improve, the killings would continue. They explained that other attempts to get the attention of the authorities had all been futile.[77]

In 1789, Mónica de la Cruz murdered her four- or five-year-old daughter María Merced in the Teranguará mine with a machete. She cried, "This is what the captain has looked for with all the violence he inflicted on me!"[78] In her testimony, she repeated these words, never showing remorse but continuing to blame the conditions in the mine. She declared she would rather be executed than suffer further violence from the captain. Her lawyer argued against the death penalty, insisting that punishment should be "softer for a weak woman and for those who are rustic," and added that to "mourn bitterly the death of her little daughter" would be punishment enough.[79] She won her appeal and was sentenced instead to be sold to another owner, a victory in that she escaped the mines alive. Whether her sentence inspired the other infanticides is not known but it is noteworthy that all of the other court cases involved men.

The accused also described the despair and rage that led to the murders. Their victims were often surrogates for the male overseers they were powerless to confront.[80] Nonetheless, some expressed the same motive as Cruz, to spare the child a life in the mines. When questioned about his attack on an eight- or nine-year-old boy, Manuel Santa Fe said he wanted to "rid him of the sorrow, [and] he considered it best that the little boy did not suffer as he did, and be free [of slavery] once and for all now when he was young."[81] Although these murderers did receive capital punishment, their publicity led to an investigation and ultimately to better regulations of the treatment of enslaved mine workers. Thus infanticide as a means of taking back control over the treatment of enslaved bodies was a strategy that sometimes worked.

Infanticide was committed in some societies for religious reasons. Some West Africans, including the Igbo of Nigeria, considered the birth of twins to be inauspicious and so disposed of them. In Igbo cosmology, spiritual tricksters and animal spirits might occupy the bodies of humans. Because animals bear litters, the arrival of multiple infants cast doubt on the humanity of the twins.[82] Disagreements about the boundaries of human existence brought cultures into conflict. The birth of twins could variously be read as a curse from a deity or as a blessing from the Christian God. Igbo parents of twins were increasingly caught between these poles, some going so far as to welcome intervention to save the lives of their offspring or to deliver them to Christian missions in Onitsha. Anecdotal evidence suggests that some pregnant women left their villages, returning with one child.

Anglican missionaries decried the practice as early as 1872 in reports from the Onitsha mission station in southeast Nigeria: "It is a fact that this people idolize their children; but when God according to their wishes gives them two at a time to swell the number, they murdered them as useless things, a base ingratitude in the sight of God."[83] Shortly after their capture of Nigeria, the British passed laws against infanticide and undertook prosecutions. When one Onitsha elder was accused, Mary Elms, one of the first women missionaries in Onitsha, brokered a compromise whereby village elders collaborated to raise funds for a safe house where twins might be left anonymously. She also made home visits to pregnant women, making them aware of the alternative to infanticide and checked in on them after they gave birth. Elms published a pamphlet around 1910 celebrating this intervention and seeking funds from Anglican patrons to support her twin house and the establishment of others. Elms hired a native matron to take care of the children, and the mission accepted responsibility for their fate. Village elders pledged an ongoing contribution to the maintenance of the house, and parents depositing children made a one-time payment. Despite her best efforts, and the good health of the newborns on arrival, they all died within the first year. Only later did Elms discover that the matron, a widow of an Onitsha king, was known to be a witch who cared for the infants with her own "potions" rather than the Western childrearing practices required by Elms.[84] The Igbo saw widows as polluted and dangerous. Her appointment to manage her similarly polluted charges thus made cosmological sense. The twin house was supported by elders as a place to dispose of, not to care for, the unwanted twins.[85] Elms then appointed the widow of a leper, also outcast and polluted, yet the children died of her neglect. Eventually, however, Elms sustained the lives of some fifty twins, some of whom became integrated members of Igbo society, dispelling former prejudices against them.[86]

Abortion

The suppression of knowledge that enabled family planning characterizes the whole era of European imperialism, but women continued to discover and transmit this knowledge. In fact, explorers in the Caribbean identified plants with abortifacient properties as early as 1705, when botanist Maria Sybilla Merian (1647–1717) traveled with her daughter from Germany to Suriname. Slave and Amerindian women spoke frankly with her about the peacock flower (*Poinciana*), subversively and widely employed to deprive masters of future slaves and to spare the offspring the cruelties of enslavement.[87] The low fecundity of slave populations on the sugar islands can be attributed to the fatal conditions of sugar production, but conception may have been less of a problem than abortion. Robert Thomas, a surgeon on the islands of Saint Kitts and Nevis during the early 1780s, listed "frequent abortions" along with "free and early intercourse" as the main cause of the decrease in the slave population.[88]

This effective act of resistance alarmed Europeans especially because peacock flower did not appear to have the deleterious effects of other plant-based abortifacients. Hence, some observers believed its availability and ease of use promoted promiscuity. Janet Schaw (1731–1801), a Scottish woman who traveled the West Indies in the 1770s, denounced the "young black wenches [who] lay themselves out for white lovers."[89] She claimed that to avoid having children interrupt their pleasure, "they have certain herbs and medicines that free them from such an incumbrance."[90] Abortion became associated with the lasciviousness of the tropics throughout the Americas. In 1799, German botanist Alexander von Humboldt (1769–1859) embarked on a voyage to study the plants along the Orinoco River in Venezuela. In his remarks on the natives of the region, Humboldt chided the young wives who averted motherhood with their "guilty practice . . . of preventing pregnancy by the use of deleterious herbs."[91]

Yet knowledge of the peacock flower, let alone its cultivation or use, does not seem to have spread to Europe in the great Columbian Exchange of animals, plants, people, and culture between the Old World and the New World. Western medicine already had other methods to induce abortion, most more interventionist. The preferred method of the eighteenth century was known as "the hand," whereby the midwife or doctor inserted his hand into the uterus and punctured the placenta.[92] Other methods included bloodletting, toxic douches, vigorous exercise, and horseback rides. These methods usually required the assistance of someone else, preventing the self-reliance and secrecy of herbal methods. This nontransference of biological exchange deprived European women of one means of abortion, ensuring their dependence on male healthcare practitioners or increasingly clandestine midwives.

Midwives helped women procure abortions legally in the Ottoman Empire as late as 1838, although local regulations such as those in the capital Istanbul came into effect earlier. In 1827, two Jewish midwives, one known as the "bloodstained midwife," were exiled for selling abortifacients.[93] Pharmacies had already been prohibited from selling plants that could induce abortion. Islamic law ordinarily did not regulate women's bodies, seeing them as adjunct to the family and under the authority of patriarchs. As long as husbands agreed, women could abort pregnancies until the era of reform from 1839 to 1876 known as the *Tanzimat* ushered in the modern state. The *Tanzimat* criminal code and other reforms were influenced by the French and Western jurisprudence. Regulating women's bodies as a way of monitoring population growth led to provisions for women's healthcare and restrictions on abortion. Penalties included two years hard labor for those who performed an abortion. A provider of tools or drugs that caused abortion was subject to a two-year prison sentence.[94] As part of a general overhaul of Ottoman administration, more highly regulated certifications ensured that midwives only delivered babies, but they were prohibited from using forceps because of their possible use for inducing abortion. Regulators also curbed access to certain pharmaceuticals with abortifacient uses such as "henna, alum, ammonia, asphodel roots, . . . citric acid or lemonade powder, and terracotta or dirt."[95]

The first class for midwives occurred in Istanbul in 1842 and was taught by European women, a French and an Austrian, recruited for their superior knowledge of modern Western obstetrics.[96] By 1845, thirty-six women earned their certificates, twenty-six Christians and ten Muslims. They were required to pledge before their respective religious officiates that they would not perform abortions. This low number of certificate holders suggests that many midwives, especially Jewish midwives, continued to practice as they always had, only now in violation of the law.[97] To prevent fraudulent credentials, police confiscated and destroyed the certificates of deceased midwives.[98] In the late nineteenth century, surveillance mechanisms proliferated, but so did the number of foreign midwives whose activities escaped detection, despite a law that penalized anyone who had knowledge of an abortion but failed to report it. One German woman doctor even ran

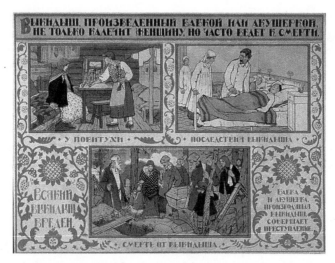

Figure 5.6.   Promoting Legal Abortion in the Soviet Union
The Soviet Union legalized abortion in 1920. This poster urges women to forego the use of granny midwives in favor of modern medical establishments run by men.

an abortion clinic in Istanbul from 1900 to 1905. Her diplomatic immunity delayed her extradition.[99]

Doctors generally enjoyed a wider scope of action—and opinion—than midwives. Some believed that abortion might be necessary to save a mother's life. Figure 5.6 illustrates the view that modern methods were superior to traditional ones that ended the mother's life. Aziz Idris Bey (1840–1878), a military physician, wrote that women who chose to have abortions lacked "shame and good manners" although allowing that "under certain circumstances, abortion is both legitimate and sometimes necessary. That is to say, the womb can have problems as opposed to its natural course, and pregnancy can put the mother's life into danger during delivery."[100] Later reformers used antiabortion sympathies to draw attention to the evils of polygamy and concubinage, explaining that women who resorted to abortion were often victims of rivalry among other wives and of "lustful" and "cowardly" men.[101] According to Namik Kemal (1840–1888), writing in 1872, "In our country, abortion is also performed due to some contemptible men who are indulged both in their wives' aggression, and their own lust. These men take concubines in secrecy, and after they impregnate them, they leave the concubines and their children to the villainy of their wives."[102] Kemal's views earned him exile. He would later return as one of the Young Turks who modernized Turkey fully after World War I. Another reformer, the secularist Salahaddin Asim, went further in his text *On the Condition of Women in Ottoman Society* (1910). He blamed the seclusion of women as a cause of abortion because secluded women supposedly preferred lesbianism. "The greatest foe of a lesbian is the child. Sometimes this animosity reaches such a degree that if pregnant, a lesbian or a woman who would like to become a lesbian tries to abort her baby, or she gives up completely the disciplining of and caring for children. . . . Abortion and refraining from birth giving harms our women, our nation, and our race at the same time."[103] Women's bodies as a resource for the nation could be marshalled to advance the perfectibility and competitiveness of the race. The idea that women might exercise autonomous control over their bodies is still contested in some cultures.

Contraception

Fears about the impact of unchecked population growth on environmental resources and on the quality of life inspired some to promote fertility control. Well into the twentieth century, proponents of contraception were known as Malthusians after eighteenth-century political economist Thomas Malthus (1766–1834). Malthus doubted human progress because of one inexorable fact: due to the universal passion to procreate, human population was bound to increase geometrically while food supply would only increase arithmetically. Malthus deduced that competition over scarce resources would result in human misery and conflict until disease, wars, and famine eliminated the surplus population. His theory on the balance of nature became known in the nineteenth century as the Malthusian nightmare of catastrophic overpopulation. Anticipating Darwin, whose theory of natural selection he influenced, Malthus credited scarcity with producing higher intelligence in northern climates: "In those countries where nature is the most redundant in spontaneous produce, the inhabitants will not be found the most remarkable for acuteness of intellect. Necessity has been with great truth called the mother of invention. Some of the noblest exertions of the human mind have been set in motion by the necessity of satisfying the wants of the body."[104] Clever and robust Europeans, desperate for resources, would then naturally make use of the human and natural resources of the Southern Hemisphere until increasingly more devastating catastrophes would check population on a global scale. Among their innovations would be contraception.

Neo-Malthusians accepted that the Malthusian nightmare had occurred in the form of famines and disease outbreaks and would continue to occur unless population growth was checked. In India, where census taking as early as 1881 revealed the rate of population growth, mathematician Raghunath Karve (1882–1953) promoted contraception through literature and the distribution of birth control devices in 1921. Although there were no laws prohibiting contraception, the subject was sufficiently controversial that Karve was dismissed from his post at Wilson College in Bombay.[105] Multiple societies nonetheless formed to promote birth control. They gradually connected to the international movement associated with Margaret Sanger (1879–1966), the American founder of Planned Parenthood. However, opposition among Catholics and Hindus was galvanized by Mahatma Gandhi's (1869–1948) condemnation of birth control: sex was reserved only for procreation and should otherwise be avoided. In 1925, Gandhi wrote in his *Young India* weekly journal that, "It is still worse for a person to indulge his animal passions and escape the consequences of his acts."[106] At the 1931 meeting of the All India Women's Conference, the religiously orthodox opposed birth control, but so did some liberal activists who did not want to stand against Gandhi. The group could only agree to focus on improving the health of women and children, with reproductive knowledge a subset of that.[107]

That same year, renowned German sexologist Magnus Hirschfeld (1868–1935) visited India as part of a world tour to promote his work at the Institute for Sexual Science in Berlin. An early champion of sexual liberation, including free love, birth control, and gay rights, Hirschfeld lauded India as the birthplace of sexology, with the *Kama Sutra* as its original text. Hirschfeld tailored his lectures to his audience, ranging from "Sex Pathology" at Calcutta's Indian Medical Association, to "Homosexuality, Inborn or Acquired?" at the Indian Psychoanalytic Society, to "Love, Sex, and Marriage" for the general public at the Taj Hotel in Bombay.[108] These seminars were popular with India's emerging middle class who believed that the adoption of Western science was the key to India's modernization and eventual independence. One letter to the *Bombay Chronicle* noted the overflow crowds and called for larger venues so that as many people as possible could take advantage of them. "In view of the fact that problems like those of sexual reforms and Birth-Control are little or hardly discussed in this city or rather country of ours, it will be no small gain to us, if we are enabled to drink deep into the cup of this branch of human knowledge by the good office of this eminent authority of Germany."[109]

Hirschfeld's tour galvanized Indian sexologists who were already promoting sexology and eugenics as the means of developing a robust Indian middle class. Their main concern was to control the sexuality of the single young people migrating into India's fast-growing cities. Narayan Phadke's (1894–1978) widely read text, *Sex Problem in India* (1927), urged sexual discipline as the way to revitalize a "declining race" for "who could deny that physical strength and military power will be for us an indispensable instrument to keep [self-rule] after it is won?"[110] In Phadke's explicitly anticolonial merger of traditional Indian asceticism with modern scientific sexology, the propagation of the most optimal semen was central to building an independent India.[111]

With Hirschfeld and Phadke opening up public debate, activists could open clinics. Dr. A. P. Pillay (1890–1956) opened clinics in Bombay's mill sector. In smaller towns, laywomen spread knowledge of birth control. In Budaon, Olive Glasgow Titus (1884–1967) described the many women who "come to me begging me to tell them something or to give them something that would release them from this slavery."[112] Sanger and her British counterpart Marie Stopes (1880–1958) promoted contraception in India in the 1930s through the magazine *Marriage Hygiene*. Stopes recommended the insertion of cotton waste, soaked in cooking oil, into the vagina as a barrier method. They also toured for years, addressing women's groups and even meeting with Gandhi.

Sanger's focus on poor women worldwide, as well as her embrace of eugenics, implicated birth control in racial politics, particularly in racially divided societies like the United States and South Africa. The Race Welfare Society of Johannesburg (RWS) and the Mothers' Clinic Committee of Cape Town (MCC) opened clinics in 1932. The RWS was determined to limit poor white women's fertility to assure that the white race was fit, while the MCC was a feminist organization dedicated to women's empowerment. The latter attracted more clients. They distributed the diaphragm, also known as the "Dutch cap," to qualifying women.[113] These whites-only clinics resembled those in the poor neighborhoods of London, despite the fact that South Africa's overcrowded slums were racially integrated. Although the number of clients was only in the hundreds, a decline in the birth rate resulted, causing the RWS concern. Clinics were only supposed to serve married mothers of many poor children, but they likely attracted a much broader spectrum of women. A member of the RWS detailed this concern in 1937: "Bearing in mind the current apprehension as to unduly falling birth rates, and the close scrutiny of [birth control] work that may result, I think we should be particularly careful that the work being done at our Clinic can be justified in detail on eugenic grounds, and is not open to a charge that the Clinic functions blindly without regard to considerations of National Welfare."[114] No birth control advocate wanted to be seen as promoting immorality, or worse, a decline in the birth rate of healthy white babies. A focus on the degeneracy of poor whites thus justified limiting their reproduction.

Johannesburg's working women were primarily factory workers who had migrated with their families to the city after the Depression. Records for the clinics indicate that the level of repeat visits fluctuated, suggesting that women may have attempted birth control but not followed through. Use of the diaphragm required advanced planning and access to privacy and water. None of this was possible in the slums, where as many as nine people might share a room.[115] Moreover husbands may not have been accommodating. Dr. Dorothea Douglas-Henry described her work in Cape Town clinics during the 1940s: "You know, one knew of women being beaten up because their husbands found that they had a cap hidden away somewhere they'd never told about."[116] In a patient ledger from the 1930s, "Husband destroyed [contraceptive] appliances and Mother had three children in three successive years, followed by mental breakdown," but then somehow managed to return to the clinic and had no more children.[117] Even a nurse at the RWS clinic insisted that "the wife should have the right to decide" when a husband came to the clinic demanding that it withhold contraception from his wife in 1939.[118] Feminists who intervened in the sphere of intimate life decried male control of women's bodies whether it be on the part of the husband or the state.

Sterilization

Empowering women to choose between different options for fertility control required education and a recognition of their competency. In the United States, where eugenics was most widely practiced, criminals, alcoholics, and the mentally disabled were deemed incompetent to make decisions about their bodies and sterilized without their consent. In the colonies, however, dependence on native labor undercut eugenicist demands to rid populations of the unfit.

The president of the British Medical Association in Kenya called for a full eugenics program in 1931, resigned to the fact that "native backwardness could never be made to disappear under the mere trappings of civilization."[119] Sterilization of the unfit would be required to achieve this goal. To determine fitness, Kenyan doctors counted brain cells and measured brain capacity among whites and blacks. Henry Laing Gordon (1865–1947), the leading eugenicist in Kenya, believed that the study of Africans, largely uncontaminated by civilization, would reveal the inborn mind. In 1933, he formed the Race Improvement Society dedicated to end the "breeding of BAD HUMAN STOCK" and promote the birth rate of "our middle classes."[120] He warned of the imminent peril to the fittest. "We are developing a *poor white group*, a *submerged Asiatic group*, and a *huge African group* of alarming potentialities."[121] He proposed further limiting immigration to pure British stock, "not retired breeders from Anglo-India or elsewhere."[122] Poor whites became menaces to society, as he attested to in one murder case in which a white man was hanged for murdering two women. He argued that the accused could not be held accountable and should have never been born in the first place, placing blame on a society that refused to impede the proliferation of idiocy.

But Gordon's major preoccupation centered on East Africans. By studying convicts, he categorized the degrees of feeble-mindedness and idiocy known as amentia. The many grades made detection of the highest functioning aments difficult. High-functioning aments in the native milieu were impossible to detect. Only when they transitioned into civilized life through schooling or employment did their abnormalities manifest. They might perform well enough on intelligence tests, but their social functioning appeared abnormal. Dr. Francis Vint (1897–unknown) obtained the brains of hundreds of cadavers from the Nairobi hospital and weighed them. He correlated brain weight with intelligence and claimed to have proven that the brain of the average native weighed five ounces less than that of the European. Vint therefore concluded that the adult African possessed the intelligence of a seven- or eight-year-old European boy.[123] In publicizing these findings, Gordon added that the divergence in brain size happened in adolescence. The native child tended to be a "bright, malleable, nice little fellow, often—as one says—quick in the uptake" but "falls away" in adolescence, quite the opposite of the European.[124] When Gordon presented these findings to the British Eugenics Society in London in 1934, some colleagues expressed skepticism, among them Julian Huxley (1894–1963), the leading social Darwinist of that era. The African Research Survey group criticized his findings. By that time, brain measurements and intelligence tests were under fire. Critics pointed out that his results were too straightforward, itself a cause for suspicion of his methods. Moreover, even some eugenicists worried over the uses to which such spurious research might be put.

Even in Germany, eugenicists occupied a broad spectrum of opinion throughout the 1920s; the diversity of their views hardly constituted a coherent movement. A preoccupation with heredity and the impulse to intervene in human reproduction may have been common to them, but how best to achieve this aim was hotly contested, some advocating negative and some positive eugenics.[125] Nazi policies merged the two approaches by promoting the birth rate of fit populations while simultaneously implementing sterilization programs, resulting in nearly 400,000 sterilizations.[126] Although most were German, French colonial troops stationed in Germany, residents of Germany's former African empire, and their mixed-race offspring were also targets. The so-called Rhineland bastards were the progeny of unions between German women and French colonial troops who occupied the Rhineland after Germany's defeat in World War I. A 1933 study of twenty-seven such children variously identified as "Moroccan" or "Annamese," in reality Afro-German and Asian-German, revealed a higher than average incidence of childhood psychoses and lower than average school performances, enough to indict racial mixing. The professor who undertook the study, Wolfgang Abel (1905–1997), was later tasked with "carrying out the discreet sterilization of the Rhineland bastards."[127]

Not all Afro-Germans were "Rhineland bastards." Immigrants from Germany's colonies in Africa had enjoyed German citizenship since the 1890s. But with the rise of the Nazis, they not only lost their rights but so did their children. Doris Reiprich (b. 1918), whose father was from Cameroon and her mother from Germany, recalled a course on race in 1935 when she was in middle school in which students were taught that "God made all whites and Blacks, half-breeds come from the Devil. Half-breeds can only inherit the bad characteristics of both races."[128] Such views underpinned the forced sterilization recalled by Reiprich's sister Erika Ngambi ul Kuo (b. 1915). "Many colored women were sterilized. Gerda, Hanna . . . Christel's mother hid her in a convent near Cologne. They got her out of there and sterilized her too. Our nephew also. After the sterilization they sent him right home; they didn't even allow him to rest."[129] Because Nazis needed their labor, they did not target Afro-Germans as a group for extermination. They could achieve their goal of racial purity by merely sterilizing them, men as well as women.

Immigration

Although racial fitness motivated population management policies in many countries, some population experts thought beyond the boundaries of their individual nations. Worry about the growth of the earth's population led some demographers to analyze the relationship between the birth rate and immigration. In 1894, the first president of the Malthusian League, Charles Robert Drysdale (1829–1907), asserted that, "Perhaps no other single cause has done more to prevent ordinary people from recognizing the necessity for a lower birth-rate than the fact of our colonial possessions."[130] The fantasy of empty land out there somewhere permitted governments and individuals alike to doubt claims about the perils of overpopulation.

To explore these issues, Margaret Sanger convened a population conference in Geneva in 1927. Geographer Marcel Aurousseau (1891–1983) wrote to the Australian High Commission in London: "This conference is deeply interested in the existence of great areas which are unoccupied or occupied by backward races and in the general questions of migration."[131] Yet these lands could not be made available to just anyone. Geographer John Walter Gregory (1864–1932) defended Australia's racially exclusive immigration policy at the same conference: "Every nation has the right to protect itself from deterioration by racial intermixture. Australia is biologically well supported in its claim to restrict immigration to the white race, and it would no doubt prefer to maintain its present British racial solidarity, but immigrants from Southern and Eastern Europe cannot be excluded as belonging to a different race."[132] Malthusians remained convinced that overpopulation was a problem even after the devastating death tolls of World War I. But they differed on what should be done to redistribute populations to lands that could better support them. Such remarks implied that Anglo-Saxon purity could not be reasonably maintained, so other Europeans, broadly defined, were admitted to whiteness.

However, with nationalism dominating discussions of immigration and population, few delegates thought globally. The French government was particularly concerned about its metropolitan birthrate, which lagged significantly behind that of Britain and Germany, its principal rivals for European and international dominance. Journalists, novelists, and demographers alike noted that French settlers living in its colonies bore more children. French women in Algeria bore thirty-seven children per thousand, compared to twenty-six in the metropole, so fears of depopulation could be allayed by promoting settlements overseas.[133] In the French colony of Madagascar, this also translated into promoting the birthrate of the native Merina, deemed by Governor Joseph Simon Gallieni (1849–1916) to be the superior race among the island's peoples. Their work ethic and above all their labor were deemed essential to creating the economic infrastructure that would entice settlers.[134] But their immigration to France unsettled white supremacy. After World War I, labor needs could only be met by the importation of foreign workers. But anxious pronatalists feared the hybridization of the French race due to the arrival of male immigrants with "excess virility."[135] Forced to accept "Kabyle street sweepers, Annamese stokers, Negro dockers, and Chinese laborers" in the immediate aftermath of the war, the National Alliance for the Increase of the French Population urged their replacement by "our usual immigrants, the Italians and the Spaniards."[136] Likened to a blood transfusion, these virile Catholic immigrants could marry French women and evolve into proper French families. But only those without "physiological flaws" should be selected. The blood must be compatible. "There exist actual blood types and one cannot, without great danger, mix the blood of different and *incompatible* groups."[137] The Alliance cited the United States to warn of the dangers of miscegenation.

In contrast to the anemic French, Southern Europeans still preserved traditional family values and fecundity. Feminism, that "individualist virus," was less influential there.[138] Southern Europe constituted an intermediate zone between the sterility of Northern Europe and the animal sexuality of Africa. Such whites would need to band together to combat the "Yellow Peril" seen in larger family sizes throughout Asia and in diasporic Asian communities worldwide.[139] Moreover, Greeks, Levantines, and Berbers were rejected as "second-rate immigrants that no country is actively seeking out."[140] Demographer Jacques Bertillon (1851–1922) concluded that "the most ignorant countries are also the most fecund ones."[141]

Perceiving that Europe would be submerged in a sea of nonwhites, Malthusian came to be a term of contempt for the promoters of birth control. Journalist Ludovic Naudeau (1872–1949) concluded that the "old, solitary, hunched up Malthusian" would "sadly vegetate" in the city with no one left to work his farm, eventually dying as a "vanquished man," the price for a life of egotistical indulgence and material pleasure.[142] Advanced civilizations limited family size to their detriment. Demographers supposed that once assimilated to Frenchness, these hybrid families would adopt French birth spacing and similarly fail to increase. Beyond the promotion of immigration, such concerns resulted in laws banning abortion and contraception and in incentive programs to reward white fecundity. French pronatalists introduced incentives for women including Medals for Mothers in 1920 where mothers of ten children earned a gold medal, eight children merited the silver, and five the bronze. In Fascist Italy, mothers of fourteen not only received the gold but also got to meet the dictator Benito Mussolini (1883–1945).[143] More substantial welfare programs provided stipends to white families in proportion to the numbers of children.

Out of these race-based policies, the welfare state emerged to support poor families regardless of race once negative eugenics disappeared from official policy after World War II. Nonetheless, access to contraception and abortion remains contested in many places, still more tolerated when matters of health rather than personal choice are at stake and still pivoting on mandates to practice individual self-control. Population as an index of national glory would always prove problematic. Populations could never be large enough or pure enough. They required large-scale management by the state, yet individual behavior could be nearly impossible to control. While governments debated abstractions like immigration policy, embodied individuals provided health care to other embodied individuals.

MANAGING ILLNESS AND HEALTH

Missionaries, soldiers, government officials, and settlers interacted with colonized people at the level of the body, bringing with them medical knowledge and interventions geared to producing greater conformity to Western sex and gender norms while also improving disease and longevity rates. Western caregivers also discovered medical remedies among native populations, brought them home, and improved on them. The transfer of knowledge therefore went both ways. The colonized—particularly the elite—often adopted Western medicine,

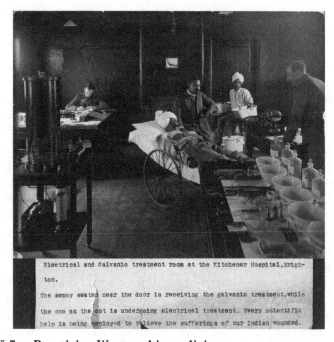

Figure 5.7. Practicing Western biomedicine
Opportunities for professional advancement in the medical field attracted Asians and Africans into medical careers.

even becoming practitioners (see Figure 5.7), although some interventions conflicted with traditional practices and understandings. Western practitioners combined multiple modalities when "Treating the Body." Nonetheless, basic conceptions of the body differed widely, bringing cultures into conflict. "Treating the Baby" was particularly contested because it pivoted on matters private—marital sexuality—and matters public: the rate of population growth. Childrearing practices were also implicated in "Treating the Mind," as Western mental health practitioners increasingly focused on infancy and childhood as critical in the formation of personality. Some local people actively sought Western healthcare, some resisted it. In most cases, people adopted Western modalities as just one among many treatment options, thus subtly subverting European efforts to manage their intimate lives.

Treating the Body

Benevolent imperialists saw their role quite differently from that of the soldier, businessman, or government official. Missionaries, and then secular medical organizations, imbued the colonized world with Western knowledge and skills, often with remarkable results. Early missionaries brought Western medicine to Asia, Africa, and other regions of the colonized world. Often they recognized only the superiority of Western practices. But knowledge transfers eventually went in multiple directions.

Two doctors, one American and one British, founded the Medical Missionary Society in 1838 with the explicit aim of bringing Western biomedicine to China. They coordinated Protestant medical mission work for the better part of the century. They only supported the work of trained professionals, by definition men, and generally scorned traditional Chinese healing. But Catholic nuns, whose gender as well as belief in divine intercession and miraculous cures built a bridge to native practices, provided a syncretic approach to healthcare. Assunta Pallotta (1878–1905), an Italian nun, worked in China in 1904–1905 at an orphanage that cared for children with typhus in the village of Dongergou in Shanxi. As the daughter of a poor farming family in central Italy, she had no dowry and was only accepted into the convent through connections. Because she entered poor, she was consigned to menial work. Even in China, she did laundry and worked in the kitchen alongside Chinese women. She learned a bit of Chinese from them, including how to say the rosary prayer. The orphanage was run by the Order of Chinese Virgins until the missionary nuns arrived from Italy and France. When Pallotta and three other nuns contracted typhus, a Chinese healer prescribed herbal remedies. When Pallotta finally succumbed, the seven missionary nuns and three women of the Order of Chinese Virgins who attended her attested to a sweet fragrance filling the room at the moment of her expiration.[144] The scent allegedly filled the village as her funeral procession passed through, attracting more and more followers, and only abated three days after her interment. Miraculous fragrance upon death was also a phenomenon known in Chinese Buddhism, thus local villagers had a framework for interpreting the event. Chinese Catholic priests confirmed the miracle. Eight years later, her body was disinterred and found to be well-preserved, further proof of her holiness. A healing cult developed around her. Scraps of her clothing were applied to the wounds of pilgrims who visited the village. After praying to Pallotta, taking iron pills, and drinking the liquid from boiled fragments of her coffin, their wounds healed. The mother superior of the convent printed cards with her image alongside a prayer and distributed them to pilgrims. When healed, they reported their stories that were then reprinted in Franciscan newsletters. Stories of Pallotta's healing powers surfaced in Syria, Tunisia, India, France, and the United States.[145]

Sufferers reported combining all forms of Western and Chinese medicine with supernatural practices to receive healing, showing the degree to which medical practice in some areas of China had become thoroughly hybrid. In 1923, a Chinese Virgin took her five-year-old niece, stricken blind by the swelling from a tumor on her neck, to the nun's clinic, a traditional Chinese healer, a government hospital, and a Protestant clinic: all to no avail. They then sought the supernatural help of martyrs from the Boxer Rebellion (1899–1901) who were also rumored to leave a sweet fragrance after they died. The girl was cured only when she wore a medal with Pallotta's image and prayed "Aunty Maria Assunta have mercy on me."[146] Faith healing through the use of relics was so common among the Chinese that even non-Catholics sought healing from Pallotta. Where Western beliefs coincided with the beliefs of local people, greater possibilities for cross-cultural exchange existed. Bodies could be healed and accounts of people actively seeking a wide range of interventions attests to their agency, but people living in colonies were more often compelled to encounter Western health care.

In British Botswana, mining companies required medical examination of Tswana men who sought employment in the gold and diamond mines. Missionary doctors, rather than state doctors, conducted the examinations, relying on mining company largesse: the more examinations the doctors completed, the more funds they earned. For greater efficiency, they examined men in groups, either naked to the waist or totally naked. The men raised their arms and turned in a circle for a simple visual check. Up to half might be dismissed for "Defective Development" generally described as: "Long, thin, young natives, whose chests and arms aren't developed in proportion to the legs."[147] Those who passed might then have their lungs inspected. Mololokane Makati recalled his first examination in 1937: "The white doctors, they just put their machines on our bodies so they were just checking from my body to see if I was healthy, but I don't know what diseases actually they were looking for . . . they were checking all things but mostly the lungs to see whether my breath was normal or what."[148] The word for breath in Tswana, *mowa*, also referred to the soul or the inner essence of the person. Tswana people such as Makati assigned *mowa* meaning beyond mere lung function. Similarly, they perceived their bodies as holistic entities. If they were fit for reproduction, they were fit for work, so they puzzled at European examinations of isolated body functions for the performance of discrete tasks.

Dr. Donald MacRae, Botswana's Principal Medical Officer in 1920, concluded that civilization had a deleterious impact on their otherwise admirable physiques, noting that the Tswana were "physically, not . . . what they were in the old days. Contact with civilisation has not benefited them in this respect, but even so in physique, as in endurance and intelligence, they are far from contemptible."[149] Ten years later, their condition had apparently degenerated further to the point where they compared unfavorably to other South African ethnic groups such as the Zulu and Xhosa. Doctors urged them to regain their physical fitness for the "economic advancement of their Territory."[150] Yet over the following decade, between 10 percent and 20 percent of all applicants for mine work were deemed unfit. By 1941, only 55 percent were deemed fit enough for military service.[151] Local chiefs blamed mine work and civilization. One explained, "In our childhood days there was no civilisation and such a disease was not known amongst us."[152] Seasonal migration to the mines meant that tuberculosis contracted there spread to the rural population as well. Recurrent drought and failed crop harvests caused malnutrition and scurvy. Modernization destroyed the admirable physiques of Tswana men and therefore their capacity for performing the manly roles required of them in the mines or by the military.

Treating the Baby

Health care workers had to combat the forces of tradition as well as modernity. Some advocated early childhood intervention before the impact of either could be irreversible. The child often stood at the nexus between the intimate lives of parents and the mandate of progress. In the eighteenth century, the poor treatment of children, especially by slave masters, ignited public opinion even among those who were not explicitly in support of abolition. Benevolent imperialists later identified the helpless child at home and abroad as in need of rescue from practices that they believed imperiled his or her health. Caring for the child inspired a wide variety of crusades in Europe and in the colonies.

During her ten-year stay in Brazil, Adèle Toussaint-Samson (1826–1911) documented her broad diversity of experiences. Living in Rio with her husband on business in the 1850s, she wrote primarily about the city where she daily observed the physical brutality to which slaves were subjected. When she visited a plantation, she expressed shock and pity at the wretched state of the children. "The little darkies of three or four years, entirely naked, were returning with their rations of *feijoes*, which their delicate stomachs could hardly digest; also did they nearly all have large stomachs, enormous heads, and lank arms and legs,—in short, all the signs of the rickets. It caused pity to see them; and I never understood, from a speculative stand-point even, that these merchants of human flesh did not take better care of their merchandise."[153] Disgust at the physical deformities of slaves punctuates her travel narrative, and in every case she attributed it to the cruelties of the slave system itself. But she also indicted childrearing practices in communities of color as another cause of deformity. Because mothers strapped their small children about their waists, they became hunched over even as their children became bow-legged.[154] By the mid-nineteenth century, European experts on infant care recommended greater separation between the bodies of mother and child. Women in many agricultural societies wore their small children by means of slings to be able to keep track of them while they worked but also to nurture them. This latter function was increasingly condemned by Europeans as a cause of poor individuation and a sign of a primitive family system.

Into the twentieth century, concerns about disparities in infant mortality between colonizing and colonized countries motivated benevolent imperialism, leading to global adoption of Western approaches to baby care (see Figure 5.8). "The startling revelations of vital statistics have aroused practically every nation to the tremendous waste which the appalling death rate of children under 5 years of age imposes upon the resources of the world," according to a US health officer in the Philippines in 1913.[155] After focusing energies on diseases that affected settlers, healthcare workers turned their attention to native populations, especially children. Governor General Leonard Wood (1860–1927) called a special conference in 1921 to address the problem. Elite Americans and Filipinos blamed "superstitious and faulty maternity practices based on the ignorance of the people."[156]

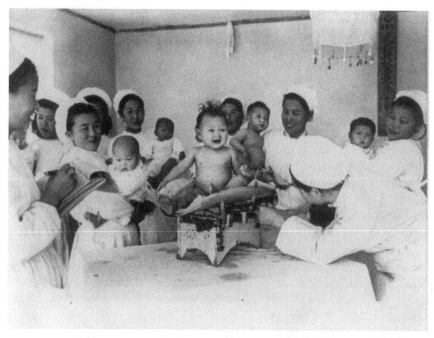

Figure 5.8. Modern baby care
Modern hospitals introduced biomedical baby care and modern nursing throughout the world, including nations like Korea that were not under direct Western
control.

These included breastfeeding the child as soon as he cried whether or not he was
hungry; rocking or dancing him to sleep; and sharing a sleeping space with him.
In addition to fostering "diseases of the digestive apparatus," these practices would
make him "nervous and spoiled."[157] In 1922, Filipino Dr. Fernando Calderon
(1866–1948) identified one "source of danger to the small children is the bad
custom common among our people of kissing the children."[158] Allowing children to kiss religious statues or crosses was also singled out as a means of spreading disease. US health workers distributed pamphlets with easy to follow feeding,
diapering, and sleeping schedules. Another precautionary measure, segregating
small children from the world of adults, meant that they would not be able to
participate in evening celebrations that would keep them up too late and put
them in contact with too many people. All of these measures appealed to more
elite Filipino families, reflecting the degree to which Western civilization was
equated to modernity, which meant regimentation and sanitation.

Proximity to adults was identified as one source of illness in children; lessening physical contact also implied diminished breastfeeding. Not only did scien-
tifically minded parenting experts see the practice of breastfeeding toddlers as
less healthy, it also impeded the birth rate. Where custom prevented intercourse

between husband and wife during the two-to-three years of breastfeeding, family size was limited. For example, extended periods of breastfeeding among sub-Saharan Africans confounded Europeans, some of whom concluded that postpartum abstinence led to abortion, adultery, and polygamy. Belgian concerns about the birth rate prompted European matrons to intervene in Congo. Félicie Vandenperre (1857–1928) opened the Drops of Milk lactation league in 1912, first in Brussels and then Kisantu. However, its services only caught on in the 1920s when colonial personnel regarded population decline with growing concern. In her 1926 addresses, Vandenperre urged intervention in African birth-spacing practices. "Without black labor, our colony would never be able to send to Europe the wealth buried in its soil. . . . To protect the child in the Congo is a duty, not only of altruism, but of patriotism."[159] In cooperation with the Catholic Church, the league launched a "crusade to combat the prejudices that separate the spouses."[160] At the Baudoinville mission station, the league saw successes where nuns raised girls. Convincing women to wean sooner required the substitution of cow and soy milk, stimulating economic growth in these areas. The early introduction of solid foods enabled women to return to work and to intercourse sooner. The league then increased its efforts around mining camps. At Union Minière, women from the league gave women at the camps food rations and other gifts in exchange for participation in the program. League women did not include vegetables in the rations so as to compel recipients to grow their own. The camps offered schooling, medical care, and even bride price to entice male miners to bring their families. After two decades, the program could boast success. In 1925, there were 41 children per 100 women in the camps; twenty years later, there were 136 children for every 100 women. Other measures of the program's success included birth weight and growth rate curves similar to European children, lower rates of infant and maternal mortality, and the prevalence of monogamy.[161]

In addition to such direct methods, the league also published "Baby in the Bush" pamphlets in the 1930s.[162] They prescribed rigorous three-hour feeding schedules and giving the infant his own bed to train him to sleep through the night. White women urged Congolese women not to spoil children, to let them cry so they would learn to deal with frustration. "Not undergoing any frustration, he lives in a climate of absolute security."[163] They advised pregnant women to avoid African medicine women and to give birth in a hospital instead. In short, European norms in these pamphlets prevailed in everything from infant care to appearance and interior decoration. Unsurprisingly, only middle-class Congolese women adopted European family norms, according to a 1950 study. Among other things, they demonstrated their European orientation by feeding their children sugared powder milk substitutes.[164] Those women who resisted the league's precepts defended tradition: "We can't let the child cry like the whites."[165] In their view, isolating the child from the mother's body disrupted fertility patterns and marriage practices in addition to traumatizing the child itself.

Women's resistance to or adoption of European child-rearing practices illustrates the multiple responses to imperialism and the ways in which intimate bodily experiences like breastfeeding became politicized.

Treating the Mind

The child's trauma could produce psychotic behavior. Some advocates of modern baby care believed that proper individuation was the goal of childrearing. The absence of proper individuation created mental and social problems. Western theories of mental health, especially with the influence of psychoanalysis, emphasized the connection between baby care and individuation, but, in the colonies, treatment seldom went beyond confinement in an institution.

In sub-Saharan Africa, British officials accepted that care for the insane was a part of the kinship system and that madness was a culturally relative term.[166] Efforts at institutional care were therefore limited and often left to missionaries. Meanwhile, psychiatrists justified nonintervention, even when desired by the individual or his family, by claiming not to understand the African mind. They associated idiocy with cultural practices like prolonged breastfeeding and thus generally did not offer treatment to adults. But they did order confinement for more dangerous sufferers of "persecutory delusions"—a common diagnosis in Nigeria.[167] Isaac O., a nineteen-year-old missionary student identified in records only by last initial, conspired to kill all Europeans in Nigeria in 1932. His hybrid situation was identified as one of the sources of his delusions and his embrace of violence taken as proof that he was a menace to society. Unsurprisingly, young men like Isaac constituted the majority of inmates whose "madness" threatened white rule. Doctors saw those Africans who could not successfully transition from rural agriculture to urban wage labor as alienated and "decultured," itself a sign of mental illness.[168] Psychiatrist John Colin Carothers (1903–1989) described Africans as a people prone to mental illness, deficient in frontal lobe development relative to Europeans. He blamed this on their poor individuation, which maintained their brains in a childlike state.[169] Reformers sought special care for the wandering insane, who were too numerous for the lunatic wards of the overcrowded prisons. A 1906 ordinance led to the creation of two asylums, Yaba and Aro. Once inside, however, dank and unhygienic cells made their situation worse than that of convicts. Moreover, neglect rather than treatment followed: for most of the colonial period there were no psychiatrists on the payroll.[170]

Whereas male mental illness manifested as opposition to colonialism in the British view, women's mental illness presented as postpartum depression. Unwed pregnant mothers sought refuge at missions when their families expelled them from their villages. It is in this context that the identification of infanticide as proof of temporary insanity changed the narrative from witchcraft to mental illness. In 1941, a Namibian court found a murdering mother innocent by reason of temporary insanity and ordered her internment in an insane asylum in South Africa, where she remained for five years.[171] Nangombe's illegitimate pregnancy would have been understood by earlier generations as an omen or even the result of witchcraft because conception should have been rendered impossible by her mother's placement of menstrual blood over her sleeping quarters, a traditional contraceptive measure. But by the 1940s, over 40 percent of Namibians had converted to Christianity, and most of those were young people. Nangombe supposedly suffered from fits, perhaps epilepsy, which was not associated with mental defect among her people. But European lawyers made that association, especially when they deemed her answers to their questions irrational.[172] The District Surgeon for Ovamboland testified, "It seems that there are times when the girl is almost sane, practically sane. At other times . . . I should say that her mental condition is not wholly normal."[173] Europeans determined sanity as they understood it and the psychiatrists of the period betrayed their assumptions that just being African was a mark of mental deficiency. By this time, Europeans rejected the traditional justification of infant murder as a cultural practice that protected communities from evil and instead assumed that no mother would lay murderous hands on her offspring unless she was insane.

In the late nineteenth century, the institutionalizing of the insane spread through much of Europe and soon thereafter into its colonies. Specialized treatments, including electric shock therapy and lobotomies, altered the body as a way of correcting the mind. Constructed as an alternative to the jails, hospitals, and poor houses, which could not adequately treat mental illness, asylums promised perfectibility at two levels: the hoped-for rehabilitation of the insane individual and, failing that, their removal from society so as to prevent their reproduction. But due to inadequate staffing and budgets, colonial facilities often served as little more than warehouses for the insane. People therefore moved in and out of asylums somewhat irregularly. This resulted in their being hybrid institutions, dependent on local knowledge, formed in a complex process of negotiation.[174] Family and community involvement sometimes undercut and other times reinforced psychiatric authority and compounded the surveillance mechanisms on which it rested. The decision whether to allow a mentally ill person to remain at home was highly contested by neighbors and relatives in addition to experts. In colonial Vietnam, testimony from relatives and neighbors as to the normalcy of the person often carried as much weight as the reports of psychiatrists. Opened in 1918, the Bien Hoa asylum in Saigon accepted patients whose family requested their internment as well as those whose internment was court ordered. An "inoffensive mad person" generally stayed with the family, but neighbors might contest this designation as they did in the case of Cac, whose act of arson in 1927 took the life of a nine-year-old child.[175] His initial confinement was court ordered, but his early release sparked controversy in his village. His release from Bien Hoa did not convince the community that he was not a threat. The prestige of white medicine only went so far. Only when village elders testified to his apparent normalcy did he transition back into village life.

Mental and physical illness might variously be understood as clinical depression, spirit possession, or a result of spoiling the child. Colonized people responded in a variety of ways to Western healthcare initiatives: some resisting, many adapting or co-opting, and others enthusiastically embracing. Benevolent imperialists might also adapt: the transfer of non-Western medical modalities to the West is still underway as greater awareness spreads of the role of family and community in producing health.

MANAGING SEXUALITY

Although managing reproduction and infant care entailed the management of sexuality, imperialists understood sexuality to be a distinct category. Specifically, the association of disease and enfeeblement with errant sexuality led to a host of interventions that combined several of the practices discussed previously. Deviant sexuality was ascribed to "Gender Variance," people who today might be identified as transgender or intersex. Imperialists studied, regulated, and forced conformity, but ultimately the forces of modernity operating within their own communities rendered them invisible. Only after the Age of Empire ended has there been gradual acceptance of gender variance in some parts of the world. Errant sexuality also produced "Sexually Transmitted Diseases." Regulators in every empire attempted to curb the spread of disease even if they could not curb prostitution. Often the prostitute was subjected to regular examinations, seen as the disease carrier. Local forms of resistance, including the noncooperation of white clients, undermined attempts to regulate the spread of disease until education prevailed over punitive measures. "Antimasturbation Campaigns" addressed another form of errant sexuality. Some went so far as to promote infant male circumcision as a way to stop masturbation, leading to widespread adoption of the practice in the English-speaking world. "Female Circumcision" attracted less attention, although the few major campaigns to abolish it prompted violent conflict with peoples who defended the practice against Western incursion. All of these movements show gradual cooperation between colonizer and colonized as Western medicalized views of sexuality prevailed.

Gender Variance

From the perspective of imperialists, the most extreme version of embodied difference presented as ambiguous gender identity. Variously termed hermaphrodites, intersex, or transgender, people with nonconforming gender identities came to represent the irreconcilability of colonized others with the European gender order. Although European imperial regimes differed in the severity of their response to gender diversity in colonial spaces, in most cases they sought to suppress the expression of transgender practices and identities.

In the late eighteenth century, explorers in the South Pacific did not hesitate to remark on gender-variant persons such as the *mahu* of Tahiti. Captain William

Bligh (1754–1817) of the HMS *Bounty* was especially intrigued by transgender Polynesians, recording his personal examination of their genitals and describing them as quite "common in this sea."[176] Bligh went on to explain that the *mahu* were "selected when Boys and kept with the Women solely for the carnesses [*sic*] of the men. . . . The Women treat him as one of their Sex . . . equally respected and esteemed."[177] By contrast, transgender persons vanished from nineteenth-century missionary records. This historical silence likely reflects difficulty situating transgender behavior into ethnographic categories as well as greater secrecy on the part of Polynesians, who were by then familiar with European contempt for gender variance.[178]

In traditional Hindu society, *hijras* were culturally defined as "neither man nor woman," being androgynous males who were castrated so as to achieve the ritual power of sexual renunciation.[179] They were usually employed as musicians or dancers at marriages or childbirth ceremonies, which they blessed for fertility and prosperity in the name of the Mother Goddess, and otherwise supported with ritual alms. One strategy to marginalize them was the removal of traditional entitlements, such as the withdrawal by the British Raj of protection by Indian states for the *hijra* caste of sacred female men. The outlawing of "begging or extorting money, whether authorized by former governments or not," along with the criminalizing of castration, was designed to target "the abominable practices of the wretches."[180] By steadily reducing their social functions, and ultimately classing them with thugs, vagrants, and gypsies in the Criminal Tribes Act (1871), British authorities succeeded in pushing *hijras* to the dishonored margins of Indian society.

A related portrayal of primitive, natural, uniform heterosexuality appeared in many nineteenth-century accounts of Africa. In 1911, German anthropologist Ferdinand Karsch (1853–1936) disputed the prevailing narrative based on his research among hunter-gatherers in Portuguese Angola. "The most unnatural vices, which we regard as the most recent ways of stimulation of an over civilized culture are practised there in the light of day, in the open, as common practice."[181] Yet most of his colleagues rejected Karsch's conclusion that homosexuality was inborn and universal rather than a condition of modern decadence. Reports of same-sex or transgender practices were generally rationalized as being misconstrued by European observers or as the corruption of naïve Africans by decadent outsiders, a contrivance that persists in Africa to the present day.

When marginalized by their own communities, gender-variant persons might escape detection, but the transgender shamanic religious beliefs of many Siberian and Amerindian peoples presented a more direct challenge to imperial rule due to their ability to inspire native resistance. A common feature of shamanism was that certain exceptional persons, or shamans, had a supernatural ability to cross into the spirit realms using the power inherent in sexual energy. As described in 1914 by Polish anthropologist Marie Czaplicka (1884–1921), "Socially, the shaman does not belong to either the class of males or to that of females, but to a third class, that of shamans [who] have special taboos comprising both male and female characters."[182] During the Tsarist period, Russian Orthodox missionaries dismissed shamanic rites as the trivial superstitions of "savages" who had no true religion, or at least none that made sense. As one missionary declared in 1901 after a failed attempt to convert the Altai people of Central Siberia

> Good Heavens! What impenetrable darkness and ignorance do these miserable nomads live in! One can observe everywhere heads of strangled and tortured sacrificed animals. Inside of their dwellings there stand all sorts of idols and hang all sorts of small rags. Around these dwellings and among birch trees there hang the same rags or ribbons on ropes. Here are these Altaian gods! It is hard to imagine that they worship all this junk![183]

Ethnologists used the lens of psychology to describe shamanism as a cultural mental disorder, an "arctic hysteria" of extreme neurosis "on the verge of insanity," induced by the severity of life in the harsh, frigid climate.[184] According to Russian anthropologist Vladimir Bogoraz (1865–1936), the most extreme form of "arctic hysteria" was transvestism, which ranged from simple cross-dressing to "complete gender transformation, perversion, and hermaphroditism," going so far as same-sex marriage to "a spiritual pederast" husband.[185]

Under the intense Russification program of the Soviet Union, transgender shamans were doubly reviled as class enemies and sexual deviants. In 1924, the Yakut Department of Justice that governed much of Eastern Siberia issued instructions to persecute shamans as subversive elements. Their spiritual rites were banned, they were refused hunting grounds, and they were forbidden from having sexual intercourse. During the 1930s, Soviet authorities succeeded in pushing shamanism underground with a program of compulsory self-denunciation and ostracism of both shamans and their relatives.[186]

The transgender two-spirit identities found among Amerindian peoples varied greatly in their roles and status within different ethnic groups. For instance, the male-bodied Zuni *lhamana* and the Navajo *nadle* engaged in typically female tasks, such as weaving baskets and crafting pottery, without a distinctive spiritual dimension to their gender-variant social roles. By contrast, the male-bodied Mohave *hwame* and the female-bodied Klamath *tw!nna'ek* were highly valued as shamans and medicine people. The male-bodied Cheyenne *heemaneh'* led the Scalp Dance after the return of a war party, and the male-bodied Lakota *winkte* played a sacred role in the Sun Dance ceremony.[187] In frontier discourses, all gender-variant Amerindians were conflated with "sodomites" regardless of their role in Native societies and were commonly referred to by the pejorative French-Canadian term *berdache*, meaning catamite, although in many cases their sexual relations were bisexual or heterosexual.[188]

From their earliest contact with gender-variant people in the New World, European conquerors, explorers, missionaries, and officials persecuted two-spirit Amerindians wherever they imposed colonial rule. In California, Spanish missionaries were outraged by widespread *berdache* customs and began a concerted effort in the 1780s to eradicate gender variance, which they often attributed to

Native peoples in general. Speaking of *"maricas"* among the Yuma in 1775, Pedro Font (d. 1781) condemned them as "sodomites, dedicated to nefarious practices . . . in this matter of incontinence there will be much to do when the Holy Faith and the Christian religion are established among them."[189] By the 1820s, the missionaries at San Juan Capistrano were able to report that although *berdaches* were once very numerous among the local natives, "at the present time this horrible custom is entirely unknown among them."[190] Subsequent accounts from the region contain no trace that even the memory of gender-variant traditions survived the Spanish encounter with Mission Indians.

As white Americans explored lands west of the Mississippi River, they were similarly confounded by two-spirit people. George Catlin (1796–1872), renowned for his paintings of the American West, featured a *berdache* in one of his works (see Figure 5.9). Catlin described the *berdache* role as "one of the most unaccountable and disgusting customs, that I have ever met in the Indian country . . . a man dressed in woman's clothes . . . driven to the most servile and degrading duties."[191] As early as the 1870s, US government agents ordered *berdaches* among the Sioux people to wear men's clothing and to cut their hair short. Prohibitions on traditional curing rituals forced gender-variant shamans into secrecy, and boys at reservation boarding schools were punished if caught secretly wearing

Figure 5.9. Cheyenne Hetaneman, a female berdache in battle, 1889
Two-spirit or third-gender persons held special status among Amerindians like the Cheyenne. Their gender variance fascinated Westerners, who sought to reform or eliminate them.

female attire. Native peoples initially resisted US efforts to force two-spirit persons to conform to white American gender norms. As recalled among the Crow, "One agent in the late 1890s . . . tried to interfere with Osh-Tisch, who was the most respected *badé*. The agent incarcerated the *badés*, cut off their hair, made them wear men's clothing. . . . The people were so upset with this that Chief Pretty Eagle came into Crow Agency, and told [the agent] to leave the reservation. It was a tragedy, trying to change them."[192]

A more effective tactic was forcing *non*-transgender Native American boys to don female attire as punishment for breaking rules at reservation boarding schools. The association of humiliation with cross-dressing soon turned Native Americans against two-spirit persons, who were now the target of contempt and persecution. Female-bodied gender variants fared even worse after two-spirit native gender roles were replaced by a Western ideology that deemed women inherently subordinate. By example, precontact Mojave venerated transgender female-bodied *hwame* as powerful shamans. When the community stopped validating the role, the last *hwame* Sahaykwisa (1845–1895) was ridiculed by Mojave men and finally abandoned the male social role after being raped. When she later expressed a longing for sexual companionship with women, she was accused of witchcraft, gang raped, and drowned in the Colorado River.[193] Ultimately, the Bureau of Indian Affairs succeeded in rendering gender variance unacceptable to Native Americans by tying economic success to their adoption of white American social norms, which included a distillation of gender into sharply defined Western roles.[194]

Sexually Transmitted Diseases

The othering of nonconforming bodies in the colonies extended to prostitutes. Concerns about public health, and especially the health of servicemen stationed in the colonies, motivated crusades to combat sexually transmitted diseases in the nineteenth century. Policies that were initially designed to regulate brothels in Hong Kong would ultimately form the basis for Contagious Diseases (CD) legislation in many parts of the British Empire. In 1857, Hong Kong Governor John Bowring (1792–1872) issued the first such Ordinance for Checking the Spread of Venereal Diseases, which set up a system of brothel licensing and a regimen for regular medical inspection of sex workers. Although its success at limiting the spread of disease was unclear at best, it became the model for similar laws enacted as far afield as Canada and South Africa. In 1864, a British Royal Navy surgeon described how the system functioned to the parliamentary committee that drafted the Contagious Diseases Acts (1864) for Great Britain: "We had a good example of prevention at Hong Kong; it is one of those places in which there are excellent sanitary regulations. All the prostitutes are registered, the brothel keepers have licences, and are under government superintendence; the colonial surgeon examines the women periodically, and if a woman is found to be diseased she is immediately signed to the Lock Hospital, and kept there till she is cured."[195]

In Great Britain, a repeal effort led by feminist social reformers Josephine Butler (1828–1906) and Florence Nightingale (1820–1910) succeeded in persuading parliament to suspend the CD Acts in 1883, arguing that they were an affront to women's liberty and that they unjustly punished the victims of prostitution rather than the perpetrators. Faced with similar calls, the Registrar-General of Hong Kong, James Russell (1843–1893), mounted a vigorous defense of the colonial version as a gesture of humanity. "The Contagious Diseases Acts in England have for their object the protection of Soldiers and Sailors. The Contagious Diseases Ordinances here have not only that object, *but have also for their object the protection of girls and women against brothel slavery* and hence it is that the Colonial Government had to adopt the 'registration' and 'licensing' of brothels, and keep up a complete Police inspection."[196] Despite such humanitarian pretenses, the main purpose and effect of the government brothel system was to cordon off the sexual partners of British soldiers, sailors, and civil servants from the sexual partners of native men in Hong Kong and Singapore. British reports on the native populace of the two island cities abound with references to filth and squalor. A typical 1897 memorandum described the cities as "two vast plague spots . . . two putrid sores . . . infecting an ever widening circle of human creatures."[197] Indeed, after Hong Kong Governor John Pope Hennessy (1834–1891) became one of the few local British officials to oppose brothel regulation, on "the principle of equal treatment for all peoples," he was dispatched to govern the far less important colony of Mauritius.[198] The prevailing view that Chinese sex workers must be protected from their own ignorance and separate from their kinfolk justified disparate treatment and kept the system intact long after the British version was repealed, until 1927 in Singapore and through World War II in Hong Kong.

For advocates of the CD Acts, Britain's Mediterranean garrisons at Malta, Gibraltar, and the Greek Ionian Islands were essential to the medical surveillance and supervision of sexual contact between British personnel and local prostitutes. Accordingly, Admiral William Martin (1801–1895) reported in 1868 on their implementation in Malta: "There should be no trifling in this matter—the disease is ruining multitudes of innocent as well as of guilty, it embarrasses the service, squanders the public money, and saps the stamina of the population."[199] On both Malta and the Greek island of Corfu, prostitutes were required to register, undergo examination by a police doctor three times each month, and were forcibly confined if showing disease symptoms. However, whereas the CD Acts were by all accounts successful at segregating and monitoring prostitution on small island possessions with easily manageable native populations, the situation on Gibraltar reflected the far greater difficulty of regulation typical of colonial spaces. On one hand, British authorities had no ability to control soldiers and sailors who set out on excursions across the isthmus connecting Gibraltar to Spain. On the other hand, as a military surgeon noted in 1867, although the laws provided "ample powers for the removal of [Spanish] aliens known to be diseased . . . those enjoying the rights of British subjects, cannot be dealt with in the same manner."[200] Although regulators were partially successful in setting up a brothel system for migrant prostitutes, they were unable to solve the intractable problem of naturalized "native" prostitutes operating out of independent lodgings. When Governor General Horace Smith-Dorrien (1858–1930) finally shut down the brothel quarter in 1922, Gibraltar's sex workers simply moved to La Linea just across the Spanish border, where they could ply their trade to British military personnel altogether beyond British jurisdiction.

If regulation of the sex trade proved untenable in the small military fortress of Gibraltar, it was virtually impossible in the fluid social expanses of colonial Africa. In 1876, the surgeon major of Sierra Leone alerted the Legislative Council of "the ravages that Venereal is making in the colony" and proposed CD legislation as a "great benefit to the Civil population, as well as to the unfortunates themselves."[201] But despite a substantial contingent of British soldiers and sailors in the West African colony, Gray's proposal was swiftly dismissed by the Executive Council and Governor Cornelius Kortright (1817–1897), who stated that prostitution in Sierra Leone was "*so* common [and] adopted at so early an age, that it would be impossible to carry out the measures recommended by Surgeon Major Gray."[202] This general attitude prevailed in nearly all of British Africa, where the sexuality of native women was deemed unmanageable barring a systematic intervention that would be far too expensive to maintain. Relative lack of regulation meant that local prostitutes kept some control over their work. In Nairobi, capital of Kenya, black women casually signaled their availability by stating they were unmarried and then discretely providing sexual services to the men who called on them at their private residences. According to Hadija Njeri, a sex worker in Nairobi during the 1920s and 1930s, most preferred European clients because they paid better and left promptly with minimal personal attachment: "White men didn't touch your breasts if they wanted you, those white people weren't looking for women to be wives to marry them, they wanted someone for a short-time."[203]

Although more consistent and sustained, German efforts to regulate prostitution in their African possessions similarly foundered due to a scarcity of resources and the impracticality of monitoring large native populations. The bans on interracial marriage issued in 1905 for German Southwest Africa (modern Namibia) and in 1906 for German East Africa (modern Tanzania) fueled the sex commerce as noted in medical reports. "In earlier years, the European more often sought a certain native woman to engage; he had a black wife. Due to the influence of public opinion in Germany . . . the European has broken himself of this habit. This has had the practical result that the white increasingly looks elsewhere for his sexual gratification, and consequently is directed to the black Venus vulgivaga [the goddess of prostitution]."[204] By 1910, German colonial authorities in East Africa and Cameroon issued orders for the "general control of prostitutes," including regular examinations and the quarantine of suspect cases.[205] However, these regulations proved unenforceable for a variety of reasons.

At the peak of the German Empire in 1914, there were only 139 physicians throughout Germany's colonial possessions, which totaled some 14 million inhabitants. Moreover, the reliance on native soldiers and police, who did not place great priority on enforcing such ordinances, made it easy for prostitutes to evade regulation by moving around or simply failing to register. Some sex workers entered marriages of convenience, which exempted them from supervision, and colonial doctors reported that many women engaged in casual "opportunity prostitution" rather than outright solicitation, which was all but impossible to identify, much less to regulate.[206] Finally, many patients left treatment before it was complete, and even scattered attempts at imprisonment were unsuccessful. As one doctor reported from the Marshall Islands, "despite all supervision those from Ebon infected with venereal disease have found the opportunity to engage in sexual intercourse among themselves in the hospital as well as [with others] outside the hospital. It has even occurred that a girl infected with gonorrhea dug under the fence in order to get outside!"[207] The failure to educate native peoples or to build local support for antivenereal campaigns doomed German efforts from the outset.

In stark contrast, a French initiative in Madagascar proved far more successful due to its focus on education and treatment rather than discipline and quarantine. In 1901, Governor Joseph Galliéni (1849–1916) implemented a comprehensive health and family policy designed to halt the spread of sexually transmitted disease. Galliéni opened a venereal hospital outside the capital of Antananarivo to treat both prostitutes and the general population, including men, that removed much of the stigma associated with such efforts elsewhere. Just as importantly, he had brochures distributed in the local Malgache language and organized weekly lectures, given by native medical assistants, on such topics as "the hygiene of pregnant women" and the "ravages of syphilis."[208] In short order, doctors from the international branch of the French Society of Health and Moral Prophylaxis (SFPSM) regularly cited Galliéni's work in Madagascar as an innovative and exemplary model for the French Empire. Although many expressed skepticism that they might actually change the "free" sexual mores of native peoples, they believed that they could appeal to their "primitive" sense of self-interest.[209] Indeed, they argued that the presumed lack of native morality or shame would assist the circulation of information on sexually transmitted disease. In 1903, a report in the SFPSM's bulletin explained, "In order to instruct our colored brothers about venereal diseases, you will not need to teach them, as you want so strongly to do in France, that they are not at all shameful diseases. On this point they are well in advance of us."[210] According to the SFPSM, the greater problem that colonial doctors needed to confront was the complacency and carelessness that resulted from the absence of shame. "In order to trouble this serenity, it requires an effort to address directly the interest in self-conservation of the individual, the family, the tribe."[211]

In Japan, Meiji authorities introduced a nationwide system for medical examination of prostitutes in 1876 that mirrored Britain's CD Acts, which was further tightened with the Regulations for the Control of Prostitutes (1900) and the Law for the Prevention of Venereal Diseases (1927). As early as the Russo-Japanese War of 1905, the Japanese military operated a brothel system where it brought the sexual activity of both soldiers and prostitutes under the surveillance and regulation of military physicians. By the 1920s, the Bureau of Hygiene operated 482 health exam offices and 223 hospitals for prostitutes covering 535 official prostitution quarters nationwide, their greater investment in the program yielding better results.[212] Regulation of prostitution was an indicator of the imperial obsession with managing native sexuality. Nations throughout the world attempted but usually failed to police interracial sex. More strenuous interventions to promote Western sexuality followed, the most successful of which survived beyond the Age of Empire.

Antimasturbation Campaigns

As modern sexologists, purity campaigners, and eugenicists worried over the health and fitness of the European population, they fixated on male masturbation as a concern of epidemic proportions. The old biblical sin of onanism, previously a dire matter of individual morality, was drawn into nineteenth-century medical models that held the fitness of the nation to be directly tied to the virility of its men. Citing American sexologist James Foster Scott (1863–1943), British purity crusader Christabel Pankhurst (1880–1958) asserted that, "The proper subjugation of the sexual impulses and the conservation of the complex seminal fluid, with its wonderfully invigorating influence, develop all that is best and noblest in men."[213] By contrast, the sexual instinct of "incontinent men" was so "perverted and corrupted" due to their exploits with prostitutes that they could no longer be satisfied by "virtuous women."[214] Such men suffered from "an excess of seminal secretions," relieved by compulsive masturbation, "a waste of vital force which impoverishes their moral nature and weakens their body."[215] These widely held views influenced sexologists around the world, including Japan, the Ottoman Empire, and India, to take measures to eradicate it, including exercise, early marriage, and even circumcision.

In Japan, reformers wrestled with the dilemma of how to tell students not to masturbate without inspiring some to try it. Much like their European counterparts, they focused on what the founder of Japan's Medical School for Women, Yoshioka Yayoi (1871–1959), described as "the most terrible ailment related to the sexual instinct."[216] By 1910, most Japanese pedagogues echoed the views of Keiō University education reformer Mukō Gunji (1865–1943) who deplored the "devastating consequences of masturbation," ranging from paleness, anorexia, and memory lapses to depression, neurasthenia, and death.[217]

In the Ottoman Empire, regulating and disciplining sexual behavior similarly became part of the public discourse on modernity. In 1895, French doctor Benoît Boyer (d. 1897) received a commission to inspect hygiene in the Lebanese city of Beirut. His report condemned "alcoholic and venereal excess, long night-outs, the emotions of gambling, the maneuvers of masturbation, repeated up to 15 times a day" as the key factors that undermined public health.[218] Although Boyer also criticized polygamy and the seclusion of women, his main focus was on the supposedly uncontrolled and degenerate sexual excesses of Lebanese men. Some Arab elites of the Ottoman Empire saw sexual discipline as a means of national regeneration. Dozens of books and journals took up the cause, the most influential of which was the revised *Manual on Health and Marriage* (1899) by Beirut sexologist Shakir al-Khuri (1847–1913). In 1907, the editor of Cairo's leading daily *The Pyramids* noted that "a few years after its publication, it became very widespread; it is seized by all hands, and I can hardly see a Syrian young man who hasn't read it and hasn't benefited from it."[219] As in Europe, the main preoccupation of authors and readers was to prevent masturbation. Al-Khuri claimed that masturbators were readily identified by their physical bearing: a hunched posture, yellowish skin, memory lapses, and, in extreme cases, madness, heart disease, and even death. The medical discourse of controlling "degenerate" male sexuality clearly filtered into Arab popular consciousness, with letters regularly printed in Egyptian and Syrian newspapers on "the harmful habit" of masturbation.[220] A typical example, from a young man in the small Nile Delta village of Malij, requested advice on how to stop his brother's masturbation. The reply in Cairo's *Digest* was to tie down the brother's hands in his sleep, to watch him constantly during the day, and to have him married as soon as possible.[221]

In the eighteenth century, men in the British military dreaded the prospect of being forcibly circumcised if captured by savages. With the nineteenth-century shift to confident colonial rule the supposed practical benefits of circumcision replaced its prior association with violation and otherness. By the 1850s, British Army doctors in India began to prescribe circumcision to relieve the distraction of caring for sensitive foreskins in hot, humid climates. As adult soldiers in British India increasingly opted for the surgery, some military officers started to promote routine infant circumcision in Britain to preempt the inconvenience for future servants of empire.[222] The idea was initially quite unwelcome in the British metropole, where Richard Burton noted in *Arabian Nights* (1886) that "Christendom . . . practically holds circumcision in horror."[223] However, it found a receptive audience among medical experts alarmed by the "nervous disorders" attributed to masturbation, and they were soon joined by allies in the social purity movement. They believed that circumcision reduced sensation to the point of halting masturbation, which strongly implies that these advocates were themselves uncircumcised.

In 1887, Eton College schoolmaster Edward Lyttelton (1855–1942) endorsed routine circumcision to prevent masturbation, asserting that "the least defilement in boyhood enormously increases the difficulty of continence in manhood."[224] The British purity campaign revived the work of French surgeon Claude-François Lallemand (1790–1854) who published three volumes between 1836 and 1842 on the imaginary disease called spermatorrhea. Lallemand held that any seminal emission, to say nothing of masturbation, drained a man of "nerve force" with devastating effects on the mind and body to the point of lunacy and paralysis.[225] His therapies included driving needles into the prostate, cauterizing the urethra with a solution of silver nitrate, and ultimately amputation of the foreskin. Because the men subjected to such treatment did not return for more, Lallemand proclaimed his regimen a success in curing an array of common maladies from eczema to indigestion. Whereas his proposals for routine circumcision were soundly rejected in Continental Europe, where genital integrity was still central to men's sexual identity, its normalization in British India assisted its later adoption by antimasturbation purity reformers in Great Britain.[226]

British regulators now viewed male circumcision as an optimal means to rein in men's sexual impulses that were viewed as corrupting and degenerative in nineteenth-century Europe. They in turn exported the recently abhorred practice to Australia, New Zealand, Canada, and the United States where its embrace as a mark of social status and upright morality soon led to its near universal adoption. As more and more middle-class whites opted for circumcising their infant sons, the intact foreskin was associated with immigrants, people of color, and a lower-class upbringing. The unmutilated penis therefore became a stigma of those who supposedly lacked culture, hygiene, intelligence, and, in short, civilization.[227] The result was a vicious cycle where a once foreign religious ritual became a ubiquitous mark of respectable society. Such was the dynamic interchange between metropole and empire that a practice dreaded by early British explorers was later endorsed by colonial officials, whose cause was taken up by metropolitan reformers and thereby imposed back into imperial dominions.

Female Circumcision

Some cultures advocated female circumcision to curb women's masturbation or sexual pleasure more generally. Practiced in some parts of Africa and the Middle East, circumcision ranges from excision of the clitoris to infibulation, a process that entails the removal of the labia and the suturing of the vulva. Missionaries and other benevolent imperialists condemned the practice and occasionally tried to prohibit it with little success.

An early attempt by Europeans to halt the practice was reported by Scottish explorer James Bruce (1730–1794) in his *Travels to Discover the Source of the Nile* (1790) an account of his journeys from 1768 to 1773 in the Red Sea coastal areas of Egypt and Arabia. Bruce initially believed that local practices of both male and female circumcision must be due to some genital deformity. He soon discovered that this did not hold for men but was led to believe that, in the case of women, "a certain disproportion is found generally to prevail among them."[228] Bruce further explained that Roman Catholic priests who settled in Egypt had initially forbidden excision among Coptic women, but later relented because "the heat of the climate, or some other natural cause, did, in that particular nation, invariably alter the formation" of women's genitals so as to impede "the consequences for which matrimony was instituted."[229]

Similarly, when the French Catholic Church in Upper Volta (modern Burkina Faso) threatened in the late nineteenth century to excommunicate converts that continued to practice clitoridectomy, the Sisters of Our Lady of Africa petitioned in favor of excision so that young girls would be accepted as "normal" in their native environment.[230] Even feminists such as Sister Marie-Andrée du Sacré-Coeur (1899–1988), who spent three months in Mali in 1936 and used her legal training to draft legislation for the protection of African women, agreed that the social stigma for women who were not excised outweighed concerns about their genital integrity.[231] In Islamic regions of French West Africa, where female genital excision was endemic and Islamic courts administered family law, French colonial officials deemed it outside the scope of their authority and expressed no desire to antagonize subject populations by opposing such local traditions. Body modification to insure marriageability extended to genital mutilation.

In the British Empire, Protestant missionaries denounced the "barbaric" practice as early as 1906, and their arguments with regard to infant and maternal mortality resonated with colonial officials who were alarmed over low population growth rates in East Africa prior to World War II.[232] The period from 1929 to 1931 was marked by a "female circumcision controversy" after Scottish missionaries in Kenya persuaded feminist groups in Britain to push for a ban.[233] In 1930, the House of Commons convened an inquiry that concluded "the best way to tackle the problem was through education and not by force of an enactment and that the best way was to leave the people concerned free to choose what custom was best suited to their changing conditions."[234] Yet local anti-excision efforts met with little success and much ridicule. For instance, when the Methodist Church of Meru enacted a loyalty oath in renunciation of female genital mutilation, its membership dropped from seventy to six. The 1930s initiative was soon abandoned having failed to garner any discernible native support

Two decades later, British officials pushed the all-male Kikuyu Council of Elders to issue a formal ban in 1956 sparking a fierce backlash among teen girls guided by their excised female elders. A movement known as *Ngaitana*, self-circumcision, spread from district to district as school girls in groups of three to twenty convened in secret and "against all previous custom, some circumcised themselves, others one another, and others were circumcised by their own mothers."[235] *Ngaitana* soon became an act of anticolonial defiance in conjunction with Kenya's nationalist Mau Mau Uprising (1952–1960). In a 1995 interview, Charity Tirindi recalled how "If you were not circumcised, [Mau Mau fighters] came for you at night, you [were] taken to the forest [and] circumcised, and you [were] roasted for what you have been circumcised [the clitoris] and you [were] told to eat it."[236] By contrast to the successful campaign against foot binding in China, the failure to forge an indigenous movement in Kenya based on native institutions led to the nationalist rejection of anti-excision efforts as an imperialist imposition of Western values.

Modern purity campaigns involving sex organs laid a medical veneer over preexisting doctrines of virtue and vice.[237] Contestations over the sexual body set rational civilization in opposition to primitive savagery or cultural degeneration. Unsurprisingly, the management of sexuality proved a battleground between nationalists and imperialists throughout the twentieth century.

CONCLUSION

Whether acting independently or on behalf of governments, missionaries, doctors, and reformers spread a particular ideology of ableism across the globe. Ability became another dimension of intersecting identity on par with, or even superseding, race, class, and gender. Ability invoked far more than the physical functioning demanded by employers and demographers. It also encompassed mental dispositions and behaviors that would reproduce the social order, especially the appropriate management of sexuality as the highest expression of self-control. Physical disability therefore became closely associated with moral degeneracy.

Colonizers attributed degeneracy in behavior and body to errant sexuality and gradually substituted Western biomedicine, with its pharmaceuticals and behavior regimes, for native forms of regulation and herbal cures. In some instances, however, knowledge transfer went the other way, or even in multiple directions. Individuals whose bodies and behaviors conformed in utility and beauty to European norms could adapt to or even modify imperial standards, whereas those least capable of conformity were ostracized, transformed, or worse. The pursuit of perfectibility succeeded in spreading ideologies of self-control across the globe. Some forms of body modification, such as scarification and clitoridectomy, generally disappeared as populations became more urban and Westernized and sexual attractiveness could be conveyed by other means. Traditional approaches to reproduction and mental illness were also generally replaced by more Western views in proportion to the degree of exposure to Christianity and economic globalization. Forms of sexual regulation such as prolonged breastfeeding or the use of contraception were expanded or reduced depending on the labor needs of communities anxious about population size. Workplaces and military recruiters inspected men's bodies for fitness while the scientific management of sexuality included fitness regimes like yoga that offered techniques to optimize semen. The end result was the suppression of practices and knowledges that could not be assimilated into Western medical and scientific constructions of embodiment.

Meanwhile, native activists campaigned to end practices that produced disabilities or that intruded on what was becoming a universal right to bodily integrity. Locating agency in these campaigns proves problematic, as native reformers might be easily dismissed as advocates of Westernization or even collaborators with the imperial project. And indeed some were. Nationalist movements emerged from conflicts over modification of cultures or bodies, with reformers more likely to seek allies among Europeans, embracing the ideology of universal rights, while separatists rejected universalism because it emanated from the European Enlightenment. Most colonized people were caught in the middle, attempting to preserve traditions that were seen as increasingly incompatible with modernity.

TIMELINE

1789	Abolitionist Olaudah Equiano publishes his autobiography
1812	Tahitian ruler Pomare II declares himself a Christian
1831	Charles Darwin begins his voyage around the South America aboard the HMS *Beagle*
1838	An American doctor cofounds the Medical Missionary Society with a British doctor
1839	Tanzimat code in Ottoman Empire criminalizes abortion
1857	Hong Kong Governor issues Ordinance for Checking the Spread of Venereal Diseases
1871	Criminal Tribes Act of India further marginalizes *hijras*
1874	Christians in China form the Heavenly Feet Society to oppose foot binding
1893	Swami Vivekananda of India gives address at the Chicago World's Fair
1901	French Madagascar's governor implements healthcare and education program to halt the spread of STDs
1905	Italian nun dies of typhus in China; healing cult develops around the miracles at her death
1905	German government bans interracial marriage in its African colonies
1906	British in Ghana pass law against witch-finding
1907	Chinese feminist and nationalist Qiu Jin executed for treason
1912	"Drops of Milk" baby-care league opens chapter in Belgian Congo
1919	Bien Hoa mental asylum opens in French Indochina city of Saigon
1920	French issue "Medals for Mothers" of large families; Italians soon follow suit
1925	Gandhi formally opposes birth control
1932	The Race Welfare Society of Johannesburg and the Mothers' Clinic Committee of Cape Town open birth control clinics in South Africa
1933	Race Improvement Society of Kenya forms

SIX

THE END OF EMPIRE

Toussaint Louverture of Haiti and France

O you Africans, my brothers . . . you whose liberty is sealed
with more than half of your own blood! How long will I have
the mortification of seeing my misled children fly the coun-
sels of a father who idolises them! . . . Is it then possible that
the labourers will always be the plaything and the instruments of vengeance of those monsters whom hell has loosed
upon this colony? . . . The blood of so many victims cries for
vengeance, and human and divine justice cannot delay to
confound the guilty.
—Toussaint Louverture, proclamation to people of Haiti, 1795

*Begun in 1791, the slave revolution in Saint-Domingue (Haiti) had evolved into a
full-scale war for control of the island by 1795. General Toussaint Louverture
(1743–1803), a former slave, attempted to impose order on his troops by evoking
mutually exclusive clichés: are Africans his brothers or his children? Are laborers,
former slaves, the instruments of white vengeance or avengers themselves?[1] Familial and embodied metaphors, frequently invoked in revolutionary crises, recall the
centrality of intimacy to modern imperial relations.*

*Louverture, and the course he steered toward the end of empire, mirrors the rise
and fall of European hegemony. Born a slave to educated parents, Louverture was
raised Catholic and developed a hybrid identity. His master employed him as a
livestock driver and coachman, positions of some authority that enabled him to
preserve his masculine identity. Freed in 1777, he had a Catholic marriage and
fathered two sons. After the slave rebellion broke out in 1791, he helped his former
master escape and then joined the revolt, quickly rising to leadership. With the abolition of slavery as his single goal, he accepted aid from the Spaniards who wanted
to use the slaves to oust the French. The revolt was therefore caught up in the*

superpower politics of the era, which drew the British into the war as well. After the French formally abolished slavery in 1794, Louverture returned his army to French control. With the plantation aristocracy defeated at home and in the colonies, Louverture saw no need for independence from France until Napoleon Bonaparte (1769–1821) restored slavery in 1802. Then the war resumed in full force as the former slaves refused re-enslavement. Although Napoleon captured Louverture and imprisoned him in France, where he died, the former slaves defeated the French and proclaimed the independence of Haiti in 1804.

The Haitian Revolution had an unlikely beginning in a hybrid religious practice infused with Enlightenment precepts, overseen by a woman who claimed to be under spirit possession. In 1791, a "green-eyed woman of African and Corsican descent named Cécile Fatiman" first mobilized the slaves into rebellion by slitting the throat of a sacrificial pig at the infamous Bois Caïman voodoo ceremony.[2] Voodoo priest and rebel leader Dutty Boukman (d. 1791) then proclaimed, "Throw away the image of the god of the whites who thirsts for our tears and listen to the voice of liberty that speaks in the hearts of all of us."[3] Natural liberty and religious ecstasy combined to mobilize thousands of slaves to rise in rebellion, to set plantations on fire, and to murder planters and their families, as seen in Figure 6.1.

In an account penned soon after the successful Haitian Revolution, French colonist Antoine Dalmas (1757–1830) described the sacrifice of the black pig. "The religious ceremony in which the nègres slit its throat, the greed with which they drank its blood, the importance they attached to owning some of its bristles which they believed would make them invincible reveal the characteristics of the Africans . . . ignorant and stupid."[4] Writing from exile in the United States, Dalmas stigmatized

Figure 6.1.   Haitian Revolution
The revolution launched by slaves in France's premiere Caribbean colony in 1791 ended slavery, established the independent nation of Haiti, and created a model for the world. Brutal violence was perpetrated on all sides.

the rituals of the victorious rebels, which reflected both the bitterness of the defeated white Creole refugees and their unshaken sense of racial superiority. His fellow exile, Moreau de Saint-Méry (1750–1819), similarly emphasized the role of dark magic in such ceremonies, as voodoo priestesses danced into a trance-like state so that spirits could communicate through them. "They spin around ceaselessly. And there are some in this species of bacchanal who tear their clothing and even bite their flesh. Others who are only deprived of their senses and have fallen in their tracks are taken, even while dancing, into the darkness of a neighboring room, where a disgusting prostitution exercises a most hideous empire."[5]

Whereas imperialist authors described slave mobilization for freedom as primitive and debauched, Haiti's leaders went to the other extreme and located citizenship in the virtuous family. After ten years of brutal war and the collapse of the economic and social orders, Haiti needed to be rebuilt, in Louverture's view, by patriarchal Catholic families. In 1801, Louverture issued a decree now known as the Dictatorial Proclamation that blamed negligent parents for debauched youth. It included surveillance, prison terms, forced labor, and death sentences as corrective measures:

> Barely are they born than we see these same children with jewels and earrings, covered in rags, their clothing filthy, wounding the eyes of decency through their nudity. . . . It is certain beyond any doubt that they will be bad citizens, vagabonds, thieves. And if they are girls, then they are prostitutes all of them ready to follow the prompting of the first conspirator who will preach murder and pillage to them. It is upon such vile mothers and fathers, on students so dangerous, that the magistrates of the people must ceaselessly keep an open eye. . . . The most holy of all institutions among men who live in society, that from which flows the greatest good, is marriage. . . . Thus a wise government must always occupy itself with surrounding happy couples with honour, respect and veneration. It should only rest after having extirpated immorality to the last root.[6]

He concluded with orders that this proclamation be read at Catholic Mass. In the 1804 Haitian Declaration of Independence, revolutionary leader Jean-Jacques Dessalines (1758–1806) called on the liberated slaves to restore their families. "Native citizens, men, women, girls, and children, let your gaze extend on all parts of this island: look there for your spouses, your husbands, your brothers, your sisters. Indeed! Look there for your children, your suckling infants, what have they become? . . . I shudder to say it . . . the prey of these vultures."[7]

Moreau associated religious ecstasy with sexual debauchery; Louverture blamed the negligence of parents among the newly freed for the corruption of youth; Dessalines romanticized the vulnerable, humble family. The thirteen-year battle for the future of the island pitted poor whites against rich, free people of color against slaves, and republicans against aristocrats. It pitted West African traditions against Enlightenment rationalism and collective identity against individual citizenship. These binaries left a legacy of division that hampered the creation of unified communities.

In this chapter, we explore this process from the eighteenth century onward, emphasizing the multiplicity of approaches to ending imperialism. Some emanated *from Enlightenment theory of natural rights, some from expressly non-Western traditions, some from the valorizing of violence. All involved knowledge transfers, hybrid formations, and a range of intimacies. Whether elitist or populist, liberal or Marxist, violent or peaceful the gendered nature of resistance exaggerated the importance of masculine prowess and resulted in rigid patriarchal family formations in many newly liberated countries. Every extension of empire met with resistance. The first set of resistance struggles shared characteristics of contained conflicts. They erupted in the eighteenth and nineteenth centuries and, except in the Americas, were generally localized and unsuccessful. World War I was a watershed event that galvanized mass movements to demand national self-determination. The global catastrophe of World War II then set the stage for the final and ultimately successful transfers of power, some peaceful and gradual, others violent and protracted.*

Imperialism led to a construction of manhood that valorized courage and virility while devaluing certain forms of femininity.[8] Moreover, colonialism translated European notions of stern discipline in the proper socialization of children into a parallel theory of social progress that equated cultural differences with primitivism and immaturity.[9] At the same time, imperial hypermasculinity damaged the humanity of the aggressor by turning mercy and kindness into signs of weakness.[10] The psychological damage was of course more intense for colonized subjects who had to not only come to terms with the indignity of defeat and conquest but also with the legacy of racist domination.[11] This "loss of self" extended to the destruction of native values and the imposition of racist norms. The corresponding "recovery of self" involved forging a new national identity, often by co-opting Western discourses and adapting them to revitalized native forms. It resulted in the eventual and often violent ouster of the colonizer.

CONTAINED CONFLICTS

The Haitian Revolution was one of a series of "Early Revolutions" that launched decolonization in the New World. From the American Revolution of 1775 through the Latin American Revolutions of the 1820s, revolutionaries called on romantic and gendered images of virtuous heroines, manly warriors, and the nation as mother to rouse support. By 1830, in part due to the increasing technology gap between colonizers and colonized, rebels were more usually defeated. "Failed Insurrections" nonetheless illustrate the agency of the colonized and, over the long run, undermined imperial rule in the French, British, and German Empires, often because of the brutality used to end them. "Millenarianism" and concepts of mystical body transformation characterize another cluster of resistance movements before World War I. Native peoples in New Zealand, Tanzania, and the United States revived or invented spiritual rituals around the turn of the nineteenth century that they believed would make them immune to bullets. These various responses to imperialism, even those that failed, attest to the resilience of the colonized and the centrality of gender.

Early Revolutions

Spanish rule in the Americas was over two hundred years old by the time sporadic uprisings broke out in the eighteenth century, culminating in the decolonization of most of Latin America in the early nineteenth century. The Túpac Amaru Rebellion (1780–1782) aimed to restore honor and dignity to the native peoples of the South American Andes who had suffered two and a half centuries of oppression since the arrival of the Spanish conquistadores in the 1530s. In 1780, the indigenous and mestizo peasantry mounted a rebellion against the Spanish Viceroyalty of Peru under the leadership of Túpac Amaru II (1742–1781), who claimed to be a direct descendent of the last Inca ruler. As was generally true of peasant rebellions, women played a crucial role both in support of the male fighters and by taking up arms themselves. At the start of the rebellion, Túpac Amaru's wife Micaela Bastidas (1744–1781) swiftly set out to recruit soldiers and distribute weapons. In council or through letters, Amaru and his wife regularly consulted and coordinated the war effort.[12] In one letter, Bastidas urged her husband not to squander his momentum, calling on him to lay siege to Cuzco, the former capital of the Inca Empire, showing a clear understanding of the tactics, logistics, and strategy of the war:

> Chepe: you will kill me with grief for you slowly go through the villages. . . . I am tired of telling you not to dally in those pueblos where there is nothing for us to do. But you occupy yourself passing through them without any consideration that our soldiers need to be fed even if one gives them money and this will also run out in due time. . . . We will also lose all those who I had rallied for our taking of Cuzco. . . . I warned you many times to go immediately to Cuzco, but you have not paid any attention. This has given them time to prepare themselves, as they have done, placing cannons on the Picchu Hill and other such dangerous machinery, so you no longer hold the advantage. . . . I guess God wants me to suffer for my sins.—Your Wife.[13]

Bastidas acted in the native Peruvian tradition of hereditary female chieftains who exercised local authority in the same manner as their male counterparts, an institution rooted in the time before the Spanish conquest. In Amaru's absence, Bastidas ruled the main rebel compound with an iron hand and was reportedly "fiercer than her husband."[14] As they moved through the countryside, they attracted thousands of followers, mostly peasants, but some Creoles as well. Gathering forces from across the continent, the Spaniards finally surrounded the insurgents and captured Bastidas and her family. In 1781, they executed her in front of Túpac Amaru and their son before executing them in turn.

A generation later, Creole revolutionaries, who often distanced themselves from both indigenous leaders and peasants, met with greater success. When Latin American independence leader Simón Bolívar (1783–1830) condemned the Spaniards during the Wars of Independence in South America (1810–1825), he often echoed Dessalines in his focus on imperial violations of women's honor. "The monsters and tigers of Spain have . . . used their infamous arms against the innocent feminine breasts of our beauties; they have shed their blood. They have killed many of them and they loaded them with chains, because they conceived the sublime plan of liberating their beloved country!"[15] Bolívar extended the concepts of male valor and courage that are at the core of nationalism to the women that had taken part in the uprisings, while using their example to inspire his men-at-arms to prove their own virility by defending their women's honor.

When speaking of the new nation of Gran Columbia at the Congress of Angostura (1818), Bolívar invoked the same Enlightenment language of a universal family of mankind that became the clarion call of modern revolution. "The greater part of the native peoples has been annihilated; the European has mingled with the American and with the African, and the African has mingled with the Indian and with the European. Born from the womb of a common mother, our fathers, different in origin and blood, are foreigners; all differ visibly in the epidermis, and this dissimilarity leaves marks of the greatest transcendence."[16] Notions of honor tied up with male virility and female virtue had an ancient pedigree long preceding the Enlightenment and had always been invoked in times of war. The change brought on by the modern concept of universal human rights was to extend this honor from the elite to all men and women so as to bind them together as one common national family.[17]

Where Túpac failed, Bolívar succeeded. Where Túpac's wife, Bastidas, co-led the revolt, Bolívar called on men to defend women's virtue and the mother country, rendering the women themselves passive. Gender dynamics influenced the contours of resistance movements even as women's opportunity for direct engagement expanded and contracted. Images of flesh and blood underscore the centrality of the body to resistance movements.

Failed Insurrections

Where they were able, local people thwarted military occupation with violent resistance throughout the nineteenth century. If they were reasonably well armed, their attacks on invaders could become full-fledged wars. Violence perpetrated on both sides typically gendered the conflicts, leaving a cult of masculine valor that would influence a people's adaptation to occupation as well as its final stand against it. Occasionally female warriors emerged who were either lauded for their enactment of roles traditionally reserved to men or as maternal figures inspiring freedom fighters. These wars took on different forms, typical of the multiplicity of responses to imperialism. Most became civil wars revealing preexisting divides among the colonized themselves as well as different relationships with the invading forces. The legacy of failure also left deep divisions within occupied territories, compromised imperial claims to benevolence, and inspired later generations to resume the fight.

The French conquest of Algeria began with the capture of the capital Algiers in 1830. As the occupiers steadily expanded their control along the Mediterranean coast, imperial speculators acquired agricultural land and subsidized large-scale settlement, triggering a land rush of French settlers. Initial resistance was fierce but decentralized. It eventually coalesced around Emir Abd el-Kader (1808–1883), elected chief of a tribal confederation in 1832. Member of a Sufi brotherhood who pledged jihad against the invaders, Abd el-Kader led bands of militants who resisted the French for over a decade. As early as 1835, Abd el-Kader worked the superpower rivalry between the French and the British to his advantage and obtained material support directly from the British consulate in Morocco.[18] His forces exacted their first victory against the French in 1835 at the Macta River in Western Algeria, twenty thousand Algerian cavalry against five thousand French. Taking advantage of the inhospitable terrain, Abd el-Kader's forces waged guerrilla war against the French for fifteen years until his capture in 1847.

The French responded with a brutal campaign of mass terror that lasted the decade. Marshal Thomas-Robert Bugeaud (1784–1849), the governor-general of French Algeria, ordered a scorched earth campaign as soon as he arrived in 1840. His troops had specific orders to burn crops, raze orchards, steal herds, and to kidnap women and children, claiming that he was merely adopting local tactics. "I am as much an Arab as you are. . . . Your vast solitudes, your steepest mountains, your crags, your deepest ravines cannot frighten me. . . . Like a river of fire I will scourge this land in all directions."[19] Bugeaud's primary tactical weapon was the *razzia*, a punitive raid into resisting villages where, according to one officer, French troops took on "a savagery that would make an honest bourgeois' hair stand on end."[20] Captured Algerian men were decapitated and their heads displayed on the ends of bayonets, mounted on pikes or walls, or hung from the saddles of cavalrymen. A cash prize was given for each pair of ears taken from the enemy, and sexual violence was understood to be a weapon of war. Interrogations to discover conspirators or hidden supplies included torture. Dr. Félix Jacquot (1819–1857), accompanying one such *razzia* in 1847, described their methods. Trying to requisition sufficient supplies for their dying horses, soldiers raided villages. During one raid, they threw an elderly woman from a balcony and stripped her naked in the streets, demanding the location of the supposedly hidden grain silos:

> Bent over with age, ruined by misery and time, stunned by her fall, besides being blinded and frozen with fear . . . half-dead, she tried to grasp anyone within reach to implore their mercy and kiss their clothing. She lavished kind names upon her young cavalier: "Sun of the days without fog, shadow near water, fountain of the desert" . . .—"Show us the silos!," they yelled even louder— "Flower of the sand, fertile palm," repeated the old lady. "All this gets us nowhere," said a soldier loading his rifle.[21]

Her response to this brutality was to recall men to their humanity by meeting violence with kindness. To no avail. The longer the war raged on, the harsher the reprisals.

Although the *razzias* pacified the population for a time, violent resistance erupted again in 1871. Seeing France's defeat by Germany in the Franco-Prussian War (1870–1871) as a sign from God, Muhammad al-Muqrani (1815–1871) mobilized several hundred thousand Berber peasants to rebel. It took French forces ten months to end the rebellion. By 1872, some three million Algerians had died from war and famine, their best lands seized by settlers, and their culture up-ended by systematic destruction of schools, libraries, and mosques.[22] The crushed Algerian resistance fragmented and went underground. It was left to another generation to finally win independence from the French Empire in 1962.

In British India, the East India Company had secured treaties with independent Mughal princes for over a century before a full-scale war of resistance broke out in 1857. Sepoys, elite Indian recruits into the British armed forces, began a mutiny in Meerut, near the capital at Delhi, after some in their ranks had been imprisoned for refusing to open cartridges greased with pig fat by mouth, a violation of Muslim dietary laws. This trigger was but one of many ways in which British imperialists, often motivated by a desire to spread Christian norms, disparaged Indian traditions. For instance, the recently-enacted Hindu Widows Remarriage Act (1856) banned the stigmatizing of widows, which included head shaving, denial of access to community wells, and otherwise being forced to live as outcasts.[23] As elsewhere, intrusions into the sphere of the intimate, including gender relations and bodily practices, provoked violence. When peasants supported the mutineers, it turned into full-scale war that spread throughout north-central India including major population centers at Lucknow, Delhi, and Kanpur. The British initially lost control of these regions and insurgents demanded the restoration of the Mughal emperor.

As the war escalated, some elite Indians joined the fray, including Lakshmibai, the Rani (queen) of independent Jhansi in North India. In the 1850s, the Rani of Jhansi (1828–1858) had mantained tolerable relations with the British even as they encroached on her territory. Her husband's death in 1853 produced a succession dispute because the British did not recognize her adopted son as the legitimate heir but instead allowed her to govern as a client ruler. This cooperation estranged her from some of her deceased husband's troops. Neither a collaborator nor a freedom fighter, the Rani of Jhansi wanted to protect the sovereignty of her state and believed that negotiating with the British would secure it. Indeed, at the start of the Indian Rebellion she sided with the British, even offering her troops to come to their aid, but they rejected her offer amid deepening mistrust. Persuaded to join the Indian Mutiny, the Rani of Jhansi embraced the freedom struggle as atrocities mounted on both sides. The sepoys accepted her leadership, as she wielded her husband's sword and dressed as a man, although legend has it that she also led warriors in battle as a mother, with her son strapped to her back in combat.[24] She won several victories but was killed in 1858 when a squadron of the King's Royal Irish Cavalry ambushed her encampment. Her heroism was celebrated across India. In the 1910s, radical nationalist Vinayak Savarkar (1883–1966) wrote in his biography of the Rani of Jhansi, "The flame of patriotism was always burning in her heart. And she was proud of her country's honour and pre-eminent in war. It is very rarely that a nation is so fortunate as to be able to claim such an angelic person as a daughter and queen."[25] Like many freedom fighters, the real Rani is lost beneath the mythology, as she was likely neither pure angel nor a pure patriot.

In 1900, the British confronted another warrior queen in Yaa Asantewaa (1840–1921), Queen Mother of Ejisu in West Africa's Asante Empire. Unlike India, West Africa had a long tradition of female participation in combat, including an "Amazon corps" of several thousand women soldiers in the neighboring Kingdom of Dahomey who were noted by the French for their remarkable speed and courage.[26] Although the Asante did not have a standing army of female warriors, they had a tradition of "female senior men" taking wartime leadership when male chiefs faltered.[27] The War of the Golden Stool (1900) began under such circumstances, when Governor Frederick Hodgson (1851–1925) of the British Gold Coast (modern Ghana) demanded to sit on the sacred Golden Stool, the throne of Asante that was left vacant after King Prempeh I (1870–1931) was exiled to the Seychelles Islands in the Indian Ocean. At a secret council held the night after Hodgson's inflammatory demand, Asantewaa called on the men to wage war against the British. "How can a proud and brave people like the Asante sit back and look while the white men took away their king and chiefs, and humiliated them with a demand for the Golden Stool. . . . If you, the chiefs of Asante, are going to behave like cowards and not fight, you should exchange your loincloths for my undergarments."[28] Asantewaa's challenge rallied the dispirited men to swear the oath of war. Within three days, her forces set siege to the main British fort at Kumasi, capital of Asante, led by the sixty-year-old queen mother who wore the leather belt and sword of a warrior chief. As a fleeing German teacher reported, Asantewaa was not merely a symbolic head but rather the supreme commander of the Asante forces:

> An old woman called Yaa Asantewaa lives in Adweso, the mother or the aunt of the chief there, a man who was sent into exile with Prempeh. Since then she has ruled the town. She has much influence in the whole of Asante, and is the soul and the head of the rebellion. When the Governor invited the chiefs to negotiate with him, she sent to tell them "I have loaded my gun, and not for nothing." She is in fact sitting quietly at Adweso, but sends her orders out from there to the different camps around Kumasi.[29]

The British defeated Asantewaa after eight months when reinforcements were dispatched from the main West African Regiment stationed at Sierra Leone. To the bitter end, Asantewaa blamed the setback on the cowardice of men. As she was escorted into exile, she turned to say "Asante women, I pity you." Someone asked, "What about us, the men?" Asantewaa replied, "Which men? The men died at the battle front."[30] Equating masculinity with willingness to die in battle, Asantewaa dismissed the male survivors as virtual women. The Asante Empire was incorporated into the Gold Coast Colony, but their fierce resistance gave them the distinction of being ranked among the so-called martial races within the British colonial hierarchy.

In all of these instances, imperialists used a divide-and-conquer strategy, exacerbating preexisting antagonisms between disparate groups of natives. Therefore, when anticolonial rebellions broke out, they often degenerated into civil wars. In German Southwest Africa (modern Namibia) the major ethnic groups—Ovambo, Nama, and Herero—became more antagonistic toward one another as German settlements infringed on their lands. The native peoples were pastoralists, raising cattle on large tracts of land. Some converted to Christianity, creating yet another divide. Even within ethnic groups, conflict rendered unified resistance to the Germans difficult; indeed, colonizers took sides in these disputes to gain advantage. When the Herero fought over who would succed Paramount Chief Maharero Tjamuaha (1820–1890), Samuel Maharero (1856–1923) relied on German support to oust the other contenders.

One of the disaffected, Daniel Kariko, acquired weapons from neighboring British Bechuanaland and was convicted of treason. Kariko wrote one last letter to his former chief and protector in 1896, evoking familial relations: "I wait as your younger brother praying, in this instance to tell you; If you kill me, then do not . . . send the very first people at hand, because you are lazy or so that you can say of those to be killed that they were not killed by you. . . . Will you have the bravery to face those, who know you to be the killer, who ask you 'Why did you kill Daniel,' to know that you killed a child of your mother."[31] Maharero confiscated their lands and supported their execution by the Germans, but Kariko escaped. Evoking the mother was intended to remind belligerents of literal and abstract ties of kinship, ties that might unify the colonized against the colonizer.

In 1897, when cattle blight decimated 90 percent of their stock, Herero and Nama began to sell their land to the Germans, something they had resisted for decades. Maharero facilitated the transactions. Disease spread and refugees fled to South Africa and Bechuanaland. Those who remained became increasingly desperate. By January 1904, some Herero rose in revolt under Maharero's leadership as a last resort against German policies that had dispossessed them of land, water, and cattle. Initially, eight thousand Herero, half of them armed with rifles, faced two thousand Germans. They attacked villages, killed settlers, and destroyed infrastructure like telegraph lines. One German reported that the Herero "beasts had raped the [German] women after murdering the men and then slaughtered them like sheep. . . . Patrols found the body parts hanging on trees like meat to be cured: excised breasts, arms, legs. And over there, the Herero women had mutilated half-grown boys with knives and then left them lying there to bleed to death!"[32] Whether the reports were true or not, they were enough to provoke a violent reaction from the Germans. By reporting that women were among the Herero combatants, Germans justified attacking Herero indiscriminately. Media coverage of the rebellion emphasized Herero ferocity, as seen in Figure 6.2.

The Germans, now armed with machine guns, responded to Herero raids with genocide. On his arrival in June 1904, General Lothar von Trotha (1848–1920) proclaimed, "I shall annihilate the revolting tribes with rivers of blood and rivers of gold. Only after a complete uprooting will something [new] emerge."[33] In an

Figure 6.2. **US news coverage of Herero Rebellion**
Fears of the contagion of anticolonial rebellion dominated newspaper coverage of the 1904 Herero uprising in German Southwest Africa (Namibia).

October 1904 letter to the German high command, known as the Extermination Order, he ordered that, "All Herero, armed or unarmed . . . will be shot dead . . . I will no longer accept women and children, but will . . . shoot at them."[34] This policy was a sharp departure from that of his immediate predecessor, Governor Theodor Leutwein (1849–1921), who was seen as too lenient by Kaiser Wilhelm II (1859–1941). Von Trotha dismissed Leutwein's objections, stating that "I deem it wiser for the entire nation to perish . . . The Herero nation must vanish from the face of the earth."[35] The Extermination Order divided officials in Berlin, endorsed by Chief General Alfred von Schlieffen (1833–1913) but opposed by Chancellor Bernhard von Bülow (1849–1929). The Kaiser finally agreed to rescind the order in December 1904.[36]

Von Trotha's actions illustrate how the power of individual imperialists on the ground could be nearly absolute. Moreover, the deliberate extermination of native peoples was far from unprecedented. Indeed, German imperialists cited the treatment of Native Americans by the US government. Bernhard Dernburg (1865–1937), in his inaugural speech as head of the German Imperial Colonial

Office, proclaimed in 1907, "There can be no doubt that some native tribes have to vanish, just as some animals perish because of the impact of civilization. . . . The history of the colonization of the United States, clearly the biggest colonial endeavor the world has ever known, had as its first act the complete annihilation of its native peoples."[37] Offered a year after the Herero War had ended, the proclamation attempted to legitimize German actions by situating them in the context of global imperialism, with US practices as the standard.

During the Herero War, noncombatants, including women and children, were herded into the arid Omaheke Desert where, "like a wounded beast," they were "tracked down from one water-hole to the next" until they died of thirst, hunger, or exposure.[38] In the words of one German missionary, the war "turned Hereroland into a desert, full of human corpses and the cadavers of livestock. Everywhere we encounter the bleaching bones of the Herero and the graves of brave German soldiers. The country has become a giant cemetery in which whites and blacks rest facing one another."[39] By the end of the conflict, some 70 to 80 percent of the Herero had perished, with most survivors confined to work camps, except for the *Bambusen*, Herero youths given as mascots to individual German soldiers.[40]

Initially, the Nama under the leadership of Hendrik Witbooi (d. 1905) supported the Germans in the war, but when they later joined the uprising the Nama used guerilla tactics that were far more successful than the open confrontation of the Herero. It took the Germans fourteen thousand troops and two years to finally suppress the rebellion. They lost two thousand troops in the conflict, compared to ten thousand Nama deaths, and at least sixty thousand Herero, a majority of the population.[41]

In the aftermath, some Herero youth pledged loyalty to the Germans. Youths in the *Otruppa* movement donned German uniforms and regalia. Although its origins are not entirely clear, the practice drew on the Herero tradition of marking a man's status and prowess on the body using ritual scarification, animal skin trophies, and colored hatbands. As one Herero informant explained the adoption of German military uniforms, "If you wear the clothes of your enemy, the spirit of the enemy is weakened. You are then wearing the spirit of his brothers and then they are weakened. Hereros did do this; there is the sense of this in wearing the German uniform."[42] The first evidence of *Otruppa* ceremonies appears in photos and accounts from the immediate aftermath of the genocide, in 1905–1908. They organized themselves into district regiments with ranking leaders taking the names and titles of former German officers. The 1923 funeral of Paramount Chief Maharero was a landmark event in this formation of a new Herero identity. The weeklong ceremony featured 2,500 uniformed Herero led by 170 officers mounted on horseback.[43] In 1940, South African colonial officials sought to understand why the Herero preserved German military orders long after the Germans departed in 1918 at the end of World War I. As one *Otruppa* informant tersely stated, "We do it so that we will be men."[44] Identifying with the victor to reclaim a masculine identity is one measure of the loss-of-self produced by imperialism. The recovery-of-self was also a gendered act, as the vanquished coopted some of the victor's power by mimicking him.

Millenarianism

Resistance movements led by armed militants in well-organized campaigns, or by guerilla fighters using whatever implements they had at their disposal, generally failed in the nineteenth and early twentieth centuries. As a response, some defeated people, like the Herero, believed in the power of wearing special clothing, including that of the enemy, to reclaim some of his power. Millenarian movements might also include the revival of spiritual belief systems and traditional cultural practices that had lapsed under pressure from European incursions. In different corners of the globe, native peoples reacted to failed military campaigns against the enemy by calling on higher powers to protect them as they ushered in the end of the world.

Violent conflict marked early British contact with the Maori of New Zealand, especially once land confiscation escalated after 1840. A series of resistance wars lasted from 1845 to 1872. In 1862, the Maori prophet Te Ua Haumene (1820s–1866) founded the syncretic Hauhau religion, which blended Christian parables with traditional Maori beliefs on the principle of Pai Mārire, goodness and peace. Te Ua claimed to have received a vision of the Archangel Gabriel, who revealed to him that the end of days was at hand, when the Europeans would be swept away and the land would be restored to its rightful Maori owners.[45] While many Maori were attracted to Hauhau pacifism, Te Ua's militant disciples embraced a more frenzied form of worship, with the revival of ancient rituals such as preserving the heads of enemy soldiers after cannibalizing their bodies. In common with similar resistance movements across the world, Maori warriors believed that the Hauhau incantation would render them invulnerable to bullets. In a 1920 interview, Te Kahupukoro, who survived the Maori attack on Sentry Hill in April 1864, described the war party's faith in the protective chant.

> There were two tiers of rifles blazing at us. We continued our advance, shooting and shouting our war-cries. Now we cried out the "*Hapa*" ("Pass over") incantation which Hepanaia had taught us, to cause the bullets to fly harmlessly over us: "*Hapa, hapa, hapa! Hau, hau, hau! Pai-marire, rire, rire—hau!*" As we did so we held our right hands uplifted, palms frontward, on a level with our heads—the sign of the *ringa-tu*. This, we believed, would ward off the enemy's bullets; it was the faith with which we all had been inspired by Te Ua and his apostles. . . . The bullets came ripping through our ranks. "*Hapa, hapa!*" our men shouted after delivering a shot, but down they fell. "*Hapa!*" a warrior would cry, with his right hand raised to avert the enemy's bullets, and with a gasp—like that—he would fall dead.[46]

In April 1865, Governor George Grey (1812–1898) officially condemned "the rites and practices of [this] fanatical sect, consisting, as they do . . . in the public parade of the cooked heads of their victims, in cannibalism, and in other revolting acts . . .

repugnant to all humanity."⁴⁷ A series of military defeats, along with the capture and imprisonment of hundreds of Hauhau warriors, brought the militant phase of the religious movement to a close in 1866.

In the early 1890s, a similar movement known as the Ghost Dance spread through Native American communities in the United States. The Lakota of the northern Great Plains defeated the US military in the Great Sioux War of 1876, but, further west, armed resistance to US expansion and land confiscation proved futile. Like the Maori, defeated Native Americans took refuge in a spiritual movement. The Paiute shaman Wovoka (1856–1932) claimed to have received a vision from the Christian God during the solar eclipse on January 1, 1889. His revelation foretold that all evils would be swept from the world, that the Earth would regenerate with plentiful game, and that the living would be reunited with the dead. Wovoka called for the ceremonial Round Dance, enacted by men and women in a circle with interlocking hands, to be performed every five days to hasten the dawn of the new era. In 1890, a Lakota Sioux delegation visited Wovoka in Nevada to receive his teachings. Wovoka's chief Lakota disciple, Kicking Bear (1846–1904), later recalled how the prophet described the new land that would be returned to the Native Americans after the white people vanished. "For my chosen people, the Indians, who are to inhabit it, and among them will be all those of their ancestors who have died. . . . The new lands will be covered with sweet-grass and running water and trees, and herds of buffalo and ponies will stray over it, that my red children may eat and drink, hunt and rejoice."⁴⁸ The Lakota adapted the Round Dance to resemble their traditional Sun Dance war ceremony, and called it the Spirit Dance, which was translated into English as the Ghost Dance.

Kicking Bear is believed to have introduced the concept of Ghost Shirts, worn by Lakota warriors during the dance to imbue them with the power to repel bullets. The movement came to a tragic end when the US military moved to suppress the "Messiah Craze" by arresting leading Lakota chiefs. Chief Sitting Bull (1831–1890) was killed by a policeman during his arrest, after which his supporters fled in fear of reprisals. A small band was surrounded by the US 7th Cavalry at Wounded Knee Creek in South Dakota. The commanding US officer gave the order to fire after a weapon discharged in the air when a young, deaf Sioux warrior refused to give up his gun. When the shooting had ended, 39 American soldiers and 153 Sioux, mostly women and children, lay dead, while a number of wounded Sioux died away from the battlefield.⁴⁹

In the aftermath, the only option was a more subtle resistance, to secretly practice their beliefs despite constant pressure from the US Indian Bureau to give up such things as healing rituals and spirit guides. As one Lakota holy man testified, "Except for the Ghost Dance, we actually gave none of these up that still were useful and essential in our lives. We simply practiced them in a quiet way and out of the government people's sight. How could we give up that which kept us close to [the Great Spirit] *Wankan-Tanka*, to Grandfather, to Grandmother Earth, and to the powers of the four directions?"⁵⁰ In contrast to the mechanistic view of nature held by many whites at the time, Lakota imagery suggests a sense of closeness to the earth that indigenous people maintained long after their subjugation.

At the turn of the twentieth century, imperial administrators in German East Africa (modern Tanzania) introduced a similar set of measures to strengthen their hold over the colony. They imposed a head tax, drafted forced labor for construction projects, and required each village to grow cotton for export. These policies disrupted the social fabric of native life by forcing men away from their villages to work and placed a severe strain on local resources. In 1904, a resistance movement emerged around spirit medium Kinjikitile Ngwale (d. 1905) who claimed to have communed with the fertility god Bokero while being possessed by a snake spirit. Kinjikitile persuaded his followers to unite the various ethnic groups in the region and rise up against the Germans, aided by a magical potion that allegedly turned bullets into water.[51] As explained by German mission inspector Alexander Merensky (1837–1918), "A new message came that in due time the earth would swallow up the whites; one should in confidence take up the battle with them; their guns would shoot water instead of bullets so that one will be able to beat the dangerous stranger to death with the Kirri, the cudgel."[52]

The ensuing Maji Maji Rebellion (1905–1907) took its name from the Swahili word for water, although the potion soon proved to be as ineffective as the Hauhau chant and the Ghost Dance. The Imperial German Army ruthlessly crushed the rebellion with a scorched earth policy similar to that perfected against the Herero, destroying villages, crops, and livestock while mowing down thousands of natives with machine guns. In *Water Rites*, a local stage act of protest to this day, the shock is still recalled to a heavy, frenetic drumbeat simulating gunfire. "When the warriors fled, they screamed, 'The *Maji* is a lie! The *Maji* is a lie!' But for my grandfather, Magwira, the *Maji* was not a lie. After all, the *Maji* had united our country."[53] Although the forced cultivation of cotton was the main cause of the Maji Maji Rebellion, a host of grievances contributed to the resentments that fueled the uprising. Indeed, Tanzania's first president, Julius Nyerere (1922–1999), suggested a strikingly different cause for the conflict. "Among the Wangindo, while they are not silent about German atrocities and the cotton system, they are much louder on the subject of German mercenaries and houseboys sleeping with their wives in circumstances which were a flagrant affront to Ngindo husbands. Adultery in Ngindo was punishable by war against offenders."[54] Colonial intimacy therefore contributed to native anger, as native men insisted on maintaining control over their women and disparaged interracial sex. Notably, German colonists agreed, which led the governor's office to issue a decree banning interracial marriage soon after the war broke out in 1905.[55]

All of these rebellions were undertaken by vanquished native peoples who had exhausted other options for resistance. Ironically, their desperate last acts contributed further to their oppression. Viewed as signs of their infantile minds and primitive cultures, millenarian movements only deepened imperial control.

In China, on the other hand, a millenarian movement hastened the fall of the Qing Empire at the hands of Chinese liberals. In the late 1890s, a militant secret society emerged known as the Righteous and Harmonious Fists, which featured many of the elements seen in other millenarian movements. The Chinese resented Western incursions after China's defeat in the Opium Wars (1839–1842; 1856–1860). The Boxers, as they were called by Western missionaries, combined martial arts training with a belief that "when a supplicant chanted the correct incantation, the god descended and possessed his body, and with much frothing at the mouth, he acquired invulnerability and superhuman skills with sword and lance."[56] The interference of Christian missionaries in local affairs was a major flashpoint for Chinese resentment, particularly when priests intervened in favor of Chinese Christians in legal disputes. This growing indignation turned violent with the Juye Incident of 1897, when Boxers killed two German missionaries from the Society of the Divine Word. In response, Kaiser Wilhelm II ordered the German East Asia Fleet to seize Jiaozhou Bay, to show the Chinese "with the most brutal ruthlessness" that he was "not to be toyed with."[57] An escalating series of attacks on Christian missions and converts finally erupted into the full-scale Boxer Rebellion (1899–1901).

In spring 1900, thousands of Boxers streamed toward Beijing carrying banners with their slogans: "Support the Ching! Destroy the Foreigner!" and "Fists of Righteous Harmony, carry out the Way on behalf of Heaven!"[58] In June, open fighting broke out after German Minister Clemens von Ketteler (1853–1900) ordered the unprovoked execution of a Boxer boy, causing thousands of Boxers to storm the city to burn down Christian churches along with any victims caught inside.[59] A multinational expedition of European, American, and Japanese marines promptly set out from the port of Tianjin to march on Beijing, as seen in Figure 6.3, leading to a declaration of war from Qing Prince Duan (1856–1922), a supporter of the Boxers. Joined by the Qing Imperial Army, the Boxers nonetheless remained a significant, though controversial, part of the Chinese confrontation with imperial powers. Even royal officials who were skeptical about Boxer mystical claims conceded that their broad populist appeal was a crucial link between the ruling Empress Dowager Cixi (1835–1908) and the Chinese masses. As one minister observed during a debate on how best to deploy the Boxers, "Perhaps their magic is not to be relied upon; but can we not rely on the hearts and minds of the people? Today China is extremely weak. We have only the people's hearts and minds to depend upon. If we cast them aside and lose the people's hearts, what can we use to sustain the country?"[60]

Boxers blamed women for the inevitable failure of Boxer magic. According to a Chinese account of the Boxer defeat at Tianjin, "Supporters of the Boxer bandits said: 'When the fighting began between the Boxers and the foreigners, the foreigners were unable to hold their own. Then, suddenly, in the midst of the foreign army there stood a naked woman. The Boxers' magical powers were thwarted, and they dared not advance.'"[61] One remarkable Boxer solution for such problems was the creation of a female unit, the Red Lanterns Shining. When Boxers

Figure 6.3.   Boxer Rebellion, 1900
China's "Society of Righteous Heavenly Fists" or Boxers believed they had special
powers to resist the bullets of their enemies, in this case the US Marines, which were
called in by the British to help restore order.

set siege to the Northern Cathedral of Beijing, with many women among the
thousands of Catholics who had taken refuge inside, they said, "We have to await
the Red Lantern Shining before we can advance. The Red Lanterns are all girls
and young women, so they do not fear dirty things."[62] Much like other societies
where women were attributed with extraordinary powers *because* they were
deemed polluted, the Red Lanterns were believed to be capable of flight, walking
on water, setting fires from a distance, and causing enemy guns to fail, powers
that the Boxers did not claim for themselves. They also engaged in far more mundane domestic tasks, such as caring for wounded Boxers and mending their
clothing. The Red Lanterns were led by a young prostitute, the Holy Mother
Lotus Huang, and provided a refuge for ambitious women seeking to escape the
confines of Confucian patriarchy.[63] The Boxer Rebellion was ultimately crushed
in a wave of rape, looting, and massacres by occupying troops, after which the
surviving Boxers simply changed their notorious outfits and faded into the populace.[64] Yet their views on gender, and especially on women's sexuality, persisted
well into the twentieth century.

MASS MOVEMENTS

Such views would increasingly come under attack. The failed wars and millenarian movements of the nineteenth and early twentieth centuries inspired moderate reformers to work within imperial systems to bring about gradual change.

"Liberal Nationalism" might eventually demand the full ouster of the colonizer but advocated adaptation of imperial institutions for postcolonial purposes. Liberal nationalists worked from within a hybridized Western ideology, exposing the contradictions between liberalism and imperialism. "Marxism" similarly worked from within a hybridized Western ideology but usually to more radical ends. Whereas both liberals and Marxists might use acts of "Civil Disobedience," some revolutionaries inflated it into an ideology, with both Western and Eastern origins. These different strategies demonstrate the multiplicity of responses to imperialism and the degree to which local conditions complicated challenges to imperial rule.

Liberal Nationalism

After the failure of millenarian movements, liberal nationalists committed to working within the imperial system for the rights of native peoples. Separatist Maori, for example, set up a ruling Grand Council in the 1890s, with a constitution, a cabinet, and a Minister of Affairs to petition Queen Victoria for self-government. In 1897, Apirana Ngata (1874–1950) helped found the Young Maori Party, from which he was elected to New Zealand's parliament in 1905 and then appointed to the cabinet in 1909. From 1928 to 1934, he served as New Zealand's Minister of Native Affairs and was the first Maori to serve as acting Deputy Prime Minister. Ngata used his positions to promote Maori cultural rejuvenation, believing that access to Western skills and power structures was the best way to advance Maori interests.

In the United States, where racial discrimination severely limited political options for the Lakota Sioux, intellectuals such as Luther Standing Bear (1868–1939), recruited for the Carlisle Indian Industrial School, performed in Buffalo Bill's Wild West shows in England and appeared in a dozen Hollywood films. He was active in the Indian Rights Association, which successfully petitioned President Franklin Roosevelt (1882–1945) to include the study of Native Americans in public school curricula and to allow tribes greater self-government. He used his writing to promote greater understanding and tolerance. In the forward to *Land of the Spotted Eagle* (1933), Standing Bear asserted the following:

> White men seem to have difficulty in realizing that people who live differently from themselves still might be traveling the upward and progressive road of life. . . . It is still popular conception, on the part of the Caucasian mind, to regard the native American as a savage, meaning that he is low in thought and feeling, and cruel in acts; that he is a heathen, meaning that he is incapable, therefore void, of high philosophical thought concerning life and life's relations. . . . The inner life of the Indian is, of course, a closed book to the white man. So from the pages of this book I speak for the Lakota—the tribe of my birth.[65]

These efforts were typical of movements throughout the colonized world in the 1920s and 1930s that sought to spread knowledge of traditional cultures and use modern institutions to gain greater autonomy.

In the immediate aftermath of the failed Boxer Rebellion, most Chinese reformers dismissed the Boxer movement as an "uprising of the superstitious
mob and of ignorant and worthless armed bandits."[66] Yet, as early as 1903,
Chinese nationalist leader Sun Yat-sen (1866–1925) praised the Boxers for their
spirited resistance, seeing them instead as heroic, if simple-minded, patriots:
"Look at the Boxers [who] rose in violent resistance to the foreigners and fought
like madmen. . . . Only they were stupid . . . and did not know the value of firearms and merely depended upon naked blades. . . . If they had cast aside these
crude weapons and changed to modern ones, it is doubtful whether the allied
expeditionary force would have achieved such quick results. . . . If the entire
country were aroused, there would be no comparison."[67]

The widespread view that Boxer patriotism and bravery was defeated by madness and ignorance convinced reformers that China's survival depended on reno-
vating Chinese gender norms along Western lines. Kang Youwei (1858–1927), a
leading Confucian political theorist and supporter of the Qing dynasty, held that
China's decline was due to the physical weakness of its men caused by their ener-
vating decadent lifestyle. Leftist social critic Lu Xun (1881–1936) also decried the
lack of Chinese manliness, casting the blame on the traditional cultivation of
gentility and the popularity of female impersonation on stage.[68] For nationalists
of all stripes, the solution was to build strong, manly Chinese bodies, rejecting
traditions that blurred gender distinctions. Physical education and military drills
became standard in China's modernized curriculum, and athletic venues and
team sports became a fixture of Chinese urban planning.[69] Many nationalist reformers also embraced women's liberation arguing that it was impossible for
China to become strong so long as half the population was excluded from schooling or work outside the home.

Sun Yat-sen's "People's Principles" of nationalism, democracy, and social
welfare were embraced by women activists such as revolutionary feminist Qiu
Jin (1875–1907). After joining Sun's group in 1905, Qiu Jin founded the radical
Chinese Women's Journal in Shanghai, writing that, "We want to unite our sisters into a solid whole. . . . We Chinese women should become the vanguard in
arousing women to welcome enlightenment."[70] To modernize Chinese gender
relations, reformers sought to ban foot binding, prostitution, and pornography.
But the Qing were threatened by such sweeping reforms and executed Qiu Jin
for her part in a conspiracy in 1907. Nonetheless, in 1911 Sun Yat-sen's Revolutionary Alliance successfully overthrew the Qing Emperor Puyi (1906–1967),
bringing China's imperial dynasty to an end. This was soon followed by civil
war between communists and nationalists, which made nation building impossible until 1949 when the nationalists fled to the island of Taiwan.

Liberal nationalists in many parts of the world formed national congresses,
believing that imperial institutions were flexible enough to gradually transfer
authority to local elites. Liberal Western institutions initially supported these congresses. In lands formerly controlled by the Ottoman Empire, defeated after World
War I, liberals initially welcomed League of Nations mandates that promised

gradual self-governance. But in Syria and Lebanon, the French Empire imposed more direct rule, creating a hierarchy of citizens that privileged a French-educated native elite while dismissing populist demands for the same rights and protections afforded to French citizens. The quest for full citizenship rights for all men remained a constant source of protest during the mandate period, with major social fault lines between those who believed the path lay in secular Pan-Arab unity and those who gravitated toward Islamist egalitarianism.

In 1920, General Henri Gouraud (1867–1946) marked his arrival in Beirut as French high commissioner of Syria by situating France's newest colonial subjects within the same rubric of paternalism as other French imperial possessions. "France has always found pleasure in this gift, to see marching by her side her adopted children like her own children. Who could believe that [the] Moroccans and Senegalese, after having spilled their blood for four years on the battlefield, would sacrifice themselves again yesterday, if France were not a true mother to them?"[71] The family metaphor continued to position Europeans as superiors, infantilizing colonial subjects. The French cultivated a native elite, primarily Christian, who ruled until independence. Although the French issued a constitution that promoted religious pluralism, it required the presidency to be held by a Christian and the prime minister's post to be held by a Sunni Muslim.

Within a generation, independence leaders turned these images on their heads. The German defeat of France in World War II signaled the illegitimacy and vulnerability of French rule. In December 1943, as independence neared, Lebanon's leading magazine *al-Dabbur* (The Wasp) celebrated with a cover titled "Here is Our New Emblem": a bare-chested warrior-citizen wielding a sword and shield to protect his glamorous female companion (see Figure 6.4).[72] Wearing the Phrygian cap, the companion represented France, now in a subordinate position, disempowered by her femininity and dependent on Lebanese male leadership. Independence leaders and the international community pressured General Charles de Gaulle (1890–1970), the leader of the French government in exile, to end the mandate.

By the 1950s, liberal nationalists who had organized in Europe's colonies since World War I convinced some European powers to take gradual steps toward exiting their colonies. Except for Algeria, most African colonies in the French Empire transitioned to independence peacefully. Liberal parties in metropole and colony alike worked together to achieve the indigenization of business, politics, and education. In French West Africa, close political, cultural, and economic connections fostered the development of African liberalism. In Ivory Coast, future first president Félix Houphouët-Boigny (1905–1993), descended from prominent Akan chieftains, was a Catholic, a doctor, and an investor in coffee plantations. Through a National Farmer's Association, he promoted agricultural development, lobbying for better prices for export products. Gaining election to the French Constituent Assembly, he sponsored legislation to abolish forced labor throughout the French Empire. He then worked through various Ivoirian democratic parties to advance the cause of national self-determination for all of French

Figure 6.4.   "Here is our New Emblem," *The Wasp,* **1943**
Reflecting the changed circumstances of the French Empire during the Nazi occupation, a newly independent Lebanese man protects his female companion.

Africa. On his appointment to the French cabinet in 1956, he evoked familial
metaphors consistent with native Akan principles of leadership: "I did not know
that in accepting this engagement . . . that I would extend my family. Today, it is
all of the Baule . . . all of Côte d'Ivoire, all of francophonic Black Africa . . . that [I]
would like to serve with all [my] soul."[73] Houphouët-Boigny positioned himself
as both leader and servant, envisioning a unity of French Africans. Less radical
than pan-Africanism, Francophonie paid homage to the Empire.

In Congo, the Liberal Party of Belgium enabled future president Patrice
Lumumba (1925–1961) to develop his own brand of Congolese Liberalism. In
speeches and writings throughout the 1950s, Lumumba insisted that women's
education was essential to Congolese progress and that women should have
equal political rights and opportunities to work outside the home. Lumumba
often focused his remarks on the so-called *évolués,* Congolese men with a Western education who were said to be "evolving" toward a European identity. For
Lumumba, the evolution of men, to say nothing of the nation as a whole, was

limited so long as women were unable to engage as equal partners in raising educated children and contributing to Congo's economic prosperity. Whereas many
évolués thought that a standard French education in the humanities and sciences
was a pointless waste of time for women, Lumumba disagreed. "Yes, they will
serve her amply! What is more pleasant than having a spouse who speaks French
and who puts all her theoretical knowledge into practice! . . . Are we not dis-
tressed each time we observe that, as soon as we start speaking French to visiting
friends, our wives suddenly become 'strangers' because they do not know the
language?"[74] Moreover, Lumumba held that women's ability to enter the workplace alongside men was not merely a matter of gender rights or of economic
benefit but also a matter of racial equality and crucial to the success of Western
societies. "If white women work in offices, why not black women? If we men
work in offices in the same way as Europeans do, why can't our women?"[75]

Lumumba criticized "little kings" who saw their wives more as servants than
companions.[76] He spoke of a new kind of manhood, one that cast aside backward
customs such as arranged marriage and bride price, holding that a proper *évolué*
man must be a caring, responsible, enlightened head of household in partnership
with his wife. Although Lumumba was unable to secure a woman's right to vote
at a time when most Belgians and Congolese agreed that politics was "a male
affair," he was remarkable for promoting women's equal civic rights at a time
when political citizenship was coded male.[77] In 1960, Lumumba became the first
elected prime minister of an independent Congo, having led the struggle for liberation from Belgium as head of the broad-based Congolese National Movement.
Despite being in office only a short six months before his assassination in January
1961, Lumumba's legacy endured due to his extensive writings on Pan-African
unity and women's rights. His emphasis on the importance of women's full citizenship was exceptional within the masculinist discourses of nationalism, best
captured in Lumumba's declaration in *Congo: My Country* (1962): "When you
civilize a man, you only civilize an individual; but when you civilize a woman,
you civilize a whole people."[78]

Liberal feminist interracial women's cooperation also resulted in anti-imperialist
agitation. In Uganda, a long tradition of higher education for African women, many
of whom studied in Britain, meant that educated African, British, and South Asian
women shared similar visions for an independent Uganda in the 1940s and 1950s.
Their commitment to nonracialism evolved out of the inclusionary efforts of
Anglican missionaries and the Girl Guides, established in 1921.[79] By 1946, women
activists believed a nonsectarian organization was needed so they founded the
Ugandan Women's Association. Their membership grew to two thousand in the
1950s and doubled again in the 1960s. Hemantini Bhatia, an organizer of Indian
descent, said "here we felt like one."[80] However, to protest the British government's
1953 exile of Buganda's king, Kabaka Mutesa II (1924–1969), black Ugandan women
allied with other African women's organizations to form the Mothers of the Nation.
Speaking in Luganda and darkening their eyes, wearing "long sashed bark cloth"
and not grooming their hair, they protested in traditional fashion outside the

British governor's mansion until eventually the king was reinstated in 1955.[81] Although strategic racial separatism was effective for certain protest actions, interracial cooperation was the norm. After Uganda achieved independence in 1962, the Ugandan Women's Association successfully lobbied for including women's rights in the constitution. They thus blended tradition in their style of protest with modernity in their women's rights agenda.

Marxism

Liberal nationalism tended to appeal to educated elites who had developed hybrid identities. Others sought a more populist and sometimes violent approach to ending imperialism and promulgated a more comprehensive critique of it. By the early twentieth century, and especially after the establishment of the Soviet Union in 1922, many anticolonial revolutionaries were drawn to the Marxist promise of radical egalitarianism. The premise of the ideology formulated by Karl Marx (1818–1883) in *The Communist Manifesto* (1848) and in *Das Kapital* (1867) was that workers, the proletariat, should control the means of economic production and equitably share in the fruits of their labor. Because the capitalist class, the bourgeoisie, would never voluntarily give up wealth and power, Marx believed that this would only come to pass after violent revolution. Vladimir Lenin (1870–1924), the leader of Russia's successful Communist Revolution (1917), extended Marx's critique of social and economic oppression to the realm of empire, which he deemed the ultimate and most exploitative form of advanced capitalism. Marx was intrigued by the notion of the premodern, clan-based, matrilineal social order, and he often ridiculed the patriarchal, colonialist, and ethnocentric assumptions of his contemporaries. Marx spoke approvingly of "the intelligent black" Australian Aboriginal, by contrast to the English civilizer, a "silly . . . gentleman . . . ass," and he attacked the British Reverends, Russian Tsars, and Indian Brahmins alike for amassing power at the expense of women.[82] Marx's creed bridged cultural and gender divides with its emphasis on class-based solidarity and was therefore especially resonant with the oppressed victims of imperial economic exploitation.

Studying at Western-oriented educational institutions or in the West itself exposed young elites from the colonies to Marxist ideas. In the 1920s and 1930s, the London School of Economics attracted ambitious students from across the British Empire. "The LSE was like a miniature UN, and the exchange of ideas with some of the most brilliant minds did help us a great deal," recalled one alumnus.[83] Many became radicalized by their exposure to shared racial prejudice. On hearing the news of the Italian invasion of Abyssinia (modern Ethiopia), Indian students in London stood in solidarity with subjugated Ethiopians. "We felt terribly shocked at the way the Italians bombed the whole of Abyssinia. And being also black, naturally that influenced us a lot."[84] Snehansu Kanta Acharya (1913–1986) was Indian, not black, but claimed membership in a community of the dispossessed. Pan-Africanism clearly mobilized anticolonial resistance among all colonized peoples, not just those of African descent.

Communism attracted Indian nationalists "because that was the one party which was talking about Indian freedom. They were trying to form groups of Indians in Cambridge, Oxford, London and some other cities to give Communist ideas to students."[85] Jyoti Basu (1914–2010) went on to a career in postindependence India as a member of the Communist Party and Minister of West Bengal. British Marxists in India also sowed the seeds of rebellion when they taught classes based on Marx's text *Wage-Labour and Capital* (1849) at Saint Paul's College in Calcutta. Professor Christopher Ackroyd was a clergyman, labor organizer, and whistle-blower who investigated the shooting of two Indian political prisoners in police custody. A new breed of radical, he "seemed more interested in winning converts to Marxism than to Christianity."[86] Radical educators might enjoy a wide sphere of action because of the limited ability of the government to crack down on subversive instructors. Some influential college administrators defended academic freedom, which included the right to criticize imperial government.

In China, Mao Zedong (1893–1976) discovered Marx's ideology during his brief time as a provincial rebel soldier in 1911–1912, inspired by Sun Yat-sen's revolution against the Qing dynasty. Given the penetration of American capitalism (see Figure 6.5), Mao was not convinced that liberalism would go far enough. By 1917,

Figure 6.5.   Keds shoes advertised in China
American capitalism destabilized traditional culture, contributing to the outbreak of the liberal revolution launched by Sun Yat-sen against the Qing dynasty in 1911.

Mao was a leading student activist at First Normal School of Hunan Province, where his first article, printed in the radical *New Youth* magazine of Shanghai, called on readers to build their physical fitness in service of revolution. When the nationalist May Fourth Movement swept China in 1919, in response to Western imperial powers endorsing the expansion of the Japanese Empire at China's expense, Mao embraced revolutionary Marxism, joining the Chinese Communist Party (CCP) at its foundation in 1921. Mao swiftly rose through the ranks to become a leading Marxist theorist by 1927 and then de facto leader of the CCP and of the People's Liberation Army (PLA) in 1935. Unlike orthodox communists, Mao held that revolution could emerge as an agrarian peasant uprising from below. For Mao, the mobilizing of peasant women to support revolution was therefore essential and displaced the usual Marxist emphasis on organizing men working in factories.

As early as 1921, Mao arranged for groups of radical Chinese women activists to study abroad in France. In 1927, Mao wrote of the "four thick ropes" of oppression that kept the Chinese peasantry in a state of feudal subservience:

> A man in China is usually subjected to the domination of three systems of authority (political authority, clan authority, and religious authority). . . . As for women, in addition to being dominated by these three systems of authority, they are also dominated by the men (the authority of the husband). These four authorities—political, clan, religious, and masculine—are the embodiment of the whole feudal-patriarchal ideology and system, and are the four thick ropes binding the Chinese people, particularly the peasants.[87]

In the Long March of 1934–1935, Mao led the PLA away from confrontation with the nationalist Kuomintang in South China to instead fight the Japanese Empire in North China. Some two thousand women joined in the PLA's baptism of fire, including Kang Keqing (1911–1992), known as the Girl Commander or the Red Amazon, who led a battalion of eight hundred men and went on to become president of the All-China Women's Federation.[88] After Mao's victory in 1949, the Red Army served as the new blueprint for Chinese society as a whole, with the strong, resolute communist soldier as the new model man.[89] The unisex Mao suit, patterned after the military uniform, was made standard attire for both men and women, extending the symbol of China's power and progress to women. By erasing gender difference in the public sphere, the Mao suit therefore became the social emblem of the Chinese Communist Party's theoretical commitment to women's emancipation and gender equality.[90]

Vietnam's independence leader Ho Chi Minh (1890–1969) came to Marxism from a rather different path, having left his village in 1911 to travel the world by working odd jobs on ships and during extended stays in London and New York. His political awakening took place after he moved to Paris in 1919, where he was radicalized by the refusal of the Western imperial powers to give Vietnam the same rights of self-determination that were proclaimed for European peoples in the Treaty of Versailles (1919). Ho also recognized early that the plight of women under colonialism could serve as a lightning rod for building opposition to French rule. In 1922, he published an article in *Le Paria*, a newspaper he founded in Paris, where he appealed to a French audience for support by highlighting the abuse of women:

> Colonization is in itself an act of violence of the stronger against the weaker. This violence becomes still more odious when it is exercised upon women and children. It is bitterly ironic to find that civilization—symbolized in its various forms, *viz.*, liberty, justice, etc., by the gentle image of woman, and run by a category of men well known to be champions of gallantry—inflicts on its living emblem the most ignoble treatment and afflicts her shamefully in her manners, her modesty, and even her life. Colonial sadism is unbelievably widespread and cruel. . . . These facts will allow our Western sisters to realize both the nature of the "civilizing mission" of capitalism, and the sufferings of their sisters in the colonies.[91]

Ho's gender politics bordered on the paternalistic, but highlighting the victimization of women by imperialists had become a standard feature of anti-imperialism. At the same time, it disempowered women as activists in their own liberation.

In 1923, Ho left Paris for the Soviet Union and later for China, where he became steeped in the ideology of revolutionary Marxism. In 1941, Ho returned to Vietnam to lead the Viet Minh guerrilla war against both the Vichy French and the Japanese Imperial Army. In 1942–43, while jailed in China, Ho wrote a series of poems known as the *Prison Diary of Ho Chi Minh*. In one poem, Ho wrote of how, "In the mountains, I met the tiger and came out unscathed."[92] In another poem, Ho wrote that "When the prison doors are opened, the real dragon will fly out."[93] Following his escape from prison, Ho consolidated his power and moved ruthlessly against any opponents, purging and executing many thousands of rival fighters, making little distinction between dissident communists and nationalist opponents: "All those who do not follow the line that I have set out will be smashed."[94]

Like Mao, Ho adapted Marxism to suit the circumstances of Indochina. Reflecting his own hybrid identity, he appropriated key features of Western liberalism into his ideology. Whereas Lenin's analysis of imperialism as a parasitic stage of capitalism first attracted Ho to communism, Ho couched Vietnam's Declaration of Independence (1948) in the Western vocabulary of rights. It began, "All men are created equal; they are endowed by their Creator with certain unalienable Rights; among these are Life, Liberty, and the pursuit of Happiness."[95] Ho then invoked the French Revolution's Declaration of the Rights of Man and of the Citizen (1789): "All men are born free and with equal rights, and must always remain free and have equal rights."[96] It went on to analyze imperialism and expose the hypocrisy of the Enlightenment thinkers who justified it. Thereafter, war consumed Indochina for two decades, ousting first the French Empire and then the United States when it intervened during the Vietnam War (1955–1975).

Civil Disobedience

Ho fought fire with fire. In the Marxist view, imperial violence could only be overthrown by the violence of the colonized. But some anti-imperialists carved out a different path. India's pacifist independence leader Mahatma Gandhi (1869–1948) charted a path toward independence that derived not from the barrel of a gun but from his asceticism and moral authority. Although he began his career as a lawyer serving the British Empire in South Africa, Gandhi abandoned liberalism in favor of Hindu asceticism, marked by the masculine ability to discipline the mind and regulate the sexual body, which he then used to subvert the foundations of the colonial order.[97] Nonetheless, some claimed he transcended the man–woman dichotomy and therefore could mobilize both men and women for the cause of Indian liberation. Gandhi developed his philosophy of nonviolent resistance from observing the passive resistance of his mother and wife. Gandhi held that women embodied the dual impulse for "obedience and rebellion against authority" that could challenge the colonial state without provoking violence. He took on these "female strengths" in his own personification of Indian nationalism.[98] Whereas other liberation movements invited women to take on masculine attributes by fighting alongside men, Gandhi feminized the usually masculinist struggle against empire by organizing men and women in acts of passive resistance. He argued that "India's salvation depends on the sacrifices and enlightenment of her women. . . . Man and woman are one, their problems must be one in essence. The soul in both is the same."[99]

While some nationalists invoked the sword or the iron forge, Gandhi invoked the *charkha* (spinning wheel) and *khadi* (homespun cloth) as symbols of India's national identity.[100] Gandhi's model for female strength was not India's warrior-princess, the Rani of Jhansi, but rather the stoic, long-suffering Princess Draupadi from the ancient Hindu epic *Mahabharata*, who called on the god Krishna to protect her from ravishment. "To me," Gandhi stated in 1921, "the female sex is not the weaker sex; it is the nobler of the two: for it is even today the embodiment of sacrifice, silent suffering, humility, faith and knowledge."[101] Gandhi's emphasis on nonviolence was crucial in persuading millions of Indian women of all castes to venture outside the domestic sphere in mass public protests (see Figure 6.6).

Gandhi also attracted people from different religions. His philosophy merged elements of Hindu renunciation of materialism and of Buddhist self-enlightenment with the pacifist Christian ethos of the Sermon on the Mount. His creed was a direct challenge to the ideology of muscular Christianity that had previously given moral force to the civilizing mission of the British Empire. When the British reacted to Gandhi's peaceful tactics with violence, they only succeeded in exposing their own savagery and thereby strengthening India's claim to civilization. Gandhi was jailed along with tens of thousands of his followers. The resulting outcry at British tactics, both in India and in the West, resulted in their release eight months later, followed by the Gandhi–Irwin Pact (1931) where the British renounced such

Figure 6.6.   Indian Women in the Salt March, 1930
Marching to protest injustice is a classic strategy of civil disobedience. As an extension of their domestic role, women answered Gandhi's call to march against British taxes on salt.

measures. This same pattern would repeat itself until India finally achieved independence in 1947.

African Nationalists also used the tactics of nonviolent civil disobedience. When Kwame Nkrumah (1909–1972) began in the 1940s to organize resistance in Ghana, his calls to "positive action" were modeled after Gandhi's techniques.[102] The resistance strategies of Kenneth Kaunda (b. 1924), Zambia's first president on independence in 1964, were similarly influenced by Gandhism. "I could not lend myself to take part in any (violent) campaigns. *I reject absolutely violence in any of its forms as a solution to our problem.*"[103] To be sure, the appeal of Gandhi's approach for African freedom fighters seems to have been more practical than philosophical, as when Kaunda expressed the view that, "Man, just like any other animal, is violent."[104] African revolutionaries did not shy away from violent opposition to the imperial state or domestic rule by European settlers, yet Gandhi's philosophy provided an alternative model of nonviolent resistance. Kaunda further merged Gandhian collective action with Marxist ideals of a classless society organized around village industry. Kaunda's biography in some ways mirrors that of Africa as a whole, vacillating between the appeal of Gandhian *Satyagraha*, or Soul Force, and the mystique of African warrior masculinity. In general, African liberation movements shifted toward violence only after first attempting to achieve their goals through peaceful means. At the 1958 All-Africa People's Conference, hosted by Nkrumah, Algerian rebels who had taken up arms against the French had a difficult time gaining legitimacy due to prevailing neo-Gandhian sentiment.

Civil disobedience took many forms. Strikes, boycotts, and marches erupted in almost every colony during World War II. Nigeria's cost of living increased 74 percent between 1939 and 1943 as labor power, access to overseas markets, and agricultural output dwindled. Yoruba women in Nigerian cities, especially the capital Lagos, were active merchants and traders. They sustained male strikers during Nigeria's general strike of 1945 by lowering prices, extending credit, or contributing directly to protest funds. During the six weeks of the strike, 150,000 government workers walked off their jobs. It came after four years of strife in which the government instituted price controls and managed food distribution. To subvert price controls, Nigerian men and women alike engaged in acts of sabotage and a brisk black market trade. By 1944, over two-thirds of Nigerians obtained their food on the black market.

Organized opposition came from the main nationalist newspaper, the *West African Pilot*, the Nigerian National Democratic Party, and the Lagos Market Women's Association, which stated, "Lagos women have not only to feed and clothe their unemployed husbands and relatives but also to pay their income tax for them, lest they are sent to prison for defaulting."[105] They achieved partial success when the government raised the taxable income level.

However, continuing food shortages inspired market women to take more dramatic action. Over one thousand gathered in August 1945, and, shouting in Yoruba, demanded an end to the government-managed markets. Refusing to speak in English was a palpable form of resistance in itself. British officials demanded they behave more like British ladies who stood patiently in ration lines.[106] Meanwhile trade unionists, although supportive of the protesters, insisted that the real casualty of wartime economic controls was the male wage earner who could not support his family. Contrary to market women's interests, male strikers demanded a family wage comparable to that earned by Europeans. Culturally relative discourses about women's labor therefore collided. They demanded government allowances on par with those granted to Europeans, but did not receive them due in part to the assumption that maintaining a European family cost more. Unionists and market women demanded an increase in the cost-of-living allowance, but the government refused, arguing that it would worsen economic conditions and that male workers should better control their women.[107]

In response, the government organized a commission that recommended increased wages for men because "The sooner the male ceases to rely upon the economic contribution of the female to the family exchequer, the sooner will the wage structure be founded upon a more correct basis."[108] Unionists welcomed the report and expected the government to enact its recommendations. But more commissions followed and another report concluded that the African family structure, where polygamy was still widely practiced, nullified universalist claims to government entitlements. African difference precluded basic justice once again. An editorial in the *Daily Service*, the organ of the more radical Nigerian Youth movement, brooked no compromise: "Until men are *treated as men and paid as men* on the basis of the services they render irrespective of their race and colour, no Nigerian would be stupid enough to regard himself sincerely as a member of the British Commonwealth of Nations."[109] Masculine honor trumped metropolitan affiliation, and wartime discrimination provoked nationalist rebellion.

TRANSFERS OF POWER

Men who served in the armed forces during World War II made even stronger claims to masculinity. World War II galvanized anti-imperialist movements, exposing the vulnerability of the European powers as well as their dependence on native labor for their very survival. The war against Nazi Germany and Imperial Japan inspired many to serve in "European Militaries" proud to defend the so-called free world. On their return, African servicemen therefore demanded greater freedom and eventually national independence. Conversely, some colonized people welcomed Japanese invaders as liberators who pledged to safeguard Asia for Asians. Japan's campaign to rally other Asians to support its expanding empire is seen in Figure 6.7. Like the Burmese who eventually broke away from Japanese sponsorship to form a truly independent force to fight imperial rule, Indonesians were motivated to defeat both the Japanese and the Dutch. They joined "Japanese-Sponsored Militaries" because they were impressed by Japan's victories but also because they felt no loyalty toward their colonial masters. Where the Japanese occupation proved brutal, as in Indonesia, "Independence Armies" formed that initially worked with the Japanese but ultimately turned against them. These differences illustrate the range of responses to European imperialism even as it was crumbling.

Figure 6.7. Manchukuo
Commemorating Japan's occupation of Manchuria in 1935, this propaganda poster promotes Asian unity in the face of Western Imperialism.

European Militaries

Of necessity, European militaries had to adapt to the cultures of their native recruits. Recruiters recognized, and even respected, military athleticism in the form of native sport and dance. The African tradition of military dance for ethnic cohesion persisted long after the advent of European empire, as described by a Swazi warrior in 1943: "The warriors dance and sing at the *Incwala* and so they do not fight, although they are many and from all parts of the country and are jealous and proud. When they dance they feel they are one and they can praise each other."[110] For African colonial soldiers in the late imperial period, Western sports replaced tribal dance as the means to promote physical fitness, a competitive spirit, unit discipline, and social cohesion. Besides its role in building the character and self-esteem of individual sportsmen, the emergence of colonial or municipal football teams produced an awareness of belonging to a broader national entity above and beyond ancient tribal divisions. The playing fields of empire also provided a rare venue where Africans met their colonial rulers on equal terms, whether in the mixed-race teams of the King's African Rifles or in the polo matches championed by Nigeria's elite officer corps.

African veterans returning from the frontlines of World War II held an iconic status in nationalist narratives of Africa's political awakening, although their actual role in revolution was often more symbolic. In 1948, British colonial police in the capital of Gold Coast (Ghana) fired on a peaceful march of veterans protesting the denial of jobs and stipends that had been promised them during the war. The resulting Accra Riots became a milestone in Africa's liberation struggle, forcing the British into a course of reforms that led to Ghana's independence in 1957. Nationalists framed the "unprovoked massacre" of veterans from the highly decorated Gold Coast Regiment as an affront to all the people of Ghana and an indictment of the colonial system as a whole.[111] The disrespect of African men in uniform, despite their wartime sacrifices, underscored the inability of the colonial order to meet the aspirations of all Africans.

This was even more apparent in colonies such as Rhodesia (modern Zimbabwe) where the large white settler population made the color line of racial inequality a daily fact of life. At the 1940 recruitment ceremony for the Rhodesian African Rifles (RAR), soldiers heard a stirring speech about how "once white and black people have stood side by side in war they will live far more happily together afterwards, remembering how they have helped each other."[112] As with the Gold Coast, promises of greater equality and social progress fell flat after the war. In 1944, one RAR lance corporal summed up the frustration of soldiers in a scathing letter: "The African has served his rulers with admirable devotedness. What is he to receive for this? A continual exclusion from human rights? If so, our rulers must be quite shameless to blame the [Nazi] enemy for his brutality and assumed racial superiority."[113] Continued racial discrimination by democratic nations and their empires made condemnation of totalitarian regimes ring hollow and empowered the colonized to fight back.

Fighting the Nazis roused many Nigerians to initially support the British war effort. Nigerian youth learned anti-Nazi songs with lyrics such as "Hitler that is throwing the world into confusion, push him with a shovel into the grave."[114] British recruiters promised young men they would learn a trade while enlisted. Isaac Fadoyebo (1925–2012) joined the Royal West African Air Force at age sixteen. Within a year he deployed to Burma along with 100,000 other Africans from Britain's colonies where his company was ambushed by the Japanese. Although badly injured, he and another African were the only survivors. He watched villagers raid their supplies but noted, "The war had impoverished them a lot and I would not blame them for picking a few things that belonged to the dead or people who were severely incapacitated."[115] Villagers loyal to the British hid them for ten months before they were finally rescued and repatriated.

The powerful image of the African soldier was essential to cracking the myth of white superiority, reclaiming the sphere of physical agency, and empowering the muscular nationalism of Africa's liberation movements.[116] When empires failed to reward the loyalty of colonial troops, the disintegration of imperial rule was soon to follow.

Japanese-Sponsored Forces

Because their countries were not occupied by enemy forces, African allegiances during World War II were relatively uncomplicated. Very few actively supported the Axis powers. In countries occupied by Japanese forces, however, Asian colonized people initially saw them as liberators. Indeed, Japan promoted insurgency in its enemies' colonies as a way to destabilize them from within and to promote pan-Asian cooperation.

In Burma, a region of disparate ethnic groups that had only been separated from the rest of British India in 1937, Japanese rule shattered the aura of white invincibility. Moreover, Japan organized local armies and promoted youth leagues and military academies in the areas under their control leading to a surge of national awakening. In 1941, at the instigation of Japanese Colonel Suzuki Keiji (1897–1967), nicknamed Bo Mogyo or Captain Thunderbolt, Burma's legendary Thirty Comrades agreed to form the Burmese Independence Army (BIA) in support of Japan's pending invasion of British India. Ba Maw (1893–1977), Burma's wartime prime minister during the Japanese occupation, described in his memoirs the deeply symbolic blood-drinking ceremony that sealed the bond of the BIA's fighting men:

> All the comrades gathered round a silver bowl, slit a finger till some blood dropped from it into the bowl, mixed it with strong liquor, and each drank his full portion of it after having repeated in unison with the others an oath "to be indissolubly bound together by this bond of blood when fighting the British enemy." It was the ancient warrior's oath and communion of the Burmese, and it left the young men taut and inflamed.[117]

The BIA's formation was a milestone in the development of Burmese national consciousness. It was the first indigenous army representing most of Burma's people, and its extensive network of soldiers was bound by wartime camaraderie that cut across different personal backgrounds and ethnic groups.[118] In 1943, when Ba Maw announced Burma's sham independence within Japan's Greater East Asia Co-prosperity Sphere, he proclaimed that it was "One Blood, One Voice, One Command."[119]

Yet the strains between Burmese nationalists and Japanese imperialists were never far from the surface. Ba Maw recalled a standoff between his fellow nationalist leader Aung San (1915–1947) and a Japanese officer: "It could be viewed as a clash between two psychoses: that of a late-coming strong race trying to impress a weak race with its new strength and superiority, and that of a weak race trying not to be impressed in order not to expose its weakness."[120] When the British reclaimed Burma in 1945, the Thirty Comrades were quick to switch allegiance, yet their radio broadcast of the liberation from Japan reaffirmed that Burma would not go meekly back under British rule. "You have known by now with what aims the Burmese Army has come into existence and of what stuff it is made. Its one and only aim is to fight for Burmese freedom and it is to that aim that practically the whole of Burmese Youth have dedicated their lives."[121] Having proven themselves in wartime, Burmese men would insist on forging their own future and soon ushered Burma to independence in 1948.

Some armies also recruited women. The Japanese sponsored the Indian National Army under the leadership of Subhas Chandra Bose (1897–1945). Originally recruited from Indian prisoners of war held by the Japanese in Malaysia, the army lacked a pan-Indian character, so Bose called for volunteers from every religion, caste, region, and gender. To this end, he organized a Rani of Jhansi regiment that would eventually include fifteen hundred young women.[122] At a rally in Singapore in 1943, Bose called for "a unit of brave Indian women to form a 'Death-defying Regiment' who will wield the sword, which the brave Rani of Jhansi wielded in India's First War of Independence in 1857."[123] They showed that women could also claim military muscularity as a path to independence.

Dr. Lakshmi Swaminadhan (1914–2012), a gynecologist and obstetrician, was one of the first recruits. After hearing Bose's call, she "spent a sleepless night . . . wondering if it could ever be done."[124] She despaired at Indian women's conservatism but agreed with Bose that "men and women were two equal halves of a whole" and must fight "shoulder to shoulder."[125] To swell the ranks of the regiment, Swaminadhan and Bose toured the Malaysian countryside to recruit rural women. They also placed ads in English-language newspapers. In Kuala Lumpur, capital of Malaya, seventeen-year-old Janaky Athi Nahappan (1925–2014) snuck out of the house to attend a rally at which Bose spoke. She was so moved by his speech in Hindustani and English that "the feeling grew in me that I must join."[126] She donated her earrings that very day and persuaded her father to sign the consent form. Once in combat, the women's gender did not matter. According to Captain Swaminadhan, "I suppose we all forgot our sex. We were just automatons. We fired, refilled, and fired again, and yet again, endlessly."[127] In 1946, Nahappan was a founding member of the Malaysian Indian Congress and later participated in the Malayan Emergency (1948–1960), a British euphemism for Malaysia's long struggle for independence.

Independence Armies

Approximately four million people died during Japan's occupation of the Dutch East Indies during World War II due to forced labor and disease. With some eighty thousand Dutch held in concentration camps and the Dutch government in exile, the time was ripe to form an independence army. Dutch captives were liberated in 1945 only to be caught up in the Indonesian war of independence (see Figure 6.8). Nationalist partisans in the Dutch East Indies embraced hypermasculinity during the Indonesian National Revolution (1945–1949) that resisted the return of Dutch colonial rule. In response to decades of subjugation by Dutch imperialists, Javanese militants elevated public displays of force, abrasive personalities, and sexual prowess into a new ideal of manhood. The newly minted Indonesian Republican Army featured wildcat militia groups with dynamic names such as Red Bears,

Figure 6.8. Dutch prisoners in Indonesia, 1945
British forces liberated Dutch concentration camp survivors just after World War II and just before the beginning of the Indonesian War of Independence.

Gorilla Guards, Wild Tigers, and Black Bulls.[128] Dutch imperialists were shocked to find that their formerly loyal subjects were capable of such martial discipline and tenacity. As one Dutch observer noted, men of the Indies had suddenly evolved into "Super-Indonesians" who exhibited fanatical bravery and sacrifice to the point of charging Sherman tanks armed only with daggers.[129] Western military advisors soon recognized the threat posed by the rugged, brash Indonesian freedom fighters. In 1946, a British military officer warned that Indonesian nationalism was not to be dismissed as "a shallow, effeminate, intellectual cult" but rather to be regarded as an "urgent affair."[130]

In 1948, an American military attaché similarly reported that the Dutch had gravely "underestimated the strength and virility of the Republic."[131] The hypermasculinity of the Indonesian militants had achieved its intended effect, not only to empower and motivate the partisans but just as importantly to replace Western derision with respect for their manhood. As one revolutionary commander stated, "the fighting spirit of the people has triumphed. Dutch enemies have misinterpreted our goodwill and peace-loving attitude . . . as a sign of weakness."[132] By the late 1940s, both Indonesian and Dutch accounts likened the freedom fighters to the macho cowboys of America's Wild West, the paragon of romanticized masculinity, a far cry from the naïve servants portrayed by Dutch imperialists just a decade earlier. In 1949, the Dutch conceded and Indonesia became independent.

World War II sparked independence movements when Japanese occupation forces emboldened insurgents to take up arms against their Dutch, French, or British masters. The tumultuous experience of Imperial Japan left a very mixed legacy for the colonized peoples of East and Southeast Asia. On one hand, Japan showed that Asian peoples could challenge the Western powers on an equal footing, and it shattered the foundations of the colonial state. On the other hand, the Japanese Empire featured many of the same excesses, including the notion of being a master race. Yet, whether forming in support of the Japanese, as with the BIA of Burma, or in opposition, as with the Viet Minh of Vietnam, wartime armies created a newfound sense of national unity, restored the pride and agency of colonized men and women, and set all of them on the path to eventual postwar independence.

ENDING SETTLER COLONIES

However, the end of World War II reinvigorated victorious empires in most places. At the same time, postwar challenges in the metropole relegated colonial issues to the periphery. This exacerbated a long-standing divide between settler and nonsettler colonies, the latter gradually transitioning to independence, the former gearing up for war. The most protracted wars for independence took place in settler colonies like "British Kenya" and "French Algeria" where the transfer of power to natives threatened local white rule, entrenched for generations. Metropolitan governments were caught between the white settler colonial lobby, the anti-imperial sentiments of their own people and of the United Nations, and the now irreconcilable contradictions within imperialism itself.

British Kenya

When tens of thousands of whites settled in British Kenya in the interwar years, they monopolized the most productive land which spurred native peoples into violent rebellion. By 1946, a resistance movement organized around traditional oathing rituals emerged first among the Kikuyu peoples and later spread to several other ethnic groups. The Mau Mau oath revived long-repressed warrior traditions with a sacred rite that merged tribal totems and Christian symbols so as to bind militants in solidarity to the liberation struggle. The rejection of imposed European norms seen in cultural revival movements elsewhere reached an extreme with the blend of sexual, martial, and atavistic elements in the Mau Mau oaths. In a report prepared by Frank Derek Corfield (1902–1968) for the colonial government of Kenya, the Mau Mau oath was described with extreme revulsion:

> There was a corresponding increase in bestiality in the ritual of the oath, thus forcing the initiate to reach the necessary pitch of blood lust and degradation to make it possible for him to pronounce the ghastly words. . . . Concoctions of the foulest and almost unimaginable ingredients were eaten and drunk. . . . For one of the more notorious concoctions, known as the "Kaberichia cocktail," semen produced in public was mixed in a bowl with menstrual and sheep's blood and drunk while repeating the oath.[133]

In another official inquiry commissioned by the British government, psychiatrist John Colin Carothers (1903–1989) characterized Mau Mau oaths as deliberately profaning Christian beliefs and tribal taboos, designed to draw initiates into ever deeper levels of obscenity, so as to detach them from civilized norms.[134] Both reports framed the "forest culture" of Mau Mau as a reversion to primitivism, wherein previously loyal servants regressed into violent resistance, reflecting the presumed schizoid pathology of African minds.[135] Indeed, the primeval symbolism of the Mau Mau oaths was designed to counter "the terror of gunfire and the terror of hellfire" that worked in tandem to subjugate Africans under British colonial rule.[136] By recovering Kikuyu warrior virility and forging a spiritual sense of military cohesion, the Mau Mau oaths countered the emasculating effects of imperial oppression and dissipated the aura of white invulnerability that maintained the colonial order.

In 1952, the movement erupted into the Mau Mau Uprising (1952–1960), a violent guerrilla campaign based in the forests around Mount Kenya. Despite the warrior ethos of oath taking, General Dedan Kimathi (1920–1957), who led the main rebel force, considered women and family life essential to the liberation struggle. Unlike Kikuyu society at large, marriages among forest fighters were monogamous and egalitarian. The Mau Mau held joint councils "where women's voices were heard," and the forest fighters claimed that there was equality among guerrillas in the bush.[137] According to Mau Mau memoirs, "killing people like [loyalist Chief] Waruhiu was the work of women and girls."[138] At the same time, Mau Mau men were proud of their virility. Sam Thebere said he joined the insurgency "to regain stolen lands and to become an adult."[139] Kikuyu who remained loyal to the British mocked the Mau Mau fighters as *ihii*, uncircumcised boys, to insult their masculinity in a society where the traditional rite of passage into manhood was a circumcision ceremony at about age fourteen. The Mau Mau rebels turned it into a badge of honor, using the term to mean "freedom fighters" with the revolution itself as the true rite of passage into manhood.[140]

To suppress the revolt, British forces heavily bombed forests that harbored Mau Mau militants and declared a "free-fire zone" where villages were burned and any African could be shot on sight. Army and police units received a bounty for Mau Mau corpses, or more often just the hands that were chopped off and gathered in piles to be sent off as proof.[141] Kimathi's capture in 1956 marked the end of the forest war, followed by his execution and unmarked burial in 1957. In the aftermath, colonizers confined over a million Kikuyu in fenced villages and reeducation camps. The detention system was designed to reconstruct Kikuyu manhood so as to transform Mau Mau warriors back into servile subjects. The British classified detainees by color code, from "black" for the hard core who refused to cooperate at all, through intermediate shades of gray, to fully reformed "white" for those pending release.[142] Forcing men to do "women's work"—cooking, laundry, sewing, and cleaning for other men—was a key facet of the camp reeducation system. All Mau Mau memoirs of camp life dwell on this process of domestication where success at doing women's work was the yardstick of rehabilitation.[143]

The suppression of the Mau Mau Uprising inflamed partisan and ethnic divisions among Kenyans and turned white settlers against independence. But after the end of the rebellion, independence proceeded through the electoral process. Jomo Kenyatta (1889–1978), Kenya's first president, was imprisoned from 1953 to 1959 after a show trial for alleged Mau Mau organizing, but newly empowered voters elected him president nonetheless. Other independence leaders distanced themselves from Mau Mau, including Daniel Moi (b. 1924), Kenyatta's vice president.[144] Their rival parties merged to pave the way for Kenya's independence in 1963.

French Algeria

With over one million European residents in 1960, Algeria was the most populous European settler colony. It enjoyed special status as a department of greater France, but that brought few benefits to the vast majority of the population. Algerian agitation against the French persisted through the nineteenth and early twentieth centuries. The 1945 Algerian uprising at Sétif, on the day that World War II ended in Europe, opened the final chapter of resistance that would last until 1962 and force the collapse of the French government. Freedom fighters and French forces alike attacked civilian populations and widely used torture in what was one of the bloodiest anticolonial revolutions.

The scale of urban guerilla warfare distinguished the Algerian War of Independence (1954–1962) from other insurgencies. Because they could move about without being suspected, Algerian women constituted some 3 percent of combatants in Algeria's National Liberation Front (FLN), about eleven thousand altogether, although some scholars argue that the numbers were far greater.[145] Young urban women were often trusted to plant bombs. Zohra Drif (b. 1934), the daughter of a judge, received a European education and dressed in Western attire. Yet she became a bomber during the freedom struggle. So did Djamila Bouazza (b. 1938), another French-oriented young woman who was noted after her arrest for wearing her bleached hair short. Their opposition to France baffled the military, as they defied the stereotype of the rural, Muslim partisan and had been so thoroughly Westernized.[146] Crediting her French education for her militance, Baya Hocine (1940–2000) explained: "The history I was taught in high school clearly showed me that nationalist and revolutionary movements were in no way considered subversive. . . . France itself, which recognizes in its constitution the 'right of peoples to dispose of themselves,' has always refused our people the right to liberate themselves."[147] In 1957, a French military tribunal sentenced her to death for planting bombs at age seventeen. Another bomber, Djamila Boupacha (b. 1938), was also sentenced to death in 1959 after being tortured and raped. Renowned feminist Simone de Beauvoir (1908–1986) turned her trial into a cause célèbre in France with a series of essays that emphasized Boupacha's youth and middle-class background but downplayed her religion. Not wishing to have accounts of the rape become fodder for pornography, Beauvoir instead indicted the hypocrisy of the French and of patriarchy in general. The negative publicity of Boupacha's trial diminished French support for the war. FLN operatives as far away as India distributed pamphlets demanding her release.[148] She was pardoned in 1962.

Rural women played different roles. Sewing uniforms was one of the many ways women could support the revolution. They also provisioned supplies and hid partisans. Some suffered retribution, from having their farms and homes razed to enduring arrest and torture:

> 'Confess! Tell us what we want to know or we'll shoot!' 'Shoot!' I said. 'It makes no difference to me! I'm a girl, I'm not a grown woman, but I'll leave men behind me! . . . Each one of them will kill a hundred of yours! Kill me!' They brought a whip. They beat me. They switched on the electricity for their machines. They tortured me. 'I don't recognize you!' I didn't feel any fear: God made these Frenchmen seem like shadows in front of my eyes! And it was true, I would have preferred to die! Suddenly one of them asked me, 'Are you a virgin?'[149]

She did not attest to being a victim of rape though the chilling question posed by her interrogator suggests that rape was standard procedure.

Not all Algerian women supported the armed resistance, preferring more gradual liberal approaches to national and personal autonomy. In 1956, women in neighboring Tunisia and Morocco had made significant gains after independence from France. Changes in personal status law enabled women's consent in marriage and property ownership and raised the age of consent. Reformers in Algeria believed that new personal status laws might win women's support against the FLN. At the beginning of the war, the French military in Algiers presided over the public unveiling of Muslim women who cast their lot with the egalitarian rhetoric of French republicanism. These women separated themselves from the Algerian liberation struggle in the belief that women's emancipation would be better secured by a French Algeria rather than a Muslim one. A powerful volley in a contest over women's allegiance, the spectacle drew over one hundred thousand onlookers in May 1958. The FLN scorned these women as prostitutes.[150]

The divide between pro-French or pro-independence failed to capture the complex position such women occupied. After decades of carving out a space for Muslim feminists in the suffrage campaign of metropolitan France, where women did not win the right to vote until 1946, Algerian women articulated the bind they found themselves in. In 1953, Fadila Ahmed wrote, "We, the women of Algeria, have two jailers: colonialism . . . and the apathetic men who hang on to customs and traditions inherited not from Islam but their ignorant fathers. The second is worse than the first."[151] Only the overthrow of both would liberate Muslim women. Muslim feminists thus formed uneasy alliances with French feminists. Algerian women drafted petitions to the now legitimized Gaullist government. They demanded reforms in marriage laws above all else. In 1959, a sixteen-year-old wrote, "I don't want to be kept like a hen in a henhouse . . . or sold like a cow. I would like to be married to someone who makes me happy. I don't want to be thrown out someday with five or six children, to be left in misery."[152] In another petition, a fifty-year-old woman agreed that "There should be a law that allows our girls to choose a husband and to be married in the [city hall] like the French; this wouldn't prevent marriages in our religion, but . . . we would see fewer abandoned women. Men, they're free—why not us?"[153] Less-educated women, often just able to sign their names, affixed them to petitions written on hand-drawn tricolor French flags.[154]

Like most colonial conflicts, the wars in Algeria and Kenya were civil wars. Because the FLN was united and well organized around the banner of Islam, Algerian liberals never gained the upper hand and the French government abandoned loyalists, some two hundred thousand in the armed forces alone.[155] Figure 6.9 underscores French attempts to win hearts and minds late in the war. In Kenya, by contrast, loyalists prevailed after the suppression of Mau Mau and negotiated a gradual transfer of power. In both cases, victory for the colonized meant a mass exodus of settlers, white and Indian in the case of Kenya, white and Arab loyalists in the case of Algeria. Settlers had claimed these colonies as their homelands for over a century, which made disentanglement that much more traumatic. Loyalists, often more educated and liberal than the populist base, had evolved Western identities for generations, making a return to a precolonial identity nonsensical. Sorting out populations in these new nations, as well as individual allegiances and hybridity, continues to trouble the postcolonial world.

Figure 6.9. French forces recruiting pamphlet, 1960
In the midst of its war to prevent Algerian independence, the French forces attempted
to recruit Algerians with a positive representation of Muslims.

POSTCOLONIALISM?

Formerly colonized people wrestled with the legacy of colonialism in the immediate aftermath of their wars for independence. The ascent of military dictators in
many new nations was perhaps unsurprising given the association between martial prowess and national regeneration. To maintain their dearly won independence, some new leaders in the 1950s formally committed themselves to policies
of "Non-Alignment," refusing to fall under the influence of either of the world's
new superpowers, the United States and the Soviet Union. As imperial powers
continued to fight colonial wars, the newly formed "United Nations" took a stand
against all forms of imperialism in 1960. But some observers worried over the
persistence of the colonization of the mind. Many postcolonial authors pondered
the enduring legacy of Western imperialism by exploring what some would call
"Westoxification."

Non-Alignment

By the early 1950s, India's first prime minister, Jawaharlal Nehru (1889–1964)
became the symbol of the new statesman who guided the transition from imperialism to independence. Nehru steered a middle course between capitalism and
communism, defining independence as freedom to exist outside of any imperial
power's sphere of influence. But it was more than the absence of support for communism or capitalism. He defined non-alignment in 1955: "The main objectives
of that policy are: the pursuit of peace, not through alignment with any major

power or group of powers but through an independent approach to each contro-versial or disputed issue, the liberation of subject peoples, the maintenance of freedom, both national and individual, the elimination of racial discrimination and the elimination of want, disease and ignorance, which afflict the greater part of the world's population."[156] The rhetoric of non-alignment shifted attention from nations as abstractions to individuals as bodies with the right to be free from disease and discrimination. Non-alignment applied to military policy, but also economic modernization, without which new cycles of dependency would ensnare new nations.

The Bandung Conference in Indonesia formally launched the Non-Alignment Movement (NAM) in 1955. African American author Richard Wright (1908–1960) was in attendance: "The scorned, insulted, offended, dispossessed, in short, the destitute people of the human race were meeting. . . . That meeting of the rejected was in itself like bringing the western world to trial!"[157] Non-alignment united a wide range of colonized people regardless of race or nationality. Leading feminists like American Pearl S. Buck (1892–1973) and Indonesian Sukina Kusima believed that the NAM understood the connection between women's issues and interna-tional development, and the recognition of what would later be captured by the phrase, "The personal is political."[158] Kusima asserted in a 1959 interview that Indonesia's advances for women were victories for Eastern women in general, but the Eastern woman must now "squash this great prison she has fallen into . . . the prison of decrepit tradition. . . . [Western woman] is lucky because of industrial advancement . . . for household appliances give her more time and energy . . . there-fore she enjoys more personal freedom."[159] Feminists in the era of decolonization saw economic modernization as essential to women's freedom, enabling the per-sonal autonomy that would then lead to reforms in marriage.

Regardless of nationality, liberals tended to value personal freedom over community identity even when it pivoted on modern consumerism. Combatting nationalism and racialism could be accomplished through the unity of the for-merly colonized. Nehru believed India had a special role to play in the liberation of Africa: "The tragedy of Africa is greater than that of any other continent, whether it is racial or political. It is up to Asia to help Africa to the best of her ability."[160] But this help was sometimes seen as paternalism or even Indian impe-rialism. Nehru's commitment to African freedom was unequivocal but compli-cated by the situation of the large population of Indians resident throughout Africa. In Kenya, the Mau Mau Uprising frightened them into supporting the British. In South Africa, they sought exceptions to apartheid segregation laws and special privileges as Indians. But Nehru was adamant in a 1953 speech that East Africa's Indians "could expect no help from us, no protection from us, if they seek any special rights in Africa which were not in the interests of Africa."[161] His insistence on their loyalty to Africa led many to immigrate to the United States and Canada. Nehru's non-alignment also alienated East African leaders who saw India's liberal economic policies as anything but neutral. Julius Nyerere of Tanzania, for example, gravitated to Maoism.

The aggressive neutrality of Egypt's Gamal Abdel Nasser (1918–1970) provided an African model of non-alignment. In 1952, the Free Officers Movement, led by Lieutenant Colonel Nasser, abolished Egypt's monarchy and proclaimed a democratic republic. The Free Officers consisted of junior military officers and civil servants from the lower middle class who chafed at the monopoly on power held by Egypt's wealthy elites. The charismatic Nasser became Egypt's prime minister in 1954 and then was elected president in 1956. Nasser's meteoric ascent to power was driven in part by calls for internal social justice and in part by a sense that Egypt's traditional ruling class was unwilling to throw off the vestiges of British imperialism, represented by Britain's continued control of the Suez Canal. In 1956, Nasser seized the canal, provoking an Anglo-French invasion to retake the Suez and topple him from power.

Western press coverage of the Suez Crisis decried "the dangerous and false nationalism of this immature leader."[162] An editorial cartoon in the *New York Daily News* depicted an ironically feminized Nasser in a harem outfit reclining on a settee, sensuously basking at the rapt attention of his masculine suitors, the United States and the Soviet Union. Nasser was both feminized and empowered by his ability to hold sway over the two superpowers. Another cartoon in *The Times-Union* of Albany, New York, depicted a brutish, primitive Nasser as a Pharaoh in a loincloth, baring his hairy arms, legs, and chest, grinning viciously with a bomb in his hand. Both cartoons hinged on portraying Nasser as gender deviant.[163] Nonetheless, the world's new superpowers, the United States and the Soviet Union, forced the British and French into a humiliating retreat barely a week into the campaign. The Suez Crisis was a watershed for decolonization, exposing the impotence of the once towering British and French Empires, emboldening nationalists the world over, and setting the United Nations squarely on the side of an end to empire. By practicing militant non-alignment, Nasser became an icon of defiance for former colonial subjects and a symbol of the newly empowered non-Western man.

The NAM was an early space for navigating postcolonial gender and race politics. The perceived paternalism of Indian elites who sought to help Africa was countered by Nasser's machismo. Because the movement was formed by independence leaders rather than imperialists, it articulated authentic aspirations of newly liberated peoples, including feminists, but the multiplicity of paths to liberation reflects the multiple responses to imperialism since its inception.

United Nations

Some NAM members distanced themselves from the United Nations, while others were devoted to both institutions. Nehru's sister, Vijaya Lakshmi Pandit (1900–1990), who became the first woman president of the United Nations General Assembly in 1953, was instrumental in the UN's founding. Pandit toured the United States in 1944 giving lectures indicting colonialism and promoting international cooperation. The press coverage surrounding her tour influenced founding meetings that year in Washington, DC, and San Francisco. Independence leaders such as Gandhi worried that the UN would be nothing more than a debating club, whereas other skeptics assumed it would merely provide cover for the old imperial order. Those who believed in its possibilities pressed it to do more to end imperialism.

Pandit demanded that the UN take action against South Africa, which in 1946 applied apartheid laws to Indian communities. She insisted: "What the world needs is not more charters, not more committees to define and courts of justice to interpret, but a more willing implementation of the Charter by all governments."[164] Occupying higher moral ground, Pandit led the Indian delegation to persuade the UN General Assembly to condemn apartheid, which it eventually did, confirming that her faith in a world assembly was not misplaced: "Mine is an appeal to a conscience, the conscience of the world, which this Assembly is."[165] But South African Prime Minister Jan Smuts (1870–1950) pointed out that hers was a "hollow victory," calling her "my child."[166] This patronizing rhetoric equated her naiveté to the idealism of the United Nations. He rightly predicted that a UN sanction would only prevent his reelection but do nothing to dent apartheid in the short term.

Newly elected heads of state decried this infantilizing rhetoric and drew attention to the colonization of the mind that they had long endured. The proceedings of the 1960 UN Declaration on the Granting of Independence to Colonial Countries and Peoples reflected a vision of egalitarian liberation, one often framed in the gendered terms of masculine dignity and global brotherhood. The delegate from Ceylon (Sri Lanka) condemned the imperial system as a grave violation, a "moral prostitution" and a "rape" that served to emasculate grown men.[167] The delegate from Liberia agreed that colonialism was "a system that takes the manhood out of those exposed to it."[168] And the delegate from Congo declared an end to European paternalism. "Not long ago we were being poisoned with the sugared venom of colonialism . . . but we have outgrown the stage of servitude, we are no longer credulous children who can be made to believe in Santa Claus forever."[169] Turning to decolonization, the delegate from Laos declared that "nearly a thousand million men have recovered their outraged dignity and freedom."[170] The delegate from Lebanon affirmed that, "Our age is one of co-operation among free and equal peoples and men. More still, it is an age of human brotherhood, association, and mutual assistance."[171]

Speaking in August 1960 on the banks of the Ubangi River at Bangui, capital of the Central African Republic, French Minister of Culture André Malraux (1901–1976) welcomed the world's newest nation with equal parts nostalgia and optimism. "An era comes to an end as night falls . . . This is not merely a transfer of attributions, but a transfer of destinies."[172] The year 1960 came to be known as the Year of Africa, when sixteen nations proclaimed independence from the British, French, and Belgian Empires, a culmination of African aspirations to international respect, dignity, and equality. In December 1960, the United Nations capped off the march to freedom by passing the Declaration on the Granting of Independence, which heralded a new international norm that saw

no legitimate place for empire. The curtains had not yet fallen on Western imperialism, but the UN Declaration clearly ushered in the final act. This chorus of
voices rising in triumph from former colonial subjects across the world had a
common refrain: that all peoples had an equal claim to humanity, and so the Age
of Empire must come to an end.

Westoxification

The liberal orientation of the United Nations, particularly its position on women's
equality, provoked opposition among Islamic intellectuals who believed European
imperialism had to be overthrown at the level of the mind. In 1962, Persian social
critic Jalal Al-e Ahmad (1923–1969) published a censored version of *Gharbzadegi*,
a term he coined with connotations of contagion and striking a blow, that has been
variously rendered in English as Weststruckness or Westoxification. Al-e Ahmad
opens his tract with a metaphor of disease, the affliction of a society disordered by
Westernization: "I say that *Gharbzadegi* is like cholera. If this seems distasteful,
I could say it's like heatstroke or frostbite. . . . In any case, we're talking about a
disease. A disease that comes from without. . . . This [Westoxification] has two
heads. One is the West, the other is ourselves who are Weststruck."[173] When the
formerly colonized evoke images of bodily decay as metaphors for the Age of
Empire, the centrality of intimate imperialism comes into sharp relief.

Gharbzadegi was one of the first attempts to examine the cultural imperialism
that persisted or even intensified in the postcolonial era, as some leaders in the
non-Western world sought by emulation to match the progress, power, and prosperity of the West. Al-e Ahmad reserves his most scathing critique for the Westernized woman, obsessed with material goods and a consumer lifestyle, and for
the Westernized man, "who's easily led, who isn't genuine, who's unprincipled,
has no roots, and is not of the soil of this land."[174] *Gharbzadegi* draws a portrait of
a vapid femininity, with a false sense of liberation that neglects maternal duties,
and of an alienated and impotent masculinity, groveling for Western approval
through mindless mimicry. "The [Westoxicated] man even describes, understands, and explains himself in the language of orientalists! . . . He has placed
himself, an imagined thing, under the orientalist's microscope, and he depends
on what the orientalist sees, not on what he is, feels, and experiences."[175] For all
his ridicule of Western machine civilization, Al-e Ahmad was not an opponent of
progress and modernity. To the contrary, his cure for Westoxification was mastery of technology, the muscle of the West, while holding on to the "precious
jewel" of Persia's heart and soul.[176] Other nationalists would also accept economic
modernity—for men only. It was left to women to be the bearers of tradition.

CONCLUSION

In May 2014, Berlin's Charité hospital returned three skeletons and eighteen
skulls that dated to the Herero Genocide to a delegation from Namibia, a
stark reminder that in many parts of the world recovery from the legacy of

imperialism continues to the present day. The trajectory of the Herero vividly captures the loss and recovery of self that for many marked the experience of empire as a whole, a course that began with resistance and was ended by resistance. Although Herero society was shattered by the German Empire, the Herero people soon began to recover a national identity with the *Otruppa* ceremony, merging precolonial traditions with new colonial practices to produce a unique hybrid. The loss of self was most acute in last-stand millenarian movements such as the Ghost Dance, which called on beliefs in mystical body transformation to resist the force of Western invaders. The failure of such movements did not extinguish the spirit of resistance that they embodied, as colonized people searched for new ways to oppose imperial rule. The shift toward more modern forms of resistance is perhaps best captured by the Haitian Revolution, which opened with the Bois Caïman ceremony and closed with modern statehood. Whether through the slave system, in the colonial prison, or by wars of attrition, the endemic violence of empire destroyed traditional social norms but at the same time created a new sense of purpose and unity among the victims of empire. Whereas modern nationalist discourses generally revolved around concepts of male honor and valor, the participation of women was indispensable to the success of anticolonial mobilization. Few bridged the gender dichotomy better than Mahatma Gandhi, whose Soul Force movement rallied millions of women to join millions of men in a mass campaign of peaceful disobedience.

The recovery of self often began with co-opting Western discourses and adapting them to native forms, as in the physical fitness movements by which colonized men reclaimed a sense of agency and vitality. The muscular nationalism that emerged was often expressed in a form of hypermasculinity that rivaled that of hegemonic imperialism. Although nationalist narratives often erase the role of women, the history of resistance includes warrior queens like the Rani of Jhansi in addition to the many thousands that took up arms in peasant rebellions or guerrilla wars. The very different treatment that women fighters received also reveals how the norms of empire shifted over time, from being torn apart by the Spaniards in the late eighteenth century to rallying public opinion against colonialism in the twentieth century.

Yet, the recovery of self was not complete with the arrival of formal independence, but instead, contested notions of citizenship and gender carried over into the postcolonial era. Meanwhile, the United Nations proclaimed new international norms of equal rights and self-determination that recognized the common humanity of all people. On the eve of Indian independence in 1947, Prime Minister Jawaharlal Nehru gave a speech in parliament on India's Tryst with Destiny. "At the stroke of the midnight hour, when the world sleeps, India will awake to life and freedom. A moment comes, which comes but rarely in history, when we step out from the old to the new, when an age ends, and when the soul of a nation, long suppressed, finds utterance."[177] A most fitting epitaph for the Age of Empire.

TIMELINE

1781	Micaela Bastidas executed for her role in the rebellion of her husband, Tupac Amaru II, against the Spanish in Peru
1791	Bois Caïman voodoo ceremony launches Haitian Revolution
1801	Dictatorial Proclamation in Haiti promotes criminalizing moral infractions
1832	Abd el-Kader coordinates Algerian resistance against the French occupation
1856	British government passes Hindu widow remarriage act, precipitating Indian Rebellion
1866	Maori Hauhau rebellion against British settlement of New Zealand
1871	Muhammad al-Muqrani leads Berber insurrection against French in Algeria
1897	Apirana Ngata helps found the Young Maori Party in New Zealand
1900	War of the Golden Stool led by Queen Asantewaa against British in Gold Coast
1904–1906	Herero and Nama of Namibia rebel against German rule and suffer genocide
1905–1907	Maji Maji uprising in German East Africa
1906	Qiu Jin executed in China for conspiracy to overthrow the Qing dynasty
1941	Nigerian Isaac Fadoyebo joins British Army in World War II; deployed to Burma
1943	Rani of Jhansi regiment formed in the Indian National Army
1959	Algerian Djamila Boupacha sentenced to death for planting bombs in the Algerian war; sentence commuted due to public outcry
1960	UN Declaration on the Granting of Independence to Colonial Countries and Peoples

CONCLUSION

The brilliant tableau that introduced this book remains on the walls of the pavilion for which it was commissioned, the only permanent building of the Paris Exposition of 1931. Today that building houses a tropical fish aquarium, boasting two albino alligators in addition to the usual aquatic attractions. So much for the Age of Empire. Slightly more relevant is the immigration history museum, now also housed there, which both celebrates diversity in France and exposes the challenges immigrants have faced. This is what matters to the French today. Gone is the arrogant boastfulness of the modern French Empire expressed in the last great imperial exposition (see Figure 1). So why bother studying it?

Since the Roman Empire, scholars and general readers alike have been fascinated by the rise and fall of empires. We search for patterns and clues. We wonder about the inevitability of decline and try to use history to predict the future. We return again and again to the roots of empires, to their various manifestations, to their legacies. Historians now investigate the most recent rise and fall of empire: the Soviet Union driven by communist ideology. Scholars, pundits, activists, and the merely curious have brought new questions to the Marxist roots of that ideology. In the 1950s and 1960s, as the liberal empires of Western Europe fell, people questioned liberalism as an ideology due to its problematic relationship to imperialism. Liberalism and imperialism, not to mention the intersection between the two, have certainly generated enormous interest in the economic, political, and diplomatic aspects of the European empires. Only recently have scholars broadened their studies with a greater focus on the cultural and the social, and more recently still, the intimate and the embodied. As this subfield grows, it becomes possible to speculate about the role of body in the decline of empire. Although we cannot offer a comprehensive theory about the rise and fall of empires, we venture to suggest a few tentative conclusions that might inspire further research.

The first of these has to do with contradictions inherent in modern liberalism, the tension between equality and freedom, for example. Many have cited the fundamental incompatibility between liberalism, with its emphasis on

Conclusion Figure 1.   1931 Colonial Exposition in Paris
The last of the great world's fairs, this exposition marked the apex of European imperialism. Representing the colonies as barely clothed women continued the long-standing
association of the body with empire.

individual autonomy, and imperialism, which requires subjugation. But rather
than dismissing liberal imperialists as mere hypocrites, we argue instead that
liberal universalism never implied rights for all, at least not all at once. Going
back to John Locke (1632–1704), the founder of modern liberalism, it is clear
that membership in the social contract pivoted on the ability to reason and the
ownership of property, both thought to be limited to privileged white men.
Married to the Enlightenment idea of progress, as typified by Condorcet,
European liberalism saw the unenlightened peoples of the world as deficient,
perhaps not inherently but as the result of despotism or ignorance, both of
which would be remedied by the spread of Enlightenment. European liberals
thus supported imperialism when its goal was to uplift rather than to dominate. Its preferred method was cooperation with local elites.

Many colonized peoples refashioned liberalism, defined as a reform project
based on reason, to address local conditions such as child marriage or polygamy.
For example, the Hindu Brahmin Raja Ram Mohan Roy (1772–1833) of India

used British law to achieve these aims as early as the 1820s. Liberals everywhere adapted the Enlightenment project, which included the extension of rights, to the political and social circumstances of their native lands, often working with colonizers. Most eventually saw national self-determination as the logical extension of political liberalism and exposed the contradiction between liberalism and imperialism. Separating the two, some but not all nationalist liberals fought for independence, fulfilling the promise of political liberalism. They less often accepted economic liberalism, the ideological basis for capitalism. Boycotts, strikes, and black markets were potent and ubiquitous forms of economic resistance, sometimes undertaken by political liberals.

The second reason for the decline of the European empires has to do with intimacies. While familiarity often breeds contempt, it just as often bred ambivalence or even love. Although stories abound of the unspeakable cruelties colonizers perpetrated against their native lovers, mixed-race offspring, and subordinates, ties of affection complicated loyalties. Law courts in the eighteenth-century Caribbean occasionally recognized interracial marriages and the rights of mixed-race children to inherit property. In German Southwest Africa, German men fought against the erosion of the rights of their mixed-race offspring in the early twentieth century. During World War I, French soldiers lobbied so that pensions for their Vietnamese families would be equal to those granted European families. In the 1930s, members of the International Boy Scouts, as young as thirteen years old, protested against South African laws that prevented black boys from joining. Women also reached across racial lines to form regional and international organizations. In the Pan-Pacific Women's Association, friendships between Maori delegates and white New Zealanders fostered an organization that has successfully lobbied for women's rights regardless of race since 1928. These examples illustrate that intimate relations between husbands and wives, between parents and children, and between activists of all ages challenged imperialism and eventually contributed to its demise.

We offer a third tentative theory about the decline of the European empires. They never really did—unless one insists on a narrow understanding of empire as the direct *political* control of one land by another. At the outset, we defined this direct control as colonialism and pointed out that imperialism is the ideology that justified it. Colonialism may have ended, but not imperialism. Liberal imperialism underpins the ideologies and institutions of economic and cultural globalization. It was instrumental in establishing international norms, including international human rights. This is only possible because of the success of liberalism itself, attested to by the number of elites within formerly colonized lands who embrace it in some version. The legacy of European empires can be seen in the many adaptations of liberal-style governing doctrines. By example, most former colonies have democratic constitutions, at least in principle if not in practice. For intimate life, the imperial heritage includes more homogenous family formations—in the worldwide decline of polygamy, for instance. Most governments also pay at least lip service to tolerance for minorities. It can also be seen in the general progress of women's rights. Indeed, some postcolonial nations have elected female heads of state whereas a number of Western nations have yet to do so. And, many developing economies, most notably Communist China, have shifted toward a "free-market" model and now compete with powerful Western corporations. The global circulation of goods, what some have called the "coca-colonization" of the world, and of health practices, such as the popularity of yoga in the West, continue trends that began in the Age of Empire.

These hypotheses only came into focus when we organized material in a thematic manner cutting across eras and empires. Studying empires separately and tracing their chronological development obscured their underlying logic. Of course every empire is distinct from every other and evolves differently over time. Each has generated an impressive, even daunting, body of scholarship. But textbooks synthesize this material and emphasize similarities rather than differences. Each chapter therefore has a distinct focus, roughly correlating to the stages of empire: from first contact to family formations, then to hybrid identities in the colonies and the metropole, and finally to reform movements and eventual independence. But several topics cut across the entire text: interracial sex and mixed-race peoples; hybrid identities and communities; the adaptability of imperial institutions; and bodies in motion.

Interracial sex is perhaps foremost among these. In the modern empires, interracial sex was not only widespread but also generated a lot of commentary. We discuss it in every chapter. In chapter 1, newly arrived British sailors encountered willing Polynesians of both sexes, at least according to the crews of the Cook voyages. Coercive and commercial interracial sex developed in the Caribbean when brothels at ports of call expanded their clientele beyond pirates. In chapter 2, we discuss how interracial sex fostered the integration of European newcomers into various communities, from the Inuit of Alaska to the Nama of Namibia. Increased anxiety about such relationships, especially in the metropole, motivated programs to encourage white women's immigration, the assumption being that men would naturally prefer to be sexually involved with someone from their own ethnic group. In chapter 3, interracial sex enabled some colonized people to become white, especially in Indonesia where marriage to a white man allowed native women and their mixed-race children to become "equated" Europeans. But interracial sex could also lead to segregation laws and curfews in the many places, such as Darwin, Australia, which experienced rape panics in the early twentieth century as a result of the proximity of Aboriginal men to white women. In chapter 4, fantasies of interracial sex fueled the legend of exotic performer Mata Hari, a Dutch woman who performed in brown face. Her independence from her Dutch husband was at least in part a result of his interracial sex with their servant. Much like her veil dances, harem erotica on postcards and paintings conveyed the widespread temptation to engage in interracial sex. In chapter 5, theories of degeneracy made governments more vigilant in their population management policies. Anxious about declining birth rates among whites, Northern and Western European governments sought to import fertile and prolific

Catholics from Poland, Spain, or Italy rather than allow large-scale immigration of people from their colonies who might reproduce themselves, or worse, might reproduce with white women. In chapter 6, some anticolonial nationalists decried miscegenation. Nationalist revolutions often demanded a rejection of all things European, whereas nation building after the colonizer's exit was often undertaken by elites with European blood or training.

Closely related, mixed-race people and communities also feature prominently throughout the text. In chapter 1, some of the first condemnations of white male sexual excess came from missionaries and officials who decried the abandonment of their mixed-race children. This featured in abolitionist tracts and slave narratives in which freed slaves expressed horror at the cruel treatment masters exacted on their own progeny. As shown in chapter 2, some white men married their slaves and legitimized the children; as such, marriages were widely tolerated in the early stages of colonial rule. More scandalous were the marriages of white women to nonwhite men, as in the case of an Australian socialite and her princely Indian husband. Gossip columnists speculated as to the coloring of the child they were expecting. In chapter 3, the fate of mixed-race children often hinged on whether their fathers recognized them. Potential allies with European governments, they were too valuable to be left to their mother's care. In some places, schools emerged to make them white and therefore to prevent them from becoming a force for resistance.

The second major theme that cuts across chapters is the hybridity of individuals and even of societies the world over. Some British explorers of the Pacific in the eighteenth century had themselves tattooed in Polynesia, while some Polynesians converted to Christianity a generation later. European children's books and sports clubs incorporated more representations of the world's peoples, and those peoples adapted European sports. Among the women considered in chapter 2, experiences of hybridity included the migration of Indian indentured servants to the Caribbean and of Chinese prostitutes to the Western United States. Dedicated to hybridity, in chapter 3 we look at the institutions that produced it, such as governments, churches, and schools, but also at personal relationships, such as the marriage of Zanzibari princess Emily Ruete to a German spice merchant. Shared foods, hybrid art forms, and global tourism are subjects of chapter 4, while we explore hybrid health regimes and bodily practices, such as the management of the insane in Vietnam by hospital and family alike, in chapter 5. In chapter 6, many resistance movements depended on the leadership of assimilated elites, such as Samuel Maharero of what is now Namibia, and often involved a rejection of cultural practices that had become too European. Elites elsewhere like the *évolués* of Belgium would successfully lobby for independence in Africa.

Third, school and church served the dual purpose of insuring white fitness for rule while training native people to be ruled, and eventually to assume rule. Imperial institutions were thus always adapting. From the sporting fields of elite boys' schools in England in chapter 1, to the Catholic schools for Eritrean mixed-race children in chapter 3, educators strived to instill self-control and devotion to duty. Nonetheless, these institutions might provide opportunities for the empowerment of white women and native men and women, even African American women missionaries in Mozambique, as we discussed in chapter 2. It could also enable the upward mobility of converts among the colonized, as seen in the case of Father Vangeke in 1930s Papua. Secular schools were less overtly disruptive, although as Assia Djebar's story shows in chapter 3, disruptions might occur at the level of the psyche. Her father's upward mobility as an Algerian teacher of French in the 1930s opened doors for her but left her estranged from Islamic traditions. The military also enabled upward mobility but demanded bodily discipline and reproduced racial hierarchies as described in chapter 1. Veterans might come back ready to enjoy the privileges of citizenship or more determined to overthrow colonial masters. On the other hand, disabled subjects were deemed unfit for conscription or mine work, as shown in chapter 5. Labor compounds, segregated neighborhoods, and hill stations were imperial institutions engineered for maintaining order. Managing space and mobility was central to the success of empires, but regulations became harder to enforce. Dalat was built in Vietnam as a hill station to recreate French life in the highlands away from the native population, yet dependence on local labor doomed the enterprise. Segregated neighborhoods generated controversy in Bulawayo, Zimbabwe, when a large population of diaspora Indians challenged the black/white divide. Sumptuary laws and curfews, designed to control movement, were also difficult to enforce. Meanwhile, wartime demands such as price controls were subverted by enterprising women, who in Nigeria launched a massive protest against the government markets of Lagos, as we described in chapter 6. Imperial institutions both stabilized and destabilized empire due to the complicated entanglements of body and gender, which necessitated constant adaptations.

Fourth, embodied performances enabled native peoples to achieve status and eventually independence. In chapter 1, we show how modern masculinity evolved a sports ethic first in Britain and then across the globe. But, as we show in chapter 3, failure at cricket could doom the career of the upwardly mobile Indian. In chapter 4, the big-game hunt produced interracial alliances as a site of male bonding, and the hunting prowess of North Indians was held in especially high regard. In chapter 5, Indian yogis spread fitness crazes with eugenic benefits. Meanwhile, Caribbean subjects of the British Empire made cricket their own. The resistance movements of chapter 6 explicitly called for athleticism to recover wounded masculinity by literally training the bodies of partisans for armed struggle. The same is true of dance. From the veil dances of Mata Hari in chapter 4 to the bacchanal that launched the Haitian Revolution in chapter 6, bodies in motion crossed cultures, simultaneously reinforcing and challenging Western stereotypes, as seen in Figure 2. In chapter 1, seductive Tahitian dancers whirled around drawing in white men who found them irresistible, and critics of creolization cited the freestyle dancing of white women who had succumbed to the "lascivious climate" in chapter 2. Conversely, the dances of Australian factory

Conclusion Figure 2.   Plantation slaves dancing
Despite the horrific conditions of plantation slavery, some communities managed to recreate West African traditions, illustrating the power of bodies in motion to resist imperialism.

women in chapter 2 convey a resilient exuberance in the face of oppression, easing their alienation through play and camaraderie. In chapter 3, Djebar was mesmerized by the dancing of her grandmother who represented the Muslim tradition from which she was estranged. On the other hand, missionaries cringed at the dancing and feasting at Ndebele weddings, which were held regardless of church sanctions. In chapter 4, we highlight how "savages" from a mélange of ethnicities danced in world's fairs and ethnographic shows. In chapter 5, dancing by both Ghanaian witches and witch-finders followed the social dislocation of rapid modernization. In chapter 6, we highlight the potency of trance-inducing ritual dances in atavistic anticolonial movements, most famously the Ghost Dance of the Lakota Sioux.

Today, cosmopolitan consumers of global popular culture enjoy embodied performances in sport and dance that are only possible because of the Age of Empire. In "La Gloria," a contemporary music video by Gotan Project, athletic mixed-race male dancers spar in the sand as an Argentine football announcer shouts calls over the bandoneón. That dance and sport are thoroughly infused by the legacy of imperialism is evident in the syncretic tango, a syncopated Argentinian dance based on African styles as well as the influence of European immigrants, including Germans who brought the bandoneón to South America in the late nineteenth century. The dancers are marked with tattoo portraits of their white team owners, while pallid female "angels" are seated on a swing from on high to keep the ball in play. The white owners, donning gangster attire from the 1930s, a throwback in time, eventually dissolve in a cloud of black dust. The players are represented as timeless and eternal, grounded in the sand of their arena, the sand glittering as it slips through their fingers. Despite their implied subjugation, they emit power. Contemporary theorists describe how power is fluid and no one is in possession of it for more than a moment, just as no one can monopolize possession of the ball. For postmodern theorists, herein lies the possibility for liberation. The desirable body in motion, self-possessed and athleticized for performance, will insist on its own liberation. In this context, contemporary choreographers stage self-ironic performances that turn imperialism on its head.

Each generation brings a new set of concerns and prospects to the study of empire. By definition, an empire is a set of economic and political arrangements with a core ruling power that controls lands formerly under the control of someone else. Historians therefore remain duly interested in state-level economic and political decisions. Of course, so do we, but our view of how power functions leads us to focus on a wider spectrum of repressions, yet also possibilities, among the colonized. By studying the intimate, from sexual relations to labor relations, personal interactions reveal complex dynamics where power emanates from multiple sites. In Michel Foucault's synthesis, modern identities are constructed by such asymmetrical yet reciprocal power relations, like that between doctor and patient, confessor and penitent, teacher and student. Among others, *Intimate Empires* adds those between performer and audience, owner and athlete, and choreographer and dancer. In Foucault's view, modernity began in the eighteenth century, at precisely the moment old authorities gave way to new and human nature was seen as malleable. Under the aegis of liberal imperialism, whole societies might be remade in the West's image but never wholesale or without resistance. Edward Said developed this point in *Orientalism* but described how orientalists preferred to perpetuate the idea of an exotic Orient, frozen in time, rather than to modernize it. They projected all that the West would deflect, in a process of identity formation that applies far beyond Asia. Most prominent is sexuality, with the decadent Oriental despot set in opposition to the restrained liberal. Yet, gradually and as a result of widespread intimacies, this binary broke down. The study of gender and sexuality therefore not only provides insight into the private lives of modern peoples thrown into close proximity, it also uncovers the foundations of modern racial and gender identities. Finally, it exposes the embodied aspects of imperial power at every level.

Which brings us back to the body. Our global world puts us in contact with people everywhere at any minute through the power of the Internet. We are troubled by an endless flow of news headlines from so many parts of the world still torn by violence, sectarian strife, and diseases that spread nearly as swiftly as does the news about them. Such news of embodied suffering, which affects us to the very core, inspires us to search for answers. We know more about the cultures of peoples who formerly lived in relative isolation than was possible in any previous era, but answers remain elusive. We enjoy diverse cuisines, clothing, film, and music, and can, in a few clicks, actually learn something meaningful about them. But how do we make sense of it all? These artifacts of material culture, often consumed by the body, are perhaps the most immediate way that many in the West encounter European imperialism. *Intimate Empires* goes beyond those few clicks and offers a deeper analysis and comparative historical perspective to students, scholars, and the merely curious. We trust that its many case studies, references to major theorists, and compelling arguments about the centrality of the body will inspire research that will further illuminate the Age of Empire.

GLOSSARY

Ableism Social discrimination or intellectual prejudice against people with disabilities. This ranges from overt physical exclusion to neglect of their concerns. It privileges abled bodies as the norm and presumes the physical and psychological conformity of disabled persons.

Age of Enlightenment The European intellectual, cultural, and political movement of the eighteenth century that urged social reforms based on scientific principles. It promoted the use of reason over faith for the advancement of knowledge and the improvement of society.

Capitalism An economic system in which private individuals and corporations own property and control the means of production. Goods and services are provided in return for profit, and society is organized around the ownership of capital and the provision of wage labor.

Citizenship From a legal standpoint, it means exercising the rights and enjoying the privileges of belonging to a particular nation-state. More broadly, a citizen is a member of a given social group who participates in or identifies with that group's daily civic life.

Colonialism Where one nation conquers another and exercises direct rule over the inhabitants of the conquered territory. This often includes the displacement of indigenous peoples by settler populations that immigrate to the colony from the conquering nation.

Complex Embodiment Emerging from disability theory, it conceptualizes the body as a blend of idealized social constructs and of actual corporeal factors. It seeks to understand the physical body as both what it actually is and how it is socially perceived.

Constructionism The view that personal identity reflects the internalization of social constructs rather than an expression of intrinsic characteristics. In the "weak" version, identity emerges from both social norms and innate traits. In the "strong" version, identity is entirely a social construct.

Discourse The symbols, ideas, practices, and attitudes that systematically construct a worldview by characterizing the subjects of which they speak. For instance, medico-legal discourses seek to instill social norms by imbuing them with the appearance of rational, scientific authority.

Dominion An autonomous state that is nominally under the sovereign rule of an imperial power. A political entity that exercises most or all of the routine functions of government while ceding some authority to another nation, usually in the sphere of international affairs.

Double Consciousness The division of personal identity between two incompatible cultures. This involves conformance to a dominant culture while concealing one's cultural heritage and leads to the psychosocial tension of being an "insider" and an "outsider" at the same time.

Essentialism The view that individual or group attributes are "hard-wired" by genetics and thus inherited from one's parents. Identity and personality are regarded as an expression of mostly immutable and predetermined characteristics that are effectively fixed at birth.

Globalization The transfer of people, goods, and ideas across international borders and cultural boundaries. It involves the functional integration of economic systems, social customs, political structures, and cultural norms across the greater part of the world.

Hegemony The power structure by which people are ruled or governed. It includes the means of coercive control and their ideological legitimacy. A hegemon refers to whoever exercises power over others, which may be an individual ruler, a governing elite, or a political state.

Homoeroticism Intimacy between persons of the same sex regardless of sexual identity or of sexual orientation. The term is used to discuss erotic behavior between persons of the same sex without imposing or presuming modern concepts of inherent homosexual attraction.

Hybridity The mixture of customs, languages, and identities that emerges from the intermingling of different cultures. It is usually associated with cultural imperialism whereby colonized peoples adapt to colonial rule by adopting the habits or values of the colonizers.

Ideology A worldview of how society functions or how it should be structured. This involves the promotion or legitimation of a set of beliefs and its underlying value system. Competing ideologies serve either to maintain or to challenge the interests of the dominant social class.

Imperialism The ideology of empire by which one nation asserts political, social, and economic domination over another. This encompasses formal sovereignty over subjugated peoples as well as informal mechanisms of control over autonomous regions.

Intersectionality A sociological concept that emphasizes the multiple identities an individual possesses and examines the degree to which overlapping power structures produce complex identities. It challenges universalisms that posit uniform race, class, or gender identities.

Materiality The conceptualization of the body as a dynamic, fluid construct of both its physical corporeality and of its perceptual positioning within society.

Cultural practices are inscribed onto bodies by social norms, which are then "naturalized" by their physical enactment.

Mercantilism An economic and political system that regards a nation's power as based on its balance of trade with other nations. It emphasizes the control of trade routes, the monopolistic exploitation of colonial possessions, and the accumulation of trade goods.

Mimicry The performance of European identity by colonized people, from the appropriation of clothing, language, and comportment to the embrace of religious or political ideologies. Mimicry subverts imperialism when it becomes mockery or parody of colonial discourses.

Nationalism A political ideology in which individuals associate their own interests with that of the nation. It is a sense of belonging to a group of people that shares a common identity and a common purpose separate from that of any other national group.

Orientalism The representation of the Orient by Western art and literature in a stereotyped and exoticized manner designed to legitimize cultural superiority. The East was portrayed as static, enervated, backward, and tyrannical versus the dynamic, virile, modern, and egalitarian West.

Ornamentalism The creation of a social hierarchy through public rituals and status-marking objects designed to situate individuals within a stratified social order. The primary factor in social positioning is individual class status rather than collective racial identity.

Othering The categorizing, marginalization, and exclusion of a person or group of people who are considered outside the boundaries of a societal norm. The process of creating the Other defines normalcy (the One) by imposing derogatory stereotypes onto the excluded group.

Pageantry The elaborate display of imperialism through public spectacles and exhibitions. Commemorative enactments function to normalize hegemonic social norms and to manage historical memory by selecting out what is celebrated versus what is marginalized.

Performativity The enactment or "performance" of social and cultural narratives of behavior, especially in reference to gender and sexuality. This creates the illusion of gender as an intrinsic attribute when it is actually a result of the internalization of socially constructed norms.

Postcolonialism The political, economic, military, and cultural legacy of imperial rule by which colonial power relations persist after formal independence. This includes the objective material conditions of postcolonial nations and the subjective effects of colonial heritage.

Queer Theory A field of subversive critical theory that emerged out of gay/lesbian studies and feminist studies. It challenges the presumption that gender and sexual identity are fixed, essential attributes and emphasizes the social attribution of meaning to particular sexual acts.

Racialization The subjective imposition of a racial interpretation on qualities or characteristics that do not inherently exhibit a racial context. It generally refers to a process by which peoples and their customs are categorized as inferior due to perceived racial traits.

Representation The imagery through which concepts are produced and given meaning. This process is inherently value-laden and reflects the nature of power relationships. The capacity to define how people, places, or things are perceived grants the ability to control them.

Scientific Racism The misuse of flawed scientific methods and concepts so as to classify racial groups as inherently superior or inferior. These are often framed in evolutionary or genetic terms, although scientific racism preceded Darwin and misrepresents Darwin's theories.

Sexuality In the broad sense it refers to the capacity of all people to have erotic attractions, behaviors, and experiences. More narrowly it refers to the specific erotic feelings of a given individual, especially whether they are oriented toward the same or the opposite sex.

Social Darwinism A discredited ideology that applied biological concepts of natural selection and "survival of the fittest" to ethnic and social groups. It classified people as "strong" or "weak" and held that over the long run, the "strong" would survive while the "weak' would perish.

Socialism Generally defined in opposition to capitalism, it holds that the economic resources of society ultimately belong to the public as a whole and not to the private sphere. Its many forms share a common concern with enacting social justice by the removal of economic inequality.

Sovereignty The ultimate authority to rule over a territory and to govern the people who reside within it. An independent nation-state is considered a sovereign entity to the extent that it is free from external interference, whether economic, military, or political.

Subaltern A member of a social group that is outside the hegemonic power structure and who therefore lacks cultural and political influence due to his or her subordinate status. Subaltern studies seek to retrieve the viewpoint of colonized peoples versus that of the colonizing elite.

Syncretism The merging of customs and beliefs from two or more cultures, which produces a novel and distinct hybrid culture. The disparate elements of the original cultures are melded together to produce a separate and unified cultural tradition or product.

Transgenderism The blending, crossing, or transgression of social gender norms by adopting the mannerisms, accessories, or appearance usually reserved to the opposite sex. This may range from cross-dressing for practical reasons all the way to a fully transsexual identity.

Transnational On the individual level, it refers to an identity or lifestyle that crosses or ignores national and cultural boundaries. As a broader social movement, transnationalism emphasizes the interconnectivity of human experience regardless of arbitrary international borders.

Universalism The principle that any given aspect of human nature or of human behavior applies to all people in all times and places. It is most frequently used in reference to a religious doctrine or philosophical tenet that the same values and standards apply to all people.

NOTES

Introduction

1. Quoted in Patricia A. Morton, "National and Colonial: The Musée des Colonies at the Colonial Exposition, Paris, 1931," *Art Bulletin* 80, no. 2 (June 1998): 357.
2. Marquis de Condorcet, "The Future Progress of the Human Mind," in *The Portable Enlightenment Reader*, ed. Isaac Kramnick (New York: Penguin Books, 1995), 30.
3. Audre Lorde, "The Master's Tools Will Never Dismantle the Master's House," in *Sister Outsider: Essays and Speeches* (Berkeley: Crossing Press, 1984), 110–114.
4. Michel Foucault, *The History of Sexuality*, trans. Robert Hurley, 3 vols. (New York: Pantheon Books, 1978–1986).
5. Ann Laura Stoler, *Race and the Education of Desire: Foucault's History of Sexuality and the Colonial Order of Things* (Durham, NC: Duke University Press, 1995).
6. Quoted in Ann Laura Stoler, *Carnal Knowledge and Imperial Power: Race and the Intimate in Colonial Rule* (Berkeley: University of California Press, 2010), 173.
7. Ibid.
8. Helen Callaway and Dorothy O. Helly, "Crusader for Empire: Flora Shaw/Lady Lugard," in *Western Women and Imperialism: Complicity and Resistance*, ed. Nupur Chaudhuri and Margaret Strobel (Bloomington: Indiana University Press, 1992), 79–97.
9. Nancy Rose Hunt, *A Colonial Lexicon: Of Birth Ritual, Medicalization, and Mobility in the Congo* (Durham, NC: Duke University Press, 1999).
10. Quoted in Nancy Rose Hunt, "'Le Bébé en Brousse': European Women, African Birth Spacing, and Colonial Intervention in Breast Feeding in the Belgian Congo," in *Tensions of Empire: Colonial Cultures in a Bourgeois World*, ed. Frederick Cooper and Ann Laura Stoler (Berkeley: University of California Press, 1997), 309.
11. Ronald Hyam, *Empire and Sexuality: The British Experience* (Manchester, UK: Manchester University Press, 1990).
12. Robert Aldrich, *Colonialism and Homosexuality* (London: Routledge, 2003).
13. Mrinalini Sinha, *Colonial Masculinity: The 'Manly Englishman' and the 'Effeminate Bengali' in the Late Nineteenth Century* (Manchester, UK: Manchester University Press, 1995).
14. Edward W. Said, *Orientalism* (New York: Vintage Books, 1978).

15. W. E. B. Du Bois, *Darkwater: Voices from within the Veil* (New York: Harcourt, Brace and Howe, 1920), 30.

16. Gayatri Chakravorty Spivak, *A Critique of Postcolonial Reason: Toward a History of the Vanishing Present* (Cambridge, MA: Harvard University Press, 1999).

17. Homi K. Bhabha, *The Location of Culture* (London: Routledge, 1994).

18. Ashis Nandy, *The Intimate Enemy: Loss and Recovery of Self under Colonialism* (Delhi: Oxford University Press, 1983).

19. Assia Djebar, *Fantasia: An Algerian Cavalcade*, trans. Dorothy S. Blair (Portsmouth, NH: Heinemann, 1993), 156–157.

Chapter One

1. William Wales, "Appendix V: Journal of William Wales," in *The Journals of Captain James Cook on His Voyages of Discovery: The Voyage of the Resolution and Adventure, 1772–1775*, ed. John C. Beaglehole (Cambridge: Cambridge University Press, 1961), 859.

2. Ibid.

3. David Buchbinder, *Performance Anxietifes: Re-Producing Masculinity* (St. Leonards, N.S.W., Australia: Allen & Unwin, 1998), 4–7.

4. Raewyn Connell, *Masculinities*, 2nd ed. (Berkeley: University of California Press, 2005), 186–192.

5. Quoted in Linda E. Merians, *Envisioning the Worst: Representations of "Hottentots" in Early-Modern England* (Newark: University of Delaware Press, 2001), 181.

6. Quoted in Harriet Guest, *Empire, Barbarism, and Civilisation: Captain Cook, William Hodges, and the Return to the Pacific* (Cambridge: Cambridge University Press, 2007), 29.

7. Kathleen Wilson, *The Island Race: Englishness, Empire, and Gender in the Eighteenth Century* (London: Routledge, 2003), 171.

8. Quoted in Wilson, *Island Race*, 172.

9. Wilson, *Island Race*, 175.

10. Ibid., 177.

11. Ibid., 184–186.

12. Quoted in Christopher B. Balme, "Sexual Spectacles: Theatricality and the Performance of Sex in Early Encounters in the Pacific," *Drama Review* 44, no. 4 (Winter 2000): 72.

13. Lewis de Bougainville, *A Voyage Round the World: Performed by Order of His Most Christian Majesty, 1766–1769*, trans. John Reinhold Forster (London: J. Nourse, 1772), 219.

14. Quoted in Wilson, *Island Race*, 192.

15. Ibid., 198.

16. Raewyn Connell, "Identity," in *Critical Terms for the Study of Gender*, ed. Catharine R. Stimpson and Gilbert Herdt (Chicago: University of Chicago Press, 2014), 169.

17. Anne Salmond, *The Trial of the Cannibal Dog: The Remarkable Story of Captain Cook's Encounters in the South Seas* (New Haven: Yale University Press, 2003), 395.

18. Quoted in Guest, *Empire, Barbarism, and Civilisation*, 103.

19. Guest, *Empire, Barbarism, and Civilisation*, 103.

20. Quoted in Brooke N. Newman, "Gender, Sexuality, and the Formation of Racial Identities in the Eighteenth-Century Anglo-Caribbean World," *Gender and History* 22, no. 3 (November 2010): 595–596.

21. Newman, "Gender, Sexuality," 597.

22. Quoted in Ronald Hyam, *Empire and Sexuality: The British Experience* (Manchester, UK: Manchester University Press, 1990), 89.

23. Quoted in Michael Khodarkovsky, "'Ignoble Savages and Unfaithful Subjects': Constructing Non-Christian Identities in Early Modern Russia," in *Russia's Orient: Imperial Borderlands and Peoples, 1700–1917*, ed. Daniel R. Brower and Edward J. Lazzerini (Bloomington: Indiana University Press, 1997), 10.

24. Quoted in Susan Layton, "Nineteenth-Century Russian Mythologies of Caucasian Savagery," in *Russia's Orient: Imperial Borderlands and Peoples, 1700–1917*, ed. Daniel R. Brower and Edward J. Lazzerini (Bloomington: Indiana University Press, 1997), 86.

25. Quoted in Susan Layton, *Russian Literature and Empire: Conquest of the Caucasus from Pushkin to Tolstoy* (Cambridge: Cambridge University Press, 1994), 183.

26. Quoted in Katya Hokanson, "Russian Women Travelers in Central Asia and India," *Russian Review* 70, no. 1 (January 2011): 10.

27. Ibid.

28. Quoted in Robert Hogg, *Men and Manliness on the Frontier: Queensland and British Columbia in the Mid-Nineteenth Century* (Basingstoke, UK: Palgrave Macmillan, 2012), 155.

29. Jock Phillips, *A Man's Country? The Image of the Pakeha Male—A History* (Auckland, N.Z.: Penguin Books, 1987), 26.

30. Quoted in Phillips, *Man's Country*, 37.

31. Marilyn Lake, "Australian Frontier Feminism and the Marauding White Man," in *Gender and Imperialism*, ed. Clare Midgley (Manchester, UK: Manchester University Press, 1998), 123–124.

32. Quoted in Phillips, *Man's Country*, 52.

33. Ibid.

34. Ibid., 37.

35. Quoted in Owen White, *Children of the French Empire: Miscegenation and Colonial Society in French West Africa, 1895–1960* (New York: Oxford University Press, 1999), 14.

36. André Thiellement, *Azawar: Illustrations de l'auteur* (Rennes, France: L'Amitié par le Livre, 1949), 38.

37. Quoted in White, *Children of the French Empire*, 14.

38. Ibid., 15.

39. Quoted in Lora Wildenthal, *German Women for Empire, 1884–1945* (Durham, NC: Duke University Press, 2001), 81.

40. Ibid.

41. Ibid., 95.

42. Quoted in Robert Aldrich, *Colonialism and Homosexuality* (London: Routledge, 2003), 305.

43. Aldrich, *Colonialism and Homosexuality*, 309.

44. Quoted in Aldrich, *Colonialism and Homosexuality*, 67.

45. Heike I. Schmidt, "Colonial Intimacy: The Rechenberg Scandal and Homosexuality in German East Africa," *Journal of the History of Sexuality* 17, no. 1 (January 2008): 26.

46. Quoted in Schmidt, "Colonial Intimacy," 35.

47. Ibid., 38.

48. Schmidt, "Colonial Intimacy," 39.

49. Ibid., 47.

50. Quoted in Schmidt, "Colonial Intimacy," 48.

51. Quoted in Daniel J. Walther, "Racializing Sex: Same-Sex Relations, German Colonial Authority, and *Deutschtum*," *Journal of the History of Sexuality* 17, no. 1 (January 2008): 14–15.

52. Walther, "Racializing Sex," 16.

53. Quoted in John Millar, *The Origin of the Distinction of Ranks; Or, an Inquiry into the Circumstances Which Give Rise to Influence and Authority in the Different Members of Society* (Basel, Switzerland: J. J. Tourneisen, 1793), 87.

54. Quoted in Johann Reinhold Forster, *Observations Made During a Voyage Round the World*, ed. Nicholas Thomas, Harriet Guest, and Michael Dettelbach (Honolulu: University of Hawai'i Press, 1996), 260.

55. Quoted in Herbert Spencer, "Domestic Retrospect and Prospect," *Popular Science Monthly*, September 1877, 521.

56. Quoted in Heike Bauer, "Measurements of Civilization: Non-Western Female Sexuality and the Fin-de-Siècle Social Body," in *Sexuality at the Fin de Siècle: The Making of a "Central Problem,"* ed. Peter Cryle and Christopher E. Forth (Newark: University of Delaware Press, 2008), 97.

57. Todd W. Reeser, *Masculinities in Theory: An Introduction* (Malden, MA: Wiley-Blackwell, 2010), 150.

58. Helen Kanitkar, "'Real True Boys': Moulding the Cadets of Imperialism," in *Dislocating Masculinity: Comparative Ethnographies*, ed. Andrea Cornwall and Nancy Lindisfarne (London: Routledge, 1994), 183.

59. Quoted in Robert A. Huttenback, "G. A. Henty and the Imperial Stereotype," *Huntington Library Quarterly* 29, no. 1 (November 1965): 64.

60. Huttenback, "G. A. Henty," 65.

61. Quoted in Huttenback, "G. A. Henty," 73.

62. Quoted in Joseph Bristow, *Empire Boys: Adventures in a Man's World* (London: HarperCollins, 1991), 197.

63. Jeff Bowersox, *Raising Germans in the Age of Empire: Youth and Colonial Culture, 1871–1914* (Oxford: Oxford University Press, 2013), 134.

64. Ibid., 135.

65. Ibid., 30–33.

66. Robert Baden-Powell, *Scouting for Boys: The Original 1908 Edition* (Mineola, NY: Dover Publications, 2007), 12.

67. Michael Rosenthal, "Knights and Retainers: The Earliest Version of Baden-Powell's Boy Scout Scheme," *Journal of Contemporary History* 15, no. 4 (October 1980): 605–606.

68. Baden-Powell, *Scouting for Boys*, 342.

69. John Tosh, *A Man's Place: Masculinity and the Middle-Class Home in Victorian England* (New Haven, CT: Yale University Press, 1999), 174–175.

70. Quoted in J. A. Mangan, *'Manufactured' Masculinity: Making Imperial Manliness, Morality, and Militarism* (London: Routledge, 2012), 84–85.

71. Ibid., 343.

72. Quoted in Christopher E. Forth, "*La Civilisation* and Its Discontents: Modernity, Manhood, and the Body in the Early Third Republic," in *French Masculinities: History, Culture, and Politics*, ed. Christopher E. Forth and Bertrand Taithe (Basingstoke, UK: Palgrave Macmillan, 2007), 96.

73. Quoted in Joan Tumblety, *Remaking the Male Body: Masculinity and the Uses of Physical Culture in Interwar and Vichy France* (Oxford: Oxford University Press, 2012), 13.

74. Ibid.

75. Quoted in Anssi Halmesvirta, "Building the *Élan Vital* of the Finnish Nation: Ivar Wilskman's Ideology of Gymnastics," *International Journal of the History of Sport* 26, no. 5 (April 2009): 623.

76. Ibid., 627.

77. Ibid., 628.

78. Quoted in Pierre Brocheux and Daniel Hémery, *Indochina: An Ambiguous Colonization, 1858–1954*, trans. Ly Lan Dill-Klein (Berkeley: University of California Press, 2009), 184.

79. Quoted in Robert Aldrich, "Colonial Man," in *French Masculinities: History, Culture, and Politics*, ed. Christopher E. Forth and Bertrand Taithe (Basingstoke, UK: Palgrave Macmillan, 2007), 124–125.

80. Quoted in Brocheux and Hémery, *Indochina*, 184.

81. Quoted in Aldrich, "Colonial Man," 128–129.

82. Ibid., 129.

83. Wildenthal, *German Women for Empire*, 80.

84. Quoted in Wildenthal, *German Women for Empire*, 100.

85. Quoted in Fouad Makki, "Imperial Fantasies, Colonial Realities: Contesting Power and Culture in Italian Eritrea," *South Atlantic Quarterly* 107, no. 4 (Fall 2008): 749–750.

86. Ibid., 750–751.

87. Quoted in Warwick Anderson, "The Trespass Speaks: White Masculinity and Colonial Breakdown," *American Historical Review* 102, no. 5 (December 1997): 1344.

88. Anderson, "Trespass Speaks," 1349.

89. Ibid., 1357.

90. Quoted in Anderson, "Trespass Speaks," 1359.

91. Ibid., 1352–1353.

92. Ibid., 1353–1354.

93. Anderson, "Trespass Speaks," 1350.

94. Quoted in Anderson, "Trespass Speaks," 1361–1362.

95. Anderson, "Trespass Speaks," 1365.

96. Robert A. Nye, "Western Masculinities in War and Peace," *American Historical Review* 112, no. 2 (April 2007): 417–438.

97. Joan B. Landes, "Republican Citizenship and Heterosocial Desire: Concepts of Masculinity in Revolutionary France," in *Masculinities in Politics and War: Gendering Modern History*, ed. Stefan Dudink, Karen Hagemann, and John Tosh (Manchester, UK: Manchester University Press, 2004): 111.

98. Leo Braudy, *From Chivalry to Terrorism: War and the Changing Nature of Masculinity* (New York: Alfred A. Knopf, 2003), 293.

99. Ibid., 294.

100. John M. MacKenzie, "Heroic Myths of Empire," *Popular Imperialism and the Military, 1850–1950*, ed. John M. MacKenzie (Manchester, UK: Manchester University Press, 1992), 114–115.

101. Graham Dawson, "The Blond Bedouin: Lawrence of Arabia, Imperial Adventure, and the Imagining of English-British Masculinity," in *Manful Assertions: Masculinities in Britain since 1800*, ed. Michael Roper and John Tosh (London: Routledge, 1991), 118.

102. Quoted in Graham Dawson, *Soldier Heroes: British Adventure, Empire, and the Imagining of Masculinities* (London: Routledge, 1994), 166.

103. Quoted in Isabel V. Hull, *Absolute Destruction: Military Culture and the Practices of War in Imperial Germany* (Ithaca, NY: Cornell University Press, 2005), 135.

104. Émile Boutroux, "Germany's Civilized Barbarism," *New York Times Current History of the European War* 1, no. 1 (December 1914): 160–169.

105. Quoted in Judy Bartel, *The Holocaust: A Primary Source History* (Milwaukee, WI: Gareth Stevens, 2006), 16.

106. Rachel Standfield, "Violence and the Intimacy of Imperial Ethnography: The *Endeavour* in the Pacific," in *Moving Subjects: Gender, Mobility, and Intimacy in an Age of Global Empire*, ed. Tony Ballantyne and Antoinette Burton (Urbana: University of Illinois Press, 2009), 32, 41.

107. Ibid., 46.

108. Quoted in Sudipta Sen, "Colonial Aversions and Domestic Desires: Blood, Race, Sex, and the Decline of Intimacy in Early British India," in *Sexual Sites, Seminal Attitudes: Sexualities, Masculinities and Culture in South Asia*, ed. Sanjay Srivastava (New Delhi: Sage Publications, 2004), 76.

109. Quoted in Linda Colley, *Captives: Britain, Empire, and the World, 1600–1850* (New York: Anchor Books, 2004), 288.

110. Colley, *Captives*, 287–292.

111. Jaap de Moor, "The Recruitment of Indonesian Soldiers for the Dutch Colonial Army, c. 1700–1950," in *Guardians of Empire: The Armed Forces of the Colonial Powers, c. 1700–1964*, ed. David Killingray and David Omissi (Manchester, UK: Manchester University Press, 1999), 59.

112. Quoted in Egodi Uchendu, "Introduction: Are African Males Men? Sketching African Masculinities," in *Masculinities in Contemporary Africa*, ed. Egodi Uchendu (Dakar, Senegal: Council for the Development of Social Science Research in Africa, 2008), 1.

113. Susan J. Rasmussen, "Veiled Self, Transparent Meanings: Tuareg Headdress as Social Expression," *Ethnology* 30, no. 2 (April 1991): 102.

114. Quoted in de Moor, "Recruitment of Indonesian Soldiers," 60.

115. Ibid.

116. Gerke Teitler, "The Mixed Company: Fighting Power and Ethnic Relations in the Dutch Colonial Army, 1890–1920," in *Colonial Armies in Southeast Asia*, ed. Karl Hack and Tobias Rettig (London: Routledge, 2006), 163.

117. Quoted in de Moor, "Recruitment of Indonesian Soldiers," 63.

118. Ibid.

119. Quoted in Allison Blakely, *Blacks in the Dutch World: The Evolution of Racial Imagery in a Modern Society* (Bloomington: Indiana University Press, 1993), 246.

120. Blakely, *Blacks in the Dutch World*, 245.

121. Quoted in Blakely, *Blacks in the Dutch World*, 251.

122. Quoted in Peter Zinoman, "Colonial Prisons and Anti-Colonial Resistance in French Indochina: The Thai Nguyen Rebellion, 1917," *Modern Asian Studies* 34, no. 1 (February 2000): 65.

123. Ibid., 65.

124. Ibid., 94.

125. Ibid., 97.

126. Quoted in May Opitz, "Racism, Sexism, and Precolonial Images of Africa in Germany," in *Showing Our Colors: Afro-German Women Speak Out*, ed. May Opitz, Katharina Oguntoye, and Dagmar Schultz, trans. Anne V. Adams (Amherst: University of Massachusetts Press, 1992), 44.

127. Quoted in David Killingray, "Gender Issues and African Colonial Armies," in *Guardians of Empire: The Armed Forces of the Colonial Powers, c. 1700-1964*, ed. David Killingray and David Omissi (Manchester, UK: Manchester University Press, 1999), 236.

128. Quoted in Timothy H. Parsons, *The African Rank-and-File: Social Implications of Colonial Military Service in the King's African Rifles, 1902-1964* (Portsmouth, NH: Heinemann, 1999), 159.

129. Anne McClintock, *Imperial Leather: Race, Gender, and Sexuality in the Colonial Contest* (New York: Routledge, 1995), 14-15.

130. Quoted in Jennifer Anne Boittin, Christina Firpo, and Emily Musil Church, "Hierarchies of Race and Gender in the French Colonial Empire, 1914-1946," *Historical Reflections* 37, no. 1 (Spring 2011): 70.

131. Hilary Beckles, "Black Masculinity in Caribbean Slavery," in *Interrogating Caribbean Masculinities: Theoretical and Empirical Analyses*, ed. Rhoda E. Reddock (Kingston, Jamaica: University of the West Indies Press, 2004), 228-230.

132. Quoted in Beckles, "Black Masculinity," 234.

133. Angela Woollacott, *Gender and Empire* (London: Palgrave Macmillan, 2006), 18.

134. Martin Meredith, *The Fortunes of Africa: A 5000-Year History of Wealth, Greed, and Endeavor* (New York: Public Affairs, 2014), 124.

135. Maurice Hall, "Negotiating Jamaican Masculinities," in *Global Masculinities and Manhood*, ed. Ronald L. Jackson II and Murali Balaji (Urbana: University of Illinois Press, 2011), 35.

136. Ronald L. Jackson II, *Scripting the Black Masculine Body: Identity, Discourse, and Racial Politics in Popular Media* (Albany: State University of New York Press, 2006), 76-85.

137. Beckles, "Black Masculinity," 229.

138. Quoted in Beckles, "Black Masculinity," 233.

139. Ibid.

140. Quoted in Maurice O. Wallace, *Constructing the Black Masculine: Identity and Ideality in African American Men's Literature and Culture, 1775-1995* (Durham, NC: Duke University Press, 2002), 90.

141. Quoted in Herbert Sussman, *Masculine Identities: The History and Meanings of Manliness* (Santa Barbara, CA: Praeger, 2012), 102.

142. Quoted in Daniel P. Black, *Dismantling Black Manhood: An Historical and Literary Analysis of the Legacy of Slavery* (New York: Garland Publishing, 1997), 103-104.

143. Quoted in Wallace, *Constructing the Black Masculine*, 89.

144. Quoted in Ibrahima Seck, *Bouki Fait Gombo: A History of the Slave Community of Habitation Haydel (Whitney Plantation) Louisiana, 1750-1860* (New Orleans, LA: University of New Orleans Press, 2014), 106.

145. Ibid., 108.

146. Ibid., 110.

147. Olaudah Equiano, *The Interesting Narrative of the Life of Olaudah Equiano, or Gustavus Vassa, the African*, 3rd ed. (London: G. Vassa, 1790), 86.

148. Ibid., 132.

149. Ibid., 250.

150. Jocelyn Stitt, "Olaudah Equiano, Englishness, and the Negotiation of Raced Gender," *Michigan Feminist Studies*, no. 14 (1999-2000), http://hdl.handle.net/2027/spo.ark5583.0014.005.

151. Quoted in Tuzyline Jita Allan, "A Retrospective: Looking for 'the African' in the Hybrid: Thoughts on Masculinity in Equiano's *The Interesting Narrative*," in *Masculinities in African Literary and Cultural Texts*, ed. Helen Nabasuta Mugambi and Tuzyline Jita Allan (Banbury, UK: Ayebia Clarke, 2010), 290.

152. Ibid.

153. Christopher L. Miller, *The French Atlantic Triangle: Literature and Culture of the Slave Trade* (Durham, NC: Duke University Press, 2008), 33–37.

154. Quoted in Sussman, *Masculine Identities*, 105.

155. W. E. B. Du Bois, *The Souls of Black Folk: Essays and Sketches*, 3rd ed. (Chicago: A. C. McClurg, 1903), 3.

156. Ibid., 4.

157. Rudyard Kipling, "The White Man's Burden," *McClure's Magazine*, February 1899, 290.

158. Quoted in Howard Zinn, *A People's History of the United States, 1492-Present* (New York: HarperCollins, 2003), 300.

159. Carolyn A. Brown, "A 'Man' in the Village Is a 'Boy' in the Workplace: Colonial Racism, Worker Militance, and Igbo Notions of Masculinity in the Nigerian Coal Industry, 1930–1945," in *Men and Masculinities in Modern Africa*, ed. Lisa A. Lindsay and Stephan F. Miescher (Portsmouth, NH: Heinemann, 2003), 160.

160. Quoted in Brown, "Man in the Village," 157.

161. Ibid.

162. Frantz Fanon, *Black Skin, White Masks*, trans. Charles Lam Markmann (New York: Grove Press, 1967), 157.

163. Ibid., 165, 177.

164. Morris Low, "The Emperor's Sons Go to War: Competing Masculinities in Modern Japan," in *Asian Masculinities: The Meaning and Practice of Manhood in China and Japan*, ed. Kam Louie and Morris Low (London: Routledge Curzon, 2003), 83.

165. Irokawa Daikichi, "Popular Movements in Modern Japanese History," in *The Japanese Trajectory: Modernization and Beyond*, ed. Gavan McCormack and Yoshio Sugimoto (Cambridge: Cambridge University Press, 1988), 69.

166. Gary P. Leupp, *Male Colors: The Construction of Homosexuality in Tokugawa Japan* (Berkeley: University of California Press, 1995), 155.

167. Barbara Sato, "Commodifying and Engendering Morality: Self-Cultivation and the Construction of the 'Ideal Woman' in 1920s Mass Women's Magazines," in *Gendering Modern Japanese History*, ed. Barbara Molony and Kathleen Uno (Cambridge, MA: Harvard University Press, 2005), 103–104.

168. Quoted in Yorimitsu Hashimoto, "Japanese Tea Party: Representations of Victorian Paradise and Playground in *The Geisha* (1896)," in *Histories of Tourism: Representation, Identity, and Conflict*, ed. John K. Walton (Clevedon, UK: Channel View Publications, 2005), 118.

169. Quoted in Theodore F. Cook Jr., "Making 'Soldiers': The Imperial Army and the Japanese Man in Meiji Society and State," in *Gendering Modern Japanese History*, ed. Barbara Molony and Kathleen Uno (Cambridge, MA: Harvard University Press, 2005), 263.

170. Quoted in Michele M. Mason, "Empowering the Would-Be Warrior: Bushidō and the Gendered Bodies of the Japanese Nation," in *Recreating Japanese Men*, ed. Sabine Frühstück and Anne Walthall (Berkeley: University of California Press, 2011), 73.

171. Quoted in Hashimoto, "Japanese Tea Party," 120.

172. Low, "Emperor's Sons," 85.

173. Ibid.

174. Quoted in Low, "Emperor's Sons," 86.

175. Ibid., 87.

176. Romit Dasgupta, "Creating Corporate Warriors: The 'Salaryman' and Masculinity in Japan," in *Asian Masculinities: The Meaning and Practice of Manhood in China and Japan*, ed. Kam Louie and Morris Low (London: Routledge Curzon, 2003), 122.

177. Quoted in David Cannadine, *Ornamentalism: How the British Saw Their Empire* (Oxford: Oxford University Press, 2001), 61.

178. Quoted in Cannadine, *Ornamentalism*, 86–88.

179. Ibid., 140.

180. Quoted in Mrinalini Sinha, *Colonial Masculinity: The 'Manly Englishman' and the 'Effeminate Bengali' in the Late Nineteenth Century* (Manchester, UK: Manchester University Press, 1995), 15–16.

181. Quoted in Revathi Krishnaswamy, "The Economy of Colonial Desire," in *The Masculinity Studies Reader*, ed. Rachel Adams and David Savran (Malden, MA: Blackwell Publishers, 2002), 297.

182. Quoted in Sikata Banerjee, *Make Me a Man! Masculinity, Hinduism, and Nationalism in India* (Albany: State University of New York Press, 2005), 33.

183. Quoted in Zareer Masani, *Indian Tales of the Raj* (Berkeley: University of California Press, 1987), 12.

184. Ibid., 10–11.

185. Quoted in Sinha, *Colonial Masculinity*, 21.

186. Quoted in Sikata Banerjee, *Muscular Nationalism: Gender, Violence, and Empire in India and Ireland, 1914–2004* (New York: New York University Press, 2012), 56.

187. Ibid.

188. Quoted in Charu Gupta, "Anxious Hindu Masculinities in Colonial North India: *Shuddhi* and *Sangathan* Movements," *CrossCurrents* 61, no. 4 (December 2011): 446.

189. Quoted in Gyanendra Pandey, *Routine Violence: Nations, Fragments, Histories* (Stanford, CA: Stanford University Press, 2006), 127.

190. Quoted in Evelyne Combeau-Mari, "Sport in the French Colonies (1880–1962): A Case Study," *Journal of Sport History* 33, no. 1 (Spring 2006): 29.

191. Ibid., 35.

192. Combeau-Mari, "Sport in the French Colonies," 41.

193. Quoted in Philip Dine, *Sport and Identity in France: Practices, Locations, Representations* (Oxford, UK: Peter Lang, 2012), 66–67.

194. Ibid., 68.

195. Sarah Radcliffe and Sallie Westwood, *Remaking the Nation: Place, Identity, and Politics in Latin America* (London: Routledge, 1996), 144.

196. Quoted in Eduardo P. Archetti, *Masculinities: Football, Polo, and the Tango in Argentina* (Oxford, UK: Berg, 1999), 96.

197. Ibid., 97.

198. Ibid., 68.

199. Quoted in Matthew Brown, *From Frontiers to Football: An Alternative History of Latin America since 1800* (London: Reaktion Books, 2014), 115.

200. Ibid., 115–116.

201. Archetti, *Masculinities*, 71–72.

202. James Cook, *The Journals of Captain Cook*, ed. Philip Edwards (London: Penguin Books, 2003), 277.

203. James MacGregor Burns, *Fire and Light: How the Enlightenment Transformed our World* (New York: Thomas Dunne, 2013), 53.

204. Quoted in Sankar Muthu, *Enlightenment against Empire* (Princeton, NJ: Princeton University Press, 2003), 74.

205. Ibid., 93.

206. Ibid., 157, 190.

207. Ibid., 75.

208. Mark Twain, "Battle Hymn of the Republic (Brought Down to Date)," in *Mark Twain's Weapons of Satire: Anti-Imperialist Writings on the Philippine-American War*, ed. Jim Zwick (Syracuse, NY: Syracuse University Press, 1992), 40.

209. Mark Twain, "A Salutation to the Twentieth Century," in *Mark Twain's Weapons of Satire: Anti-Imperialist Writings on the Philippine-American War*, ed. Jim Zwick (Syracuse, NY: Syracuse University Press, 1992), 12–13.

210. Quoted in Philip S. Foner, *Mark Twain: Social Critic*, 2nd ed. (New York: International Publishers, 1972), 377.

211. Quoted in Gail Lumet Buckley, *American Patriots: The Story of Blacks in the Military from the Revolution to Desert Storm* (New York: Random House, 2001), 143.

212. Henry T. Johnson, *The Black Man's Burden* (Philadelphia: A. M. E. Church, 1899), n.p.

213. Michele Mitchell, *Righteous Propagation: African Americans and the Politics of Racial Destiny after Reconstruction* (Chapel Hill: University of North Carolina Press, 2004), 69.

214. Quoted in Mitchell, *Righteous Propagation*, 69.

215. Ibid., 68.

216. Frantz Fanon, *The Wretched of the Earth*, trans. Richard Philcox (New York: Grove Press, 2004), 5.

217. Ibid., 50–51.

218. Ibid., 237.

219. Ibid., 49–50.

Chapter Two

1. Quoted in Tracey Rizzo, "'A Lascivious Climate': Representations of Colonial Subjectivity in the *Causes Célèbres* of Eighteenth-Century France," *Journal of Caribbean History* 34, no. 1/2 (2000): 172.

2. Ibid., 171.

3. Rizzo, "Lascivious Climate," 170–172.

4. Quoted in Tracey Rizzo, *A Certain Emancipation of Women: Gender, Citizenship, and the* Causes Célèbres *of Eighteenth-Century France* (Selinsgrove, PA: Susquehanna University Press, 2004), 46.

5. Joan W. Scott, "Gender: A Useful Category of Historical Analysis," *American Historical Review* 91, no. 5 (December 1986): 1053–1075.

6. Thomas Paine, "Women, Adored and Oppressed," in *The Portable Enlightenment Reader*, ed. Isaac Kramnick (New York: Penguin Books, 1995), 588.

7. Quoted in Bonnie G. Smith, *Imperialism: A History in Documents* (Oxford: Oxford University Press, 2000), 22–23.

8. Rifa'a Tahtawi, "Rifa'a Tahtawi Reflects on Paris, Its People, Their Ideas, and Lives in the 1820s," in *Sources in the History of the Modern Middle East*, ed. Akram Fouad Khater, 2nd ed. (Boston: Wadsworth Cengage Learning, 2011), 60.

9. Ibid., 61.

10. Françoise de Graffigny, *Letters from a Peruvian Woman*, trans. David Kornacker (New York: Modern Language Association of America, 1993), 70.

11. Ibid., 57.

12. Claire de Duras, *Ourika: An English Translation*, trans. John Fowles (New York: Modern Language Association of America, 1994), 39.

13. Ibid., 33.

14. Gertrudis Gómez de Avellaneda, *Sab* and *Autobiography*, trans. Nina M. Scott (Austin: University of Texas Press, 1993), 125.

15. Ibid., 144–145.

16. Michael A. McDonnell, "'Il a Epousé une Sauvagesse': Indian and Métis Persistence across Imperial and National Borders," in *Moving Subjects: Gender, Mobility, and Intimacy in an Age of Global Empire*, ed. Tony Ballantyne and Antoinette Burton (Urbana: University of Illinois Press, 2009), 161.

17. Richard Godbeer, "Eroticizing the Middle Ground: Anglo-Indian Sexual Relations along the Eighteenth-Century Frontier," in *Sex, Love, Race: Crossing Boundaries in North American History*, ed. Martha Hodes (New York: New York University Press, 1999), 95–96.

18. Quoted in Godbeer, "Eroticizing the Middle Ground," 102.

19. Godbeer, "Eroticizing the Middle Ground," 103.

20. Quoted in Godbeer, "Eroticizing the Middle Ground," 105.

21. Ibid.

22. Quoted in Gwenn A. Miller, "'The Perfect Mistress of Russian Economy': Sighting the Intimate on a Colonial Alaskan Terrain, 1784–1821," in *Haunted by Empire: Geographies of Intimacy in North American History*, ed. Ann Laura Stoler (Durham, NC: Duke University Press, 2006), 306.

23. Miller, "Perfect Mistress of Russian Economy," 311.

24. Quoted in Miller, "Perfect Mistress of Russian Economy," 313.

25. Lisa Frink, "Storage and Status in Precolonial and Colonial Coastal Western Alaska," *Current Anthropology* 48, no. 3 (June 2007): 354.

26. Ursula Trüper, *The Invisible Woman: Zara Schmelen, African Mission Assistant at the Cape and in Namaland* (Basel, Switzerland: Basler Afrika Bibliographien, 2006), 39.

27. Quoted in Lora Wildenthal, *German Women for Empire, 1884–1945* (Durham, NC: Duke University Press, 2001), 86–87.

28. Ibid., 86.

29. Ibid., 87.

30. George Steinmetz, *The Devil's Handwriting: Precoloniality and the German Colonial State in Qingdao, Samoa, and Southwest Africa* (Chicago: University of Chicago Press, 2007), 133.

31. Quoted in Lora Wildenthal, "Race, Gender, and Citizenship in the German Colonial Empire," in *Tensions of Empire: Colonial Cultures in a Bourgeois World*, ed. Frederick Cooper and Ann Laura Stoler (Berkeley: University of California Press, 1997), 269.

32. Quoted in Katie Pickles and Angela Wanhalla, "Embodying the Colonial Encounter: Explaining New Zealand's 'Grace Darling,' Huria Matenga," *Gender and History* 22, no. 2 (August 2010): 362.

33. Ibid., 370.

34. Quoted in Mary Prince, *The History of Mary Prince: A West Indian Slave*, 3rd ed. (London: F. Westley and A. H. Davis, 1831), 32.

35. Rizzo, "Lascivious Climate," 167–169.

36. Quoted in Sara Salih, *Representing Mixed Race in Jamaica and England from the Abolition Era to the Present* (New York: Routledge, 2011), 47.

37. Quoted in Brooke N. Newman, "Gender, Sexuality, and the Formation of Racial Identities in the Eighteenth-Century Anglo-Caribbean World," *Gender and History* 22, no. 3 (November 2010): 587.

38. Ibid.

39. Maria Nugent, *Lady Nugent's Journal: Jamaica One Hundred Years Ago*, ed. Frank Cundall (Cambridge: Cambridge University Press, 2010), 76, 125.

40. Quoted in Jane Robinson, *Parrot Pie for Breakfast: An Anthology of Women Pioneers* (Oxford: Oxford University Press, 1999), 114.

41. Hilary McD. Beckles, "Historicizing Slavery in West Indian Feminisms," *Feminist Review* 59 (Summer 1998): 42.

42. Ibid., 43–44.

43. Ibid., 45.

44. Ibid., 46.

45. Malte Fuhrmann, "'Western Perversions' at the Threshold of Felicity: The European Prostitutes of Galata-Pera (1870–1915)," *History and Anthropology* 21, no. 2 (June 2010): 160.

46. Ehud R. Toledano, *As If Silent and Absent: Bonds of Enslavement in the Islamic Middle East* (New Haven, CT: Yale University Press, 2007), 86.

47. Ehud R. Toledano, "Late Ottoman Concepts of Slavery (1830s–1880s)," *Poetics Today* 14, no. 3 (Autumn 1993): 492–493.

48. Ibid., 500.

49. Toledano, *As If Silent*, 87.

50. Quoted in Trevor R. Getz and Liz Clarke, *Abina and the Important Men: A Graphic History* (New York: Oxford University Press, 2012), 88.

51. Martin Klein and Richard Roberts, "Gender and Emancipation in French West Africa," in *Gender and Slave Emancipation in the Atlantic World*, ed. Pamela Scully and Diana Paton (Durham, NC: Duke University Press, 2005), 167–168.

52. Ibid., 173.

53. Ibid., 174.

54. Nils Johan Ringdal, *Love for Sale: A World History of Prostitution*, trans. Richard Daly (New York: Grove Press, 2004), 229.

55. Ibid., 239.

56. Philippa Levine, *Prostitution, Race, and Politics: Policing Venereal Disease in the British Empire* (New York: Routledge, 2003), 244, 311.

57. Quoted in Philippa Levine, "Sexuality, Gender, and Empire," in *Gender and Empire*, ed. Philippa Levine (Oxford: Oxford University Press, 2004), 144.

58. Elizabeth Sinn, "Women at Work: Chinese Brothel Keepers in Nineteenth-Century Hong Kong," *Journal of Women's History* 19, no. 3 (Fall 2007): 88.

59. Quoted in Sinn, "Women at Work," 87.

60. Sinn, "Women at Work," 96.

61. George M. Blackburn and Sherman L. Ricards, "The Prostitutes and Gamblers of Virginia City, Nevada: 1870," *Pacific Historical Review* 48, no. 2 (May 1979): 240.

62. Quoted in Blackburn and Ricards, "Prostitutes and Gamblers," 244.

63. Blackburn and Ricards, "Prostitutes and Gamblers," 243.

64. Quoted in Kazuhiro Oharazeki, "Listening to the Voices of 'Other' Women in Japanese North America: Japanese Prostitutes and Barmaids in the American West, 1887–1920," *Journal of American Ethnic History* 32, no. 4 (Summer 2013): 8.

65. Oharazeki, "Listening to the Voices," 9.

66. Quoted in Oharazeki, "Listening to the Voices," 10.

67. Oharazeki, "Listening to the Voices," 11.

68. Sandra Ponzanesi, "The Color of Love: *Madamismo* and Interracial Relationships in the Italian Colonies," *Research in African Literatures* 43, no. 2 (Summer 2012): 161.

69. Quoted in Ponzanesi, "Color of Love," 161.

70. Ruth Ben-Ghiat, *Fascist Modernities: Italy, 1922–1945* (Berkeley: University of California Press, 2001), 129.

71. Quoted in Joy Damousi, *Depraved and Disorderly: Female Convicts, Sexuality, and Gender in Colonial Australia* (Cambridge: Cambridge University Press, 1997), 37.

72. Quoted in Anne Summers, *Damned Whores and God's Police: The Colonization of Women in Australia* (New York: Penguin Books, 1975), 267.

73. Quoted in Damousi, *Depraved and Disorderly*, 60.

74. Ibid.

75. Quoted in Marilyn Lake, "Australian Frontier Feminism and the Marauding White Man," in *Gender and Imperialism*, ed. Clare Midgley (Manchester, UK: Manchester University Press, 1998), 126.

76. Quoted in Angela Woollacott, *Gender and Empire* (London: Palgrave Macmillan, 2006), 30.

77. Emma Robertson, *Chocolate, Women, and Empire: A Social and Cultural History* (Manchester, UK: Manchester University Press, 2009), 93–94.

78. Quoted in Robertson, *Chocolate, Women, and Empire*, 95.

79. Ibid., 97.

80. Ibid., 98.

81. Quoted in Allyson M. Poska, "Babies on Board: Women, Children, and Imperial Policy in the Spanish Empire," *Gender and History* 22, no. 2 (August 2010): 270.

82. Poska, "Babies on Board," 271–272.

83. Ibid., 273.

84. Quoted in Rizzo, "Lascivious Climate," 162.

85. Ibid., 166.

86. Ibid.

87. Quoted in Summers, *Damned Whores and God's Police*, 291.

88. Georgiana Molloy and John Molloy, "Georgiana Molloy and Captain John Molloy to Mrs. Helen Story, 8 December 1834," in *Women Writing Home, 1700–1920: Female Correspondence across the British Empire*, ed. Klaus Stierstorfer, Vol. 2, ed. Deirdre Coleman (London: Pickering and Chatto, 2006), 160.

89. Ibid., 161.

90. H. A. Lindsay, "The World's First Policewoman," *Quadrant* 3, no. 2 (Autumn 1959): 76.

91. Quoted in Lake, "Australian Frontier Feminism," 127.

92. Quoted in Simon Dagut, "Gender, Colonial 'Women's History,' and the Construction of Social Distance: Middle-Class British Women in Later Nineteenth-Century South Africa," *Journal of Southern African Studies* 26, no. 3 (September 2000): 563.

93. Ibid., 564.

94. Ibid., 566.

95. Quoted in Sarah Steinbock-Pratt, "'We Were All Robinson Crusoes': American Women Teachers in the Philippines," *Women's Studies* 41, no. 4 (June 2012): 384.

96. Ibid.

97. Ibid., 385.

98. Quoted in Elsbeth Locher-Scholten, *Women and the Colonial State: Essays on Gender and Modernity in the Netherlands Indies 1900–1942* (Amsterdam: Amsterdam University Press, 2000), 31.

99. Ibid., 97.

100. Ibid., 156–157.

101. Ibid., 98.

102. Quoted in Denise K. Comer, "'White Child Is Good, Black Child His [or Her] Slave': Women, Children, and Empire in Early Nineteenth-Century India," *European Romantic Review* 16, no. 1 (January 2005): 39.

103. Quoted in Swapna M. Banerjee, "Blurring Boundaries, Distant Companions: Non-Kin Female Caregivers for Children in Colonial India (Nineteenth and Twentieth Centuries)," *Paedagogica Historica* 46, no. 6 (December 2010): 780.

104. Quoted in Ann Laura Stoler, *Carnal Knowledge and Imperial Power: Race and the Intimate in Colonial Rule* (Berkeley: University of California Press, 2010), 173.

105. Ibid., 164.

106. Ibid., 173.

107. Locher-Scholten, *Women and the Colonial State*, 91–92.

108. Stoler, *Carnal Knowledge*, 183–184.

109. Quoted in Stoler, *Carnal Knowledge*, 182.

110. Ibid., 133.

111. Quoted in Dea Birkett, "The 'White Woman's Burden' in the 'White Man's Grave': The Introduction of British Nurses in Colonial West Africa," in *Western Women and Imperialism: Complicity and Resistance*, ed. Nupur Chaudhuri and Margaret Strobel (Bloomington: Indiana University Press, 1992), 178.

112. Ibid., 181–182.

113. Ibid., 182.

114. Ibid., 184.

115. Quoted in Wildenthal, *German Women for Empire*, 32.

116. Quoted in Lora Wildenthal, "'When Men Are Weak': The Imperial Feminism of Frieda von Bülow," *Gender and History* 10, no. 1 (April 1998): 58.

117. Ibid., 60.

118. Ibid., 61.

119. Quoted in Steinbock-Pratt, "We Were All Robinson Crusoes," 372.

120. Steinbock-Pratt, "We Were All Robinson Crusoes," 373–374.

121. Ibid., 388.

122. Ibid., 376.

123. Quoted in Steinbock-Pratt, "We Were All Robinson Crusoes," 377.

124. Steinbock-Pratt, "We Were All Robinson Crusoes," 390.

125. Sister Nivedita, *Letters of Sister Nivedita*, Vol. 2 (Calcutta, India: Nababharat Publishers, 1982), 661.

126. Barbara N. Ramusack, "Cultural Missionaries, Maternal Imperialists, Feminist Allies: British Women Activists in India, 1865–1945," in *Western Women and*

Imperialism: Complicity and Resistance, ed. Nupur Chaudhuri and Margaret Strobel (Bloomington: Indiana University Press, 1992), 125.

127. Sister Nivedita, *The Complete Works of Sister Nivedita*, Vol. 1 (Calcutta, India: Sister Nivedita Girls' School, 1967), 469.

128. Ramusack, "Cultural Missionaries," 124–125.

129. Margaret Fountaine, *Butterflies and Late Loves: The Further Travels and Adventures of a Victorian Lady*, ed. W. F. Cater (Topsfield, MA: Salem House, 1986), 16.

130. Quoted in Smith, *Imperialism*, 82.

131. Fountaine, *Butterflies and Late Loves*, 132.

132. Quoted in Susan L. Blake, "A Woman's Trek: What Difference Does Gender Make?" in *Western Women and Imperialism: Complicity and Resistance*, ed. Nupur Chaudhuri and Margaret Strobel (Bloomington: Indiana University Press, 1992), 27.

133. Ibid., 29.

134. Ibid.

135. Ibid., 28.

136. Ibid., 29.

137. Ibid., 31.

138. R. E. Cheesman, review of *"Behold Our New Empire"–Mussolini*, by Louise Diel, *International Affairs* 18, no. 5 (September–October 1939): 706.

139. Louise Diel, *"Behold Our New Empire"–Mussolini*, trans. Kenneth Kirkness (London: Hurst and Blackett, 1939), 13.

140. Ibid., 66–67.

141. Eric S. Roubinek, "Re-Imagined Communities: National, Racial, and Colonial Visions in Nazi Germany and Fascist Italy, 1922–1943" (PhD diss., University of Minnesota, 2014), 4–16.

142. Quoted in Marie-Paule Ha, *French Women and the Empire: The Case of Indochina* (Oxford: Oxford University Press, 2014), 39.

143. Quoted in Nikki Cooper, "(En)Gendering Indochina: Feminisation and Female Figurings in French Colonial Discourses," *Women's Studies International Forum* 23, no. 6 (November–December 2000): 756.

144. Ibid., 757.

145. Edward A. Tiryakian, "White Women in Darkest Africa: Marginals as Observers in No-Woman's Land," *Civilisations* 41, no. 1/2 (September 1993): 215.

146. Julia Clancy-Smith, "The 'Passionate Nomad' Reconsidered: A European Woman in *L'Algérie Française* (Isabelle Eberhardt, 1877–1904)," in *Western Women and Imperialism: Complicity and Resistance*, ed. Nupur Chaudhuri and Margaret Strobel (Bloomington: Indiana University Press, 1992), 64–71.

147. Marguerite Duras, *The Lover*, trans. Barbara Bray (New York: Pantheon Books, 1985), 23.

148. Ibid., 24.

149. Ibid., 16.

150. Ibid., 37.

151. Ibid., 49.

152. Ibid., 59.

153. Ian Littlewood, *Sultry Climates: Travel and Sex Since the Grand Tour* (London: Thistle Publishing, 2013), 62.

154. Klaus de Albuquerque, "In Search of the Big Bamboo: Among the Sex Tourists of the Caribbean," *Transition*, no. 77 (1998): 50.

155. Quoted in Maurizio Peleggi, "The Social and Material Life of Colonial Hotels: Comfort Zones as Contact Zones in British Colombo and Singapore, ca. 1870–1930," *Journal of Social History* 46, no. 1 (Fall 2012): 143.

156. The Ladies Letter, *Melbourne Punch*, November 4, 1915.

157. Jacqueline Lo, "Miscegenation's 'Dusky Human Consequences,'" *Postcolonial Studies* 5, no. 3 (2002): 298–299.

158. Raden Adjeng Kartini, "Javanese Aristocracy and the Dutch," in *Southeast Asian History: Essential Readings*, ed. D. R. SarDesai, 2nd ed. (Boulder, CO: Westview Press, 2013), 149–150.

159. Ibid., 150.

160. Ibid., 151.

161. Ibid., 148.

162. Ibid., 151.

163. Ibid.

164. Quoted in Fiona Paisley, "Performing 'Interracial Harmony': Settler Colonialism at the 1934 Pan-Pacific Women's Conference in Hawai'i," in *Moving Subjects: Gender, Mobility, and Intimacy in an Age of Global Empire*, ed. Tony Ballantyne and Antoinette Burton (Urbana: University of Illinois Press, 2009), 136.

165. Quoted in Fiona Paisley, *Glamour in the Pacific: Cultural Internationalism and Race Politics in the Women's Pan-Pacific* (Honolulu: University of Hawai'i Press, 2009), 118.

166. T. Damon I. Salesa, "'Travel-Happy' Samoa: Colonialism, Samoan Migration, and a 'Brown Pacific,'" *New Zealand Journal of History* 37, no. 2 (October 2003): 172.

167. Quoted in Paisley, *Glamour in the Pacific*, 119.

168. Paisley, "Performing Interracial Harmony," 138.

169. Rokeya Sakhawat Hossain, *Sultana's Dream: A Feminist Utopia and Selections from the Secluded Ones*, ed. and trans. Roushan Jahan (New York: Feminist Press, 1988), 34.

170. Ibid., 35.

171. Roushan Jahan, "*The Secluded Ones*: Purdah Observed," in Hossain, *Sultana's Dream*, 22.

172. Roushan Jahan, "Rokeya: An Introduction to Her Life," in Hossain, *Sultana's Dream*, 45.

173. Hossain, *Sultana's Dream*, 17–18.

174. Quoted in Siobhan Lambert Hurley, "Out of India: The Journeys of the Begam of Bhopal, 1901–1930," in *Bodies in Contact: Rethinking Colonial Encounters in World History*, ed. Tony Ballantyne and Antoinette Burton (Durham, NC: Duke University Press, 2005), 304.

175. Sarojini Naidu, *The Bird of Time: Songs of Life, Death, and the Spring* (New York: John Lane, 1912), 41–42.

176. Edmund Gosse, "Introduction," in Naidu, *The Bird of Time*, 4–5.

177. Ibid., 5.

178. Ibid., 6.

179. Quoted in Patricia van der Spuy and Lindsay Clowes, "'A Living Testimony of the Heights to Which a Woman Can Rise': Sarojini Naidu, Cissie Gool, and the Politics of Women's Leadership in South Africa in the 1920s," *South African Historical Journal* 64, no. 2 (June 2012): 346.

180. Ibid.

181. Sita Anantha Raman, "Crossing Cultural Boundaries: Indian Matriarchs and Sisters in Service," *Journal of Third World Studies* 18, no. 2 (Fall 2001): 139.

182. Ibid., 140.

183. Quoted in Mytheli Sreenivas, "Creating Conjugal Subjects: Devadasis and the Politics of Marriage in Colonial Madras Presidency," *Feminist Studies* 37, no. 1 (Spring 2011): 70.

184. Ibid.

185. Sreenivas, "Creating Conjugal Subjects," 65.

186. Quoted in Sreenivas, "Creating Conjugal Subjects," 69.

187. Ibid., 71.

188. Ibid., 87.

189. Deniz Kandiyoti, "End of Empire: Islam, Nationalism, and Women in Turkey," in *Women, Islam, and the State*, ed. Deniz Kandiyoti (Philadelphia: Temple University Press, 1991), 26–27.

190. Quoted in Andrew Mango, *Atatürk: The Biography of the Founder of Modern Turkey* (Woodstock, NY: Overlook Press, 1999), 164.

191. Mango, *Atatürk*, 381.

192. Quoted in Mango, *Atatürk*, 434.

193. Quoted in Jennifer Anne Boittin, "Feminist Mediations of the Exotic: French Algeria, Morocco, and Tunisia, 1921–39," *Gender and History* 22, no. 1 (April 2010): 136.

194. Ibid., 137.

195. Ibid., 138.

196. Boittin, "Feminist Mediations," 142.

197. Quoted in Boittin, "Feminist Mediations," 143.

198. Quoted in Adrienne Edgar, "Bolshevism, Patriarchy, and the Nation: The Soviet 'Emancipation' of Muslim Women in Pan-Islamic Perspective," *Slavic Review* 65, no. 2 (Summer 2006): 256.

199. Ibid., 252.

200. Edgar, "Bolshevism, Patriarchy," 260.

201. Ibid., 252.

202. Ibid., 266–267.

Chapter Three

1. Quoted in Roxanne L. Euben, *Journeys to the Other Shore: Muslim and Western Travelers in Search of Knowledge* (Princeton, NJ: Princeton University Press, 2006), 158.

2. Emily Ruete, *Memoirs of an Arabian Princess: An Autobiography*, trans. unknown (New York: D. Appleton, 1888), 146–147.

3. Emily Ruete, *An Arabian Princess between Two Worlds: Memoirs, Letters Home, Sequels to the Memoirs, Syrian Customs and Usages*, ed. Emeri van Donzel (Leiden: E. J. Brill, 1993), 422.

4. Peter Wade, "Hybridity Theory and Kinship Thinking," *Cultural Studies* 19, no. 5 (September 2005): 602–621.

5. Ibid., 605.

6. Emily Ruete, *Memoirs of an Arabian Princess*, trans. Lionel Strachey (New York: Doubleday, Page, and Co., 1907), 9.

7. Ibid., 10.

8. Ibid., 89.

9. Ruete, *An Arabian Princess*, 455.

10. Ibid., 460.
11. Pew Research, "Religion and Public Life Project," Pewforum.org, 2011.
12. Jeremy Rich, "Javouhey, Anne-Marie," in *Dictionary of African Biography*, ed. Emmanuel K. Akyeampong and Henry Louis Gates Jr. (Oxford: Oxford University Press, 2012), 199.
13. Sarah A. Curtis, *Civilizing Habits: Women Missionaries and the Revival of French Empire* (Oxford: Oxford University Press, 2010), 209–210.
14. Quoted in Curtis, *Civilizing Habits*, 215.
15. Ibid., 218.
16. Ibid., 219.
17. Ibid.
18. Ibid., 220.
19. Quoted in Nola Cooke, "Early Nineteenth-Century Vietnamese Catholics and Others in the Pages of the *Annales de la Propagation de la Foi*," *Journal of Southeast Asian Studies* 35, no. 2 (June 2004): 265.
20. Quoted in Cooke, "Early Nineteenth-Century Vietnamese Catholics," 283.
21. Cooke, "Early Nineteenth-Century Vietnamese Catholics," 281.
22. Ibid., 274.
23. Quoted in Cooke, "Early Nineteenth-Century Vietnamese Catholics," 279.
24. Cooke, "Early Nineteenth-Century Vietnamese Catholics," 278.
25. Quoted in Cooke, "Early Nineteenth-Century Vietnamese Catholics," 280.
26. Quoted in Lisa Curtis-Wendlandt, "Missionary Wives and the Sexual Narratives of German Lutheran Missions among Australian Aborigines," *Journal of the History of Sexuality* 20, no. 3 (September 2011): 508.
27. Ibid., 507.
28. Ibid., 509.
29. Ibid., 513.
30. Ibid.
31. Quoted in Margaret Allen, "'White Already to Harvest': South Australian Women Missionaries in India," *Feminist Review*, no. 65 (Summer 2000): 103.
32. Allen, "White Already to Harvest," 97.
33. Ibid., 98.
34. Quoted in Allen, "White Already to Harvest," 103.
35. Ibid., 95.
36. Ibid., 103.
37. Sylvia M. Jacobs, "Give a Thought to Africa: Black Women Missionaries in Southern Africa," in *Western Women and Imperialism: Complicity and Resistance*, ed. Nupur Chaudhuri and Margaret Strobel (Bloomington: Indiana University Press, 1992), 211.
38. Quoted in Jacobs, "Give a Thought to Africa," 211.
39. Ibid., 212.
40. Quoted in Adam Hochschild, *King Leopold's Ghost: A Story of Greed, Terror, and Heroism in Colonial Africa* (Boston: Houghton Mifflin, 1998), 154.
41. Quoted in T. Lynn Smith, "Three Specimens of Religious Syncretism in Latin America," in *Sociology in Latin America*, ed. Man Singh Das (New Delhi: MD Publications, 1994), 62.
42. Quoted in Smith, "Three Specimens," 63.
43. Smith, "Three Specimens," 67–68.

44. Quoted in Zareer Masani, *Indian Tales of the Raj* (Berkeley: University of California Press, 1987), 73.

45. Ibid., 72.

46. Quoted in Padma Anagol, "Indian Christian Women and Indigenous Feminism, c.1850-c.1920," in *Gender and Imperialism*, ed. Clare Midgley (Manchester, UK: Manchester University Press, 1998), 88.

47. Ibid., 92.

48. Anagol, "Indian Christian Women," 85.

49. Quoted in Meera Kosambi, "Returning the American Gaze: Situating Pandita Ramabai's American Encounter," in Pandita Ramabai, *Pandita Ramabai's American Encounter: The Peoples of the United States (1889)*, ed. and trans. Meera Kosambi (Bloomington: Indiana University Press, 2003), 4.

50. Kosambi, "Returning the American Gaze," 6–7.

51. Quoted in Anagol, "Indian Christian Women," 96.

52. Quoted in Anne Dickson-Waiko, "Colonial Enclaves and Domestic Spaces in British New Guinea," in *Britishness Abroad: Transnational Movements and Imperial Cultures*, ed. Kate Darian-Smith, Patricia Grimshaw, and Stuart Macintyre (Carlton: Melbourne University Press, 2007), 225.

53. Dickson-Waiko, "Colonial Enclaves," 218.

54. Deborah Gaitskell, "Devout Domesticity? A Century of African Women's Christianity in South Africa," in *Readings in Gender in Africa*, ed. Andrea Cornwall (London: International African Institute, 2005), 178.

55. Ibid., 185.

56. Quoted in Gaitskell, "Devout Domesticity," 180.

57. Gaitskell, "Devout Domesticity," 184.

58. Quoted in Gaitskell, "Devout Domesticity," 183.

59. Ibid., 181.

60. Ibid., 179.

61. Gaitskell, "Devout Domesticity," 185.

62. Quoted in Wendy Urban-Mead, "Negotiating 'Plainness' and Gender: Dancing and Apparel at Christian Weddings in Matabeleland, Zimbabwe, 1913–1944," *Journal of Religion in Africa* 38, no. 2 (May 2008): 230.

63. Ibid., 231.

64. Ibid., 223.

65. Ibid., 214.

66. Urban-Mead, "Negotiating 'Plainness' and Gender," 217.

67. Quoted in Urban-Mead, "Negotiating 'Plainness' and Gender," 220.

68. Ibid., 233.

69. Quoted in Tammy M. Proctor, "'A Separate Path': Scouting and Guiding in Interwar South Africa," *Comparative Studies in Society and History* 42, no. 3 (July 2000): 606.

70. Ibid., 613.

71. Quoted in Timothy H. Parsons, *Race, Resistance, and the Boy Scout Movement in British Colonial Africa* (Athens: Ohio University Press, 2004), 259.

72. Quoted in Proctor, "Separate Path," 616.

73. Proctor, "Separate Path," 615.

74. Ibid., 617.

75. Quoted in Proctor, "Separate Path," 618.

76. Ibid., 619.
77. Ibid., 620.
78. Ibid., 613.
79. Quoted in David H. Anthony III, "Max Yergan in South Africa: From Evangelical Pan-Africanist to Revolutionary Socialist," *African Studies Review* 34, no. 2 (September 1991): 28.
80. Ibid., 29.
81. Ibid., 35.
82. Ibid., 42.
83. Ibid., 46.
84. Ouarda Merrouche, *The Long Term Impact of French Settlement on Education in Algeria* (Uppsala, Sweden: Uppsala University Department of Economics, 2007), 2.
85. Elsbeth Locher-Scholten, *Women and the Colonial State: Essays on Gender and Modernity in the Netherlands Indies, 1900–1942* (Amsterdam: Amsterdam University Press, 2000), 19.
86. Hardik Brata Biswas, "Wanton Women and Cheap Prints: Farces, Other Genres, and the Reading Publics in Colonial Calcutta," in *Sexuality Studies*, ed. Sanjay Srivastava (New Delhi: Oxford University Press, 2013), 47.
87. Quoted in Larry Prochner, Helen May, and Baljit Kaur, "'The Blessings of Civilisation': Nineteenth-Century Missionary Infant Schools for Young Native Children in Three Colonial Settings—India, Canada and New Zealand 1820s–1840s," *Paedagogica Historica* 45, no. 1/2 (February 2009): 87.
88. Ibid., 88.
89. Ibid., 95.
90. Ibid., 96–97.
91. Ibid., 96.
92. Ibid., 100.
93. Adèle Toussaint-Samson, *A Parisian in Brazil: The Travel Account of a Frenchwoman in Nineteenth-Century Rio de Janeiro*, trans. Emma Toussaint (Wilmington, DE: Scholarly Resources, 2001), 38.
94. Ibid., 36.
95. Raden Adjeng Kartini, "Javanese Aristocracy and the Dutch," in *Southeast Asian History: Essential Readings*, ed. D. R. SarDesai, 2nd ed. (Boulder, CO: Westview Press, 2013), 151.
96. Ibid., 149.
97. Assia Djebar, *Fantasia: An Algerian Cavalcade*, trans. Dorothy S. Blair (Portsmouth, NH: Heinemann, 1993), 156–157.
98. Ibid., 179.
99. Ibid., 215.
100. Quoted in Masani, *Indian Tales of the Raj*, 88.
101. Ibid., 86.
102. Ibid.
103. Ibid., 10–11.
104. Ibid., 11.
105. Ibid., 155.
106. Djebar, *Fantasia*, 185.
107. Ibid.

108. Quoted in Bonnie G. Smith, *Imperialism: A History in Documents* (Oxford: Oxford University Press, 2000), 101.

109. Ibid., 101.

110. Ibid., 51.

111. Djebar, *Fantasia*, 195.

112. Quoted in Fanny Colonna, "Educating Conformity in French Colonial Algeria," trans. Barbara Harshav, in *Tensions of Empire: Colonial Cultures in a Bourgeois World*, ed. Frederick Cooper and Ann Laura Stoler (Berkeley: University of California Press, 1997), 358.

113. Djebar, *Fantasia*, 145.

114. Ibid., 213.

115. Quoted in Colonna, "Educating Conformity," 365.

116. Ibid.

117. Mervat Hatem, "Through Each Other's Eyes: The Impact on the Colonial Encounter of the Images of Egyptian, Levantine-Egyptian, and European Women, 1862–1920," in *Western Women and Imperialism: Complicity and Resistance*, ed. Nupur Chaudhuri and Margaret Strobel (Bloomington: Indiana University Press, 1992), 38.

118. Quoted in Warwick Anderson, "States of Hygiene: Race 'Improvement' and Biomedical Citizenship in Australia and the Colonial Philippines," in *Haunted by Empire: Geographies of Intimacy in North American History*, ed. Ann Laura Stoler (Durham, NC: Duke University Press, 2006), 103.

119. Ibid., 105.

120. Ibid., 106.

121. Ibid.

122. Ibid., 106–107.

123. Anderson, "States of Hygiene," 105.

124. Quoted in Anderson, "States of Hygiene," 107.

125. Robert Manne, "Aboriginal Child Removal and the Question of Genocide, 1900–1940," in *Genocide and Settler Society: Frontier Violence and Stolen Indigenous Children in Australian History*, ed. A. Dirk Moses (New York: Berghahn Books, 2004), 225.

126. Quoted in Anderson, "States of Hygiene," 108.

127. Ibid., 107–108.

128. Quoted in Owen White, *Children of the French Empire: Miscegenation and Colonial Society in French West Africa, 1895–1960* (New York: Oxford University Press, 1999), 54.

129. Ibid., 67.

130. Ibid., 60.

131. Quoted in Fouad Makki, "Imperial Fantasies, Colonial Realities: Contesting Power and Culture in Italian Eritrea," *South Atlantic Quarterly* 107, no. 4 (Fall 2008): 745.

132. Makki, "Imperial Fantasies, Colonial Realities," 746.

133. Quoted in Sandra Ponzanesi, "The Color of Love: *Madamismo* and Interracial Relationships in the Italian Colonies," *Research in African Literatures* 43, no. 2 (Summer 2012): 162.

134. Adele Perry, "Reproducing Colonialism in British Columbia, 1849–1871," in *Bodies in Contact: Rethinking Colonial Encounters in World History*, ed. Tony Ballantyne and Antoinette Burton (Durham, NC: Duke University Press, 2005), 149–155.

135. Quoted in Enakshi Dua, "Racialising Imperial Canada: Indian Women and the Making of Ethnic Communities," in *Gender, Sexuality, and Colonial Modernities*, ed. Antoinette Burton (London: Routledge, 1999), 128.
136. Ibid., 125.
137. Ibid., 124.
138. Ibid., 125.
139. Quoted in Mrinalini Sinha, "Britishness, Clubbability, and the Colonial Public Sphere," in *Bodies in Contact: Rethinking Colonial Encounters in World History*, ed. Tony Ballantyne and Antoinette Burton (Durham, NC: Duke University Press, 2005), 192.
140. Ibid.
141. Sinha, "Britishness, Clubbability," 195.
142. Quoted in Masani, *Indian Tales of the Raj*, 17.
143. Ibid., 16.
144. Jan-Georg Deutsch, "Celebrating Power in Everyday Life: The Administration of Law and the Public Sphere in Colonial Tanzania, 1890–1914," *Journal of African Cultural Studies* 15, no. 1 (June 2002): 96.
145. Quoted in Deutsch, "Celebrating Power," 100.
146. Quoted in Lora Wildenthal, *German Women for Empire, 1884–1945* (Durham, NC: Duke University Press, 2001), 125–126.
147. Ibid., 125.
148. Ibid.
149. Ibid., 127.
150. Damon Salesa, "Samoa's Half-Castes and Some Frontiers of Comparison," in *Haunted by Empire: Geographies of Intimacy in North American History*, ed. Ann Laura Stoler (Durham, NC: Duke University Press, 2006), 85.
151. Ibid., 86.
152. Ibid., 80.
153. Ibid., 87.
154. Quoted in Tamara Loos, "A History of Sex and the State in Southeast Asia: Class, Intimacy, and Invisibility," *Citizenship Studies* 12, no. 1 (February 2008): 32.
155. Loos, "History of Sex and the State," 35.
156. Quoted in Ann Laura Stoler, "Sexual Affronts and Racial Frontiers: European Identities and the Cultural Politics of Exclusion in Colonial Southeast Asia," in *Tensions of Empire: Colonial Cultures in a Bourgeois World*, ed. Frederick Cooper and Ann Laura Stoler (Berkeley: University of California Press, 1997), 215.
157. Bart Luttikhuis, "Beyond Race: Constructions of 'Europeanness' in Late-Colonial Legal Practice in the Dutch East Indies," *European Review of History* 20, no. 4 (August 2013): 541–542.
158. Ibid., 546.
159. Ibid., 547.
160. Quoted in Luttikhuis, "Beyond Race," 548.
161. Luttikhuis, "Beyond Race," 550.
162. Quoted in White, *Children of the French Empire*, 78.
163. Ibid., 80.
164. White, *Children of the French Empire*, 145.
165. Eric T. Jennings, "Hill Stations, Spas, Clubs, Safaris, and Colonial Life," in *The Routledge History of Western Empires*, ed. Robert Aldrich and Kirsten McKenzie (New York: Routledge, 2014), 352.

166. Quoted in Dane Kennedy, *The Magic Mountains: Hill Stations and the British Raj* (Berkeley: University of California Press, 1996), 100.

167. Kennedy, *The Magic Mountains*, 14–15.

168. Quoted in Eric T. Jennings, *Imperial Heights: Dalat and the Making and Undoing of French Indochina* (Berkeley: University of California Press, 2011), 73.

169. Ibid., 72.

170. Ibid., 84.

171. Ibid.

172. Quoted in White, *Children of the French Empire*, 28.

173. Dickson-Waiko, "Colonial Enclaves," 217.

174. Ibid., 219.

175. Quoted in Dickson-Waiko, "Colonial Enclaves," 218.

176. Dickson-Waiko, "Colonial Enclaves," 222.

177. Ibid., 221.

178. Angela Woollacott, *Gender and Empire* (London: Palgrave Macmillan, 2006), 52.

179. Fiona Paisley, "Race Hysteria, Darwin, 1938," in *Bodies in Contact: Rethinking Colonial Encounters in World History*, ed. Tony Ballantyne and Antoinette Burton (Durham, NC: Duke University Press, 2005), 236.

180. Ibid., 246–247.

181. Quoted in Paisley, "Race Hysteria," 241.

182. Paisley, "Race Hysteria," 238.

183. Busani Mpofu, "'Undesirable' Indians, Residential Segregation, and the Ill-Fated Rise of the White 'Housing Covenanters' in Bulawayo, Colonial Zimbabwe, 1930–1973," *South African Historical Journal* 63, no. 4 (December 2011): 553.

184. Quoted in Mpofu, "'Undesirable' Indians," 564.

185. Ibid.

186. Ibid.

187. Ibid., 566.

188. Ibid., 567.

189. Ibid.

190. Ruete, *An Arabian Princess*, 114.

191. Beryl Satter, "Marcus Garvey, Father Divine, and the Gender Politics of Race Difference and Race Neutrality," *American Quarterly* 48, no. 1 (March 1996): 44.

192. Marcus Garvey, *The Philosophy and Opinions of Marcus Garvey: Or, Africa for the Africans*, ed. Amy Jacques Garvey (Fitchburg, MA: Majority Press, 1986), 86.

193. Quoted in Satter, "Marcus Garvey," 43.

194. Ibid., 60.

195. Quoted in Barbara Sòrgoni, "'Defending the Race': The Italian Reinvention of the Hottentot Venus During Fascism," *Journal of Modern Italian Studies* 8, no. 3 (Fall 2003): 412.

196. Quoted in White, *Children of the French Empire*, 153.

197. White, *Children of the French Empire*, 153.

198. Quoted in White, *Children of the French Empire*, 155.

199. Ibid., 156.

200. Ibid.

201. Ibid., 176.

202. Ibid.

Chapter Four

1. Quoted in Pat Shipman, *Femme Fatale: Love, Lies, and the Unknown Life of Mata Hari* (New York: HarperCollins, 2007), 152.
2. Ibid.
3. Ibid., 149.
4. Ibid., 165.
5. Quoted in Rhonda K. Garelick, *Electric Salome: Loie Fuller's Performance of Modernism* (Princeton, NJ: Princeton University Press, 2007), 68.
6. Ibid., 69.
7. Ibid., 104.
8. Christin J. Mamiya, "Nineteenth-Century French Women, the Home, and the Colonial Vision: *Les Sauvages de la Mer Pacifique* Wallpaper," *Frontiers* 28, no. 1/2 (2007): 100.
9. Quoted in Mamiya, "Nineteenth-Century French Women," 102.
10. Ibid., 115.
11. Ibid., 104.
12. Ibid., 106.
13. Deepika Ahlawat, "Empire of Glass: F. & C. Osler in India, 1840–1930," *Journal of Design History* 21, no. 2 (Summer 2008): 156.
14. Quoted in Ahlawat, "Empire of Glass," 162.
15. Ahlawat, "Empire of Glass," 157.
16. Ibid., 158.
17. Quoted in Ahlawat, "Empire of Glass," 159.
18. Quoted in Willem Floor, "A Note on Persian Cats," *Iranian Studies* 36, no. 1 (March 2003): 32.
19. Ibid.
20. Ibid., 36–37.
21. Floor, "Note on Persian Cats," 41.
22. Quoted in Floor, "Note on Persian Cats," 33.
23. Ibid., 38.
24. Ibid.
25. Ibid., 39.
26. Ibid., 40.
27. Floor, "Note on Persian Cats," 41.
28. Sarah Cheang, "Women, Pets, and Imperialism: The British Pekingese Dog and Nostalgia for Old China," *Journal of British Studies* 45, no. 2 (April 2006): 360–361.
29. Ibid., 363.
30. Quoted in Cheang, "Women, Pets, and Imperialism," 363–364.
31. Cheang, "Women, Pets, and Imperialism," 364.
32. Quoted in Cheang, "Women, Pets, and Imperialism," 365.
33. Ibid., 370.
34. Ibid.
35. Ibid., 384.
36. Brett L. Shadle, "Cruelty and Empathy, Animals and Race, in Colonial Kenya," *Journal of Social History* 45, no. 4 (Summer 2012): 1100.
37. Quoted in Shadle, "Cruelty and Empathy," 1101.
38. Ibid., 1103.

39. Ibid., 1104.
40. Ibid., 1105.
41. Shadle, "Cruelty and Empathy," 1106.
42. Quoted in Nupur Chaudhuri, "Shawls, Jewelry, Curry, and Rice in Victorian Britain," in *Western Women and Imperialism: Complicity and Resistance*, ed. Nupur Chaudhuri and Margaret Strobel (Bloomington: Indiana University Press, 1992), 234.
43. Charles Stuart, *The Ladies' Monitor: Being a Series of Letters* (London: Brettel, 1809), 28.
44. Mrs. Hugh Fraser, *A Diplomatist's Wife in Japan: Letters from Home to Home* (London: Hutchinson, 1904), 175–176.
45. Quoted in Anna Marie Kirk, "Japonisme and Femininity: A Study of Japanese Dress in British and French Art and Society, c. 1860-c. 1899," *Costume* 42 (2008): 123.
46. Elsbeth Locher-Scholten, *Women and the Colonial State: Essays on Gender and Modernity in the Netherlands Indies, 1900–1942* (Amsterdam: Amsterdam University Press, 2000), 129.
47. Ibid., 130–131.
48. Ibid., 139.
49. Ibid., 142.
50. Quoted in Zareer Masani, *Indian Tales of the Raj* (Berkeley: University of California Press, 1987), 91.
51. Quoted in Bonnie G. Smith, *Imperialism: A History in Documents* (Oxford: Oxford University Press, 2000), 86.
52. Malathi de Alwis, "'Respectability,' 'Modernity,' and the Policing of 'Culture' in Colonial Ceylon," in *Gender, Sexuality, and Colonial Modernities*, ed. Antoinette Burton (London: Routledge, 1999), 183.
53. Quoted in Alwis, "Respectability, Modernity," 185.
54. Ibid., 184.
55. Ibid., 184–185.
56. Ibid., 187.
57. Quoted in Maria Suriano, "Clothing and the Changing Identities of Tanganyikan Urban Youths, 1920s–1950s," *Journal of African Cultural Studies* 20, no. 1 (June 2008): 99.
58. Ibid., 100.
59. Ibid.
60. Ibid., 103.
61. Ibid.
62. Ibid., 101.
63. Suriano, "Clothing and the Changing Identities," 101.
64. Ndabaningi Sithole, *African Nationalism* (Cape Town: Oxford University Press, 1959), 146–147.
65. Alys Eve Weinbaum et al., "The Modern Girl Around the World: Cosmetics Advertising and the Politics of Race and Style," in *The Modern Girl around the World: Consumption, Modernity, and Globalization*, ed. Alys Eve Weinbaum et al. (Durham, NC: Duke University Press, 2008), 27–28.
66. Ibid., 33–35.
67. Ibid., 42–43.
68. Quoted in Weinbaum et al., "Modern Girl," 44.

69. Mona Russell, "Marketing the Modern Egyptian Girl: Whitewashing Soap and Clothes from the Late Nineteenth Century to 1936," *Journal of Middle East Women's Studies* 6, no. 3 (Fall 2010): 25–26.

70. Ibid., 28.

71. Quoted in Russell, "Marketing the Modern Egyptian Girl," 29–30.

72. Ibid., 32.

73. Russell, "Marketing the Modern Egyptian Girl," 34.

74. Ibid., 38.

75. Ibid., 42–43.

76. Olaudah Equiano, *The Interesting Narrative of the Life of Olaudah Equiano, or Gustavus Vassa, the African*, 3rd ed. (London: G. Vassa, 1790), 355–356.

77. Quoted in Pernille Røge, "An Early Scramble for Africa: British, Danish, and French Colonial Projects on the Coast of West Africa, 1780s and 1790s," in *The Routledge History of Western Empires*, ed. Robert Aldrich and Kirsten McKenzie (New York: Routledge, 2014), 77.

78. Ibid., 78.

79. Quoted in Colleen Taylor Sen, *Curry: A Global History* (London: Reaktion Books, 2009), 38.

80. Chaudhuri, "Shawls, Jewelry, Curry, and Rice," 238.

81. Quoted in Sen, *Curry*, 43.

82. Ibid.

83. Ibid.

84. Quoted in Kristin Hoganson, "Food and Entertainment from Every Corner of the Globe: Bourgeois U.S. Households as Points of Encounter, 1870–1920," *Amerikastudien / American Studies* 48, no. 1 (2003): 119.

85. Ibid.

86. Ibid., 120.

87. Ibid., 123.

88. Ibid., 126.

89. Quoted in Eric T. Jennings, *Imperial Heights: Dalat and the Making and Undoing of French Indochina* (Berkeley: University of California Press, 2011), 72.

90. Ibid., 79.

91. Jennings, *Imperial Heights*, 79.

92. Ibid., 80.

93. Ibid., 84.

94. Quoted in Smith, *Imperialism*, 91.

95. Quoted in Julie Livingston, "Physical Fitness and Economic Opportunity in the Bechuanaland Protectorate in the 1930s and 1940s," *Journal of Southern African Studies* 27, no. 4 (December 2001): 811.

96. Richard Meinertzhagen, *Kenya Diary: 1902–1906* (Edinburgh: Oliver and Boyd, 1957), 178.

97. Quoted in Tracey Rizzo, "A Lascivious Climate: Representations of Colonial Subjectivity in the *Causes Célèbres* of Eighteenth-Century France," *Journal of Caribbean History* 34, no. 1/2 (2000): 166.

98. Alvis E. Dunn, "'A Sponge Soaking up All the Money': Alcohol, Taverns, Vinaterías, and the Bourbon Reforms in Mid-Eighteenth-Century Santiago de los Caballeros, Guatemala," in *Distilling the Influence of Alcohol: Aguardiente in Guatemalan History*, ed. David Carey Jr. (Gainesville: University Press of Florida, 2012), 75.

99. Quoted in Dunn, "Sponge Soaking up All the Money," 81.

100. Susan Diduk, "European Alcohol, History, and the State in Cameroon," *African Studies Review* 36, no. 1 (April 1993): 3.

101. Ibid., 2–3.

102. Quoted in Diduk, "European Alcohol, History, and the State," 7.

103. Quoted in Owen White, "Drunken States: Temperance and French Rule in Côte d'Ivoire, 1908–1916," *Journal of Social History* 40, no. 3 (Spring 2007): 671.

104. Ibid., 672.

105. Gerard Sasges, "State, Enterprise, and the Alcohol Monopoly in Colonial Vietnam," *Journal of Southeast Asian Studies* 43, no. 1 (February 2012): 137.

106. Quoted in Sasges, "State, Enterprise, and the Alcohol Monopoly," 148.

107. Sasges, "State, Enterprise, and the Alcohol Monopoly," 155.

108. David T. Courtwright, *Forces of Habit: Drugs and the Making of the Modern World* (Cambridge, MA: Harvard University Press, 2001), 75.

109. "Absinthe Mata Hari Bohemian," Absinthe Mata Hari website, http://absinthematahari .com/?q=content/absinthe-mata-hari-bohemian (emphasis added).

110. Chris Carlsson, "Absinthe Mata Hari," *Spirits Review*, http://www.spiritsreview .com/reviews-absinthe-mata-hari.html.

111. Rachel Holmes, *African Queen: The Real Life of the Hottentot Venus* (New York: Random House, 2007), 106.

112. Lora Wildenthal, *German Women for Empire, 1884–1945* (Durham, NC: Duke University Press, 2001), 51.

113. Quoted in Wildenthal, *German Women for Empire*, 51.

114. Quoted in Alice L. Conklin, *In the Museum of Man: Race, Anthropology, and Empire in France, 1850–1950* (Ithaca, NY: Cornell University Press, 2013), 33.

115. Conklin, *In the Museum of Man*, 150.

116. Ibid., 154.

117. Quoted in Conklin, *In the Museum of Man*, 169.

118. Ibid., 171.

119. Quoted in Bluford Adams, "'A Stupendous Mirror of Departed Empires': The Barnum Hippodromes and Circuses, 1874–1891," *American Literary History* 8, no. 1 (Spring 1996): 43.

120. Ibid., 44.

121. Ibid.

122. Ibid., 45.

123. Ibid., 46.

124. Ibid., 47.

125. Quoted in Smith, *Imperialism*, 108.

126. Quoted in Rosalind H. Williams, *Dream Worlds: Mass Consumption in Late Nineteenth-Century France* (Berkeley: University of California Press, 1982), 60.

127. Jennifer Kopf, "Picturing Difference: Writing the Races in the 1896 Berlin Trade Exposition's Souvenir Album," *Historical Geography* 36 (2008): 116–117.

128. Ibid., 118.

129. Quoted in Kopf, "Picturing Difference," 126.

130. Ibid., 130.

131. Maria Grever and Berteke Waaldijk, "Women's Labor at Display: Feminist Claims to Dutch Citizenship and Colonial Politics around 1900," *Journal of Women's History* 15, no. 4 (Winter 2004): 12–14.

132. Ibid., 16.

133. Seiji Nagata, *Hokusai: Genius of the Japanese Ukiyo-e*, trans. John Bester (Tokyo: Kodansha International, 1995), 81–82.

134. Quoted in Ricard Bru, "Tentacles of Love and Death: From Hokusai to Picasso," in *Secret Images: Picasso and the Japanese Erotic Print*, ed. Museu Picasso de Barcelona (New York: Thames and Hudson, 2010), 59.

135. Ibid.

136. Quoted in Debora L. Silverman, *Art Nouveau in Fin-de-Siècle France: Politics, Psychology, and Style* (Berkeley: University of California Press, 1989), 261.

137. Susan J. Napier, *From Impressionism to Anime: Japan as Fantasy and Fan Cult in the Mind of the West* (New York: Palgrave Macmillan, 2007), 30–35.

138. Quoted in Lionel Lambourne, *Japonisme: Cultural Crossings between Japan and the West* (London: Phaidon Press, 2005), 44.

139. Ibid.

140. Quoted in Cynthia Saltzman, *Portrait of Dr. Gachet: The Story of a Van Gogh Masterpiece, Money, Politics, Collectors, Greed, and Loss* (New York: Penguin Books, 1998), 316.

141. Quoted in Lambourne, *Japonisme*, 51.

142. Quoted in Nathalia Brodskaïa, *Post-Impressionism* (New York: Parkstone Press International, 2007), 170.

143. Ibid., 177.

144. Ibid., 179.

145. Malén Gual, "Dialogue with Japanese Art," in *Secret Images: Picasso and the Japanese Erotic Print*, ed. Museu Picasso de Barcelona (New York: Thames and Hudson, 2010), 83.

146. Quoted in Sieglinde Lemke, *Primitivist Modernism: Black Culture and the Origins of Transatlantic Modernism* (Oxford: Oxford University Press, 1998), 36.

147. Ibid., 36.

148. Ibid., 37.

149. Wolfgang Amadeus Mozart, "The Abduction from the Seraglio," *OperaFolio*, http://www.operafolio.com/opera.asp?n=Die_Entfuhrung_aus_dem_Serail.

150. Quoted in Timothy D. Taylor, *Beyond Exoticism: Western Music and the World* (Durham, NC: Duke University Press, 2007), 60.

151. John M. MacKenzie, *Orientalism: History, Theory, and the Arts* (Manchester, UK: Manchester University Press, 1995), 155–156.

152. Giacomo Puccini, *Madam Butterfly: A Japanese Tragedy*, trans. R. H. Elkin (New York: Boosey, 1906), 12.

153. Roberta Di Carmine, *Italy Meets Africa: Colonial Discourses in Italian Cinema* (New York: Peter Lang, 2011), 39–40.

154. Quoted in Di Carmine, *Italy Meets Africa*, 41.

155. James Chapman and Nicholas J. Cull, *Projecting Empire: Imperialism and Popular Cinema* (London: I. B. Tauris, 2009), 20.

156. Quoted in Richard Dyer, *Heavenly Bodies: Film Stars and Society*, 2nd ed. (London: Routledge, 2004), 95.

157. Quoted in Deborah Willis, "The Image and Paul Robeson," in *Paul Robeson: Artist and Citizen*, ed. Jeffrey C. Stewart (New Brunswick, NJ: Rutgers University Press, 1998), 78.

158. Quoted in Martin Bauml Duberman, *Paul Robeson* (New York: Alfred A. Knopf, 1988), 179.

159. Ibid., 180.

160. May Opitz, "Racism, Sexism, and Precolonial Images of Africa in Germany," in *Showing Our Colors: Afro-German Women Speak Out*, trans. Anne V. Adams, ed. May Opitz, Katharina Oguntoye, and Dagmar Schultz (Amherst: University of Massachusetts Press, 1992), 34.

161. Quoted in Opitz, "Racism, Sexism, and Precolonial Images," 69.

162. Ibid., 70.

163. Ibid.

164. Opitz, "Racism, Sexism, and Precolonial Images," 72.

165. Karsten Linne, *Deutschland jenseits des Äquators? Die NS-Kolonialplanungen für Afrika* (Berlin: Christoph Links Verlag, 2008), 79.

166. Eleanor M. Hight, "The Many Lives of Beato's 'Beauties,'" in *Colonialist Photography: Imag(in)ing Race and Place*, ed. Eleanor M. Hight and Gary D. Sampson (London: Routledge, 2004), 130–131.

167. Ibid., 138.

168. Quoted in Hight, "Many Lives," 138–139.

169. Hight, "Many Lives," 148.

170. Lisa Z. Sigel, *Governing Pleasures: Pornography and Social Change in England, 1815–1914* (New Brunswick, NJ: Rutgers University Press, 2002), 152.

171. Patricia Johnston, "Advertising Paradise: Hawai'i in Art, Anthropology, and Commercial Photography," in *Colonialist Photography: Imag(in)ing Race and Place*, ed. Eleanor M. Hight and Gary D. Sampson (London: Routledge, 2004), 202–203.

172. Quoted in Sigel, *Governing Pleasures*, 152.

173. Ibid., 153.

174. Dane Kennedy, *The Highly Civilized Man: Richard Burton and the Victorian World* (Cambridge, MA: Harvard University Press, 2005), 15–22.

175. Deborah Lutz, *Pleasure Bound: Victorian Sex Rebels and the New Eroticism* (New York: W. W. Norton, 2011), 137.

176. Richard F. Burton, *A Plain and Literal Translation of the Arabian Nights Entertainments, Now Entituled: The Book of the Thousand Nights and a Night*, Vol 1. (London: Burton Club, 1885), xviii.

177. Quoted in Anjali Arondekar, *For the Record: On Sexuality and the Colonial Archive in India* (Durham, NC: Duke University Press, 2009), 27.

178. Kennedy, *Highly Civilized Man*, 237–243.

179. Leela Gandhi, *Affective Communities: Anticolonial Thought, Fin-de-Siècle Radicalism, and the Politics of Friendship* (Durham, NC: Duke University Press, 2006), 52.

180. John Lauritsen and David Thorstad, *The Early Homosexual Rights Movement (1864–1935)* (Ojai, CA: Times Change Press, 1995), 88.

181. Quoted in Colette Colligan, *The Traffic in Obscenity from Byron to Beardsley: Sexuality and Exoticism in Nineteenth-Century Print Culture* (New York: Palgrave Macmillan, 2006), 64.

182. Burton, *Plain and Literal Translation*, xxiii.

183. Richard Phillips, *Sex, Politics, and Empire: A Postcolonial Geography* (Manchester, UK: Manchester University Press, 2006), 130.

184. Quoted in Richard Bernstein, *The East, the West, and Sex: A History* (New York: Vintage Books, 2009), 116.

185. Havelock Ellis, *Studies in the Psychology of Sex: Sexual Inversion*, 2nd ed. (Philadelphia: F. A. Davis Company, 1901), 16.

186. Quoted in Robin Hackett, *Sapphic Primitivism: Productions of Race, Class, and Sexuality in Key Works of Modern Fiction* (New Brunswick, NJ: Rutgers University Press, 2004), 26.

187. Hackett, *Sapphic Primitivism*, 24.

188. Richard von Krafft-Ebing, *Psychopathia Sexualis: A Medico-Forensic Study*, 12th ed., trans. F. J. Rebman (New York: Rebman Company, 1906), 2, 25.

189. Quoted in Hackett, *Sapphic Primitivism*, 24.

190. Jacobus X [pseud.], *The Erogenous Zones of the World*, ed. Norman Lockridge (New York: Bridgehead Books, 1964), 441.

191. Ibid.

192. Ibid.

Chapter Five

1. Olaudah Equiano, *The Interesting Narrative of the Life of Olaudah Equiano, or Gustavus Vassa, the African*, 3rd ed. (London: G. Vassa, 1790), 70.

2. Ibid., 4.

3. Ibid., 71.

4. Ibid., 14.

5. Ibid., 28.

6. Ibid., 28–29.

7. Ibid., 25.

8. Ibid., 28.

9. Marquis de Condorcet, "The Future Progress of the Human Mind," in *The Portable Enlightenment Reader*, ed. Isaac Kramnick (New York: Penguin Books, 1995), 27.

10. Ibid., 36.

11. Quoted in Clara Pinto-Correia and João Lourenço Monteiro, "Science in Support of Racial Mixture: Charles-Augustin Vandermonde's Enlightenment Program for Improving the Health and Beauty of the Human Species," *Endeavour* 38, no. 1 (March 2014): 24.

12. Ibid., 25.

13. Ibid., 24.

14. Ibid., 25.

15. Quoted in William Max Nelson, "Making Men: Enlightenment Ideas of Racial Engineering," *American Historical Review* 115, no. 5 (December 2010): 1364.

16. Nelson, "Making Men," 1380.

17. Ibid., 1369.

18. Ibid., 1377.

19. Quoted in Stephen Jay Gould, *The Mismeasure of Man* (New York: W. W. Norton, 1996), 411.

20. Ibid., 407.

21. Gould, *Mismeasure of Man*, 409.

22. Quoted in Gould, *Mismeasure of Man*, 407.

23. Ibid., 408.

24. Charles Darwin, *Charles Darwin's Beagle Diary*, ed. R. D. Keynes (Cambridge: Cambridge University Press, 1988), 223.
25. Ibid., 222.
26. Charles Darwin, *The Descent of Man, and Selection in Relation to Sex*, Vol. 1 (London: John Murray, 1871), 232.
27. Gould, *Mismeasure of Man*, 107–109.
28. Charles Darwin, *Descent of Man*, 172.
29. Quoted in Gould, *Mismeasure of Man*, 424.
30. Quoted in Makiko Kuwahara, *Tattoo: An Anthropology* (New York: Berg, 2005), 49.
31. Ibid., 55.
32. Ibid., 56.
33. Kuwahara, *Tattoo*, 53.
34. Quoted in Kuwahara, *Tattoo*, 58.
35. Quoted in Heidi Gengenbach, "Tattooed Secrets: Women's History in Magude District, Southern Mozambique," in *Bodies in Contact: Rethinking Colonial Encounters in World History*, ed. Tony Ballantyne and Antoinette Burton (Durham, NC: Duke University Press, 2005), 258.
36. Gengenbach, "Tattooed Secrets," 255.
37. Ibid., 266.
38. Quoted in Gengenbach, "Tattooed Secrets," 253.
39. Ibid., 258–259.
40. Gengenbach, "Tattooed Secrets," 264–265.
41. Quoted in Gengenbach, "Tattooed Secrets," 265.
42. Gengenbach, "Tattooed Secrets," 269–270.
43. Olatunji Ojo, "Beyond Diversity: Women, Scarification, and Yoruba Identity," *History in Africa* 35 (2008): 351.
44. Quoted in Ojo, "Beyond Diversity," 368.
45. Ojo, "Beyond Diversity," 368.
46. Quoted in Ojo, "Beyond Diversity," 372.
47. Ibid., 370.
48. John Macgowan, *How England Saved China* (London: T. F. Unwin, 1913), 18–19.
49. Angela Zito, "Secularizing the Pain of Footbinding in China: Missionary and Medical Stagings of the Universal Body," *Journal of the American Academy of Religion* 75, no. 1 (March 2007): 12.
50. Ibid., 15.
51. Quoted in Zito, "Secularizing the Pain," 16n21.
52. Qiu Jin, "Random Feelings," in *Women Imagine Change: A Global Anthology of Women's Resistance from 600 B.C.E. to Present*, ed. Eugenia C. DeLamotte, Natania Meeker, and Jean F. O'Barr (New York: Routledge, 1997), 494.
53. Quoted in William C. Olsen, "'Children for Death': Money, Wealth, and Witchcraft Suspicion in Colonial Asante," *Cahiers d'Études Africaines* 42, no. 167 (2002): 532.
54. Ibid., 538.
55. Ibid.
56. Ibid., 533.
57. Olsen, "Children for Death," 529.
58. Quoted in Olsen, "Children for Death," 534.
59. Mark Singleton, *Yoga Body: The Origins of Modern Posture Practice* (Oxford: Oxford University Press, 2010), 56–57.

60. Quoted in Nile Green, "Breathing in India, c. 1890," *Modern Asian Studies* 42, no. 2/3 (March–May 2008): 302.

61. Green, "Breathing in India," 301.

62. Ibid., 303–304.

63. Ibid., 289.

64. Ibid., 290.

65. Ibid., 291.

66. Mark Singleton, "Yoga, Eugenics, and Spiritual Darwinism in the Early Twentieth Century," *International Journal of Hindu Studies* 11, no. 2 (August 2007): 128.

67. Quoted in Singleton, "Yoga, Eugenics," 132.

68. Singleton, "Yoga, Eugenics," 131.

69. Quoted in Singleton, "Yoga, Eugenics," 133.

70. Ibid., 135–136.

71. Quoted in Raymond F. Piper, "In Support of Altruism in Hinduism," *Journal of Bible and Religion* 22, no. 3 (July 1954): 181.

72. Quoted in Wilson Chacko Jacob, *Working Out Egypt: Effendi Masculinity and Subject Formation in Colonial Modernity, 1870–1940* (Durham, NC: Duke University Press, 2011), 78.

73. Jacob, *Working Out Egypt*, 73.

74. Quoted in Jacob, *Working Out Egypt*, 81.

75. Jacob, *Working Out Egypt*, 87.

76. Tracey Rizzo, "Between Dishonor and Death: Infanticides in the *Causes Célèbres* of Eighteenth-Century France," *Women's History Review* 13, no. 1 (2004): 5–21.

77. Marcela Echeverri, "'Enraged to the Limit of Despair': Infanticide and Slave Judicial Strategies in Barbacoas, 1788–98," *Slavery and Abolition* 30, no. 3 (September 2009): 404.

78. Quoted in Echeverri, "Enraged to the Limit," 406.

79. Ibid., 410.

80. Echeverri, "Enraged to the Limit," 411.

81. Quoted in Echeverri, "Enraged to the Limit," 416.

82. Misty L. Bastian, "'The Demon Superstition': Abominable Twins and Mission Culture in Onitsha History," *Ethnology* 40, no. 1 (Winter 2001): 16.

83. Quoted in Bastian, "Demon Superstition," 15.

84. Bastian, "Demon Superstition," 21.

85. Ibid., 22.

86. Ibid., 23.

87. Londa Schiebinger, "Feminist History of Colonial Science," *Hypatia* 19, no. 1 (Winter 2004): 236.

88. Quoted in Schiebinger, "Feminist History," 244.

89. Ibid., 243.

90. Ibid.

91. Ibid., 241.

92. Schiebinger, "Feminist History," 240.

93. Tuba Demirci and Selçuk Akşin Somel, "Women's Bodies, Demography, and Public Health: Abortion Policy and Perspectives in the Ottoman Empire of the Nineteenth Century," *Journal of the History of Sexuality* 17, no. 3 (September 2008): 386.

94. Ibid., 392.

95. Ibid., 416.

96. Ibid., 395.

97. Ibid., 397.

98. Ibid., 399.

99. Ibid., 404.

100. Quoted in Demirci and Somel, "Women's Bodies," 406.

101. Ibid., 409.

102. Ibid., 410.

103. Ibid., 414.

104. Thomas Malthus, *An Essay on the Principle of Population* (Oxford: Oxford University Press, 1993), 144.

105. Barbara N. Ramusack, "Embattled Advocates: The Debate over Birth Control in India, 1920–40," *Journal of Women's History* 1, no. 2 (Fall 1989): 36.

106. Quoted in Ramusack, "Embattled Advocates," 38.

107. Ramusack, "Embattled Advocates," 43.

108. Veronika Fuechtner, "Indians, Jews, and Sex: Magnus Hirschfeld and Indian Sexology," in *Imagining Germany Imagining Asia: Essays in Asian-German Studies*, ed. Veronika Fuechtner and Mary Rhiel (Rochester, NY: Camden House, 2013), 113.

109. Quoted in Fuechtner, "Indians, Jews, and Sex," 113.

110. Quoted in Sanjay Srivastava, "'Sane Sex,' the Five-Year Plan Hero, and Men on Footpaths and in Gated Communities: On the Cultures of Twentieth-Century Masculinity," in *Masculinity and Its Challenges in India: Essays on Changing Perceptions*, ed. Rohit K. Dasgupta and K. Moti Gokulsing (Jefferson, NC: McFarland, 2014), 36.

111. Srivastava, "Sane Sex," 36–38.

112. Quoted in Ramusack, "Embattled Advocates," 40.

113. Susanne Klausen, "Women's Resistance to Eugenic Birth Control in Johannesburg, 1930–39," *South African Historical Journal* 50, no. 1 (May 2004): 153.

114. Quoted in Klausen, "Women's Resistance," 161.

115. Klausen, "Women's Resistance," 162.

116. Quoted in Klausen, "Women's Resistance," 163.

117. Ibid.

118. Ibid.

119. Quoted in Chloe Campbell, *Race and Empire: Eugenics in Colonial Kenya* (Manchester, UK: Manchester University Press, 2007), 39.

120. Ibid., 46.

121. Ibid., 46.

122. Ibid., 47.

123. Campbell, *Race and Empire*, 54.

124. Quoted in Campbell, *Race and Empire*, 57.

125. Edward Ross Dickinson, "Biopolitics, Fascism, Democracy: Some Reflections on Our Discourse about 'Modernity,'" *Central European History* 37, no. 1 (2004): 8–9.

126. Ibid., 17.

127. Quoted in May Opitz, "Racism, Sexism, and Precolonial Images of Africa in Germany," in *Showing Our Colors: Afro-German Women Speak Out*, trans. Anne V. Adams, ed. May Opitz, Katharina Oguntoye, and Dagmar Schultz (Amherst: University of Massachusetts Press, 1992), 52.

128. Ibid., 61.

129. Ibid., 66.

130. Quoted in Alison Bashford, "Nation, Empire, Globe: The Spaces of Population Debate in the Interwar Years," *Comparative Studies in Society and History* 49, no. 1 (January 2007): 183–184.
131. Ibid., 186.
132. Ibid., 187.
133. Margaret Cook Andersen, "Creating French Settlements Overseas: Pronatalism and Colonial Medicine in Madagascar," *French Historical Studies* 33, no. 3 (Summer 2010): 423.
134. Ibid., 430.
135. Quoted in Elisa Camiscioli, "Reproducing the 'French Race': Immigration and Pronatalism in Early-Twentieth-Century France," in *Bodies in Contact: Rethinking Colonial Encounters in World History*, ed. Tony Ballantyne and Antoinette Burton (Durham, NC: Duke University Press, 2005), 225.
136. Ibid.
137. Ibid., 224.
138. Ibid.
139. Ibid., 223.
140. Ibid., 227.
141. Ibid., 222.
142. Ibid., 229.
143. Bonnie S. Anderson and Judith P. Zinsser, *A History of Their Own: Women in Europe from Prehistory to the Present*, Vol. 2 (New York: Oxford University Press, 2000), 209–210.
144. Henrietta Harrison, "Rethinking Missionaries and Medicine in China: The Miracles of Assunta Pallotta, 1905–2005," *Journal of Asian Studies* 71, no. 1 (February 2012): 129–130.
145. Ibid., 138–139.
146. Quoted in Harrison, "Rethinking Missionaries," 140.
147. Quoted in Julie Livingston, "Physical Fitness and Economic Opportunity in the Bechuanaland Protectorate in the 1930s and 1940s," *Journal of Southern African Studies* 27, no. 4 (December 2001): 801.
148. Ibid., 807.
149. Ibid., 793.
150. Ibid., 794.
151. Livingston, "Physical Fitness," 794.
152. Quoted in Livingston, "Physical Fitness," 811.
153. Adèle Toussaint-Samson, *A Parisian in Brazil: The Travel Account of a French-woman in Nineteenth-Century Rio de Janeiro*, trans. Emma Toussaint (Wilmington, DE: Scholarly Resources, 2001), 60–61.
154. Ibid., 29.
155. Quoted in Bonnie McElhinny, "'Kissing a Baby Is Not at All Good for Him': Infant Mortality, Medicine, and Colonial Modernity in the U.S.-Occupied Philippines," *American Anthropologist* 107, no. 2 (June 2005): 187.
156. Ibid.
157. Ibid., 188.
158. Ibid.
159. Quoted in Nancy Rose Hunt, "'Le Bébé en Brousse': European Women, African Birth Spacing, and Colonial Intervention in Breast Feeding in the Belgian Congo,"

in *Tensions of Empire: Colonial Cultures in a Bourgeois World*, ed. Frederick Cooper and Ann Laura Stoler (Berkeley: University of California Press, 1997), 289.

160. Ibid., 293.
161. Hunt, "Le Bébé en Brousse," 300.
162. Ibid., 296.
163. Quoted in Hunt, "Le Bébé en Brousse," 303.
164. Hunt, "Le Bébé en Brousse," 306.
165. Quoted in Hunt, "Le Bébé en Brousse," 309.
166. Jonathan Sadowsky, "The Social World and the Reality of Mental Illness: Lessons from Colonial Psychiatry," *Harvard Review of Psychiatry* 11, no. 4 (July–August 2003): 212.
167. Ibid., 213.
168. Richard Keller, "Madness and Colonization: Psychiatry in the British and French Empires, 1800–1962," *Journal of Social History* 35, no. 2 (Winter 2001): 308.
169. Ibid.
170. Ibid., 310.
171. Meredith McKittrick, "Faithful Daughter, Murdering Mother: Transgression and Social Control in Colonial Namibia," *Journal of African History* 40, no. 2 (1999): 265.
172. Ibid., 278.
173. Quoted in McKittrick, "Faithful Daughter," 279.
174. Claire Edington, "Going in and Getting out of the Colonial Asylum: Families and Psychiatric Care in French Indochina," *Comparative Studies in Society and History* 55, no. 3 (July 2013): 728.
175. Ibid., 733.
176. Quoted in Lee Wallace, *Sexual Encounters: Pacific Texts, Modern Sexualities* (Ithaca, NY: Cornell University Press, 2003), 13.
177. Ibid., 14.
178. Niko Besnier, "Polynesian Gender Liminality through Time and Space," in *Third Sex, Third Gender: Beyond Sexual Dimorphism in Culture and History*, ed. Gilbert Herdt (New York: Zone Books, 1994), 294.
179. Serena Nanda, *Gender Diversity: Crosscultural Variations*, 2nd ed. (Long Grove, IL: Waveland Press, 2014), 28.
180. Quoted in Serena Nanda, "Hijras: An Alternative Sex and Gender Role in India," in *Third Sex, Third Gender: Beyond Sexual Dimorphism in Culture and History*, ed. Gilbert Herdt (New York: Zone Books, 1994), 414.
181. Quoted in Marc Epprecht, *Heterosexual Africa? The History of an Idea from the Age of Exploration to the Age of AIDS* (Athens: Ohio University Press, 2008), 45.
182. Quoted in Sandra E. Hollimon, "The Gendered Peopling of North America: Addressing the Antiquity of Systems of Multiple Genders," in *The Archeology of Shamanism*, ed. Neil S. Price (London: Routledge, 2001), 124.
183. Quoted in Andrei A. Znamenski, *Shamanism and Christianity: Native Encounters with Russian Orthodox Missions in Siberia and Alaska, 1820–1917* (Westport, CT: Greenwood Press, 1999), 76.
184. Quoted in Andrei A. Znamenski, *The Beauty of the Primitive: Shamanism and the Western Imagination* (Oxford: Oxford University Press, 2007), 80–81.
185. Quoted in Andrei A. Znamenski, *Shamanism in Siberia: Russian Records of Indigenous Spirituality* (Dordrecht, Netherlands: Kluwer Academic, 2003), 76.

186. Znamenski, *Shamanism in Siberia*, 307.

187. Sabine Lang, *Men as Women, Women as Men: Changing Gender in Native American Cultures*, trans. John L. Vantine (Austin: University of Texas Press, 1998), 176–180.

188. Will Roscoe, *Changing Ones: Third and Fourth Genders in Native North America* (New York: St. Martin's Press, 1998), 17–18.

189. Quoted in Walter L. Williams, *The Spirit and the Flesh: Sexual Diversity in American Indian Culture* (Boston: Beacon Press, 1992), 138.

190. Ibid., 139.

191. Quoted in Roger M. Carpenter, "Womanish Men and Manlike Women: The Native American Two-Spirit as Warrior," in *Gender and Sexuality in Indigenous North America, 1400–1850*, ed. Sandra Slater and Fay A. Yarbrough (Columbia: University of South Carolina Press, 2011), 155.

192. Quoted in Leslie Feinberg, *Transgender Warriors: Making History from Joan of Arc to RuPaul* (Boston: Beacon Press, 1996), 25.

193. Lang, *Men as Women*, 294.

194. Williams, *Spirit and the Flesh*, 190–192.

195. Quoted in Philip Howell, *Geographies of Regulation: Policing Prostitution in Nineteenth-Century Britain and the Empire* (Cambridge: Cambridge University Press, 2009), 201.

196. Quoted in Philippa Levine, "Modernity, Medicine, and Colonialism: The Contagious Diseases Ordinances in Hong Kong and the Straits Settlements," in *Gender, Sexuality, and Colonial Modernities*, ed. Antoinette Burton (London: Routledge, 1999), 37–38.

197. Ibid., 40.

198. Levine, "Modernity, Medicine," 41.

199. Quoted in Howell, *Geographies of Regulation*, 154.

200. Ibid., 180.

201. Quoted in Richard Phillips, *Sex, Politics, and Empire: A Postcolonial Geography* (Manchester, UK: Manchester University Press, 2006), 116.

202. Ibid., 122.

203. Quoted in Luise White, *The Comforts of Home: Prostitution in Colonial Nairobi* (Chicago: University of Chicago Press, 1990), 91.

204. Quoted in Daniel J. Walther, "Sex, Public Health, and Colonial Control: The Campaign against Venereal Diseases in Germany's Overseas Possessions, 1884–1914," *Social History of Medicine* 26, no. 2 (May 2013): 191.

205. Ibid., 201.

206. Ibid.

207. Ibid., 202.

208. Quoted in Judith Surkis, *Sexing the Citizen: Morality and Masculinity in France, 1870–1920* (Ithaca, NY: Cornell University Press, 2006), 228.

209. Ibid.

210. Ibid.

211. Ibid.

212. Sabine Frühstück, *Colonizing Sex: Sexology and Social Control in Modern Japan* (Berkeley: University of California Press, 2003), 44.

213. Christabel Pankhurst, "The Need for Chastity in Males," in *Sexuality*, ed. Robert A. Nye (Oxford: Oxford University Press, 1999), 135.

214. Ibid., 134–135.

215. Ibid., 135.

216. Quoted in Frühstück, *Colonizing Sex*, 62.

217. Ibid., 62–63.

218. Quoted in Liat Kozma, "'We, the Sexologists…': Arabic Medical Writing on Sexuality, 1879–1943," *Journal of the History of Sexuality* 22, no. 3 (September 2013): 428.

219. Ibid., 437.

220. Ibid., 426.

221. Kozma, "We, the Sexologists," 442.

222. Ronald Hyam, *Empire and Sexuality: The British Experience* (Manchester, UK: Manchester University Press, 1990), 77.

223. Richard F. Burton, *A Plain and Literal Translation of the Arabian Nights Entertainments, Now Entituled: The Book of the Thousand Nights and a Night*, Vol. 2 (London: Burton Club, 1885), 13n.

224. Quoted in Robert Darby, *A Surgical Temptation: The Demonization of the Foreskin and the Rise of Circumcision in Britain* (Chicago: University of Chicago Press, 2005), 195.

225. Darby, *Surgical Temptation*, 64–65.

226. Ibid., 7–8.

227. David L. Gollaher, *Circumcision: A History of the World's Most Controversial Surgery* (New York: Basic Books, 2000), 106–108.

228. Quoted in Lilian Passmore Sanderson, *Against the Mutilation of Women: The Struggle to End Unnecessary Suffering* (London: Ithaca Press, 1981), 64.

229. Ibid., 65.

230. Eloïse A. Brière, "Confronting the Western Gaze," in *Female Circumcision and the Politics of Knowledge: African Women in Imperialist Discourses*, ed. Obioma Nnaemeka (Westport, CT: Praeger, 2005), 167.

231. Catherine Coquery-Vidrovitch, *African Women: A Modern History*, trans. Beth Gillian Raps (Boulder, CO: Westview Press, 1994), 209.

232. Lynn Thomas, "'Ngaitana (I Will Circumcise Myself)': Lessons from Colonial Campaigns to Ban Excision in Meru, Kenya," in *Female "Circumcision" in Africa: Culture, Controversy, and Change*, ed. Bettina Shell-Duncan and Ylva Hernlund (Boulder, CO: Lynne Rienner, 2000), 132.

233. Ibid.

234. Quoted in Brière, "Confronting the Western Gaze," 167–168.

235. Quoted in Thomas, "*Ngaitana*," 138.

236. Ibid., 141.

237. Robert A. Nye, *Sexuality* (Oxford: Oxford University Press, 1999), 113–114.

Chapter Six

1. Quoted in C. L. R. James, *The Black Jacobins: Toussaint L'Ouverture and the San Domingo Revolution*, 2nd ed. (New York: Vintage, 1989), 152.

2. Laurent Dubois, *Avengers of the New World: The Story of the Haitian Revolution* (Cambridge, MA: Harvard University Press, 2004), 100.

3. Quoted in Dubois, *Avengers of the New World*, 100.

4. Antoine Dalmas, "History of the Revolution of Saint-Domingue," in *Slave Revolution in the Caribbean, 1789–1804: A Brief History with Documents*, ed. Laurent Dubois and John D. Garrigus (Boston: Bedford/St. Martin's, 2006), 90.

5. Médéric-Louis-Élie Moreau de Saint-Méry, *A Civilization That Perished: The Last Years of White Colonial Rule in Haiti*, trans. Ivor D. Spencer (Lanham, MD: University Press of America, 1985), 5.

6. Toussaint L'Ouverture, *The Haitian Revolution*, ed. Nick Nesbitt (London: Verso, 2008), 66–68.

7. Jean-Jacques Dessalines, "The Haitian Declaration of Independence," in *Slave Revolution in the Caribbean, 1789–1804: A Brief History with Documents*, ed. Laurent Dubois and John D. Garrigus (Boston: Bedford/St. Martin's, 2006), 189.

8. Ashis Nandy, *The Intimate Enemy: Loss and Recovery of Self under Colonialism* (Delhi: Oxford University Press, 1983), 43.

9. Ibid., 15.

10. Ibid., 69.

11. Raewyn Connell, *Southern Theory: The Global Dynamics of Knowledge in Social Science* (Cambridge, UK: Polity Press, 2007), 184.

12. Jerome R. Adams, *Notable Latin American Women: Twenty-Nine Leaders, Rebels, Poets, Battlers, and Spies, 1500–1900* (Jefferson, NC: McFarland, 1995), 72.

13. Micaela Bastidas, "Micaela Bastidas Admonishes Her Husband, Tupac Amaru," in *The Tupac Amaru and Catarista Rebellions: An Anthology of Sources*, ed. Ward Stavig and Ella Schmidt (Indianapolis: Hackett Publishing, 2008), 109–110.

14. Blanca Tovias, "Native Women of the Americas in Power (c. 1530–1880)," in *The Routledge History of Western Empires*, ed. Robert Aldrich and Kirsten McKenzie (New York: Routledge, 2014), 186.

15. Quoted in Evelyn Cherpak, "The Participation of Women in the Independence Movement in Gran Columbia, 1780–1830," in *Latin American Women: Historical Perspectives*, ed. Asunción Lavrin (Westport, CT: Greenwood Press, 1978), 222.

16. Quoted in Roberto Fernández Retamar, "Caliban: Notes Toward a Discussion of Culture in Our America," in *The Latin American Cultural Studies Reader*, ed. Ana del Sarto, Alicia Ríos, and Abril Trigo (Durham, NC: Duke University Press, 2004), 85.

17. Victor M. Uribe-Uran, "The Changing Meaning of Honor, Status, and Class: The *Letrados* and Bureaucrats of New Granada in the Late Colonial and Early Postcolonial Period," in *State and Society in Spanish America during the Age of Revolution*, ed. Victor M. Uribe-Uran (Wilmington, DE: Scholarly Resources, 2001), 59–60.

18. John King, "Arms and the Man: Abd el-Kader," *History Today* 40, no. 8 (August 1990): 23.

19. Quoted in Benjamin Claude Brower, *A Desert Named Peace: The Violence of France's Empire in the Algerian Sahara, 1844–1902* (New York: Columbia University Press, 2009), 35.

20. Quoted in Jennifer Sessions, *By Sword and Plow: France and the Conquest of Algeria* (Ithaca, NY: Cornell University Press, 2011), 163.

21. Quoted in Brower, *Desert Named Peace*, 80.

22. Edmund Burke III, "The Terror and Religion: Brittany and Algeria," in *Colonialism and the Modern World: Selected Studies*, ed. Gregory Blue, Martin Bunton, and Ralph Croizier (Armonk, NY: M. E. Sharpe, 2002), 46–48.

23. Clare Anderson, *The Indian Uprising of 1857-8: Prisons, Prisoners, and Rebellion* (London: Anthem Press, 2007), 5.

24. Tobias Rettig, "Recruiting the All-Female Rani of Jhansi Regiment: Subhas Chandra Bose and Dr. Lakshmi Swaminadhan," *South East Asia Research* 21, no. 4 (December 2013): 630.

25. Quoted in Adrian Shubert, "Women Warriors and National Heroes: Agustina de Aragón and Her Indian Sisters," *Journal of World History* 23, no. 2 (June 2012): 284.

26. Joshua S. Goldstein, *War and Gender: How Gender Shapes the War System and Vice Versa* (Cambridge: Cambridge University Press, 2001), 63.

27. Pashington Obeng, "Gendered Nationalism: Forms of Masculinity in Modern Asante of Ghana," in *Men and Masculinities in Modern Africa*, ed. Lisa A. Lindsay and Stephan F. Miescher (Portsmouth, NH: Heinemann, 2003), 196–197.

28. Quoted in Obeng, "Gendered Nationalism," 198.

29. Quoted in Emmanuel Akyeampong and Pashington Obeng, "Spirituality, Gender, and Power in Asante History," *International Journal of African Historical Studies* 28, no. 3 (1995): 505.

30. Ibid., 506.

31. Quoted in Jan-Bart Gewald, *Herero Heroes: A Socio-Political History of the Herero of Namibia, 1890–1923* (Oxford: James Currey, 1999), 100.

32. Quoted in George Steinmetz, *The Devil's Handwriting: Precoloniality and the German Colonial State in Qingdao, Samoa, and Southwest Africa* (Chicago: University of Chicago Press, 2007), 201.

33. Quoted in Mark Cocker, *Rivers of Blood, Rivers of Gold: Europe's Conquest of Indigenous Peoples* (New York: Grove Press, 1998), 328.

34. Quoted in Steinmetz, *Devil's Handwriting*, 179–180.

35. Quoted in Sabelo J. Ndlovu-Gatsheni, *Coloniality of Power in Postcolonial Africa: Myths of Decolonization* (Dakar, Senegal: Council for the Development of Social Science Research in Africa, 2013), 136.

36. David Olusoga and Casper W. Erichsen, *The Kaiser's Holocaust: Germany's Forgotten Genocide and the Colonial Roots of Nazism* (London: Faber and Faber, 2010), 156–158.

37. Quoted in Jens-Uwe Guettel, "From the Frontier to German South-West Africa: German Colonialism, Indians, and American Westward Expansion," *Modern Intellectual History* 7, no. 3 (November 2010): 524.

38. Quoted in Helmut Bley, *South-West Africa under German Rule, 1894–1914*, trans. Hugh Ridley (Evanston, IL: Northwestern University Press, 1971), 162.

39. Quoted in Steinmetz, *Devil's Handwriting*, 195.

40. Steinmetz, *Devil's Handwriting*, 211.

41. Dominik J. Schaller, "'Every Herero Will Be Shot': Genocide, Concentration Camps, and Slave Labor in German South-West Africa," in *Forgotten Genocides: Oblivion, Denial, and Memory*, ed. René Lemarchand (Philadelphia: University of Pennsylvania Press, 2011), 63.

42. Quoted in Hildi Hendrickson, "Bodies and Flags: The Representation of Herero Identity in Colonial Namibia," in *Clothing and Difference: Embodied Identities in Colonial and Post-Colonial Africa*, ed. Hildi Hendrickson (Durham, NC: Duke University Press, 1996), 227.

43. Jim Naughten, *Conflict and Costume: The Herero Tribe of Namibia* (London: Merrell, 2013), 16–17.

44. Quoted in Molly McCullers, "'We Do It So That We Will Be Men': Masculinity Politics in Colonial Namibia, 1915–49," *Journal of African History* 52, no. 1 (March 2011): 49.

45. James O. Gump, "A Spirit of Resistance: Sioux, Xhosa, and Maori Responses to Western Dominance, 1840–1920," *Pacific Historical Review* 66, no. 1 (February 1997): 33.

46. Quoted in James Cowan, *The New Zealand Wars: A History of the Maori Campaigns and the Pioneering Period*, Vol. 2 (Wellington, New Zealand: R. E. Owen, 1923), 24–25.

47. Quoted in Stuart Barton Babbage, *Hauhauism: An Episode in the Maori Wars, 1863–1866* (Wellington, New Zealand: Reed Publishing, 1937), 61.

48. Quoted in Gump, "Spirit of Resistance," 34.

49. Alice Beck Kehoe, *The Ghost Dance: Ethnohistory and Revitalization*, 2nd ed. (Long Grove, IL: Waveland Press, 2006), 24.

50. Quoted in Gump, "Spirit of Resistance," 48.

51. Jamie Monson, "War of Words: The Narrative Efficacy of Medicine in the Maji Maji War," in *Maji Maji: Lifting the Fog of War*, ed. James Giblin and Jamie Monson (Leiden, Netherlands: E. J. Brill, 2010), 44–46.

52. Quoted in Arthur J. Knoll and Hermann J. Hiery, eds., *The German Colonial Experience: Select Documents on German Rule in Africa, China, and the Pacific, 1884–1914* (Lanham, MD: University Press of America, 2010), 476.

53. Quoted in D. Soyini Madison, *Acts of Activism: Human Rights as Radical Performance* (Cambridge: Cambridge University Press, 2010), 294.

54. Quoted in Knoll and Hiery, *German Colonial Experience*, 475.

55. Lora Wildenthal, *German Women for Empire, 1884–1945* (Durham, NC: Duke University Press, 2001), 107–108.

56. Larry Clinton Thompson, *William Scott Ament and the Boxer Rebellion: Heroism, Hubris, and the "Ideal Missionary"* (Jefferson, NC: McFarland, 2009), 7.

57. Quoted in Steinmetz, *Devil's Handwriting*, 434.

58. Quoted in Thompson, *William Scott Ament*, 44.

59. Joseph W. Esherick, *The Origins of the Boxer Uprising* (Berkeley: University of California Press, 1987), 302–303.

60. Quoted in Esherick, *Origins of the Boxer Uprising*, 289.

61. Quoted in Paul A. Cohen, *History in Three Keys: The Boxers as Event, Experience, and Myth* (New York: Columbia University Press, 1997), 119.

62. Quoted in Esherick, *Origins of the Boxer Uprising*, 297.

63. Esherick, *Origins of the Boxer Uprising*, 298.

64. Cohen, *History in Three Keys*, 181.

65. Luther Standing Bear, *Land of the Spotted Eagle* (Lincoln: University of Nebraska Press, 1978), xv.

66. Quoted in Cohen, *History in Three Keys*, 239.

67. Ibid., 240.

68. Bret Hinsch, *Masculinities in Chinese History* (Lanham, MD: Rowman and Littlefield, 2013), 139.

69. Ibid.

70. Quoted in Kumari Jayawardena, *Feminism and Nationalism in the Third World* (London: Zed Books, 1986), 182.

71. Quoted in Elizabeth Thompson, *Colonial Citizens: Republican Rights, Paternal Privilege, and Gender in French Syria and Lebanon* (New York: Columbia University Press, 2000), 40.

72. Thompson, *Colonial Citizens*, 247.

73. Quoted in Jeanne Maddox Toungara, "The Apotheosis of Côte d'Ivoire's Nana Houphouët-Boigny," *Journal of Modern African Studies* 28, no. 1 (March 1990): 28.

74. Quoted in Karen Bauwer, *Gender and Decolonization in Congo: The Legacy of Patrice Lumumba* (New York: Palgrave Macmillan, 2010), 23.

75. Ibid., 24.

76. Bauwer, *Gender and Decolonization in Congo*, 18.

77. Quoted in Bauwer, *Gender and Decolonization in Congo*, 28.

78. Patrice Lumumba, *Congo: My Country*, trans. Graham Heath (New York: Praeger, 1962), 116.

79. Aili Mari Tripp, "Women's Mobilization in Uganda: Nonracial Ideologies in European-African-Asian Encounters, 1945–1962," *International Journal of African Historical Studies* 34, no. 3 (2001): 548.

80. Quoted in Tripp, "Women's Mobilization in Uganda," 551.

81. Tripp, "Women's Mobilization in Uganda," 562.

82. Quoted in Kevin B. Anderson, *Marx at the Margins: On Nationalism, Ethnicity, and Non-Western Societies* (Chicago: University of Chicago Press, 2010), 204–208.

83. Quoted in Zareer Masani, *Indian Tales of the Raj* (Berkeley: University of California Press, 1987), 96.

84. Ibid., 98.

85. Ibid., 97.

86. Masani, *Indian Tales of the Raj*, 95.

87. Quoted in Jayawardena, *Feminism and Nationalism*, 192.

88. Lily Xiao Hong Lee and Sue Wiles, *Women of the Long March* (St. Leonards, NSW: Allen and Unwin, 1999), 151.

89. Hinsch, *Masculinities in Chinese History*, 152.

90. Susan L. Mann, *Gender and Sexuality in Modern Chinese History* (Cambridge: Cambridge University Press, 2011), 119–120.

91. Ho Chi Minh, "Annamese Women and French Domination," in *Ho Chi Minh on Revolution: Selected Writings, 1920–66*, ed. Bernard B. Fall (New York: Praeger, 1967), 13.

92. Ho Chi Minh, "Poems from Prison Diary," in *Ho Chi Minh on Revolution: Selected Writings, 1920–66*, ed. Bernard B. Fall (New York: Praeger, 1967), 135.

93. Ibid., 137.

94. Quoted in William J. Duiker, *Ho Chi Minh: A Life* (New York: Hyperion, 2000), 371.

95. Ho Chi Minh, "Declaration of Independence of the Democratic Republic of Viet-Nam (September 2, 1945)," in *Ho Chi Minh on Revolution: Selected Writings, 1920–66*, ed. Bernard B. Fall (New York: Praeger, 1967), 143.

96. Ibid.

97. Joseph S. Alter, "Celibacy, Sexuality, and Nationalism in North India," in *Bodies in Contact: Rethinking Colonial Encounters in World History*, ed. Tony Ballantyne and Antoinette Burton (Durham, NC: Duke University Press, 2005), 318–320.

98. Ketu H. Katrak, "Indian Nationalism, Gandhian 'Satyagraha,' and Representations of Female Sexuality," in *Nationalisms and Sexualities*, ed. Andrew Parker et al. (New York: Routledge, 1992), 396.

99. Quoted in Peter N. Stearns, *Gender in World History*, 2nd ed. (New York: Routledge, 2006), 92.

100. Katrak, "Indian Nationalism," 397.

101. Quoted in Katrak, "Indian Nationalism," 398.

102. Quoted in Ali A. Mazrui, "Gandhi, Marx, and the Warrior Tradition in African Resistance: Towards Androgynous Liberation," in *The Warrior Tradition in Modern Africa*, ed. Ali A. Mazrui (Leiden, Netherlands: E. J. Brill, 1977), 194.

103. Ibid., 187.

104. Ibid.

105. Quoted in Lisa Lindsay, "Domesticity and Difference: Male Breadwinners, Working Women, and Colonial Citizenship in the 1945 Nigerian General Strike," *American Historical Review* 104, no. 3 (June 1999): 791.

106. Lindsay, "Domesticity and Difference," 792–793.

107. Ibid., 795.

108. Quoted in Lindsay, "Domesticity and Difference," 805.

109. Ibid., 812.

110. Quoted in Judith Lynne Hanna, "African Dance and the Warrior Tradition," in *The Warrior Tradition in Modern Africa*, ed. Ali A. Mazrui (Leiden, Netherlands: E. J. Brill, 1977), 119.

111. Quoted in Henry S. Wilson, *African Decolonization* (London: Edward Arnold, 1994), 140.

112. Quoted in Timothy Stapleton, *African Police and Soldiers in Colonial Zimbabwe, 1923–80* (Rochester, NY: University of Rochester Press, 2011), 167.

113. Ibid., 167.

114. Quoted in Saheed Aderinto, "Isaac Fadoyebo at the Battle of Nyron: African Voices of the First and Second World Wars, ca. 1914–1945," in *African Voices of the Global Past: 1500 to the Present*, ed. Trevor R. Getz (Boulder, CO: Westview Press, 2014), 116.

115. Ibid., 131.

116. Michael Adas, "Contested Hegemony: The Great War and the Afro-Asian Assault on the Civilizing Mission Ideology," in *Decolonization: Perspectives from Now and Then*, ed. Prasenjit Duara (London: Routledge, 2004), 84.

117. Ba Maw, *Breakthrough in Burma: Memoirs of a Revolution, 1939–1946* (New Haven, CT: Yale University Press, 1968), 139.

118. Michael Aung-Thwin and Maitrii Aung-Thwin, *A History of Myanmar since Ancient Times: Traditions and Transformations* (London: Reaktion Books, 2012), 232.

119. Quoted in U Maung Maung, *Burmese Nationalist Movements, 1940–1948* (Honolulu: University of Hawai'i Press, 1990), 50.

120. Maw, *Breakthrough in Burma*, 156.

121. Quoted in Robert H. Taylor, *General Ne Win: A Political Biography* (Singapore: Institute of Southeast Asian Studies, 2015), 565.

122. Carol Hills and Daniel C. Silverman, "Nationalism and Feminism in Late Colonial India: The Rani of Jhansi Regiment, 1943–1945," *Modern Asian Studies* 27, no. 4 (October 1993): 741.

123. Quoted in Nilanjana Sengupta, *A Gentleman's Word: The Legacy of Subhas Chandra Bose in Southeast Asia* (Singapore: Institute of Southeast Asian Studies, 2012), 204.

124. Quoted in Rettig, "Recruiting the All-Female," 632.

125. Ibid., 633.

126. Ibid., 635.

127. Quoted in Hills and Silverman, "Nationalism and Feminism," 746.

128. Frances Gouda, "Gender and 'Hyper-Masculinity' as Post-Colonial Modernity during Indonesia's Struggle for Independence, 1945 to 1949," in *Gender, Sexuality, and Colonial Modernities*, ed. Antoinette Burton (London: Routledge, 1999), 164.

129. Quoted in Gouda, "Gender and Hyper-Masculinity," 164.

130. Ibid., 167.

131. Ibid.

132. Ibid., 171.

133. Frank Derek Corfield, *The Origins and Growth of Mau Mau: An Historical Survey* (Nairobi: Colony and Protectorate of Kenya, 1960), 167.

134. John Colin Carothers, *The Psychology of Mau Mau* (Nairobi: Government Printer, 1954), 16.

135. Jock McCulloch, *Colonial Psychiatry and "The African Mind"* (Cambridge: Cambridge University Press, 1995), 72.

136. Mazrui, "Gandhi, Marx," 181.

137. Quoted in Luise White, "Matrimony and Rebellion: Masculinity in Mau Mau," in *Men and Masculinities in Modern Africa*, ed. Lisa A. Lindsay and Stephan F. Miescher (Portsmouth, NH: Heinemann, 2003), 181.

138. Ibid.

139. Quoted in Daniel Branch, "The Enemy Within: Loyalists and the War against Mau Mau in Kenya," *Journal of African History* 48, no. 2 (2007): 299.

140. Brendon Nicholls, *Ngugi wa Thiong'o, Gender, and the Ethics of Postcolonial Reading* (Burlington, VT: Ashgate, 2010), 78–79.

141. David P. Sandgren, *Mau Mau's Children: The Making of Kenya's Postcolonial Elite* (Madison: University of Wisconsin Press, 2012), 33.

142. White, "Matrimony and Rebellion," 186.

143. Ibid., 187–188.

144. Denis Judd, *Empire: The British Imperial Experience from 1765 to the Present* (New York: Basic Books, 1996), 351–352.

145. Meredeth Turshen, "Algerian Women in the Liberation Struggle and the Civil War: From Active Participants to Passive Victims?" *Social Research* 69, no. 3 (Fall 2002): 890.

146. Natalya Vince, "Transgressing Boundaries: Gender, Race, Religion, and 'Françaises Musulmanes' during the Algerian War of Independence," *French Historical Studies* 33, no. 3 (Summer 2010): 452.

147. Quoted in Vince, "Transgressing Boundaries," 453.

148. Julien Murphy, "Beauvoir and the Algerian War: Toward a Postcolonial Ethics," in *Feminist Interpretations of Simone de Beauvoir*, ed. Margaret A. Simons (University Park: Pennsylvania State University Press, 1995), 288.

149. Quoted in Assia Djebar, *Fantasia: An Algerian Cavalcade*, trans. Dorothy S. Blair (Portsmouth, NH: Heinemann, 1993), 135.

150. Jaime Wadowiec, "Muslim Algerian Women and the Rights of Man: Islam and Gendered Citizenship in French Algeria at the End of Empire," *French Historical Studies* 36, no. 4 (Fall 2013): 655.

151. Quoted in Wadowiec, "Muslim Algerian Women," 654.

152. Ibid., 660.

153. Ibid., 661.

154. Wadowiec, "Muslim Algerian Women," 663.

155. Martin Shipway, *Decolonization and Its Impact: A Comparative Approach to the End of the Colonial Empires* (Malden, MA: Blackwell, 2008), 217.

156. Quoted in Devaki Jain and Shubha Chacko, "Walking Together: The Journey of the Non-Aligned Movement and the Women's Movement," *Development in Practice* 19, no. 7 (September 2009): 903.

157. Ibid., 896.

158. Carol Hanisch, "The Personal is Political," in *Notes from the Second Year: Women's Liberation*, ed. Shulamith Firestone and Anne Koedt (New York: Radical Feminism, 1970), 76–78.

159. Quoted in Laura Bier, "Modernity and the Other Woman: Gender and National Identity in the Egyptian Woman's Press, 1952–1967," *Gender and History* 16, no. 1 (April 2004): 99.

160. Quoted in Gerard McCann, "From Diaspora to Third Worldism and the United Nations: India and the Politics of Decolonizing Africa," *Past and Present* 218, sup. 8 (May 2013): 265.

161. Ibid., 268.

162. Quoted in Michelle Hart, *Eye on Israel: How America Came to View Israel as an Ally* (Albany: State University of New York Press, 2006), 150.

163. Peter Gottschalk and Gabriel Greenberg, *Islamophobia: Making Muslims the Enemy* (Lanham, MD: Rowman and Littlefield, 2008), 117.

164. Quoted in Manu Bhagavan, "A New Hope: India, the United Nations, and the Making of the Universal Declaration of Human Rights," *Modern Asian Studies* 44, no. 2 (March 2010): 323.

165. Ibid., 324.

166. Ibid.

167. Quoted in Vrushali Patil, "Contending Masculinities: The Gendered (Re) Negotiation of Colonial Hierarchy in the United Nations Debates on Decolonization," *Theory and Society* 38, no. 2 (March 2009): 208.

168. Ibid.

169. Ibid., 209.

170. Ibid., 208.

171. Ibid., 209.

172. Quoted in Martin Shipway, "'Transfer of Destinies,' or Business as Usual? Republican Invented Tradition and the Problem of 'Independence' at the End of the French Empire," *The Round Table* 97, no. 398 (October 2008): 747.

173. Jalal Al-e Ahmad, *Gharbzadegi [Weststruckness]*, trans. John Green and Ahmad Alizadeh (Costa Mesa, CA: Mazda Publishers, 1997), 11.

174. Ibid., 116.

175. Ibid., 121.

176. Ibid., 61.

177. Jawaharlal Nehru, "Tryst with Destiny," in *Great Speeches of Modern India*, ed. Rudrangshu Mukherjee (New Delhi: Random House India, 2007), 185.

BIBLIOGRAPHY

Introduction

Aldrich, Robert. *Colonialism and Homosexuality*. 2003.

Bhabha, Homi K. *The Location of Culture*. 1994.

Chaudhuri, Nupur, and Margaret Strobel, eds. *Western Women and Imperialism: Complicity and Resistance*. 1992.

Cooper, Frederick, and Ann Laura Stoler, eds. *Tensions of Empire: Colonial Cultures in a Bourgeois World*. 1997.

Djebar, Assia. *Fantasia: An Algerian Cavalcade*. Translated by Dorothy S. Blair. 1993.

Du Bois, W. E. B. *Darkwater: Voices from within the Veil*. 1920.

Foucault, Michel. *The History of Sexuality*. Translated by Robert Hurley. 3 vols. 1978–1986.

Hunt, Nancy Rose. *A Colonial Lexicon: Of Birth Ritual, Medicalization, and Mobility in the Congo*. 1999.

Hyam, Ronald. *Empire and Sexuality: The British Experience*. 1990.

Kramnick, Isaac, ed. *The Portable Enlightenment Reader*. 1995.

Lorde, Audre. *Sister Outsider: Essays and Speeches*. 1984.

Morton, Patricia A. "National and Colonial: The Musée des Colonies at the Colonial Exposition, Paris, 1931." *Art Bulletin* 80, no. 2 (June 1998): 357–377.

Nandy, Ashis. *The Intimate Enemy: Loss and Recovery of Self under Colonialism*. 1983.

Said, Edward W. *Orientalism*. 1978.

Sinha, Mrinalini. *Colonial Masculinity: The 'Manly Englishman' and the 'Effeminate Bengali' in the Late Nineteenth Century*. 1995.

Spivak, Gayatri Chakravorty. *A Critique of Postcolonial Reason: Toward a History of the Vanishing Present*. 1999.

Stoler, Ann Laura. *Carnal Knowledge and Imperial Power: Race and the Intimate in Colonial Rule*. 2010.

Stoler, Ann Laura. *Race and the Education of Desire: Foucault's* History of Sexuality *and the Colonial Order of Things*. 1995.

Chapter One

Adams, Rachel, and David Savran, eds. *The Masculinity Studies Reader.* 2002.

Aldrich, Robert. *Colonialism and Homosexuality.* 2003.

Anderson, Warwick. "The Trespass Speaks: White Masculinity and Colonial Break-down." *American Historical Review* 102, no. 5 (December 1997): 1343–1370.

Archetti, Eduardo P. *Masculinities: Football, Polo, and the Tango in Argentina.* 1999.

Baden-Powell, Robert. *Scouting for Boys: The Original 1908 Edition.* 2007.

Ballantyne, Tony, and Antoinette Burton, eds. *Moving Subjects: Gender, Mobility, and Intimacy in an Age of Global Empire.* 2009.

Balme, Christopher B. "Sexual Spectacles: Theatricality and the Performance of Sex in Early Encounters in the Pacific." *Drama Review* 44, no. 4 (Winter 2000): 67–85.

Banerjee, Sikata. *Make Me a Man! Masculinity, Hinduism, and Nationalism in India.* 2005.

Banerjee, Sikata. *Muscular Nationalism: Gender, Violence, and Empire in India and Ireland, 1914–2004.* 2012.

Bartel, Judy. *The Holocaust: A Primary Source History.* 2006.

Beaglehole, John C., ed. *The Journals of Captain James Cook on His Voyages of Discovery: The Voyage of the* Resolution *and* Adventure, *1772–1775.* 1961.

Black, Daniel P. *Dismantling Black Manhood: An Historical and Literary Analysis of the Legacy of Slavery.* 1997.

Blakely, Allison. *Blacks in the Dutch World: The Evolution of Racial Imagery in a Modern Society.* 1993.

Boittin, Jennifer Anne, Christina Firpo, and Emily Musil Church. "Hierarchies of Race and Gender in the French Colonial Empire, 1914–1946." *Historical Reflections* 37, no. 1 (Spring 2011): 60–90.

Bougainville, Lewis de. *A Voyage Round the World: Performed by Order of His Most Christian Majesty, 1766–1769.* Translated by John Reinhold Forster. 1772.

Boutroux, Émile. "Germany's Civilized Barbarism." *New York Times Current History of the European War* 1, no. 1 (December 1914): 160–169.

Bowersox, Jeff. *Raising Germans in the Age of Empire: Youth and Colonial Culture, 1871–1914.* 2013.

Braudy, Leo. *From Chivalry to Terrorism: War and the Changing Nature of Masculinity.* 2003.

Bristow, Joseph. *Empire Boys: Adventures in a Man's World.* 1991.

Brocheux, Pierre, and Daniel Hémery. *Indochina: An Ambiguous Colonization, 1858–1954.* Translated by Ly Lan Dill-Klein. 2009.

Brower, Daniel R., and Edward J. Lazzerini, eds. *Russia's Orient: Imperial Borderlands and Peoples, 1700–1917.* 1997.

Brown, Matthew. *From Frontiers to Football: An Alternative History of Latin America since 1800.* 2014.

Buchbinder, David. *Performance Anxieties: Re-Producing Masculinity.* 1998.

Buckley, Gail Lumet. *American Patriots: The Story of Blacks in the Military from the Revolution to Desert Storm.* 2001.

Burns, James MacGregor. *Fire and Light: How the Enlightenment Transformed our World.* 2013.

Cannadine, David. *Ornamentalism: How the British Saw Their Empire.* 2001.

Colley, Linda. *Captives Britain, Empire, and the World, 1600–1850.* 2004.

Combeau-Mari, Evelyne. "Sport in the French Colonies (1880–1962): A Case Study." *Journal of Sport History* 33, no. 1 (Spring 2006): 27–57.

Connell, Raewyn. *Masculinities*. 2nd ed. 2005.

Cook, James. *The Journals of Captain Cook*. Edited by Philip Edwards. 2003.

Cornwall, Andrea, and Nancy Lindisfarne, eds. *Dislocating Masculinity: Comparative Ethnographies*. 1994.

Cryle, Peter, and Christopher E. Forth, eds. *Sexuality at the Fin de Siècle: The Making of a "Central Problem."* 2008.

Dawson, Graham. *Soldier Heroes: British Adventure, Empire, and the Imagining of Masculinities*. London: Routledge, 1994.

Dine, Philip. *Sport and Identity in France: Practices, Locations, Representations*. 2012.

Du Bois, W. E. B. *The Souls of Black Folk: Essays and Sketches*. 3rd ed. 1903.

Dudink, Stefan, Karen Hagemann, and John Tosh, eds. *Masculinities in Politics and War: Gendering Modern History*. 2004.

Equiano, Olaudah. *The Interesting Narrative of the Life of Olaudah Equiano, or Gustavus Vassa, the African*. 3rd ed. 1790.

Fanon, Frantz. *Black Skin, White Masks*. Translated by Charles Lam Markmann. 1967.

Fanon, Frantz. *The Wretched of the Earth*. Translated by Richard Philcox. 2004.

Foner, Philip S. *Mark Twain: Social Critic*. 2nd ed. 1972.

Forster, Johann Reinhold. *Observations Made during a Voyage Round the World*. Edited by Nicholas Thomas, Harriet Guest, and Michael Dettelbach. 1996.

Forth, Christopher E., and Bertrand Taithe, eds. *French Masculinities: History, Culture, and Politics*. 2007.

Frühstück, Sabine, and Anne Walthall, eds. *Recreating Japanese Men*. 2011.

Guest, Harriet. *Empire, Barbarism, and Civilization: Captain Cook, William Hodges, and the Return to the Pacific*. 2007.

Gupta, Charu. "Anxious Hindu Masculinities in Colonial North India: *Shuddhi* and *Sangathan* Movements." *CrossCurrents* 61, no. 4 (December 2011): 441–454.

Hack, Karl, and Tobias Rettig, eds. *Colonial Armies in Southeast Asia*. 2006.

Halmesvirta, Anssi. "Building the *Élan Vital* of the Finnish Nation: Ivar Wilskman's Ideology of Gymnastics." *International Journal of the History of Sport* 26, no. 5 (April 2009): 621–639.

Hogg, Robert. *Men and Manliness on the Frontier: Queensland and British Columbia in the Mid-Nineteenth Century*. 2012.

Hokanson, Katya. "Russian Women Travelers in Central Asia and India." *Russian Review* 70, no. 1 (January 2011): 1–19.

Hull, Isabel V. *Absolute Destruction: Military Culture and the Practices of War in Imperial Germany*. 2005.

Huttenback, Robert A. "G. A. Henty and the Imperial Stereotype." *Huntington Library Quarterly* 29, no. 1 (November 1965): 63–75.

Hyam, Ronald. *Empire and Sexuality: The British Experience*. 1990.

Jackson, Ronald L., II. *Scripting the Black Masculine Body: Identity, Discourse, and Racial Politics in Popular Media*. 2006.

Jackson, Ronald L., II, and Murali Balaji, eds. *Global Masculinities and Manhood*. 2011.

Johnson, Henry T. *The Black Man's Burden*. 1899.

Killingray, David, and David Omissi, eds. *Guardians of Empire: The Armed Forces of the Colonial Powers, c. 1700–1964*. 1999.

Kipling, Rudyard. "The White Man's Burden." *McClure's Magazine*, February 1899.

Layton, Susan. *Russian Literature and Empire: Conquest of the Caucasus from Pushkin to Tolstoy.* 1994.

Leupp, Gary P. *Male Colors: The Construction of Homosexuality in Tokugawa Japan.* 1995.

Lindsay, Lisa A., and Stephan F. Miescher, eds. *Men and Masculinities in Modern Africa.* 2003.

Louie, Kam, and Morris Low, eds. *Asian Masculinities: The Meaning and Practice of Manhood in China and Japan.* 2003.

MacKenzie, John M., ed. *Popular Imperialism and the Military, 1850–1950.* 1992.

Makki, Fouad. "Imperial Fantasies, Colonial Realities: Contesting Power and Culture in Italian Eritrea." *South Atlantic Quarterly* 107, no. 4 (Fall 2008): 735–754.

Mangan, J. A. *'Manufactured' Masculinity: Making Imperial Manliness, Morality, and Militarism.* 2012.

Masani, Zareer. *Indian Tales of the Raj.* 1987.

McClintock, Anne. *Imperial Leather: Race, Gender, and Sexuality in the Colonial Contest.* 1995.

McCormack, Gavan, and Yoshio Sugimoto, eds. *The Japanese Trajectory: Modernization and Beyond.* 1988.

Meredith, Martin. *The Fortunes of Africa: A 5000-Year History of Wealth, Greed, and Endeavor.* 2014.

Merians, Linda E. *Envisioning the Worst: Representations of "Hottentots" in Early-Modern England.* 2001.

Midgley, Clare, ed. *Gender and Imperialism.* 1998.

Millar, John. *The Origin of the Distinction of Ranks: Or, an Inquiry into the Circumstances Which Give Rise to Influence and Authority in the Different Members of Society.* 1793.

Miller, Christopher L. *The French Atlantic Triangle: Literature and Culture of the Slave Trade.* 2008.

Mitchell, Michele. *Righteous Propagation: African Americans and the Politics of Racial Destiny after Reconstruction.* 2004.

Molony, Barbara, and Kathleen Uno, eds. *Gendering Modern Japanese History.* 2005.

Mugambi, Helen Nabasuta, and Tuzyline Jita Allan, eds. *Masculinities in African Literary and Cultural Texts.* 2010.

Muthu, Sankar. *Enlightenment against Empire.* 2003.

Newman, Brooke N. "Gender, Sexuality, and the Formation of Racial Identities in the Eighteenth-Century Anglo-Caribbean World." *Gender and History* 22, no. 3 (November 2010): 585–602.

Nye, Robert A. "Western Masculinities in War and Peace." *American Historical Review* 112, no. 2 (April 2007): 417–438.

Opitz, May, Katharina Oguntoye, and Dagmar Schultz, eds. *Showing Our Colors: Afro-German Women Speak Out.* Translated by Anne V. Adams. 1992.

Pandey, Gyanendra. *Routine Violence: Nations, Fragments, Histories.* 2006.

Parsons, Timothy H. *The African Rank-and-File: Social Implications of Colonial Military Service in the King's African Rifles, 1902–1964.* 1999.

Phillips, Jock. *A Man's Country? The Image of the Pakeha Male—A History.* 1987.

Radcliffe, Sarah, and Sallie Westwood. *Remaking the Nation: Place, Identity, and Politics in Latin America.* 1996.

Rasmussen, Susan J. "Veiled Self, Transparent Meanings: Tuareg Headdress as Social Expression." *Ethnology* 30, no. 2 (April 1991): 101–117.

Reddock, Rhoda E., ed. *Interrogating Caribbean Masculinities: Theoretical and Empirical Analyses.* 2004.

Reeser, Todd W. *Masculinities in Theory: An Introduction.* 2010.

Roper, Michael, and John Tosh, eds. *Manful Assertions: Masculinities in Britain since 1800.* 1991.

Rosenthal, Michael. "Knights and Retainers: The Earliest Version of Baden-Powell's Boy Scout Scheme." *Journal of Contemporary History* 15, no. 4 (October 1980): 603–617.

Salmond, Anne. *The Trial of the Cannibal Dog: The Remarkable Story of Captain Cook's Encounters in the South Seas.* 2003.

Schmidt, Heike I. "Colonial Intimacy: The Rechenberg Scandal and Homosexuality in German East Africa." *Journal of the History of Sexuality* 17, no. 1 (January 2008): 25–59.

Seck, Ibrahima. *Bouki Fait Gombo: A History of the Slave Community of Habitation Haydel (Whitney Plantation), Louisiana, 1750–1860.* 2014.

Sinha, Mrinalini. *Colonial Masculinity: The 'Manly Englishman' and the 'Effeminate Bengali' in the Late Nineteenth Century.* 1995.

Spencer, Herbert. "Domestic Retrospect and Prospect." *Popular Science Monthly,* September 1877.

Srivastava, Sanjay, ed. *Sexual Sites, Seminal Attitudes: Sexualities, Masculinities, and Culture in South Asia.* 2004.

Stimpson, Catharine R., and Gilbert Herdt, eds. *Critical Terms for the Study of Gender.* 2014.

Stitt, Jocelyn. "Olaudah Equiano, Englishness, and the Negotiation of Raced Gender." *Michigan Feminist Studies,* no. 14 (1999-2000). http://hdl.handle.net/2027/spo.ark5583.0014.005.

Sussman, Herbert. *Masculine Identities: The History and Meanings of Manliness.* 2012.

Tosh, John. *A Man's Place: Masculinity and the Middle-Class Home in Victorian England.* 1999.

Thiellement, André. *Azawar: Illustrations de l'auteur.* 1949.

Tumblety, Joan. *Remaking the Male Body: Masculinity and the Uses of Physical Culture in Interwar and Vichy France.* 2012.

Uchendu, Egodi, ed. *Masculinities in Contemporary Africa.* 2008.

Wallace, Maurice O. *Constructing the Black Masculine: Identity and Ideality in African American Men's Literature and Culture, 1775–1995.* 2002.

Walther, Daniel J. "Racializing Sex: Same-Sex Relations, German Colonial Authority, and *Deutschtum.*" *Journal of the History of Sexuality* 17, no. 1 (January 2008): 11–24.

Walton, John K., ed. *Histories of Tourism: Representation, Identity, and Conflict.* 2005.

White, Owen. *Children of the French Empire: Miscegenation and Colonial Society in French West Africa, 1895–1960.* 1999.

Wildenthal, Lora. *German Women for Empire, 1884–1945.* 2001.

Wilson, Kathleen. *The Island Race: Englishness, Empire, and Gender in the Eighteenth Century.* 2003.

Woollacott, Angela. *Gender and Empire.* 2006.

Zinn, Howard. *A People's History of the United States, 1492-Present.* 2003.

Zinoman, Peter. "Colonial Prisons and Anti-Colonial Resistance in French Indochina: The Thai Nguyen Rebellion, 1917." *Modern Asian Studies* 34, no. 1 (February 2000): 57–98.

Zwick, Jim, ed. *Mark Twain's Weapons of Satire: Anti-Imperialist Writings on the Philippine-American War.* 1992.

Chapter Two

Albuquerque, Klaus de. "In Search of the Big Bamboo: Among the Sex Tourists of the Caribbean." *Transition*, no. 77 (1998): 48–57.

Ballantyne, Tony, and Antoinette Burton, eds. *Bodies in Contact: Rethinking Colonial Encounters in World History*. 2005.

Ballantyne, Tony, and Antoinette Burton, eds. *Moving Subjects: Gender, Mobility, and Intimacy in an Age of Global Empire*. 2009.

Banerjee, Swapna M. "Blurring Boundaries, Distant Companions: Non-Kin Female Caregivers for Children in Colonial India (Nineteenth and Twentieth Centuries)." *Paedagogica Historica* 46, no. 6 (December 2010): 775–788.

Beckles, Hilary McD. "Historicizing Slavery in West Indian Feminisms." *Feminist Review* 59 (Summer 1998): 34–56.

Ben-Ghiat, Ruth. *Fascist Modernities: Italy, 1922–1945*. 2001.

Blackburn, George M., and Sherman L. Ricards. "The Prostitutes and Gamblers of Virginia City, Nevada: 1870." *Pacific Historical Review* 48, no. 2 (May 1979): 239–258.

Boittin, Jennifer Anne. "Feminist Mediations of the Exotic: French Algeria, Morocco, and Tunisia, 1921–39." *Gender and History* 22, no. 1 (April 2010): 131–150.

Chaudhuri, Nupur, and Margaret Strobel, eds. *Western Women and Imperialism: Complicity and Resistance*. 1992.

Comer, Denise K. "'White Child Is Good, Black Child His [or Her] Slave': Women, Children, and Empire in Early Nineteenth-Century India," *European Romantic Review* 16, no. 1 (January 2005): 39–58.

Cooper, Frederick, and Ann Laura Stoler, eds. *Tensions of Empire: Colonial Cultures in a Bourgeois World*. 1997.

Cooper, Nikki. "(En)Gendering Indochina: Feminisation and Female Figurings in French Colonial Discourses." *Women's Studies International Forum* 23, no. 6 (November–December 2000): 749–759.

Dagut, Simon. "Gender, Colonial 'Women's History,' and the Construction of Social Distance: Middle-Class British Women in Later Nineteenth-Century South Africa." *Journal of Southern African Studies* 26, no. 3 (September 2000): 555–572.

Damousi, Joy. *Depraved and Disorderly: Female Convicts, Sexuality, and Gender in Colonial Australia*. 1997.

Diel, Louise. *"Behold Our New Empire"–Mussolini*. Translated by Kenneth Kirkness. 1939.

Duras, Claire de. *Ourika: An English Translation*. Translated by John Fowles. 1994.

Duras, Marguerite. *The Lover*. Translated by Barbara Bray. 1985.

Edgar, Adrienne. "Bolshevism, Patriarchy, and the Nation: The Soviet 'Emancipation' of Muslim Women in Pan-Islamic Perspective." *Slavic Review* 65, no. 2 (Summer 2006): 252–272.

Fountaine, Margaret. *Butterflies and Late Loves: The Further Travels and Adventures of a Victorian Lady*. Edited by W. F. Cater. 1986.

Frink, Lisa. "Storage and Status in Precolonial and Colonial Coastal Western Alaska." *Current Anthropology* 48, no. 3 (June 2007): 349–374.

Fuhrmann, Malte. "'Western Perversions' at the Threshold of Felicity: The European Prostitutes of Galata-Pera (1870–1915)." *History and Anthropology* 21, no. 2 (June 2010): 159–172.

Getz, Trevor R., and Liz Clarke. *Abina and the Important Men: A Graphic History.* 2012.

Gómez de Avellaneda, Gertrudis. *Sab and Autobiography.* Translated by Nina M. Scott. 1993.

Graffigny, Françoise de. *Letters from a Peruvian Woman.* Translated by David Kornacker. 1993.

Ha, Marie-Paule. *French Women and the Empire: The Case of Indochina.* 2014.

Hodes, Martha, ed. *Sex, Love, Race: Crossing Boundaries in North American History.* 1999.

Hossain, Rokeya Sakhawat. *Sultana's Dream: A Feminist Utopia and Selections from the Secluded Ones.* Edited and translated by Roushan Jahan. 1988.

Kandiyoti, Deniz, ed. *Women, Islam, and the State.* 1991.

Khater, Akram Fouad, ed. *Sources in the History of the Modern Middle East.* 2nd ed. 2011.

Kramnick, Isaac, ed. *The Portable Enlightenment Reader.* 1995.

Levine, Philippa, ed. *Gender and Empire.* 2004.

Levine, Philippa. *Prostitution, Race, and Politics: Policing Venereal Disease in the British Empire.* 2003.

Lindsay, H. A. "The World's First Policewoman." *Quadrant* 3, no. 2 (Autumn 1959): 75–77.

Littlewood, Ian. *Sultry Climates: Travel and Sex since the Grand Tour.* 2013.

Lo, Jacqueline. "Miscegenation's 'Dusky Human Consequences.'" *Postcolonial Studies* 5, no. 3 (2002): 297–307.

Locher-Scholten, Elsbeth. *Women and the Colonial State: Essays on Gender and Modernity in the Netherlands Indies, 1900–1942.* 2000.

Mango, Andrew. *Atatürk: The Biography of the Founder of Modern Turkey.* 1999.

Midgley, Clare, ed. *Gender and Imperialism.* 1998.

Naidu, Sarojini. *The Bird of Time: Songs of Life, Death, and the Spring.* 1912.

Newman, Brooke N. "Gender, Sexuality, and the Formation of Racial Identities in the Eighteenth-Century Anglo-Caribbean World." *Gender and History* 22, no. 3 (November 2010): 585–602.

Nivedita, Sister. *The Complete Works of Sister Nivedita.* Vol. 1. 1967.

Nivedita, Sister. *Letters of Sister Nivedita.* Vol. 2. 1982.

Nugent, Maria. *Lady Nugent's Journal: Jamaica One Hundred Years Ago.* Edited by Frank Cundall. 2010.

Oharazeki, Kazuhiro. "Listening to the Voices of 'Other' Women in Japanese North America: Japanese Prostitutes and Barmaids in the American West, 1887–1920." *Journal of American Ethnic History* 32, no. 4 (Summer 2013): 5–40.

Paisley, Fiona. *Glamour in the Pacific: Cultural Internationalism and Race Politics in the Women's Pan-Pacific.* 2009.

Peleggi, Maurizio. "The Social and Material Life of Colonial Hotels: Comfort Zones as Contact Zones in British Colombo and Singapore, ca. 1870–1930." *Journal of Social History* 46, no. 1 (Fall 2012): 124–153.

Pickles, Katie, and Angela Wanhalla. "Embodying the Colonial Encounter: Explaining New Zealand's 'Grace Darling,' Huria Matenga." *Gender and History* 22, no. 2 (August 2010): 361–381.

Ponzanesi, Sandra. "The Color of Love: *Madamismo* and Interracial Relationships in the Italian Colonies." *Research in African Literatures* 43, no. 2 (Summer 2012): 155–172.

Poska, Allyson M. "Babies on Board: Women, Children, and Imperial Policy in the Spanish Empire." *Gender and History* 22, no. 2 (August 2010): 269–283.

Prince, Mary. *The History of Mary Prince: A West Indian Slave*. 3rd ed. 1831.

Raman, Sita Anantha. "Crossing Cultural Boundaries: Indian Matriarchs and Sisters in Service." *Journal of Third World Studies* 18, no. 2 (Fall 2001): 131–148.

Ringdal, Nils Johan. *Love for Sale: A World History of Prostitution*. Translated by Richard Daly. 2004.

Rizzo, Tracey. *A Certain Emancipation of Women: Gender, Citizenship, and the Causes Célèbres of Eighteenth-Century France*. 2004.

Rizzo, Tracey. "'A Lascivious Climate': Representations of Colonial Subjectivity in the *Causes Célèbres* of Eighteenth-Century France." *Journal of Caribbean History* 34, no. 1/2 (2000): 157–177.

Robertson, Emma. *Chocolate, Women, and Empire: A Social and Cultural History*. 2009.

Robinson, Jane. *Parrot Pie for Breakfast: An Anthology of Women Pioneers*. 1999.

Roubinek, Eric S. "Re-Imagined Communities: National, Racial, and Colonial Visions in Nazi Germany and Fascist Italy, 1922–1943." PhD diss., University of Minnesota, 2014.

Salesa, T. Damon I. "'Travel-Happy' Samoa: Colonialism, Samoan Migration, and a 'Brown Pacific.'" *New Zealand Journal of History* 37, no. 2 (October 2003): 171–188.

Salih, Sara. *Representing Mixed Race in Jamaica and England from the Abolition Era to the Present*. 2011.

SarDesai, D. R., ed. *Southeast Asian History: Essential Readings*. 2nd ed. 2013.

Scott, Joan W. "Gender: A Useful Category of Historical Analysis." *American Historical Review* 91, no. 5 (December 1986): 1053–1075.

Scully, Pamela, and Diana Paton, eds. *Gender and Slave Emancipation in the Atlantic World*. 2005.

Sinn, Elizabeth. "Women at Work: Chinese Brothel Keepers in Nineteenth-Century Hong Kong." *Journal of Women's History* 19, no. 3 (Fall 2007): 87–111.

Smith, Bonnie G. *Imperialism: A History in Documents*. 2000.

Sreenivas, Mytheli. "Creating Conjugal Subjects: Devadasis and the Politics of Marriage in Colonial Madras Presidency." *Feminist Studies* 37, no. 1 (Spring 2011): 63–92.

Steinbock-Pratt, Sarah. "'We Were All Robinson Crusoes': American Women Teachers in the Philippines." *Women's Studies* 41, no. 4 (June 2012): 372–392.

Steinmetz, George. *The Devil's Handwriting: Precoloniality and the German Colonial State in Qingdao, Samoa, and Southwest Africa*. 2007.

Stierstorfer, Klaus, ed. *Women Writing Home, 1700–1920: Female Correspondence across the British Empire*. Vol. 2. 2006.

Stoler, Ann Laura. *Carnal Knowledge and Imperial Power: Race and the Intimate in Colonial Rule*. 2010.

Stoler, Ann Laura, ed. *Haunted by Empire: Geographies of Intimacy in North American History*. 2006.

Summers, Anne. *Damned Whores and God's Police: The Colonization of Women in Australia*. 1975.

Tiryakian, Edward A. "White Women in Darkest Africa: Marginals as Observers in No-Woman's Land." *Civilisations* 41, no. 1–2 (September 1993): 209–238.

Toledano, Ehud R. *As If Silent and Absent: Bonds of Enslavement in the Islamic Middle East*. 2007.

Toledano, Ehud R. "Late Ottoman Concepts of Slavery (1830s–1880s)." *Poetics Today* 14, no. 3 (Autumn 1993): 477–506.

Trüper, Ursula. *The Invisible Woman: Zara Schmelen, African Mission Assistant at the Cape and in Namaland*. 2006.

Van der Spuy, Patricia, and Lindsay Clowes. "'A Living Testimony of the Heights to Which a Woman Can Rise': Sarojini Naidu, Cissie Gool, and the Politics of Women's Leadership in South Africa in the 1920s." *South African Historical Journal* 64, no. 2 (June 2012): 343–363.

Wildenthal, Lora. *German Women for Empire, 1884–1945*. 2001.

Wildenthal, Lora. "'When Men Are Weak': The Imperial Feminism of Frieda von Bülow." *Gender and History* 10, no. 1 (April 1998): 53–77.

Woollacott, Angela. *Gender and Empire*. 2006.

Chapter Three

Akyeampong, Emmanuel K., and Henry Louis Gates, Jr., eds. *Dictionary of African Biography*. 2012.

Aldrich, Robert, and Kirsten McKenzie, eds. *The Routledge History of Western Empires*. 2014.

Allen, Margaret. "'White Already to Harvest': South Australian Women Missionaries in India." *Feminist Review*, no. 65 (Summer 2000): 92–107.

Anthony, David H., III. "Max Yergan in South Africa: From Evangelical Pan-Africanist to Revolutionary Socialist." *African Studies Review* 34, no. 2 (September 1991): pp. 27–55.

Ballantyne, Tony, and Antoinette Burton, eds. *Bodies in Contact: Rethinking Colonial Encounters in World History*. 2005.

Burton, Antionette, ed. *Gender, Sexuality, and Colonial Modernities*. 1999.

Chaudhuri, Nupur, and Margaret Strobel, eds. *Western Women and Imperialism: Complicity and Resistance*. 1992.

Cooke, Nola. "Early Nineteenth-Century Vietnamese Catholics and Others in the Pages of the *Annales de la Propagation de la Foi*." *Journal of Southeast Asian Studies* 35, no. 2 (June 2004): 261–285.

Cooper, Frederick, and Ann Laura Stoler, eds. *Tensions of Empire: Colonial Cultures in a Bourgeois World*. 1997.

Cornwall, Andrea, ed. *Readings in Gender in Africa*. 2005.

Curtis, Sarah A. *Civilizing Habits: Women Missionaries and the Revival of French Empire*. 2010.

Curtis-Wendlandt, Lisa. "Missionary Wives and the Sexual Narratives of German Lutheran Missions among Australian Aborigines." *Journal of the History of Sexuality* 20, no. 3 (September 2011): 498–519.

Darian-Smith, Kate, Patricia Grimshaw, and Stuart Macintyre, eds. *Britishness Abroad: Transnational Movements and Imperial Cultures*. 2007.

Das, Man Singh, ed. *Sociology in Latin America*. 1994.

Deutsch, Jan-Georg. "Celebrating Power in Everyday Life: The Administration of Law and the Public Sphere in Colonial Tanzania, 1890–1914." *Journal of African Cultural Studies* 15, no. 1 (June 2002): 93–103.

Djebar, Assia. *Fantasia: An Algerian Cavalcade*. Translated by Dorothy S. Blair. 1993.

Euben, Roxanne L. *Journeys to the Other Shore: Muslim and Western Travelers in Search of Knowledge*. 2006.

Garvey, Marcus. *The Philosophy and Opinions of Marcus Garvey: Or, Africa for the Africans*. Edited by Amy Jacques Garvey. 1986.

Hochschild, Adam. *King Leopold's Ghost: A Story of Greed, Terror, and Heroism in Colonial Africa*. 1998.

Jennings, Eric T. *Imperial Heights: Dalat and the Making and Undoing of French Indochina*. 2011.

Kennedy, Dane. *The Magic Mountains: Hill Stations and the British Raj*. 1996.

Locher-Scholten, Elsbeth. *Women and the Colonial State: Essays on Gender and Modernity in the Netherlands Indies, 1900–1942*. 2000.

Loos, Tamara. "A History of Sex and the State in Southeast Asia: Class, Intimacy, and Invisibility." *Citizenship Studies* 12, no. 1 (February 2008): 27–43.

Luttikhuis, Bart. "Beyond Race: Constructions of 'Europeanness' in Late-Colonial Legal Practice in the Dutch East Indies." *European Review of History* 20, no. 4 (August 2013): 539–558.

Makki, Fouad. "Imperial Fantasies, Colonial Realities: Contesting Power and Culture in Italian Eritrea." *South Atlantic Quarterly* 107, no. 4 (Fall 2008): 735–754.

Masani, Zareer. *Indian Tales of the Raj*. 1987.

Merrouche, Ouarda, *The Long Term Impact of French Settlement on Education in Algeria*. 2007.

Midgley, Clare, ed. *Gender and Imperialism*. 1998.

Moses, A. Dirk, ed. *Genocide and Settler Society: Frontier Violence and Stolen Indigenous Children in Australian History*. 2004.

Mpofu, Busani. "'Undesirable' Indians, Residential Segregation, and the Ill-Fated Rise of the White 'Housing Covenanters' in Bulawayo, Colonial Zimbabwe, 1930–1973." *South African Historical Journal* 63, no. 4 (December 2011): 553–580.

Parsons, Timothy H. *Race, Resistance, and the Boy Scout Movement in British Colonial Africa*. 2004.

Ponzanesi, Sandra. "The Color of Love: *Madamismo* and Interracial Relationships in the Italian Colonies." *Research in African Literatures* 43, no. 2 (Summer 2012): 155–172.

Prochner, Larry, Helen May, and Baljit Kaur. "'The Blessings of Civilisation': Nineteenth-Century Missionary Infant Schools for Young Native Children in Three Colonial Settings—India, Canada, and New Zealand, 1820s–1840s." *Paedagogica Historica* 45, no. 1/2 (February 2009): 83–102.

Proctor, Tammy M. "'A Separate Path': Scouting and Guiding in Interwar South Africa." *Comparative Studies in Society and History* 42, no. 3 (July 2000): 605–631.

Ramabai, Pandita. *Pandita Ramabai's American Encounter: The Peoples of the United States (1889)*. Translated by Meera Kosambi. 2003.

Ruete, Emily. *An Arabian Princess between Two Worlds: Memoirs, Letters Home, Sequels to the Memoirs, Syrian Customs and Usages*. Edited by Emeri van Donzel. 1993.

Ruete, Emily. *Memoirs of an Arabian Princess*. Translated by Lionel Strachey. 1907.

Ruete, Emily. *Memoirs of an Arabian Princess: An Autobiography*. Translated by unknown. 1888.

SarDesai, D. R., ed., *Southeast Asian History: Essential Readings*. 2nd ed. 2013.

Satter, Beryl. "Marcus Garvey, Father Divine, and the Gender Politics of Race Difference and Race Neutrality." *American Quarterly* 48, no. 1 (March 1996): 43–76.

Smith, Bonnie G. *Imperialism: A History in Documents*. 2000.

Sòrgoni, Barbara. "'Defending the Race': The Italian Reinvention of the Hottentot Venus during Fascism." *Journal of Modern Italian Studies* 8, no. 3 (Fall 2003): 411–424.

Srivastava, Sanjay, ed. *Sexuality Studies.* 2013.

Stoler, Ann Laura, ed. *Haunted by Empire: Geographies of Intimacy in North American History.* 2006.

Toussaint-Samson, Adèle. *A Parisian in Brazil: The Travel Account of a Frenchwoman in Nineteenth-Century Rio de Janeiro.* Translated by Emma Toussaint. 2001.

Urban-Mead, Wendy. "Negotiating 'Plainness' and Gender: Dancing and Apparel at Christian Weddings in Matabeleland, Zimbabwe, 1913–1944." *Journal of Religion in Africa* 38, no. 2 (May 2008): 209–246.

Wade, Peter. "Hybridity Theory and Kinship Thinking." *Cultural Studies* 19, no. 5 (September 2005): 602–621.

White, Owen. *Children of the French Empire: Miscegenation and Colonial Society in French West Africa, 1895–1960.* 1999.

Wildenthal, Lora. *German Women for Empire, 1884–1945.* 2001.

Woollacott, Angela. *Gender and Empire.* 2006.

Chapter Four

"Absinthe Mata Hari Bohemian." Absinthe Mata Hari website. http://absinthematahari .com/?q=content/absinthe-mata-hari-bohemian.

Adams, Bluford. "'A Stupendous Mirror of Departed Empires': The Barnum Hippo-dromes and Circuses, 1874–1891." *American Literary History* 8, no.1 (Spring, 1996): 34–56.

Ahlawat, Deepika. "Empire of Glass: F. & C. Osler in India, 1840–1930." *Journal of Design History* 21, no. 2 (Summer 2008): 155–170.

Aldrich, Robert, and Kirsten McKenzie, eds. *The Routledge History of Western Empires.* 2014.

Arondekar, Anjali. *For the Record: On Sexuality and the Colonial Archive in India.* 2009.

Bernstein, Richard. *The East, the West, and Sex: A History.* 2009.

Brodskaïa, Nathalia. *Post-Impressionism.* 2007.

Burton, Antoinette, ed. *Gender, Sexuality, and Colonial Modernities.* 1999.

Burton, Richard F. *A Plain and Literal Translation of the Arabian Nights Entertainments, Now Entituled: The Book of the Thousand Nights and a Night.* Vol. 1. 1885.

Carey, David, Jr., ed. *Distilling the Influence of Alcohol: Aguardiente in Guatemalan History.* 2012.

Carlsson, Chris. "Absinthe Mata Hari." *Spirits Review.* http://www.spiritsreview.com/ reviews-absinthe-mata-hari.html.

Chapman, James, and Nicholas J. Cull. *Projecting Empire: Imperialism and Popular Cinema.* 2009.

Chaudhuri, Nupur, and Margaret Strobel, eds. *Western Women and Imperialism: Complicity and Resistance.* 1992.

Cheang, Sarah. "Women, Pets, and Imperialism: The British Pekingese Dog and Nostalgia for Old China." *Journal of British Studies* 45, no. 2 (April 2006): 359–387.

Colligan, Colette. *The Traffic in Obscenity from Byron to Beardsley: Sexuality and Exoticism in Nineteenth-Century Print Culture.* 2006.

Conklin, Alice L. *In the Museum of Man: Race, Anthropology, and Empire in France, 1850–1950.* 2013.

Courtwright, David T. *Forces of Habit: Drugs and the Making of the Modern World.* 2001.

Di Carmine, Roberta. *Italy Meets Africa: Colonial Discourses in Italian Cinema.* 2011.

Diduk, Susan. "European Alcohol, History, and the State in Cameroon." *African Studies Review* 36, no. 1 (April 1993): 1–42.

Duberman, Martin Bauml. *Paul Robeson.* 1988.

Dyer, Richard. *Heavenly Bodies: Film Stars and Society.* 2nd ed. 2004.

Ellis, Havelock. *Studies in the Psychology of Sex: Sexual Inversion.* 2nd ed. 1901.

Equiano, Olaudah. *The Interesting Narrative of the Life of Olaudah Equiano, or Gustavus Vassa, the African.* 3rd ed. 1790.

Floor, Willem. "A Note on Persian Cats." *Iranian Studies* 36, no. 1 (March 2003): 27–42.

Fraser, Mrs. Hugh. *A Diplomatist's Wife in Japan: Letters from Home to Home.* 4th ed. 1904.

Gandhi, Leela. *Affective Communities: Anticolonial Thought, Fin-de-Siècle Radicalism, and the Politics of Friendship.* 2006.

Garelick, Rhonda K. *Electric Salome: Loie Fuller's Performance of Modernism.* 2007.

Grever, Maria, and Berteke Waaldijk. "Women's Labor at Display: Feminist Claims to Dutch Citizenship and Colonial Politics around 1900." *Journal of Women's History* 15, no. 4 (Winter 2004): 11–18.

Hackett, Robin. *Sapphic Primitivism: Productions of Race, Class, and Sexuality in Key Works of Modern Fiction.* 2004.

Hight, Eleanor M., and Gary D. Sampson, eds. *Colonialist Photography: Imag(in)ing Race and Place.* 2004.

Hoganson, Kristin. "Food and Entertainment from Every Corner of the Globe: Bourgeois U.S. Households as Points of Encounter, 1870–1920." *Amerikastudien / American Studies* 48, no. 1 (2003): 115–135.

Holmes, Rachel. *African Queen: The Real Life of the Hottentot Venus.* 2007.

Jacobus X [pseud.]. *The Erogenous Zones of the World.* Edited by Norman Lockridge. 1964.

Jennings, Eric T. *Imperial Heights: Dalat and the Making and Undoing of French Indochina.* 2011.

Kennedy, Dane. *The Highly Civilized Man: Richard Burton and the Victorian World.* 2005.

Kirk, Anna Marie. "Japonisme and Femininity: A Study of Japanese Dress in British and French Art and Society, c. 1860-c. 1899." *Costume* 42 (2008): 111–129.

Kopf, Jennifer. "Picturing Difference: Writing the Races in the 1896 Berlin Trade Exposition's Souvenir Album." *Historical Geography* 36 (2008): 112–138.

Krafft-Ebing, Richard von. *Psychopathia Sexualis: A Medico-Forensic Study.* 12th ed. Translated by F. J. Rebman. 1906.

Lambourne, Lionel. *Japonisme: Cultural Crossings between Japan and the West.* 2005.

Lauritsen, John, and David Thorstad. *The Early Homosexual Rights Movement (1864–1935).* 1995.

Lemke, Sieglinde. *Primitivist Modernism: Black Culture and the Origins of Transatlantic Modernism.* 1998.

Linne, Karsten. *Deutschland jenseits des Äquators? Die NS-Kolonialplanungen für Afrika.* 2008.

Livingston, Julie. "Physical Fitness and Economic Opportunity in the Bechuanaland Protectorate in the 1930s and 1940s." *Journal of Southern African Studies* 27, no. 4 (December 2001): 793–811.

Locher-Scholten, Elsbeth. *Women and the Colonial State: Essays on Gender and Modernity in the Netherlands Indies, 1900–1942.* 2000.

Lutz, Deborah. *Pleasure Bound: Victorian Sex Rebels and the New Eroticism.* 2011.

MacKenzie, John M. *Orientalism: History, Theory, and the Arts.* 1995.

Mamiya, Christin J. "Nineteenth-Century French Women, the Home, and the Colonial Vision: *Les Sauvages de la Mer Pacifique* Wallpaper." *Frontiers* 28, no. 1/2 (2007): 100–120.

Masani, Zareer. *Indian Tales of the Raj.* 1987.

Meinertzhagen, Richard. *Kenya Diary: 1902–1906.* 1957.

Mozart, Wolfgang Amadeus. "The Abduction from the Seraglio." *OperaFolio.* http://www.operafolio.com/opera.asp?n=Die_Entfuhrung_aus_dem_Serail.

Museu Picasso de Barcelona, ed. *Images: Picasso and the Japanese Erotic Print.* 2010.

Nagata, Seiji. *Hokusai: Genius of the Japanese Ukiyo-e.* Translated by John Bester. 1995.

Napier, Susan J. *From Impressionism to Anime: Japan as Fantasy and Fan Cult in the Mind of the West.* 2007.

Opitz, May, Katharina Oguntoye, and Dagmar Schultz, eds. *Showing Our Colors: Afro-German Women Speak Out.* Translated by Anne V. Adams. 1992.

Phillips, Richard. *Sex, Politics, and Empire: A Postcolonial Geography.* 2006.

Puccini, Giacomo. *Madam Butterfly: A Japanese Tragedy.* Translated by R. H. Elkin. 1906.

Rizzo, Tracey. "'A Lascivious Climate': Representations of Colonial Subjectivity in the *Causes Célèbres* of Eighteenth-Century France." *Journal of Caribbean History* 34, no. 1/2 (2000): 157–177.

Russell, Mona. "Marketing the Modern Egyptian Girl: Whitewashing Soap and Clothes from the Late Nineteenth Century to 1936." *Journal of Middle East Women's Studies* 6, no. 3 (Fall 2010): 19–57.

Saltzman, Cynthia. *Portrait of Dr. Gachet: The Story of a Van Gogh Masterpiece, Money, Politics, Collectors, Greed, and Loss.* 1998.

Sasges, Gerard. "State, Enterprise, and the Alcohol Monopoly in Colonial Vietnam." *Journal of Southeast Asian Studies* 43, no. 1 (February 2012): 133–157.

Sen, Colleen Taylor. *Curry: A Global History.* 2009.

Shadle, Brett L. "Cruelty and Empathy, Animals and Race, in Colonial Kenya." *Journal of Social History* 45, no. 4 (Summer 2012): 1097–1116.

Shipman, Pat. *Femme Fatale: Love, Lies, and the Unknown Life of Mata Hari.* 2007.

Sigel, Lisa Z. *Governing Pleasures: Pornography and Social Change in England, 1815–1914.* 2002.

Silverman, Debora L. *Art Nouveau in Fin-de-Siècle France: Politics, Psychology, and Style.* 1989.

Sithole, Ndabaningi. *African Nationalism.* 1959.

Smith, Bonnie G. *Imperialism: A History in Documents.* 2000.

Stewart, Jeffrey C., ed. *Paul Robeson: Artist and Citizen.* 1998.

Stuart, Charles. *The Ladies' Monitor: Being a Series of Letters.* 1809.

Suriano, Maria. "Clothing and the Changing Identities of Tanganyikan Urban Youths, 1920s–1950s." *Journal of African Cultural Studies* 20, no. 1 (June 2008): 95–115.

Taylor, Timothy D. *Beyond Exoticism: Western Music and the World.* 2007.

Weinbaum, Alys Eve, Lynn M. Thomas, Priti Ramamurthy, Uta G. Poiger, Madeleine Yue Dong, and Tani E. Barlow, eds. *The Modern Girl around the World: Consumption, Modernity, and Globalization.* 2008.

White, Owen. "Drunken States: Temperance and French Rule in Côte d'Ivoire, 1908–1916." *Journal of Social History* 40, no. 3 (Spring 2007): 663–684.

Wildenthal, Lora. *German Women for Empire, 1884–1945.* 2001.

Williams, Rosalind H. *Dream Worlds: Mass Consumption in Late Nineteenth-Century France.* 1982.

Chapter Five

Anderson, Bonnie S., and Judith P. Zinsser. *A History of Their Own: Women in Europe from Prehistory to the Present.* Vol. 2. 2000.

Andersen, Margaret Cook. "Creating French Settlements Overseas: Pronatalism and Colonial Medicine in Madagascar." *French Historical Studies* 33, no. 3 (Summer 2010): 417–444.

Ballantyne, Tony, and Antoinette Burton, eds. *Bodies in Contact: Rethinking Colonial Encounters in World History.* 2005.

Bashford, Alison. "Nation, Empire, Globe: The Spaces of Population Debate in the Interwar Years." *Comparative Studies in Society and History* 49, no. 1 (January 2007): 170–201.

Bastian, Misty L. "'The Demon Superstition': Abominable Twins and Mission Culture in Onitsha History." *Ethnology* 40, no. 1 (Winter 2001): 13–27.

Burton, Antoinette, ed. *Gender, Sexuality, and Colonial Modernities.* 1999.

Burton, Richard F. *A Plain and Literal Translation of the Arabian Nights Entertainments, Now Entituled: The Book of the Thousand Nights and a Night.* Vol. 2. 1885.

Campbell, Chloe. *Race and Empire: Eugenics in Colonial Kenya.* 2007.

Cooper, Frederick, and Ann Laura Stoler, eds. *Tensions of Empire: Colonial Cultures in a Bourgeois World.* 1997.

Coquery-Vidrovitch, Catherine. *African Women: A Modern History.* Translated by Beth Gillian Raps. 1994.

Darby, Robert. *A Surgical Temptation: The Demonization of the Foreskin and the Rise of Circumcision in Britain.* 2005.

Darwin, Charles. *Charles Darwin's Beagle Diary.* Edited by R. D. Keynes. 1988.

Darwin, Charles. *The Descent of Man, and Selection in Relation to Sex.* Vol. 1. 1871.

Dasgupta, Rohit K., and K. Moti Gokulsing, eds. *Masculinity and Its Challenges in India: Essays on Changing Perceptions.* 2014.

DeLamotte, Eugenia C., Natania Meeker, and Jean F. O'Barr, eds. *Women Imagine Change: A Global Anthology of Women's Resistance from 600 B.C.E. to Present.* 1997.

Demirci, Tuba, and Selçuk Akşin Somel. "Women's Bodies, Demography, and Public Health: Abortion Policy and Perspectives in the Ottoman Empire of the Nineteenth Century." *Journal of the History of Sexuality* 17, no. 3 (September 2008): 377–420.

Dickinson, Edward Ross. "Biopolitics, Fascism, Democracy: Some Reflections on Our Discourse about 'Modernity.'" *Central European History* 37, no. 1 (2004): 1–48.

Echeverri, Marcela. "'Enraged to the Limit of Despair': Infanticide and Slave Judicial Strategies in Barbacoas, 1788–98." *Slavery and Abolition* 30, no. 3 (September 2009): 403–426.

Edington, Claire. "Going in and Getting out of the Colonial Asylum: Families and Psychiatric Care in French Indochina." *Comparative Studies in Society and History* 55, no. 3 (July 2013): 725–755.

Epprecht, Marc. *Heterosexual Africa? The History of an Idea from the Age of Exploration to the Age of AIDS.* 2008.

Equiano, Olaudah. *The Interesting Narrative of the Life of Olaudah Equiano, or Gustavus Vassa, the African.* 3rd ed. 1790.

Feinberg, Leslie. *Transgender Warriors: Making History from Joan of Arc to RuPaul.* 1996.

Frühstück, Sabine. *Colonizing Sex: Sexology and Social Control in Modern Japan.* 2003.

Fuechtner, Veronika, and Mary Rhiel, eds. *Imagining Germany Imagining Asia: Essays in Asian-German Studies.* 2013.

Gollaher, David L. *Circumcision: A History of the World's Most Controversial Surgery.* 2000.

Gould, Stephen Jay. *The Mismeasure of Man.* 1996.

Green, Nile. "Breathing in India, c. 1890." *Modern Asian Studies* 42, no. 2/3 (March–May 2008): 283–315.

Harrison, Henrietta. "Rethinking Missionaries and Medicine in China: The Miracles of Assunta Pallotta, 1905–2005." *Journal of Asian Studies* 71, no. 1 (February 2012): 127–148.

Herdt, Gilbert, ed. *Third Sex, Third Gender: Beyond Sexual Dimorphism in Culture and History.* 1994.

Howell, Philip. *Geographies of Regulation: Policing Prostitution in Nineteenth-Century Britain and the Empire.* 2009.

Hyam, Ronald. *Empire and Sexuality: The British Experience.* 1990.

Jacob, Wilson Chacko. *Working Out Egypt: Effendi Masculinity and Subject Formation in Colonial Modernity, 1870–1940.* 2011.

Keller, Richard. "Madness and Colonization: Psychiatry in the British and French Empires, 1800–1962." *Journal of Social History* 35, no. 2 (Winter 2001): 295–326.

Klausen, Susanne. "Women's Resistance to Eugenic Birth Control in Johannesburg, 1930–39." *South African Historical Journal* 50, no. 1 (May 2004): 152–169.

Kozma, Liat. "'We, the Sexologists …': Arabic Medical Writing on Sexuality, 1879–1943." *Journal of the History of Sexuality* 22, no. 3 (September 2013): 426–445.

Kramnick, Isaac, ed. *The Portable Enlightenment Reader.* 1995.

Kuwahara, Makiko. *Tattoo: An Anthropology.* 2005.

Lang, Sabine. *Men as Women, Women as Men: Changing Gender in Native American Cultures.* Translated by John L. Vantine. 1998.

Livingston, Julie. "Physical Fitness and Economic Opportunity in the Bechuanaland Protectorate in the 1930s and 1940s." *Journal of Southern African Studies* 27, no. 4 (December 2001): 793–811.

Macgowan, John. *How England Saved China.* 1913.

Malthus, Thomas. *An Essay on the Principle of Population.* 1993.

McElhinny, Bonnie. "'Kissing a Baby Is Not at All Good for Him': Infant Mortality, Medicine, and Colonial Modernity in the U.S.-Occupied Philippines." *American Anthropologist* 107, no. 2 (June 2005): 183–194.

McKittrick, Meredith. "Faithful Daughter, Murdering Mother: Transgression and Social Control in Colonial Namibia." *Journal of African History* 40, no. 2 (1999): 265–283.

Nanda, Serena. *Gender Diversity: Crosscultural Variations.* 2nd ed. 2014.

Nelson, William Max. "Making Men: Enlightenment Ideas of Racial Engineering." *American Historical Review* 115, no. 5 (December 2010): 1364–1394.

Nnaemeka, Obioma, ed. *Female Circumcision and the Politics of Knowledge: African Women in Imperialist Discourses.* 2005.

Nye, Robert A., ed. *Sexuality.* 1999.

Ojo, Olatunji. "Beyond Diversity: Women, Scarification, and Yoruba Identity." *History in Africa* 35 (2008): 347–374.

Olsen, William C. "'Children for Death': Money, Wealth, and Witchcraft Suspicion in Colonial Asante." *Cahiers d'Études Africaines* 42, no. 167 (2002): 521–550.

Opitz, May, Katharina Oguntoye, and Dagmar Schultz, eds. *Showing Our Colors: Afro-German Women Speak Out.* Translated by Anne V. Adams. 1992.

Phillips, Richard. *Sex, Politics, and Empire: A Postcolonial Geography.* 2006.

Pinto-Correia, Clara, and João Lourenço Monteiro. "Science in Support of Racial Mixture: Charles-Augustin Vandermonde's Enlightenment Program for Improving the Health and Beauty of the Human Species." *Endeavour* 38, no. 1 (March 2014): 19–26.

Piper, Raymond F. "In Support of Altruism in Hinduism." *Journal of Bible and Religion* 22, no. 3 (July 1954): 178–183.

Price, Neil S., ed. *The Archaeology of Shamanism.* 2001.

Ramusack, Barbara N. "Embattled Advocates: The Debate over Birth Control in India, 1920–1940." *Journal of Women's History* 1, no. 2 (Fall 1989): 34–64.

Rizzo, Tracey. "Between Dishonor and Death: Infanticides in the *Causes Célèbres* of Eighteenth-Century France." *Women's History Review* 13, no. 1 (2004): 5–21.

Roscoe, Will. *Changing Ones: Third and Fourth Genders in Native North America.* 1998.

Sadowsky, Jonathan. "The Social World and the Reality of Mental Illness: Lessons from Colonial Psychiatry." *Harvard Review of Psychiatry* 11, no. 4 (July–August 2003): 210–215.

Sanderson, Lilian Passmore. *Against the Mutilation of Women: The Struggle to End Unnecessary Suffering.* 1981.

Schiebinger, Londa. "Feminist History of Colonial Science." *Hypatia* 19, no. 1 (Winter 2004): 233–254.

Shell-Duncan, Bettina, and Ylva Hernlund, eds. *Female "Circumcision" in Africa: Culture, Controversy, and Change.* 2000.

Singleton, Mark. *Yoga Body: The Origins of Modern Posture Practice.* 2010.

Singleton, Mark. "Yoga, Eugenics, and Spiritual Darwinism in the Early Twentieth Century." *International Journal of Hindu Studies* 11, no. 2 (August 2007): 125–146.

Slater, Sandra, and Fay A. Yarbrough, eds. *Gender and Sexuality in Indigenous North America, 1400–1850.* 2011.

Surkis, Judith. *Sexing the Citizen: Morality and Masculinity in France, 1870–1920.* 2006.

Toussaint-Samson, Adèle. *A Parisian in Brazil: The Travel Account of a Frenchwoman in Nineteenth-Century Rio de Janeiro.* Translated by Emma Toussaint. 2001.

Wallace, Lee. *Sexual Encounters: Pacific Texts, Modern Sexualities.* 2003.

Walther, Daniel J. "Sex, Public Health, and Colonial Control: The Campaign against Venereal Diseases in Germany's Overseas Possessions, 1884–1914." *Social History of Medicine* 26, no. 2 (May 2013): 182–203.

White, Luise. *The Comforts of Home: Prostitution in Colonial Nairobi.* 1990.

Williams, Walter L. *The Spirit and the Flesh: Sexual Diversity in American Indian Culture.* 1986.

Zito, Angela. "Secularizing the Pain of Footbinding in China: Missionary and Medical Stagings of the Universal Body." *Journal of the American Academy of Religion* 75, no. 1 (March 2007): 1–24.

Znamenski, Andrei A. *The Beauty of the Primitive: Shamanism and the Western Imagination.* 2007.

Znamenski, Andrei A. *Shamanism and Christianity: Native Encounters with Russian Orthodox Missions in Siberia and Alaska, 1820–1917.* 1999.

Znamenski, Andrei A. *Shamanism in Siberia: Russian Records of Indigenous Spirituality.* 2003.

Chapter Six

Adams, Jerome R. *Notable Latin American Women: Twenty-Nine Leaders, Rebels, Poets, Battlers, and Spies, 1500–1900.* 1995.

Akyeampong, Emmanuel, and Pashington Obeng. "Spirituality, Gender, and Power in Asante History." *International Journal of African Historical Studies* 28, no. 3 (1995): 481–508.

Aldrich, Robert, and Kirsten McKenzie, eds. *The Routledge History of Western Empires.* 2014.

Al-e Ahmad, Jalal. *Gharbzadegi [Weststruckness].* Translated by John Green and Ahmad Alizadeh. 1997.

Anderson, Clare. *The Indian Uprising of 1857-8: Prisons, Prisoners, and Rebellion.* 2007.

Anderson, Kevin B. *Marx at the Margins: On Nationalism, Ethnicity, and Non-Western Societies.* 2010.

Aung-Thwin, Michael, and Maitrii Aung-Thwin. *A History of Myanmar since Ancient Times: Traditions and Transformations.* 2012.

Babbage, Stuart Barton. *Hauhauism: An Episode in the Maori Wars, 1863–1866.* 1937.

Ballantyne, Tony, and Antoinette Burton, eds. *Bodies in Contact: Rethinking Colonial Encounters in World History.* 2005.

Bauwer, Karen. *Gender and Decolonization in Congo: The Legacy of Patrice Lumumba.* 2010.

Bhagavan, Manu. "A New Hope: India, the United Nations, and the Making of the Universal Declaration of Human Rights." *Modern Asian Studies* 44, no. 2 (March 2010): 311–347.

Bier, Laura. "Modernity and the Other Woman: Gender and National Identity in the Egyptian Woman's Press, 1952–1967." *Gender and History* 16, no. 1 (April 2004): 99–112.

Bley, Helmut. *South-West Africa under German Rule, 1894–1914.* Translated by Hugh Ridley. 1971.

Blue, Gregory, Martin Bunton, and Ralph Croizier, eds. *Colonialism and the Modern World: Selected Studies.* 2002.

Branch, Daniel. "The Enemy Within: Loyalists and the War against Mau Mau in Kenya." *Journal of African History* 48, no. 2 (2007): 291–315.

Brower, Benjamin Claude. *A Desert Named Peace: The Violence of France's Empire in the Algerian Sahara, 1844–1902.* 2009.

Burton, Antionette, ed. *Gender, Sexuality, and Colonial Modernities.* 1999.

Carothers, John Colin. *The Psychology of Mau Mau.* 1954.

Cocker, Mark. *Rivers of Blood, Rivers of Gold: Europe's Conquest of Indigenous Peoples.* 1998.

Cohen, Paul A. *History in Three Keys: The Boxers as Event, Experience, and Myth.* 1997.

Connell, Raewyn. *Southern Theory: The Global Dynamics of Knowledge in Social Science.* 2007.

Corfield, Frank Derek. *The Origins and Growth of Mau Mau: An Historical Survey.* 1960.

Cowan, James. *The New Zealand Wars: A History of the Maori Campaigns and the Pioneering Period.* Vol. 2. 1923.

Del Sarto, Ana, Alicia Ríos, and Abril Trigo, eds. *The Latin American Cultural Studies Reader.* 2004.

Djebar, Assia. *Fantasia: An Algerian Cavalcade.* Translated by Dorothy S. Blair. 1993.

Duara, Prasenjit, ed. *Decolonization: Perspectives from Now and Then*. 2004.

Dubois, Laurent. *Avengers of the New World: The Story of the Haitian Revolution*. 2004.

Dubois, Laurent, and John D. Garrigus, eds. *Slave Revolution in the Caribbean, 1789–1804: A Brief History with Documents*. 2006.

Duiker, William J. *Ho Chi Minh: A Life*. 2000.

Esherick, Joseph W. *The Origins of the Boxer Uprising*. 1987.

Fall, Bernard B., ed. *Ho Chi Minh on Revolution: Selected Writings, 1920–66*. 1967.

Firestone, Shulamith, and Anne Koedt, eds. *Notes from the Second Year: Women's Liberation*. 1970.

Getz, Trevor R., ed. *African Voices of the Global Past: 1500 to the Present*. 2014.

Gewald, Jan-Bart. *Herero Heroes: A Socio-Political History of the Herero of Namibia, 1890–1923*. 1999.

Giblin, James, and Jamie Monson. *Maji Maji: Lifting the Fog of War*. 2010.

Goldstein, Joshua S. *War and Gender: How Gender Shapes the War System and Vice Versa*. 2001.

Gottschalk, Peter, and Gabriel Greenberg. *Islamophobia: Making Muslims the Enemy*. 2008.

Guettel, Jens-Uwe. "From the Frontier to German South-West Africa: German Colonialism, Indians, and American Westward Expansion." *Modern Intellectual History* 7, no. 3 (November 2010): 523–552.

Gump, James O. "A Spirit of Resistance: Sioux, Xhosa, and Maori Responses to Western Dominance, 1840–1920." *Pacific Historical Review* 66, no. 1 (February 1997): 21–52.

Hart, Michelle. *Eye on Israel: How America Came to View Israel as an Ally*. 2006.

Hendrickson, Hildi, ed. *Clothing and Difference: Embodied Identities in Colonial and Post-Colonial Africa*. 1996.

Hills, Carol, and Daniel C. Silverman. "Nationalism and Feminism in Late Colonial India: The Rani of Jhansi Regiment, 1943–1945." *Modern Asian Studies* 27, no. 4 (October 1993): 741–760.

Hinsch, Bret. *Masculinities in Chinese History*. 2013.

Jain, Devaki, and Shubha Chacko. "Walking Together: The Journey of the Non-Aligned Movement and the Women's Movement." *Development in Practice* 19, no. 7 (September 2009): 895–905.

James, C. L. R. *The Black Jacobins: Toussaint L'Ouverture and the San Domingo Revolution*. 2nd ed. 1989.

Jayawardena, Kumari. *Feminism and Nationalism in the Third World*. 1986.

Judd, Denis. *Empire: The British Imperial Experience from 1965 to the Present*. 1996.

Kehoe, Alice Beck. *The Ghost Dance: Ethnohistory and Revitalization*. 2nd ed. 2006.

King, John. "Arms and the Man: Abd el-Kader." *History Today* 40, no. 8 (August 1990): 22–28.

Knoll, Arthur J., and Hermann J. Hiery, eds. *The German Colonial Experience: Select Documents on German Rule in Africa, China, and the Pacific, 1884–1914*. 2010.

Lavrin, Asunción, ed. *Latin American Women: Historical Perspectives*. 1978.

Lee, Lily Xiao Hong, and Sue Wiles. *Women of the Long March*. 1999.

Lemarchand, René, ed. *Forgotten Genocides: Oblivion, Denial, and Memory*. 2011.

Lindsay, Lisa. "Domesticity and Difference: Male Breadwinners, Working Women, and Colonial Citizenship in the 1945 Nigerian General Strike." *American Historical Review* 104, no. 3 (June 1999): 783–812.

Lindsay, Lisa A., and Stephan F. Miescher, eds. *Men and Masculinities in Modern Africa*. 2003.

L'Ouverture, Toussaint. *The Haitian Revolution*. Edited by Nick Nesbitt. 2008.

Lumumba, Patrice. *Congo: My Country*. Translated by Graham Heath. 1962.

Madison, D. Soyini. *Acts of Activism: Human Rights as Radical Performance*. 2010.

Mann, Susan L. *Gender and Sexuality in Modern Chinese History*. 2011.

Masani, Zareer. *Indian Tales of the Raj*. 1987.

Maung Maung, U. *Burmese Nationalist Movements, 1940–1948*. 1990.

Maw, Ba. *Breakthrough in Burma: Memoirs of a Revolution, 1939–1946*. 1968.

Mazrui, Ali A. *The Warrior Tradition in Modern Africa*. 1977.

McCann, Gerard. "From Diaspora to Third Worldism and the United Nations: India and the Politics of Decolonizing Africa." *Past and Present* 218, sup. 8 (May 2013): 258–280.

McCullers, Molly. "'We Do It So That We Will Be Men': Masculinity Politics in Colonial Namibia, 1915–49." *Journal of African History* 52, no. 1 (March 2011): 43–62.

McCulloch, Jock. *Colonial Psychiatry and 'The African Mind.'* 1995.

Moreau de Saint-Méry, Médéric Louis Élie. *A Civilization That Perished: The Last Years of White Colonial Rule in Haiti. 1797–1798*. Translated by Ivor D. Spencer. 1985.

Mukherjee, Rudrangshu, ed. *Great Speeches of Modern India*. 2007.

Nandy, Ashis. *The Intimate Enemy: Loss and Recovery of Self under Colonialism*. 1983.

Naughten, Jim. *Conflict and Costume: The Herero Tribe of Namibia*. 2013.

Ndlovu-Gatsheni, Sabelo J. *Coloniality of Power in Postcolonial Africa: Myths of Decolonization*. 2013.

Nicholls, Brendon. *Ngugi wa Thiong'o, Gender, and the Ethics of Postcolonial Reading*. 2010.

Olusoga, David, and Casper W. Erichsen. *The Kaiser's Holocaust: Germany's Forgotten Genocide and the Colonial Roots of Nazism*. 2010.

Parker, Andrew, Mary Russo, Doris Sommer, and Patricia Yaeger, eds. *Nationalisms and Sexualities*. 1992.

Patil, Vrushali. "Contending Masculinities: The Gendered (Re) Negotiation of Colonial Hierarchy in the United Nations Debates on Decolonization." *Theory and Society* 38, no. 2 (March 2009): 195–215.

Rettig, Tobias. "Recruiting the All-Female Rani of Jhansi Regiment: Subhas Chandra Bose and Dr. Lakshmi Swaminadhan." *South East Asia Research* 21, no. 4 (December 2013): 627–638.

Sandgren, David P. *Mau Mau's Children: The Making of Kenya's Postcolonial Elite*. 2012.

Sengupta, Nilanjana. *A Gentleman's Word: The Legacy of Subhas Chandra Bose in Southeast Asia*. 2012.

Sessions, Jennifer. *By Sword and Plow: France and the Conquest of Algeria*. 2011.

Shipway, Martin. *Decolonization and Its Impact: A Comparative Approach to the End of the Colonial Empires*. 2008.

Shipway, Martin. "'Transfer of Destinies,' or Business as Usual? Republican Invented Tradition and the Problem of 'Independence' at the End of the French Empire." *Round Table* 97, no. 398 (October 2008): 747–759.

Shubert, Adrian. "Women Warriors and National Heroes: Agustina de Aragón and Her Indian Sisters." *Journal of World History* 23, no. 2 (June 2012): 279–313.

Simons, Margaret A., ed. *Feminist Interpretations of Simone de Beauvoir*. 1995.

Standing Bear, Luther. *Land of the Spotted Eagle*. 1978.

Stapleton, Timothy. *African Police and Soldiers in Colonial Zimbabwe, 1923–80*. 2011.

Stavig, Ward, and Ella Schmidt, eds. *The Tupac Amaru and Catarista Rebellions: An Anthology of Sources*. 2008.

Stearns, Peter N. *Gender in World History.* 2nd ed. 2006.

Steinmetz, George. *The Devil's Handwriting: Precoloniality and the German Colonial State in Qingdao, Samoa, and Southwest Africa.* 2007.

Taylor, Robert H. *General Ne Win: A Political Biography.* 2015.

Thompson, Elizabeth. *Colonial Citizens: Republican Rights, Paternal Privilege, and Gender in French Syria and Lebanon.* 2000.

Thompson, Larry Clinton. *William Scott Ament and the Boxer Rebellion: Heroism, Hubris, and the "Ideal Missionary."* 2009.

Toungara, Jeanne Maddox. "The Apotheosis of Côte d'Ivoire's Nana Houphouët-Boigny." *Journal of Modern African Studies* 28, no. 1 (March 1990): 23–55.

Tripp, Aili Mari. "Women's Mobilization in Uganda: Nonracial Ideologies in European-African-Asian Encounters, 1945–1962." *International Journal of African Historical Studies* 34, no. 3 (2001): 543–564.

Turshen, Meredeth. "Algerian Women in the Liberation Struggle and the Civil War: From Active Participants to Passive Victims?" *Social Research* 69, no. 3 (Fall 2002): 889–911.

Uribe-Uran, Victor M., ed. *State and Society in Spanish America during the Age of Revolution.* 2001.

Vince, Natalya. "Transgressing Boundaries: Gender, Race, Religion, and 'Françaises Musulmanes' during the Algerian War of Independence." *French Historical Studies* 33, no. 3 (Summer 2010): 445–474.

Wadowiec, Jaime. "Muslim Algerian Women and the Rights of Man: Islam and Gendered Citizenship in French Algeria at the End of Empire." *French Historical Studies* 36, no. 4 (Fall 2013): 649–676.

Wildenthal, Lora. *German Women for Empire, 1884–1945.* 2001.

Wilson, Henry S. *African Decolonization.* 1994.

CREDITS

Page 163: Courtesy of the Library of Congress.
Page 175: LC-USZ62-93243, Library of Congress Prints and Photographs Division Washington, D.C. 20540 USA.
Page 186: Courtesy of the Library of Congress.
Page 188: LC-USZ62-100043, Library of Congress Prints and Photographs Division Washington, D.C. 20540 USA.
Page 191: © Heritage Image Partnership Ltd/Alamy.
Page 195: Mary Evans Picture Library.
Page 208: Bridgeman-Giraudon/Art Resource, NY.
Page 212: © World History Archive/Alamy.
Page 220: General Research Division, The New York Public Library, Astor, Lenox and Tilden Foundations.
Page 235: British Library, B20029-90.
Page 239: Courtesy of the Library of Congress.
Page 246: Manuscript 166032, National Anthropological Archives, Smithsonian Institution.
Page 273: Picture by John Clymer/Lightroom Photos/fotolibra.
Page 280: LC-USZ62-96939, Library of Congress Prints and Photographs Division Washington, D.C. 20540 USA.
Page 284: LC-USZ62-116140, Library of Congress Prints and Photographs Division Washington, D.C. 20540 USA.
Page 286: Image courtesy of Chapman University, Orange, California.
Page 290: Imperial War Museums, SE5898.
Page 296: Musee d'Histoire Contemporaine, B.D.I.C., Paris, France/Archives Charmet/ Bridgeman Images.
Page 304: Conc. 1 - Bibliotheque Historique de la Ville de Paris, Paris, France/Archives Charmet/Bridgeman Images.
Page 309: Conc. 2 - Courtesy of the Library of Congress.

INDEX

A

Abd el-Kader, 263

Abduction from the Seraglio (Mozart), 194

Abel, Wolfgang, 232

abolitionism; Avellaneda, 67–68; Blumenbach, 210–11; Darwin, 211–12; Duras, 67; Equiano, 43–44, 176, 205–6; Douglass, 42, 44; Grigg, 75; Hart Gilbert, 75; Hart Thwaites, 75; in Africa, 76–77, 176–77; Jacobs, 42; Mana community, 114–15; Mansah, 76; Northup, 42; Prince, 73, 75

abortion, 219, 225–28, 227f

absinthe, 182–83

Abyssinia. *See* Ethiopia

An Account of Jamaica (Stewart), 42

Accra Riots, 287

Acharya, Snehansu Kanta, 279

Ackroyd, Christopher, 280

Adair, James, 69

Adiseshiah, Malcolm, 121

Afghan Snow, 173

Afghanistan, 108, 164, 201

African Methodist Episcopal Church (AME), 123

Age of Enlightenment, 5; and abolition, 44, 62; and anti-imperialism, 56–57, 282; and liberty, 255, 258–60, 262; and progress, 206, 208, 208f. *See also* liberalism

Aguinaldo, Emilio, 57

Al-e Ahmad, Jalal, 300

Alaska, 69–70

Algeria, 28, 54, 97, 107f, 107–8, 130, 132–35, 134f, 175f, 233, 262–64, 276, 285, 293–95, 296f

Ahmed, Fadila, 295

Ahyssa of Senegal and Saint-Domingue, 62–64, 65

Aida (Verdi), 194, 195f

āikane (warrior acolytes), 16

alcohol, 180–83

Aldrich, Robert, 9

Algerian resistance, 262–64

Algerian War of Independence, 294

All-Africa People's Conference, 285

all-India feminism, 101–5, 102f

Alquier, Jeanne, 108

al-riyada, (ancient Islamic tradition of mental training and physical discipline), 222

altered bodies; body marking, 213–16, 215f; foot binding, 216–18, 217f; overview, 213; perfectibility and, 213–23; witchcraft and, 218–20; yoga and, 220–23, 220f

Alutiiq, 69–70

Amaru II, Túpac, 261

Ambonese, 36

AME. *See* African Methodist Episcopal Church

American Anti-Imperialist League, 57

American Revolution, 4, 65

ancient texts, 199–201

Andrews, Elsie, 100–101

Andrews, Julia C., 178

Angola, 244

anthropology, 184–85, 200–202

anti-imperialism, 38–39, 51–52, 56–59, 132, 136, 141; in Belgian Empire, 277–78; in British Empire, 51–53, 170–71, 254, 264–65, 269–70, 274, 278–80, 283–89, 292–93; in Dutch Empire, 290–91; in French Empire, 38–39, 257–59, 262–64, 275–77, 281–82, 293–96; in German Empire, 266–68, 271; in Ottoman Empire, 32, 97, 105–6, 195–96; in Qing Empire, 272–75, 280–81; in Spanish Empire, 261–62, 274; in United States, 270–71. *See also* nationalism

Antigua, 64*f*, 75

antimasturbation campaigns, 251–53

Arabia, 253

Arabian Nights (Burton), 199–201, 252

Argentina, 54–55

Armenian Genocide, 7*f*

Army of the Greater Japanese Empire, 49

Arnold, Ellen, 117, 118

Asantewaa, Yaa, 265

Asim, Salahaddin, 227–28

Atatürk, Kemal, 106

Aung San, 289

Aurousseau, Marcel, 233

Australia, 18–19, 25, 81, 85–86, 99, 116–18, 136–37, 147*f*, 149–50, 233, 253

Austria, 24, 183

B

Baartman, Saartjie "Sara," 183–84, 185

babies, treatment of, 238–41, 239*f*

Baden-Powell, Olave, 126–27

Baden-Powell, Robert, 25–26, 126

Bailey, Henrietta, 119

Ba Maw, 288–89

Banks, Joseph, 13, 14, 213

Barbados, 73, 75

Barker, June, 136–37

Barker, Mary Anne, 87

Barnum, Phineas Taylor, 186–87

Barot, Louis, 19–20, 28

Bartram, William, 69

Bastidas, Micaela, 261

Basu, Jyoti, 280

BBIA. *See* Bulawayo British Indian Association

Beato, Felice, 198

Beauvoir, Simone de, 294

Bechuanaland. *See* Botswana

Becker, Carl, 70–71

Begum, Shahjahan, 103

"Behold Our New Empire"–Mussolini (Diel), 96

Belgium, 4, 119, 240, 277–78

Bell, John, 19

Ben Cheikh, Tawhida, 107

Bengal, 51–52, 93, 101–3, 117, 163, 170–71, 221, 280

Bennett, Victoria Amohau, 100–101

berdache (catamite), 245–46, 246*f*

Berlin Conference, 4

Berlin Trade Show, 189

Bertheaume, Marthe, 106–7

Bertillon, Jacques, 234

Besant, Annie, 126, 221

Bestuzhev, Alexander, 18

Bey, Aziz Idris, 227

Bhabha, Homi, 10

Bhatia, Hemantini, 278

BIA. *See* Burmese Independence Army

BICC. *See* Brethren in Christ Church

Bismarck, Otto von, 4

Black Hollanders, 37–38

"The Black Man's Burden" (Johnson), 58

Black Skin, White Masks (Fanon), 47

Bligh, William, 243–44

Blumenbach, Johann Friedrich, 210–11

Blunt, Wilfred Scawen, 141

boarding schools, 136–39

Bogoraz, Vladimir, 245

Bois Caïman voodoo ceremony, 258

Bolívar, Simón, 261–62

Bonaparte, Napoleon, 32, 258

Bonnin, Gertrude. *See* Zitkala-Sa

Bory, Gabriel de, 210

Bose, Subhas Chandra, 289

Botswana (Bechuanaland), 237, 266

Bouazza, Djamila, 294

Bougainville, Louis Antoine de, 16

Boukman, Dutty, 258

Boupacha, Djamila, 294

Bowring, John, 247

Boxer Rebellion, 272–73, 273*f*, 275

Boyer, Benoît, 251–52

Boy Scouts, 25–26, 28, 126–27

Bracquemond, Félix, 190

Brazil, 55, 64*f*, 113, 120–21, 131, 238

Brethren in Christ Church (BICC), 124–25, 124*f*

Britain, 3–5, 24–25, 35, 75, 103, 121, 126, 133, 164–66, 169, 177–78, 183–84, 187, 200–201, 205–6, 211–12, 221, 231, 247–48, 252–53, 254, 279–81
British Columbia, 139
British Raj, 51–52, 133, 140–41, 147–48, 171, 244
Brown, William, 131
Bruce, James, 253
Buchner, Max, 20
Buck, Pearl S., 297
Buffon, Comte de, 209–10
Bugeaud, Thomas-Robert, 263
Bulawayo British Indian Association (BBIA), 150–51
Bülow, Frieda von, 91–92
Burkina Faso, 153, 254. *See also* French West Africa
Burma, 187, 288–89
Burmese Independence Army (BIA), 288
Burton, Richard, 199–201, 252
Bushidō: Soul of Japan (Nitobe), 49
Butler, Josephine, 248
Büttner, Carl, 70

C

Calcutta Club, 141
Calderon, Fernando, 239
California, 245–46
Callaway, Helen, 8
Calmette, Albert, 182
Camerini, Mario, 195–96
Cameroon, 20, 22, 181, 189, 232, 249
Canada, 139–40, 187, 247, 253, 297
capitalism; defined, 313; economics and, 13, 14*f*; *Wage-Labour and Capital* and, 280
Caribbean, 17, 37, 41, 64*f*, 73–75, 81–85, 98, 114, 139, 176, 180, 205, 225, 258*f*
Carnegie, Mabel, 167
Carothers, John Colin, 241
Cassarouy, Joseph, 63
Castle, Agnes, 166
Castle, Egerton, 166
Catlin, George, 246, 246*f*
cats, 164–65, 165*f*
CCP. *See* Chinese Communist Party
Central African Republic, 299
Ceylon. *See* Sri Lanka
Chamberlain, Mary, 91
Chamier, George, 19

charkha (spinning wheel), 283
Chatterjee, Bankim, 51
Chattopadhyay, Harindranath, 132
Chaudhuri, Nupur, 8
Chaupin, Barthélémy, 138
Chérie (Goncourt), 192
Cheyenne *heemaneh'*, 245
children, 88–90, 89*f*, 238–41, 239*f*
China, 33, 50, 79, 144*f*, 164–66, 167*f*, 170, 174*f*, 216–18, 217*f*, 236–37, 272–73, 273*f*, 275, 280*f*, 280–82
Chinese Communist Party (CCP), 281
Chinese Women's Journal, 275
Chisholm, Caroline, 85–86
Christian denominations; African Methodist Episcopal (AME), 119, 123; Anglican, 121, 123, 130, 279; Baptist, 117–18; Brethren in Christ (BICC), 124–25; Catholic, 68, 74, 114–16, 120–22, 138, 180, 233, 235–36, 240, 254–55, 259; Lutheran, 70–71, 116; Methodist, 75, 123; Moravian, 75
Christianity, 5; animism and, 128, 214, 219, 224–25; converts, 69, 77, 112–13, 115–16, 121–22, 120–25, 213–14; education, 130; healthcare, 235–37; missions, 113–19; reform movements, 76–77, 104, 181–82, 214, 216–17, 254; YMCA, 127–28; YWCA, 100–101, 104
circumcision; female, 253–55; male, 35, 252–53; *Ngaitana*, 254
circuses, 186–90, 188*f*
citizenship; cultural competencies and, 143–46, 154, 259, 276; feminism and, 63, 99, 189; masculinity and, 32, 278; racial qualifications for, 7, 20, 70–71, 80, 232; reward for service, 31, 37–38; through marriage, 97, 145–46
civil disobedience; forms of, 285; Gandhi and, 283–85, 284*f*; Gandhism influencing, 284–85; mass movements and, 283–86, 284*f*
Clark, Ralph, 81
class status; body discipline and, 238–40, 253; clothing and, 123, 128, 169–70; consumerism and, 162, 216; eugenics and, 229, 231; femininity and, 83, 91, 95, 171; immigration and, 29, 96; Marxism and, 279, 284; masculinity and, 13, 18, 23–27, 32, 86; mimicry and, 48; race and, 100, 118, 128, 145; rebellion and,

294, 298; scouting and, 126–27; sexual deviance and, 81, 201–2, 245; upward mobility, 28–29, 55, 87–88, 135

climate; circumcision and, 252–53; clothing and, 170; illness and, 30, 60, 88, 146, 245; theories of gender difference and, 63, 85; theories of racial difference and, 10, 51, 206–12, 228; reliance on native labor and, 87; sexuality and, 116–17, 180, 200

clothing; assimilation and, 32–33, 69, 97; gender non-conformity and, 246–47; as evidence of hybridity, 124–25, 125f, 136; as marker of civilization, 18, 114–15, 176, 214; as marker of cultural difference, 89, 107f, 112; as defense of tradition, 122; as orientalism, 158–59, 167f, 170; for anthropological display, 185, 189; sumptuary laws, 122–23

collectibles; artifacts, of empire, and, 160–68; furnishings in colonies, 162–63, 163f; furnishings in metropole, 160–62; overview, 160; pets, 164–68, 165f, 167f

Colonial Exposition, 1–2, 303, 304f

Colonialism and Homosexuality (Aldrich), 9

A Colonial Lexicon (Hunt), 9

Colonial Masculinity (Sinha), 9

colonial militaries, 36–40, 37f, 40f

Columbia, 120, 223–24, 262

communism; Christianity and, 128; feminism and, 99, 108; fear of, 145–46; in China 218, 275, 280–81; in France, 54; in India, 280; in Soviet Union, 108, 227f, 245, 279, 282, 296, 298; in Vietnam, 281–82; theorists, 181, 279–82

The Communist Manifesto (Marx), 279

Condorcet, Marquis de, 5, 208–9

Congo, 119, 172, 240, 277–78, 299

Congo: My Country (Lumumba), 278

Congress of Angostura, 262

Connolly, Amelia, 139

Contagious Diseases Acts, 247–49

contraception, 152, 234, 228–30, 255

converts; AME and, 123; BICC and, 124–25, 124f; clothing and, 122–23; global Christianity and, 120–25, 124f; overview, 120; segregationist policies and, 122; Shrovetide festival and, 120–21

Cook, Cecil, 136, 150

Cook, James, 12, 15, 56

Corbyn, Frederick, 88

Corday, Michel, 188–89

Cornide, José, 84

cosmetics, 97, 173–75, 174f, 175f

Côte d'Ivoire, 182, 276–77. See also French West Africa

Coubertin, Pierre de, 53

Cruz, Mónica de la, 223–24

crystal, 162, 163f

Cuba, 45, 58, 67–68, 178

Cumming, Constance, 147

curriculum; geography, 133–34; language, 131–32

Cuvier, Georges, 184

Czaplicka, Marie, 244–45

D

al-Dabbur magazine, 276, 277f

Dahomey, 145, 265. See also French West Africa

Dalat, 148

Dalmas, Antoine, 258–59

dance, 86, 101, 105, 124–25, 141, 157–59, 171–73, 194, 197, 244–45, 259, 280, 286–87, 308–9, 309f

Danish Guinea, 176–77

Dark-Lanthorn, 69

Darles, Auguste, 39

Darwin, Charles, 185, 211, 212, 212f

Das Kapital (Marx), 279

Davidson, Frances, 124

Debussy, Claude, 187–88

Declaration on the Granting of Independence, UN, 299–300

Delavignette, Robert, 148

Dernburg, Bernhard, 267–68

The Dervish's Secrets (Sufi pamphlet), 221

The Descent of Man (Darwin), 211, 212

Dessalines, Jean-Jacques, 259

devadasis (low-caste girls dedicated to ritual service), 104–5

Dharmapala, Anagarika, 171

Dictatorial Proclamation, 259

Diderot, Denis, 56, 57

Diel, Louise, 95–96

al-Din Shah, Nasir, 164–65

A Diplomatist's Wife in Japan (Fraser), 169

disability, 104, 187, 216, 237–38

divide-and-conquer strategy, 265–66

Dixey, Annie Coath, 165

Djebar, Assia, 10, 132, 133, 135

Dominica, 17, 60

Donnadieu, Marie, 97

Doten, Alfred, 79

double consciousness, 45, 128, 314

Douglas, James, 139

Douglas-Henry, Dorothea, 230

Douglass, Frederick, 42, 44

Dream of the Fisherman's Wife (Hokusai), 191, 191*f*

Drif, Zohra, 294

drink, 82*f*, 115, 123, 180–83

Drops of Milk lactation league, 240

Drysdale, Charles Robert, 232

Du Bois, W. E. B., 10, 45, 128

Ducos de la Haille, Pierre, 1–2, 6

Duff-Gordon, Lucie, 86

Dufour, Joseph, 161

Dunn, Henry, 181

Duras, Claire de, 67

Duras, Marguerite, 97–98

Dutch concentration camp survivors, 290, 290*f*

Dutch East Indies. *See* Indonesia

E

early childhood education, 130–31

Earthy, Emily Dora, 214, 215*f*

Eberhardt, Isabelle, 97

economics; agricultural labor, 82*f*; capitalism, 13, 14*f*, 280; dislocation produced by imperialism, 219; global circulation of food and drink, 176–77; globalization, 6, 11, 63, 158, 171, 203, 220, 255, 305–6; immigration and, 233; indigenization of, 276, 278, 297; labor exploitation,119, 285, 297; London School of Economics, 279; Marxism, 279; masculinity and, 13, 50, 124; motive for imperialism, 3; nationalism and, 174; prostitution and, 78

Efendi, Ahmet Mithat, 105

Egypt, 32, 66, 75, 135–36, 162, 174–75, 189, 194, 195*f*, 201, 222, 252–53, 298

Eiffel, Gustave, 187

Eigo Fukai, 48–49

"Electricity for Darkest Africa" (poster), 14*f*

Ellis, Havelock, 201

Elms, Mary, 224–25

Elphinstone, Mountstuart, 164

embodiment. *See also specific practice of;* complex, 313; overview of, 308–10, 309*f*; select practices of, xxiii

empire. *See also* artifacts, of empire; colonialism; end of empire; imperialism; institutions, of empire; race, of empire; coverage of, 6–8; democracy and, 305–6; European empires, 1936, xxiv; European overseas, in Atlantic, ca. 1750, xix; historiography of, 8–10; intimacies and, 305; legacy of, 11; liberalism contradictions and, 303–5; patterns of world trade, 1914, xx; persistence of, 305–6; as playground, xxii, 15–17; as playground map, xxii; reasons for rise and fall of, 303–6; topics covered about, 6–8

Empire and Sexuality (Hyam), 9

Empire films, 196–97, 196*f*

Engels, Friedrich, 181–82

Engle, Adda, 124

Equiano, Olaudah, 43–44, 176, 205–6

Eritrea (Italian East Africa), 29–30, 80, 138

The Erogenous Zones of the World (Jacobus X), 202

erotica, 198–203

Essay on the Manner of Perfecting the Human Species (Vandermonde), 209–10

Ethiopia (*Italian East Africa*), 4, 80, 95–96, 194, 279

eugenics, 27, 212, 221–22, 230–32

European militaries, 286–88

European overseas empires, in Atlantic, ca. 1750, xix

évolués (evolving toward European identity), 277–78

evolution, 121*f*, 210–12

expositions; Paris Exposition, 1–2, 303, 304*f*; spectacle and, 186–90, 188*f*

F

Fadoyebo, Isaac, 288

fairs, 186–90, 188*f*

The Faithful Comrade (youth journal), 25

Fales, Louis, 30

Fanon, Frantz, 47, 58–59

Fantasia (Djebar), 10

Fargue, Nicolas de la, 73–74
Fatiman, Cécile, 258
F. & C. Osler, 162–63
Fee, Mary Helen, 92
femininities; Ahyssa of Senegal and
    Saint-Domingue and, 62–64; colonial
    household, 83–90; colonized women,
    72–83; conclusions about, 109–10; East
    versus West and, 64–65; independent
    women, 90–99, 95f; interracial
    romance and, 68–72, 72f; melodramas
    and, 66–68; timeline, 110; virtue in
    cross-cultural contexts, 64–72
feminism, 306; abolition and, 44; in Algeria,
    294–95; in China, 218, 275; in Egypt, 175;
    Enlightenment and, 65; in India, 121–22;
    non-alignment and, 297–98; Pekingese
    dog and, 166; population and, 233; in
    New Zealand, 99–101; in South Africa,
    104, 230; in Sri Lanka, 171–72; in Turkey,
    105–6; in Uganda, 278; women's health
    and, 104, 230, 248, 254
Ferguson, Dugald, 18–19
Ferry, Jules, 27, 159
Fiji, 50
Fink, Molly, 99
Finland, 27
FitzRoy, Robert, 211, 212f
FLN. See National Liberation Front
food, 69–70, 74, 83, 86, 88, 122, 170, 176–80,
    219, 240, 285
football, 55
foot binding, 216–18, 217f
Forster, E. M., 20–21
Forster, George, 15
Forster, Johann Reinhold, 23–24
Foucault, Michel, 8, 310
Fountaine, Margaret, 94–95, 94f
France, 1–2, 3–5, 27–29, 39–40, 54, 66–67,
    97–98, 114–15, 145, 157–59, 164–65, 182,
    184–85, 187–88, 192–94, 233, 258, 276,
    281–82, 294–95, 303
France Offering the Dove of Peace to Five
    Continents (Haille), 1–2, 6
Fraser, Mary Crawford, 169
Free Officers Movement, 298
French Guiana, 114
French Revolution, 31, 114–15, 187, 282
French Revolution's Declaration of the
    Rights of Man and of the Citizen, 282

French Society of Health and Moral
    Prophylaxis (SFPSM), 250
French Union for Women's Suffrage, 106
French West Africa, 19, 28–29, 35, 76–77,
    96, 130, 137, 145–46, 148, 254, 276
Freud, Sigmund, 31
Freyre, Gilberto, 55
Fuegians, 211, 212f
Fuller, Loie, 159–60
furnishings; in colonies, 162–63, 163f; in
    metropole, 160–62

G

Gallieni, Joseph Simon, 233, 250
Galton, Francis, 211–12
Gandhi, Mahatma, 170; civil disobedience
    and, 283–85, 284f; contraception and,
    228–29; East African Indian Congress
    and, 104; Reddi and, 105; women and,
    283, 284f
Gandhi–Irwin Pact, 283–84
Garde Indigène, 38–39
Garrison, Fielding, 30–31
Garvey, Marcus, 128, 151–52, 152f
gaucho horseman, 54–55
Gauguin, Paul, 192–93
Gaulle, Charles de, 276
gender. See also femininities; masculinities;
    women; women, colonized; women,
    independent; slavery and, 63–64, 64f;
    transgenderism, 316; variance,
    243–47, 246f
geography curriculum, 133–34
German East Africa. See Tanzania
German Southwest Africa. See Namibia
Germany, 4–5, 21f, 25, 33–34, 39, 95–96,
    111–13, 133–34, 181, 184, 189, 197–98,
    231–32, 267
Ghana (Gold Coast), 35, 37, 76, 91, 177,
    218–19, 265, 284, 287
Gharbzadegi (Al-e Ahmad), 300
al-Ghazzāl, Ahmad, 65
Ghose, Aurobindo, 221
Ghost Dance movement, 270–71, 301
Gibraltar, 248–49
Gilbert, Marie, 117, 118
Gill, Sarah Ann, 75
Girault, Arthur, 145
Girl Guides, 126, 278

La Gloria (Gotan Project), 309
Golden Stool. *See* War of the Golden Stool
Gómez de Avellaneda, Gertrudis, 67–68
Goncourt, Edmond de, 191–92
Gool, Zainunnisa "Cissie," 104
Gordon, Henry Laing, 231
Gosse, Edmund, 103
Gotan Project, 309
Gouraud, Henri, 276
Graffigny, Françoise de, 66–67
Greece, 200, 202, 248
Gregory, John Walter, 233
Grey, George, 269–70
Grigg, Nanny, 75
Guam, 45, 46*f*
Guatemala, 180–81
Guerre, Jean, 73–74
Guimet, Emile, 158
Guinea, 146. *See also* French West Africa
Gutiérrez, Alonso, 180
Gutiérrez, Rufino, 120
Guyana, 83, 139
gymnastics, 27

H

Hairy Family of Burma, 187
Haiti (Saint-Domingue), 62–63, 73–74,
    84–85, 145, 210, 257–59, 258*f*
Haitian Revolution, 257–60, 258*f*
Hall, Mary, 95
hammock tradition, 47
hapa (pass over), 269
Hardy, Georges, 138
Harrington, Peter, 182
Hart Gilbert, Anne, 75
Hart Thwaites, Elizabeth, 75
Hauhau movement, 269–70
d'Haussonville, Gabriel, 96
Hawaii, 2, 12, 16, 58, 101, 110
health management; French Society of
    Health and Moral Prophylaxis, 250;
    Manual on Health and Marriage, 252;
    overview, 234–35, 235*f*; perfectibility
    and, 234–43; treating baby and, 238–41,
    239*f*; treating body and, 235–37; treating
    mind, 241–43
Heavenly Feet Society, 216–17
Heiser, Victor, 30
Helly, Dorothy, 8

Hendricks, Zara, 70
Hennessy, John Pope, 248
Henty, G. A., 24–25
"Here is our New Emblem" (*al-Dabbur*),
    276, 277*f*
Herero Rebellion, 266–68, 267*f*, 300–301
hijras (neither man nor woman), 244
Hillen, Ernest, 89–90
Hindu Mahasabha, 52–53
Hindu Widows Remarriage Act, 264
Hinduism, 93, 103–5, 121, 220, 244, 264, 283
Hintrager, Oskar, 20
Hirakawa Tōkichi, 79
Hirschfeld, Magnus, 229
Hitler, Adolf, 34, 287
Ho Chi Minh, 281–82
Hocine, Baya, 294
Hodges, William, 13–14
Hodgson, Frederick, 265
Hokusai, Katsushika, 190–91, 191*f*, 192
Hokusai Sketches, 190–91, 191*f*, 192
Holland. *See* Netherlands
homespun cloth. *See khadi*
homosexuality, 9, 16, 20, 22–23, 31, 66, 81,
    101, 200–202, 227–29, 241, 244
Hong Kong, 78, 247–48
Hossain, Rokeya Sakhawat, 101–3
Hottentots, 13, 14
Houphouët-Boigny, Félix, 276–77
How England Saved China (Macgowan), 217
Humboldt, Alexander von, 225
Hume, James, 140
"Hun Speech" (Wilhelm II), 33
Hunt, Nancy Rose, 9
Husen, Bayume Mohamed, 197
Hutchinson, John, 81
Hyam, Ronald, 9
hypermasculinity, 34, 260, 290–91

I

ICS. *See* Indian Civil Service
illness. *See* health management
Imalhayène, Tahar, 135
immigration, 28–29, 55, 79, 81–82, 88, 90,
    96, 99, 139, 143–44; 144*f*, 178, 232–34
Incidents in the Life of a Slave Girl
    (Jacobs), 42
indentured servants, 80–83, 82*f*
independence armies, 288, 290–91, 290*f*

India, 17, 20, 25, 34–35, 51–52, 78, 88, 93, 101–5, 102*f*, 117–18, 121–22, 130, 132–33, 140–41, 147–48, 162–64, 163*f*, 169–71, 177–78, 199–201, 220–22, 228–29, 244, 252–53, 264, 279–80, 283–84, 284*f*, 289, 296–97, 301
India Club, 140–41
Indian Civil Service (ICS), 51
Indian National Army, 289
Indian Rebellion, 264–65
Indian Rights Association, 274
Indochina. *See* Vietnam
Indonesia (Dutch East Indies), 36–38, 88–90, 89*f*, 99–100, 131–132, 143–145, 144*f*, 157–58, 159*f*, 170, 188*f*, 189–90, 290–91, 297
Indonesian National Revolution, 290–91
infanticide, 223–25
"In Love as in War" (McGirt), 58
insurrections; Algerian resistance, 262–64; divide-and-conquer strategy and, 265–66; failed, 262–69, 267*f*; Herero Rebellion, 266–68, 267*f*; Indian Rebellion, 264–65; overview, 262; War of the Golden Stool, 265
The Interesting Narrative (Equiano), 43–44, 176, 205–6
interracial sex, 2, 7, 14–17, 117; as cause for rebellion, 271; in fiction, 67–68; German regulation of, 29, 39, 142–43, 271; proponents of, 19–20, 137, 210; prostitution and, 78–80, 249, 251; rape panics and, 140, 150; with native women, 17, 19–20, 21*f*, 69–72; with white women, 94, 98
In the Shadow of the Bush (Bell), 19
intimacies, 305
Intimate China (Little), 218
The Intimate Enemy (Nandy), 10
Ionian Islands, 248
Iran (Persia), 164–65, 165*f*, 201, 300
Isert, Paul Erdmann, 176–77
Islam; abortion and, 226; *al-riyada*, 222; consumerism and, 174–75; female circumcision and, 254; feminism and, 101–3, 107–8, 295; slavery and, 76; converts to, 97; defense of tradition for women, 64–66, 103, 135, 300; in Turkey, 106
Italy, 4–5, 80, 96, 113, 153, 195, 197, 234, 236
Ivory Coast. *See* Côte d'Ivoire

Iyer, Krishna, 221–22

J

Jacobs, Harriett, 42
Jacobus X, 202
Jacquot, Félix, 263
Jamaica, 41–42, 74, 81–82, 126, 151–52
Jamets, 74
Japan, 4–5, 47–50, 49*f*, 79, 169, 187, 190–92, 191*f*, 194–95, 198, 218, 250–51, 286*f*, 291
Japanese spirit, Western science. *See wakon yôsai*
Japanese-sponsored forces, 288–89
japonisme, 190–93, 198
Java. *See* Indonesia
Javouhey, Anne-Marie, 114–15
Jhansi. *See* Rani of Jhansi
Johnson, Henry, 58
Jones, Nancy, 119
"Jumbo" (poster), 39, 40*f*
Junod, Henri Alexandre, 214
Juye Incident, 272

K

Kama Sutra, 201
Kang Keqing, 281
Kang Youwei, 275
Kant, Immanuel, 56–57
Kariko, Daniel, 266
Karsch, Ferdinand, 244
Kartini, Raden Ajeng, 99–100, 131–32
Karve, Raghunath, 228
Kasai Rubber Company, 119
Kaunda, Kenneth, 284
Kawānanakoa, Abigail, 101
Keds shoes, 280*f*
Kemal, Namik, 227
Kenya, 35, 39, 104, 166–68, 179–80, 196*f*, 231, 249, 254, 292–93, 295, 297
Kenya Diary (Meinertzhagen), 179–80
A Kenyan Farm Diary (Carnegie), 167
Kenyatta, Jomo, 196*f*, 293
Ketteler, Clemens von, 272
Keysser, Frieda, 116–17
khadi (homespun cloth), 283
Khan, Inayat, 158
al-Khuri, Shakir, 252
Kicking Bear, 270

Kif Tebbi (Camerini), 195–96
Kim (Kipling), 25
kimono, 169–70
King, James, 16
Kinjikitile Ngwale, 271
Kipling, Rudyard, 24, 25, 45–46
Klamath *tw!nna'ek*, 245
Korea, 4, 239f
Kortright, Cornelius, 249
Krafft-Ebing, Richard von, 24, 201–2
Kusima, Sukina, 297

L

Laban, William, 143
Lady Lugard. *See* Shaw, Flora
Lagos Market Women's Association, 285
Lakota *winkte*, 245
Lakshmibai. *See* Rani of Jhansi
Lallemand, Claude-François, 252–53
Lamarck, Jean-Baptiste, 211
Land of the Spotted Eagle (Standing
    Bear), 274
language curriculum, 131–32
Laos, 299
Law for the Prevention of Venereal
    Diseases, 250–51
Lawrence, T. E., 32–33, 33f
Lebanon, 112, 276, 277f, 299
Lenin, Vladimir, 279, 282
Le Page du Pratz, Antoine-Simon, 42–43
Le Pichon, Jean, 148
Letters from a Peruvian Woman
    (Graffigny), 66–67
Leutwein, Theodor, 267
liberalism, 5–7; communism and, 108;
    critique of imperialism, 56–57;
    democracy, 31, 63, 115, 122, 275–76, 287,
    305–6; Enlightenment, 304; feminism,
    100, 102, 218; imperialism and, 5–6;
    nationalism and, 276; non-alignment
    and, 297; Ottoman reforms, 105;
    segregation and, 128
Liberia, 181, 299
Libya, 96, 195
The *Lion Dog of Peking* (Dixey), 165
Little, Alicia, 217–18
Liu Zhang, 78
The Location of Culture (Bhabha), 10
Locke, John, 304

London School of Economics, 279
Lotus Huang, 273
Lougheed, James, 140
Louisiana, 42–43
Louverture, Toussaint, 257–59
Lumumba, Patrice, 277–78
Lu Xun, 275
Lyautey, Hubert, 21, 28
Lyttelton, Edward, 252

M

Macaulay, Thomas Babington, 51
Macdonald, Claude, 50
Macgowan, John, 217
MacRae, Donald, 237
Madagascar, 114, 233, 250
Madame Butterfly (Puccini), 194–95
Madame N, 84–85
madamismo (high-class prostitution), 80
Maharero, Samuel, 266
Mahomed, Sake Dean, 177
mahu (Tahitian natives), 243–44
Maji Maji Rebellion, 271
Makati, Mololokane, 237
Malawi, 95
Malaysia (Malaya), 50, 126, 147, 289
Mali, 254. *See also* French West Africa
Malraux, André, 299
Malta, 248
Malthus, Thomas, 228
*Management and Diseases of Infants under
    the Influence of the Climate of India*
    (Corbyn), 88
Mansah, Abina, 76
Manual on Health and Marriage
    (al-Khuri), 252
Maori, 34, 71, 100–101, 269–70
Mao Zedong, 280–81
maps; decolonization in Asia and Africa,
    1945–1999, xxvi; embodiment
    practices, xxiii; empire, as playground,
    xxii; empires and patterns of world
    trade, 1914, xx; European empires,
    1936, xxiv; European overseas empires,
    in Atlantic, ca. 1750, xix; European
    population movements, 1750–1914, xxi;
    migration routes from China to India,
    19th century, xxi; resistance and
    revolution, xxv

Marie-Andrée du Sacré-Coeur, 254
maroon settlements, 43
Marquesas Islands, 193
marriage; Hindu Widows Remarriage Act,
    264; *Manual on Health and Marriage*,
    252; missions and, 116–17; Mixed
    Marriage Law, 143
Marshall Islands, 250
martial races, 34–36
Martin, Julia. *See* Matenga, Huria
Martin, William, 248
Martini, Ferdinando, 138
Martinique, 47, 62
Marx, Karl, 279, 280
Marxism; Ackroyd and, 280;
    establishment of, 279; Ho and, 281–82;
    Keds and, 280*f*; Mao and, 280–81
masculinities; anti-imperialism and, 56–59;
    boys made into men, 24–28; bridging
    divide, 53–59; capitalist economics and,
    13, 14*f*; *Colonial Masculinity*, 9;
    colonized elites and, 47–53; colonized
    masses and, 40–47; conclusions about,
    59–61; imperial men and, 23–31;
    interracial sex and, 14–23; men turned
    into colonists, 28–31; overview, 2, 13;
    Pacific explorers and, 12–14; social
    Darwinism and, 23–24; timeline, 60–61;
    warriors, 31–40
Masood, Syed Ross, 20–21
Massey, Cromwell, 35
masturbation. *See* antimasturbation
    campaigns
Mata Hari, 157–59, 159*f*, 183
Matenga, Huria, 71
Mathews, Joseph, 131
Mathews, Mary, 79
Mauclair, Camille, 159–60
Mauritius, 248
May, Karl, 25
Mayne, Francis, 78
MCC. *See* Mothers' Clinic Committee of
    Cape Town
McGirt, James, 58
McKeurtan, Mary, 150–51
Mehmet, Deli, 75
Meiji Restoration program, 48–49
Meinertzhagen, Richard, 179–80
Meli, Rashidi Ali, 172
melodramas, 66–68

Memoirs of an Arabian Princess (Ruete),
    111–12
men. *See also* masculinities; colonialism
    and, 28–31; imperial, 23–31; making
    boys into, 24–28; YMCA, 127–28
Merensky, Alexander, 271
Merian, Maria Sybilla, 225
La Meschachébé newspaper, 43
Middle East, 5, 9, 170, 200, 253
migration routes, from China to India, 19th
    century, xxi
Millar, John, 23
millenarianism; Boxer Rebellion, 272–73,
    273*f*; contained conflicts and, 269–73,
    273*f*; Ghost Dance movement, 270–71;
    Hauhau movement, 269–70; Maji Maji
    Rebellion, 271
Millingen, Frederick, 164
Minh Mang, 115
missions; global Christianity and, 113–19;
    Javouhey and, 114–15; Mana, 114–15;
    marriage and, 116–17; overview, 113;
    personality of missionary and, 116
Mitchell, Samuel, 136
Mixed Marriage Law, 143
mixed-race populations, 7; African
    rejection of, 152–53; boarding schools for,
    136–38; eugenics and, 232; immigration
    and, 233; on the frontiers, 69–70; white
    mothers of, 99; white fathers of 73–74,
    117; in diverse societies, 143–44;
    proponents of, 209–10
Mohave *hwame*, 245
Molloy, Georgiana, 86
Monsieur N, 84–85
Montandon, George, 185–86
Monts, Clara von, 184
"More Like His Dad Everyday"
    (cartoon), 46*f*
Morley, John, 200
Morocco, 21, 65, 97, 186*f*, 263, 294
Mothers' Clinic Committee of Cape Town
    (MCC), 230
Mott, John, 127–28
Mozambique, 118–19, 214
Mozart, Wolfgang Amadeus, 194
Mpofu, Dlodlo, 125
Mtendeje, Andrew Kunguru, 172
Mughals, 34–35, 162, 264
Mukhopadhyay, Mokshodayani, 170–71

Mukō Gunji, 251
al-Muqrani, Muhammad, 263–64
Musa, Nabawiya, 135–36
Museum of Man, 185
Mussolini, Benito, 95–96, 234
Mutesa II, Kabaka, 278–79
Myanmar. *See* Burma

N

Nahappan, Janaky Athi, 289
Naidu, Sarojini, 103–4
NAM. *See* Non-Alignment Movement
Namibia (German Southwest Africa), 20,
    29, 70, 189, 249, 266–67, 267*f*, 300, 305
Nandy, Ashis, 10
Nangombe, 241–42
Narrative of the Life of Frederick Douglass
    (Douglass), 42
Nasi, Guglielmo, 80
Nasser, Gamal Abdel, 298
National Afro-American Council, 58
National Exhibition of Women's Labor,
    189–90
nationalism; Black Nationalism, 58, 152,
    173; economic nationalism, 174;
    imperial nationalism, 15, 17, 28, 50,
    91–92, 134; masculinity and, 24, 26–28,
    222, 252; military service and, 38;
    population question and, 233–34; sports
    and, 51–55. *See also* anti-imperialism
National Liberation Front (FLN), 294, 295
Natural Feet Society, 217–18
Naudeau, Ludovic, 234
Navajo *nadle*, 245
Nazism, 34, 95–96, 153, 186, 197, 232, 286–87
Nederburgh, Izak Alexander, 144
Nehru, Jawaharlal, 296–97, 301
Neimy, Khalil, 94–95, 94*f*
Nelson, Horatio, 32
Netherlands, 37–38, 158, 170, 192
neurasthenia, 22, 30–31, 251
Neuville, Henri, 185
Nevada, 79
Neville, Octavius, 137
New Guinea. *See* Papua New Guinea
New York, 186–87
New Zealand, 18–19, 34, 71, 83, 100–101,
    131, 171, 187, 253, 269–70, 274
Ngaitana (selfcircumcision), 254

Ngambi ul Kuo, Erika, 197, 232
Ngata, Apirana, 274
Ngatata, Wi Tako, 171
Niger, 137, 148. *See also* French West Africa
Nigeria, 8, 43, 47, 50, 113, 181, 196*f*, 196–97,
    205, 216, 224–25, 241, 285–87
Nightingale, Florence, 91, 248
Nitobe Inazō, 49
Nittel-de Wolff van Westerrode, Maria, 87
Njeri, Hadija, 249
Nkrumah, Kwame, 284, 285
Noble, Margaret, 93
non-alignment, 296–98
Non-Alignment Movement (NAM),
    297, 298
North Carolina, 69
Northern Territory Aboriginal
    Ordinance, 149
Northup, Solomon, 42
Nsumbane, Lise, 214
Nugent, Maria, 74
nurses, 91–93
Nyerere, Julius, 271

O

O., Isaac, 241
Olympics, 27, 53–54
*On the Condition of Women in Ottoman
    Society* (Asim), 227–28
Order of Saint Michael and Saint
    George, 50
Ordinance for Checking the Spread of
    Venereal Diseases, 247
Orientalism (Said), 9, 310
The Origin of the Distinction of Ranks
    (Millar), 23
Orsmond, John Muggridge, 213
Osifekunde, 216
Osler. *See* F. & C. Osler
Osundina, 216
Otruppa movement, 268–69, 301
Ottoman Empire, 5, 32, 75–76, 105–106,
    194, 195, 226–27, 251–52, 275–76. *See
    also* Egypt
El Ouafi, Boughèra, 54
Ourika (Duras), 67
Our Sentimental Garden (Castle & Castle),
    166
Ousley, Benjamin, 118–19

P

Pacific explorers vignette, 12–14
Packsaddle (Aboriginal laborer), 149–50
Paine, Thomas, 65
painting, 190–93, 191*f*
Pallotta, Assunta, 236–37
Pandit, Vijaya Lakshmi, 298–99
pan-Islamic feminism, 105–8, 107*f*
Pankhurst, Christabel, 251
Papua New Guinea, 22, 120, 122, 129*f*, 148–49
Paris Exposition, 1–2, 303, 304*f*
A *Paris Profile* (al-Tahtawi), 66
Paris World's Fair, 187–89
Pasha, Ibrahim, 162
Pasha, Mehmet Ali, 105
A *Passage to India* (Forster), 20
Patterson, Albert, 43
peacock flower, 225–26
Pekingese lapdogs, 165–66, 167*f*
People's Liberation Army (PLA), 281
"People's Principles" (Sun), 275
perfectibility; ableism and, 207; altered bodies
   and, 213–23; climate, and evolution and,
   121*f*, 210–12; conclusions about, 255–56;
   *Essay on the Manner of Perfecting the
   Human Species*, 209–10; health
   management and, 234–43; overview,
   207–8, 208*f*; progress theories and, 208–10;
   race and, 121*f*, 207–12; reproduction
   management, 223–34; sexuality
   management, 243–55; timeline, 256
performing arts, 194–98, 195*f*, 196*f*
Perry, Matthew, 48, 198
Persia. *See* Iran
Peru, 66–67, 261
Peters, Carl, 92
Petite-Nanon, 73–74
pets, 164–68, 165*f*, 167*f*
Phadke, Narayan, 229
Philip, John, 130
Philippines, 30–31, 45, 57–58, 87, 92–93,
   178, 238
Philippinitis, 30
Philosopher Dick (Chamier), 19
Picasso, Pablo, 193
Pillay, A. P., 229
Piper, Raymond, 222
Piyaseeli, Rupa, 172
PLA. *See* People's Liberation Army

Pomare II, 213–14
Portrait of Père Tanguy (van Gogh), 192
Portugal, 4, 209
postcards, 198–99
postcolonialism; defined, 315; non-
   alignment and, 296–98; overview, 9–10,
   296; United Nations and, 298–300;
   Westoxification and, 300
postpartum depression, 241–42
"Power of Habit" (cartoon), 21*f*
Prashad, Jagannath, 221
Pratt, Henry, 162
The Present State of Egyptians (Umar), 222
Prince, Mary, 73, 75
Prison Diary of Ho Chi Minh (Ho), 282
Prisoner of the Caucasus (Pushkin), 17–18
progress theories, 5, 14*f*, 25, 65, 185, 188,
   208–10, 304
prostitution, 22, 40, 49, 77–81, 105, 148,
   193, 201, 247–51. *See also* sexually
   transmitted diseases
Psychopathia Sexualis (Krafft-Ebing), 24
Puccini, Giacomo, 194–95
punitive raid. *See* razzia
Pushkin, Alexander, 17–18
Puyi, Qing Emperor, 275
pygmies, 184

Q

Qing Empire. *See* China
Qiu Jin, 218, 275
Quashee, 42, 44
Quyen, Luong Ngoc, 38, 39

R

race, of empire; climate and evolution and,
   121*f*, 210–12; Equiano and, 205–6;
   mixed-race people, 307; overview, 2–3,
   207; perfectibility and, 121*f*, 207–12
Race and the Education of Desire (Stoler), 8
Race Welfare Society of Johannesburg
   (RWS), 230
Rajagopalachari, Chakravarti, 222
Ramabai, Pandita, 121–22
ramzanis (dancing boys with female
   costumes), 35
Rand, Philinda, 87
"Random Feelings" (Qiu), 218

Rani of Jhansi, 264–65, 289

RAR. *See* Rhodesian African Rifles

Raza, Roustam, 32

razzia (punitive raid), 263

Rechenberg, Albrecht von, 22

Reddi, Muthulakshmi, 104–5

Red Lanterns Shining, 273

Regulations for the Control of Prostitutes, 250

Reiprich, Doris, 197, 232

reproduction; abortion, 225–28, 227*f*; contraception, 228–30; immigration, 232–34; infanticide, 223–25; overview, 223; perfectibility and, 223–34; sterilization, 230–32

Reunion, 114

revolutions; Bolívar and, 261–62; early, 257–60, 258*f*, 261–62; French Revolution's Declaration of the Rights of Man and of the Citizen, 282; Haitian Revolution, 257–60, 258*f*; Indonesian National Revolution, 290–91; map, xxv; Túpac Amaru Rebellion, 261

Rhodesia. *See* Zimbabwe

Rhodesian African Rifles (RAR), 287

Righteous and Harmonious Fists, 272–73, 273*f*

Rigonaux, Nicolas, 154

Robertson, George, 15

Robeson, Paul, 128, 196, 196*f*, 197

Roche, Harriet, 87

Rodin, Auguste, 191, 192

Rohrbach, Paul, 29

Roosevelt, Nicholas, 30

Roosevelt, Theodore, 45–46, 57, 92

Roy, Raja Ram Mohan, 304–5

Roy, Willy von, 22

Rubi, Ibu, 8

Ruddick, Daisy, 137

Ruete, Emily, 111–12, 151

Russell, James, 248

Russia, 4–5, 17–18, 25, 27, 75, 164, 245, 279. *See also* Soviet Union

RWS. *See* Race Welfare Society of Johannesburg

S

Sab (Gómez de Avellaneda), 67–68

Sahaykwisa, 247

Sahetmiradov, Halmirad, 108

Said, Edward, 9, 310

Said-Ruete, Rudolph, 151

Saint-Domingue. *See* Haiti

Saint Kitts and Nevis, 225

Saint-Méry, Moreau de, 62–64, 180, 259

salt march, 284*f*

Samoa, 142–43

Sanders of the River (Empire films), 196–97, 196*f*

Sanger, Margaret, 228, 229, 233

Santa Fe, Manuel, 224

sari, 169

Sastro, Ibu, 90

Satyagraha (Soul Force), 284

Satthianadhan, Krupabai, 121, 122

Saturday Review, 26

Scarborough, William, 58

scarification, 205–6, 216

Schaw, Janet, 225

Schmelen, Heinrich, 70

Schnee, Heinrich, 143

Scholte, Lin, 89

schools; boarding schools, 72*f*, 136–39, 155, 247; Cambridge, 133; communism and, 108, 279, 281; curriculum, 131–34; destruction of, 264; discrimination in, 100; early childhood education, 130–31; for British boys, 26–27; geography and, 133–34; for housekeeping, 87, 107; in India, 93, 101, 104; in Japan, 49; language and, 87–88 131–32; London School of Economics, 279; mission schools, 119; Oxford, 133; as subversive, 294; teachers, 87, 91–93, 134–36, 182; upward mobility and, 51, 136

scientific racism, 184–85, 211–12, 316

Scott, James Foster, 251

Scouting for Boys (Baden-Powell), 25–26

Scouts. *See* Boy Scouts

Scramble for Africa, 4, 50, 57

The Secluded Ones (Hossain), 102

segregation, 57, 78–80, 104, 119, 122–23, 126–27, 134, 139–41, 142–43, 149–51, 174, 297

Seidensticker, Lisette, 92

Self-Help (Smiles), 48

Sellon, Edward, 17

Semsigul, 75

Senegal, 62–63, 67, 114, 153. *See also* French West Africa

Senghor, Léopold, 153–54

separatist movements, 151–54, 152*f*

sepoys, 36, 264

Serène, Raoul, 28

Seven Years War, 3–4

Sex Problem in India (Phadke), 229

sexuality. *See also* interracial sex; antimasturbation campaigns, 251–53; *Colonialism and Homosexuality,* 9; defined, 316; *Empire and Sexuality,* 9; female circumcision, 253–55; gender variance, 243–47, 246*f*; overview, 243; perfectibility and, 243–55; *Psychopathia Sexualis,* 24

sexually transmitted diseases (STDs), 17, 78, 247–51

Seychelles Islands, 265

SFPSM. *See* French Society of Health and Moral Prophylaxis

Sha'arawi, Huda, 174–75

shamanism, 244–45

Shaw, Flora, 8

shawl, 169

Sheppard, William Henry, 119

Sherwood, Mary Martha, 88

Shrovetide festival, 120–21

Siberia, 70, 244–45

Sierra Leone, 206, 249, 265

Sinasi, Ibrahim, 105

Singapore, 78, 248, 289

Singh, Khushwant, 132

Sinha, Mrinalini, 9

Sithole, Ndabaningi, 173

Sitting Bull, 270

Sketch for a Historical Picture of the Progress of the Human Mind (Condorcet), 208–9

The Slave Caravan (May), 25

slavery; abortion and, 75, 225; cruelty and, 41–42; food and, 176–77; infanticide and, 223–24; in Africa, 25, 76–77, 215–16; in Caribbean, 62–64, 67–68, 73–75, 114–15, 257–59; in Ottoman Empire, 75–76; in South America, 223–24, 238; masculinity, and, 41–42; maroon communities, 43; Petite-Nanon, 73–74; Semsigul, 75; slave rebellion, 257–59; in United States, 42–43. *See also* abolitionism

Smiles, Samuel, 48

Smith-Dorrien, Horace, 249

Smuts, Jan, 299

social Darwinism, 23–26, 185, 231

Society for the Prevention of Cruelty to Animals (SPCA), 166–68

Solf, Wilhelm, 142

Somalia, 199

Sotadic Zone, 200

Soul Force. *See* Satyagraha

The *Souls of Black Folk* (Du Bois), 45

South Africa, 13–14, 35, 75, 86–87, 95, 104, 123, 126–28, 130, 174, 183–84, 199, 214–15, 230, 242, 247, 266, 268, 283, 297, 299

South Dakota, 270

Spain, 3–4, 44, 65, 84, 193, 248–49, 261–62

Soviet Union, 108, 227*f*, 245, 279, 282, 298

SPCA. *See* Society for the Prevention of Cruelty to Animals

spectacle; artifacts, of empire, and, 183–90; circuses, fairs, and expositions, 186–90, 188*f*; overview, 183; people, as objects of study, 183–86, 186*f*

Spencer, Herbert, 24, 212

spinning wheel. *See* charkha

Spivak, Gayatri, 10

sports, 24, 26–27, 51–52, 148, 197, 222, 275, 286–87

Sri Lanka (Ceylon), 98, 171, 299

Standing Bear, Luther, 274

Stanhope, Lovell, 74

Stanley, Henry Morton, 14*f*

STDs. *See* sexually transmitted diseases

sterilization, 230–32

Stewart, John, 42

Stileman, Charles, 164, 165*f*

Stoler, Ann Laura, 8

Stopes, Marie, 229

Strehlow, Carl, 116–17

Strobel, Margaret, 8

Stuart, Charles "Hindoo," 169

Stuhlmann, Franz, 184

subaltern; colonized elites and, 51–53, 52*f*; defined, 316; *The Location of Culture* and, 10

The Subjects of the Shah (Stileman), 164, 165*f*

Sudan, 50–51, 153

Suez Canal, 298

Sultana's Dream (Hossain), 102–3

Sun Yat-sen, 275

Surier, Albert, 27
Suriname, 225
Suzuki Keiji, 288
Swaminadhan, Lakshmi, 289
Swaziland, 287
Symonds, John Addington, 201
Syria, 76, 94, 236, 252, 276

T

Tahiti, 15–16, 60, 114, 192–93, 202, 213–14, 243–44
Tahitian Pastorals (Gauguin), 193
al-Tahtawi, Rifa'a, 66
Tanzania (German East Africa), 22, 31, 91–92, 141*f*, 142, 172–73, 179, 189, 197, 249, 271, 297
Tanzimat reform period, 105–6, 226
tattooing, 34, 171, 213–15
Tchitchelle, Stéphane, 153
teachers, 91–93, 134–36, 134*f*
Te Kahupukoro, 269
"Terminal Essay" (Burton), 200, 201
Te Ua Haumene, 269
Thackeray, William Makepeace, 177–78
Thai Nguyen Uprising, 38–39
Thailand (Siam), 4
Thapar, Romesh, 132
The Thinker (Rodin), 192
Thistlewood, Thomas, 41
Thomas, Robert, 225
Tierra del Fuego, 211
Tirindi, Charity, 254
Titus, Olive Glasgow, 229
Tjamuaha, Maharero, 266
Toby, Jean-François, 137
Togo, 133, 189
Topuz, Fatma Aliye, 106
Toussaint-Samson, Adèle, 131, 238
toy sets, 25
transgressing boundaries. *See* boundaries, transgressing
trans-Pacific feminism, 99–101
travelers, female, 94–96, 95*f*
Travels to Discover the Source of the Nile (Bruce), 253
treatment; of baby, 238–41, 239*f*; of body, 235–37; of mind, 241–43
Trinidad, 83, 94
Trocadero Palace, 185

Trotha, Lothar von, 266–67
Troup, Jonathan, 17
Tuareg, 35–36
Túpac Amaru Rebellion, 261
Turkey, 105–106. *See also* Ottoman Empire
Turkmenistan, 108
Tunisia, 107, 236, 294
Turner, John, 130–31
Twain, Mark, 57
Twelve Years a Slave (Northup), 42
twins, 224–25
Two Tahitian Women (Gauguin), 193

U

Uganda, 278–79
Ugandan Women's Association, 278–79
Umar, Muhammad, 222
United Nations, 298–300
United States, 3, 4–5, 25, 30, 37, 42–43, 45–46, 46*f*, 57–58, 60, 79–80, 83, 92, 110, 118–19, 121–22, 130, 132, 140, 142, 152, 156, 171, 178, 185, 186–87, 230, 233, 236, 246–47, 253, 258, 260, 268, 270, 274, 282, 296, 297, 298, 307
Untrodden Fields of Anthropology (Jacobus X), 202
Upper Volta. *See* Burkina Faso
Uruguay, 84
Uzbekistan, 108

V

Vancouver, George, 69
Vandenperre, Félicie, 240
Vandermonde, Charles-Augustin, 209–10
Vangeke, Louis, 122
van Gogh, Vincent, 192
van Helsdingen-Schoevers, Beata, 87
Vanuatu, 12–13, 17, 60
veiling, 35
Venezuela, 225
Verdi, Giuseppe, 194, 195*f*
Vicissitudes of Bush Life in Australia and New Zealand (Ferguson), 18–19
Viet Minh guerrilla war, 282
Vietnam (Indochina), 28, 38–39, 54, 97–98, 115–16, 148, 178–79, 182, 242, 281–82, 291
Vietnam's Declaration of Independence, 282

Vint, Francis, 231
Vivekananda, Swami, 51, 220–21

W

Waal-Hirèna, 153
Wage-Labour and Capital (Marx), 280
wakon yôsai (Japanese spirit, Western science), 48
Wales, William, 12
Walker, C. J., 174
wallpaper, 161
War of the Golden Stool, 265
Wars of Independence in South America, 261–62
Washington, Booker T., 128
The Wasp. See al-Dabbur magazine
Watts, William, 34
wearables; artifacts, of empire, and, 168–75; in colonies, 170–73; cosmetics, 173–75, 174f, 175f; in metropole, 168–70; overview, 168
Welldon, James, 26–27
Western militaries, 31–34, 33f
Western Women and Imperialism (Chaudhuri & Strobel, eds.), 8
Westoxification, 300
"The White Man's Burden" (Kipling), 45–46
White Women's Protection Ordinance, 149
Wilhelm II, Kaiser, 33, 267, 272
Wills, Charles James, 164
Wilskman, Ivar, 27
Wimpffen, Baron de, 210
Witbooi, Hendrik, 268
witchcraft, 218–20, 241
Wollstonecraft, Mary, 44
women. *See also* femininities; circumcision and, 253–55; *On the Condition of Women in Ottoman Society*, 227–28; French Algeria and, 294–95; French Union for Women's Suffrage, 106; Gandhi and, 283, 284f; Indian National Army and, 289; Lagos Market Women's Association, 285; National Exhibition of Women's Labor, 189–90; *Two Tahitian Women*, 193; Ugandan Women's Association, 278–79;

Western Women and Imperialism, 8;
White Women's Protection Ordinance, 149
women, independent; collectors, 94–96, 95f; nurses and teachers, 91–93; overview, 90; pleasure seekers, 96–99; travelers, 94–96, 95f
Women of Islam (Topuz), 106
Women's Christian Temperance Union, 122, 150
Wood, Leonard, 238
World Renewal cult, 48
World War I, 5, 32, 33f, 37f, 38–40, 54, 106, 159, 182, 197, 232–33, 275
World War II, 34, 38–39, 47, 50, 53, 90, 153, 276, 285–90, 293
Wovoka, 270
The Wretched of the Earth (Fanon), 59
Wright, Richard, 297

Y

Yamada Waka, 79
Yellow Peril, 140, 234
Yergan, Max, 127–28, 151
Yergan, Susie Wiseman, 128
yoga, 220–23, 220f
Yogendra, Swami Sri, 222
Yoshioka Yayoi, 251
The Young Ladies of Avignon (Picasso), 193
Young Men's Christian Association (YMCA), 127–28
Young Women's Christian Association (YWCA), 100–101, 104
Yup'ik, 70

Z

Zambia, 284
Zanzibar, 111–12
Zeehandelaar, Estella, 99–100
Zelle, Margaretha. *See* Mata Hari
Zimbabwe (Rhodesia), 119, 124–125, 124f, 150–51, 173, 287
Zinder, 148
Zitkala-Sa, 72f
Zulu, 35
Zuni *lhamana*, 245